Bonds of Wool

Studies in Medieval and Early Modern Canon Law

Kenneth Pennington, General Editor

Editorial Advisory Board

Uta-Renate Blumenthal, The Catholic University of America

Giles Constable, Institute for Advanced Study

Richard Helmholz, University of Chicago

John E. Lynch, The Catholic University of America

Robert Somerville, Columbia University

Brian Tierney, Cornell University

Studies in Medieval and Early Modern Canon Law

VOLUME 15

Bonds of Wool
The Pallium and Papal Power in the Middle Ages

Steven A. Schoenig, SJ

The Catholic University of America Press
Washington, D.C.

Copyright © 2016
The Catholic University of America Press
All rights reserved
The paper used in this publication meets the
minimum requirements of American National
Standards for Information Science—Permanence
of Paper for Printed Library Materials,
ANSI Z39.48-1984.
∞

Design and composition by Kachergis Book Design

Cataloging-in-Publication data available from the
Library of Congress
ISBN 978-0-8132-3370-3

in honorem magistri Roberti Somerville,
in gratam memoriam Rogerii Reynolds,
et ad maiorem Dei gloriam

Contents

List of Illustrations	viii
Acknowledgments	ix
List of Abbreviations	xi
Introduction	1
Part 1: Weaving the Pattern (741–882)	**21**
1. Obtaining the Pallium	27
2. Bestowing the Pallium	73
3. Using the Pallium	117
4. Interpreting the Pallium	151
Part 2: A Well-Worn Garment (882–1046)	**179**
5. Carelessness	193
6. Creativity	227
Part 3: The Reformer's Badge (1046–1119)	**275**
7. A Tool of the Reform: The Ends	279
8. A Tool of the Reform: The Means	321
9. New Meanings for a New Age	363
Epilogue: The Pallium in Classical Medieval Jurisprudence (ca.1140–ca. 1271)	**397**
1. *Decretum* and Decretists	401
2. Decretals and Decretalists	440
Conclusion	483
Selected Bibliography	489
Index of Papal Letters	517
Index of Canonical Works	522
General Index	525

Illustrations

Figure 1. Sees of Western Palligers	2
Figure 2. The Development of the Pallium	3
Figure 3. A Bishop Being Vested with the Pallium	22
Figure 4. Heribert of Cologne Receives the Pallium	181
Figure 5. Emperor Henry V and Pope Paschal II	276
Figure 6. An Emperor and an Archbishop	398

Acknowledgments

First and foremost I offer my deepest thanks to Robert Somerville for the meticulous care, patience, wisdom, and good humor shown to me during the research and writing of this book. I also wish to thank Susan Boynton, Euan Cameron, Adam Kosto, and the much missed Roger Reynolds, who encouraged this project from its inception. I have not been able to do justice to all their helpful suggestions, but the book is better for their involvement.

During my research I was moved by the ready generosity with which scholars around the world responded to my pleas and provided advice and information. I gratefully acknowledge the useful assistance of Greta Austin, Bruce Brasington, Martin Brett, Giles Constable, Bernard D'Alteroche, Louis Hamilton, Klaus Herbers, Eric Knibbs, Maureen Miller, Jörg Müller, Przemysław Nowak, Jane Rosenthal, Herbert Schneider, Neslihan Senocak, Anders Winroth, and Thomas Zotz. More recently I have enjoyed fruitful conversations with scholars who have been equally helpful: Courtney Booker, Carolyn Carty, Celia Chazelle, James Ginther, Wilfried Hartmann, John Osborne, Kriston Rennie, Joanna Story, and Francesca Tinti. All of them have my respect and my thanks.

Through their unstinting support, Philip Gavitt, Thomas Madden, and the rest of the faculty and staff in the Department of History and the Center for Medieval and Renaissance Studies at Saint Louis University showed humbling confidence in me and reassured me that the whole effort was worthwhile. I am privileged to be their colleague. Daniel Webb rendered valuable assistance with indexing and proofreading. In addition, several magnanimous souls read the manuscript in whole or in part, gave me valuable comments and criticism, and saved me from errors and from despair. I am particularly and deeply grateful to the anonymous readers and to Brenda Bolton, Anne Duggan, Atria Larson, John Padberg, SJ, and especially my trusted counselor, Damian Smith, for their truly heroic labors on my behalf. Of course, they should not be blamed for the deficiencies that remain.

I am gratified that my book has found a home well suited to it at the Catholic University of America Press, and I thank Trevor Lipscombe and the editorial committee for welcoming it. Heartfelt appreciation is due to series editor Kenneth Pennington, who enthusiastically supported the book from the moment he saw it and displayed much kindness along the way.

I am immeasurably thankful to my family, who have upheld me through thick and thin and buoyed me with their interest and their love.

Finally, I owe a large debt of gratitude to my brothers in the Society of Jesus. My Jesuit superiors, who missioned me to the academic apostolate, sustained me with the guidance and resources I needed in order to thrive in it. My confreres at the Xavier Jesuit Community in New York and the Sacred Heart Jesuit Community in St. Louis, and many others beyond, accompanied me with fraternal friendship and constant intellectual stimulation. There are also a number of Jesuit scholars in this book's bibliography. I hope that, in my own small way, I am carrying on the tradition.

Et de pallio quidem tantum nos dixisse sufficiat.
(Bruno of Segni, *De Sacramentis Ecclesiae*)

Abbreviations

AASS	*Acta Sanctorum*
BF	*Papstregesten, 1024–1058* (Frech)
BH	*Papstregesten, 844–872* (Herbers)
BU	*Papstregesten, 872–882* (Unger)
BZ	*Papstregesten, 911–1024* (Zimmermann)
Clavis	*Clavis Canonum: Selected Canon Law Collections before 1140* (ed. Fowler-Magerl): database component
CCCM	*Corpus Christianorum: Continuatio Mediaevalis*
CCSL	*Corpus Christianorum: Series Latina*
GaP	*Gallia Pontificia*
GP	*Germania Pontificia*
HEOJ	*Histoire de l'église depuis les origines jusqu'a nos jours*
IP	*Italia Pontificia*
JK, JE, JL	*Regesta Pontificum Romanorum ab Condita Ecclesia ad Annum post Christum Natum MCXCVIII* (Jaffé)
MGH Auct. ant.	*Monumenta Germaniae Historica: Auctores Antiquissimi*
MGH Briefe	*Monumenta Germaniae Historica: Briefe der deutschen Kaiserzeit*
MGH Conc.	*Monumenta Germaniae Historica: Concilia*
MGH Const.	*Monumenta Germaniae Historica: Constitutiones et Acta Publica Imperatorum et Regum*
MGH Epp.	*Monumenta Germaniae Historica: Epistolae*
MGH Epp. sel.	*Monumenta Germaniae Historica: Epistolae Selectae*
MGH Font.	*Monumenta Germaniae Historica: Fontes Iuris Germanici Antiqui in usum scholarum separatim editi*
MGH LdL	*Monumenta Germaniae Historica: Libelli de Lite Imperatorum et Pontificum*

MGH Poet. *Monumenta Germaniae Historica: Poetae Latini Medii Aevi*
MGH SS *Monumenta Germaniae Historica: Scriptores*
MGH SSRG *Monumenta Germaniae Historica: Scriptores Rerum Germanicarum in usum scholarum separatim editi*
MGH SSRG n.s. *Monumenta Germaniae Historica: Scriptores Rerum Germanicarum, nova series*
PL *Patrologiae Cursus Completus: Series Latina* (ed. Migne)
Potthast *Regesta Pontificum Romanorum inde ab Anno post Christum Natum MCXCVIII ad Annum MCCCIV* (Potthast)
Rolls *Rerum Britannicarum Medii Aevi Scriptores*
WH *Walther-Holtzmann-Kartei* (Holtzmann)
ZPUU *Papsturkunden, 896–1046* (ed. Zimmermann)
* A papal letter no longer extant (*deperditum*)
† A papal letter considered inauthentic (*spurium*)

Citations of Classical Medieval Canonical Sources

C. *causa* (case) in the second part of the *Decretum*
c. *capitulum* (chapter) in the *Decretum*
1Comp, 2Comp, etc. *Compilationes Antiquae* (*Prima, Secunda*, etc.)
D. *distinctio* (distinction) in the first and third parts of the *Decretum*
d.a.c. *dictum* (comment) of Gratian before a chapter in the *Decretum*
De cons. *De consecratione*, the third part of the *Decretum*
d.p.c. *dictum* (comment) of Gratian after a chapter in the *Decretum*
q. *quaestio* (question) in the second part of the *Decretum*
X *Liber Extra* or the *Decretals of Gregory IX*

Decretist and Decretalist Works

Animal *Animal est substantia* (ed. Coppens)
BernParm *Corpus Iuris Canonici*, vol. 2, *Decretales Domini Gregorii Papae IX* (*Glossa Ordinaria in Decretales*)
Casus Fuldenses *Constitutiones Concilii Quarti Lateranensis una cum Commentariis Glossatorum* (ed. García y García)
Casus Parisienses *Constitutiones Concilii Quarti Lateranensis una cum Commentariis Glossatorum* (ed. García y García)

Abbreviations   xiii

Elegantius	Summa *"Elegantius in iure divino" seu Coloniensis* (ed. Fransen and Kuttner)
Glossa Ordinaria	*Corpus Iuris Canonici*, vol. 1, *Decretum Gratiani (Glossa Ordinaria in Decretum)*
Honorius	*Magistri Honorii Summa "De iure canonico tractaturus"* (ed. Weigand et al.)
HostAurea	*Henrici de Segusio Cardinalis Hostiensis Summa Aurea*
HostLect	*Lectura sive Apparatus Domini Hostiensis super Quinque Libris Decretalium*
Huguccio	Lons-Le-Saunier, Archive Dép., Ms. 12 F.16
JohTeut	*Johannis Teutonici Apparatus Glossarum in Compilationem Tertiam* (ed. Pennington)
Magister	*The Summa Parisiensis on the Decretum Gratiani* (ed. McLaughlin)
Omnibonus	Cologne, Stadtarchiv, Ms. W folio 248
Omnis	Summa *"Omnis qui iuste iudicat" sive Lipsiensis* (ed. Weigand et al.)
Paucapalea	*Die Summa [des Paucapalea] über das Decretum Gratiani* (ed. Schulte)
Roland	*Summa Magistri Rolandi* (ed. Thaner)
Rufinus	*Summa Decretorum* (ed. Singer)
SimonBis	*Summa in Decretum Simonis Bisinianensis* (ed. Aimone)
Sinibaldo	*Commentaria Innocentii Quarti Pontificis Maximi super Libros Quinque Decretalium*
StephTourn	*Stephan von Doornick (Étienne de Tournai, Stephanus Tornacensis): Die Summa über das Decretum Gratiani* (ed. Schulte)

Introduction

When Pope Symmachus wrote to Bishop Caesarius of Arles in 513, expounding certain points that he wished his vicar to promulgate throughout Gaul, he also allowed him a rare privilege. After closing the letter, as if belatedly inspired, he added a brief line in which he bestowed "the faculty of using the pallium."[1] This honorific gesture was the first extant papal grant (however informal) of that ecclesiastical vestment in the Western church. Over half a millennium later, in 1081, Pope Gregory VII sent a blistering letter to William of Rouen, chastising him for failing to request the pallium from the apostolic see in accord with custom and canon law. He extolled the vestment as "the very splendid insigne of your dignity" and "the supplement of your honor." He threatened the archbishop with a severe judgment if he continued to disobey, and even forbade him to perform ordinations and consecrations until he had gained the pallium.[2] What had happened in the intervening centuries? The

---

1. Philippus Jaffé, *Regesta Pontificum Romanorum ab Condita Ecclesia ad Annum post Christum Natum MCXCVIII*, ed. Gulielmus Wattenbach, S. Loewenfeld, F. Kaltenbrunner, and P. Ewald, 2nd rev. ed., vol. 1 (Leipzig: Veit, 1885; reprinted in Graz: Akademische Druck- und Verlagsanstalt, 1956), no. 764 [hereafter "JK," "JE," or "JL"; in this case, "JK"], *Monumenta Germaniae Historica: Epistolae* (Berlin: Weidmann, etc., 1891–), 3:40 [hereafter "MGH Epp."].

2. JL 5204, Leo Santifaller, ed., *Quellen und Forschungen zum Urkunden- und Kanz-*

2   Introduction

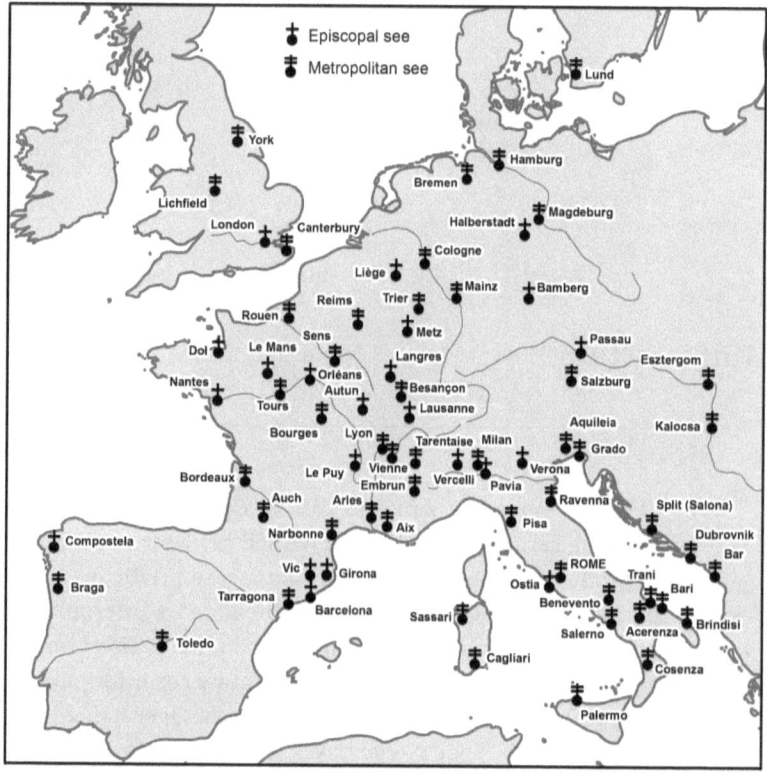

Figure 1. Sees of Western bishops who claimed or received the pallium from the eighth to the early twelfth century. Map drawn by Tristan Nelson.

change was stunning: the vestment had gone from afterthought to crux, from gift to requirement, from honorary adornment to official badge, from sign of friendship to means of control. Along with this transformation, the papacy itself had been transformed, and the pallium was instrumental in that evolution.

These are only two of a myriad references to the pallium in texts from the Middle Ages. In this simple material object an array of litur-

---

leiwesen Papst Gregors VII, part 1, Studi e testi 190 (Vatican City: Biblioteca Apostolica Vaticana, 1957), 223.

Introduction   3

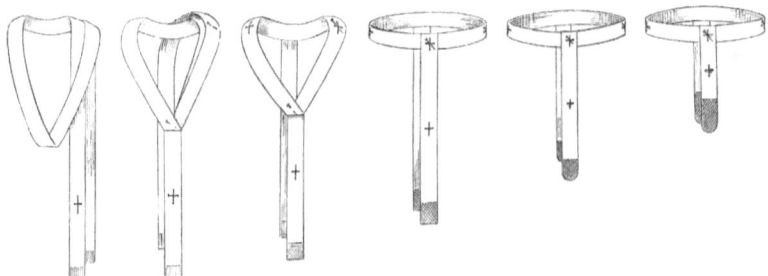

Figure 2. The development of the form of the pallium. Reprinted from Joseph Braun, *Die liturgische Gewandung im Occident und Orient: nach Ursprung und Entwicklung, Verwendung und Symbolik* (Freiburg: Herder, 1907), 649.

gical usages, canonical requirements, political relationships, and religious interpretations intersected. As the medieval popes got into the habit of distributing this garment to chosen bishops throughout the West, they gradually realized that something more than a woolen stole was at stake: it functioned as an instrument of papal influence.[3] Through adroit manipulation of its use and understanding, the papacy harnessed this customary gift as a means of exercising control over far-flung bishops and subordinating them more effectively to Rome. The right to wear the pallium became a prerogative through which the papacy shared authority with other prelates—and simultaneously wielded authority over them. Following the story of this artifact sheds light on papal history, and also on the ways in which medieval people structured their society, exercised power, and communicated ideas and values.

The pallium (or pall) was a band of white wool that encircled the shoulders and fell in two strips on the chest and back.[4] It was usu-

---

3. Maureen C. Miller cites the pallium alongside the maniple, the dalmatic, and the sandals as distinctively Roman garb shared with others as a privilege by the popes, who sought to control their use and through them forge relationships and facilitate collaboration. See her *Clothing the Clergy: Virtue and Power in Medieval Europe, c. 800–1200* (Ithaca, N.Y.: Cornell University Press, 2014), 26–29.

4. The custom of weaving pallia from the wool of lambs blessed on St. Agnes's day (January 21) at the church of Sant'Agnese fuori le mura in Rome, which is still the case today, cannot be traced back before the fifteenth century. See Amato Pietro

4   Introduction

ally embroidered with crosses and affixed with three pins. Its form underwent gradual change over the centuries.[5] The loop (*circulus*) was the segment that surrounded the shoulders, originally falling from shoulder to shoulder in loose arcs to both front and back, later woven in a tighter, more circular form. The strips (*lineae* or *vittae*) were originally the segments that hung in front and back from the left shoulder (where the band crossed itself) almost to the ground, often ending in fringes. Later, each was drawn over to the lowest point of the loop and attached there, at the center of breast and back. The pins (*acus* or *spinulae*) at first held the garb together, two at the meeting points on breast and back, where the strips were attached to the loop, and the third on the left shoulder, where the strips began. Even after the pallium was woven as a single piece, in a Y-shape or T-shape, the pins were retained as decorations, sometimes passing through eyelets attached to the vestment beneath to keep the garment in place. The crosses (*cruces*), which seem to have varied in number (usually two, four, or six), color (usually black, purple, or red), and placement (at least at the ends of the strips), were additional decorations. Although images of the pallium survive from the Middle Ages in works of art, few physical pallia remain, since by custom they were buried with their wearers.[6]

Frutaz, *Il complesso monumentale di Sant'Agnese*, 6th ed. (Rome: Nova Officina Poligrafica Laziale, 2001), 32–37.

5. See Ch. Rohault de Fleury, continued by his son, *La messe: études archéologiques sur ses monuments* (Paris: Morel, 1889), 8:47–68, with plates 630–37; Herbert Thurston, "The Pallium," in *Historical Papers*, ed. John Morris (London: Catholic Truth Society, 1892), 1:97–100; and Joseph Braun, *Die liturgische Gewandung im Occident und Orient: nach Ursprung und Entwicklung, Verwendung und Symbolik* (Freiburg: Herder, 1907), 642–51, with fig. 297 on 649. The Latin terms above are taken from medieval liturgical commentators.

6. Among the handful extant from the premodern era, the best preserved are two from Arles, dating to late antiquity; two from Cologne, belonging to the eleventh-century archbishops Heribert and Anno II; and two from the thirteenth century, buried with Rodrigo Jiménez de Rada of Toledo and Pope Boniface VIII. See Braun, *Liturgische Gewandung*, 643; Félix J. Martínez Llorente, "El palio: consideraciones histórico-canónicas en torno a un emblema pontificio," *Anales Melitenses* 1 (2004): 426n136; and Miller, *Clothing the Clergy*, 106–8. Adam of Bremen reported that the tomb of Hoger of Hamburg, who had died in 915, was opened around 1035, and nothing was found but his pillow and his pallium's crosses; see *Gesta Hammaburgensis Ecclesiae Pontificum*, in *Monumenta Germaniae Historica: Scriptores Rerum Germanicarum*

An article of religious attire in the Latin church since the fourth or fifth century, the pallium was used as a liturgical vestment and a papal insigne. Over the next millennium it grew in prominence as popes began to bestow it regularly on other bishops as a mark of distinction and a sign of their bond to the Roman church. In a culture that often understood symbols as both signifying realities and bringing them about—a concept most clearly seen in the sacraments—the pallium both reflected and created status and authority for Christendom's chief shepherds. The vestment was mentioned in sources of nearly every genre, period, and region in the medieval West, for by its zenith in the central Middle Ages, it touched on many overlapping areas of medieval life and thought. It was the subject of documents, such as petitions for and grants of the privilege of wearing it. It carried juridical effects, such as the rights to consecrate bishops and convoke synods. It became a tool in power relations among popes, kings, and bishops, all of whom used it to further their interests. It was seen as a token of holiness, laid upon Peter's tomb before its conferral and offering a measure of his sacred prestige. It could be worn only in church, during the Mass, on specific days and within a given jurisdiction. And it was charged with value and meaning, witnessed by the many moralistic and figurative explanations applied to it. This study thus examines the medieval pallium from a number of interconnecting standpoints. By focusing on the papacy as the primary thread in the story, it aims to discover what bound these elements together into an effective instrument of papal power. But by approaching the subject as a many-sided cultural reality, it also seeks to determine exactly how this subtle tool worked.[7]

---

in usum scholarum separatim editi (Hannover: Hahn, etc., 1841–), 2:53–54 [hereafter "MGH SSRG"]. These objects must have been made of a material more resistant to decay than the pallium's wool. But he said nothing about the pins, which may have been saved for Hoger's successors (especially if they were set with precious stones, as was true in the high Middle Ages).

7. Scholars have long approached gift-giving as a "total social phenomenon," with many aspects and multiple meanings affecting society as a whole. Only a holistic approach can attempt to grasp the complementarity of these factors. See Arnoud-Jan A. Bijsterveld, Do ut des: *Gift Giving,* Memoria, *and Conflict Management in the Medieval Low Countries,* Middeleeuwse studies en bronnen 104 (Hilversum: Verloren, 2007), 22, 29, 53.

The beginnings of the pallium are lost in obscurity, but various theories have provided fodder for scholarly debates.[8] Some theories are no longer seriously entertained.[9] A connection to the high priestly vestments designed for Aaron in the Old Testament may be attributed to the typological mindset of medieval liturgists, who approached the question more from a theological than a historical viewpoint.[10] A derivation from a mantle worn by Peter and passed down to his successors, for which other garments were substituted over time, may have arisen from a misunderstanding of the custom of laying pallia on Peter's tomb, so that they were said to be "taken from the body of blessed Peter." Hypotheses that the pallium was a rearranged version of some sacred or everyday apparel involve too many suppositions and rely too heavily on a superficial association with the classical garment of the same name, nor do they adequately account for the fact that it was originally reserved to the pope or worn only by his leave.

Two opposing theories have received the most attention: one defends the papal origin of the pallium, the other the imperial. Joseph Braun presents the former argument.[11] He rejects a secular source because, from the earliest times, the garment was a liturgical vestment, restricted to sacred functions, and an ecclesiastical honor, granted by the popes on their own authority and with Peter's blessing. Rather than a product of a gradual transformation in form and purpose, he proposes that it was created from the start as a specifically papal insigne. The Romans were accustomed to using sashes to distinguish persons of high standing. In an age when liturgical vestments did not yet differ from ordinary clothes, and Christians were no longer persecuted, such garb for the chief Western bishop may have seemed appropriate. Perhaps the Eastern version of the pallium, the *omophorion*, similar in form and use, influenced the adoption

---

8. On the origins of liturgical vestments generally, see Miller, *Clothing the Clergy*, 13–23.

9. See Braun, *Liturgische Gewandung*, 653–61.

10. See Johan Chydenius, *Medieval Institutions and the Old Testament*, Societas Scientiarum Fennica: Commentationes Humanarum Litterarum 37.2 (Helsinki: Helsingfors, 1965).

11. See Braun, *Liturgische Gewandung*, 652–53, 661–64.

of this Roman attire.¹² Or perhaps the church copied a kind of civil distinction for its own use.

In contrast, supporters of an imperial source, among them Louis Duchesne, hold that the Roman emperor originally granted the pallium to the bishop of Rome.¹³ It was, in their view, an ornamental insigne, perhaps a refashioned remnant of the toga, which became part of the costume of imperial officials. Indeed, in a law of 382, Emperor Theodosius I allowed certain functionaries the privilege of wearing *pallia discolora* upon their outer clothes.¹⁴ Consular diptychs offered examples of a kind of sash resembling the pallium, which in its most ornate form became the lorum sported by Byzantine emperors.¹⁵ Though an eighth-century Roman forgery, the Donation of Constantine may have preserved an echo of the imperial origin of the papal insignia when it included the lorum among those prerogatives.¹⁶ The tradition of Ravenna, in addition, maintained that its bishop had received the pallium from the emperor rather than the pope on several occasions.¹⁷ Also, during the sixth century the popes sought imperial approval for, or at least collaboration in, several pallium grants.¹⁸

12. See ibid., 664–74.
13. See L. Duchesne, *Origines du culte chrétien: étude sur la liturgie latine avant Charlemagne*, 5th ed. (Paris: de Boccard, 1925), 404–10.
14. See Joseph Wilpert, "Das 'Pallium discolor' der 'Officiales' im Kleidergesetz vom Jahre 382," *Bessarione*, ser. 2, 9 (1905): 215–18.
15. See Richard Delbrueck, *Die Consulardiptychen und verwandte Denkmäler*, Studien zur spätantiken Kunstgeschichte 2 (Berlin: de Gruyter, 1929), 43–66, and Percy Ernst Schramm, "Von der Trabea triumphalis des römischen Kaisers über das byzantinische Lorum zur Stola der abendländischen Herrscher: ein Beispiel für den Wandel von Form und Bedeutung im Laufe der Jahrhunderte und bei der Übertragung von einem Land in das andere," in *Herrschaftszeichen und Staatssymbolik: Beiträge zu ihrer Geschichte vom dritten bis zum sechszehnten Jahrhundert*, ed. Percy Ernst Schramm, Monumenta Germaniae Historica Schriften 13 (Stuttgart: Hiersemann, 1954), 1:26–28.
16. *Monumenta Germaniae Historica: Fontes Iuris Germanici Antiqui in usum scholarum separatim editi* (Hannover: Hahn, etc., 1869–), 10:87 [hereafter "MGH Font."].
17. Agnellus of Ravenna, *Liber Pontificalis Ecclesiae Ravennatis*, in Claudia Nauerth, ed., based on the edition of O. Holder-Egger, *Agnellus von Ravenna: Bischofsbuch*, Fontes Christiani 21 (Freiburg: Herder, 1996), 206, 302, 412. Cf. John Albert Eidenschink, *The Election of Bishops in the Letters of Gregory the Great: With an Appendix on the Pallium*, The Catholic University of America Canon Law Studies 215 (Washington, D.C.: The Catholic University of America Press, 1945), 110–14, 123–25.
18. Cf. the counterarguments of Braun, *Liturgische Gewandung*, 634–39, and Odilo Engels, "Der Pontifikatsantritt und seine Zeichen," in *Segni e riti nella chiesa altome-*

8   Introduction

Theodor Klauser has breathed fresh life into the imperial theory by pointing out that Christian bishops were incorporated into the structures of the late Roman Empire, with positions of civil rank and responsibility.[19] Naturally, they too would have merited the honorific rights and specific insignia enjoyed by their secular counterparts, to whom they were assimilated. In the strict imperial hierarchy of the day, each grade of ecclesiastical official received its identifying sash, which gave rise not only to the pallium but also to the stoles of priests and deacons. But how these garments became liturgical vestments, with their worldly roots soon forgotten, remains murky. In the end, most scholars view the secular parallels of the pallium as too striking to be coincidental. Bernhard Schimmelpfennig sums up recent opinion when he posits that either the emperor ceded the insigne to the pope as a mark of honor, or the pope usurped it when imperial influence over Rome receded, probably during the fifth century.[20]

It was not until the early sixth century that extant textual testimonies to the pallium began to appear.[21] The biography of Pope Mark (336) in the *Liber Pontificalis* claimed that he had permitted the suburbicarian bishop of Ostia to wear it, in view of his right to consecrate the bishop of Rome.[22] This source often attributed later practices to early popes in a bid to increase these practices' authority, but this statement would not have been believable if the pallium's use had been a recent innovation. It was thus evidence that it had

---

dievale occidentale, Settimane di studio del Centro italiano di studi sull'alto medioevo 33 (Spoleto: Sede del Centro, 1987), 2:740–44.

19. See Theodor Klauser, *Der Ursprung der bischöflichen Insignien und Ehrenrechte*, Bonner akademische Reden 1 (Krefeld: Scherpe, 1948).

20. See Bernhard Schimmelpfennig, "Vestments, Pope's Liturgical: Pallium," in *The Papacy: An Encyclopedia*, ed. Philippe Levillain (New York: Routledge, 2002), 3:1607.

21. See José María Martí Bonet, *El palio: insignia pastoral de los papas y arzobispos* (Madrid: Biblioteca de Autores Cristianos, 2008), 12–18. This book is a slightly revised and expanded version of Martí, *Roma y las iglesias particulares en la concesión del palio a los obispos y arzobispos de occidente, año 513–1143*, Colectánea San Paciano 21 (Barcelona: Herder, 1976).

22. Louis Duchesne, ed., *Le Liber pontificalis*, Bibliothèque des écoles françaises d'Athènes et de Rome, ser. 2, 3 (Paris: Thorin, 1886), 1:202.

been worn in Rome as soon as the early fifth century, perhaps not too long after the empire came to accept Christianity. It also seemed clear that the pallium became the particular insigne of the papal office. When Pope Felix IV lay dying in 530, he attempted to designate his successor, Boniface II, by handing him his pallium—to the outrage of the senate.[23] And when Pope Silverius was deposed by the Byzantine general Belisarius in 537, he was stripped of his pallium and clothed in a monk's habit.[24]

The first known pallium grants also hailed from the sixth century. On four occasions popes offered the vestment to bishops of Arles.[25] At first it may have been a special favor, reflecting intimate ties to the Roman church, but soon it was habitually requested and bestowed because of these bishops' role as papal vicars in Gaul. Invoking a longstanding custom, Pope John III conferred the pallium on Peter of Ravenna in 569.[26] Since this city was the Byzantine exarch's seat, its bishops probably wished to imitate Eastern prelates who wore the *omophorion*. As former suffragans of Rome, they were still ordained by the pope, who retained some sway over them, and so they looked to him for this privilege.[27] There was even evidence at this time of a suspension of the vestment's use. Pope Pelagius I instructed his representative in Sicily to withdraw the prerogative from Secundus of Taormina in 559, due to his neglect of the duties of his office.[28] Sicilian bishops, who were Roman suffragans, were often administrators

---

23. To the Roman clergy and people, JK —, Adalbert Hamman, ed., *Patrologiae Cursus Completus: Series Latina, Supplementum* (Paris: Garnier, 1958–74), 3:1280–81. Felix asked Boniface to return his pallium if he recovered, but he perished.

24. Duchesne, *Liber pontificalis*, 1:293.

25. Symmachus to Caesarius in 513, JK 764, MGH Epp. 3:37–40 (cf. JK *766); Vigilius to Auxanius in 545, JK 913, MGH Epp. 3:60–62; Vigilius to Aurelian in 546, JK 918, MGH Epp. 3:64–66; and Pelagius I to Sapaudus in 557, JK 944, Pius M. Gassó and Columba M. Batlle, eds., *Pelagii I Papae: Epistulae quae Supersunt (556–561)*, Scripta et Documenta 8 (Montserrat: Abbatia Montisserrati, 1956), 14–17 (cf. JK 945).

26. JK 1041, *Italia Pontificia*, Regesta Pontificum Romanorum (Berlin and Zurich: Weidmann, 1906–75), 5:23 no. 22 [hereafter "IP"], *Corpus Christianorum: Series Latina* (Turnhout: Brepols, 1953–), 140A:1100 [hereafter "CCSL"].

27. See 69n148 below.

28. To John the *defensor*, JK 1000, IP 10:194 no. 1, Gassó and Batlle, *Epistulae*, 114–15.

10   Introduction

of the Roman church's property on the island, and so remained under close papal oversight. They too may have been influenced by the use of the *omophorion* in the nearby East.

Thanks to his papal register's survival, but also to the creative activity of his pivotal pontificate, surviving evidence of the pallium mushrooms under Pope Gregory the Great at the turn of the seventh century.[29] Gregory made no fewer than fourteen pallium grants. He endowed prelates in positions similar to those just surveyed: the bishop of Arles, two bishops of Ravenna, and the Sicilian bishops of Messina, Syracuse, and Palermo.[30] But he also palliated another Italian bishop (of Milan, similar in civil and ecclesiastical importance to Ravenna) and bishops in Eastern areas under Roman jurisdiction, such as Illyricum (Prima Justiniana and Salona) and Greece (Corinth and Nicopolis).[31] The last four were metropolitans and, in Eastern fashion, may have looked to their patriarch for their insignia; Prima Justiniana was also a papal vicariate.

Finally, there were three special cases. Secular rulers influenced two of them. Gregory decorated Leander of Seville with the pallium in 599, partly to honor his friend and partly to favor the Visigothic King Reccared after his conversion to the catholic faith.[32] In the

---

29. See Eidenschink, *Election*, 109–43; Martí, *Palio*, 19–46; Alan Thacker, "Gallic or Greek? Archbishops in England from Theodore to Ecgberht," in *Frankland: The Franks and the World of Early Medieval Europe*, ed. Paul Fouracre and David Ganz (Manchester: Manchester University Press, 2008), 52–55; and Karine Merlin, "La concession du pallium dans la correspondance de Grégoire le Grand," in *Correspondances: documents pour l'histoire de l'antiquité tardive*, ed. Roland Delmaire, Janine Desmulliez, and Pierre-Louis Gatier, Collection de la maison de l'orient et de la Méditerranée 40, série littéraire et philosophique 13 (Lyon: Maison de l'Orient et de la Méditerranée, 2009), 349–57.

30. Virgilius of Arles in 595, JE 1374, CCSL 140:354–357; John of Ravenna in 594, JE 1326, IP 5:25 no. 31, CCSL 140:277; Marinian of Ravenna in 595, JE 1377, IP 5:26–27 no. 38, CCSL 140:363; Donus of Messina in 595, JE 1388, IP 10:335 no. 8, CCSL 140:377; John of Syracuse in 595, JE 1397, IP 10:306–7 no. 24, CCSL 140:388; and John of Palermo in 603, JE 1905, IP 10:227 no. 14, CCSL 140A:1041.

31. Constantius of Milan in 593, JE 1272, IP 6.1:33 no. 25, CCSL 140:217–18; John of Prima Justiniana in 594, JE 1164, CCSL 140:282–83; Maximus of Salona in 599, JE 1761, CCSL 140A:816–17; John of Corinth in 595, JE 1378, CCSL 140:364–66; and Andrew of Nicopolis in 595, JE 1387, CCSL 140:375–76. The last was a notice to the Epiran bishops; the actual grant has been lost.

32. JE 1756, CCSL 140A:802–5.

Introduction   11

same year, after some hesitations, the pope acceded to the Frankish Queen Brunhild's request to give the vestment to her favorite, Syagrius of Autun, especially since that bishop was furthering papal projects in Gaul and England.[33] Most important was Gregory's grant to his missionary to England, Augustine of Canterbury, in 601, as he was establishing the English church.[34] The pope required Augustine's successors, as well as the future bishops of York, each to seek the pallium from the apostolic see, and he attached to the vestment the rank of metropolitan and the power to consecrate suffragan bishops. It would be a model of far-reaching influence.

Other texts in Gregory's register and beyond, as many as twenty-three, mentioned the pallium and provided future canonical collections with relevant material for a variety of situations. A group of contentious letters between Rome and Ravenna dealt with the proper times and places in which the vestment should be worn.[35] A pair of documents relating to Syagrius of Autun offered directives on the procedure and qualifications for obtaining the pallium.[36] A letter that denied the privilege to Desiderius of Vienne demonstrated the necessity of precedent (and the possibility of refusal).[37] Interchanges with Salona depicted the vestment as a sign of communion, to be withdrawn as a punishment or permitted when good relations were restored.[38] The remaining letters were notices concerning the grants

33. JE 1751, CCSL 140A:794–97.
34. JE 1829, CCSL 140A:934–35.
35. To John of Ravenna in 593, JE 1259, IP 5:25 no. 29, CCSL 140:200–203, and again in 594, JE 1330, IP 5:25–26 no. 32, CCSL 140:280–81; and to the papal emissary Castorius in 596, JE 1411, IP 5:74 no. 3, CCSL 140:403–4, and again in 599, JE 1694, IP 5:75 no. 9, CCSL 140A:726–27. There were also copies of John III's grant to Peter of Ravenna in 569 (JK 1041, IP 5:23 no. 22, CCSL 140A:1100) and a letter from John of Ravenna to Gregory after 593 (CCSL 140A:1097–99).
36. To Brunhild in 597, JE 1491, CCSL 140A:518–21; and to Aregius of Gap in 599, JE 1748, CCSL 140A:790–92.
37. In 599, JE 1749, *Gallia Pontificia, Regesta Pontificum Romanorum* (Göttingen: Vandenhoeck and Ruprecht, 1998–), 3.1:81–82 no. 57 [hereafter "GaP"], CCSL 140A:793.
38. To Natalis of Salona in 592, JE 1173, CCSL 140:102–3; to the Dalmatian bishops in 592, JE 1174, CCSL 140:104–5; to the papal emissary Antoninus in 592, JE 1175, CCSL 140:105–7; a notice in the register, CCSL 140A:1096–97; and to Maximus of Salona in 599, JE 1703, CCSL 140A:734.

12 Introduction

discussed above and correspondence discussing Eastern affairs.[39] Finally, in a decree from the Roman synod of 595, Gregory was insistent that no payment should be demanded for the acquisition of the pallium.[40]

The less plentiful evidence of the seventh and early eighth centuries revealed that the popes mostly adhered to the pattern set by their predecessors, especially Gregory.[41] Pope Boniface IV continued the tradition for Arles, although there was no longer any talk of a papal vicariate; in fact, its old rival, Vienne, eventually procured the vestment from Pope Gregory III.[42] Nicopolis resurfaced in 625, when Pope Honorius I refused the pallium until Bishop Hypatius came to Rome and swore that he had not been involved in the death of his predecessor.[43] After Ravenna, ever a thorn in Rome's side, gave up its pretensions to independence, Pope Leo II declared that its bishops would never have to pay to receive their pallia when they came to Rome for ordination.[44] Elsewhere in Italy, Grado and Aquileia, initially claiming the same territory but divided by political, theological, and ecclesiastical allegiances, acquired the vestment in 628 and 723, respectively, forming one more element in their competition.[45]

---

39. To the Illyrian bishops in 594, JE 1165, CCSL 140:276; to Childebert in 595, JE 1376, CCSL 140:360–62; to the Greek bishops in 595, JE 1379, CCSL 140:366–68; to Brunhild in 599, JE 1743, CCSL 140A:772–75; to Reccared in 599, JE 1757, CCSL 140A:805–11; to Augustine of Canterbury in 601, JE 1843, MGH Epp. 2:331–43, at 337; to Anastasius of Antioch in 590, JE 1074, CCSL 140:9–10; and to Sebastian of Risan in 591, JE 1096, CCSL 140:35.

40. MGH Epp. 1:364–65, c. 5 (JE post 1365).

41. See Martí, *Palio*, 63–84.

42. To Florian of Arles in 614, JE 2001, MGH Epp. 3:453–55 (cf. JE 2002); and to Wilchar of Vienne between 731 and 741, mentioned in the *Liber Pontificalis*, in Duchesne, *Liber pontificalis*, 1:421 (JE post 2253). Wilchar may have come from Boniface's circle and represented a first attempt to restore the metropolitan structure of the Frankish church. See Beate Schilling, "Wilchar von Vienne und das Pallium," in *Inquirens Subtilia Diversa*, ed. Horst Kranz and Ludwig Falkenstein (Aachen: Shaker, 2002), 23–30.

43. Transmitted in Deusdedit's canonical collection, JE 2010, Victor Wolf von Glanvell, ed., *Die Kanonessammlung des Kardinals Deusdedit* (Paderborn: Schöningh, 1905; reprinted in Aalen: Scientia, 1967), 137.

44. Duchesne, *Liber pontificalis*, 1:360 (JE *2123, IP 5:34 no. *71). The act implied that Gregory the Great's regulation of 595 had been forgotten or ignored.

45. Honorius I to Primogenius of Grado, JE 2016, IP 7.2:33–34 no. 8, MGH Epp.

Introduction   13

In accord with the Gregorian plan, archbishops in Augustine's see, Canterbury, continued receiving the pallium, although the nascent English church took time to be consolidated; a century passed between York's first and second pallium.⁴⁶ More significant because of their future impact were English missionaries who traveled to the Continent to evangelize the Germanic tribes. Following Gregory the Great's example for England, the popes enhanced their efforts by vesting them with the pallium and granting them the power to erect dioceses: Sergius I did so for Willibrord in 695, and Gregory III for Boniface in 732.⁴⁷ As was true for their English forebears, the right to consecrate bishops accompanied possession of the vestment.

3:694–96; and Gregory II to Serenus of Aquileia, JE 2166, IP 7.2:35 no. 12, MGH Epp. 3:698–99. See 94–95 below. Both continued receiving the pallium in the early eighth century: see Gregory III to Antoninus of Grado in 731, mentioned in the *Chronica de Singulis Patriarchis Novae Aquileiae*, in Giovanni Monticolo, ed., *Cronache veneziane antichissime*, Fonti per la storia d'Italia 9 (Rome: Forzani, 1890), 1:10–11 (JE *2231, IP 7.2:36 no. *16); and Gregory III to Calixtus of Aquileia between 731 and 733, JE 2240, IP 7.2:37–38 no. 19, MGH Epp. 3:707–8.

46. Boniface V to Justus of Canterbury in 624, JE 2006, Arthur West Haddan and William Stubbs, eds., *Councils and Ecclesiastical Documents relating to Great Britain and Ireland* (Oxford: Clarendon, 1871), 3:72–73; Honorius I to Honorius of Canterbury (and Paulinus of York) in 634, JE 2020, Haddan and Stubbs, *Councils*, 3:84–85 (cf. JE 2019); Zachary to Boniface in 748 regarding Theodore of Canterbury, JE 2286, Reinhold Rau, ed., based on the editions of Michael Tangl and Wilhelm Levison, *Briefe des Bonifatius, Willibalds Leben des Bonifatius: nebst einigen zeitgenössischen Dokumenten*, Ausgewählte Quellen zur deutschen Geschichte des Mittelalters 4b (Darmstadt: Wissenschaftliche Buchgesellschaft, 1968), 258; and regarding Egbert of York in the *Versus de Patribus Regibus et Sanctis Euboricensis Ecclesiae*, in Peter Godman, ed., *Alcuin: The Bishops, Kings, and Saints of York*, Oxford Medieval Texts (Oxford: Clarendon, 1982), 100. Other English metropolitans than those attested here probably received the pallium in this period, but later chronicles and interpolated documents were unreliable witnesses (e.g., JE 2133, 2243). See Martí, *Palio*, 47–61, and Joanna Story, "Bede, Willibrord and the Letters of Pope Honorius I on the Genesis of the Archbishopric of York," *English Historical Review* 127 (2012): 783–818. The earliest English metropolitans were not styled "archbishops," but the model of stronger, Eastern-style archiepiscopal authority under Theodore caused the English by the early eighth century—e.g., Bede—to interpret Gregory's plan accordingly (Thacker, "Gallic or Greek," 55–67).

47. Alcuin, *Vita Willibrordi*, in Hans-Joachim Reischmann, ed., based on the edition of W. Levison, *Willibrord, Apostel der Friesen: seine Vita nach Alkuin und Thiofrid* (Sigmaringendorf: Glock und Lutz, 1989), 58, and JE 2239, *Germania Pontificia*, Regesta Pontificum Romanorum (Berlin: Weidmann, and Göttingen: Vandenhoeck and Ruprecht, 1911–), 4:13 no. 24 [hereafter "GP"], Rau, *Briefe*, 96–102. Also, the

In its first three centuries, then, the pallium, which was first and foremost the pope's insigne, was shared with other bishops only sporadically. When it was conferred, it was treated as an honorary distinction, usually because of a close relationship with the Roman church. Bishops allowed to dress as the pope included papal vicars; Roman suffragans, when they enjoyed special positions of responsibility; and subject prelates under the Eastern Empire's influence, perhaps by analogy to the *omophorion*, the relative of the pallium worn by all Eastern bishops. In addition, in the wake of Lombard invasions and ecclesiastical schisms, the popes consolidated their power on the Italian peninsula and linked its chief bishops to Rome through the grant of the pallium. On occasion the vestment was a pawn in relations with secular rulers, or a token of regard for friendship or collaboration with the apostolic see. Many palligers were metropolitans, but not all, and except in England there was no explicit connection between that rank and the garb.[48]

As yet there were only hints that this liturgical ornament, a sign of favor implying intimacy with Peter's successor, would help to transform the Latin church. Gregory the Great took the first step when he tied the pallium into the English church's constitution, and that example spread through English missionaries to the Continent. Various popes encouraged it, for treating these new outposts of Christianity as close dependencies, much like the Italian churches, extended the Roman church's influence. Its general oversight of the West spurred the papacy to a particular care for evangelization. But something crucial occurred in 741: the palliated missionary Boniface, with his English ideas, turned from his foundational activities in Germany to the reform of the older churches in Gaul. In that endeavor the pallium would assume a new and larger role.

Frankish missionary Corbinian supposedly received the pallium from Gregory II (Arbeo of Freising, *Vita Prima Corbiniani*, in MGH SSRG 13:197).

48. *Palliger*, meaning one who wears or is permitted to wear the pallium, was a medieval neologism that seems to have been coined in Hildesheim. See Thangmar of Hildesheim, *Vita Bernwardi*, in *Monumenta Germaniae Historica: Scriptores* (Hannover: Hahn, etc., 1826–), 4:764, 775 [hereafter "MGH SS"]; Wolfherr of Hildesheim, *Vita Godehardi Prior, Posterior*, in MGH SS 11:185, 205; *Annales Hildesheimenses*, in MGH SSRG 8:28; and Annalista Saxo, *Chronicon*, in MGH SS 37:246, 288.

The aim of this study is to map the papacy's exercise of power through the pallium. What did popes hope to achieve with it? Precisely how was it employed to realize those aims? What sort of reception did it enjoy, and what were the consequences? To the extent that it was successful, what made the pallium a suitable instrument? What were its pitfalls? And how did the answers to these questions vary over centuries and circumstances? To examine these issues adequately, the investigation draws on the widest possible range of evidence, from Roman sources and those beyond Rome. It also delves into a multitude of complex political situations and touches, sometimes glancingly, on figures and ideas from a large swath of medieval history. Although it cannot do full justice to these episodes, the endeavor is worthwhile because it puts them all together for the first time and elucidates the larger patterns at work.

This study centers on the Latin church, the patriarchate of the West, in which the pallium was worn by the pope alone *ex officio* and by other bishops to whom he granted the right (usually, but not always, metropolitans with jurisdiction over ecclesiastical provinces). Except in passing, it does not discuss the Eastern *omophorion*, which diverged in meaning from its Western counterpart. Nor does it explore the shadowy evidence in early Western churches of non-Roman "pallia," which had no association with the papacy.[49] The main analysis spans the years 741 to 1119, from the time when Boniface began to reform the Frankish church, and the pallium began

---

49. These garments, of which some evidence exists in early medieval Gaul, Spain, and Africa, may have been lesser liturgical stoles, versions of *omophoria*, or forerunners of the rational. See Braun, *Liturgische Gewandung*, 674–76; Klaus Gamber, "Das Superhumerale der Regensburger Bischöfe in seiner liturgiegeschichtlichen Entwicklung," in his *Ecclesia Reginensis: Studien zur Geschichte und Liturgie der Regensburger Kirche im Mittelalter*, Studia Patristica et Liturgica 8 (Regensburg: Pustet, 1979), 184–93; Helmut Beumann, "Das Rationale der Bischöfe von Halberstadt und seine Folgen," in *Kirche und Reich: Beiträge zur früh- und hochmittelalterlichen Kloster-, Bistums- und Missionsgeschichte*, ed. Irmgard Fees, Bibliotheca Eruditorum 33 (Goldbach: Keip, 2004), 235–38; and Thacker, "Gallic or Greek," 51–52. An oft-cited example is c. 6 of the Council of Mâcon (581/83), which obliged bishops to use the *pallium* when celebrating Mass (CCSL 148A:224). Since it was required for every bishop at every Mass, it was surely not the papally conferred pallium. A ninth- or tenth-century copyist did not understand the difference and substituted "archbishop" for "bishop," to conform the canon to the usage of his day.

to be employed regularly in ecclesiastical government, to the time when the Gregorian revolution was coming to a close, and the pallium helped to foster the emergence of the high medieval papal monarchy. This span is divided into three periods: the Carolingian age, the age of ecclesiastical reform, and the oft-ignored age between the two. These nearly four centuries formed the heyday of the pallium, when it was a significant feature of hierarchical relationships and was exploited by the papacy in ingenious ways to bind local churches to Roman authority. An epilogue examines the impact that the ideas and patterns of behavior developed during this heyday had on the Latin church's legal tradition in the twelfth and thirteenth centuries.

Within these limits, references to the pallium have been gathered from as many written sources as possible.[50] Such references are diverse and plentiful, found in almost every kind of text, including saints' lives, annals and chronicles, royal and episcopal letters, conciliar decrees and canonical collections, polemical and theological treatises, liturgical commentaries and service-books, and hundreds of papal letters.[51] To capture contemporary attitudes accurately, sources from before this era are introduced only when, and in the forms

---

50. In addition to the sacred pallium, *pallium* could refer to a monastic habit, an altar cloth, a tapestry, a quantity of fabric, various kinds of textiles, or a liturgical vestment of another sort, not to mention its use in the Latin Bible, where it usually meant a cloak. See Charles Du Fresne Du Cange, supplemented by Léopold Favre, *Glossarium Mediae et Infimae Latinitatis*, 2nd ed. (Niort: Favre, 1883–87; reprinted in Graz: Akademische Druck- und Verlagsanstalt, 1954), 6:113–19.

51. All translations from primary sources are my own. Canonical collections are titled, dated, and located, and their canons numbered, in accord with Linda Fowler-Magerl, *Clavis Canonum: Selected Canon Law Collections before 1140*, Monumenta Germaniae Historica Hilfsmittel 21 (Hannover: Hahn, 2005). The *Clavis* database provides inscriptions, rubrics, incipits, and explicits for the texts of the many unpublished collections. Papal letters are identified by their entries, whenever present, in JK, JE, and JL; in the IP, GaP, and GP series; and in Karl Augustin Frech, *Papstregesten, 1024–1058*, 2 vols., J. F. Böhmer, Regesta Imperii 3.5.1–2 (Cologne: Böhlau, 2006–11); Klaus Herbers, *Papstregesten, 844–872*, 2 vols., J. F. Böhmer, Regesta Imperii 1.4.2.1–2 (Cologne and Vienna: Böhlau, 1999–2012); Veronika Unger, *Papstregesten, 872–882*, J. F. Böhmer, Regesta Imperii 1.4.3 (Cologne: Böhlau, 2013); and Harald Zimmermann, *Papstregesten, 911–1024*, 2nd ed., J. F. Böhmer, Regesta Imperii 2.5 (Cologne: Böhlau, 1998) [hereafter "BF," "BH," "BU," and "BZ," respectively]. But the texts are taken, whenever possible, from the most recent critical editions, whether or not cited in these *regesta*.

in which, they were repeated by later authors who found them interesting or useful. Thus, for instance, precedents from Gregory the Great's letters are discussed through their occurrence in histories, canonical collections, and John the Deacon's biography of the pope.[52] Those Gregorian letters which did not make it into such works are downplayed, since there is no clear indication of their relevance to later thinkers. Conversely, some events were described in accounts written after the period in which they had occurred. Because the distance between event and account raises questions of reliability, and because a later account reflected the differing biases of its own period, such evidence is generally omitted.

The sources themselves drive this investigation, and the recurring themes within them determine its shape. It is divided into three parts, according to chronology, and subdivided into nine chapters, according to themes; the two chapters of the epilogue treat the themes of the previous chapters as they came to be expressed in high medieval canon law. Because the fundamental approach is thematic, the same sources may be covered from different angles in different chapters within a given period. As a result, episodes are frequently revisited to extract new insights according to the topic being discussed. This method is useful for gaining a more comprehensive, systematic view of a multifaceted phenomenon, as opposed to a catena of case studies, each isolated from its larger context.

Part 1 covers the period 741–882, the heart of the Carolingian era. At this time the basic contours of the papacy's use of the pallium and its understanding by the wider church were established, as it became a regular systematized feature of ecclesiastical relationships. Chapter 1 explores the mechanics of the gift—what conditions the popes placed on the transaction—as they impinged upon the recip-

52. See Detlev Jasper and Horst Fuhrmann, *Papal Letters in the Early Middle Ages* (Washington, D.C.: The Catholic University of America Press, 2001), 70–81. Although Gregory's original register survived at least until the ninth century, it is only when it can be shown to have been used in this period (e.g., by John the Deacon) that it is discussed here. While the register was copied during Hadrian I's pontificate (772–95), within the bounds of this study, a simple copy of most of the register's contents did not reveal the same degree of contemporary relevance or involve the same degree of creativity as the incorporation of specific letters into historiographical or canonical contexts.

ient. Chapter 2 shifts its view to the dynamics of the gift as intended by the donors, with attention to the ecclesiastical and secular relationships affected by the grant. Chapter 3 reveals that the papacy's control during the gift-giving process continued beyond the grant and kept the recipient in a subordinate position. Chapter 4 examines the array of meanings assigned to the gift, which made it desirable and inculcated certain ideals in its recipient.

Part 2 concerns the period 882–1046, a middle stage between the more dramatic changes of two periods of renewal. Yet it was not inert, for it actively preserved and left its own marks on the Carolingian inheritance, sometimes for the better, sometimes for the worse. Chapter 5 describes aspects of the model that began to break down, at times due to papal neglect and mismanagement, which produced ambiguity in the vestment's control. But chapter 6 demonstrates that some popes were also innovative in finding ways to enlarge and adapt its use, in order to exercise more effective influence over its wearers.

Part 3 embraces the period 1046–1119, when the papacy took on the leadership of a movement for church-wide reform. In these years the pallium became a tool in an ambitious endeavor to restructure the values and behavior of Christendom and to subject it firmly to papal oversight, and its use was refined accordingly. Chapter 7 shows the range of reform-oriented purposes to which the vestment was put, and its companion, chapter 8, explains the practices introduced by the reform popes to make it a more useful instrument of control and allegiance. Given the potency now expected of the pallium, chapter 9 probes the conceptual underpinnings of its role, manifested in expressions and ruminations that supported its place in ecclesiastical affairs and advanced the reform in less tangible ways.

Finally, the epilogue encompasses the period ca. 1140 to ca. 1271, when developing law schools and the evolution of the scholastic method made the study of canon law into a science. The compilation of old law, the formation of new law, and subtle, creative efforts to interpret and harmonize the canons consolidated the traditions of the past centuries into a coherent system that defined the role of the pallium in ecclesiastical relationships. The first chapter of the epilogue discusses the appearance of the vestment in Gratian's *Decretum*, the acknowledged textbook of the *ius antiquum*, and in the commentaries of those who studied it. The second chapter of the epilogue, in turn, considers the treatment of the pallium in the decretal collections of the *ius novum*, particularly the *Liber Extra*, and in the works of the commentators who delved into this growing papal law.

This simple woolen band, carefully invested with worth and import, became a subtle but powerful instrument. It heightened Rome's renown, while justifying papal involvement in local churches. It established close connections with key churchmen throughout the provinces, but also subordinated them to the Roman pontiff. It was a gift, but one with strings attached, which helped to build the papally centralized church of the high Middle Ages. This thematic analysis illuminates the mechanics of power relations in this era, and shows that the pallium merits a place alongside the other tools that extended papal oversight. Ultimately, this study is an attempt to understand more deeply how medieval culture expressed beliefs and relationships through customs and artifacts, and an effort to retrieve the aims and attitudes underlying rituals and symbols.[53]

---

53. Miller investigates the import of clerical clothing more generally, and likewise finds that it could forge relationships, express status and holiness, and communicate virtue and power (*Clothing the Clergy*, 2–5). Her focus, however, is on the change (beginning in the mid-ninth century and culminating in the reform era) to an ornate style of vestments, in which the pallium by and large did not participate. Nevertheless, the results she observes from these trends—a stronger association of the garb with the wearer and his holiness, a stricter distinction between dress inside and outside the liturgy, and an increased emphasis on vesting as constitutive in ordination rites (ibid., 12–13, 87)—may have partly been shaped by similar practices characteristic of the pallium.

PART 1

WEAVING THE PATTERN (741–882)

The story of the medieval pallium begins in the Carolingian era. Building on the foundations laid in late antiquity and the precedents forged by Pope Gregory the Great, Western churchmen of the eighth and ninth centuries developed the pallium's role in new and important ways. This period may be bounded at one end in 741, when Pope Zachary ascended Peter's chair and the Anglo-Saxon missionary Boniface turned to the reform of the Frankish church. It was a turning point in the formation of Western Christendom.[1] At the other end lay 882, marking the deaths of two prelates crucial to the pallium's history: Hincmar, archbishop of Reims, whose canonical brilliance and notorious controversies shaped the exercise of metropolitan rights, and John VIII, the last of a line of strong-willed popes who employed the vestment to realize Roman sway over the Latin church. In the creative ferment between these years, the pallium was transformed from a mark of distinction, given to bishops with special ties to the apostolic see, to a badge of office, required of all metropolitans in order to perform their functions.

This startling evolution can best be understood as a series of gradual attempts to increase papal control of the Western hierarchy. Their

---

1. See Theodor Schieffer, *Winfrid-Bonifatius und die christliche Grundlegung Europas* (Freiburg: Herder, 1954), 186.

Figure 3. A bishop being vested with the pallium at a synod (possibly Ebo of Reims at the Council of Ingelheim in 840). From the Utrecht Psalter, ca. 845–55. Utrecht, University Library. Ms. 32, fol. 90v. Used with permission.

implementation can be mapped by examining the demands made of prospective recipients (chapter 1), the relationships effected and affected by conferrals (chapter 2), the constraints imposed on palligers (chapter 3), and the meanings attached to this value-laden vestment (chapter 4). Even so, the story is sometimes wooly. There was no fully coherent or consistent theory that guided either the use of the pallium or the exercise of papal authority in the early Middle Ages. Some visionary popes had theories in mind, but they did not always successfully carry them out. At times ecclesiastical figures other than the popes took the lead in developing pallium practices. Many developments responded to particular events, pressing problems, and political and cultural situations. There was no one papal plan, beyond some general Petrine convictions and the accumulation of precedents in handling the vestment. Nevertheless, the emerging patterns indicated that the popes, however vaguely, fitfully, and instinctively, were realizing the pallium's potential for increasing their influence, for the sake of their pastoral care of the church.

These patterns of usage often had a theme that can aid their understanding. As a papal prerogative shared with certain bishops at the pope's discretion, the pallium was first and foremost a gift.[2] This term, deceptively straightforward to modern ears, described a powerful tool at the donor's disposal. Spurred by the theories of cultural anthropologists, historians over the last half-century have probed the social complexities and consequences of gift-giving.[3] These kinds of transactions in medieval society, such as nobles' donations of land

2. Various authors of this period called it a *munus* or *donum* (Nicholas I to Festinian of Dol in 866, JE 2806, BH 798, MGH Epp. 6:649; Nicholas I to Charles the Bald in 865/66, JE 2810, BH 767, MGH Epp. 6:646; Hadrian II to Charles the Bald in 868, JE 2902, MGH Epp. 6:706; John VIII to Willibert of Cologne in 873, JE 2986, BU 96, MGH Epp. 7:314; and even a forged papal letter by Ado of Vienne, JE †2146, MGH Epp. 3:92).

3. The foundational anthropological study is Marcel Mauss's 1923–24 *Essai sur le don* (*The Gift: The Form and Reason for Exchange in Archaic Societies*, trans. W. D. Halls [London: Routledge, 1990]), whose usefulness is qualified by Patrick J. Geary, "Gift Exchange and Social Science Modeling: The Limitations of a Construct," in *Negotiating the Gift: Pre-Modern Figurations of Exchange*, ed. Gadi Algazi, Valentin Groebner, and Bernhard Jussen, Veröffentlichungen des Max-Planck-Instituts für Geschichte 188 (Göttingen: Vandenhoeck and Ruprecht, 2003), 129–40. Historians began to employ gift-giving theory in their investigations thirty years after Mauss, and the resultant literature since then is vast; Bijsterveld, *Do ut des*, 17–50, provides a helpful overview.

to monastic communities, could create, maintain, or restore relationships. The often enduring bonds that resulted among the parties, driven by overlapping motives (from economic to religious) and serving both social and ideological functions, worked as a mechanism of societal integration.[4] While most scholarly attention has focused on gifts of property, smaller gifts that were economically insignificant could be just as important to social networks. In this period, furthermore, gift-giving was a political phenomenon, often taking public, ceremonial forms, with ramifications for power relations among the parties and for the array of personal alliances that composed public authority.[5] The reciprocity involved in gift-giving—the recipient's obligation to offer a countergift—gave the donor political leverage, even when the reciprocal activity was neither specified nor immediate.[6] Nevertheless, sometimes, as in the case of the pallium, one could never comparably reciprocate, which left the donor in a superior position and the recipient lastingly in his debt.[7]

In recent years historians have deemphasized anthropological theory, which never provided a wholly adequate model, and have concentrated on the meanings and contexts of particular gift-giving practices.[8] At times such transactions had only some of the features associated with gift-giving. Indeed, the "cultural template" of gift-giving could have a range of variations and uses, and could draw on a "repertoire of cultural forms" for perceiving and shaping identities and relationships.[9] As a result, the historian must attend to the "pragmatic rationality of actors," who chose, as their socio-political rela-

---

4. See Bijsterveld, *Do ut des*, 18, 23, 28–29. These bonds ranged from cordial relationships to subordination, as articulated by the disparity of the exchanges; see Patrick J. Geary, "Sacred Commodities: The Circulation of Medieval Relics," in *The Social Life of Things: Commodities in Cultural Perspective*, ed. Arjun Appadurai (Cambridge: Cambridge University Press, 1986), 173.

5. See Florin Curta, "Merovingian and Carolingian Gift-giving," *Speculum* 81 (2006): 677, 698–99.

6. See Timothy Reuter, "Gifts and Simony," in *Medieval Transformations: Texts, Power, and Gifts in Context*, ed. Esther Cohen and Mayke B. de Jong, Cultures, Beliefs and Traditions: Medieval and Early Modern Peoples 11 (Leiden: Brill, 2001), 158.

7. See Curta, "Merovingian and Carolingian Gift-giving," 675–76.

8. See Gadi Algazi, "Introduction: Doing Things with Gifts," in *Negotiating the Gift*, ed. Algazi et al., 9, and Bijsterveld, *Do ut des*, 42, 48.

9. See Algazi, "Introduction," 12, 15.

tions and goals demanded, from among diverse customs, concepts, rules, and rituals as they engaged in gift-giving.[10] When expectations differed from one party to another, the significance of the gift—not always obvious from the transaction itself—had to be negotiated, and so it is accurate to call gifts, and the ties that arose from them, contested constructions.[11] The bestowal of the pallium was a rather rarefied instance of gift-giving in the Middle Ages, and interpreting it as gift-giving cannot fully explain its nuances. But applying this template can help to illuminate how this practice was approached and understood, and how the popes made strategic use of social conventions as they negotiated their role in particular circumstances. In addition, the pallium's centrality to the interactions of key churchmen suggests its usefulness in investigating the exercise, forms, and rationales of power in the medieval church.

While the use of apparel in the display of status and authority is widely acknowledged, few scholars have considered clothing itself as a gift and simultaneously a political instrument. An exception is Stewart Gordon, who traces the history of honorific investiture as a means of personalizing and solidifying relations between superiors and subjects in various cultures.[12] As he demonstrates, robes could be highly visible signs of honor, often previously worn by the potentate himself. Bestowing them was a way to reward and retain loyalty, and they acquired meanings that varied according to the situation and were sometimes challenged. These meanings could define identities, legitimate the donor, and subordinate the recipient. The present study extends this thinking to the medieval church. Indeed, essential to the pallium's use, from papal viewpoints, was not the fact that it was worn, but the fact that it was given.[13]

10. See ibid., 14, and Bijsterveld, *Do ut des*, 54, 56.
11. See Stephen D. White, "The Politics of Exchange: Gifts, Fiefs, and Feudalism," in *Medieval Transformations*, ed. Cohen and de Jong, 185, and Algazi, "Introduction," 10–12.
12. See Stewart Gordon, "A World of Investiture," in *Robes and Honor: The Medieval World of Investiture*, ed. Stewart Gordon (New York: Palgrave Macmillan, 2001), 1–19. The robes Gordon examines were luxury items, but the pallium derived its worth from immaterial factors.
13. Since gift-giving expressed power and prestige, the act was more important than the gift (Bijsterveld, *Do ut des*, 33).

Ideas about gift-giving can thus be used for conceptually organizing the patterns of medieval thought and behavior surrounding the pallium. They offer an interpretive framework for explaining how the popes, implicitly taking advantage of such cultural models, were able to manipulate the vestment to suit the circumstances and accomplish their goals. In the Carolingians they found, for the most part, a receptive audience. Frankish esteem for Rome and Frankish fascination with vestments combined to make Francia and its sphere of influence an ideal venue for these developments.[14] The people of this age have often seemed hidebound by their adherence to tradition, but in reality they drew on their inheritance selectively, in new combinations and contexts, to produce subtle, conservative, but no less creative innovations. Similarly, in this decisive epoch in the pallium's history, which molded the assumptions underlying its use for centuries, the papacy succeeded in refashioning an old tradition and furnishing itself with an instrument of power.

14. See Miller, *Clothing the Clergy*, 31–35.

1

Obtaining the Pallium

Nicholas I was an exacting pope. Regarding the pallium, his expectations were firmly expressed, often in unusual detail. For the bishop of Dol, he laid out specific regulations on how to request, deserve, and receive the pallium.[1] He articulated misgivings about the archbishop of Vienne's orthodoxy and the archbishop of Sens's election when they sought the vestment.[2] And he did not hesitate to threaten prelates, from the Frankish heartland to the northern missions, with removal of the privilege if they wandered from his instructions.[3] His efforts crystallized trends that had been developing for many years, but his forceful statements revealed more clearly than before that the conferral of this gift was a chance not only to show favor, but also to exercise control.

Uncoerced gift-giving places the donor in a position of power over the recipient. A discretionary gift can be put to use to control anoth-

---

1. To Solomon of Brittany in 865, JE 2789, BH 764, MGH Epp. 6:640; and to Festinian of Dol in 866, JE 2806, BH 798, MGH Epp. 6:648.

2. To Ado of Vienne in 861, JE 2693, GaP 3.1:99–100 no. †84b, BH †541, MGH Epp. 6:669; to Egilo of Sens in 865/66, JE 2809, BH 766, MGH Epp. 6:644; and to Charles the Bald in 865/66, JE 2810, BH 767, MGH Epp. 6:645–46.

3. To Ansgar in 864, JE 2759, GP 6:31–32 no. 21, BH 706, Fritz Curschmann, ed., *Die älteren Papsturkunden des Erzbistums Hamburg: eine diplomatische Untersuchung* (Hamburg: Voss, 1909), 23; and to Hincmar of Reims in 866, JE 2823, BH 838, MGH Epp. 6:431.

er's behavior, for by defining the gift's meaning, the donor puts the recipient in his debt. The transaction thus expresses an asymmetrical power relationship that obliges the recipient to conform to the donor's wishes.[4] From this position of power, demands can be made and conditions attached. The donor may establish prerequisites to be met before bestowing the gift. He may deny the gift (conditionally or absolutely) in order to compel or punish certain kinds of behavior. He may use the gift's reception as an opportunity to shape a relationship. The popes of this period took important steps to exploit the grant of the pallium in all three of these manners—through prerequisites, occasional denials, and the act of reception itself.

Prerequisites

As the customary practice evolved, the popes typically demanded the fulfillment of four requirements before they consented to present the pallium to a bishop. The future recipient was expected to submit a personal request, a profession of his faith, testimony to his good character, and evidence of his canonical promotion to office. In this way the popes demonstrated their interest in supplication, orthodoxy, worthiness, and regularity from the bishops they deigned to favor. Pope John VIII's regulations of the 870s, which fixed the petition and profession as serious obligations laid upon all metropolitans, were a key step in implementing this program.

Supplication

In its earliest days the Western pallium was a gift conferred by papal initiative, but the prestige of the vestment soon prompted some bishops, especially those whose predecessors had worn it or whose sees had special ties to the Roman church, to be so bold as to request it from the pope.[5] Pope Gregory the Great encouraged this practice

---

4. See White, "Politics," 178–79, and Curta, "Merovingian and Carolingian Gift-giving," 682, 697–98.
5. Gregory the Great claimed that a preceding request was normative (to Brunhild in 597, JE 1491, CCSL 140A:519); nevertheless, he continued to grant the vestment to some bishops apparently *motu proprio* (Eidenschink, *Election*, 141).

when he bestowed the pallium on Augustine, his missionary to the English. In the accompanying letter, which dealt with the organization of the nascent church, he intended Augustine's successors (meant to be bishops of London) and the bishops of York (the other planned metropolitan see) to receive the pallium from then on.[6] Petitioning popes for pallia thus became a matter of course for English metropolitans, each of whom had to send notification of his consecration to Rome. Drawing on this tradition of his homeland, the missionary Boniface, entrusted with the task of restoring discipline among the bishops of Gaul, attempted to reorganize the Frankish church along similar lines.[7] The Roman provincial structure with *metropolitae* set over *episcopi comprovinciales*, which had fallen into desuetude, was to be restored.[8] These metropolitans were to maintain a link to the papacy, made concrete in their appeal for and recep-

6. In 601, JE 1829, CCSL 140A:935. On Gregory's plan for England and its reshaping under the influence of Theodore of Canterbury, see Thacker, "Gallic or Greek." On the pivotal example of England for the future, see ibid., 67–69, and Wilhelm Levison, *England and the Continent in the Eighth Century* (Oxford: Clarendon, 1946), 18–22.

7. Boniface adopted Gregory as "Norm und Kraftquell" for his reform of the Frankish church, and by 745 he acquired copies of letters from Gregory's register (Schieffer, *Winfrid-Bonifatius*, 204, 232). On the transfer of the English pattern to the Continent by Willibrord and Boniface, see Emile Lesne, *La hiérarchie épiscopale: provinces, métropolitains, primats en Gaule et Germanie depuis la réforme de saint Boniface jusqu'à la mort d'Hincmar, 742–882*, Mémoires et travaux des facultés catholiques de Lille 1 (Lille: Facultés Catholiques, 1905), 30–37; Levison, *England*, 59, 62, 73, 89; Friedrich Kempf, "Primatiale und episkopal-synodale Struktur der Kirche vor der gregorianischen Reform," *Archivum Historiae Pontificiae* 16 (1978): 47–50; J. M. Wallace-Hadrill, *The Frankish Church* (Oxford: Clarendon, 1983), 157; and Story, "Bede," 809–13.

8. In 742 Boniface told Zachary that the Frankish church had not had an archbishop or held a synod for more than eighty years (Rau, *Briefe*, 142). See Lesne, *Hiérarchie*, 8–29, and Matthias Schrör, *Metropolitangewalt und papstgeschichtliche Wende*, Historische Studien 494 (Husum: Matthiesen, 2009), 32–38. On the church's metropolitan constitution, see Lesne, *Hiérarchie*, 1–8; Johanne Heydenreich, *Die Metropolitangewalt der Erzbischöfe von Trier bis auf Baldewin*, Marburger Studien zur älteren deutschen Geschichte 2.5 (Marburg: Elwert, 1938), 1–3; Jean Gaudemet, *L'église dans l'empire romain (IVe–Ve siècles)*, Histoire du droit et des institutions de l'église en occident 3 (Paris: Sirey, 1958), 380–89; Roger E. Reynolds, "The Organisation, Law and Liturgy of the Western Church, 700–900," in *The New Cambridge Medieval History*, ed. Rosamond McKitterick (Cambridge: Cambridge University Press, 1995), 2:587–601; and Schrör, *Metropolitangewalt*, 16–31.

tion of the pallium. Such a link, and such a mark of honor, might increase other bishops' respect for what had become a mostly meaningless rank.[9]

Boniface's intent to establish English-style pallium-wearing metropolitans was evident in his reforming activities of the 740s.[10] At the Council of Soissons (744), at Boniface's prompting, Pippin the Short appointed *archiepiscopi* for Reims and Sens, cities in his territory that had been metropoles since late antiquity.[11] Around the same time Boniface, as papal legate, supported by Pippin and his brother Carloman, asked Pope Zachary to send pallia to these prelates and to the newly appointed archbishop of Rouen.[12] Unfortunately, the transaction did not go smoothly. After Zachary had assented, Boniface altered his original request, without explanation, to a pallium for Rouen alone, much to the pope's "bewilderment and great amazement."[13] Zachary was relying on his legate to reform the church in those regions, and since the pallia apparently had already been sent, he was likely worried that some churchmen had been unsuitably

    9. See Schrör, *Metropolitangewalt*, 39–40.
    10. See Lesne, *Hiérarchie*, 37–50; Levison, *England*, 78–93; Schieffer, *Winfrid-Bonifatius*, 205–22; and Schrör, *Metropolitangewalt*, 45–51.
    11. *Monumenta Germaniae Historica: Concilia* (Hannover: Hahn, etc., 1893–), 2.1:34 [hereafter "MGH Conc."]. On the synod, see Wilfried Hartmann, *Die Synoden der Karolingerzeit im Frankenreich und in Italien* (Paderborn: Schöningh, 1989), 56–59. Heinz Joachim Schüssler suggests that Pippin was imitating Carloman's kingdom (with its two archbishops, Boniface and Grimo of Rouen), rather than attempting a full-scale restoration of the old metropoles. See his "Die fränkische Reichsteilung von Vieux-Poitiers (742) und die Reform der Kirche in den Teilreichen Karlmanns und Pippins: zu den Grenzen der Wirksamkeit des Bonifatius," *Francia* 13 (1985): 94–95.
    12. JE 2270, GP 4:23 no. 55, Rau, *Briefe*, 166; and JE 2271, GP 4:24 no. 58, Rau, *Briefe*, 170. Paul Speck dates these letters to 743, before the Council of Soissons, so that the 744 synodal appointment of Abel and Hartbert was meant to overcome resistance to Boniface's original appointment of them ("Artabasdos, Bonifatius und die drei Pallia," *Zeitschrift für Kirchengeschichte* 96 [1985]: 179–95). Schüssler also places the request for the three pallia in 743 ("Fränkische Reichsteilung," 94). Each of the three cities was listed as *metropolis civitas* in the *Notitia Galliarum*, the catalogue of the provinces and cities of Gaul from the late fourth or early fifth century, which became a paradigm for the medieval ecclesiastical organization of western Europe. The same was true of Cologne, the see initially provided for Boniface himself; see *Monumenta Germaniae Historica: Auctores Antiquissimi* (Berlin: Weidmann, etc., 1877–), 9:585, 588, 590, 595 [hereafter "MGH Auct. ant."].
    13. JE 2271, GP 4:24 no. 58, Rau, *Briefe*, 170.

honored with the vestment. The only extant reply from Boniface, sent in 751, offered this excuse:

> About that which I made known to your Holiness at a time now past, concerning the archbishops and requesting pallia from the Roman church according to the promises of the Franks, I entreat the indulgence of the apostolic see. For they delay and have not fulfilled what they promised, and still it is being postponed and discussed. It is unknown what they wish to accomplish from this. But if it were up to me, the promise [made by the Franks to establish the palliated archbishops] would have been fulfilled.[14]

The details of this snag in Boniface's reorganization of the Frankish church are unclear, but apparently the local powers, whether secular or ecclesiastical, had refused the pallia for Reims and Sens.[15] Zachary's brief response somewhat helplessly offered praise if the Frankish leaders cooperated, and unspecified consequences if they did not.[16] This rough patch in Boniface's relationship with the papacy arose from a *faux pas* connected to the pallium. It may well have led future popes to stress the need for individual petitions directly from the candidates.[17]

Boniface's design for the future of the Frankish church was enun-

---

14. Rau, *Briefe*, 290.

15. Older literature tends to blame the problem of simony in connection to donations for the pallia, discussed in the same correspondence between Boniface and Zachary: e.g., G. Morin, "Le pallium," *Le messager des fidèles (Revue bénédictine)* 6 (1889): 262, and Lesne, *Hiérarchie*, 42–47. More recent scholars point to the resistance of anti-reform bishops such as Milo of Reims/Trier: e.g., Schieffer, *Winfrid-Bonifatius*, 222, 228–29; Jörg Jarnut, "Bonifatius und die fränkischen Reformkonzilien (743–748)," *Zeitschrift der Savigny-Stiftung für Rechtsgeschichte, kanonistische Abteilung* 66 (1979): 8–9; Schüssler, "Fränkische Reichsteilung," 83–84; and Speck, "Artabasdos," 187–89. Josef Semmler believes that Boniface realized, and was hesitant to admit to the pope, that he had illicitly consecrated Abel and Hartbert for already occupied sees ("Bonifatius, die Karolinger und 'die Franken,'" in *Mönchtum, Kirche, Herrschaft, 750–1000*, ed. Dieter R. Bauer, Rudolf Hiestand, Brigitte Kasten, and Sönke Lorenz [Sigmaringen: Thorbecke, 1998], 34). Schrör proposes that Pippin and Carloman found Boniface more useful as a sort of *Hoferzbischof* and sole palliger after Grimo's death (*Metropolitangewalt*, 49–50).

16. JE 2291, GP 4:35–36 no. 88, Rau, *Briefe*, 294. In his *vita* of Boniface in the 1060s, Othlo of St. Emmeram modified part of the letter to place the blame squarely on uncooperative secular rulers (MGH SSRG 57:196).

17. E.g., Nicholas I to Festinian of Dol in 866, JE 2806, BH 798, MGH Epp. 6:648.

ciated most clearly in the reform synod of 747, for which no records survive except an account Boniface sent to Archbishop Cuthbert of Canterbury:

We decreed in our synodal assembly and confessed that we were willing to keep the catholic faith, and unity with and subjection to the Roman church, till the end of our lives; that we were willing to be subject to St. Peter and his vicar, to assemble a synod every year, and (for metropolitans) to seek pallia from that see; and that we desired to canonically follow the instructions of St. Peter in all things.[18]

Such a resolution envisioned a hierarchy closely bound through its *metropolitani* to the apostolic see, a bond expressed in part by a general obligation to request the pallium from the pope. In this way the bishops were put in the humbling position of having to ask for a gift. Boniface's ideal may have set the stage and influenced perceptions, but it remained an ideal, and the provincial reorganization he sought developed only slowly.[19] A universal requirement to seek the pallium would take even longer to come about.

In Charlemagne's court a half-century later, the Englishman Alcuin may well have kept alive the principle of *pallia quaerere*; at least, he was certainly familiar with the practice. He described the embassy sent by Archbishop Eanbald II of York to Rome for the pallium

---

18. Rau, *Briefe*, 240. On the synod, see Hartmann, *Synoden*, 59–62. On its importance as a statement of goals, but with little effect, see Schieffer, *Winfrid-Bonifatius*, 241–43. Schüssler believes that it was not a general synod of Frankish bishops, but only an assembly in Carloman's kingdom, where a more thorough commitment to the metropolitan reform perdured ("Fränkische Reichsteilung," 97). According to Jarnut, there was no separate council in 747, and Boniface's letter to Cuthbert referred instead to the reform councils of 742–44 ("Bonifatius," 16–22).

19. Wallace-Hadrill calls Boniface's conciliar decrees "statements of intent, not of achievement" (*Frankish Church*, 156). On the opposition faced by Boniface and his eventual disappointment, see Lesne, *Hiérarchie*, 50–56, and Schieffer, *Winfrid-Bonifatius*, 226–28, 232–36, 250–55. The Lateran synod of 769, attended by a broad array of Frankish prelates, gave only Wilchar of Sens the title "archbishop of the province of Gaul" and lumped the bishops of other metropoles among the other bishops (Hartmann, *Synoden*, 84); see Lesne, *Hiérarchie*, 57–61. This was probably the same Wilchar who had previously been palliated as archbishop in Vienne (Duchesne, *Liber pontificalis*, 1:421) and now, according to Schilling, was able to continue his work of restoring the Frankish metropolitan structure as archbishop in Sens ("Wilchar," 33–36). It is unknown whether he retained his old pallium or was given a new one.

in 797 as envoys "who came from my country and my city to plead for the dignity of the sacred pallium in the canonical manner and by the apostolic instruction of blessed Gregory, our preacher."[20] Gregory the Great's ordinance for England was well known, but Alcuin also referred to unidentified canons that required or regulated the request. In any case, the provincial restructuring seeded by Boniface bore fruit under Charlemagne. The king adopted Boniface's program and, in the capitulary of Herstal (779), ordered *suffraganei episcopi* to be canonically obedient to their metropolitans.[21] His will, drawn up in 811, specified twenty-one *metropolitanae civitates* in his realm.[22] In the course of his reign, he sought the pallium for several of these metropolitans, including Tilpin of Reims, Ermenbert of Bourges, and, in the newly erected ecclesiastical province of Bavaria, Arno of Salzburg.[23] To these petitions the popes, eager to cooperate with their powerful Frankish ally, responded favorably. For example, Charlemagne told Hadrian I that he "should grant to the aforesaid Bishop Ermenbert the pallium of apostolic authority, adorned with priestly festoons, because the city that is called Bourges seems to be the metropolis in the country of Aquitaine." In reply the pope admitted

20. To Leo III, MGH Epp. 4:184.
21. *Monumenta Germaniae Historica: Capitularia Regum Francorum* (Hannover: Hahn, etc., 1883–), 1:47 (c. 1). On the synod, see Hartmann, *Synoden*, 99–101. On the reestablishment of metropolitans under Charlemagne, see Lesne, *Hiérarchie*, 61–71; Heinrich Büttner, "Mission und Kirchenorganisation des Frankenreiches bis zum Tode Karls des Großen," in *Karl der Große: Lebenswerk und Nachleben*, vol. 1, *Persönlichkeit und Geschichte*, ed. Helmut Beumann (Düsseldorf: Schwann, 1965), 482–86; and Schrör, *Metropolitangewalt*, 52–59.
22. MGH SSRG 25:38–39. The Carolingian metropoles were listed as Rome, Ravenna, Milan, Aquileia, Grado, Cologne, Mainz, Salzburg, Trier, Sens, Besançon, Lyon, Rouen, Reims, Arles, Vienne, Tarentaise, Embrun, Bordeaux, Tours, and Bourges. On Charlemagne's and Louis's archbishops, see Lesne, *Hiérarchie*, 71–86.
23. Cf. Hadrian I to Tilpin ca. 780, JE 2411, GP 4:61 no. 22, Emile Lesne, ed., "La lettre interpolée d'Hadrien I à Tilpin et l'eglise de Reims au IXe siècle," *Le moyen âge* 26 (1913): 349; Hadrian I to Charlemagne between 784 and 791, JE 2475, MGH Epp. 3:628; and Leo III to Charlemagne in 798, JE 2496, GP 1:9 no. 9, Heinz Dopsch, ed., "Papst Leo III. schreibt an König Karl den Großen, daß er in dessen Auftrag den Bischof Arn von Salzburg zum Erzbischof und Metropoliten der bayerischen Kirchenprovinz erhoben und ihm das Pallium verliehen habe (798 April)," in *1200 Jahre Erzbistum Salzburg: Dom und Geschichte*, ed. Johannes Neuhardt (Salzburg: Dom und Metropolitankapitel von Salzburg, 1998), 23.

his uncertainty: "Thus far being ignorant if provinces had already been canonically arranged in those regions, whether by our predecessors or by us, we took care for it to be investigated more precisely," but eventually he appointed him archbishop "as was once the custom" and offered him the pallium.[24] The conferral of the pallium went hand-in-hand with the halting reconstruction of metropolitan authority, a project dear to a king who wished to gain divine favor and unify his realm by reforming and organizing its church.

The popes had at their disposal four formulas for pallium grants. They were found in a formulary known as the *Liber Diurnus*, which probably attained the form in which it is known today during the reign of Charlemagne. Although the extant manuscripts represent private, northern Italian versions of the book, the papal chancery used many of the same formulas in a very similar Roman version, for both the training of notaries and the drafting of documents.[25]

---

24. JE 2475, MGH Epp. 3:628. *Infula* could refer to various types of priestly costume (Du Cange, *Glossarium*, 4:358–59, and Braun, *Liturgische Gewandung*, 426–28), but its basic meaning was a band of cloth. In classical usage it was a "sacred fillet," a woolen band worn "as a sign of religious consecration and of inviolability," or more broadly "an ornament, mark of distinction, badge of honor," even "the insignia of an office" (Charlton T. Lewis and Charles Short, *A Latin Dictionary* [Oxford: Clarendon, 1879], 949). This meaning carried over to the Middle Ages, when the word indicated the "symbol of a dignity in the form of a *ribbon*" (J. F. Niermeyer, completed by C. Van de Kieft, *Mediae Latinitatis Lexicon Minus* [Leiden: Brill, 2001], 535). See Rupert Berger, "Liturgische Gewänder und Insignien," in *Gottesdienst der Kirche: Handbuch der Liturgiewissenschaft*, vol. 3, *Gestalt des Gottesdienstes: sprachliche und nichtsprachliche Ausdrucksformen*, ed. Hans Bernhard Meyer et al. (Regensburg: Pustet, 1987), 341. From these definitions it was a short step to the pallium, and sometimes the words were synonymous; Flodoard of Reims mentioned the "archiepiscopal festoon that is named the pallium" (Philippe Lauer, ed., *Les annales de Flodoard*, Collection de textes pour servir a l'étude et a l'enseignement de l'histoire 39 [Paris: Picard et Fils, 1905], 19). *Infula* occurred frequently in the salutations found in the Bonifacian letter collection, almost always applied to addressees who were palligers; see Rau, *Briefe*, 102, 108, 140, 238, 288, 308, 324, 328, and *Monumenta Germaniae Historica: Epistolae Selectae* (Berlin: Weidmann, etc., 1916–), 1:262 [hereafter "MGH Epp. sel."], with an exception at 266. Occasionally it was used in the plural, perhaps to describe the vestment's two strips. The translation chosen in this study, "festoon," evokes a decorative band, typically suspended in a loop or curve.

25. See Leo Santifaller, *Liber Diurnus: Studien und Forschungen*, ed. Harald Zimmermann, Päpste und Papsttum 10 (Stuttgart: Hiersemann, 1976), and Hans-Henning Kortüm, *Zur päpstlichen Urkundensprache im frühen Mittelalter: die päpstlichen Privilegien, 896–1046*, Beiträge zur Geschichte und Quellenkunde des Mittelalters 17 (Sigmaringen: Thorbecke, 1995), 312–87.

One pallium formula in this book, *Pallii usum*, presumed a preceding request: "The use of the pallium," it began, "you have requested from the apostolic see, as was fitting."²⁶ Submitting a petition was endorsed, and, indeed, reference to it in a formula meant that it was expected. Pope Paschal I used this formula in a pallium grant to Bernard of Vienne in 817, and Pope Eugene II did the same for Adalram of Salzburg in 824. It may therefore be assumed that both archbishops had previously asked for the gift of the pallium.²⁷ Examples of genuine petitions submitted to the apostolic see by the prospective palligers themselves, however, no longer exist. Roman officials may not have regarded such letters as worth saving, once they had accomplished their goal.

It was not until Pope Leo IV in the late 840s that the papacy began to emphasize the petition and to insist that it come from the hopeful recipient himself. In a letter to Lothar I, Leo flouted the imperial will: "You commanded us to furnish Bishop Altheus [of Autun] with a privilege and the pallium. Therefore, we request your Greatness not to be offended about this, because we could not do what we recall was not done by that most holy pope, Gregory, up to these our own times, nor could we change the fixed bounds of the fathers."²⁸ Gregory the Great had indeed been hesitant to grant the pallium to Altheus's predecessor Syagrius of Autun for several reasons, especially that he did not request the favor personally from the pope (the petition came rather from Brunhild, queen of the Franks).²⁹ Perhaps Leo, searching the papal archives for a precedent

26. V47, Hans Foerster, ed., *Liber Diurnus Romanorum Pontificum* (Bern: Francke, 1958), 106, with slight variants C46 on 204 and A41 on 307. Instead of a critical edition, Foerster provides separate transcriptions of the three principal manuscripts of the *Liber Diurnus*, which vary in small ways. Rather than drawing on only one of the manuscripts, the present translations are based on a preliminary edition of all three: those variants are chosen which seem to make the most sense of these sometimes obscure texts.

27. The authenticity of the two privileges (JE 2549, GaP 3.1:96–97 no. 81, MGH Epp. 3:97–98; and JE †2558, GP 1:10 no. 13, Willibald Hauthaler and Franz Martin, eds., *Salzburger Urkundenbuch* [Salzburg: Gesellschaft für Salzburger Landeskunde, 1916], 2:19–20) has been doubted, but they followed the formula closely and are accepted as genuine in GaP and GP.

28. JE 2603, BH 116, MGH Epp. 5:604.

29. To Brunhild in 597, JE 1491, CCSL 140A:519. Despite his hesitations, the pope eventually agreed (to Syagrius in 599, JE 1751, CCSL 140A:794–97).

for conferring the pallium on the bishop of Autun (an unusual candidate, as a non-metropolitan), had come across Gregory's reply to Brunhild and its mention of the "individual petition" or *postulatio* required for "such a great cause." He could well have been impressed by the "old custom" later enshrined in the canonical tradition—that "the honor of the pallium ought not to be given except as the merits of cases demand and to one who vigorously requests it"—enough to withhold the pallium from Altheus and to claim that such had been the unbroken tradition since Gregory's era.[30] That does not seem to have been the case, but more and more it would become so.

Pope Nicholas I, who actively strove to assert papal primacy in the Latin church, took a lively interest in pallium petitions. In 861 he complimented Ado, archbishop of Vienne, for submitting a request: "Complying with the canonical sanction and instruction, you took care to send a letter of your Belovedness."[31] Appealing to unidentified canons, the pope considered this practice legally required. He was not so pleased, however, with the Breton attempt to acquire the pallium for the bishop of Dol in 865.[32] King Solomon's endeavor was fundamentally flawed: "No solemn petition for the sake of such a great dignity seems to have been sent, and no request observed according to a legitimate, suitable procedure."[33] This *ordo* probably involved a request from the bishop of Dol himself. Moreover, skepti-

---

30. Yet Boniface had interceded with the pope for the three pallia only a century before. The specification that the request should be made "vigorously" emphasized that the petition was to be earnest, genuinely precatory, and not *pro forma*.

31. JE 2693, GaP 3.1:99–100 no. †84b, BH †541, MGH Epp. 6:669. The authenticity of this letter has been doubted; GaP classifies it as a forgery meant to bestow a sort of papal vicariate on the archbishops of Vienne and dating after 878. Although it may be interpolated, especially in its last two sentences, its content matches the tenor of other letters of Nicholas, and the reason GaP offers for the proposed date is unconvincing (since the profession of faith was a staple of pallium petitions long before 878). It also seems odd for a forger from Vienne to have invented a problem in Ado's acquisition of the pallium.

32. This move was aimed at the erection of an ecclesiastical province, with its metropolitan see at Dol, independent of the Frankish church. See Julia M. H. Smith, "The 'Archbishopric' of Dol and the Ecclesiastical Politics of Ninth-Century Brittany," in *Religion and National Identity*, ed. Stuart Mews, Studies in Church History 18 (Oxford: Blackwell, 1982), 59–70.

33. Apparently a petition was eventually sent to Rome (cf. Nicholas I to Festinian of Dol in 866, JE 2806, BH 798, MGH Epp. 6:648).

cal of the see's claim to the vestment, the pope sought the backing of precedent: "Let him who longs to be of such great merit before us and desires to acquire such a gift with the Lord's assistance be zealous to send those writings that his predecessors received from the apostolic see at the reception of the pallium. Thus, having diligently inspected the same writings that were given by my predecessors, we too may walk with unobstructed paces in their footsteps."[34] This additional requirement would make certain that the petition arose not from ambition but from tradition. The provision of documented precedents was not a standard part of procuring the pallium, but in dubious situations it could identify traditional metropoles or determine papally approved customs.[35]

Later, in his instructions to King Lothar II in 867—after the archbishops of Trier and Cologne had been deposed in 863 for their approval of Lothar's controversial divorce—Nicholas ordered elections for the vacant sees, the consecration of the elect, and, as a final step, the acquisition of pallia for the prelates: "They should strive to obtain pallia solemnly from us."[36] The use of a word (*contendere*) with overtones of eagerness cautioned against any delay in meeting this obligation, and the word *sollempniter* perhaps referred to the form of the request. Both candidates, not installed until 870, eventually complied. As Pope John VIII wrote in 873, Bertulf of Trier had requested the pallium, and Willibert of Cologne had likewise sent a

---

34. To Solomon of Brittany, JE 2789, BH 764, MGH Epp. 6:640. The bishop dragged his feet, and the precedents he produced could not be verified in the papal *gesta,* i.e., the *Liber Pontificalis* (cf. Nicholas I to Festinian of Dol in 866, JE 2806, BH 798, MGH Epp. 6:649).

35. During the Carolingian ecclesiastical reorganization the popes themselves were sometimes unsure which cities were metropoles (e.g., Hadrian I to Charlemagne between 784 and 791, JE 2475, MGH Epp. 3:628). Probably to avoid competition between the bishops of Arles (who had the pallium) and Vienne, Gregory the Great had used lack of precedent as grounds for denying the pallium to Desiderius of Vienne (in 599, JE 1749, GaP 3.1:81–82 no. 57, CCSL 140A:793).

36. JE 2878, GP 7.1:27–28 no. 44, GP 10.1:34–35 no. 40, BH 855, MGH Epp. 6:334. On Lothar's divorce of his barren wife, Teutberga, and the pope's actions against Trier and Cologne, see Ernst Perels, *Papst Nikolaus I. und Anastasius Bibliothecarius: ein Beitrag zur Geschichte des Papsttums im neunten Jahrhundert* (Berlin: Weidmann, 1920), 53–99, 142–51, and Karl Heidecker, *The Divorce of Lothar II: Christian Marriage and Political Power in the Carolingian World,* trans. Tanis M. Guest (Ithaca, N.Y.: Cornell University Press, 2010).

"letter earnestly requesting the use of the pallium to be bestowed."[37] By this period, seeking the vestment from the apostolic see was a duty imposed on metropolitans.

Why did the simple making of a request assume such significance? As Boniface's synod of 747 hinted, a petition by its nature created a relationship of dependence binding the supplicant to the gift-giver, on whom he relied for the realization of his aspiration.[38] It seems that the popes wished to engender such dependence in the episcopate, for the sake of right order and due respect for the see of Peter. Receiving personal pleas for the gift of the pallium provided one means of doing so. By extension, secular rulers, who were intimately involved in the appointment of bishops in their areas, might supplement—but theoretically could not replace—their bishops' requests. The popes welcomed these gestures of submission as well.

Orthodoxy

A petition was not the only thing required of the would-be recipients of the pallium. The popes were keenly interested in ascertaining the orthodoxy of these key members of the hierarchy, in order to safeguard the purity of the faith and ensure the unity of the church.[39] Rome already had the reputation of a touchstone and

---

37. JE 2982, GP 10.1:37 no. 49, BU 87, MGH Epp. 7:288; and JE 2986, GP 7.1:34 no. 66, BU 96, MGH Epp. 7:314. The use of "earnestly" in the latter may have been meant to correspond to "vigorously" in the Gregorian dictum; or it may have reflected the difficulties of Willibert's quest for the pallium. Although Willibert's petition is not extant, several other parties added their earnest pleas to his: his consecrator, Liudbert of Mainz (MGH Epp. 6:244), his king, Louis the German (MGH Epp. 6:249), and even his deposed predecessor, Gunther of Cologne (MGH Epp. 6:247). The parallel wording in the first two suggests a concerted effort, and Willibert's petition possibly looked similar. It may have been included in the letter introducing his profession, only partially preserved (MGH Epp. 6:255). Dorothee Arnold suggests that Bertulf and Willibert may each have submitted two petitions: a fruitless one to Hadrian II after their election, and another to John VIII after Hadrian's death (*Johannes VIII.: päpstliche Herrschaft in den karolingischen Teilreichen am Ende des 9. Jahrhunderts*, Europäische Hochschulschriften, ser. 23, 797 [Frankfurt: Lang, 2005], 158, 162–63).

38. See Geoffrey Koziol, *Begging Pardon and Favor: Ritual and Political Order in Early Medieval France* (Ithaca, N.Y.: Cornell University Press, 1992), 45.

39. See Theodor Gottlob, *Der kirchliche Amtseid der Bischöfe*, Kanonistische Studien und Texte 9 (Bonn: Röhrscheid, 1936; reprinted in Amsterdam: Schippers, 1963), 26–41.

guardian of correct belief, but now the dialogue initiated by the petition permitted the popes to act as examiners and enforcers, without having to wait for a crisis to do so. As witnessed in two of the formulas for pallium grants in the *Liber Diurnus*, a profession of faith was expected as part of the request. These formulas included clauses meant to be used if the mandatory profession was found lacking in some respect. *Si pastores ovium* averred: "Although you should have explained more extensively the [profession of] faith that you briefly added in your letter, nevertheless we thank our Redeemer because we have learned that it is correct, even in its very brevity."[40] *Officium sacerdotis* put it similarly: "Although you should have explained in detail the faith of your Fraternity in the letter that you sent, nevertheless we rejoice in the Lord because we have learned from the solemn confession of the creed that it is correct."[41] The profession was important enough to warrant a formulaic response, and reproducing a creed was apparently considered insufficient. Worrisomely brief statements of faith, it appears, formed a common problem, and these clauses revealed the exacting approach taken by the papacy to questions of doctrine. As early as the 740s, Pope Zachary highlighted this concern in his reply to Boniface's request for the three pallia: "We have sent [the recipients instructions on] what the custom of the pallium is, and how those who are granted permission to use the pallium ought to explain their faith."[42] Receiving the pallium went hand-in-hand with the obligation *fidem exponere*.

When necessary, this custom could amount to a full doctrinal examination of candidates for high ecclesiastical office. Around 780 Pope Hadrian I wrote to Archbishop Tilpin of Reims and recalled that he had sent him the pallium after a royal envoy had provided "good testimony about your holiness and teaching." Now he instructed Tilpin to examine Lull of Mainz and "investigate his faith and teach-

---

40. V45, Foerster, *Liber Diurnus*, 103, with slight variants C44 on 202 and A39 on 302–3.

41. V46, ibid., 104–5, with slight variants C45 on 203 and A40 on 305.

42. JE 2270, GP 4:23 no. 55, Rau, *Briefe*, 166. The documents sent by Zachary are not extant (JE *2269). A similar juxtaposition of receiving the pallium and professing the faith was enunciated by Boniface's synod of 747 (Boniface to Cuthbert of Canterbury in 747, Rau, *Briefe*, 240).

ing and lifestyle and behavior and life. Thus, if he is fit and worthy to govern the episcopal cathedra, he should send to us through his envoys his catholic and orthodox faith, explained and written and signed by his own hand, along with your letter and testimony.... Then we may send him the pallium according to custom."[43] The pope sent a trusted archbishop, whose pallium was proof of his sound *doctrina*, to test the faith of a fellow prelate and determine his suitability for office. Final judgment, however, was reserved to Rome, where the pope would review Lull's profession before conferring the pallium. This profession, which has been preserved, contained a patchwork of statements from earlier creeds. It then added: "Likewise, in accord with the instruction of his Holiness, I have promised, by oath on the four gospels of Christ, fidelity to that holy church of God over which, with God's assent, the holiness of Pope Hadrian presides."[44] Treating Lull much as his predecessor Boniface had been treated, as a Roman suffragan, the pope had demanded not only a declaration of Lull's beliefs, but also a vow of loyalty to the Roman church. The entire process formed a means by which the distant Roman pontiff exercised doctrinal and disciplinary control over the burgeoning German hierarchy, and Lull submitted to this control.

Subsequent pallium grants according to the formulas *Si pastores ovium* and *Officium sacerdotis* showed that the requirement of a profession of faith persisted. Since Arno of Salzburg was personally present in Rome, a variation in the profession clause in Leo III's grant in 798 specified that the statement had been given orally rather than in writing (yet in brief, so that the pope retained the traditional wish for further detail).[45] Frequently popes chose to omit the clause—in-

---

43. JE 2411, GP 4:61 no. 22, Lesne, "Lettre," 349, 351. The quotation is not part of the interpolated section from the time of Hincmar of Reims.

44. Levison, *England*, 240, and, for the various creeds that composed this profession, 237. Gottlob finds Lull's ready compliance proof that such a procedure imposed on a petitioner was not seen as unusual (*Kirchlicher Amtseid*, 29–30).

45. JE 2498, GP 1:8 no. 7, Heinz Dopsch, ed., "Papst Leo III. verleiht Arn, dem Erzbischof und Metropoliten der bayerischen Kirchenprovinz, das Pallium (798 April 20)," in *1200 Jahre Erzbistum Salzburg*, ed. Neuhardt, 18. Why could the pope not have asked Arno to expand on his words during the oral profession? Maybe the power of precedent was such that parts of the formula were maintained even if inappropriate. Perhaps something similar occurred in Leo's grant to Fortunatus of Grado

cluding Gregory IV for Liudpram of Salzburg (837), Leo IV for Victor of Grado (852), Benedict III for Vitalis of Grado (858), and Nicholas I for Adalwin of Salzburg (860)—presumably because the submitted professions had been found satisfactory.[46] It is unlikely that they had forgotten about the obligation, for sometimes the clause was inserted; for example, in 865 it occurred in Nicholas I's grant to Rimbert of Hamburg, a see in the process of foundation, whose prelate may not have had much guidance in composing a proper profession.[47] The profession made by Hincmar of Reims at his consecration in 845 and then sent to Rome as part of his pallium petition has been preserved and was later used as a formula. It attested to the bishop's adherence to credal teachings and synodal decisions (especially those of the first four ecumenical councils), repudiation of heresies and schisms, and "due subjection and obedience to blessed Peter and his vicar," the pope.[48] Like Lull's profession, this one was more than a testimonial to correct doctrine; it expressly involved submission to papal authority.

Pope Nicholas I, who was so particular about the form of pallium petitions, proved likewise fastidious about the profession of faith. To Archbishop Ado of Vienne in 861 he wrote:

---

in 803: although the pallium was received in person, the reference to the usual written profession, sent by letter, was retained. See JE 2512, IP 7.2:40–41 no. 28, Roberto Cessi, ed., *Documenti relativi alla storia di Venezia anteriori al mille*, Testi e documenti di storia e di letteratura latina medioevale 1 (Padua: Gregoriana, 1940; reprinted in Venice: Deputazione di Storia Patria per le Venezie, 1991), 1:57.

46. JE 2580, GP 1:10 no. 14, Hauthaler and Martin, *Salzburger Urkundenbuch*, 2:27–29; JE 2616, IP 7.2:43 no. 37, BH 253, Curt-Bogislav Graf von Hacke, *Die Palliumverleihungen bis 1143: eine diplomatisch-historische Untersuchung* (Marburg: Elwert, 1898), 148–50 (*pace* Martí, *Palio*, 101); JE 2672, IP 7.2:43 no. 38, BH 419, Hacke, *Palliumverleihungen*, 150–53 (*pace* Martí, *Palio*, 101); and JE 2681, GP 1:11 no. 17, BH 512, Hauthaler and Martin, *Salzburger Urkundenbuch*, 2:35–36. Another explanation, given the recurrence of the two sees, is that a church's previous documents were used as exemplars for further grants; yet such a practice does not imply that the required profession ceased.

47. JE 2798, GP 6:35 no. 26, BH 785, Curschmann, *Ältere Papsturkunden*, 27. See Eric Knibbs, *Ansgar, Rimbert and the Forged Foundations of Hamburg-Bremen* (Farnham: Ashgate, 2011), 179–81.

48. *Monumenta Germaniae Historica: Formulae Merowingici et Karolini Aevi* (Hannover: Hahn, etc., 1886–), 555–56, and MGH Epp. 8.1:1–2. See Gottlob, *Kirchlicher Amtseid*, 31.

Because of [your petition] we have given over our apostolic heart to happiness—although, having read through the same, we were saddened because, observing the four synods, you omitted the fifth and sixth. For we are favorable to you in your petition for the pallium. Nevertheless, for a reason of this sort, your request was not to be fulfilled unless, having reviewed the intent of the composition you sent, we had learned that you were willing in all things to hold what the holy church teaches as dogma. And so we wish and likewise ask your Holiness to send, with all swiftness, [a statement of] how you feel about those fifth and sixth synods.[49]

The pope found a seemingly minor flaw in the archbishop's profession: the first four ecumenical councils had been mentioned, but not the next two, also regarded as authoritative.[50] The petition provided Nicholas with an *occasio* to verify Ado's compliance with the church's teaching, and he would not grant it until a more explicit profession had been sent—more elaborate than the statements exacted from Lull (who mentioned no such councils by name) and Hincmar (who referred only to the first four).

In 864 Nicholas also instructed Ansgar, missionary archbishop to the Danes and Swedes, regarding proper procedure: "We grant you to use the pallium only in the manner of the apostolic see, namely such that your successors ... profess in writing and by oath that they hold the faith with us, and accept the six holy synods, and will venerably observe and carry out the decrees of all the prelates of the Roman see, and the letters that have been brought to them, for all their days."[51] Now the written statement of faith had to be con-

---

49. JE 2693, GaP 3.1:99–100 no. †84b, BH †541, MGH Epp. 6:669.

50. The Councils of Nicaea I (325), Constantinople I (381), Ephesus (431), and Chalcedon (451) had long been recognized as preeminent. By the ninth century many authorities had added the Councils of Constantinople II (553) and III (680–81) to the list. Although the Council of Nicaea II (787), later regarded as the seventh, had already taken place, its reception was slow in the West due to the Carolingian misunderstanding of its decrees. See Francis Dvornik, *The Photian Schism: History and Legend* (Cambridge: Cambridge University Press, 1948), 309–19. According to the papal profession of faith found in the *Liber Diurnus* and continually revised as further ecumenical councils were accepted in Rome, six were recognized in Nicholas's time, and the seventh was probably not officially acknowledged until after 880 (ibid., 442–47). Ado's own chronicle, finished some years after this letter, recognized six councils (J.-P. Migne, ed., *Patrologiae Cursus Completus: Series Latina* [Paris: J.-P. Migne, 1844–65], 123:115) [hereafter "PL"].

51. JE 2759, GP 6:31–32 no. 21, BH 706, Curschmann, *Ältere Papsturkunden*, 23.

firmed by oath and included a promise to adhere to papal dictates. Only under these conditions, which guaranteed orthodoxy in union with and under the guidance of the papacy, would the pallium be given. Similarly, he demanded the bishop of Dol's submission if he desired to gain the pallium, as the pope told the Breton king in 865: "Let him also send ... written proofs of the catholic faith and public promises to observe the decretal sanctions of the cathedra of blessed Peter.... For thus is the authority of the apostolic see and the unopposable observance of the holy Roman church."[52] For Nicholas, the pallium was a tool for, among other things, enforcing orthodoxy and obedience among the senior clergy, in the service of papal primacy.[53]

It fell to Pope John VIII to confirm the prelates chosen to occupy the sees of Trier and Cologne after Nicholas I's depositions in the wake of Lothar II's divorce, and in this he showed himself as firm as his predecessor. In 873 he commanded Bertulf of Trier or his legates to appear before him and bear witness to his rule of faith, among other things; then, after papal approval, he would deserve to receive the pallium.[54] Willibert of Cologne had sent a profession of faith to Hadrian II, and his consecrator, Liudbert of Mainz, had testified to his orthodoxy: "Perfected in the faith of the holy and undivided Trinity, he can instruct those living under him in no small way."[55] Nevertheless, in 873 Hadrian's successor John informed Willibert that he could not

---

Knibbs argues convincingly that, although the letter in its present condition was largely forged by Ansgar's successor Rimbert, these words form most of what remains of a genuine pallium grant to Ansgar (*Ansgar*, 158–63). Indeed, they fit well with the tenor of Nicholas's treatment of the pallium elsewhere.

52. JE 2789, BH 764, MGH Epp. 6:640.

53. On Nicholas's ecclesiology, see Perels, *Papst Nikolaus*; *Histoire de l'église depuis les origines jusqu'a nos jours* (Paris: Bloud and Gay, 1934–64), 6:367–95 [hereafter "HEOJ"]; Karl-Ulrich Betz, *Hinkmar von Reims, Nikolaus I., Pseudo-Isidor: fränkisches Landeskirchentum und römischer Machtanspruch im 9. Jahrhundert* (Bonn: Rheinische Friedrich-Wilhelms-Universität, 1965), esp. 76–90; and Y. M.-J. Congar, *L'ecclésiologie du haut moyen âge: de Saint Grégoire le Grand à la désunion entre Byzance et Rome* (Paris: Cerf, 1968), 206–26.

54. JE 2982, GP 10.1:37 no. 49, BU 87, MGH Epp. 7:288.

55. MGH Epp. 6:244. Willibert's profession is not extant, but the letter introducing it is. There he described himself as "firm in the catholic faith in every way" and committed himself to obey the pope, to whom he professed canonical subjection (MGH Epp. 6:255).

yet confer the pallium on him for two reasons, one of which continued a trend enforced by Nicholas: "We have discovered that the page of your faith contains less than it ought, that is, since you made no mention in it, according to custom, of the holy universal synods, in which the creed of our faith is contained, nor of the decretal constitutions of the Roman pontiffs. You neither fortified it with your own signature nor indicated at all that you sent anyone to confirm it by oath."[56] The archbishop's *fidei pagina,* deficient in both form and content, failed to satisfy what was required by custom. Only through the pallium applicant's duly attested embrace of conciliar creeds and Roman rulings could the pope rest assured in his fidelity.

The Johannine Law

The duties thus far examined—both petition and profession—finally became the object of general papal legislation shortly afterwards. At the Roman synod of 875, Pope John VIII issued a canon, *Quoniam quidam,* meant to expedite episcopal consecrations:

> Since certain metropolitans, refusing to explain their faith to the holy apostolic see according to the old custom, neither request nor receive the use of the pallium, and thereby the consecration of bishops for widowed churches is prolonged (not without danger), it has pleased us [to decree] that whatever metropolitan does not send to explain his faith and receive the pallium from the apostolic see for more than three months from his consecration should lack the dignity entrusted to him. And, after a second and a third admonition, there should be permission for other metropolitans to come to the aid of the widowed churches by ordaining a bishop, with the counsel of the Roman pontiff.[57]

---

56. JE 2986, GP 7.1:34 no. 66, BU 96, MGH Epp. 7:314.

57. MGH Conc. 5:9–10 (c. 2). On the synod, see Hartmann, *Synoden,* 344–46. The date of 875 is hypothetical, but Friedrich Maassen argues for it persuasively ("Eine römische Synode aus der Zeit von 871 bis 878," *Sitzungsberichte der philosophisch-historischen Classe der kaiserlichen Akademie der Wissenschaften* 91 [1878]: 774–80). The pallium rule was issued directly after a canon on the primacy of the Roman church, probably meant to legitimize Charles the Bald's imperial coronation, which occurred just after this synod (Arnold, *Johannes,* 179–81). The juxtaposition of the two canons suggests that the pallium regulation was seen as an expression or exercise of papal primacy. Indeed, John VIII continued the main lines of Nicholas I's ecclesiology (Congar, *L'écclesiologie,* 232–46).

Obtaining the Pallium   45

The law addressed a pastoral problem caused by the apparent reluctance of metropolitans to follow the *prisca consuetudo* and tender their petitions and professions to the pope. Perhaps they found it burdensome or the occasion of unneeded papal interference, or they may have realized the position of dependence in which such a practice placed them. Whatever the case, without the addition of the pallium, they were supposedly unable to ordain bishops for their vacant suffragan sees (*viduatae ecclesiae*), which then remained without shepherds for extended periods. Thus John decided to impose the three-month deadline, after which a metropolitan would lose his office (*commissa sibi dignitas*) if he had not complied.[58]

This canon, which represented the first time that the pallium became an explicit obligation imposed upon all metropolitans, assumed two requirements as non-negotiable: the profession of faith for the pallium, and the pallium for the consecration of bishops. Due to the lack of the profession, it implied, the pallium was withheld, and due to the lack of the pallium, episcopal consecrations were deferred. The ruling was modeled on canon 25 of the Council of Chalcedon (451), which did not mention the pallium but dealt with a similar problem (delays in episcopal ordinations) and responded with a similar measure (a three-month deadline); even the incipits were similar.[59] Consequently, the present canon was seen as an update of the Chalcedonian regulation for a church that had come to associate the pallium with the power to consecrate. The innovative measures of Gregory the Great regarding Augustine of Canterbury and the English church had taken root and shaped ecclesiastical law.

Two years later at the Council of Ravenna (877), John revised this legislation.[60] The new canon, *Quisquis metropolitanus*, reflected

58. Strictly speaking, the deadline applied to the sending of the petition and profession. It did not imply that the envoys would make it to Rome, much less return home with the pallium, so quickly. Knibbs suggests that John was prompted to issue this deadline because of Willibert of Cologne's irregular installation (870) and long delayed reception of the pallium (874) after papal hesitations and royal negotiations (*Ansgar*, 143n11).

59. Chalcedon's exception for "unavoidable necessity" did not occur in this Roman canon but came up at the Council of Ravenna (877).

60. On the synod, see Hartmann, *Synoden*, 347–49. As Maassen observes, there

three changes. The initial explanatory clause, with its elucidation of the motivating problem, was omitted (but the appeal to custom, *priscus mos*, was retained and set later in the text). Next, the exception "with no unavoidable need looming" was inserted. Finally, the clause "such that he withdraws from that episcopal see and lacks all permission to consecrate for as long as he disregards the old custom to explain the faith and seek the pallium" was added to the sanction.[61] Further consideration since 875, points made by the fathers at Ravenna, or experience gained from attempting to implement this rule for two years had thus resulted in some basic shifts. First, the focus of the legislation moved from providing for timely episcopal consecrations to simply enforcing the pallium obligation. This shift may have occurred because the synod was repeating older legislation rather than responding to a new situation. Second, the consequences of noncompliance were softened by allowing for delays due to *inevitabilis necessitas* and by revising the penalty from deposition to suspension. One must wonder whether the pope had run into problems while trying to enforce the more stringent demand of 875 or had encountered resistance from the bishops gathered at Ravenna (a city not known for its willing embrace of Roman demands). Whatever the case, both the Roman and the Ravennese versions of the Johannine edict eventually entered the canonical tradition.[62]

---

were substantial similarities between these canons and those of the Council of Rome (875), which implies a close relationship ("Römische Synode," 778–80). This connection was strengthened by the similar political circumstances of the two synods, both seeking to confirm Charles the Bald's imperial dignity. Perhaps materials from the first synod were brought to Ravenna for the second, and so the earlier canons were repeated—with modifications, mostly explicable on the basis of the changed context, as Maassen details. Yet not all the changes may have been intended by the fathers; it is unknown who transcribed the canons, or why, and so alterations may have been editorial or even casual in nature.

61. MGH Conc. 5:68 (c. 1).

62. This analysis accepts the common assumption that the two councils were in fact two, distinct in time, place, and (to some extent) canonical output (see, e.g., Hartmann, *Synoden*, 344–49, and Arnold, *Johannes*, 179–81)—i.e., that the Roman texts (found in a canonical manuscript of the late ninth or early tenth century) and the Ravennese (edited by Holste, who does not identify his manuscript source) represent two different sources with two different traditions. However, these traditions overlapped strikingly and displayed significant but unpredictable variants; the most important witnesses were Burchard's *Decretum*, Deusdedit's canonical collection, and

When John traveled to Francia in the following year to celebrate a general synod, he brought these developments with him. As he granted the pallium to Rostagnus of Arles and appointed him papal vicar in Gaul, he urged his new representative to enforce the pallium obligation among the Frankish bishops, "to warn, stir, and command [metropolitans] to hurry to seek [the pallium] according to ancient custom."[63] This grant otherwise copied a previous grant by Gregory the Great to Virgilius of Arles, but John deliberately inserted this instruction as an object of special concern, with the familiar (if rather misleading) appeal to *antiquus mos*.[64] A few months later John presided at the Council of Troyes (878), which accepted the decisions of Ravenna wholesale and promulgated them north of the Alps.[65] The subscriptions of eight West Frankish metropolitans witnessed to their reception of the papal rules binding them, under threat of serious penalties, to clarify their faith and ask for the pallium.

John VIII's pontificate, then, was the culmination and consolidation of decades of development. At the same time, it revealed an am-

---

Pseudo-Liutprand's papal history, all from the eleventh century. Perhaps they went back to an earlier source that had attempted to combine the two sets of canons, or perhaps they were confused traces of a single council that had been variously recorded. If there was only one council, the differing tenor discussed here would have to be reframed, not as papal backpedaling or fine-tuning between 875 and 877, but as divergent receptions by those who wrote down the canons, or as corruption in transmission.

63. JE 3148, BU 353, MGH Epp. 7:110.

64. Philip Grierson, "Rostagnus of Arles and the Pallium," *The English Historical Review* 49 (1934): 75–76, compares this letter to the exemplar (from 595, JE 1374, CCSL 140:354–57). Arnold finds in John's use of the Gregorian text an effort to portray himself as heir to the great pope's authority (*Johannes*, 153). Or it was simply common sense, if John wished to revive the late antique papal vicariate of Arles, to use the privilege granted to the last vicar. But a more practical explanation is possible: away from Rome on the pope's trip through Gaul, the papal notaries, without their usual materials at hand, copied from Gregory's original document, perhaps still preserved in Arles.

65. MGH Conc. 5:103 (c. 3). On the synod, see Hartmann, *Synoden*, 336–40. Grierson theorizes that John disguised this "innovation" as a confirmation of practices already accepted elsewhere ("Rostagnus," 82). The application of the Ravennese decisions to the Frankish church was part of a general reform project; see Hubert Mordek and Gerhard Schmitz, "Papst Johannes VIII. und das Konzil von Troyes (878)," in *Geschichtsschreibung und geistiges Leben im Mittelalter*, ed. Karl Hauck and Hubert Mordek (Cologne: Böhlau, 1978), 193–94.

biguity in the conferral of the pallium: what was initially an honor, bestowed by the donor's choice, was now also a requirement, fulfilled at the recipient's initiative. Gracious gift (on the one side) and enforced reliance (on the other) were not wholly exclusive of each other, as any beggar knows, and both aspects contributed to the papacy's efforts to control the episcopate. With greater or lesser success over the coming centuries, the popes would attempt this balancing act between privilege and obligation.

Worthiness

The obligatory request for the pallium accomplished even more than submission to papal authority and assurance of doctrinal purity: through it the popes could test the virtue and worthiness of men proposed for high office in the church. As previously noted, Pope Hadrian I, already convinced of the holiness of Tilpin of Reims, instructed him to probe Lull of Mainz's *conversatio et mores ac vita* as part of Lull's application for the pallium.[66] The same pope took into consideration that Ermenbert of Bourges seemed "to exercise pastoral care devoutly" when he granted him the pallium between 784 and 791.[67] Pope Nicholas I agreed to send Egilo of Sens the pallium in 865/66, despite problems with his election, only because the archbishop showed outstanding virtue: "We praise the fact that you have humbly wished to evade the weights of pastoral care, but then again we approve that you have obediently bent the shoulders of your mind to bear them.... This fact, together with the praise of your holiness, has inclined our Pontificate, though with difficulty, nevertheless to send the pallium for your confirmation."[68] It was a grand tribute indeed, since the wording imitated certain passages of Gregory the Great's *Regula Pastoralis*.[69] Likewise, the pope lauded Egilo to King Charles the Bald: "We were filled with enormous exultation about him, since his reputation proclaims that he is the sort of man that the apostle indicates ought

---

66. JE 2411, GP 4:61 no. 22, Lesne, "Lettre," 349, 351.
67. As he told Charlemagne, JE 2475, MGH Epp. 3:628.
68. JE 2809, BH 766, MGH Epp. 6:644.
69. Floribert Rommel, Bruno Judic, and Charles Morel, eds., *Grégoire le Grand: règle pastorale*, Sources chrétiennes 381 (Paris: Cerf, 1992), 1:124, 150.

to be a bishop."⁷⁰ Charles, in turn, took a page from the pope's book in 867 when he begged him for the pallium for Wulfhad, archbishop of Bourges, whom he called "both vigorous in character and upright in behavior," despite the irregularity of his promotion.⁷¹ In these cases personal merit was the deciding factor in bestowing the pallium.

Pope John VIII continued the scrutiny of virtue that had become commonplace for those who would wear the vestment. To King Charles the Bald in 876 he praised Adalgar of Autun, "whom, behold, not undeservedly moved by reason of your love and by the uprightness of his behavior, we have sent back to you palliated." Elsewhere in the letter he described the bishop as "most holy," "gracious," "the son of salvation."⁷² The pope was likewise exuberant regarding Rostagnus of Arles in 878: "Of this virtue [charity], dearest brother, I discovered that you are full, when I had shown my bodily presence in the city of Arles for the restoration of the holy churches of God, as the true report of many testimonies far and wide told me about you."⁷³ While he borrowed the first clause from his Gregorian exemplar, John's insertion of the following two clauses likely reflected the impression the archbishop's *fama* had made upon him.⁷⁴ Justification could be found for ascertaining the good character expected of the palliger. When John the Deacon compiled his life of Gregory the Great around 876, he included a letter in which the revered pope would not even discuss granting the pallium to Desiderius of Vienne until he was "secure and without any doubt" regarding rumors that the bishop had been studying pagan books—"nonsense and secular literature" containing "the blasphemous praises of the heinous."⁷⁵ Such a patristic precedent reinforced the papal mindset.

The acclaim that reached the ears of Pope Hadrian II regarding

---

70. JE 2810, BH 767, MGH Epp. 6:645.
71. PL 124:874.
72. JE 3063, BU 213, MGH Epp. 7:23–24.
73. JE 3148, BU 353, MGH Epp. 7:109.
74. Dietrich Lohrmann identifies this insertion as the pope's own dictation (*Das Register Papst Johannes' VIII. (872–882): neue Studien zur Abschrift Reg. Vat. 1, zum verlorenen Originalregister und zum Diktat der Briefe*, Bibliothek des deutschen historischen Instituts in Rom 30 [Tübingen: Niemeyer, 1968], 281).
75. PL 75:148, quoting JE 1824. Since Gregory did not mention the pallium here, and had rejected Desiderius's petition for it two years before (in 599, JE 1749,

Willibert of Cologne attempted to gloss over problems with his election by citing his integrity. According to his consecrator, he seemed "beyond a doubt to have the grace of purpose in holiness and of knowledge in eloquence."[76] Even to his deposed predecessor, Gunther, Willibert was "a man clearly noble, well educated, mature, and (we believe) very suited to this office; if perhaps anyone wishes to say anything unfavorable about him, you should believe that it is nothing else but ill will, since he is also known to be good."[77] Yet the pope still had reservations, shared at first by his successor, John VIII. Such concern formed the context of a papal letter to Willibert in 873, which seems to bear the fingerprints of Anastasius the Librarian. It provided a full-fledged rationale for relating the pallium to merit: "The use of the pallium is, among other things, of such great virtue that, after it is conferred, it removes from him on whom it is conferred all calumny from past transgressions—not that it purges crimes, but that the caution of the one conferring it ought to be so great that only on one lacking them does he attempt to confer such a great gift."[78] The pallium's *tanta virtus* (depicted here as a sort of inner power) cleared the one obtaining it of all false accusations from the past. Since the pope was prudent enough not to grant it to a criminal, it bore witness to papal authority's judgment of the recipient's innocence. Given such a presumption, the grant of the pallium had to be approached cautiously, or even denied to the unworthy.

GaP 3.1:81–82 no. 57, CCSL 140A:793), it is unlikely that this letter was a reply to such a petition. But John the Deacon thought so, and thus soundness of character as a prerequisite for the vestment was conceivable in his time. John was not always accurate in details, and his narration sometimes reflected his late Carolingian Roman context and his desire to glorify Gregory. But most of his text was based on a copy of Gregory's register, with extensive quotations from papal letters. See Hans-Albert Wilhelmi, *Die "Vita Gregorii Magni" des Johannes Diaconus: Schwerpunkte ihrer Wirkungsgeschichte*, Deutsche Hochschuledition 76 (Neuried: Ars Una, 1998), 2–12. Excerpts from John's *vita* in this study are checked against those letters, and unless otherwise noted (as here), its accuracy can be accepted.

76. Liudbert of Mainz to Hadrian II in 870, MGH Epp. 6:244.

77. MGH Epp. 6:247. The reference to a possible naysayer brings to mind the accuser who complained to the pope (cf. John VIII to Willibert of Cologne in 873, JE 2986, GP 7.1:34 no. 66, BU 96, MGH Epp. 7:314).

78. JE 2986, GP 7.1:34 no. 66, BU 96, MGH Epp. 7:314. See Lohrmann, *Register*, 249–50.

Regularity

Although good moral fiber could cover a multitude of reservations, another consistent concern centered on the proper accession to office of the candidate for the pallium. Pope Hadrian I asked Tilpin of Reims to investigate not only Lull of Mainz's faith and morals, but also the circumstances behind his installation: "We also enjoin your Fraternity, because certain things have reached us ... to examine everything about his ordination diligently ... so that we may send him the pallium according to custom, and judge his ordination firm, and cause him to be established as archbishop."[79] The pope was probably bothered by reports that Lull had accepted the see uncanonically, while his predecessor Boniface was still alive. But once the circumstances had been scrutinized and excused, the pallium would confirm his position.[80]

A similar concern haunted the elevation of Hincmar, who replaced the deposed Ebo as archbishop of Reims.[81] Emperor Lothar I's letter to Pope Leo IV seeking the pallium for Hincmar in the late 840s carefully justified his promotion: the see was vacant, the candidate qualified, and his election and ordination canonical. Although Ebo complained, "unfairly pretending that a successor had been assigned to him while he still survived," representation had been made to Rome, and the synodal acts of the *plenitudo episcoporum* (presumably the Council of Beauvais in 845) supported Hincmar's appointment.[82] Apparently the petition succeeded, for the Council of Soissons (853), adjudicating the status of the clergy ordained by Ebo, affirmed Hinc-

---

79. JE 2411, GP 4:61 no. 22, Lesne, "Lettre," 351.
80. See Lesne, "Lettre," 333; Levison, *England*, 234; and, with a different view, Knibbs, *Ansgar*, 41n103.
81. On Hincmar's accession and the controversy regarding the claims of Ebo and the clerics he ordained, see Heinrich Schrörs, *Hinkmar, Erzbischof von Reims: sein Leben und seine Schriften* (Freiburg: Herder, 1884), 27–39, 61–71, 270–92, and Jean Devisse, *Hincmar, archevêque de Reims, 845–882*, Travaux d'histoire ethico-politique 29 (Geneva: Droz, 1975–76), 1:31–40, 71–97, 2:600–628. Celia Chazelle interprets the illustration on fol. 90v of the Utrecht Psalter (see 22 above) as reflecting Hincmar's concern around 850 to establish his archiepiscopal authority and right to the pallium ("Archbishops Ebo and Hincmar of Reims and the Utrecht Psalter," *Speculum* 72 [1997]: 1069–71); but see 97n85 below.
82. MGH Epp. 5:610. On the synod, see Hartmann, *Synoden*, 205–8.

mar's rank: "It was shown by the most obvious proofs and decreed by synodal judgment that Archbishop Hincmar had been canonically acquired from a neighboring diocese, canonically elected and canonically ordained and canonically completed with the pallium of the apostolic see, his ordination having been approved, and confirmed on the pinnacle of the primacy with metropolitan authority, in every respect and in all things."[83] Here the pallium formed the canonical completion of the installation process through papal approval, which cemented the legitimacy of Hincmar's succession. Nevertheless, the Ebonian clerics who were Hincmar's enemies claimed that, before bestowing the pallium on him, the pope had first required him to swear that Ebo (alive at the time as bishop of Hildesheim) was in fact dead. They implied that the pope would not have granted Hincmar the pallium, and thus confirmation, until Ebo's claim had passed away with him, and that he did so only after Hincmar had perjured himself.[84] As late as 866, at another Council of Soissons, Hincmar was still defending his position by pointing to, among other things, the *usus pallii* that he had gained from Leo IV as a mark of papal consent.[85] By demanding evidence of licit induction as a prerequisite, the popes turned the pallium's reception into a necessary act of papal confirmation of archiepiscopal office.

The attention to canonical promotion occasioned by a pallium request gave the papacy an opening to show either strictness or leniency. Pope Nicholas I castigated Egilo, archbishop of Sens, in 865/66 because he had been elected not from that church but from a monastery in another province: this act amounted to "trampling on the sacred canons and disdain for the clerics" who had advanced in the *cursus honorum* of the church of Sens.[86] Similarly, the pope com-

---

83. MGH Conc. 3:273. The use of "primacy" reflected Hincmar's view of the exalted, nearly autonomous position of metropolitans. On the synod, see Hartmann, *Synoden*, 245–49. In the mid-tenth century Flodoard of Reims recalled the bestowal of the pallium as a symbol of resolution: only after Ebo had ceded claim to Reims and Hincmar had sent his profession of faith to Rome was Hincmar approved as archbishop through the vestment (*Historia Remensis Ecclesiae*, in MGH SS 36:193).

84. *Narratio Clericorum Remensium,* in MGH Conc. 2.2:812–13.

85. MGH Epp. 8.1:181. On the synod, see Hartmann, *Synoden*, 318–19.

86. JE 2809, BH 766, MGH Epp. 6:644.

plained to King Charles the Bald, who had selected Egilo, that his appointment was "unseemly, or rather illicit," carried out "hardly rightfully" and "irregularly," to be compared with seizing the command of a camp in which he had not served, or eating the fruits of others' labor.[87] Although, as observed above, Egilo's exemplary virtue prompted Nicholas to overlook the abnormality and approve his accession, the conferral of the pallium provided the pope opportunity and leverage to express his dismay.[88] Charles also named Wulfhad, one of the controversial Ebonian clerics whose ordinations Hincmar asserted were invalid, as archbishop of Bourges before receiving the pope's judgment on his contested status. The king addressed an obsequious letter to Nicholas in 867 that apologized for this premature promotion and begged him for "the pallium of apostolic authority."[89] The Council of Troyes added a likewise obsequious appeal to the pope "to confirm and adorn the ordination of our brother and fellow priest Wulfhad, to whose restoration and promotion you have deigned to be favorable, with the bestowal of the use of the pallium."[90] Nicholas had since died, but his successor, Pope Hadrian II, responded favorably in 868 and granted Wulfhad the pallium "for his fuller confirmation," despite the hastiness of his consecration.[91] Even in its indulgence the papacy exercised power, for refusal of the pallium loomed as a real possibility.

Indeed, Hadrian did not show himself so lenient with Louis the German. When that king, without consulting the apostolic see, appointed Willibert as archbishop of Cologne in 870 to replace Gunther, deposed after Lothar II's divorce, he met with stubborn papal opposition.[92] Willibert's consecrator, Liudbert of Mainz, guaranteed

87. JE 2810, BH 767, MGH Epp. 6:645–46.
88. JE 2809, BH 766, MGH Epp. 6:644.
89. PL 124:875.
90. MGH Conc. 4:238. On the synod, see Hartmann, *Synoden*, 320–21.
91. JE 2894, MGH Epp. 6:699. The comparative "fuller" perhaps implied that Wulfhad had already received confirmation from local authorities, now corroborated by papal authority through the pallium.
92. See Günther Ullrich, "Die Kölner Bischofswahl von 870 und die Praxis der Bistumsbesetzung im Karolingerreich," *Rheinische Vierteljahrsblätter* 11 (1941): 254–62, and Boris Bigott, *Ludwig der Deutsche und die Reichskirche im Ostfränkischen Reich (826–876)*, Historische Studien 470 (Husum: Matthiesen, 2002), 202–8. The reasons

to Hadrian that the new archbishop had taken office "with the election and agreement of the clergy and people" and had been ordained "with diligent consideration, having examined the sacred canons and the decretals of your predecessors, as well as the legal rights of the divine scriptures, after questioning, reasoning, judging, confirming."[93] Louis and even Gunther himself added their assurances that the process had been canonical and had involved all necessary parties.[94] The pope, however, opted to withhold the pallium until he found out more about "the manner of Willibert's substitution," that is, how he had come to office.[95] Progress in the case was slow, and in 873 Hadrian's successor, John VIII, had even more reason to hesitate, as he told the archbishop: "One of the sons of the church of Cologne, of which you seem to be in charge, approached our see and accuses the origins of your promotion in words and writing.... The origins of your advancement are reported to be very blameworthy, and ought to be purified by immediate satisfaction."[96] Willibert's old age and sickness prevented him from traveling to Rome as the pope had ordered, but insistent royal intervention persuaded John to confer the pallium anyway—as he simultaneously promised to send a legate to look into the matter and take appropriate action.[97]

---

for papal displeasure were several: Nicholas I had demanded that the apostolic see be consulted before replacements for the deposed archbishops were elected (to Lothar II in 863, JE 2753, BH 678, MGH Epp. 6:288); Charles the Bald had already appointed a claimant, Hilduin, to Cologne (*Annales Xantenses*, in MGH SSRG 12:29); Hadrian II had commanded that no one be ordained without the consent of the new emperor, Louis II (Hugh of Flavigny, *Chronicon*, in MGH SS 8:354 [JE *2922]); and Hadrian had promised to rehear Gunther's case before a successor was named (to Louis the German in 870, JE 2930, MGH Epp. 6:731).

93. MGH Epp. 6:243–44.
94. MGH Epp. 6:247, 249–51.
95. To Liudbert of Mainz in 870, JE 2932, GP 4:66 no. 37, GP 7.1:31 no. 57, MGH Epp. 6:733. Cf. Hadrian II to Louis the German in 870, JE 2930, MGH Epp. 6:731.
96. JE 2986, GP 7.1:34 no. 66, BU 96, MGH Epp. 7:314. Arnold distinguishes between the circumstances of the election, which resulted in the initial denial of the pallium, and the personal accusation, which demanded papal intervention (justified on Pseudo-Isidorian grounds). Both matters concerned Willibert's accession, but even without the accusation, the pallium, which had become "a constitutive element of episcopal lordship," could not at first be given (*Johannes*, 164–65).
97. To Willibert in 874, JE 2988, GP 7.1:34–35 no. 67, BU 120, Erich Wisplinghoff, ed., *Rheinisches Urkundenbuch: Ältere Urkunden bis 1100*, Publikationen der Gesellschaft für Rheinische Geschichtskunde 57 (Düsseldorf: Droste, 1994), 2:159.

The other archbishop appointed after Lothar's divorce, Bertulf of Trier, also vexed the pope, as John wrote to him in 873: "Learning that your Religiosity had been promoted against the prohibition of the apostolic see, we have proposed that you must not be counted among the bishops until, put on the spot, you are shown to have been canonically consecrated." The pope thus summoned him to Rome to render an account, "so that at a canonical examination, in which we have decided your case in a spirit of mildness, you may appear blamelessly promoted and without any delay receive the pallium, which you request from us."[98] In the situations of both Trier and Cologne, the pallium supplied the pope with a tool—the more effective because the more sought—for ensuring the choice of acceptable prelates, and for influencing a procedure usually dominated by secular lords and ambitious clerics. It gave the pope a reason to intervene and a definite say.[99]

By this period, obtaining the pallium had taken its place, among the other steps of the installation process, as a necessary ingredient in the making of the highest churchmen. In canon 27, the Fourth Council of Constantinople (869–70) sanctioned the use of the pallium: "According to the norms handed down throughout each province and region and city, we decree that those things which are proofs and signs of the order that each person is seen to have should be retained in ecclesiastical promotions and consecrations. Thus bishops to whom it has been granted to use pallia at certain times should be clothed with them at the same times and places."[100] Allowing for

---

98. JE 2982, GP 10.1:37 no. 49, BU 87, MGH Epp. 7:288. Some of the reasons for papal irritation were the same as in Willibert's case. For the "prohibition of the apostolic see," see Nicholas I's dictate (to Lothar II in 863, JE 2753, BH 678, MGH Epp. 6:288), to which his successors remained faithful by claiming authority for papal involvement in these cases (Arnold, *Johannes*, 166). Perhaps the popes were trying to make such involvement a general rule (Ullrich, "Kölner Bischofswahl," 262).

99. As Louis the German admitted to Louis II in 870, Willibert's appointment had canonically taken place "save the peace of the Roman church" (MGH Epp. 6:250).

100. G. Alberigo, J. A. Dossetti, P.-P. Joannou, C. Leonardi, and P. Prodi, eds., *Conciliorum Oecumenicorum Decreta*, 3rd ed. (Bologna: Istituto per le Scienze Religiose, 1973), 185. This assembly came to be viewed in the West as the eighth ecumenical council. Although it was a council occasioned by Eastern problems, dealing with Eastern affairs, and attended by Eastern bishops, its canons should be

local variations (probably the differing treatment of the pallium in East and West), this canon encouraged the use of the vestment as a badge of office, *indicium et signum ordinis,* acquired during elevation. In the Western church the sole patriarch, the bishop of Rome, distributed this gift as the crowning of a canonical succession, and so its reception also played an important role in maintaining union with the apostolic see. Accordingly John VIII reminded the Dalmatian bishops in 879 to "willingly pay heed to return to the lap of the holy Roman church, your mother. Thus an archbishop canonically elected by you, with the agreement and will of all of you, should come to us and receive the grace of episcopal consecration and the sacred pallium from us unhesitatingly, according to the original custom."[101] By making the vestment an essential part of creating an archbishop, the popes ensured that this middle level between themselves and the bishops of a province was tightly bound to Rome.

Denial

Implicit in the insistence on prerequisites was the threat that the pope would withhold the gift of the pallium if those qualifications were not met. It was a real possibility; examples of pallium denials have already been encountered. Pope Leo IV bucked a trend of cooperating with the demands of secular powers by refusing the pallium to Altheus of Autun, probably because the bishop did not make the request himself.[102] Pope Nicholas I resisted the attempts of Festinian of Dol to gain the vestment by withholding it unless presented with documented precedents (which, as he discovered, did not exist).[103]

---

scrutinized for Western influence—because it was convoked, shaped, and confirmed by Western authority—and Western impact, because its decrees were brought to Rome and translated into Latin by Anastasius the Librarian, whence they could have influenced canon law or papal thinking in a crucial period for the pallium. This remains true even though John VIII seems to have annulled the council a decade later (Dvornik, *Photian Schism,* 202–10). On the council and its reception, see ibid., 132–58, 279–330.

101. JE 3262, BU 530, MGH Epp. 7:157. On the relationship of Dalmatia to the Roman church, see HEOJ 4:537–38.

102. To Lothar I, JE 2603, BH 116, MGH Epp. 5:604.

103. To Solomon of Brittany, JE 2789, BH 764, MGH Epp. 6:640.

Similar to these cases, instances of conditional grants have been examined. Nicholas stipulated a more exact profession of faith from Ado of Vienne before the archbishop deserved to receive the pallium.[104] And Popes Hadrian II and John VIII wanted to know more about the accessions of Bertulf of Trier and Willibert of Cologne before they conceded the vestment to those prelates.[105] By the mid-ninth century, then, the popes were using the threat of denial to exert pressure and enforce their oversight of the episcopate.

Perhaps they were inspired by the example of Pope Gregory the Great, whose deeds were kept alive in this century. In the 870s the *gesta* of the bishops of Auxerre, mistaking Desiderius of Vienne for his contemporary Desiderius of Auxerre, repeated a letter of Gregory to the former in which he balked at his request for the *pallium pontificale*. As with Festinian of Dol, the bishop's claim "that certain privileges were once granted to [his] church by the apostolic see and that her priests had the use of the pallium from of old" could not be verified in the papal *scrinium*, and so the pope instructed him to search the charters of his church and submit any pertinent precedents.[106] About the same time, John the Deacon peppered his life of Gregory with anecdotes and letters that depicted the pope denying, placing conditions on, and even removing the pallium. He refused it to Syagrius of Autun until the bishop and the Frankish rulers agreed to work against certain prevalent abuses under the supervision of a papal legate.[107] He instructed his legate to prohibit Natalis of Salona from using it until the bishop restored those advanced to higher ranks against their will.[108] As mentioned above, he withheld it from

104. JE 2693, GaP 3.1:99–100 no. †84b, BH †541, MGH Epp. 6:669.
105. To Liudbert of Mainz, JE 2932, GP 4:66 no. 37, GP 7.1:31 no. 57, MGH Epp. 6:733; to Bertulf, JE 2982, GP 10.1:37 no. 49, BU 87, MGH Epp. 7:288; and to Willibert, JE 2986, GP 7.1:34 no. 66, BU 96, MGH Epp. 7:314.
106. Michel Sot, Guy Lobrichon, Monique Goullet, and Pierre Bonnerue, eds., *Les gestes des évêques d'Auxerre*, Les classiques de l'histoire de France au moyen âge 42 (Paris: Belles Lettres, 2002), 87, quoting JE 1749.
107. PL 75:126, referring to JE 1748 and JE 1751.
108. PL 75:134, quoting JE 1175. The pope was not wresting the vestment away from the bishop, but rather withdrawing his permission to use it, which constituted the privilege *per se*. As often happened with other medieval gifts (e.g., donations of land to monasteries), the pallium retained ties to its donor, such that it never

Desiderius of Vienne until he put to rest reports that the bishop had been perusing pagan literature.[109] And he entered a protracted controversy with John of Ravenna over the latter's use of the pallium during litanies outside of church: the pope forbade this practice under a stern threat of deprivation, "lest you begin not to have even at Mass that which you boldly usurp also on the streets."[110] There was no doubt, at least in Gregory's mind, that he could take away the misused privilege. These historical instances provided later popes with support for controlling the pallium to accomplish their agenda.

Yet the Gregorian inheritance could also be wielded to object to such control. After Hadrian II had denied the pallium to Willibert of Cologne in 870, the clergy and people of that city (probably prompted by Louis the German, since royal legates brought their letter to the pope) replied with a carefully argued protest on the archbishop's behalf.[111] They professed themselves "not without scruple of amazement" and wondered why the pope put off bestowing the pallium according to custom. They invoked historical examples:

> Prior to all satisfaction, your predecessor, blessed Gregory, mercifully sent the pallium to Bishop Syagrius [of Autun] with a sacred admonition of reproof, as is read. And your Industry knows how clemently he acted towards Maximus, bishop of Salona, in the giving of the pallium. To him, among other things, he writes: "For just as we do not suffer illicit things to [be perpetrated], so we do not deny things that are customary."

---

passed into the recipient's independent possession, but relied on the donor's continued good will. Cf. Geary, "Sacred Commodities," 183.

109. PL 75:148, quoting JE 1824. As noted above, John the Deacon may have been confused here.

110. PL 75:172, quoting JE 1259.

111. This letter is traditionally considered to begin *Officio piae subiectionis* and end *scripsit pietati vestrae* (MGH Epp. 6:244–46). But the final sentence forms an abrupt termination and seems rather to introduce the following letter in the manuscript, that of Gunther (ibid., 6:246–48). It thus seems likely that Gunther's letter was originally reproduced as an insertion within the clergy and people's letter. Beginning with a salutation and the words *Scit vestra beatitudo*, Gunther's letter arguably continues through the words *semper inlustrare dignetur*, which offers a typical closing benediction. If so, the remainder, beginning *Igitur ut veridice* and ending *per saecula praestet*, actually comprises the conclusion of the clergy and people's letter. This reconstruction is adopted here.

Obtaining the Pallium   59

The pope's guiding principles, from the perspective of Cologne, should have been mercy and custom, rather than taking the shocking step of refusing the vestment. Nevertheless, they closed by acknowledging the pope's power to do as he saw fit, and even attempted to take the blame upon themselves.[112] While not challenging Hadrian's right to withhold the pallium, this letter revealed that some local churches had come to desire and expect the vestment and would apply whatever pressure they could to acquire it.

Even so, Gregory's successors continued to employ the pallium—or the lack thereof—to enforce ecclesiastical discipline. The chronicle of the patriarchs of Grado in the 820s or 830s recorded a letter of Pope Gregory II to Serenus of Aquileia that forbade him to trespass upon Grado's jurisdiction, "so that you may show that you have not unjustly received the grace of the conferred pallium from presumption—and thus, if you are proven disobedient, be judged unworthy by the vigor of an apostolic council."[113] This pope was more explicit about the danger to Serenus's pallium in his letter to the Istrian bishops, also preserved in the chronicle: he had enjoined Serenus "never to surpass his boundary or invade another's rights, but to be willing to be content in what he has possessed till now. And you should know, most beloved, that the pallium has been granted to him under this condition."[114] In addition, a variant of the *Liber Diurnus* formula *Si pastores ovium* that was apparently conceived under Gregory IV drew a minatory clause from a letter of Gregory the Great to John of Ravenna. After instructing the recipient on the proper wearing of the pallium, it warned: "[Your Fraternity should] claim nothing further for yourself by the daring of rash presumption, lest, when a matter of external dress is irregularly seized, even matters that could be regularly allowed should be lost."[115] This version of *Si pastores ovium*, sent to

112. Ibid., 6:248, referring to JE 1751 and quoting JE 1703.
113. Monticolo, *Cronache*, 1:12–13, quoting JE 2166.
114. Ibid., 1:13, quoting JE 2167.
115. Gregory IV to Liudpram of Salzburg in 837, JE 2580, GP 1:10 no. 14, Hauthaler and Martin, *Salzburger Urkundenbuch*, 2:28, quoting JE 1326. This letter appears to be the earliest extant example of this form of *Si pastores ovium*. It was followed in this period by Leo IV to Victor of Grado in 852, JE 2616, IP 7.2:43 no. 37, BH 253, Hacke, *Palliumverleihungen*, 149; Benedict III to Vitalis of Grado in 858,

numerous palligers for over a century, cited Gregorian authority for its thinly veiled threat that abuse of the vestment could well result in its removal.

The deposition of Archbishop Ebo of Reims engendered a long-lasting tumult in which the giving and withholding of the pallium played a significant part.[116] Ousted from his see in 835 due to his support of Lothar I against the latter's father Louis the Pious, Ebo was briefly reinstated in 840 before being expelled again the following year. In 844, with Emperor Lothar's backing, he and Bartholomew of Narbonne (who shared Ebo's predicament) approached Pope Sergius II and asked to be restored to their sees. The *Liber Pontificalis* recounted the episode: "A certain Ebo and Bartholomew, archbishops who had been driven out of the church for their crimes, deprived of their honor, requested the most holy pontiff to deign to reconcile them and bestow the pallium on them. And [Sergius] said that they were not worthy to receive communion among the clergy, but only had permission to receive communion among the common folk."[117] The pallium was a tangible sign of the dignity from which they had been deposed. To receive it again would have meant regaining their archbishoprics and thus the clerical state (*communio inter clericos*), but the

---

JE 2672, IP 7.2:43 no. 38, BH 419, Hacke, *Palliumverleihungen*, 151; Nicholas I to Adalwin of Salzburg in 860, JE 2681, GP 1:11 no. 17, BH 512, Hauthaler and Martin, *Salzburger Urkundenbuch*, 2:36; and Nicholas I to Rimbert of Hamburg in 865, JE 2798, GP 6:35 no. 26, BH 785, Curschmann, *Ältere Papsturkunden*, 27. Possibly, however, this was the form present in the version of the *Liber Diurnus* actually used in the ninth-century papal chancery, while the form known today as the standard *Si pastores ovium* was a variant preserved in the extant manuscripts, which were school-books from outside Rome. The first time the "standard" version was used (though with some changes) in an authentic pallium grant in this period was not until 878 (John VIII to Wala of Metz, JE 3183, BU 427, PL 126:798–99), although the *Liber Diurnus* manuscript containing this version of the formula seems to date from the late eighth or early ninth century.

116. See Courtney M. Booker, *Past Convictions: The Penance of Louis the Pious and the Decline of the Carolingians* (Philadelphia: University of Pennsylvania Press, 2009), 183–209.

117. Duchesne, *Liber pontificalis*, 2:90. Hincmar repeated this story around 860 as evidence of his own legitimacy as archbishop of Reims (*De Praedestinatione Dei et Libero Arbitrio*, in PL 125:392). According to the tenth-century account of Flodoard of Reims, Ebo had the backing of the papal vicar, Drogo of Metz, though to no avail (*Historia Remensis Ecclesiae*, in MGH SS 36:189).

pope decided to readmit them only to lay communion and to punish them by withholding the pallium. Later, in 866, when opinion was shifting in Ebo's favor, Pope Nicholas I felt bound to defend his predecessor's treatment of the overthrown prelate. He depicted Ebo as unreasonable in his claims, "urged by obstinate men and joined to them, suddenly seeking both to be reconciled by [the apostolic see] and to be adorned with the pallium, and, as if a bishop among bishops, with no preceding discussion of his case, demanding to be given communion."[118] Given the history of the vestment, *pallio decorari* meant being specially honored and attaining (or regaining) a position of power. The pope thus painted Ebo as a proud, overreaching man who wanted not merely to be forgiven, but even to be exalted.

The popes were not much easier on Hincmar, Ebo's successor at Reims from 845. As seen above, the Ebonian clerics whose validity Hincmar questioned asserted around 866 that he had obtained his pallium under false pretenses and that Pope Leo IV had placed a proviso on its reception: "In that letter of apostolic authority, by which the use of the pallium was granted to the same Hincmar, one reads a cautious insertion, as can be found in the archives of the holy Roman mother church: 'We grant you the use of the pallium—except, however, for the struggle that exists between you and Ebo.'"[119] Unless this fragment had been fabricated, the pope seems to have intended that the outcome of the quarrel could reverse the privilege if unfavorable to Hincmar, whose position he appeared hesitant to confirm. Following the policy of Gregory the Great, moreover, Pope Nicholas I bristled at rumors that Hincmar was wearing the pallium

---

118. To the Council of Soissons, JE 2822, BH 837, MGH Epp. 6:422.

119. *Narratio Clericorum Remensium*, in MGH Conc. 2.2:813. If authentic, this fragment is the sole witness to a document thought to be lost (JE *2596, BH 138). Ludwig Falkenstein suggests that it was a later interpolation; see "Zu verlorenen päpstlichen Privilegien und Schreiben: Palliumverleihungen an die Erzbischöfe von Reims (8.–12. Jahrhundert)," in *Eloquentia copiosus: Festschrift für Max Kerner zum 65. Geburtstag*, ed. Lotte Kéry (Aachen: Thouet, 2006), 187n35. But the fact that Leo suggested, in two letters between 847 and 855, that Hincmar had usurped the see of Reims makes such a proviso unsurprising (to the bishops of Gaul and Lothar I, JE 2618–19, BH 134–35, MGH Epp. 5:604–6). For further clues about Hincmar's pallium grant, see 136n75, 167 below.

beyond the permitted times. Ominously, in 866, he warned him of the consequences: "He deserves to lose a privilege (as Pope St. Simplicius writes) who abuses the power granted him."[120] Failing to observe restrictions on the pallium's use was seen not merely as an abuse of a symbol, but as an abuse of power. In the end, the pope did not deprive Hincmar of his privilege, but he admonished him to avoid pride, bragging, and vainglory. Sometimes a hint of the pallium's loss alone was enough to keep churchmen in line, for Hincmar seems to have caused no further trouble on this front.

Nicholas made ample use of such threats in his efforts to compel the churches to recognize a strong papal authority. After granting the missionary Ansgar the right to wear the pallium in 864, the pope appended the following terms:

Nevertheless, recognize that all these things added above are granted by the apostolic see to your Beatitude if you deviate in nothing at all from the faith and decrees of the holy catholic and apostolic Roman church. But if you eagerly presume to deviate from the faith and instructions or sanctions of the apostolic see, which is exalting you with such a great honor, you shall lack these our favors granted to you.[121]

To wear what the pope wore meant being the pope's man. The papal character of the pallium implied a loyalty to the convictions and dictates of the papacy, which was its source, and violating that loyalty would result in losing the honor. Similarly, when Pope Hadrian II awarded the pallium to Actard, the exiled bishop of Nantes, in 868, he included a cautionary clause: "With God's assent, use the pallium, granted to you by us from the affection of pity and comfort alone, and, unless you are ungrateful to the prelates of the apostolic see, be decorated with honor while you live."[122] The otherwise praiseworthy tone of the letter ruled out any specific concern about Actard's obedience, but the imposed condition ("unless you are ungrateful ..."), in the tradition of Nicholas I, made the pallium a tool for enforcing

---

120. JE 2823, BH 838, MGH Epp. 6:431, quoting JK 583.
121. JE 2759, GP 6:31–32 no. 21, BH 706, Curschmann, *Ältere Papsturkunden*, 23. The favors (plural) included not only the pallium, but probably also Ansgar's legation.
122. JE 2904, MGH Epp. 6:709.

Obtaining the Pallium   63

faithful submission to the papacy. By this period the vestment had certainly become a gift with strings attached.

It is not surprising, therefore, that the possibility of the deprivation of the pallium reared its head at Pope John VIII's Councils of Rome (875) and Ravenna (877), which were foundational for pallium law. In a canon concerning the proper "use of the pallium, that it should not be used presumptuously by metropolitans," the penalty for infringement was the loss of the use of the vestment ("let him lack that honor"), a sanction that went back to Gregory the Great's dispute with John of Ravenna.[123] Indeed, the canon quoted letters of that pope: "He who defends this heavy yoke and bond of the neck, not as an ecclesiastical, but as a certain secular dignity"—that is, not as a sign of the burdens of pastoral office, but as a worldly decoration, possibly a cause of conceit—"should lack the permitted dignity that he abuses. For by right he deserves to lose a privilege who boldly usurps illicit things."[124] In fact, this quotation was reworded from passages in a letter of Gregory to John of Ravenna and in a letter of Pope Simplicius to an earlier John of Ravenna (the same letter as was previously used by Nicholas I); it was shaped as well by some degree of free composition.[125] But the intent seems clear: one who misused a *permissa dignitas* or *privilegium* was to be stripped of it.

---

123. MGH Conc. 5:10. The penalty was mistakenly omitted from the manuscript containing the Roman canon (c. 3, *Quicumque sane*), but is supplied from the Ravennese canon (c. 3, *Quicumque sane*), which repeated the sentence verbatim (ibid., 5:68).

124. Ibid., 5:10. The Ravennese version of this quotation was almost exactly the same (ibid., 5:68).

125. The Roman canon attributed it to letters of Gregory "to John and Marinian, bishops of Ravenna" (ibid., 5:10), and the Ravennese to letters of Gregory "to John, bishop of Palermo, and Marinian, bishop of Ravenna" (ibid., 5:68). Neither was wholly correct. The first half of the quotation was borrowed partly from JE 1259 (IP 5:25 no. 29, CCSL 140:201) and partly from sentiments in the same letter and in JE 1326 (IP 5:25 no. 31, CCSL 140:277), both to John of Ravenna. The mention of Marinian may have been an error, since the only extant letter to Marinian about the pallium (JE 1377, IP 5:26–27 no. 38, CCSL 140:363) does not seem similar. As for John of Palermo, Gregory granted him the pallium (JE 1905, IP 10:227 no. 14, CCSL 140A:1041), but apart from a warning not to be presumptuous, the content does not seem relevant. The source of the second half of the quotation was Simplicius to John of Ravenna in 482 (JK 583, IP 5:21 no. 7, PL 58:36), also cited by Nicholas to Hincmar in 866 (JE 2823, BH 838, MGH Epp. 6:431).

The pallium, after all, was not a right but a gift, and the privilege of wearing it could justly be withdrawn if its wearer broke the law that defined it. Though tightly bound to the acquisition and exercise of metropolitan office, it was not equivalent to the office, and deprivation did not automatically mean deposition.[126] Nevertheless, the loss of so visible and prestigious a sign of authority left the prelate handicapped, at least, and so the denial of the pallium was a potent weapon in the papal arsenal.

Reception

Once the prerequisites had been met and the pope had agreed to confer the pallium, there remained the practical matter of receiving it. Acquiring this gift from the bishop of Rome required, in most cases, a trip to the Eternal City. This was certainly the expectation of Gregory the Great, in a letter that John the Deacon inserted in his late ninth-century *vita,* when the pope instructed Maximus of Salona to "send a person to us who may receive the pallium, to be brought to you, according to custom."[127] This visit provided opportunities for papal goals to be pursued, and the manner of the vestment's reception became yet another way in which the papacy exercised control over its recipients. There were two basic ways of getting the pallium: sending for it, and fetching it personally.

Legates and Letters

In this period, the lengthy, difficult journey was usually delegated. The pallium was ordinarily obtained through envoys sent from a local church with the bishop's written request and profession of faith. As usual, England offered an example of proper procedure dating back to Gregory the Great. Alcuin bore witness to that pope's intent in a letter to King Offa of Mercia in 792/93:

---

126. The later cases of Harold of Salzburg and Aribo of Mainz manifested the ambiguity in the connection between office and vestment.

127. PL 75:180, quoting JE 1703.

Obtaining the Pallium   65

Pope Gregory, our preacher of blessed memory, determined that there are two metropolitan cities in Britain and wished for the same to be honored with the dignity of the pallium.... In place of the deceased, [a new archbishop] should be ordained by the surviving archbishop. Nevertheless, when the pallium is sent to him by the lord pope, he first ought to receive it in his own church from those subject to him, just as some very experienced Romans have handed down to me.[128]

This practice entailed the pallium's dispatch from Rome to England, where an archbishop was vested with it in his cathedral by his subordinates (perhaps his suffragan bishops or the cathedral clergy).[129] As his *vita* made clear in the 820s, Alcuin himself had once fulfilled the role of envoy in Archbishop Eanbald I of York's quest for the pallium, and on the way home he had chanced to meet Charlemagne in Parma.[130] It was a historic encounter with lasting consequences, for the king persuaded Alcuin to join his court after the completion of his errand. In the royal court Alcuin was then able to intercede with the pope for further pallium embassies.[131] Such trips enabled significant contacts to be made, and thus the vestment played a part in weaving a web of personal connections across Europe.

Pope Nicholas I spelled out the correct practice in 865 for the Breton king and the bishop of Dol, a new claimant to the pallium. Envoys from a local church were more than messengers; they were to attest to the would-be palliger's fitness: "Let him also send ... a suitable legate from his own clergy ... who, by swearing with his hands placed upon the sacred codex of the gospels, may affirm that his bishop believes, and henceforth is going to observe, just as those writings sent to us by him are known to bear witness and contain."[132] Apparently the profession of faith submitted by the candidate did not suffice. It was reinforced by the oath of a personal representative,

---

128. Paul Lehmann, ed., *Holländische Reisefrüchte I–III*, Sitzungsberichte der bayerischen Akademie der Wissenschaften, philosophisch-philologische und historische Klasse 13 (Munich: Bayerische Akademie der Wissenschaften, 1921), 33–34.

129. See ibid., 31.

130. MGH SS 15.1:189–90.

131. E.g., Alcuin pled on behalf of the legates sent by Eanbald II of York to Rome for his pallium, and framed its acquisition as an "ecclesiastical necessity" (to Leo III in 797, MGH Epp. 4:184).

132. JE 2789, BH 764, MGH Epp. 6:640.

providing testimony at the risk of his eternal salvation.[133] His obligation extended even further, for his presence afforded an opportunity for the pope to influence the local church's affairs: "If necessary, he should be able to stay here at least thirty days, so that an inclination to depart may not take away from what advantage and ecclesiastical custom dictate.... Send such a man ... who is spurred by no restlessness, but lingers among us until we are able to write back, with prudent consideration and at sufficient length, about the things on which you consult [us]."[134] Clearly, in the interest of *utilitas*, the pope intended to use the pallium trip to create lines of communication between the provinces and the papacy, and he realized its potential significance by answering questions and issuing instructions, to be sent home with the envoy. Two years later the same pope charged King Lothar II to replace the deposed archbishops of Trier and Cologne: those who were elected and consecrated, "sending famous and prudent legates," had to procure pallia from the apostolic see.[135] In this era a personal appearance by the petitioner was not required, but the task and its implications were taken quite seriously and demanded prestigious, trustworthy executors.

As in other areas related to the pallium, Nicholas enforced his injunctions strictly. In 868 his successor, Pope Hadrian II, wrote to the fathers of the Council of Troyes (867), who had requested the pallium for Wulfhad as archbishop of Bourges. Nicholas had postponed the decision and died before it could be resolved, and Hadrian explained the reason for the delay: his predecessor "would have long since gladly assented ... if he who tried to receive [the pallium] had been proven to have been sent from the church of Bourges."[136] One papal reservation, then, had revolved around the synodal emissary, Actard of Nantes, who sought the vestment for Wulfhad of Bourges but did not represent that church (*ex proprio clero*, as Nicholas had written in the

---

133. Gottlob observes that the envoy swore not only as a witness to what the bishop believed and intended, but also as a stand-in for the bishop (*Kirchlicher Amtseid*, 32).

134. JE 2789, BH 764, MGH Epp. 6:640.

135. JE 2878, GP 7.1:27–28 no. 44, GP 10.1:34–35 no. 40, BH 855, MGH Epp. 6:334.

136. JE 2894, MGH Epp. 6:699.

case of Dol). Hadrian, however, showed himself more indulgent. As he mentioned in a later letter, his esteem for Actard convinced him to commit the pallium to his care.¹³⁷ The implication of the whole affair was that even bearing the vestment for another was a token of papal favor, and one not lightly consigned.

Prelates as Pilgrims

Despite the prevailing practice, a personal appearance was never discouraged. When Emperor Lothar I beseeched Pope Leo IV in the late 840s to grant the pallium to Hincmar as archbishop of Reims, he envisioned two possible manners of reception:

> We confidently entreat and earnestly request from your Paternity that, whether the mentioned archbishop approaches your Holiness himself or sends legates of his church, you do not deny them the most complete abundance of your affability and conversation and familiarity, but treat both him and his men most kindly for the sake of our love, and fulfill whatever he requests of you with suitable reason, including the bestowal of the pallium.¹³⁸

Whether in person or through envoys, the encounter between the provincials and the papacy was a key moment in establishing a relationship. The pope's welcome was crucial as an outward gesture of his acceptance of the archiepiscopal candidate. In addition, Pope Nicholas I explicitly authorized the same two alternatives when he explained the necessary profession of faith to the missionary Ansgar in 864: his successors were required to submit it "themselves or through their legates and letter."¹³⁹ In fact, although the formula *Si pastores ovium* used the word *transmisimus*, "we have sent [the pallium]," the variant formula preferred from the pontificate of Gregory IV onward substituted the less specific, more flexible word *concedimus*, "we grant."¹⁴⁰ This deviation and its implied leeway indicated that the popes val-

---

137. To the Council of Soissons in 868, JE 2903, MGH Epp. 6:707.
138. MGH Epp. 5:611.
139. JE 2759, GP 6:31–32 no. 21, BH 706, Curschmann, *Ältere Papsturkunden*, 23.
140. V45, Foerster, *Liber Diurnus*, 101, with parallels C44 on 200 and A39 on 300; and, e.g., Gregory IV to Liudpram of Salzburg in 837, JE 2580, GP 1:10 no. 14, Hauthaler and Martin, *Salzburger Urkundenbuch*, 2:27.

ued the chance to meet applicants for the pallium personally, when possible.

Instances of the personal reception of the pallium were not rare, as certain bishops found it necessary or advantageous to make the journey themselves. One common occasion in this period was that of a political embassy, a task often performed by high-ranking churchmen. Between 784 and 791, Ermenbert of Bourges came to Rome to bring certain matters to Pope Hadrian I's attention on behalf of Charlemagne, one of which was the procurement of the pallium for himself.[141] Similarly, in 798 Arno of Salzburg, one of a delegation sent by Charlemagne to Rome, brought back from Pope Leo III not only papal messages for the king, but also the pallium for himself.[142] That Arno received the vestment in person may also be deduced from his pallium grant: though based on the formula *Officium sacerdotis*, it substituted *dedimus*, "we have given [the pallium]," for the standard *transmisimus*, "we have sent."[143]

Two years later Leo conferred the pallium on Theodulf of Orléans, one of Charlemagne's closest advisors, after he had accompanied the king to Rome and there defended the pope at a synod convoked to examine charges against him. In a later poem he recalled "the Roman prelate ... / From whose hand I received the holy pallium."[144]

141. Hadrian I to Charlemagne, JE 2475, MGH Epp. 3:628.

142. *Conversio Bagoariorum et Carantanorum*, in Fritz Lošek, ed., *Die* Conversio Bagoariorum et Carantanorum *und der Brief des Erzbischofs Theotmar von Salzburg*, Monumenta Germaniae Historica Studien und Texte 15 (Hannover: Hahn, 1997), 114, and *Annales Iuvavenses Antiqui*, in MGH SS 30.2:736–37.

143. V46, Foerster, *Liber Diurnus*, 104, with parallels C45 on 203 and A40 on 305; and Leo III to Arno in 798, JE 2498, GP 1:8 no. 7, Dopsch, "Papst Leo III. verleiht," 18. The document also referred to an oral rather than written profession of faith.

144. *De Suo Exilio*, in Dieter Schaller, ed., "Philologische Untersuchungen zu den Gedichten Theodulfs von Orléans," *Deutsches Archiv für Erforschung des Mittelalters* 18 (1962): 45. Cf. Alcuin to Theodulf in 801, MGH Epp. 4:368–69. See Ann Freeman and Paul Meyvaert, "The Meaning of Theodulf's Apse Mosaic at Germigny-des-Prés," *Gesta* 40 (2001): 126. In poetry it was not unusual to refer to the pallium in the plural, probably due to metrical demands; cf. Alcuin, *Versus de Patribus Regibus et Sanctis Euboricensis Ecclesiae*, in Godman, *Bishops*, 100, and *Epitaphium Chrodegangi*, in *Monumenta Germaniae Historica: Poetae Latini Medii Aevi* (Berlin: Weidmann, etc., 1881–), 1:108 [hereafter "MGH Poet."]. On the synod, see Hartmann, *Synoden*, 122–23.

Indeed, from time to time the pope spontaneously granted the pallium to a royal emissary as a gesture of benevolence. Actard, exiled bishop of Nantes, acted as Charles the Bald's envoy to Pope Hadrian II in 868 in the ongoing case of Ebo of Reims, and the tale of Actard's persecutions by Vikings and Bretons so moved the pope that the bishop came away bedecked with the pallium.[145] And when Pope John VIII sent another envoy of Charles the Bald, Bishop Adalgar of Autun, back to his master with the pallium in 876, it was intended as a sign of friendship with the emperor.[146] In these varied political contexts, the arrival of a prelate in Rome offered a chance for diplomacy, and the bestowal of the pallium itself could sometimes play a role in ecclesiastical-secular relations, for example, as a gift meant to please a bishop's lord and gain his good will. The last three cases involved suffragan bishops, that is, non-metropolitans, who were not bound to obtain the vestment and did not usually possess it. Thus its character as a special favor was pronounced.

For some bishops the journey was religiously motivated. In 824 Arno's successor, Adalram of Salzburg, had the opportunity to be palliated when he visited Rome to pray at its shrines.[147] Any trip to the Eternal City, teeming with the relics of ancient martyrs, could be framed as a pilgrimage, but a trip to obtain the pallium—which itself, taken from the tomb of Peter, had the characteristics of a relic—was especially suited to that interpretation. For other bishops the journey was a customary part of installation. Some Italian and Dalmatian archbishops, lying under the immediate jurisdiction of the apostolic see, came to Rome both for consecration and for the pallium.[148] Pope

145. Hadrian II to Charles the Bald, JE 2902, MGH Epp. 6:704, 706.
146. John VIII to Charles the Bald, JE 3063, BU 213, MGH Epp. 7:23.
147. Louis the Pious to Eugene II, MGH Epp. 5:313. A later account implied that Adalram had been part of an imperial deputation (*Annales Iuvavenses Antiqui*, in MGH SS 30.2:740).
148. The metropolitans of northern Italy (Milan, Aquileia, Grado, and Ravenna) often traveled to Rome to take part in papal synods alongside Roman suffragans; this custom curbed their independence and resulting rivalry with the apostolic see (Januarius Pater, *Die bischöfliche visitatio liminum ss. apostolorum: eine historisch-kanonistische Studie*, Görres-Gesellschaft zur Pflege der Wissenschaft im katholischen Deutschland Veröffentlichungen der Sektion für Rechts- und Sozialwissenschaft 19 [Paderborn: Schöningh, 1914], 11–18). The prefecture of Illyricum, which included Dalmatia,

Leo III's pallium grant for Fortunatus of Grado in 803, like the one for Arno, chose *dedimus* over *transmisimus* and so hinted of the patriarch's personal presence at the time of reception.[149] Around 846 Agnellus of Ravenna recorded that, already two centuries before, Archbishop Maurus had tried to buck the tradition that Ravennese prelates traveled to Rome for episcopal ordination and the pallium.[150] And in 879 Pope John VIII encouraged the archbishop of Split to approach him after election for consecration and the pallium, in accord with *mos pristinus*.[151] Whether to venerate the holy places or to show subjection to the chief bishop of Italy, drawing near the *limina apostolorum* was an act that recognized the unique standing of the Roman church.

As another way of ensuring papal oversight, bishops might be compelled to appear before the pope in difficult cases, when he was hesitant to grant the confirmation symbolized by the pallium. John VIII seems to have been the first to issue such a summons, presumably meant to permit an intensive examination that could not be achieved through letters or legates. The situation was Lothar II's divorce, which plunged the sees of Trier and Cologne into chaos following the deposition of their pastors, whose replacements were subjected to severe scrutiny. In 873, amid questions about the appointment and orthodoxy of Bertulf of Trier, the pope was resolute: "We command your Devotion by apostolic authority in no way to postpone coming to

---

pertained to the direct jurisdiction of the pope, who exercised special rights over it (HEOJ 4:537–38). In Gregory the Great's time, the archbishop of Ravenna behaved as a Roman suffragan and received consecration from the pope, and the archbishops of Milan and Salona required papal consent before consecration (Eidenschink, *Election*, 7–9, 67). See Gaudemet, *L'église*, 445–46, and Ludo Moritz Hartmann, *Geschichte Italiens im Mittelalter*, vol. 2.1, *Römer und Langobarden bis zur Theilung Italiens* (Leipzig: Wigand, 1900), 164–66, 176–79.

149. JE 2512, IP 7.2:40–41 no. 28, Cessi, *Documenti*, 57. John VIII, who was in Gaul in 878 and must have given pallia to Rostagnus of Arles and Wala of Metz in person, replaced "we have sent" in his models with "we have granted" (JE 3148, BU 353, MGH Epp. 7:110; and JE 3183, BU 427, PL 126:798). Given its earlier use (e.g., Gregory IV to Liudpram of Salzburg in 837, JE 2580, GP 1:10 no. 14, Hauthaler and Martin, *Salzburger Urkundenbuch*, 2:27), the verb "grant" (*concedere*), reflecting "condescension," was not a sign of "new regard" for the pallium in papal thought of the late ninth century, as Grierson supposes ("Rostagnus," 75).

150. *Liber Pontificalis Ecclesiae Ravennatis*, in Nauerth, *Bischofsbuch*, 412.

151. To the Dalmatian bishops, JE 3262, BU 530, MGH Epp. 7:157.

Rome, except by reason of physical impairment. But if, held back by illness, you are unable to come yourself, we wish you, remaining both devout and faithful to the holy Roman church and the empire of our most beloved son [Louis II], to send conscientious legates of your church who may prevail to satisfy us in your place."[152] The deadline imposed was October of the same year, although the allowance of an excuse for illness showed a degree of flexibility.

With Willibert of Cologne John was even sterner, for the letter and legate he had sent to Rome did not suffice to quell the protests of complainants who had come to the pope in person:

> Having spurned all the irksomeness of resentment and sluggishness, hurry to the apostolic see, so prepared that you yourself, in person, may be able to respond to your accusers, who will certainly be found in person, and may, God willing, refute all their objections with suitable reasoning.... We are afraid that, if you are weakened by the double-talk of certain flatteries, or perhaps excuses, and consider that these words of ours do not have to be obeyed, and withdraw your presence from the hearing of our particular examination, you will produce an unfavorable impression of yourself, which we do not desire—or rather, what is more serious, you will prove the things that have been said about you, if you do not show your presence to us to wash them away.[153]

The archbishop had to appear in order to defend himself, face-to-face with his opponents. To judge from John's worry that the summons would be refused, for causes both internal (*rancor, torpor*) and external (*adulationes, excusationes*), personal presence was not easy to enforce. Undoubtedly the trip was arduous and expensive. Thus the pope added teeth to his order by threatening suspension if Willibert did not appear within a month or two.[154] Despite these vigorous efforts, the resolution of the tense situation in 874 was something of an anticlimax: John, "providing for [the archbishop's] old age and sickness," sent the pallium to Willibert.[155] However imperfectly realized, the journey to Rome for the pallium was a tool the pope could

---

152. JE 2982, GP 10.1:37 no. 49, BU 87, MGH Epp. 7:288.

153. JE 2986, GP 7.1:34 no. 66, BU 96, MGH Epp. 7:314–15. One witness, here adopted, reads "irksomeness" (*tedio*) instead of "hatred" (*odio*).

154. Ibid., 7:314.

155. JE 2988, GP 7.1:34–35 no. 67, BU 120, Wisplinghoff, *Rheinisches Urkundenbuch*, 2:158–59.

employ to implement his oversight of the Latin hierarchy in problematic situations. This idea had a rich history ahead of it.

Conclusion

Once it had become customary, and then obligatory, to request the pallium from the pope, many of the most important bishops in the Latin church submitted to papal authority in order to obtain the vestment. The process of seeking and receiving the pallium became an opportunity for the papacy, a pretext for direct papal intervention in the examination and installation of churchmen near and far. With the leverage supplied by this gift, the popes were able to demand certain kinds of belief and conduct on the part of candidates, to oversee their succession in the church's most significant sees, to correct and punish behavior at odds with Roman precepts, and to take advantage of contacts made during the acquisition of the pallium. As effective as this manipulation of the old practice could be, it was only the beginning. Beyond the rather direct, short-term use of the pallium lay the more nebulous but broader impact of its conferral on the sphere of relationships. The following chapter will explore the ways in which the gift, by affecting how the key players stood in relation to one another, was a truly political instrument, with echoes beyond its initial reception.

2

Bestowing the Pallium

For Boniface, the gift of the pallium, which Pope Gregory III sent him around 732, was a tangible sign of his closeness to Rome. According to Willibald's life of the saint, written shortly after his death in 754/55, the missionary to Germany had dispatched envoys to the pontiff to recount the "pacts of previous friendship" extended by the last pope, to express his "devoted subjection of humility" to the papacy, and to request his continued participation in the "familiarity and communion" of the apostolic see. In reply Gregory readily granted him and his subjects "communion of familiarity and friendship," conferred the pallium on him, and sent the envoys home laden with gifts and relics. Boniface was overjoyed by the "support of the apostolic see's devotion."[1] These ties of intimacy between pope and prelate, partly created and represented by the pallium, relied both on papal favor and on the recipient's submission.

Whereas the previous chapter studied the mechanics of receiving the pallium, the present chapter looks at the dynamics of conferring it, that is, the larger forces at work through the transaction. Many of the sources are the same, but the focus is now on the relationships formed when the vestment was granted. How were the popes

1. Rau, *Briefe*, 498.

hoping to finesse social and political connections within their world? How did others perceive and react to these interventions?

The communication of a significant gift creates a bond between donor and recipient. Through it the donor can make and keep friends, recruit followers, win support, fine-tune political relations, maintain his own rule—in short, make and manage social networks of alliances.[2] As Mauss observed, to make a gift is to give part of oneself, and this close association between two parties can refashion identities and reimagine relationships.[3] At the same time, this friendship is lopsided because it is unequal in power, and so loyalty blurs into submission.[4] A gift shapes the exercise of power not only between donor and recipient, but also among all who participate in the transaction or are affected by its consequences. As a result, the donor may frame or supplement the gift so as to imply a particular relationship between himself and the recipient. He may employ the gift in his interactions with interested third parties by encouraging or discouraging their involvement. And he may influence the balance of power within a network of recipients, each enjoying a similar gift. In all three of these ways, the popes of this period astutely handled the conferral of the pallium in order to manipulate ecclesio-political relations.

Relationship with the Recipient

The bond established between pope and palliger was strong and multivalent. It drew the two parties closer together through the sharing of a prized insigne, while also emphasizing the superiority of the one at whose discretion the gift was given. In addition, the recipient of papal garb benefited from the added prestige and often assumed important functions on behalf of the papacy. All these aims—intimacy and subjection, authority and representation—increased the influence of Rome, even as they privileged the local bishop.

---

2. See White, "Politics," 171–72, and Bijsterveld, *Do ut des*, 49.
3. See Mauss, "Gift," 12, and Algazi, "Introduction," 16–18, 24.
4. See White, "Politics," 179, and Curta, "Merovingian and Carolingian Gift-giving," 684, 692–93.

Intimacy and Subjection

Receiving a gift of such import as the pallium, which was first and foremost the badge of the pope himself, united the recipient more closely to the papacy while simultaneously placing him in the papacy's debt. This lopsided relationship, an intimacy between unequals, was made manifest from the start of the Carolingian era. Pope Zachary assented to Boniface's request in 744 for pallia for Rouen, Reims, and Sens "for the unification and reform of the churches of Christ."[5] It is hard to say what the pope meant. The *reformatio* probably referred to the restoration of the provincial structure, but the *adunatio* may well have indicated the unity under Rome that the reception of the Roman vestments entailed. Boniface certainly shared this sentiment. His reform synod of 747 promised to observe "unity with and subjection to the Roman church" alongside the obligation for metropolitans to obtain pallia and obey papal orders. When this promise was delivered to the apostolic see, the Roman bishop and clergy, unsurprisingly, rejoiced.[6]

Two of the formulas provided by the *Liber Diurnus* for pallium grants, *Apostolicae sedis* and *Pallii usum*, presumed that the conferral reflected or resulted in a friendly relationship. The first, intended "for the bishops of Sicily," began by acknowledging an affectionate bond: "Stirred by the good will of the apostolic see," the pope decided to bestow the pallium.[7] Such favor might be expected for the Sicilian bishops, who were immediately subject to the pope and administered large tracts of property for the Roman church.[8] But the other

---

5. JE 2271, GP 4:24 no. 58, Rau, *Briefe*, 170.
6. Boniface to Cuthbert of Canterbury, Rau, *Briefe*, 240.
7. V48, Foerster, *Liber Diurnus*, 106, with slight variants C47 on 205 and A42 on 308. A formula dedicated to Sicilian recipients probably reflected the unusual frequency with which Sicilian bishops received the pallium at the time the *Liber Diurnus* was put together.
8. See IP 10:167, 193–94, 214; Merlin, "Concession"; and Hartmann, *Geschichte*, 2.1:161–62. Some theorize that Sicilian bishops followed the Eastern custom, according to which even simple bishops regularly received the pallium (e.g., H. Grisar, "Das römische Pallium und die ältesten liturgischen Schärpen," in *Festschrift zum elfhundertjährigen Jubiläum des deutschen Campo Santo in Rom*, ed. Stephan Ehses [Freiburg: Herder, 1897], 110–11). Hacke observes that this formula mentioned no

formula spoke more broadly. In this geographically non-specific text, the gift of the pallium arose from papal fondness, "to show you and your church the charity of the same apostolic see ... [in consideration of] the good will and affection of the apostolic see for you." On this account the pope shared with the palliger his own vesture and prerogative: "We have sent the pallium from our use also to you." Its purpose was "to show the unanimity with blessed Peter the apostle that the whole flock of the Lord's sheep entrusted to him doubtlessly has."[9] The vestment was an expression of spiritual union with Peter, and thus his successor, to whom the universal church was committed.[10] Although these two formulas enjoyed scanty use in this period, their conception and continuing availability in the papal chancery illuminated a Roman attitude towards the pallium. In such thinking, the woolen band became a tie to the mother church of Rome and a thread in the tapestry that knit together the Western church.

This mindset took root early in the Roman church and was widely recognized by the ninth century. John the Deacon reproduced a letter in which Gregory the Great addressed Maximus of Salona during the latter's reconciliation with Rome: "When you have finally taken wholesome advice and humbly submitted yourself to the yoke of obedience ... understand that the grace of brotherly charity has been returned to you, and rejoice that you have been received in our fellowship.... Therefore, after your Fraternity learns that he has recovered the communion of the apostolic see, he should send us a person who may receive the pallium."[11] Obedience springing from submission permitted the reception of favor born of *fraterna caritas,* as well as ecclesial communion with the pope. This state subsequently allowed, and was signified by, the acquisition of the pallium.

---

preceding petition, which indicated special treatment of the Sicilians (*Palliumverleihungen,* 62).

9. V47, Foerster, *Liber Diurnus,* 106, with slight variants C46 on 204–5 and A41 on 307–8. The phrase "from our use" probably referred to the pope's wearing (*usus*) of the pallium, a right now shared with the recipient, but it may have simply meant "according to our custom."

10. Hacke finds in this union an effective dependence and subjection (*Palliumverleihungen,* 61).

11. PL 75:180, quoting JE 1703.

Similarly, the chronicle of the patriarchs of Grado from the 820s/30s linked the pallium to union with the Roman church. It looked back to a crucial papal intervention after a heretic had seized the see: condemning the invader, Pope Honorius I had appointed a Roman deacon, Primogenius, as metropolitan, "and till today the pontiff of the city of Grado has merited the blessing of the pallium from the supreme apostolic see."[12] Although the language made the bond sound more like a well-deserved gift than a tool of papal influence, the account served to justify Roman influence over Grado, independent-minded and in Honorius's time only recently returned to communion with the papacy.[13] Also, when Ado of Vienne or his circle forged support for their church's claim to apostolicity, their invented papal letter coupled their alleged Roman ties to a pallium grant: "Your church, which took the foundation of its holy condition from [Rome]," it read, "ought to keep [Roman] custom and instructions. Not wishing you to be deprived of the ancient gift of blessed Peter, we have sent you the use of the venerable pallium ... at the same time sending some of St. Paul's hairs."[14] Imitating the Roman church in its liturgy and its relics, Vienne also boasted the pallium as a sign of Roman prestige—even while such a derivative sign implicitly subordinated Vienne to Rome.

Even when a petitioner for the pallium offered a countergift, in an effort to retain some control in the exchange and to persuade the pope to acquiesce to the grant, he was left in an ancillary position. The two prelates who intervened with Pope Hadrian II on behalf of Willibert of Cologne in 870 attempted this kind of reciprocation. Liudbert of Mainz requested the pallium for him so that, "wreathed with it as long as he lives, he may, along with us, implore almighty God for you."[15] Gunther of Cologne, Willibert's predecessor, also sought the pallium for him "so that it may delight both us and him

12. Monticolo, *Cronache*, 1:10–11. Antoninus acquired the pallium from Gregory III "according to the example of his predecessors," as did Fortunatus from Leo III (ibid., 1:14).
13. Grado participated in the schism of the Three Chapters from about 553 to 607 (IP 7.1:13).
14. JE †2146, GaP 3.1:85–86 no. †63b, MGH Epp. 3:92.
15. MGH Epp. 6:244.

equally to love, praise, and venerate, and to visit with due services, such a great pontiff, namely you, Lord Hadrian."[16] The gifts proffered in return—lifelong prayer, devoted respect, and future service—came at great cost. The palliger remained at a subsidiary level, in the papacy's debt, obliged to admit and assist Roman preeminence. Nor was the pope persuaded by the countergifts, for it required several more years of negotiations and a change of popes before Willibert received his pallium.[17]

The implications of this bond were not always willingly acknowledged. Notwithstanding the pallium's prestige, the subjection it entailed could chafe. The Annals of Xanten observed that Archbishops Gunther of Cologne and Thietgaud of Trier, angry because of an adverse papal judgment concerning Lothar II's divorce, violated the submission implied by their vestments: "Those bishops again sent rash compositions back to Pope Nicholas [I] ... promising that, without his grace, they wished to boast equally in their places as he did in Rome, and that their rank was in no way lower than his rank—not recalling that they received the pallium of dignity from him."[18] They had accepted the sign of their *dignitas* (and, in an age when the clothes made the man, in a sense the *dignitas* itself) as a gift from the papacy, which *ipso facto* relegated them to a subordinate position, that of recipient.[19] This repercussion was even more stridently resisted by the archbishops of Ravenna, traditional rivals of the papacy in northern Italy. Around 846 Agnellus of Ravenna recounted the archbishops' efforts to wrest their freedom from Rome. That program had included the substitution of an imperial pallium for a papal one:

---

16. MGH Epp. 6:247.

17. Willibert finally obtained the pallium from John VIII in 874 (JE 2988, GP 7.1:34–35 no. 67, BU 120, Wisplinghoff, *Rheinisches Urkundenbuch*, 2:158–59).

18. MGH SSRG 12:22. In this study *dignitas* is usually translated simply as "dignity," in order to allow room for the various connotations of the Latin, including "worthiness," "authority," and "rank" (Lewis and Short, *Latin Dictionary*, 577–78), "high office," "prerogative," and "the rights and possessions forming the base of a lord's power" (Niermeyer, *Mediae Latinitatis Lexicon*, 331–32), and "right, privilege" (Du Cange, *Glossarium*, 3:117–18).

19. In the central Middle Ages, essence and appearance, the office and the representation of the office, coincided. See Heinrich Fichtenau, *Living in the Tenth Century: Mentalities and Social Orders*, trans. Patrick J. Geary (Chicago: University of Chicago Press, 1991), 50.

Many times [Archbishop Maurus] approached Constantinople in order to throw off from his church the yoke of or dependence on the Romans. And so it happened, and the church of Ravenna was removed, so that nevermore should a future shepherd of the church of Ravenna go to Rome for consecration.... Nor would she ever be under the jurisdiction of that Roman pontiff, but she would consecrate her elect here, by three of her own bishops, and get the pallium from the emperor of Constantinople.[20]

The issue was twofold: by whom was the archbishop of Ravenna consecrated, and from whom did he obtain the pallium? While the Ravennese could carry out their own consecration, they assumed that they could not make their own pallium (as the Romans did) but had to resort to a higher authority, and so had recourse to the emperor.[21] Thus the pallium, formerly the *iugum Romanorum*, might become an expression of independence from Roman rule.

The popes too were sensitive to the origin of their own pallia. Around 853 Pope Leo IV politely declined the pallium sent to him by Patriarch Ignatius of Constantinople: "It is not the custom of this church, since she is seen to be the mistress and head of all the churches, to accept a pallium bequeathed from elsewhere, but to hand it out through the whole of Europe to those to whom it is assigned."[22] Even though the pope did not interpret the gift as a bid to exert control, but only as a gesture of friendship, he sent back the unsought vestment. Receiving it would have indicated a reliance that would have made the Roman church beholden to Constantinople, in stark contrast to papal self-understanding. Instead, Rome

20. *Liber Pontificalis Ecclesiae Ravennatis*, in Nauerth, *Bischofsbuch*, 412. Cf. the archbishop's dying admonition (ibid., 420).

21. Agnellus's accounts, especially concerning the rights of Ravenna, are not always reliable, but an apparently genuine privilege of Emperor Constans II for Maurus in 666 granted autocephaly to that church and promised to confer the pallium on its archbishops (*Monumenta Germaniae Historica: Scriptores Rerum Langobardicarum et Italicarum* [Hannover: Hahn, etc., 1878–], 1:351n). The pallium would come from the emperor himself, not the patriarch of Constantinople.

22. JE 2647, BH 113, MGH Epp. 5:607. The pope ignored the case of Ravenna and the possibility that the Roman pontiff himself had originally received the pallium from the emperor. Although he called Rome the chief "of all the churches," he said that its role to distribute pallia was exercised "through the whole of Europe," which was a more limited area that left room to Eastern patriarchs to bestow *omophoria* on their own bishops. Cf. K. J. Leyser, "Concepts of Europe in the Early and High Middle Ages," *Past and Present* 137 (1992): 40.

portrayed herself as the great donor of pallia, which contributed to her role as *magistra et caput*.[23] Indeed, Pope John VIII did not hesitate to send a pallium to Ignatius's successor, Patriarch Photius, as a sign of unity: "That our lord the pope holds the Lord Photius himself, the most holy patriarch, as his own soul, and is one spirit and one body with him, and reckons him a brother and fellow minister," the papal legate announced before the Council of Constantinople (879–80), "the priestly stole sent by him itself also bears witness." Then he presented "the pontifical stole sent by the most holy Pope John, the pallium, tunic, chasuble, and sandals."[24] The gift was a concrete manifestation of communion, a way of making an invisible relationship visible. Examining this evidence, the fathers came to believe the papal declarations of friendship that were formerly mere words.[25] The Eastern mentality may not have grasped the inequality that Western eyes saw in the bond, but both sides valued the expression of closeness.[26]

John VIII hammered home the special relationship between pope and palliger in many of his letters. He gave the pallium to Thietmar I

---

23. Gift-giving asserts the donor's status, and he defines his rank by giving; indeed, the range of a leader's network of alliances, forged through gift-giving, determines his sphere of power (Reuter, "Gifts," 164, and Bijsterveld, *Do ut des*, 39).

24. *Acta Pseudo-Synodi Photianae*, in Joannes Dominicus Mansi, ed., *Sacrorum Conciliorum Nova et Amplissima Collectio* (Florence and Venice, 1759–93), 17:389. Was "pallium" (*omophoron*) in apposition to "stole," or meant as a separate vestment? Since the stole was specified as "pontifical," it was likely the pallium. Its inclusion in a set of pontifical vestments may have made it more palatable to the Greeks: rather than being accentuated as an instrument of power, as in the West, it was placed in the context of other liturgical vestments, its primary significance in the East. On the acts of this council and their authenticity, see Johan Meijer, *A Successful Council of Union: A Theological Analysis of the Photian Synod of 879–880*, Analecta Vlatadon 23 (Thessaloniki: Patriarchal Institute for Patristic Studies, 1975), 49–56.

25. *Acta Pseudo-Synodi Photianae*, in Mansi, *Sacrorum Conciliorum Collectio*, 17:389.

26. In response to the pope's recognition of him as "brother and fellow minister," Photius called John not only the same, but also "spiritual father"; yet it is uncertain to what degree the patriarch intended to embrace the pope's superiority. Dvornik holds that the Byzantines saw the presented pallium only as a token of friendship (*Photian Schism*, 199). According to Meijer, the gift was equivalent to papal recognition of the patriarch's restoration (*Successful Council*, 59). Still, in c. 17 of the Council of Constantinople ten years before, the (mostly Eastern) fathers had associated the bestowal of the vestment with the exercise of supervision (Alberigo et al., *Conciliorum Oecumenicorum Decreta*, 179).

of Salzburg in 877, he said, so that "you may be ever faithful, devoted to the holy Roman church, from which you take a drink from a splendid cup and have been made her partner for the future, on whose foundations the whole earth is forever based."[27] The metaphorical chalice offered to the archbishop produced an intimate communion, as if he became an honorary member of the Roman church, or at least its close collaborator (*particeps*). When Rostagnus of Arles sought the pallium in 878, in accord with the privileges of his predecessors, the pope characterized it as a form of filial loyalty: "When your Fraternity repeats the old custom of the apostolic see, what else but a good offspring returns to the lap of its mother?"[28] Likewise, for Dalmatian archbishops to resume coming to Rome for consecration and the pallium, as in olden times, meant, in John's words from 879, "to turn back wholeheartedly and willingly to the see of blessed Peter the apostle, which is the head and mistress of all the churches of God, and to us." Acknowledging the competition for Dalmatia's allegiance "on the part of the Greeks and Slavs," the pope forbade future archbishops to accept a foreign pallium.[29] Non-Latin churches with designs on Dalmatia might well object to the restored relations with the pope represented in part by the Roman pallium and attempt to confer their own *omophorion* in its place.

This kind of struggle, a tug-of-war with ropes of wool, was exemplified in the jurisdictional contest between the Latin and Greek churches over the newly converted nation of Bulgaria in the 860s and 870s.[30] In 879, while negotiating with the Byzantine emperor about the restoration of Photius of Constantinople, John VIII agreed to recognize him "if that patriarch from now on presumes by no means to lay claim to or keep hold of the diocese of the Bulgarians for his own jurisdiction ... and does no ordination of whatever honor in the same place ... and does not presume to send the sa-

---

27. JE 3115, GP 1:12–13 no. 24, BU 290, MGH Epp. 7:58.
28. JE 3148, BU 353, MGH Epp. 7:109, quoting JE 1374.
29. To the Dalmatian bishops, JE 3262, BU 530, MGH Epp. 7:157.
30. See Dvornik, *Photian Schism*, and A. P. Vlasto, *The Entry of the Slavs into Christendom: An Introduction to the Medieval History of the Slavs* (Cambridge: Cambridge University Press, 1970), 158–64.

cred pallium."[31] His message to Photius himself was more forceful: Greek missionaries "should withdraw from there and altogether curb themselves from the invasion of our Bulgarian diocese. If you either give them the pallium, or do an ordination of any sort there, or communicate with them, you will be held bound with them by an equal excommunication, until they obey us."[32] The Byzantine patriarch's bestowal of the pallium in Roman territory was an excommunicable offense: it intruded upon the pope's jurisdiction, for it created a bond of subjection to a patriarch other than himself. It erected a local hierarchy independent of its true superior and thereby annulled his authority. The omission of this passage in the version of the letter that Photius presented to the so-called Photian Synod (879–80) arose from the Eastern conviction that the question belonged to the competence of the emperor, not the patriarch.[33] The council accordingly avoided the Bulgarian matter, despite John's instructions to his legates to warn the patriarch *coram synodo* of the canonical consequences of sending the pallium to Bulgaria.[34] Far from a trivial gesture, the pope's dispatch of pallia to the provinces secured them as members of the Western church and adherents of papal authority—strands in a web centered on Rome.

31. To Basil I, JE 3271, BU 551, MGH Epp. 7:173–74. On the altered Greek version of this letter (prepared in Constantinople for the council), which softened the pope's demand to a request, see Meijer, *Successful Council*, 41–42, 45–49, 74–96.

32. JE 3273, BU 553, MGH Epp. 7:185–86. On the altered Greek version of this letter (prepared in Constantinople for the council), which omitted this passage, see Meijer, *Successful Council*, 42–43, 45–49, 96–106.

33. Through negotiations with the papal legates, resulting in the alterations to the papal letters, Photius worked out a compromise between Roman and Byzantine claims, an understanding accepted by John VIII: while Greek clergy could continue to minister in Bulgaria, the Bulgarian archbishop would apply to Rome for the pallium. Culturally it remained Greek, while pertaining to Roman jurisdiction. Neither side won, however, for meanwhile the Bulgarian king laid the foundations for a national, autocephalous church (Dvornik, *Photian Schism*, 210–15).

34. JE 3276, BU 555, MGH Epp. 7:189n. On the Greek version of this *commonitorium*, prepared in Constantinople for the council and presumably altered (though not in this passage) from the lost Latin original, see Meijer, *Successful Council*, 44–49, 112–20.

Authority and Representation

Since its recipients often willingly sought and valued the pallium, they must not have seen it merely as an obligation or a sign of subordination. Indeed, the relationship it represented came with significant advantages. One benefit was the backing provided by this symbol of papal authority—the added influence arising from this visible attachment to the successor of Peter. Alcuin alluded to it in 797 when he begged the pope to grant the pallium to Eanbald II of York: "The authority of the sacred pallium is very necessary in those regions to oppress the perversity of the dishonest and preserve the authority of holy church. On that account, most holy father and best shepherd, have mercy on the sons of your Paternity, and multiply the flock entrusted to you."[35] Perhaps a palliger commanded more respect from friends and foes because he possessed papal support, made manifest in his apparel.

Likewise, when he interceded with Pope Eugene II in 824, Emperor Louis the Pious recognized the help that the pallium would furnish Adalram of Salzburg. He requested "the pallium of your holy authority ... so that the same archbishop, strengthened and fortified by the authority and blessing of your Holiness, may be able henceforth by sacred teachings and exhortations to guide the people ... to the condition of a better life."[36] It is unclear how the pallium could aid Adalram's preaching and reinforce his leadership, except by inclining his listeners to regard him with greater esteem. After all, it was here described as the pope's own badge of authority, now to be shared with the archbishop. Similar sentiments surfaced when Gunther of Cologne solicited the pallium for his successor, Willibert, in 870. As the new archbishop was "most devoted" to the apostolic see, Gunther asked the pope for the "support of apostolic authority and approval" that came with the vestment, for the good of the church of Cologne.[37] Also interceding for Willibert, King Louis the German told the pope that, wearing the pallium, the archbishop would be "fes-

---

35. To Leo III, MGH Epp. 4:184. 36. MGH Epp. 5:313.
37. To Hadrian II, MGH Epp. 6:247.

tooned with your authority."³⁸ Apparently, a metropolitan's native prestige did not suffice; it had to be buttressed by that of the Roman church in order to be fully effective.

The common theme in these examples—that the pallium signified or conveyed papal *auctoritas*—was more formally incarnated in the position of official papal representative. The vestment had sometimes been the emblem of papal vicars in antiquity, and this practice was expanded in this period.³⁹ In the eighth century the phenomenon of palliated missionaries with papal backing came to the fore. Corbinian was consecrated, granted the vestment, and sent forth to evangelize: "Having received the pallium with the sanction of blessed Peter, prince of the apostles, from the report of such a great father [Pope Gregory II], he had the power to exercise the office of preaching everywhere he could through the whole world."⁴⁰ Willibrord, though already enjoying great missionary success, was sent to Rome to add papal support to his efforts: "[Pope Sergius I] clothed him with his own priestly vestments and the holy pallium of dignity ... and confirmed him with the glory of his garment ... and sent him back again, confirmed with his blessing and enriched with gifts, along with salvific instructions, for the work of the Gospel."⁴¹ As observed above, Willibrord's successor, Boniface, followed a similar pattern.⁴²

---

38. MGH Epp. 6:249.

39. An example of the ancient custom, namely the pallium and vicariate for John of Prima Justiniana, was remembered in John the Deacon's life of Gregory the Great (PL 75:144). Similarly, John VIII recalled that several late antique bishops of Arles had acted as papal vicars in Gaul and received the pallium. He revived the custom, and even the old Gregorian form of the accompanying privilege, for Rostagnus of Arles in 878 (JE 3148, BU 353, MGH Epp. 7:109–10). On the development of papal legation, see Kriston R. Rennie, *The Foundations of Medieval Papal Legation* (Basingstoke: Palgrave Macmillan, 2013), esp. 159–61, where he compares palligers in certain respects to the later phenomenon of *legati nati*.

40. Arbeo of Freising, *Vita Prima Corbiniani*, in MGH SSRG 13:197. However, the author of this *vita* may have embellished Corbinian's career by modeling him upon Boniface (Ian Wood, *The Missionary Life: Saints and the Evangelisation of Europe, 400–1050* [Harlow: Longman, 2001], 157–58).

41. Alcuin, *Vita Willibrordi*, in Reischmann, *Willibrord*, 58. Sergius may have vested Willibrord with his own pallium as a sign of special favor, an act not unknown to future generations.

42. Willibald, *Vita S. Bonifacii*, in Rau, *Briefe*, 498. Willibrord and Boniface may

A palliated metropolitan, moreover, could act as the pope's agent. Pope Hadrian I commissioned Tilpin of Reims to look into the problematic election of Lull of Mainz.[43] Boniface, explaining the acts of the reform synod (747) that had obligated metropolitans to request pallia from the apostolic see, depicted them as papal liaisons: "All bishops ought to make it known to the metropolitan, and he himself to the Roman pontiff, if anything in regard to correcting the peoples is impossible for them."[44] In a new twist on their old role, metropolitans were now seen as mid-level overseers, provincial intermediaries between pope and bishops.[45] Accordingly, in 819 Rabanus Maurus, in his textbook for the clergy, *De Institutione Clericorum*, viewed the papally conferred pallium as the sign of an ongoing link with the pope: "The honor of the pallium is decreed for a supreme pontiff, who is called an archbishop, because of his apostolic vicariate."[46] In this scheme, archbishops functioned as local representatives of Roman authority, which justified their use of a papal vestment. They

---

well have imitated the earlier English models of Augustine and Theodore of Canterbury; Pope Zachary succinctly characterized the latter as "educated in Athens, ordained in Rome, exalted with the pallium, sent to Britain" (to Boniface in 748, JE 2286, Rau, *Briefe*, 258).

43. JE 2411, GP 4:61 no. 22, Lesne, "Lettre," 351.

44. To Cuthbert of Canterbury, Rau, *Briefe*, 242.

45. Originally a metropolitan, whose role was confined to his province, acted in union with his comprovincial bishops, as the coordinator of a body and not with autonomous authority; his function as a distinct superior and a papal agent developed in England and was transferred to the Continent by Boniface (Lesne, *Hiérarchie*, 1–8, 30–37).

46. Detlev Zimpel, ed., *Hrabanus Maurus: De Institutione Clericorum Libri Tres* (Frankfurt: Lang, 1996), 315. Rabanus borrowed some of this language from Isidore of Seville's *Etymologiae*, but Isidore did not mention the pallium (W. M. Lindsay, ed., *Isidori Hispalensis Episcopi Etymologiarum sive Originum Libri XX* [Oxford: Clarendon, 1911], 1:7.12.6). Zimpel sees no reference to the pope here and interprets *apostolicam vicem* as service or office in the apostolic tradition (*De Institutione*, 19). Although Rabanus elsewhere seemed to apply this trait to all bishops (ibid., 299), his assertion that the pallium was granted to archbishops *because of* the *apostolicam vicem* implied that this function was different from other bishops' *apostolorum vicem*—otherwise, all bishops would receive the pallium. Perhaps *apostolorum vicem* referred to apostolic succession, while *apostolicam vicem* referred to representation of the pope (*apostolicus*). The pallium intrinsically evoked a close connection to the papacy, and its association with papal vicariates had clear precedents. At Fulda, where this work was written, remembrance of Boniface, a palliger and papal legate, was strong. Thus the interpretation above, also favored by Braun (*Liturgische Gewandung*, 641), seems preferable.

could implement the papacy's theoretical power and extend its scope in an era of difficult travel and slow communication.

Later papal vicars were also palliated, even if not metropolitans. In 864 King Charles the Bald reminded Pope Nicholas I that Bishop Drogo of Metz had been honored with "surpassing splendor," including both "the use of the pallium" and "the ministry of the apostolic see" as "ambassador of the apostolic see."[47] For this reason, when Emperor Lothar I had previously asked Pope Leo IV to grant Hincmar of Reims not only the pallium, but also "special authority and power in [the pope's] place, and permission to judge the other archbishops or bishops and abbots of that area," the pope refused. Since Sergius II had already granted Drogo the vicariate, Leo would not withdraw it now, as he clarified to Lothar in 851: "We have gladly granted Archbishop Hincmar the use of the pallium.... In that region, however, we have not appointed him vicar in our place, as your Majesty commands, for we cannot justly change the sentence of our predecessor and corrupt his decree without peril to souls."[48] The reference to judging prelates and the repeated phrase *vice nostra* indicated the nature of Drogo's authority: he acted as the pope's local deputy, with the power to settle cases as the pope himself would do if he were not so distant. A palliated metropolitan like Hincmar might enjoy the implicit provincial vicariate described by Rabanus, but an explicitly appointed vicar like Drogo, supported not by a metropolis but by the pallium alone, had broader responsibilities.

47. MGH Epp. 6:223. Drogo received the pallium during Louis the Pious's reign, and as archchaplain served as go-between for emperor and pope, even though an official papal vicariate was not granted until 844 (Sergius II to the transalpine bishops, JE 2586, BH 35, MGH Epp. 5:583–84); see Josef Fleckenstein, *Die Hofkapelle der deutschen Könige*, Monumenta Germaniae Historica Schriften 16.1 (Stuttgart: Hiersemann, 1959), 1:55–56, 119–21. Drogo consecrated Ansgar as bishop (Knibbs, *Ansgar*, 88–91) and, alongside three metropolitans, was supposed to judge between Ebo and Hincmar regarding the see of Reims (*Narratio Clericorum Remensium*, in MGH Conc. 2.2:812). In the mid-tenth century John of St. Arnulf said that Drogo's status as papal vicar in Gaul had made him, though not a metropolitan, a churchman of very high standing, who had enjoyed both the pallium and the title of archbishop, or even chief of archbishops (*Historia Translationis S. Glodesindis*, in PL 137:224).

48. JE 2607, BH †?239, MGH Epp. 5:591. On the authenticity of this fragment, see 106n121 below; it is here accepted as basically genuine, though interpolated in regard to the daily use of the pallium.

Other forms of vicariate may be glimpsed in the letters of Pope John VIII. Sending the pallium to Thietmar I of Salzburg in 877, he simultaneously set him over papal possessions in Bavaria.[49] As the most important bishop in the province, but also as a palliger, the metropolitan was the natural figure to administer the Roman church's affairs locally.[50] In the next year John agreed to Archbishop Rostagnus of Arles's request for "the use of the pallium and the vicariate of the apostolic see": "We entrust to your Fraternity our place in the churches that are within the kingdom of Gaul, indeed with each metropolitan keeping his own honor, according to the old custom." The proviso respecting metropolitan power was retained from the letter's Gregorian exemplar, but the current pope was not really interested in deference to the local hierarchy. Rostagnus's duties involved the supervision and coordination of the Gallican episcopate, as well as a specific task. John wanted him to enforce the ruling of the Councils of Rome (875) and Ravenna (877) that required metropolitans to obtain the pallium before consecrating bishops: "We encourage your holy Fraternity, holding our place throughout Gaul, to show concern about [noncompliance], and to forbid it by your authority, lest it grow.... Whether they obey or not, you should not delay to make everything known to our Apostolate by accurate letters, always (if you can) on the feast of the apostles, either yourself or through any legate of ours."[51] Here the vicar was not only an enforcer but an informant, a line of communication between the Gallican churches and Rome at a time when John was keenly interested in executing his new pallium regulations.[52] Whether missionaries

49. JE 3115, GP 1:12–13 no. 24, BU 290, MGH Epp. 7:58.
50. While it was not necessary to possess the pallium in order to administer Roman interests, there was a conceptual link: in this letter the grant of the pallium, the oversight of Roman property, and special devotion to and partnership with the Roman church were juxtaposed.
51. JE 3148, BU 353, MGH Epp. 7:109–10. The feast of Sts. Peter and Paul (June 29) was an appropriate time to reinforce bonds with the pope (Peter's successor), especially regarding the pallium (taken from Peter's tomb).
52. Grierson argues that the reason for the revival of the Arles vicariate was not any real power to be wielded by Rostagnus, so much as the promulgation of the Johannine pallium law in a document that could pass into the canonical tradition ("Rostagnus," 82–83).

or judges, administrators or supervisors, all papal vicars, bolstered by the badge of the pallium, spoke with the pope's voice in situations vital to his interests but beyond his reach.

A final consequence of the closeness between the papacy and the wearer of the pallium was a juridical status that may be called judicial exemption: the pope reserved judgment of the palliger to himself in any disputes that might arise. Theodulf, bishop of Orléans, made this claim when complaining to a friend in 820 about his unjust exile by Emperor Louis the Pious: "There is no witness, nor any suitable judge; / I myself had not admitted any crime. / If I had admitted it, whose censure would be able / To apply fitting reins of judgment to me? / That work belongs to the Roman prelate alone, / From whose hand I received the holy pallium."[53] Loyal advisor of the emperor, he could nevertheless appeal beyond his judgment—in theory, if not in practice—to the pope, the only "suitable judge." Perhaps at this early time it was only Theodulf's theory, but by 863 Pope Nicholas I expounded the prerogative to Hincmar of Reims. Having recalled Hincmar's confirmation through the conferral of the pallium, the pope declared:

You shall be held bound by the sentence of no excommunication or obligation or condemnation without the decree of the Roman pontiff. But if you are arraigned to be judged by whomever or from whatever source, we decree by our, or rather blessed Peter the apostle's, authority that you are reserved to the judgment of the apostolic pope, and you are not subject to the jurisdiction or judgment of anyone else, except the power of the pontiff of the Roman see.[54]

As ever, Nicholas was clear and forceful in explaining the effects, but they seem to have been a personal privilege for Hincmar, rather than a general policy.

In the following year, however, Hincmar projected his status upon others like him: "Concerning a metropolitan appointed through the

---

53. *De Suo Exilio*, in Schaller, "Philologische Untersuchungen," 45 (using the poetic plural). See Peter Godman, *Poets and Emperors: Frankish Politics and Carolingian Poetry* (Oxford: Clarendon, 1987), 100–102.

54. JE 2720, BH 626, MGH Epp. 6:366. The briefer form of these clauses in Benedict III's 855 privilege for Hincmar (JE 2664, MGH Epp. 6:368)—which did not mention the pallium—framed it as a right of appeal rather than a legal status.

sacred rules, who from ancient custom receives the pallium from the apostolic see ... the sentence of the pontiff of that see must also be awaited before judgment."[55] A legitimate archbishop's position was lofty enough that the disposition of his case required recourse to the pope, who (through the pallium) had confirmed his authority and with whom (through the pallium) close ties had been knit. But was this special status primarily due to metropolitan rank or possession of the vestment? The answer was the latter, as proven by the case of a suffragan. After Bishop Actard of Nantes had been driven from his see and merited the pallium for his plight, Pope Hadrian II attached a similar prerogative to his grant in 868: "We resolve, and by the authority of apostolic ordinance we determine, that ... you are reserved to be examined or judged without delay only by the judgment of the apostolic see, by whose decree and generosity you are known to be incardinated in a vacant church and palliated."[56] Both these acts—approval of his translation to a new see and bestowal of the pallium—needed the papacy's favor, and this special regard resulted also in papal protection.[57] Of course, as with all forms of exemption, this protection exalted papal power even as it privileged its clients.[58]

55. To Nicholas I, MGH Epp. 8.1:147–48. Cf. Flodoard of Reims, *Historia Remensis Ecclesiae*, in MGH SS 36:223.
56. JE 2904, MGH Epp. 6:710.
57. See Sebastian Scholz, *Transmigration und Translation: Studien zum Bistumswechsel der Bischöfe von der Spätantike bis zum hohen Mittelalter*, Kölner historische Abhandlungen 37 (Cologne: Böhlau, 1992), 102–17, and Mary E. Sommar, "Hincmar of Reims and the Canon Law of Episcopal Translation," *The Catholic Historical Review* 88 (2002): 429–45. Because he possessed the pallium, the Council of Douzy (871) was hesitant to place Actard in the see of Tours without papal approval (MGH Conc. 4:528). On the synod, see Hartmann, *Synoden*, 325–27.
58. See Otto Vehse, "Bistumsexemtionen bis zum Ausgang des 12. Jahrhunderts," *Zeitschrift der Savigny-Stiftung für Rechtsgeschichte, kanonistische Abteilung* 26 (1937): 86–160; Brigitte Szabó-Bechstein, *Libertas ecclesiae: ein Schlüsselbegriff des Investiturstreits und seine Vorgeschichte, 4.–11. Jahrhundert*, Studi gregoriani 12 (Rome: Ateneo Salesiano, 1985); Ludwig Falkenstein, *La papauté et les abbayes françaises aux XIe et XIIe siècles: exemption et protection apostolique*, Bibliothèque de l'École des hautes études, sciences historiques et philologiques 336 (Paris: Champion, 1997); and Barbara H. Rosenwein, *Negotiating Space: Power, Restraint, and Privileges of Immunity in Early Medieval Europe* (Ithaca, N.Y.: Cornell University Press, 1999).

Relationships with Secular Rulers

In an age when kings felt it their responsibility to protect and provide for the churches of their lands, even to the extent of appointing bishops, it is no surprise to find that they frequently intervened in the process of requesting and receiving the pallium. The popes never wholly rejected such interference; indeed, they often tried to harness it to their advantage, by treating the vestment as a favor to be awarded or denied within the complex interplay of political relations. In this period such relations ran the gamut. Cooperation between popes and secular rulers was occasionally marred by tensions, which eventually resulted in a firm stance that consolidated papal control of the vestment.

Cooperation

Certainly, the pallium was not foreign to secular politics. The garment may have been descended from a sash granted to high-ranking officials in the Christianized Roman Empire.[59] The so-called Donation of Constantine, a Roman forgery from the second half of the eighth century, corroborated such an origin. Emperor Constantine I was said to have handed over to Pope Sylvester I and his successors various vestments and insignia, including "the superhumeral, namely the lorum, which is accustomed to surround the imperial neck."[60] As imperial garb that had become a papal badge, this superhumeral or lorum, commonly identified with the pallium, supported the idea that the pope held the place in the West of the emperor, who had withdrawn to the East.[61] While the story was meant to bolster

---

59. See 8 above.

60. MGH Font. 10:87. *Pallium vel mitram* at PL 130:249 (which reprints Merlin's edition of the Pseudo-Isidorian decretals, which included the Donation) is a mistake for the reading found in two Pseudo-Isidorian manuscripts (Vatican City, Biblioteca Apostolica Vaticana, Vat. lat. 630, and Wolfenbüttel, Herzog-August-Bibliothek, Gud. lat. 212), viz., *pilleum vel mitram,* referring to headgear. On the Donation within the Pseudo-Isidorian tradition, see Horst Fuhrmann, *Einfluß und Verbreitung der pseudoisidorischen Fälschungen: von ihrem Auftauchen bis in die neuere Zeit,* Monumenta Germaniae Historica Schriften 24 (Stuttgart: Hiersemann, 1973), 2:354–407.

61. See Du Cange, *Glossarium,* 5:143, 7:663, and Johannes Fried, Donation of Constantine *and* Constitutum Constantini: *The Misinterpretation of a Fiction and its*

papal authority, it also pointed to an escape route for those wishing to evade it, as when the church of Ravenna turned to the emperor in Constantinople for the pallium, as a way of casting off the Roman yoke.[62]

In addition, stories of Pope Gregory the Great circulating in this period cited the continual presence of secular rulers in cases involving the pallium. Leander of Seville received it partly as a tribute to King Reccared, who had regained the Visigoths for orthodoxy; John of Ravenna was allowed to wear it at certain litanies only after powerful nobles intervened in his favor; Marinian of Ravenna, in contrast, failed to obtain a broader use of the pallium despite wide-ranging secular intercession; and Maximus of Salona was reconciled to the papacy after the exarch asked Gregory to be gentle with him.[63] There was no clear demarcation between secular and ecclesiastical interests in Gregory's world or for long thereafter, and the pallium mattered to the powerful. In the late eighth century Alcuin even likened the vestment to a worldly insigne as he looked back to York's

---

Original Meaning, Millennium-Studien 3 (Berlin: de Gruyter, 2007), 7–10, 39, 49–51. Fried's hypothesis (ibid., 59) that the forgery confused the pallium with the amice (sometimes called *superhumerale*) and thus could not have been the work of a Roman author does not seem persuasive. *Superhumerale* was in fact used for the pallium in this period, not only in Francia (e.g., Alcuin to Arno of Salzburg in 799, MGH Epp. 4:286–87, and to Riculf of Mainz in 800/801, MGH Epp. 4:353), but also in Rome, at least when dealing with the Eastern church (e.g., Leo IV to Ignatius of Constantinople between 847 and 853, JE 2647, BH 113, MGH Epp. 5:607). Anastasius the Librarian, translating c. 16 of Constantinople IV into Latin, glossed *superhumeralia* with *pallia*, which suggested that the word corresponded to the Greek *omophorion* (Alberigo et al., *Conciliorum Oecumenicorum Decreta*, 178). A Roman attempting to replicate a Constantinian document may well have used *superhumerale* and *lorum* as exotic, antique ways of referring to the pallium.

62. Agnellus of Ravenna, *Liber Pontificalis Ecclesiae Ravennatis*, in Nauerth, *Bischofsbuch*, 412.

63. Transmitted in a Pseudo-Isidorian decretal, Karl-Georg Schon and Klaus Zechiel-Eckes, eds., *Projekt Pseudoisidor: Text der falschen Dekretalen*, 2010, at http://www.pseudoisidor.mgh.de/html/305.htm, quoting JE 1757. This online edition is preferred to Hinschius's printed edition, which is seriously misleading, particularly concerning the genuine Pseudo-Isidorian material that is of most interest to this study (Jasper and Fuhrmann, *Papal Letters*, 155–59). For the other three cases: transmitted in John the Deacon's life of Gregory, PL 75:173, quoting JE 1326; transmitted in ibid., PL 75:175, quoting JE 1411; and transmitted in ibid., PL 75:180, quoting JE 1703.

golden age: "The times of this nation were happy then; / King and prelate were ruling it with harmonious law: / The latter the rights of the church, the former the affairs of the realm. / The latter bears on his shoulders the pallium sent by the pope, / The former lifts onto his head the crown of his ancient fathers."[64] In this view, which drew parallels between secular and ecclesiastical rule, the differences seemed incidental before the complementarity of the two powers, working in peaceful cooperation.

This openness to lay collaboration permeated the first century of this period. The popes were in need of Frankish defense, and strong Carolingian rulers, eventually given the Roman imperial title, strove to extend and consolidate their realm both physically and religiously. As already reviewed, Pippin the Short and his brother Carloman were involved in Boniface's request for pallia in Rouen, Reims, and Sens, and Charlemagne interceded for the pallium for Tilpin of Reims, Ermenbert of Bourges, and Arno of Salzburg.[65] Pope Hadrian I agreed to the request for Ermenbert "for the sake of your exceeding royal love, from the depth of our heart"; it was either a favor out of affection for Charlemagne or a means of gaining his affection.[66] Pope Leo III agreed to the request for Arno as fitting recompense for Charlemagne's efforts on behalf of the papacy: "Since through your laborious royal struggles the holy catholic and apostolic Roman church

---

64. *Versus de Patribus Regibus et Sanctis Euboricensis Ecclesiae*, in Godman, *Bishops*, 100 (using the poetic plural). See Godman, *Poets*, 41–42. The use of plurals for the insignia may have been patterned after *sceptra* (also used in the poem), which as a plural meant not "scepters" but "kingship, dominion, authority"; thus *pallia* could connote "archiepiscopacy, pastoral rule, canonical authority."

65. Zachary to Boniface ca. 744, JE 2271, GP 4:24 no. 58, Rau, *Briefe*, 170; Hadrian I to Tilpin ca. 780, JE 2411, GP 4:61 no. 22, Lesne, "Lettre," 349; Hadrian I to Charlemagne between 784 and 791, JE 2475, MGH Epp. 3:628; and Leo III to Charlemagne in 798, JE 2496, GP 1:9 no. 9, Dopsch, "Papst Leo III. schreibt an König Karl," 23. According to Hincmar of Reims in 863, Theodulf of Orléans also received the pallium at Charlemagne's intercession (MGH Epp. 8.1:128). In the case of Tilpin, Flodoard of Reims in 952/54 attributed so much initiative to Charlemagne that he, rather than the archbishop, was said to have acquired the pallium (*Historia Remensis Ecclesiae*, in MGH SS 36:171 [JE *2410]). In the case of Arno, some of the language—*familiariter, viva voce, intonuit* (unless this is a mistake for *innotuit*), *mandasset, demandationem*—suggests that Charlemagne made a forceful request and the pope responded with deference.

66. JE 2475, MGH Epp. 3:628.

exults, enriched with all good things, it befits us to fulfill your licit wishes in all things."[67] In this case the pallium became a pawn in a *quid pro quo* exchange between pope and king.

Charlemagne's successors followed his lead. Adalram of Salzburg first sought Louis the Pious's leave to visit Rome, and then the emperor commended him to the pope and requested the pallium for him.[68] Louis also used his influence to obtain the pallium for his brother and archchaplain, Drogo of Metz.[69] Hincmar of Reims asked Lothar I, as that emperor relayed to Pope Leo IV, "to acquire the pallium for him from your Paternity by our intercession." Lothar tried to persuade the pope with vague promises of rewards: "Wholly entrusting the petition of the aforesaid archbishop (very devoted and beloved to us) to your judgment and sentence, we undoubtedly assert that, if you decide to imitate the custom and good will of your fathers and predecessors in giving him honors and confirming his condition, you will more fully and easily receive worthy respects and most pleasing recompense."[70] Although he claimed to be leaving the decision to the pope, Lothar, uncertain of the outcome of Hincmar's delicate situation, resorted to what sounds like bribery. The precise mix of Leo's motives is unknown, but he acceded to the imperial plea.[71]

The ideal at this time envisioned pope and king working hand-in-hand for the good of the church.[72] This ideal, it was believed, had been exemplified in England during Gregory the Great's era, as Frechulf of Lisieux narrated in 829/30: the king appointed bishops, while the pope conferred metropolitan status through the pallium.[73] A similar spirit was attested when contemporary popes bestowed the

67. JE 2496, GP 1:9 no. 9, Dopsch, "Papst Leo III. schreibt an König Karl," 23.
68. Louis the Pious to Eugene II in 824, MGH Epp. 5:313.
69. Cf. Charles the Bald to Nicholas I in 864, MGH Epp. 6:223.
70. In 847, MGH Epp. 5:610–11.
71. But see *Narratio Clericorum Remensium*, in MGH Conc. 2.2:813.
72. Steffen Patzold charts the emergence of a model of episcopal *ministerium* in which bishops were imagined as ruling jointly with the king as complementary caretakers of Christendom. It was especially articulated by the Council of Paris (829) and supported in various legal, hagiographical, and historiographical texts, including Frechulf of Lisieux's chronicle. See his *Episcopus: Wissen über Bischöfe im Frankenreich des späten 8. bis frühen 10. Jahrhunderts*, Mittelalter-Forschungen 25 (Ostfildern: Thorbecke, 2008), 105–84.
73. *Historiae*, in CCCM 169A:721.

vestment. For example, the Bavarian bishops were to accept Arno of Salzburg as their metropolitan, not merely by papal command, but because of their loyalty to the king, who deserved a heavenly reward for helping to erect that province.[74] Also, the forged privileges for Ansgar of Hamburg, attributed to Gregory IV in 832 and Nicholas I in 864, described the founding of that archbishopric as the result of Charlemagne's conversion of its peoples and Louis the Pious's and Louis the German's organization of its hierarchy; the popes simply offered their seal of approval to the royal zeal.[75] Louis the Pious, moreover, was given broad leeway in the further management of the new church: the consecration of future archbishops was entrusted to the "sacred palatine providence" (the emperor's discretion) as long as Hamburg lacked sufficient suffragans, and all the arrangements of the "venerable prince" were confirmed.[76] In some minds, then, the pope might be relegated to a reactive role, as a lesser partner wielding a rubber stamp.

Tensions

The chronicler of Grado knew that secular rulers could abuse their sway over the papacy. The metropolitan see of Aquileia in northern Italy had been relocated to Grado after the Lombard invasions of the sixth century, but differing attitudes regarding the schism of the Three Chapters led to the erection of a rival see back in Old Aquileia (later moved to Cividale del Friuli).[77] There were thus two claim-

---

74. Leo III to Charlemagne in 798, JE 2496, GP 1:9 no. 9, Dopsch, "Papst Leo III. schreibt an König Karl," 24.

75. JE 2574, GP 6:25–26 no. 11, Curschmann, *Ältere Papsturkunden*, 13–15; and JE 2759, GP 6:31–32 no. 21, BH 706, Curschmann, *Ältere Papsturkunden*, 19–24. Rimbert's life of Ansgar similarly consigned the popes to acts of confirmation (MGH SSRG 55:34–35, 49). Indeed, Knibbs remarks that no early medieval popes directly founded archbishoprics through written acts (*Ansgar*, 94); but the pallium's involvement would allow the papacy to begin to take the lead (Kempf, "Primatiale und episkopal-synodale Struktur," 52, 61). Knibbs has thoroughly examined these privileges and judged them inauthentic creations of Ansgar and his successor Rimbert, meant to shore up the failing northern mission.

76. JE 2574, GP 6:25–26 no. 11, Curschmann, *Ältere Papsturkunden*, 14. Cf. JE 2759, GP 6:31–32 no. 21, BH 706, Curschmann, *Ältere Papsturkunden*, 22–23.

77. See IP 7.1:13, 7.2:27–28, and Heinrich Schmidinger, *Patriarch und Landesherr:*

ants to the patriarchate of Aquileia, and the chronicler described the moment when Rome recognized Old Aquileia (until then schismatic) alongside Aquileia in Grado (already a Roman ally).[78] At that time "the Lombards first brought the pallium by force from the supreme apostolic see for Serenus, archbishop of the church of Friuli."[79] This maneuver secured the vestment for the archbishop of Cividale, whose claim to be the true patriarch of Aquileia thereby gained credibility, even as it intensified his rivalry with the metropolitan of Grado. The authority behind this act may have been the papacy, but its legitimacy was compromised because the favor had allegedly been acquired through pressure. In the depiction of this episode, however accurate, the pallium was a tool employed by kings and bishops to increase their standing *vis-à-vis* neighboring powers, and the pope seemed more manipulated than manipulator.

Indeed, it was dangerous for the papacy to rely too readily on secular partnership. The matter of the short-lived archbishopric of Lichfield caused a headache for the popes. In order to give his own land ecclesiastical independence, King Offa of Mercia had divided the province of Canterbury by erecting a metropolitan see at Lichfield.[80] His contrary-minded successor, Cenwulf, writing to Pope Leo III in 797/98, explained the ecclesiastical organization of England decreed by Gregory the Great, as opposed to the violence Offa had done to it: "Because of enmity incurred with the venerable Jaenbert [arch-

---

die weltliche Herrschaft der Patriarchen von Aquileja bis zum Ende der Staufer, Publikationen des österreichischen Kulturinstituts in Rom, Abhandlungen 1 (Graz: Böhlau, 1954), 2–17.

78. Both sees had been schismatic; Grado was reconciled with Rome in 607, but Aquileia not for nearly another century (Schmidinger, *Patriarch*, 8–9, and HEOJ 5:396, 408–9).

79. *Chronica de Singulis Patriarchis Novae Aquileiae*, in Monticolo, *Cronache*, 1:11. Similarly, around 1008 John of Venice attributed Serenus's pallium to royal insistence alone, not the patriarch's worthiness or right (Luigi Andrea Berto, ed., *Giovanni Diacono: Istoria Veneticorum*, Fonti per la storia dell'Italia medievale 2 [Bologna: Zanichelli, 1999], 100). Ironically, Grado's early eleventh-century chronicle attributed the establishment of its own metropolitan status to the pleas of various nobles, to whom (not to the patriarch) the pope had issued the privilege (*Chronicon Gradense*, in Monticolo, *Cronache*, 1:37–38, 40).

80. See Nicholas Brooks, *The Early History of the Church of Canterbury: Christ Church from 597 to 1066* (Leicester: Leicester University Press, 1984), 111–27.

bishop of Canterbury] and the nation of the Kentish, King Offa first strove to divert the honor of his dignity and disperse it into two dioceses. And your most pious fellow bishop and predecessor, Hadrian, at the request of the aforesaid king, began to do what nobody previously presumed, and elevated the prelate of the Mercians with the pallium."[81] Heeding a royal request born of political ambitions, Pope Hadrian I had made the bishop of Lichfield equal to Canterbury as a metropolitan, but Cenwulf now asked Leo to reverse that unprecedented deviation. In defense of Hadrian, the pope replied: "He would not have done this except for the fact that your preeminent king, Offa, testified by his letter that the petition for it was the one and unanimous will of you all [the Mercian bishops and nobles], and was due to the vastness of your lands and the extension of your kingdom, as well as for very many other reasons and advantages."[82] The papacy's willingness to grant the pallium through the intercession of secular princes had come back to haunt it. Tossed about by shifting political forces, Leo resorted to blaming the last king.

Worse yet, some in this era tried to leave the pope out of the pallium equation altogether. If a ruler could choose the incumbent of a metropolitan see, the vestment effectively became his to distribute—once the pope had sent it, as usually happened without much ado. In his *gesta* of Louis the Pious in the mid-830s, Thegan upbraided Ebo of Reims for repaying the emperor evil for good: "He vested you with the purple and the pallium, but you clothed him with sackcloth. He dragged you undeserving to the pontifical pinnacle, but you wished to expel him by a false judgment from the throne of his fathers."[83] Of course, Louis had not literally vested Ebo with

---

81. Found in R. A. B. Mynors, R. M. Thomson, and M. Winterbottom, eds., *William of Malmesbury:* Gesta Regum Anglorum, *The History of the English Kings*, Oxford Medieval Texts (Oxford: Clarendon Press, 1998), 128. "The honor of his dignity" is obscure: *honor* could mean "competence," "well-established legal condition," "territory," or "sovereignty" (Niermeyer, *Mediae Latinitatis Lexicon*, 495–98). The phrase probably meant "the competence of his office."

82. JE 2494, MGH Epp. 4:188.

83. MGH SSRG 64:232. "Purple," the color of the robes worn by emperors, kings, and magistrates, came to mean "lofty station, high dignity" (Lewis and Short, *Latin Dictionary*, 1493).

either purple or pallium, but he had nominated him archbishop of Reims and so obtained those honors for him. In this light, receiving the pallium seemed an automatic accompaniment to gaining the see. This phenomenon was nothing unique to Ebo, but the bald way in which Thegan described it reflected the dominant role of the ruler at the height of the Carolingian monarchy. The emperor later deposed Ebo for plotting against him, and Ebo thereby lost the right to use the pallium. But Louis's son, Lothar I, restored Ebo at the Council of Ingelheim (840).[84] The edict published there spoke of the vestment as a papal gift, now returned to the archbishop as an imperial gift: "We restore to you, Ebo, the see and diocese of the city of Reims, so that, clothed with the original pallium of holy apostolic bestowal, you may perform the harmony and grace of the divine office with us. Now that you have completed humble satisfaction, you receive [the pallium] from our solemn bestowal."[85] By reinvesting Ebo with the pallium previously granted by the pope, Lothar arrogated a papal right to himself and interfered in the process of papal approbation ordinarily signified by the vestment.

Similarly, Ravennese legend downplayed reliance on the pope when the pallium was at stake. According to Agnellus around 846, the first archbishop of Ravenna had acquired the metropolitan dignity and more from Valentinian III: "He first received from that emperor the pallium of white wool (as is the custom for the pontiff of the Romans to put on over the mantle), which he and his successors have used until the present day."[86] Whether the story reflected the pallium's origin as a sash granted by the emperors or merely conveyed the author's anti-Roman bias, it posited that the vestment,

---

84. On the synod, see Hartmann, *Synoden*, 197–98.
85. MGH Conc. 2.2:792. The implied object of "receive" is unclear, but the parallel between papal and imperial "bestowal" suggests the pallium itself. Perhaps there was a ceremony (*sollemnis largitas*) at the council, in which Ebo was clothed with his old pallium. Chazelle suggests that the Utrecht Psalter was made at this time, and although she is reluctant, due to Lothar's absence, to claim that fol. 90v (see 22 above) is an illustration of this council, the depiction of a bishop being vested with the pallium in the midst of a synod fits the circumstances well ("Archbishops Ebo and Hincmar," 1068).
86. *Liber Pontificalis Ecclesiae Ravennatis*, in Nauerth, *Bischofsbuch*, 206.

though customarily associated with the popes, did not have to come from the Roman church. At least one later archbishop of Ravenna was said to have obtained his pallium from the emperor, and such a practice encouraged the see's inclination toward independence from its former metropolitan.[87] Indeed, Archbishop Maurus urged his successors to resort to the emperor rather than the pope on a regular basis.[88] The question thus emerges: how much control did the popes of this time really have over this insigne?

Control

Given these competitors, it is not surprising that the bishops of Rome began to assert themselves as soon as Carolingian power began to fragment. The first examples of flouting the will of secular rulers occurred in the 840s, in the wake of the Frankish civil war. After Ebo had lost the see of Reims again in 841, Pope Sergius II declined to restore the pallium to him in 844, despite Emperor Lothar I's support of the deposed archbishop. This papal decision—to readmit Ebo to the church, but not to his office—echoed the pope's attitude to an oath of fealty described just before in the *Liber Pontificalis*: he agreed to swear fidelity to Lothar as emperor, but not to his son Louis as king of Italy.[89] In both cases Sergius yielded to the emperor in one way, while resisting in another, as if to demonstrate that he was no puppet. His successor, Leo IV, denied Lothar's petition for the pallium for Altheus of Autun a few years later, probably because the bishop himself had not requested it.[90] The same pope heeded Lothar's demand for the pallium for Hincmar of Reims, but refused to appoint him papal vicar, since Drogo of Metz already held that position. Once again the pope thwarted the imperial will, although this time

---

87. Agnellus described the installation of Maximian as directed almost wholly by the imperial will (ibid., 302). Although the donor in this passage is not entirely clear, it seems obvious from the context that the emperor granted the pallium as a sign of approval (*pace* JK post 919).

88. Nauerth, *Bischofsbuch*, 420.

89. Duchesne, *Liber pontificalis*, 2:90.

90. JE 2603, BH 116, MGH Epp. 5:604. According to the pope, the emperor had "commanded" him to grant the pallium. Although *mandare* could mean something softer, e.g., "send word," it still had the sense of ordering.

he used the pallium—granted "out of love and honor for you"—as a sop to avert complete disappointment.[91]

In a similar vein, Pope Nicholas I rejected King Solomon of Brittany's attempt to gain the pallium for Dol in 865.[92] Understanding that the demand was really a bid to erect a separate ecclesiastical province for an independent Breton kingdom, the pope resisted the insistent royal requests and scolded the king for his stubborn ambitions:

> You sent word asking us what you have also asked often before, namely to send the pallium to Festinian, the venerable bishop of Dol.... We wrote quite often to you, and at the same time to the metropolis of Tours, things that are reasonable. But, as we read again in your letter, you have inclined your ear, not your heart, to our writings.... For your metropolis is the church of Tours, as we have long since made known to you.... It seems blameworthy that, on account of the division of the kingdom, anyone should strive to claim such things for himself.[93]

Nicholas found fault with the logic that Breton political independence (*divisio regni*) necessitated a Breton archbishop, palliated and not answerable to Tours. More important to the pope were precedent and the established hierarchy. In all the foregoing situations the papacy flexed its growing muscle against secular manipulation and was able to maintain both its authority and the larger principles it considered important.[94]

From this strengthened position the popes engaged more often in *do ut des* exchanges involving the pallium.[95] Despite the irregularity of Egilo of Sens's promotion, Nicholas I agreed to Charles the Bald's petition in 865/66 as a means of extracting a favor from the king: "We ask that, just as we have heard you and granted [the pallium] to him, so your Piety may deign to lavish on him with generous sumptuousness what we beg for his sake, namely the proper-

---

91. In 851, JE 2607, BH †?239, MGH Epp. 5:591.
92. JE 2789, BH 764, MGH Epp. 6:640.
93. Nicholas to Solomon in 865/66, JE 2807, BH 770, MGH Epp. 6:647.
94. Schrör suggests that the pallium was the "decisive instrument" that permitted the papacy to wrest control of some Frankish ecclesiastical affairs from the early Carolingian kings (*Metropolitangewalt*, 58–59).
95. Gregory the Great had done the same, as John the Deacon illustrated in his *vita* (PL 75:126, referring to JE 1748 and JE 1751).

ty and all the things known to have been stolen from the church of Sens in whatever way. Thus, just as the same man is adorned on the outside with such a great gift granted by us, so too he may rejoice on the inside from the revenues of the church entrusted to him by your Clemency."[96] As in the past, the various aspects of the office, both ecclesiastical and secular, benefited from the joint activity of pope and king, but now the pope did more than follow the royal lead. Charles seemed to get the message, for in 867 he framed his petition for the pallium for Wulfhad of Bourges in ingratiating terms, and he justified the archbishop's premature appointment as a response to the needs of the region, which was suffering persecution.[97]

Nicholas died too soon to fulfill that request, but his successor, Hadrian II, was willing to do so in 868 because Charles had cooperated with the papacy in another matter, the restoration of the Ebonian clerics after years of controversy:

> We render no small thanks to your Kindness. For you too took care ... to stretch out your hand with lively zeal to restore the aforesaid clerics, to whom you perceived that the apostolic see was stretching out its hand. On that account, as you now request that the first of them, namely our brother and fellow bishop Wulfhad, be adorned by the generosity of our authority with the use of the pallium in the manner of his [predecessors], we have deservedly applied the ears of condescension.[98]

The king had done the papacy a favor by collaborating in a difficult matter, and so the pope did the king a favor in return. Hadrian's successor, John VIII, continued to use the gift of the pallium as a negotiating tool. He heeded King Carloman of Bavaria's petition for Thietmar I of Salzburg in 877, but simultaneously required royal assent to an arrangement concerning papal property in his land.[99] The pope was indebted to Carloman for his favors to the Roman church and planned to work closely with him in the future, and so Thietmar's pallium formed one step in a political dance of give-and-take.

By John's pontificate the papacy was dealing forcefully with is-

---

96. JE 2810, BH 767, MGH Epp. 6:646.
97. PL 124:874–75.
98. JE 2902, MGH Epp. 6:705.
99. JE 3114, BU 289, MGH Epp. 7:58.

sues surrounding the pallium—taking into account the pleas of princes, but not allowing them to determine papal policy. Such an attitude appeared after the problematic accessions of Bertulf of Trier and Willibert of Cologne following Lothar II's divorce.[100] John felt bound to examine Bertulf's promotion, but in 873 reluctantly allowed imperial prayers to soften his approach: "Because we put up with our beloved son, the emperor [Louis II], exceedingly insistent in his daily petitions for the sake of your business, we have recognized that the origins of your advancement must be scrutinized gently indeed—though by no means left undiscussed."[101] Soon after, despite Willibert's noncompliance with a papal summons, John bestowed the pallium on him, "as our most beloved son, Lord Louis the august emperor, and his most kind uncle, King Louis, have also very much intervened," with a mere promise to send a legate to examine the charges against him.[102] In both instances the pope bowed to imperial pressure, while refusing to drop the matter altogether. Something comparable occurred with the Byzantine emperor, as observed above, when John agreed to recognize Patriarch Photius of Constantinople, but only if the Bulgarian church was returned to Roman jurisdiction and Eastern pallia were no longer sent there.[103] Attaching such conditions in negotiations with powerful leaders reflected not only the confidence of a robust papacy, but also the importance of the pallium to all parties.

John VIII was also keen to employ palligers as go-betweens. Having palliated Adalgar of Autun, an imperial envoy, as a sign of favor to Charles the Bald in 876, the pope went beyond this one-time gesture and proposed a more permanent role for the bishop: "When we had learned that the oft-mentioned bishop was so faithful to you ... on that account we decided that he would be a mediator between

---

100. Royal influence had been brought to bear on Willibert's case since his election in 870. Not only did Louis the German plead with Hadrian II for the pallium, but he also begged Emperor Louis II and Empress Engelberga for their help in commending Willibert to the pope (MGH Epp. 6:249–51).

101. JE 2982, GP 10.1:37 no. 49, BU 87, MGH Epp. 7:288.

102. JE 2988, GP 7.1:34–35 no. 67, BU 120, Wisplinghoff, *Rheinisches Urkundenbuch*, 2:158.

103. To Basil I in 879, JE 3271, BU 551, MGH Epp. 7:173–74.

our pontifical power and your imperial power. In this way he would be like an instrument of both voices, and would report your concerns to us and announce our concerns to you."[104] Likewise, the pallium grant for Thietmar I of Salzburg in the following year seemed appropriate, John said, so that he might become "a daily intercessor for the Roman church before King Carloman."[105] Such intermediaries, powerful local figures in their own right yet also clothed with the pope's own vestment, permitted the bishop of Rome to be involved in courtly affairs throughout Europe.

Relationships among Palligers

Western bishops enjoyed precedence and exercised power within the church according to a complicated set of criteria, including the historic importance of their sees, seniority according to consecration, and political preferment. Into this mix was injected the grant of the pallium, a mark of distinction that reflected special ties to the papacy and imparted not only prestige but also juridical effects (examined in the next chapter). The vestment could thus reinforce or upset the balance of power within the hierarchy. Moreover, as the use of the pallium became more common, how palligers related to each other began to receive attention. As a result of the way the vestment had been integrated into the church's constitution, most of these churchmen were metropolitans. But the popes were interested in controlling others, not themselves, and so they continued to honor non-metropolitans on occasion. Thus there were two kinds of palliger, with differing ecclesio-political impact: palliated metropolitans and palliated suffragans.

Palliated Metropolitans

The pope had to be careful—especially when embryonic provinces still stood on uncertain footing—that his gift did not create chaos. That concern directed Pope Hadrian I between 784 and 791, when he cautiously attempted to discover whether a pallium for Ermen-

---

104. JE 3063, BU 213, MGH Epp. 7:24.
105. JE 3115, GP 1:12–13 no. 24, BU 290, MGH Epp. 7:58.

bert of Bourges would tread on another metropolitan's feet: "No room for usurpation in another's [territory] should be granted to priests. This aforesaid most holy man confessed to us that he seemed to be under no archbishop's jurisdiction."[106] Responding to the undesirability both of bishops lacking metropolitans and of competing archbishops in the same province, the pope was willing to confer the pallium as long as the promotion did not usurp another's office. Perhaps Hadrian had in mind the ongoing strife between the patriarchs of Aquileia and Grado, which had taken a turn for the worse earlier in the century. The Grado chronicle in the 820s or 830s did not forget the threat posed by Aquileia when it had first gained the pallium from Gregory II. Nevertheless, the pope had written to Patriarch Serenus and forbidden him "ever to invade another's rights, or by the daring of rashness usurp anyone's jurisdiction, but to be content in those things that he had possessed until then. [Gregory] commanded him not to surpass in any manner the bounds possessed by Donatus, prelate of Grado."[107] Since their quarrel centered on which was the true patriarch of Aquileia, the addition of the pallium seemed to Grado to lend credence to the cause of Old Aquileia. The pope, however, did not want it to be an excuse for ascendancy, but rather wished for both palligers to remain equal and distinct. The vestment could be interpreted in either sense, as engendering competition or coexistence.

It was Hincmar of Reims, that champion of metropolitan rights, who formed a coherent theory of the relationships among palliated metropolitans.[108] Canonical materials touching on the question and providing him with precedents certainly circulated at the time. The Pseudo-Isidorian decretals, which probably originated near Reims during Hincmar's archiepiscopate,[109] included among its genuine let-

---

106. To Charlemagne, JE 2475, MGH Epp. 3:628.
107. Monticolo, *Cronache*, 1:11–12. Around 1008 John of Venice claimed that Serenus's motive had been not righteousness (*iustitia*) but seizure (*usurpatio*); see *Historia Veneticorum*, in Berto, *Istoria*, 100.
108. See Schrörs, *Hinkmar*, 331–34, 366–70; Lesne, *Hiérarchie*, 171–84; Betz, *Hinkmar*; Congar, *L'écclesiologie*, 166–77; Devisse, *Hincmar*, 2:635–69; and Schrör, *Metropolitangewalt*, 60–75.
109. The Pseudo-Isidorian corpus did not dwell on the pallium, since one of its

ters Gregory the Great's reply to certain questions of Augustine after his elevation as archbishop of Canterbury. To an inquiry concerning Augustine's relationship with Gaul, the pope answered:

> Among the bishops of Gaul we bestow no authority on you, for, from the ancient times of my predecessors, the bishop of Arles has received the pallium, and we hardly ought to deprive him of the authority he has received.... You yourself, moreover, from your own authority will not be able to judge the bishops of Gaul. But by urging, coaxing, and also showing your good works for their imitation, reform the minds of the wicked to enthusiasm for holiness.... But whatever must be done from authority, let it be done with the aforesaid bishop of Arles, lest what the ancient institution of the fathers founded could be disregarded.[110]

The pallium of Arles precluded external interference. For Gregory, possession of the vestment was a sign or vehicle of authority, connected to the power to discipline bishops, but strictly limited to a given area of jurisdiction. John the Deacon's *vita* of the great pope, written during John VIII's pontificate, recounted Gregory's organization of the hierarchy in England: "He also sent [Augustine] the pallium and ordered him to ordain twelve bishops under his metropolis of Canterbury and to send bishops to both London and York. Consecrating twelve bishops under themselves, they no less would receive the pallium from the apostolic see. And after the death of Augustine, he should be held first among them who had deserved to be conse-

---

purposes was to downplay the rights and privileges of metropolitans. Still, the vestment crept into these works through Spanish material adopted from earlier canonical collections (JE 1756–57) and through groups of canonical regulations adopted wholesale (JE 1843 and the Roman synod of 595). All these texts were genuine—i.e., did not belong to the "False Decretals," the forgeries for which Pseudo-Isidore is better known—and stemmed from Gregory the Great, the effective founder of medieval pallium practice. This study, therefore, uses the Pseudo-Isidorian decretals primarily as evidence that certain Gregorian precedents were considered significant and kept alive.

110. Schon and Zechiel-Eckes, *Projekt Pseudoisidor,* at http://www.pseudo isidor.mgh.de/html/307.htm, quoting JE 1843. This canon was also found in the eighth-century *Collectio Herovalliana* (Linda Fowler-Magerl, ed., *Clavis Canonum: Selected Canon Law Collections before 1140,* Monumenta Germaniae Historica Hilfsmittel 21 [Hannover: Hahn, 2005], HV72.08 in the database component, also available at http://www.mgh.de/ext/clavis/ [hereafter "*Clavis*"]), but it is less clear that Hincmar had access to this collection.

crated first."¹¹¹ The biographer misunderstood the papal instructions, which had intended Augustine to become archbishop of London, and so he counted three English metropolitans—whereas Augustine had never moved his see to London.¹¹² In any event, Gregory's treatment of London and York implied that palliated metropolitans were essentially equal and required another factor, in this case seniority by date of consecration, to determine priority among them.

Drawing on these and other sources to formulate his own view of the position of metropolitans and provinces within the church, Hincmar articulated his theory first in his *Opusculum LV Capitulorum* (870), a response to the claims of his nephew and suffragan, Hincmar of Laon.¹¹³ He repeated and expanded his argument in his treatise *De Iure Metropolitanorum* (876), which protested against the infringement of metropolitan prerogatives presented by the appointment of Ansegis of Sens as papal vicar in Gaul and Germany.¹¹⁴ In his defense of their rights, Hincmar defined metropolitans, "who are also called primates many times in the sacred canons," as archbishops ordained "by the bishops of each province without the examination of another primate," and "who can ordain bishops in their own province ... without the decree or permission of another primate."¹¹⁵ In other words, such prelates possessed independent jurisdiction within their own provinces. Moreover, "from the law of ancient custom, they are accustomed to be distinguished with the splendor of the pallium by the apostolic see."¹¹⁶ Metropolitans did not bow to any extraprovin-

111. PL 75:100, referring to JE 1829.
112. Frechulf of Lisieux made a similar error (*Historiae*, in *Corpus Christianorum: Continuatio Mediaevalis* [Turnhout: Brepols, 1966–], 169A:721 [hereafter "CCCM"]).
113. MGH Conc. 4 supp. 2:198–99. Cf. Council of Douzy (871), in MGH Conc. 4:563. The younger Hincmar was trying to free himself from the authority of his uncle and metropolitan. See Schrörs, *Hinkmar*, 315–53, and Devisse, *Hincmar*, 2:738–85.
114. This work may have been written for, or in response to, the Council of Ponthion (876). See Schrörs, *Hinkmar*, 358–72, and Devisse, *Hincmar*, 2:810–15. On the synod, see Hartmann, *Synoden*, 333–36.
115. PL 126:191. The term "primate" was drawn from Pseudo-Isidorian sources, which invented that rank in order to reduce the power of metropolitans (Fuhrmann, *Einfluß*, 1:120–22). Hincmar called metropolitans "primates of their own provinces," and so collapsed the distinction.
116. PL 126:191. In his earlier *Opusculum* Hincmar seemed to distinguish between unpalliated metropolitans or archbishops, who were subject to primates or

cial primate because they were fully primates in their own provinces, and so it was implied that the insigne of the pallium represented or conveyed the fullness of jurisdiction.[117] Hincmar appreciated Gregory's answer to Augustine's question about Gaul, which he glossed with the precept: "That no metropolitan may presume any right in the province of another metropolitan without consulting him." Having repeated the pope's words about the pallium of Arles, he concluded: "And what he said about this one Gallican primate, who had received the pallium from the apostolic see, is certainly also to be understood about the remaining primates of the Gallicans and the Belgians and the Germans."[118] The only precedence among these metropolitans or "primates" was that found in Gregory's instructions concerning London and York, which gave priority to him "who is ordained first."[119] Solidly grounded in canon law, Hincmar argued for the inviolable rights of palliated metropolitans.[120]

Ironically, Hincmar himself in the 850s or 860s may have tried to make some pallia better than others. A fragment of a letter attributed to Pope Leo IV and addressed to Hincmar, preserved only in the eleventh-century *Collectio Britannica,* was probably forged or interpolated by the archbishop's circle (or by his enemies).[121] In it, referring

---

patriarchs, and palliated metropolitans or archbishops, who possessed independent authority as primates of their provinces (MGH Conc. 4 supp. 2:198).

117. Cf. the epithet that later became attached to the pallium, *plenitudo pontificalis officii.*

118. PL 126:197–98. Textual variants indicate that Hincmar was probably using the Pseudo-Isidorian decretals as his formal source.

119. PL 126:198.

120. Furthermore, Hincmar took Gregory's privilege appointing Virgilius of Arles as papal vicar in Gaul and quoted it, either from misunderstanding or from cunning, in such a way as to support his thesis; cf. JE 1374, CCSL 140:357, and PL 126:196. The new, anachronistic meaning was that the pope had sent the pallium, in accord with custom, not only to Virgilius but to all metropolitans, in order to preserve the honor proper to them. Two years later, John VIII's privilege for Rostagnus of Arles followed JE 1374's original wording (JE 3148, BU 353, MGH Epp. 7:109–10).

121. See Klaus Herbers, *Leo IV. und das Papsttum in der Mitte des 9. Jahrhunderts: Möglichkeiten und Grenzen päpstlicher Herrschaft in der späten Karolingerzeit,* Päpste und Papsttum 27 (Stuttgart: Hiersemann, 1996), 344–48. The interpolation of a few words in JE 2608, as Herbers suggests (ibid., 347–48n255), does not seem to suffice; he rightly adds that the original may not have been a pallium grant, but rather a privilege increasing the days on which the vestment could be worn, and in any case

to his previous pallium grant to Hincmar, the pope now supposedly appended an extraordinary privilege: the right to wear the vestment daily.[122] Such a license would have distinguished Hincmar from other metropolitans, as the text deliberately pointed out, in order to impress the gravity of the favor: "From the very beginning of our pontificate, we have granted a similar favor to no archbishop at all as we have to you, and you should not suspect that we will in any way grant [such a favor] henceforth."[123] The only other bishop who possessed this right was the pope himself, and so Hincmar would have enjoyed preeminence as a sort of transalpine pope. When Pope Nicholas I got wind of this claim in 866, he objected to the inequality of power the privilege would create among palligers: "It has been made known to our ears that your Fraternity does not use the pallium granted by the apostolic see at specific times and according to the custom defined for other metropolitan bishops. This is very displeasing if it has been committed by your Holiness proudly, such that, forgetful of humility, you are eager to seem loftier than the rest of your brothers."[124] The pope feared envy and discord among archbishops, and arrogance and independence on the part of Hincmar. Hincmar insistently denied the charge of pallium abuse.[125] If he was the forger, his trick had been uncovered under Nicholas's watchful eyes.

For the most part, Hincmar's theory of metropolitan rights, as expounded in the 870s, meshed well with the "equal and distinct" treatment proposed by the papacy. Pope John VIII, nevertheless, wished to bind the status of metropolitans even more closely to the pallium. His legislation at the Councils of Rome (875) and Ravenna (877) provided a solution if a metropolitan ignored the three-month deadline for requesting the pallium. He would forfeit jurisdiction over his province, for outside metropolitans could intervene and

---

the extant text is fragmentary. The hypothesis of interpolation works better for the accompanying fragment, JE 2607: the removal of two words, *cotidianum* and *cotidie*, renders it mostly unobjectionable.

122. Traditionally, the use of the granted pallium was restricted to certain solemn occasions.
123. JE 2608, BH †?240, MGH Epp. 5:592.
124. JE 2823, BH 838, MGH Epp. 6:430.
125. To Nicholas I in 867, MGH Epp. 8.1:216–17.

consecrate his suffragans—at least, under two conditions: the offender first had to be warned three times (which implied that repentance and restoration were permitted), and the pope had to be consulted (presumably because metropolitans would be stepping beyond their own jurisdictions).[126] One may guess that Hincmar did not like this compromise of the independent position of metropolitans in their own provinces. But it allowed the pope to check these potent figures by requiring papal approval (made manifest in the pallium) before they could exercise their rights, and by managing the involvement of peers in their supervision.

Palliated Suffragans

Most bearers of the pallium in this period were metropolitans, but not all were, and palliated suffragans presented special, sometimes difficult problems in relationships among palligers.[127] Papally backed missionaries in the early eighth century, such as Corbinian and Willibrord, wore the vestment without ever becoming metropolitans.[128] Even Boniface never stably occupied a metropolis and only acquired an episcopal see relatively late, around 746, some fifteen years after receiving the pallium.[129] But these pioneers were dealing with inchoate hierarchies in new territories, and hence their honorary distinction did not disrupt ecclesiastical structures.

True suffragans, in contrast, were anomalies when they enjoyed a prerogative ordinarily used by their superiors.[130] The best known in-

126. MGH Conc. 5:9–10. The Ravennese version of this clause was almost exactly the same (MGH Conc. 5:68).
127. In the early 870s the clergy and people of Cologne, as if in disbelief that Hadrian II had denied the pallium to their archbishop, Willibert, reminded the pope that his predecessors had bestowed the vestment "not only on archbishops, but even on suffragan bishops" (MGH Epp. 6:248).
128. Arbeo of Freising, *Vita Prima Corbiniani*, in MGH SSRG 13:197, and Alcuin, *Vita Willibrordi*, in Reischmann, *Willibrord*, 58.
129. Boniface was first assigned to Cologne in 745 but, in the face of opposition, was soon moved to Mainz, not yet recognized as a metropolitan see (Schieffer, *Winfrid-Bonifatius*, 230, 232–33; Levison, *England*, 86–87; Lesne, *Hiérarchie*, 47–48, 51; and Schüssler, "Fränkische Reichsteilung," 96–97).
130. Gifts may be diverted from their usual trajectories, with ramifications on social dynamics; nevertheless, these new paths can be institutionalized and come to define groups and relationships (Algazi, "Introduction," 26–27).

stance in this era was the bishop of Metz, a see with close ties to the Carolingians as the heartland of the family's power and the capital of Austrasia.[131] Bishop Chrodegang, a staunch ally of Pippin the Short and an influential Frankish reformer, facilitated Pope Stephen II's journey to Francia in 753–54.[132] By this time Boniface had fallen out of favor at the Frankish court and would soon be martyred in Frisia. The pope thus decided to honor the bishop of Metz, as the *Liber Pontificalis* narrated: "While he was located in Francia, he bestowed the pallium on Bishop Chrodegang, a most holy man, and ordained him archbishop."[133] Whether Stephen brought a pallium from Rome or gave him his own vestment, he likely wanted to thank Chrodegang for his efforts and name a new papal legate who held the king's confidence and could continue the reform of the Frankish church.[134] Although Chrodegang now possessed the title of archbishop, there was no indication that the status of Metz, a suffragan of Trier, had been elevated.[135] Still, his epitaph, composed perhaps by Theodulf

131. See Ch. Abel, "Étude sur le pallium et le titre d'archevêque jadis portés par les évêques de Metz," *Mémoires de la Société d'archéologie et d'histoire de la Moselle* 9 (1867): 53–129; Pierre Riché, *The Carolingians: A Family who Forged Europe*, trans. Michael Idomir Allen (Philadelphia: University of Pennsylvania Press, 1993), 13–17, 22–23; and M. A. Claussen, *The Reform of the Frankish Church: Chrodegang of Metz and the* Regula canonicorum *in the Eighth Century* (Cambridge: Cambridge University Press, 2004), 37–45.

132. See Riché, *Carolingians*, 65–66, 70, and Claussen, *Reform*, 26–28.

133. Duchesne, *Liber pontificalis*, 1:456 (JE *2314). See Riché, *Carolingians*, 75–78. The mid-tenth-century life of Chrodegang attributed to John of Gorze made grandiose claims: Chrodegang was permitted to ordain bishops throughout Gaul (it is uncertain whether such a wide-ranging faculty was exercised), to wear the *stola* (probably the pallium) wherever he went (even outside his church, an unusually broad freedom), and to use the processional cross (a prerogative often added to later pallium grants, but here likely an anachronism) (MGH SS 10:568).

134. See Schieffer, *Winfrid-Bonifatius*, 256, 276–80, who goes too far when he calls Chrodegang a metropolitan (Schüssler, "Fränkische Reichsteilung," 102). The popes sometimes vested especially favored bishops with their own pallia.

135. The *Notitia Galliarum* listed Trier as a *metropolis civitas* and Metz as a *civitas* below it (MGH Auct. ant. 9:589). But Isidore of Seville explained that an archbishop wielded apostolic or vicarial authority over other bishops, even metropolitans (Lindsay, *Etymologiarum Libri*, 1:7.12.6). Only in the ninth century did "archbishop" become synonymous with "metropolitan," as Rabanus Maurus indicated when he reworked his Isidorian source (Zimpel, *De Institutione*, 297–98). Hincmar too considered the words synonyms (*Opusculum LV Capitulorum*, in MGH Conc. 4 supp. 2:198);

of Orléans in 766, honored him as a high priest: "The holy pallium, given to him from the Romulan see, / He bore, and that father of fathers [the pope] exalted him. / ... In him the pontifical summit amply thrived."[136] Indeed, Chrodegang functioned as the leading bishop of the kingdom, though still hierarchically inferior to his metropolitan.

Later bishops of Metz followed in Chrodegang's footsteps. As noted above, Drogo, imperial archchaplain and eventually papal vicar, was adorned with the pallium.[137] Again, the vestment in this case was not connected with metropolitan authority, but was a sign of favor for a key player in the empire, who mediated between pope and emperor. The example of Metz may well have inspired the unknown writer who doctored the *acta* of the bishops of Le Mans around 860, with the goal of diluting the influence of metropolitans and strengthening episcopal authority.[138] Long ago, in the reign of the seventh-century Merovingian Theoderic III, he wrote, the bishop of Le Mans had been a Drogo-like figure: "Aiglibert was archchaplain and prince of the bishops of the whole kingdom.... [He] was archbishop and master of all the bishops of the whole kingdom, through teaching and governing and wearing the pallium (as is the custom of metropolitans)."[139] The forger admitted that the pallium was ordinarily metropolitan garb, yet this suffragan had allegedly attained

---

he may have been relying on a Pseudo-Isidorian forgery attributed to Anacletus I (JK †4, Schon and Zechiel-Eckes, *Projekt Pseudoisidor*, at http://www.pseudoisidor. mgh.de/html/014.htm). The conflation of terms may have partly resulted from the English model created by Gregory the Great and revised by Theodore of Canterbury (Thacker, "Gallic or Greek").

136. MGH Poet. 1:108–9 (using the poetic plural). The wordplay compared his wearing (*efferre*) of the vestment to the pope's elevation (*efferre*) of him.

137. Charles the Bald to Nicholas I in 864, MGH Epp. 6:223.

138. See Walter Goffart, *The Le Mans Forgeries: A Chapter from the History of Church Property in the Ninth Century*, Harvard Historical Studies 76 (Cambridge, Mass.: Harvard University Press, 1966).

139. Margarete Weidemann, ed., *Geschichte des Bistums Le Mans von der Spätantike bis zur Karolingerzeit: Actus Pontificum Cenomannis in Urbe Degentium und Gesta Aldrici*, Römisch-germanisches Zentralmuseum Forschungsinstitut für Vor- und Frühgeschichte Monographien 56 (Mainz: Römisch-germanisches Zentralmuseum, 2002), 1:82. The forger gave the same status to an earlier bishop of Le Mans, Bertichram (ibid., 1:62). See Goffart, *Le Mans Forgeries*, 197–200.

it, along with the archiepiscopal title and a sort of primatial position. Aiglibert, like Drogo, was supposedly a royal favorite whose influence far exceeded his bishopric. Near the end of this period, John VIII—the pope who made the pallium essential to metropolitan office—bestowed it on Wala of Metz, but not without a caution: "Neither bishop nor archbishop should stir up a quarrel of dispute against you for this reason [having received the pallium]."[140] The local metropolitan and nearby unpalliated suffragans could easily be provoked by this gift, which, by raising the recipient's status, could upset customary relationships. Fellow suffragans might feel envious of a peer lifted above them, and a metropolitan might feel threatened by a subordinate with pretensions to near-equality.[141]

This threat was not an idle one, for the association of the pallium with metropolitan rank meant that possession of the vestment was a way for a suffragan to wrest independence from his master and erect a new ecclesiastical province. Such was the plight of Vienne, which during the archiepiscopate of Ado (860–75) was still smarting over the loss of Tarentaise. That city had been a suffragan of Vienne since late antiquity, but in the Carolingian era it became an archbishopric, apparently gaining the pallium.[142] Vienne fought this reduction to its jurisdiction and strove to reclaim Tarentaise.[143] A forgery by Ado or his circle, attributed to Hadrian I and addressed to Berther of Vienne, cleverly set this goal within the context of the last century's restoration of the provincial structure. As the pope supposedly de-

140. In 878, JE 3183, BU 427, PL 126:799.
141. E.g., *Gesta Treverorum*, in MGH SS 8:165–66.
142. Leo the Great had declared Tarentaise a suffragan of Vienne in 450 (JK 450, GaP 3.1:63–64 no. 22b, MGH Epp. 3:20–21). It is unknown when it was elevated to metropolitan status, but c. 8 of the Council of Frankfurt (794) alluded to a dispute concerning Tarentaise (MGH Conc. 2.1:167); on the synod, see Hartmann, *Synoden*, 105–15. The *Notitia Galliarum* listed Tarentaise (*civitas Ceutronum*) as the first city (but not as metropolis) in the *provincia Alpium Graiarum et Poeninarum* (MGH Auct. ant. 9:598–99). By 811 its metropolitan status was mentioned in Charlemagne's will (MGH SSRG 25:38–39), and Nicholas I confirmed it in 867, though with a lingering subjection to Vienne as its primate (to Ado of Vienne, JE 2876, GaP 3.1:109–10 no. 104, BH 846, MGH Epp. 6:667–68).
143. See GaP 3.1:28, and Beate Schilling, *Guido von Vienne: Papst Calixt II*, Monumenta Germaniae Historica Schriften 45 (Hannover: Hahn, 1998), 269–79.

creed, all metropoles (such as Vienne) were to be confirmed, which entailed the subjection of suffragan sees in keeping with ancient custom; "nor, furthermore, should any metropolis suffer prejudice if either we or our predecessors have bestowed the pallium on any of its suffragans, at the request of the pious dukes of the Franks."[144] Pallium grants to suffragans (such as Tarentaise) happened as political favors, but were not meant to overturn the local hierarchy—or so it was hoped. Since they could cause resentment among metropolitans or allow suffragans to lord it over their superiors, the forgery framed such pallia as dangers that would enfeeble the provincial restoration.

More notoriously, as Brittany broke away from Frankish dominion in the mid-ninth century, its kings and the bishops of Dol sought the pallium to procure their independence as an ecclesiastical province. Their petitions to Pope Nicholas I, however, met with resistance for many reasons, especially Dol's past subjection to Tours. To King Solomon in 865/66 the pope explained: "It finally remains for you to consider what the metropolis among you is from of old. For your metropolis is, as we once pointed out to you, the church of Tours, as the charters of our predecessors say and the examples of our forefathers show.... If you have any authorities that make clear that there was a metropolis among the Bretons, or if you retain any documents at all of our pontifical predecessors that show it, send them to us."[145] To Bishop Festinian of Dol the pope clarified what sort of *auctoritates* would prove his see's metropolitan status: "You should not be called a metropolitan until you send us the documents of your episcopal predecessors, the ones which your predecessors received at the acceptance of the pallium. For if your church deserved the gift of the pallium from this holy see, a gift of such great dignity was hardly granted to you without documents, which you ought to have stored in your archives."[146] The pope's tone hinted of his suspicion that Dol had no such proofs. Festinian claimed that Pope Severinus had consecrated his predecessor Restwald "as an archbishop," and Pope Hadrian I had granted the pallium to a certain Juthinael, but Nich-

---

144. JE †2412, GaP 3.1:91–92 no. †72b, MGH Epp. 3:96.
145. JE 2807, BH 770, MGH Epp. 6:647.
146. In 866, JE 2806, BH 798, MGH Epp. 6:649.

olas could find no evidence of either act in the *gesta* of those popes. Dol was seemingly reduced to making unsubstantiated historical allusions.[147] In this case, implicit in the interweaving of the two issues—Dol's pallium request and its relationship with Tours—was the presumption that both Dol and Tours could not have pallia unless both were metropoles and thus heads of separate provinces. The idea of a palliated suffragan, harmless to his metropolitan's rights, did not seem to occur.

However, the great theoretician of metropolitan power, Hincmar of Reims, stepped forward to present a reasoned, canonically founded account of the position of palliated suffragans—one that kept them firmly under the thumb of their metropolitans. He first composed his argument in 863, as part of his case for the deposition of Rothad of Soissons.[148] Citing the Council of Nicaea's ruling on the see of Jerusalem (325)—that it had a special place of honor or an honorary precedence (*honoris consequentia*), but without disturbance to the rights of its metropolitan in Caesarea (*salva metropoli* [*propria*] *dignitate*)—Hincmar applied this thinking to Western suffragans who wore pallia. Gregory the Great, he said, had granted the pallium to Syagrius of Autun with the provision "that, with its metropolis keeping its place and honor in all things, the city of the church of Autun ... ought to be after the church of Lyon and claim this place and order for itself from the indulgence of our authority. And we decree that the rest of the bishops keep their own places according to the time of their ordination." Hincmar added two further examples, Theodulf of Orléans and Drogo of Metz, each of whom, at the prayer of an emperor (Charlemagne and Louis the Pious, respectively), had obtained the privilege "that in receiving the pallium he may be sec-

---

147. The reference to Severinus and Restwald was a corrupt or mistaken reading of the *Liber Pontificalis*, which reported that Sergius I had ordained Bertwald as "archbishop of Britain," i.e., Canterbury, not Brittany. Juthinael was not clearly identified as bishop of Dol, and anyway it was unlikely that Hadrian I had honored the Bretons, enemies of his friend Charlemagne (L. Duchesne, *Fastes épiscopaux de l'ancienne Gaule*, 2nd ed. [Paris: Fontemoing, 1910], 2:271–74).

148. This conflict was centered on the competing rights of metropolitans and suffragans. See Perels, *Papst Nikolaus*, 99–113; Schrörs, *Hinkmar*, 237–70; and Devisse, *Hincmar*, 2:583–600.

ond after the metropolitan." Suffragans acquired this status "save the privileges, according to the sacred canons, of the metropolitan cities, to whose dignity and privilege these 'secondary metropolitans' cannot attain, such that they can be treated as equal to them—much less given priority."[149] In these situations, the pallium represented an honorary distinction for a bishop, but did not affect the fundamental (and to Hincmar, all-important) standing of his metropolitan.

Hincmar revised this argument in 870 and combined it with his theory of metropolitan rights in his *Opusculum LV Capitulorum*, as part of his case against Hincmar of Laon.[150] There he reiterated that "those who obtained privileges of this sort, whether through imperial pragmatic form or through the bestowal of the pallium by the apostolic see, the Greeks call 'secondary metropolitans.'" On this account he made an important distinction. On the one hand were metropolitans regarded as "primates, one for each province, who, from ancient custom and apostolic tradition, as we said before, according to the sacred Nicene canons, can both convoke synods and ordain bishops, and be ordained by comprovincial bishops without the examination of any other primate, and are able to arrange all things regularly throughout their provinces." On the other hand were "archbishops" or metropolitans "who cannot carry out these things without the decree of the primate" and were regarded "as archbishops or metropolitans only," rather than primates.[151] Paradoxically, in Hincmar's analysis, the metropolitan pallium was a sign of primatial authority, but the suffragan or honorary pallium did not impinge on that authority.

Indeed, the suffragan's pallium could be treated as a mark of honor without juridical import. After the death of Offa, king of Mercia, who had raised Lichfield to an archbishopric at Canterbury's expense, Alcuin wrote to Archbishop Aethelhard of Canterbury in 797 with advice on undoing the hierarchical confusion: "If it can happen for [the church of Canterbury] to be peacefully united and the

---

149. MGH Epp. 8.1:128, quoting JE 1751.
150. In this treatise Hincmar added the case of Constantinople (metropolis, Heraclea) to that of Jerusalem (metropolis, Caesarea), and he removed the cases of Theodulf and Drogo while leaving that of Syagrius.
151. MGH Conc. 4 supp. 2:202.

tear mended, it seems to be good ... that the pious father [Higbert of Lichfield] not be stripped of the pallium in his days, although the ordination of bishops should return to the holy and first see [Canterbury] ... so that the harmony of charity may be produced among the primary shepherds of the churches of Christ."[152] Three things—metropolitan standing, the right to consecrate bishops, and the pallium—commonly went together, but here Alcuin proposed removing the first two from Lichfield's bishop, while allowing him the use of his pallium for life, in order to smooth ruffled feathers and promote concord.

In 868 Pope Hadrian II palliated Actard of Nantes out of sympathy for the bishop's tribulations, as he told King Charles the Bald: "Having compassion for his many sufferings and long exile and continuous grief, we have also conferred the glory of the pallium on him, from a feeling of pity alone."[153] As the pope made clear to Actard, it was an exceptional situation:

> We would not otherwise grant this [pallium] to you (or to anyone apart from metropolitans), except that you have suffered exiles, the sea, and bonds many times and have also been frequently dragged to a capital sentence, according to the testimony of your metropolitan, who also made it known to us by letter and certified that hope did not survive for you in your own see. Your great losses, or rather merits, demanded this [pallium] as the relief of very swift comfort.[154]

The support of Actard's metropolitan may have been necessary, not only to remove a legal obstacle to his future translation, but also to show that this pallium grant to a suffragan did not impede his superior's authority.[155] The pallium here was a reward, a consolation, a well-deserved honor, without being linked to metropolitan prerogatives. Even so, the pope desired for Actard to be incardinated soon in

---

152. MGH Epp. 4:190.
153. JE 2902, MGH Epp. 6:706. Scholz adds that the new pope's desire for good relations with Charles probably also influenced his treatment of Actard (*Transmigration*, 133).
154. JE 2904, MGH Epp. 6:709.
155. In 871 Hadrian used a Pseudo-Isidorian text (JK †90), which maintained that a bishop could be translated only when driven from his see by force and compelled by necessity, to justify Actard's translation (Scholz, *Transmigration*, 110–12).

a new see, preferably a metropolis.[156] Perhaps Hadrian felt that such a see better befit a palliger's dignity, or that possessing it would regularize Actard's anomalous status. By this time, despite the old phenomenon of palliated suffragans, it was growing harder to separate the vestment from the metropolitan rank.

Conclusion

Through the astute use of the pallium, the distant papacy became a more present and active player in the relationships of power—the politics—of Latin Christendom. Bestowing the vestment on certain recipients and in certain manners was a strategic decision, with effects beyond simple reward and punishment, because palligers were seen differently from other bishops. The impact of possessing the pallium was considerable but paradoxical: it invested the wearer with Roman authority, while rendering him Rome's servant; it provided an occasion for *imperium* and *sacerdotium* to collaborate, or to contend, with each other; and it changed the face of the hierarchical landscape by spurring prelates to coexistence, or to competition. By sharing their insigne, and hence their power, the popes simultaneously exercised power over all involved in the transaction. Yet they had to make sure that this extension of their influence did not escape their control. Bishops sporting the papal badge could not become rival popes, and the provincial pallium had to remain inferior to the Roman version. The next chapter will examine the safeties that popes built into the conferral of the pallium, in order to ensure the dependence and subordination of those who had the honor of wearing it.

---

156. JE 2902, MGH Epp. 6:706. Actard was eventually given the see of Tours, as requested by the Council of Douzy (871) (MGH Conc. 4:527–28). See Scholz, *Transmigration*, 130–47. It is unknown whether, as archbishop of Tours, he was allowed to continue wearing this pallium or was given another.

3

Using the Pallium

The towering figure of Archbishop Hincmar of Reims was involved in many of the most important affairs, political and intellectual, secular and ecclesiastical, of his lifetime (806–82). His feelings on the papal gift of the pallium were complex. As a vociferous proponent of metropolitan rights, he valued it as the distinctive badge that separated an archbishop from his suffragans and confirmed his supreme authority within his province.[1] If only this privilege were not reliant on the will of a donor, who decided who wore the vestment, when, and to what effect! Indeed, Hincmar's sometimes testy correspondence with Pope Nicholas I disclosed several occasions when the archbishop seemed to be vying for control of the pallium. By framing it as the expected, customary right of a metropolitan, and by apparently trying to finagle its unlimited use, he showed himself dissatisfied with the terms of the gift.[2] Having to receive the vestment from outside his province and abide by someone else's rules vexed him.

While the pallium was a gift, its significance did not lie solely in

---

1. In 863, MGH Epp. 8.1:137, and to Nicholas I in 867, MGH Epp. 8.1:216.
2. Twice to Nicholas I in 867, MGH Epp. 8.1:216, 222; *De Iure Metropolitanorum*, in PL 126:191; and Nicholas I to Hincmar in 866, JE 2823, BH 838, MGH Epp. 6:430–31.

the one-time act of giving and receiving it. A phenomenon scholars have called "inalienability" suggests that a gift bestowing identity may be so intimately connected to its donor that he retains a claim on it even after he has given it. Due to its origin, history, or significance, it symbolizes the donor, and the transaction confirms his identity and status even while conferring a derived status and power on the recipient.[3] The pallium seems to have functioned as an inalienable gift. The papal donors expressed their ongoing claim on it through the nuances of the grant—details that implied relative status between donor and recipient, within an implicit competition for power.[4] Thus the popes instilled the pallium with canonical and liturgical consequences that continued to affect the recipients once they possessed it. These consequences served primarily to remind the palliger of his subsidiary status. The limitation of the pallium to its papally designated beneficiary, the limitation of its appearance to specifically determined times and places, and the limitations placed on a prelate's power when lacking the vestment—all these limits reinforced his dependence on the Roman pontiff. On the surface a sign of prestige as the pope's own garb, the pallium's practical impact made its wearers partial, subordinate reflections of the one who had deigned to bestow it. Popes in this period achieved this effect by putting conditions on the use of their gift.

Personal Privilege

The conferral of the right to wear the pallium was meant as a personal privilege, that is, a privilege given specifically and individually to the recipient as a person, rather than to his office, his church, or his successors. Still, as requesting and receiving the pallium became standard practice in metropolitan sees, these churches came to expect it for their pastors. In order to maintain the character of the vestment as a free gift, the popes had to keep control of it by stressing the role of their own discretion. They did so chiefly in two man-

---

3. See Bijsterveld, *Do ut des*, 19, 28–29, 86.
4. See Curta, "Merovingian and Carolingian Gift-giving," 698.

ners: by carefully restricting the grants, and by counteracting the force of custom with an emphasis on favor.

Restricted Grants

The pallium was not the prerogative of a church. Three of the four formulas for pallium grants in the *Liber Diurnus* included a clause underscoring the fact that the local church's status was left unchanged by the gift. In *Si pastores ovium*, the clause occurred at the heart of the document: "with the privileges of your church remaining in their condition," as also in *Officium sacerdotis*: "with the integrity of your privileges preserved."[5] In *Apostolicae sedis* it formed an appendix: "Also, we confirm by our authority and decree to continue undiminished all the privileges that are known to have been previously granted to your church."[6] The notion must have seemed crucial, for a variant of the last clause was tacked onto the end of a grant that otherwise followed the one formula that lacked such a clause, *Pallii usum*.[7] The precise import of these clauses is difficult to determine, but the general intent—that the bestowal of the pallium did not alter the standing of a church, as expressed in its previous *privilegia*—seems clear.[8]

Nor was the pallium the prerogative of all the incumbents of a see, to be handed down from bishop to bishop. It became customary, no matter the formula, for the phrase *diebus vitae tuae tantummodo*, "only for the days of your life," to be attached to the protocol in a pallium grant.[9] It occurred, for example, in a grant that followed

---

5. V45, Foerster, *Liber Diurnus*, 101, with parallels C44 on 200 and A39 on 300; and V46, ibid., 104, with slight variants C45 on 203 and A40 on 305.

6. V48, ibid., 107, with slight variants C47 on 205 and A42 on 309.

7. Paschal I to Bernard of Vienne in 817, JE 2549, GaP 3.1:96–97 no. 81, MGH Epp. 3:98.

8. See Hacke, *Palliumverleihungen*, 58–59. Helmut Beumann, however, interprets the mentioned privileges as previous pallium grants regulating the use of the vestment (*Theutonum nova metropolis: Studien zur Geschichte des Erzbistums Magdeburg in ottonischer Zeit*, ed. Jutta Krimm-Beumann, Quellen und Forschungen zur Geschichte Sachsen-Anhalts 1 [Cologne: Böhlau, 2000], 21).

9. Occasionally (e.g., JE †2558, 2580, 2681, and GP 1:10–11 no. 13, 14, 17) the phrase is mistakenly cited as the incipit of a document. Paul Rabikauskas, however, correctly describes it as part of the protocol (*Diplomatica Pontificia (Praelectionum*

the formula *Officium sacerdotis*, from Leo III to Fortunatus of Grado (803); in one that followed *Pallii usum*, from Eugene II to Adalram of Salzburg (824); in the several that followed the version of *Si pastores ovium* popular at this time, beginning with Gregory IV to Liudpram of Salzburg (837); and even in one that followed no formula, from Hadrian II to Actard of Nantes (868).[10] The phrase indicated that the pallium was bestowed for the duration of the recipient's life and could not be automatically transferred to his successor.[11] Although it does not appear in the sources of this period, the custom of burying the vestment with its owner would give cultural expression to this legal principle.[12]

Despite the fact that precedents were occasionally required as part of a petition, the popes did not wish to be bound by them. They generally were careful not to create perpetual entitlements, which suggests that pallium grants were sometimes taken as such. Their efforts were clearest in the case of suffragans. By the end of this period, when the pallium had become the obligatory insigne of metropolitan rank, palliated suffragans came to seem more anomalous. The danger that their successors would also expect the vestment threatened to broaden its use beyond certain specially selected bishops—causing exceptions to become rules. Thus the popes placed restrictions on pallium grants to suffragans in more explicit terms than usual. In his grant to the exiled Actard of Nantes, besides the addition to the protocol mentioned above, Pope Hadrian II conferred the vestment "not as an everlasting decree for your church, but for your use particularly, for a

---

Lineamenta), 6th rev. ed. [Rome: Pontificia Università Gregoriana, 1998], 32). The wording may well have echoed passages in the Old Testament (e.g., Ps 128:5).

10. Citations are as follows: JE 2512, IP 7.2:40–41 no. 28, Cessi, *Documenti*, 1:56; JE †2558, GP 1:10 no. 13 (where it is accepted as authentic), Hauthaler and Martin, *Salzburger Urkundenbuch*, 2:19 (*tantummodo* was missing, probably by accident in transmission); JE 2580, GP 1:10 no. 14, Hauthaler and Martin, *Salzburger Urkundenbuch*, 2:27, although one grant of this type (Nicholas I to Rimbert of Hamburg in 865, JE 2798, GP 6:35 no. 26, BH 785, Curschmann, *Ältere Papsturkunden*, 27) lacked the phrase, perhaps by accident in transmission; and JE 2904, MGH Epp. 6:709.

11. Alcuin was possibly echoing this phrase from Higbert of Lichfield's lost pallium grant (JE *2456) when he proposed that the ex-archbishop be allowed to retain the vestment *diebus suis* (to Aethelhard of Canterbury in 797, MGH Epp. 4:190).

12. See 234–35 below. The discovery of the pallia of Caesarius of Arles suggests an early inception for this custom (Miller, *Clothing the Clergy*, 106–8).

certain time and during the present life.... Be decorated with honor while you live."¹³ It was a privilege specifically for Actard, unconnected to the see he had lost or the one he would eventually gain.¹⁴

When Pope John VIII gave the pallium to another suffragan, Wala of Metz, in 878, he was unusually exact in limiting the scope of the grant. The vestment was conceded "only for the days of your life, and we grant you, not your church, to use it, with [your church's] privileges otherwise remaining in their condition.... You may have permission [to use the pallium] for the days of your life under our right and jurisdiction, as we have said. We have resolved for your successors to have no usage or custom through this our apostolic privilege granted to you."¹⁵ Although the pope followed the *Si pastores ovium* formula for the most part, these repetitious interventions stipulated that it was a personal prerogative, given for the duration of Wala's life, not to his successors, and pertaining to the bishop, not to the bishopric. The pope seemed anxious that the favor, dependent upon papal authority alone, not become customary for the see of Metz.¹⁶ It was a reasonable concern: several bishops of Metz, including Chrodegang and Drogo, had received the pallium in the past. John had recently taken steps at the Councils of Rome (875) and Ravenna (877) to associate the vestment with metropolitan status and power, and so he approached palliated suffragans cautiously. But even in the case of metropolitans, he stressed that using the pallium was a privilege, not a right, and hence could be withdrawn as easily as it had been bestowed, as he pronounced at the same two councils.¹⁷ These sorts of restrictions were a means of keeping a firm grip on the vestment's distribution.

13. JE 2904, MGH Epp. 6:709.
14. Cf. Hadrian II to Charles the Bald in 868, JE 2902, MGH Epp. 6:706.
15. JE 3183, BU 427, PL 126:798–99.
16. The falsified privileges for Ansgar of Hamburg attributed to Gregory IV and Nicholas I contained, imbedded within them, pallium grants of a strange form (JE 2574, GP 6:25–28 no. 11, Curschmann, *Ältere Papsturkunden*, 14; and JE 2759, GP 6:31–33 no. 21, BH 706, Curschmann, *Ältere Papsturkunden*, 23). Knibbs argues persuasively that these portions of the privileges were forgeries derived from a document similar to John's privilege for Wala; in the clumsy rewording he sees an attempt to surpass the bounds of a personal privilege (*Ansgar*, 147–49).
17. MGH Conc. 5:10, 68.

Custom vs. Favor

While papal pleasure determined the recipients of the pallium, that pleasure was not wholly arbitrary. Balancing the emphasis on papal choice was, paradoxically, an emphasis on custom.[18] Wearing the vestment was a personal privilege, but the power of precedent and the increasingly strong link between the pallium and metropolitan status caused certain persons to request and receive it as a matter of course. This attitude was found already in the letters of Gregory the Great. His late ninth-century biographer, John the Deacon, repeated his words to Maximus of Salona, who had mended relations with the pope and then gained the pallium: "Just as we do not suffer illicit things to be perpetrated," Gregory affirmed, "so we do not deny those which are customary."[19] For the bishops of Salona (a metropolis) to receive the vestment was regarded as routine, as long as they behaved well and preserved harmony with the apostolic see. Gregory initiated such a custom himself when he decreed that London and York would be metropoles and their incumbents would receive pallia.[20] As Alcuin poetically described it, the pope "immediate-

---

18. References to custom (*mos, consuetudo*) are ubiquitous in pallium-related sources. Usually the phrase "according to custom" occurred alone and is difficult to interpret. More rarely its meaning seems clear, but the results are by no means uniform. "Custom" could signify the papal practice of giving the pallium (e.g., Leo IV to Ignatius of Constantinople between 847 and 853, JE 2647, BH 113, MGH Epp. 5:607); the tendency for the bishops of certain sees to receive the pallium (e.g., John VIII to the Dalmatian bishops in 879, JE 3262, BU 530, MGH Epp. 7:157); the tendency for metropolitans to receive the pallium (e.g., Hincmar of Reims to Nicholas I in 864, MGH Epp. 8.1:147); the particular ways in which the pallium was used (e.g., Nicholas I to Hincmar of Reims in 866, JE 2823, BH 838, MGH Epp. 6:430–31); the request for the pallium (e.g., Council of Ravenna [877] c. 1, MGH Conc. 5:68); the profession of faith required to gain the pallium (e.g., Council of Rome [875] c. 2, MGH Conc. 5:9); the vicarial powers often attached to the pallium (e.g., John VIII to Rostagnus of Arles in 878, JE 3148, BU 353, MGH Epp. 7:109); the document accompanying the pallium (e.g., Zachary to Boniface ca. 744, JE 2271, GP 4:24 no. 58, Rau, *Briefe*, 172); the papal practice of wearing the pallium (e.g., Agnellus of Ravenna, *Liber Pontificalis Ecclesiae Ravennatis*, in Nauerth, *Bischofsbuch*, 206); or even the pallium itself (e.g., Zachary to Boniface ca. 744, JE 2270, GP 4:23 no. 55, Rau, *Briefe*, 166).
19. PL 75:180, quoting JE 1703.
20. To Augustine of Canterbury in 601, JE 1829, CCSL 140A:935.

ly commanded that [York] / Be held as capital of the churches and pinnacle of honor / And that pallia should clothe the consecrated pontiffs in it."[21] Here the pallium was bound to the pastors of a particular see, meant for each one after he had been ordained. The custom thus arose from a series of bishops acquiring the pallium, one after the other.

Later times witnessed the same phenomenon. The patriarch of Grado, as the see's chronicle stated in several places, obtained the vestment "according to the example of his predecessors."[22] Emperor Louis the Pious employed identical logic in 824, when he asked the pope for the pallium on behalf of Adalram, archbishop of Salzburg: "His predecessors who were in charge of this holy see, over which he presides by God's authority, were accustomed to receive the pallium of apostolic authority from your predecessors."[23] As justification for his request, the emperor appealed to precedent; yet he was exaggerating, for only Adalram's immediate predecessor, Arno, had been a palliger.[24] In any event, custom could seem to force the pope's hand and so impinge upon the central notion of papal choice.

Indeed, once the bishops of certain sees began to receive the pallium regularly, some claimed it as customarily *due* to them. Whiffs of this idea once emanated even from the apostolic see. The formula *Apostolicae sedis* in the *Liber Diurnus*, intended for Sicilian bishops, imagined that they would obtain the pallium simply by virtue of having taken office: "We have provided to grant your Fraternity the use of the pallium, because it is known that you have received the office of governance in the church of N."[25] In a sense, the pallium was attached to certain churches, such that it was automatically granted when their bishops had been installed. Likewise unexpectedly, Pope Paschal I issued a pallium grant for Bernard of Vienne in 817 that followed the formula *Pallii usum* for the most part, but

---

21. *Versus de Patribus Regibus et Sanctis Euboricensis Ecclesiae*, in Godman, *Bishops*, 20.
22. *Chronica de Singulis Patriarchis Novae Aquileiae*, in Monticolo, *Cronache*, 1:14.
23. To Eugene II, MGH Epp. 5:313.
24. See GP 1:4.
25. V48, Foerster, *Liber Diurnus*, 106–7, with slight variants C47 on 205 and A42 on 308.

added "to you and to your church of Vienne" after "we have gladly granted the use of the pallium."[26] This language made the grant not so much a personal privilege as an ecclesial one, although it was exceptional and could have resulted from carelessness in the papal chancery or corruption in transmission.[27] These early sources hinted that custom was not yet considered a threat to papal control of the pallium, and that there was as yet no clear doctrine on this matter.

But the threat became clearer in the course of the ninth century. The caption affixed to Emperor Lothar I's intercessory letter for Hincmar of Reims's pallium appealed to "the custom of his church."[28] Though added later (the manuscript dates to the tenth century), this caption drew on a passage in the letter that urged the pope to bow to the custom of his predecessors. It was traditional for archbishops of Reims to receive the vestment, and so it must be traditional for the popes to give it. Hincmar himself preferred to associate the pallium with his see rather than his person, as he declared to Pope Nicholas I in 867 when staving off accusations of pride: "I do not think that the use of the pallium belongs to my own dignity, but I recognize that it belongs to the splendor [*genius*] of the metropolitan see."[29] He repeated this line in another letter to the pope, along with patristic support: "Pope Leo the Great says that, even if the merits of bishops are sometimes various, nevertheless the rights of their sees continue."[30] He also argued elsewhere that all metropolitans, "from the law of ancient custom, are accustomed to be distinguished with the splendor of the pallium by the apostolic see."[31] In metropoles, he alleged, reception had become *de rigueur*. Probably not coincidentally,

---

26. JE 2549, GaP 3.1:96–97 no. 81, MGH Epp. 3:97–98. The document seems to claim that Vienne was founded by Peter and Paul, which has led some to see it as a forged attempt to exalt the church's pedigree; however, one witness retained a missing word that associated the apostles with the Roman church, as in the original *Pallii usum*, and so the letter's authenticity is not impugned.

27. Another witness added the standard mark of a personal privilege, *diebus vitae tuae tantummodo*, to the end of the protocol, but GaP calls it a copyist's error, without explanation.

28. To Leo IV in 847, MGH Epp. 5:609.
29. MGH Epp. 8.1:216.
30. MGH Epp. 8.1:222, quoting JK 495.
31. *De Iure Metropolitanorum*, in PL 126:191.

this position served the agenda of this staunch defender of metropolitan rights by loosening the pope's control over the insigne.

Against such arguments for a customary "right" to receive the pallium, the popes began to accentuate their role as discretionary gift-givers, limiting the vestment to select recipients.[32] Despite his blandishments, Emperor Lothar I admitted that the decision regarding Hincmar's pallium rested with Pope Leo IV.[33] The same pope maintained that it was the Roman church's right to dole out the pallium to others, indeed to anyone whom it appointed.[34] In 864 Pope Nicholas I consented for the pallium to be worn on Maundy Thursday: "To use the apostolic pallium on the same day is permitted to those alone to whom it has been allowed by the apostolic see."[35] Although he was issuing a general liturgical regulation, Nicholas stressed that it applied only to a chosen few, the papally privileged. A year later he described a bishop who sought the pallium as one "who longs to be of such great merit before us and desires to acquire such a gift," that is, one who necessarily threw himself upon papal judgment of his deserts.[36] The next pope, Hadrian II, showed "condescension" to a royal request in 868 for Wulfhad of Bourges to be "adorned with the use of the pallium by the generosity of our authority."[37] The language evoked the pope's freedom to give or refuse

32. One is reminded of insistence on the revocability of fiefs in the face of their evolving inheritance. Yet, whatever the customary rights claimed by archbishops, the pallium was saved from sheer inheritability because its wearers could have no legitimate heirs and because the garment was buried with them. Gifts, in fact, may be simultaneously voluntary and obligatory, for both donor and recipient, and in the Middle Ages customary claims existed alongside lordly grants in ambiguity (White, "Politics," 180–82, and Geary, "Gift Exchange," 134).

33. To Leo IV in 847, MGH Epp. 5:610–11.

34. To Ignatius of Constantinople between 847 and 853, JE 2647, BH 113, MGH Epp. 5:607.

35. To Ralph of Bourges, JE 2765, BH 711, MGH Epp. 6:636. It is unclear whether this license was given to all palligers, or only to those in whose grants Maundy Thursday was specified; since the latter verges on a tautology, the former is preferable. The letter exists in both genuine and interpolated forms (Fedor Schneider, "Ein interpolierter Brief Papst Nikolaus' I. und der Primat von Bourges," *Neues Archiv der Gesellschaft für ältere deutsche Geschichtskunde* 32 [1907]: 476–92); the latter lacks "alone," but it is unclear whether this omission affects the meaning.

36. To Solomon of Brittany, JE 2789, BH 764, MGH Epp. 6:640.

37. To Charles the Bald, JE 2902, MGH Epp. 6:705.

the gift, and his graciousness in ultimately opting to give it—even in the case of a metropolitan see, Bourges, whose incumbents had traditionally received it. Again and again in this period, the motivation behind the bestowal—variously expressed as good will, grace, comforting compassion, or beneficent piety—highlighted papal *favor*: the pallium was a favor granted by the pope, for it conveyed his favor for the recipient.[38] The Roman pontiffs thus made clear that the pallium could never be taken for granted.

Limited Use

Though eventually regarded as a badge of office, the pallium was never intended as an item of everyday vesture. Its papal donors deliberately restricted the times, places, and contexts in which it was supposed to be worn, often in ways that did not apply to themselves. They thus hoped not only to keep ongoing control of the vestment, but also to make clear, in a publicly manifest fashion, that the use of the pallium was not the recipient's by right or in its fullness. After all, the recipient was not the pope; instead, he relied on the pope to partake of this honor, to the extent that he was permitted. The limitations on wearing the pallium were realized both by issuing regulations and by battling the abuses that arose when those regulations were ignored.

Regulation

Circumscribing the ways in which the pallium was allowed to be worn was a longstanding practice. Pope Zachary vaguely alluded to it in 744, when he informed Boniface that he had sent pallia to the archbishops of Rouen, Reims, and Sens and instructed them "that they should know what the use of the pallium is."[39] All four formulas for pallium grants found in the *Liber Diurnus* indicated that this

---

38. E.g., *Apostolicae sedis*, V48, Foerster, *Liber Diurnus*, 106–7, with slight variants C47 on 205 and A42 on 308; *Annales Xantenses*, in MGH SSRG 12:22; Hadrian II to Charles the Bald in 868, JE 2902, MGH Epp. 6:706; Hadrian II to Actard of Nantes in 868, JE 2904, MGH Epp. 6:709; and John VIII to Willibert of Cologne in 874, JE 2988, GP 7.1:34–35 no. 67, BU 120, Wisplinghoff, *Rheinisches Urkundenbuch*, 2:158.

39. JE 2270, GP 4:23 no. 55, Rau, *Briefe*, 166.

usus was established by custom: each conferred the pallium, "which we grant you to use ... not otherwise than you know that your predecessors and forerunners used it" (in *Si pastores ovium*); "which you should remember to use as our predecessors granted to your predecessors" (in *Officium sacerdotis*); "which you can use according to the custom of your church" (in *Pallii usum*); and "at those times and according to that order in which you do not doubt that your predecessor also used it" (in *Apostolicae sedis*).[40] The gist was clear, but no details were provided, perhaps because the manner of use—the *tempora* when it was permitted and the *ordo* according to which it was worn—originally varied from church to church.

Traces of this tradition appeared in the ninth century. As late as 865/66, Pope Nicholas I invoked the same terms when notifying King Charles the Bald about his gift of the pallium to Egilo of Sens, "to be used according to the custom of his predecessors."[41] And in canon 27 the Fourth Council of Constantinople (869–70) authorized the use of the pallium "according to the norms handed down throughout each province and region and city."[42] This all-encompassing phrase allowed for a wide disparity in how the vestment was worn, especially that which probably existed between the Eastern and Western churches.[43]

In Rome, the pope wore the pallium on many occasions. *Ordo Romanus XXXIV*, composed around 750, had him put it on before sitting in his chair to receive envoys from a nearby city who had come to

40. Citations are as follows: V45, Foerster, *Liber Diurnus*, 101, with slight variants C44 on 200–201 and A39 on 300; V46, ibid., 104, with slight variants C45 on 203 and A40 on 305; V47, ibid., 106, with slight variants C46 on 204 and A41 on 307; and V48, ibid., 106–7, with slight variants C47 on 205 and A42 on 308. The exact meaning of "according to that order" (*eo ordine*) is unclear. Given the ritual connotations of *ordo*, it may have referred to the liturgical regulations that governed the wearing of the pallium.

41. JE 2810, BH 767, MGH Epp. 6:646.

42. Alberigo et al., *Conciliorum Oecumenicorum Decreta*, 185.

43. On the use of the *omophorion* in the East, see Braun, *Liturgische Gewandung*, 666–68; Eidenschink, *Election*, 107–9; and Robert F. Taft, "The Case of the Missing Vestment: The Byzantine Omophorion Great and Small," *Bollettino della Badia Greca di Grottaferrata*, ser. 3, 1 (2004): 273–301. Taft doubts that all Byzantine bishops originally wore it (ibid., 281–82), but his reliance on Constantinople IV (c. 27) does not account for Western influence. See 55n100 above.

request consecration for their new bishop.⁴⁴ The entry for Hadrian II in the *Liber Pontificalis* described several visions that foretold his elevation as pope. In each, Hadrian was pictured looking and acting as a pope—wearing the pallium (the most recognizable papal emblem of the period) in a procession, during the Mass, and while seated on the cathedra (perhaps at a synod).⁴⁵ *Ordo Romanus VIII*, from the second half of the ninth century, included the pallium among the liturgical vestments the pope donned even "on ordinary days."⁴⁶ Since it was his proper insigne, wearing it reinforced his identity and authority before all who saw him. And since it was subject to nobody else's oversight, he naturally enjoyed great latitude in its use.

That freedom, however, did not extend to those who shared the garment by the pope's leave. Recipients were reminded that the pallium was restricted to the eucharistic liturgy: as the formula *Si pastores ovium* put it, "for celebrating the solemnities of the Mass."⁴⁷ That the Mass was not merely the principal occasion but the only permitted one could be deduced from the mid-ninth-century Pseudo-Isidorian decretals, which reproduced Gregory the Great's genuine letter concerning Leander of Seville's pallium, "to be used at the solemnities of the Mass *alone*."⁴⁸ Likewise, Pope Hadrian II added the word *tantum* in his 868 privilege for Actard of Nantes.⁴⁹ Several documents detailed exactly what constituted this liturgical occasion. In his grant to Arno of Salzburg in 798, Pope Leo III inserted a clause into the *Officium sacerdotis* formula: "You should use that pallium from the sacristy up to the sacred altar and from the altar down to the sacristy."⁵⁰ Eighty

---

44. Michel Andrieu, ed., *Les Ordines romani du haut moyen âge*, Spicilegium Sacrum Lovaniense, études et documents 24 (Louvain: Spicilegium Sacrum Lovaniense, 1951), 3:608. Cf. the derivative text in the tenth-century *Ordo Romanus XXXV* (ibid., 4:41). The episcopal consecration would have been that of a Roman suffragan. On the Roman ecclesiastical province, see HEOJ 3:477–78; Gaudemet, *L'église*, 445–46; and Hartmann, *Geschichte*, 2.1:161–63.

45. Duchesne, *Liber pontificalis*, 2:174.

46. Andrieu, *Ordines*, 2:321–22.

47. V45, Foerster, *Liber Diurnus*, 101, with parallels C44 on 200 and A39 on 300.

48. Schon and Zechiel-Eckes, *Projekt Pseudoisidor*, at http://www.pseudoisidor.mgh.de/html/304.htm, quoting JE 1756; emphasis added.

49. JE 2904, MGH Epp. 6:709.

50. JE 2498, GP 1:8 no. 7, Dopsch, "Papst Leo III. verleiht," 18.

years later Pope John VIII said that Wala of Metz should do the same, "as is the old custom for the palliated."[51] Thus the pallium was worn only from the time the prelate vested for the liturgy until the time he removed his vestments afterwards, including opening and closing processions within the church and the action of the Mass itself. The mention of *prisca consuetudo* probably recalled Gregory the Great's dispute with the archbishop of Ravenna regarding the proper wearing of the pallium.[52]

All in all, the regulation seems to have sunk in. Alcuin described the use of the vestment to his former student, then archbishop of York, Eanbald II, in 796: "You will never be clothed with the pallium of sacred blessing apart from the ministry of assisting deacons."[53] Since deacons customarily helped bishops vest in the sacristy and escorted them during solemn pontifical Mass, Alcuin was likely describing the pallium's limitation to such a liturgy.[54] At the Council of Ingelheim (840) Emperor Lothar I restored the see of Reims and the pallium to Ebo so that he could "perform the harmony and grace of the divine office with us."[55] In other words, vested in his recovered pallium, Ebo would once again celebrate the liturgy in communion with the emperor and his bishops. Several of the testimonial letters written on behalf of Willibert of Cologne in the early 870s alluded to the vestment's liturgical use. King Louis the German asked Pope Hadrian II to send the pallium to the archbishop "for sanctifying, so that, festooned with your authority, he may embellish the sacrament

---

51. JE 3183, BU 427, PL 126:799.

52. Gregory used language similar to the foregoing quotations in a letter to John of Ravenna (in 594, JE 1326, IP 5:25 no. 31, CCSL 140:277).

53. MGH Epp. 4:168.

54. Cf. *Ordo Romanus I*, in Andrieu, *Ordines*, 2:79, 81.

55. MGH Conc. 2.2:792. In a coda—apparently forged by Ebo himself and found in only one version of the decree (Albert Werminghoff, "Ein neuer Text des Apologeticum Ebonis," *Neues Archiv der Gesellschaft für ältere deutsche Geschichtskunde* 25 [1900]: 374–75)—Drogo of Metz recalled Ebo "to the divine offices with the pallium of holy and apostolic authority" (MGH Conc. 2.2:804–5). Wearing the pallium was not required for celebrating Mass, since it could not ordinarily be worn at every Mass. Rather, these texts, which focused on Ebo's restoration, envisioned him once more vested in the sign of his office during the Mass.

of the holy and undivided Trinity with us."[56] The same king requested Emperor Louis II's help in obtaining the pallium "for sanctifying, wreathed with which [Willibert] may offer a sacrifice of praise [Ps 50:14, 23; 107:22] every day by praying for us all."[57] Also, the clergy and people of Cologne begged the pope to fortify the archbishop "with the bestowal of the pallium and the protection of sanctification, for consecrating."[58] The terms *sanctificando* and *sacrando* in these letters must have referred to celebrating sacred rites. By the end of this period, writing to Eastern Christians in 879, Pope John VIII could invoke the tradition of "the sacred pallium, which it is usual for pontiffs to use during the sacred solemnities of the Mass," as something typical and uncontested.[59]

Yet this vestment was not to be worn at every Mass. As the pallium grew in prominence, nebulous appeals to local custom usually yielded to more precise specifications. Nicholas I, Hincmar of Reims, Hadrian II, and the Fourth Council of Constantinople all bore witness in the late 860s that the pallium was conceded for use "at certain times."[60] What were these occasions? *Ordo Romanus VIII*, though composed in Gaul between 850 and 900, probably testified to an older tradition when it provided a rudimentary list during its discussion of episcopal vesting: "The chasuble [is put on], and the pallium is put on top of it. For on these days—the birthday of the Lord, Easter,

---

56. MGH Epp. 6:249. The odd wording brings baptism to mind, but since the king expected to join the archbishop in the rite, it was probably the eucharist.

57. MGH Epp. 6:250. "Every day" should not be taken as an expectation that Willibert would be granted the daily use of the pallium, for which there is no evidence, but rather as a mistake by secular lords unfamiliar with the usual practice. Liudbert of Mainz's letter to Hadrian II in support of Willibert used very similar language but, in place of "every day," substituted a more typical proviso, "as long as he lives" (MGH Epp. 6:244).

58. MGH Epp. 6:248.

59. To Basil I, JE 3271, BU 551, MGH Epp. 7:174.

60. Nicholas I to Hincmar of Reims in 866, JE 2823, BH 838, MGH Epp. 6:430; Hincmar of Reims to Nicholas I in 867, MGH Epp. 8.1:216; Hadrian II to Actard of Nantes in 868, JE 2904, MGH Epp. 6:709; and Council of Constantinople (869–70) c. 27, Alberigo et al., *Conciliorum Oecumenicorum Decreta*, 185. The canonist who compiled the *Collectio Anselmo Dedicata* a quarter-century later used the same phrase in a rubric (Canon 1.127, J. C. Besse, ed., "Collectionis *Anselmo Dedicata* Liber Primus," *Revue de droit canonique* 9 [1959]: 291).

St. Peter's, and the day of his ordination—he is clothed with a chasuble of another color."[61] When a bishop was permitted to wear the pallium, on Christmas, Easter, the feast of St. Peter (June 29), and the anniversary of his consecration, its use necessitated a different color for the chasuble, perhaps so that the white wool would stand out conspicuously. These days were fitting: the two holiest solemnities of the liturgical year, the feast of the saint whose vicar had granted the vestment, and the memorial of the recipient's assumption of pastoral office. They reminded the wearer of the importance of the gift, his special relationship with its donor, and its nature as a personal honor.

A similar list began to appear in pallium grants using the revised form of *Si pastores ovium*, apparently introduced in the pontificate of Gregory IV. Here the phrase "according to custom" and the reference to the usages of predecessors were omitted from the original formula, since those customary regulations were now abrogated in favor of the list that followed. According to it, the pallium was allowed

> only on the day of the holy and venerable resurrection of our Lord Jesus Christ, and on the anniversaries of the holy apostles, and of blessed John the Baptist, as well as on the assumption of blessed Mary, Mother of God, and similarly on the day of the birth of the Lord our God, and equally on the day of the solemnity of your church, but also on the anniversary day of your ordination.[62]

The occasions catalogued in *Ordo Romanus VIII* were now augmented with the chief solemnities of two widely venerated saints with ancient cults and close connections to Christ, John the Baptist (June 24) and the blessed Virgin Mary (August 15). The feast of St. Peter was broadened to include all the feasts of the twelve apostles.[63] And

---

61. Andrieu, *Ordines*, 2:321.
62. Gregory IV to Liudpram of Salzburg in 837, JE 2580, GP 1:10 no. 14, Hauthaler and Martin, *Salzburger Urkundenbuch*, 2:27. The archbishop's anniversary of consecration was omitted in one grant of this kind (Benedict III to Vitalis of Grado in 858, JE 2672, IP 7.2:43 no. 38, BH 419, Hacke, *Palliumverleihungen*, 151), but the copyist's eye had probably skipped from one *die* to the next.
63. Some maintain that there was a single feast honoring all the apostles. See, e.g., Thomas Zotz, "*Pallium et alia quaedam archiepiscopatus insignia*: zum Beziehungsgefüge und zu Rangfragen der Reichskirchen im Spiegel der päpstlichen Privilegierung des 10. und 11. Jahrhunderts," in *Festschrift für Berent Schwineköper*, ed.

the anniversary of the dedication of the bishop's cathedral, a memorial of great local significance, was added. In short, the most solemn celebrations in a particular church were considered appropriate for the display of so great an honor. This generous list increased the visibility of the pallium, precisely at the times when the largest number of the faithful were gathered. Its role on such occasions—often enough to be recognized, but seldom enough to be marked as special—must have intensified its importance, the wearer's distinctiveness and standing, and (for those who knew its origin) his association with Rome.

The acceptable way of using the pallium changed very little after Gregory IV's modification of *Si pastores ovium*. Only three known alterations to the usual list of pallium days occurred in this period. First, Hincmar of Reims requested, and perhaps received, license to don the pallium when consecrating his suffragan bishops.[64] It is not surprising that the vestment seemed suited to this fundamental act of metropolitan power, especially to a defender of metropolitan rights such as Hincmar. Second, as mentioned above, Pope Nicholas I, replying to Archbishop Ralph of Bourges's queries in 864, added Maundy Thursday (*in cena Domini*) to the feasts on which the pallium could be worn.[65] This permission followed another for bishops to

---

Helmut Maurer and Hans Patze (Sigmaringen: Thorbecke, 1982), 172n107, and Georg Gresser, *Clemens II.: der erste deutsche Reformpapst* (Paderborn: Schöningh, 2007), 89, 91. However, in nearly all pallium grants that mention it, the plural, "*feasts* of the apostles," was used. See Lorenz Weinrich, "Laurentius-Verehrung in ottonischer Zeit," *Jahrbuch für die Geschichte Mittel- und Ostdeutschlands* 21 (1972): 51.

64. Mentioned in a letter to Nicholas I in 867, MGH Epp. 8.1:216. A letter of Leo IV in 851 seemed to grant this request, but it was at least partially falsified (JE 2608, BH †?240, MGH Epp. 5:591–92). Yet there was certainly precedent, for Gregory III had allowed this occasion to Boniface in 732 (JE 2239, GP 4:13 no. 24, Rau, *Briefe*, 98).

65. JE 2765, BH 711, MGH Epp. 6:636. The first time Maundy Thursday occurred in a pallium grant dates to the mid-tenth century, when the standard list of pallium days yielded to longer lists, tailored to their recipients (John XII to Henry of Trier in 957, JL 3682, GP 10.1:42 no. 62, BZ 275, Harald Zimmermann, ed., *Papsturkunden, 896–1046*, Österreichische Akademie der Wissenschaften, philosophisch-historische Klasse, Denkschriften 174, Veröffentlichungen der historischen Kommission 3 [Vienna: Österreichische Akademie der Wissenschaften, 1984], 1:263 [hereafter "ZPUU"]). Thus this decree is best understood as a general addition to the standard list of this era.

sing the *Gloria* during the Mass on that day, as in Rome. In both, the pope was extending Roman usages to other bishops, in recognition of the special solemnity of the Mass of the Lord's Supper. Third, in his pallium grant to Actard of Nantes in 868, which followed no formula because of its atypical circumstances, Pope Hadrian II included the list of pallium days from the modified *Si pastores ovium*. But he inserted two further occasions, until now unprecedented: the feasts of the Ascension and of St. Martin (November 11).[66] The former was an important solemnity of Christ, and the latter honored the patron saint of Tours, the metropolis of Actard's province (and, as it would turn out, the see to which he was translated). Since Hadrian intended this pallium as a special favor to a heroically suffering pastor, he may have decided to add the two days as a gesture of kindness. In sum, all these fastidious regulations must have both heightened appreciation for the pallium when it was worn and, at the same time, emphasized the dependence on papal authority felt by its wearers.

Abuse

Perhaps the popes had judged that it was now necessary to specify pallium days in their grants in order to prevent overreaching by palligers.[67] For this reason, presumably, the updated *Si pastores ovium* formula of Gregory IV renewed an injunction of Gregory the Great: "We grant [the pallium] as was sanctioned by our most blessed predecessor, Lord Gregory, bishop of this bountiful see: 'Your Fraternity should put on the pallium in the sacristy and so proceed to the solemnities of the Mass, and claim nothing further for yourself by the daring of rash presumption, lest, when a matter of external dress is irregularly seized, even matters that could be regularly allowed

---

66. JE 2904, MGH Epp. 6:710.
67. In John VIII's 878 grant to Rostagnus of Arles (JE 3148, BU 353, MGH Epp. 7:110), which copied Gregory the Great's 595 grant to Virgilius of Arles (JE 1374, CCSL 140:354–57), the scribe left a blank space where the original had "should use within the church for the solemnities of the Mass alone." Perhaps a list of pallium days was meant to have been inserted instead of, or in addition to, the vaguer regulation of an elder era. It seems hardly likely that Rostagnus was allowed a blank check to wear the vestment however he liked.

should be lost.'"⁶⁸ As Gregory had once warned John of Ravenna, under threat of deprivation, the pallium could be worn only when preparing for and performing the liturgy, and subsequent popes found it useful to remind recipients of this rule.

Indeed, Gregory's dispute with Ravenna over the correct use of the pallium lingered in the minds of medieval churchmen—it occupied six chapters of John the Deacon's biography, which reproduced six of the pope's letters on the matter—and influenced notions of what constituted pallium abuse.⁶⁹ The affair had begun when John of Ravenna was discovered to be wearing the pallium "in the vanity of pride," but defended his actions as "granted to him from custom or privilege." The practices in question involved the use of the pallium "on the streets" (during litanies in processions outside the church) and "in the sacristy" (while sitting to receive prominent members of the church in a sort of audience before Mass). After contradictory testimonies had been gathered, it seemed clear that the bishop had the backing neither of papal privilege nor of incontestable local custom. However, when Ravennese nobles interceded, the pope allowed John to wear the pallium "at solemn litanies" four times a year, on the feasts of Sts. John the Baptist, Peter, and Apollinaris, the first bishop of Ravenna (July 23), and on the anniversary of his consecration. The pope also instructed him to don the vestment in the sacristy—but only after the audience—and then to process to the sanctuary to celebrate Mass. He remarked that using the pallium "outside the church" was an abuse unprecedented in the times of his and John's predecessors. Yet the bishop did so often and boldly, which showed that his honor lay "wholly on the outside, in display, not in the mind." He was trying to seem more than he was, perhaps by imitating the pope, who could legitimately wear the

---

68. To Liudpram of Salzburg in 837, JE 2580, GP 1:10 no. 14, Hauthaler and Martin, *Salzburger Urkundenbuch*, 2:27–28, quoting JE 1326.

69. PL 75:172–76, quoting JE 1259, 1326, 1330, 1377, 1411, and 1694. On Ravenna's fraught relationship with Rome, see IP 5:15; Hartmann, *Geschichte*, 2.1:164–66; and Eidenschink, *Election*, 110–15. John's narration of these events, when he was not quoting Gregory, may have been influenced by this ongoing rivalry, which persisted into the ninth century, as Agnellus of Ravenna's *Liber Pontificalis Ecclesiae Ravennatis* made clear.

vestment more freely. John refused to change his arrogant ways and died suddenly, and Gregory sent the pallium to his successor Marinian with directions to wear it exactly as he had ordered John.[70]

Bolstered by such a precedent and eager to exert control over all matters pertaining to the pallium, Pope Nicholas I vigorously confronted Hincmar of Reims over an apparent case of pallium abuse. Someone seems to have tampered with papal letters concerning Hincmar's use of the vestment: they now appeared to grant him the extraordinary right of *cotidianus usus*.[71] By allowing it, Leo IV had supposedly followed the will of Lothar I, according to one altered text: "Out of love and honor for you, we have gladly granted Archbishop Hincmar the use of the pallium ... that he may use it every day when performing the sacred office."[72] The favor was "the daily use of the sacred pallium," as opposed to a precise set of pallium days; still, the tradition that the pallium was a liturgical vestment, to be worn during the Mass only, was retained. The fragments that remain of Leo's letter to Hincmar himself showed a greater degree of reworking: "We recall, dearest brother, that we already sent you the pallium and indicated on how many festivities or days you should use it.... On feast days and at the consecration of your bishops, or at another time, whenever you desire to use the pallium, let permission be granted to you.... Use the pallium, which we have allowed you for daily use, with honor and reverence for almighty God."[73] The pope had allegedly permitted Hincmar to wear the vestment not only on the originally specified occasions, but now also when ordaining his suffragans (one of the chief acts of metropolitan authority, as Hincmar would have been conscious), and even whenever he liked. Such a privilege would have gone against centuries of papal

---

70. The clergy swayed Marinian to attempt to regain a broader use of the pallium through the intercession of the powerful, and testimonies were gathered again, all disagreeing among themselves. In the end the Ravennese could not prove their alleged custom, and Gregory apparently persisted in his original decision.

71. See 106n121 above.

72. JE 2607, BH †?239, MGH Epp. 5:591. The falsifier had to add only two words, *cotidianum* and *cotidie*, to the purported original.

73. JE 2608, BH †?240, MGH Epp. 5:591–92. The falsifier had to add the phrases *aut alio quocumque tempore* and *cotidianis usibus* to the purported original.

tradition and put the archbishop on par with the pope, who wore his own insigne whenever he saw fit.

When whispers of the forgeries reached Nicholas, he addressed Hincmar head-on in 866 and strove to nip the abuse in the bud. He accused him of wearing the pallium beyond the customary occasions, as defined for other metropolitans, and suspected that the cause was pride and ambition to outrank his brethren. Even if Hincmar had a special privilege—which Nicholas opposed in principle—it should not be trumpeted: "If its use at all times was granted to your Fraternity by the apostolic see (although it was received beyond the custom of the church, and thereby reasonably ought to be lost) ... nevertheless, fittingly admonished by these our allocutions, be zealous to use it discreetly, such that ... you do not surpass the measure of your own dignity."[74] The pope seemed unaware of Leo IV's supposed privilege for the archbishop, but he could at least conceive of the possibility. Even so, a pallium without restrictions was not only uncustomary but dangerous. Nicholas counseled Hincmar to remember his limited authority, which the unlimited use of the pallium obscured; he added a not too subtle threat to revoke such a right. The archbishop, tellingly, made no appeal to the falsified privilege, but simply denied the accusations:

> I truthfully admit to your Authority that, even in these regions, you will be able to find out through others, if it please you, that I scarcely use the same pallium during the whole year, except on the day of the Lord's birth and on the day of his holy resurrection.... Because of the many engagements and needs of the church and the kingdom, it is rarely allowed for me to be in my see on the decreed festivities when it is granted to metropolitans to use the pallium. And, except when I am in the same see on the decreed festivities, not only do I not use the same pallium as often as it has been granted to me, but scarcely or never. For its use I have asked nothing from the apostolic see, except as my predecessors and forerunners were accustomed to use it, and at the ordination of a bishop.[75]

---

74. JE 2823, BH 838, MGH Epp. 6:430–31.
75. MGH Epp. 8.1:216. Hincmar was possibly quoting from his lost pallium grant: "as my predecessors and forerunners were accustomed to use it" suggests the formula *Si pastores ovium*, and the addition of "at the ordination of a bishop" may have been a further papal concession (whose traces are detectable in JE 2608).

Obligatory travel, Hincmar claimed, frequently denied him opportunity to wear the pallium. His words implied that it could be used only in his own church and on the appointed days, and he maintained that he had not requested any other days than the feasts customary to the church of Reims, as well as episcopal consecrations.[76] The proud archbishop had backed down, and Nicholas had successfully enforced the idea that the pope controlled and restricted, had given and could take away again, the badge of the authority Hincmar held so dear.

Ecclesiastical authorities remained on the lookout for all forms of pallium abuse. In canon 16 the Fourth Council of Constantinople (869–70) denounced a recent travesty in which senators had arrayed themselves as priests: they were seen "to assume, as it were, a priestly rank through certain priestly clothes and vestments and, as it was supposed, to appoint bishops wrapped round with superhumerals, that is, pallia, and clothed with every other pontifical stole." This misuse was roundly condemned as "such a great injury to the divine priesthood."[77] Pseudo-bishops with mock pallia were reprehensible, for to misappropriate the badge of office was to bring the office itself into confusion or contempt. In canon 27, moreover, the council censured bishops who wore the pallium improperly and threatened sanctions against them:

Bishops to whom it has been granted to use pallia at certain times should be clothed with them at the same times and places, and not abuse such and so great a garment because of vanity and vainglory and human contentment and love of self, namely [by] inappropriately wearing it at all times of the divine sacrifice and of every other ecclesiastical mystery.... The continuous wearing of pallia shows a bishop pompous and dedicated to his own glory.... Therefore, whatever bishop clothes himself with the

---

76. This letter casts grave doubt on the authenticity of JE 2608: if Leo IV had granted Hincmar the extraordinary privilege of daily use, Hincmar would surely have brought it up here in self-defense. He either did not know about JE 2608 or, caught red-handed, gave up any attempt to pass it off as genuine.

77. Alberigo et al., *Conciliorum Oecumenicorum Decreta*, 178. The original Greek is lost, but *superhumerale* was probably a literal translation of *omophorion*, and *pallia* was probably a gloss by the translator, Anastasius the Librarian, intending to equate the Eastern vestment with the Western. Both were "priestly vestments" or "pontifical stoles" signifying the "priestly rank," and "wrapped round" depicted the way the pallium was worn.

pallium beyond the times defined for him in writing ... should be either corrected or deposed by his own patriarch.[78]

The law may have principally referred to the Eastern custom of doffing the pallium during the Gospel reading in the liturgy, but regulations of use and strictures of *tempus et locus* were certainly not unknown in the West as well.[79] Indeed, the warning about patriarchal discipline was a sentiment shared in Rome, and the mention of times specified for each bishop in writing called to mind the lists of feasts in pallium grants.[80]

This canon was translated into Latin in 871/72, and within a few years Pope John VIII promulgated his own version. At the Councils of Rome (875) and Ravenna (877), after the obligation for all metropolitans to seek the pallium had been decreed, a canon penalized pallium abuse in terms that hearkened back to Gregory the Great's difficulties with Ravenna: "Of course, whatsoever metropolitan presumes to use the pallium through the streets or at litanies, and not only on special festivities and times published by the apostolic see, for the solemnities of the Mass only, should lack that honor."[81] There followed a quotation from Gregory that justified the loss of a privilege because of its abuse, and particularly of the pallium when treated as a secular distinction, rather than one reserved for sacred contexts.[82] The canon stipulated that the pallium was to be worn only during the Mass, in church, on high holy days and the occasions named by the pope in the recipient's privilege. Apart from the case of Hincmar, instances of abuse in this era are unknown. But such general laws indicated either that problems were not uncommon, or

78. Ibid., 185–86.
79. In the fourth or fifth century Isidore of Pelusion had described this custom; see his letter to Herminus in J.-P. Migne, ed., *Patrologiae Cursus Completus: Series Graeca* (Paris: J.-P. Migne, 1857–66), 78:272.
80. The Greek version of this canon allowed for both written and unwritten regulations, but the Latin translator, Anastasius the Librarian, apparently felt no need to translate "unwritten" in his Western context, in which papal privileges with lists of pallium days had become so important (Alberigo et al., *Conciliorum Oecumenicorum Decreta*, 186). This is evidence that Anastasius, at least, viewed the canon as applicable to the Western church.
81. MGH Conc. 5:10. Cf. ibid., 5:68.
82. See 63 above.

that the papacy found it useful to restate its regulation of the pallium, and thereby to tighten its control.

Conditional Authority

In the course of its history, the pallium became so intertwined with metropolitan authority that eventually such authority could not be exercised without it. This evolution started with a simple association—that the vestment usually marked a bishop set above other bishops—and reached a turning point when it passed from a declarative sign (expressing the authority of its wearer) to a constitutive one (conveying authority to its wearer). By the end of this period, an archbishop was dependent on the pallium to perform certain functions related to his office. Thus, at least in theory, centralizing popes effectively "made" the most important prelates in the Latin church, who operated only at papal behest.

A Bishop over Bishops

The memory of how Pope Gregory the Great had erected the English hierarchy, with pallia connected to metropoles, lived on in Francia. Both Frechulf of Lisieux in 829/30 and Ado of Vienne forty years later described Gregory's work as establishing metropolitan sees and attaching the reception of the pallium to their status.[83] In a similar spirit, Pope Hadrian I mentioned the pallium around 780 to Tilpin of Reims in the same breath as the rank of his see: "We well remember that we sent you the pallium according to custom, with a privilege that the church of Reims should remain in its condition as a metropolis."[84] What was true for metropoles was also true for metropolitans. The Council of Soissons (853) ruled that Hincmar of Reims's installation was canonical and that he possessed full metropolitan authority after his acquisition of the pallium from Rome.[85]

---

83. *Historiae*, in CCCM 169A:721, and *Chronicon de Sex Mundi Aetatibus*, in PL 123:112.

84. JE 2411, GP 4:61 no. 22, Lesne, "Lettre," 349. This wording was probably drawn from the lost privilege.

85. MGH Conc. 3:273.

Conversely, Pope Nicholas I refused to allow Dol's claim to metropolitan rank and title without seeing the pallium grants given to its previous bishops.[86]

The liturgical commentators of the era agreed that palligers enjoyed a lofty distinction, but they described it somewhat differently. In 819 Rabanus Maurus asserted that the pallium was bestowed on "a supreme pontiff, who is called an archbishop."[87] In 835/36 Amalar of Metz attributed the pallium to "our [a Christian] supreme pontiff," for "by it an archbishop is distinguished from the rest of bishops."[88] And in 840/42 Walafrid Strabo maintained that "supreme shepherds only" used the pallium.[89] What did it mean for a palliger to be a *summus pontifex* or an *archiepiscopus*? At root it meant that he was a bishop set over other bishops. Again, such was the pattern Gregory the Great left in England. In 797/98 King Cenwulf of Mercia told Pope Leo III about Gregory's plan for his missionary Augustine, "to whose jurisdiction, as the same father commands, twelve bishops ought to be subject.... But first that pontifical summit, which at the time had been prescribed for London under the honor and decoration of the pallium, was offered and granted to Canterbury instead."[90] The vestment was meant to express the supreme ecclesias-

---

86. To Festinian of Dol in 866, JE 2806, BH 798, MGH Epp. 6:649.

87. Zimpel, *De Institutione*, 315. The proportion of new (as opposed to borrowed) material was especially high in this passage, and Rabanus's language was not wholly clear. It is not surprising that he had to produce original ideas here, since the pallium, as used and understood in the ninth century, was something rather new. He may have been formulating his thoughts out of whole cloth, without a patristic guide and thus unsure of his footing. Indeed, he concluded this section on vestments with a disclaimer admitting the shortcomings of his talent.

88. Ioannes Michael Hanssens, ed., *Amalarii Episcopi Opera Liturgica Omnia*, vol. 2, *Liber Officialis*, Studi e testi 139 (Vatican City: Biblioteca Apostolica Vaticana, 1948), 247–48. Either Amalar was unfamiliar with (or chose to ignore) the exceptional phenomenon of palliated suffragans, or the term "archbishop" was not yet synonymous with "metropolitan," and any palliger, even a suffragan, possessed the former title (e.g., Duchesne, *Liber pontificalis*, 1:456).

89. Alice L. Harting-Correa, ed., based on the edition of Victor Krause, *Walahfrid Strabo's* Libellus de exordiis et incrementis quarundam in observationibus ecclesiasticis rerum: *A Translation and Liturgical Commentary*, Mittellateinische Studien und Texte 19 (Leiden: Brill, 1996), 152.

90. Found in William of Malmesbury, *Gesta Regum Anglorum*, in Mynors et al., *Gesta*, 126. In a letter to Aethelhard of Canterbury in 802 (later revised to support

tical position of Augustine's see over its twelve suffragans. The same applied to York, which, as Alcuin versified, Gregory had established as "capital of the churches and pinnacle of honor," and whose prelates wore the pallium.[91] Its preeminence, made manifest by the vestment, thus signaled not only honor but jurisdiction.

With these examples from his homeland likely in mind, Boniface described the responsibility that came with the pallium in a letter to Cuthbert of Canterbury in 747: "A greater concern for the churches and care for the peoples is incumbent on us, because of the pallia that have been entrusted and received, than on other bishops, for they take care of their own dioceses only."[92] Palligers, he implied, had larger jurisdictions; they oversaw the churches of other bishops, who thus owed them submission. For this and other reasons, in 797/98 Leo III declined King Cenwulf's request to palliate the bishop of London, who (despite Gregory's original intent) had always been a suffragan of Canterbury: "We by no means dare to bestow on them the authority of the supreme pontificate. But rather we grant, approve, and promulgate that primacy as it was established at Canterbury as the first see. For our holy and venerable predecessor, Pope Celestine [I], taught us, saying: 'Let there be no vain boasting. Let those who are bishops follow the palliated, by episcopal custom.'"[93]

---

that see's primatial claims), Leo accepted the Gregorian precedent and saw the pallium as a sign, or even an instrument, of power, by virtue of which other churches were subject to its wearer (JE 2510, Haddan and Stubbs, *Councils*, 3:537).

91. *Versus de Patribus Regibus et Sanctis Euboricensis Ecclesiae*, in Godman, *Bishops*, 20.

92. Rau, *Briefe*, 240; cf. ibid., 242. Boniface's words echoed those of Pope Siricius to Himerius of Tarragona in 385 (JK 255, Pierre Coustant, ed., *Epistolae Romanorum Pontificum* [Paris: Delatour and Coustelier, 1721], 1:624, 630). These observations about the papal office were applied to the palliger's position: like the pope himself, whose insigne he shared, he was obliged to greater evangelical zeal and broader pastoral care. Alcuin similarly instructed Arno of Salzburg in 800 about the "greater burden" of pastoral responsibility required by the pallium (MGH Epp. 4:321).

93. JE 2494, MGH Epp. 4:188. See Brooks, *Early History*, 123–25. Probably Celestine was referring, not to bishops who wore pallia, but to monastic clerics whose habits (*pallia*) became a cause of vanity, or to clerics who retained classical philosopher's garb (*pallia*), or to bishops hiding in obscurity (*palliati*) who boasted that they had escaped with their illicit ordinations intact (in 428, JK 369, GaP 3.1:59–60 no. 14, PL 50:429–36). See Miller, *Clothing the Clergy*, 16–18. That Leo interpreted his words as pertaining to palligers is unsurprising: the references to episcopal consecrations, to vanity, and to custom were typical of pallium-related sources. In translating the quo-

Suspecting that London wanted the vestment out of vanity, the pope reaffirmed that suffragans should keep their customary subordination. The risk of pride may have dissuaded him from considering the possibility of an honorary pallium, such as Alcuin was proposing for Lichfield at this same time.[94]

In all corners of the continent, the pallium's use was associated with authority over bishops. When Leo erected the ecclesiastical province of Bavaria in 798, he elevated Arno of Salzburg as metropolitan over the Bavarian bishops: "He was once your fellow bishop, but now our brother and fellow bishop, and your archbishop. And considering his venerable see metropolitan, and bestowing on holy Arno, your archbishop, the use of the pallium for it, we have commanded him ... to impart support to all your churches, subject to him in their dioceses."[95] As he shared his own garb with him, the pope placed Arno above his suffragans, on a level similar to his own. The suffragans in turn had to acknowledge him as their superior, who would oversee them according to canon law. Around 835 Hilduin of St.-Denis sent Emperor Louis the Pious a report on his patron saint, Dionysius of Paris, and argued that he was the same as Dionysius the Areopagite, the first bishop of Athens. In recognition of Dionysius's association with Athens, Hilduin said, the patriarch of Constantinople

restored to the same city of the Athenians the archiepiscopal pallium, which had been removed from it for a long time after a certain tension arose, and by synodal agreement he honored it with the authority of a metropolis, which it had exercised before. For, from the foregoing years up to that time, neither was the bishop of the same city under another (except the patriarch), nor were the bishops of the cities owed to it put under its jurisdiction.[96]

---

tation as Leo would have understood it, the lead of Dorothy Whitelock is followed (*English Historical Documents, c. 500–1042*, 2nd ed., English Historical Documents 1 [London: Eyre Methuen, 1979], 1:861).

94. To Aethelhard of Canterbury in 797, MGH Epp. 4:190.

95. JE 2495, GP 1:8–9 no. 8, Heinz Dopsch, ed., "Papst Leo III. schreibt an die Bischöfe Bayerns, daß er auf ihre Bitte den Bischof Arn von Salzburg zum Erzbischof der bayerischen Kirchenprovinz bestellt und ihm das Pallium verliehen habe (798 April)," in *1200 Jahre Erzbistum Salzburg*, ed. Neuhardt, 26.

96. MGH Epp. 5:332. The Eastern *omophorion* was not necessarily "archiepiscopal" or a badge of metropolitan authority. Either Hilduin (or his source) was reading

According to this Western writer, Athens had been in a sort of half-metropolitan position, which the grant of the pallium, closely linked with the archiepiscopal title and metropolitan authority, brought back to fullness.

Likewise, around 846 Agnellus of Ravenna declared that Emperor Valentinian III had subjugated suffragan sees to the authority of the first archbishop of Ravenna: he put "fourteen cities with their churches under the consecration of blessed Bishop John by his archhieratic power," and then granted him the pallium.[97] Acquisition of the vestment, then, accompanied the establishment of Ravenna as a metropolitan (*archigeratica*) see. Finally, Hincmar of Reims, writing to Pope Nicholas I in 867, contended that the pallium marked its wearer's rank as the highest churchman in a province: "In the eyes of men the use of the pallium demonstrates that the metropolitan see is more excellent than the rest of the sees of the province of Reims."[98] In all these cases the pallium indicated a prelate who was a shepherd of shepherds.[99] This recurring association sat awkwardly side by side with the fact that suffragans sometimes were palligers too. But that contradiction was not often acknowledged, and did not seem to change what had become the dominant meaning of the vestment.

A Constitutive Sign

Declarative signs make status known; constitutive signs produce that status. It is not surprising when a declarative sign comes to assume constitutive qualities, since power depends on a social order created by shared knowledge, assumptions, and expectations.[100] Commonly accepted understandings of what an archbishop was and what he could do shaped the scope of archiepiscopal power, and as the pallium pointed out the office, so it came to be linked to the activities attributed to the officeholder.

Western practice onto the situation, or Athens's pre-732 attachment to the Western patriarchate was still remembered in his day (see HEOJ 5:456–57).

97. *Liber Pontificalis Ecclesiae Ravennatis*, in Nauerth, *Bischofsbuch*, 204, 206.

98. MGH Epp. 8.1:216.

99. In a later era the vestment would also become involved in situations concerning the jurisdiction of primates, i.e., archbishops set over other archbishops.

100. See Patzold, *Episcopus*, 37–45.

Having pastoral responsibility for other bishops entailed various kinds of supervisory power over them. Such power seems to have come with the pallium. Gregory the Great had implied as much when cautioning Augustine of Canterbury not to invade the bailiwick of the bishop of Arles: "The bishop of Arles has received the pallium, and we hardly ought to deprive him of the authority he has received. If, therefore, it happens that your Fraternity crosses to the province of Gaul, you ought to discuss with the same bishop of Arles, if there are any vices among the bishops, how they may be corrected."[101] In the same spirit, Boniface laid out the duties of the palliger in 747, when he recounted the results of a recent synod: "We decreed that a metropolitan who has been elevated with the pallium should encourage and admonish the rest [of the bishops], and investigate who among them is careful for the salvation of the people, and who neglectful.... We established that it is proper to the metropolitan to investigate the behavior of the bishops subject to him and their concern for the peoples, according to the statutes of the canons."[102] The palliated metropolitan was called to exhort his suffragans, to caution them, to assess the quality of their pastoral care, and to supervise the execution of their office.

The compiler of the False Capitularies of Benedict the Deacon, a Pseudo-Isidorian collection, included the beginning of this Bonifacian passage but varied it slightly: "It is worthy that the metropolitan, who has been elevated with the pallium, should be honored and should admonish the rest."[103] The alterations created a general principle meant to heighten esteem for metropolitans.[104] In this way the pallium played its typical role as both a decoration of honor and

---

101. Transmitted in a Pseudo-Isidorian decretal, Schon and Zechiel-Eckes, *Projekt Pseudoisidor*, at http://www.pseudoisidor.mgh.de/html/307.htm, quoting JE 1843.

102. To Cuthbert of Canterbury, Rau, *Briefe*, 240, 242.

103. Canon 2.79, Gerhard Schmitz, ed., *Edition der falschen Kapitularien des Benedictus Levita*, version 2014-12-10, at http://www.benedictus.mgh.de/edition/archiv/bl_20041007/ben2tar.pdf.

104. The main variant may simply have been a mistaken reading of *hortetur* as *honoretur*, but Emil Seckel finds it a possibly tendentious interpolation ("Studien zu Benedictus Levita (Studie VII, Teil I)," *Neues Archiv der Gesellschaft für ältere deutsche Geschichtskunde* 34 [1909]: 341).

a sign of hierarchical supervision. A final witness to the English perspective was provided by Alcuin, who advised Aethelhard of Canterbury in the early ninth century to reprimand bishops who failed to carry out their tasks: "If perhaps they be found in the seat of ecclesiastical dignity, your most holy censure should trustworthily chastise such as these, excellent father, so that you alone may have a reward from the labor of them all, for you alone are seen to surpass them all by the honor of the pallium and the dignity of the most famous see."[105] As one with responsibility for a province—visibly superior by the pallium and legally superior by his archiepiscopal office—the metropolitan was expected to discipline the prelates in his charge.

Churchmen and laymen alike assumed that metropolitans ensigned with the pallium had the prerogative to intervene in their suffragan dioceses. In 798 Pope Leo III notified King Charlemagne that he had palliated Arno of Salzburg and made him archbishop. He had then informed his suffragan bishops that Arno had "the rights of the archiepiscopate in their dioceses in the aforesaid province of the Bavarians, to teach and to preach, according to the precepts of the holy fathers.... Just as we have granted him to [the province] as its own priestly head, they should thoroughly hurry to obey canonically and to be subject, by ecclesiastical custom."[106] In addition, King Charles the Bald, begging Nicholas I in 867 to consent to the expedited consecration of Wulfhad as archbishop of Bourges by granting him the pallium, appealed to Wulfhad's role in his province as an excuse: "The bishops of that kingdom [Aquitaine] were roused by that pressing need, lest greater evils increase and present ones [not] be calmed. And because that see [Bourges] has the sovereignty of that area, they relied on the prudence and vigor and also the authority of that see, in order more easily to check the evils that had arisen."[107] Since the metropolitan possessed the *principatus* in Aquitaine, his suffragans depended on his judgment, activity, and *auctoritas* on their behalf. The pallium, then, distinguished the linchpin of the province,

---

105. MGH Epp. 4:480.
106. JE 2496, GP 1:9 no. 9, Dopsch, "Papst Leo III. schreibt an König Karl," 24.
107. PL 124:874–75.

the pastor of its pastors, on whose shoulders rested not only the vestment itself, but also the active oversight of the regional churches.

That a metropolitan had a key position and function in the care of an ecclesiastical province was becoming accepted in this period. As Boniface commiserated with Cuthbert of Canterbury, "You know that an equal labor and a greater danger presses on us than on other priests, for the ancient canons instruct that all bishops should know that a metropolitan exercises concern for a whole province."[108] But alongside this notion was the increasing extent to which this position and function were now connected to possession of the pallium. Hincmar of Reims enunciated this connection most clearly. In 863, during the proceedings surrounding Rothad of Soissons's deposition, he summed up his case: "Metropolitans, from ancient custom and canonical authority, have had the primacy of the provinces and, in the reception of the pallium, have been confirmed by the apostolic see as primates of their provinces. Only by common agreement do they consult any other primate of another province about the cases of their own province."[109] The vestment thus permitted this independent authority in their own jurisdictions. Nicholas I seems to have approved of Hincmar's ideas. When the pope wrote to him later that year, he even employed some of his language: "Our predecessors, prelates of holy memory—namely, Leo [IV] in the bestowal of the use of the pallium and Benedict [III] by the privilege of his corroboration—as their predecessors also did for your predecessors, confirmed [you] as primate of that province by canonical authority and ancient custom, for the splendor of the metropolitan church of Reims."[110] In this light, the gift of the pallium was a papal act that confirmed an archbishop as the true head of his province.[111] The vestment carried with it an authority manifested in his immunity from other bishops' power over himself and his suffragans.

---

108. In 747, Rau, *Briefe*, 242.
109. MGH Epp. 8.1:137.
110. JE 2720, BH 626, MGH Epp. 6:366.
111. Despite the shared language, Hincmar and Nicholas may well have disagreed about whether this "confirmation" merely approved what already existed or actually created a new status—i.e., how indispensable the pallium was.

The most obvious juridical consequence of this development was the attachment of the power to ordain bishops to the pallium itself. Indeed, Gregory the Great's dispatch of the pallium to England went hand-in-hand with instructions to consecrate suffragans, as well as to establish other palliated metropolitans who could in turn consecrate their own suffragans.[112] As already seen, Alcuin advocated the suppression of the archbishopric of Lichfield, while leaving its prelate the pallium as an honor. Yet, he hastened to add, Lichfield would not be able to ordain bishops, for that power should return to Canterbury, the traditional metropolitan see.[113] His train of thought witnessed that the power usually accompanied the vestment, and that Lichfield would be an exceptional case. Other evidence implicitly supported this link between power and vestment. In 870 the *Conversio Bagoariorum et Carantanorum*, a local history that defended the church of Salzburg's sphere of influence, depicted the newly palliated Archbishop Arno consecrating a bishop for the Slavs, subject to Salzburg. His successor Adalram did the same, once he had received the pallium.[114]

It was Pope Nicholas I who made the link between consecrating suffragans and possessing the pallium explicit, and even necessary, by conditioning the former on the latter. In 866, after the conversion of the Bulgarians and their apparent submission to Roman authority, the pope answered their questions and issued guidelines for the organization of the new church. One chapter of his letter dealt with the ordination of the proposed Bulgarian patriarch:

> In a place where a patriarch or archbishop has never been appointed, he is to be instituted at first by someone greater, for, according to the apostle, the lesser is blessed by the greater [Heb 7:7]. But then, having received permission and the use of the pallium, he himself from then on ordains bishops for himself.... Because of the length of the journey, he who has been elected [his successor] should no longer come here [to Rome] to be consecrated. Rather, the bishops who were consecrated by the dying archbishop, gathered together, should appoint [the next one]. In the meantime, of course, he does not sit on the throne and does not consecrate

---

112. John the Deacon, *Vita Gregorii Magni*, in PL 75:100, referring to JE 1829.
113. To Aethelhard of Canterbury in 797, MGH Epp. 4:190.
114. Lošek, *Conversio*, 116.

(except for the body of Christ) before he receives the pallium from the Roman see, as all the archbishops of Gaul and Germany and other areas are proven to do.[115]

Once planted by the papacy, the local hierarchy was self-perpetuating, with one major condition: the chief bishop had to have the pallium before he could ordain his subordinate bishops. It was the Roman pontiff's right to confer the "privileges of the archiepiscopate," including, and signified by, the pallium.[116] Indeed, before he received the vestment from the pope, an archbishop could not even perform certain acts allowed to simple bishops who needed no pallium. Nicholas claimed—whether it was fact, or rather an ideal he was trying to enforce—that it was universal practice in the Western church for new archbishops to await the vestment before fully exercising their office. The pallium was now treated as a constitutive sign. It carried metropolitan rights or powers, for without it an archbishop could not discharge certain functions proper to his state.[117]

It fell to Pope John VIII to implement Nicholas's advance, which effectively tied the office of metropolitan to the will of the papacy. His letter to Willibert of Cologne in 873, which may have been the composition of Anastasius the Librarian, provided a theoretical foundation for the necessity of possessing the pallium before ordaining bishops: "He is incomplete from whom such a great gift is taken away, nor can he be firm or complete who is not firm and whole by the conferral of this sacred apparel. And for this reason he certainly cannot stabilize anybody or establish gifts of any dignity if, deprived of the gift of this religious habit, he has not deserved to attain the privilege of such great perfection."[118] Drawing on the well-established equation of the reception of the pallium with confirma-

---

115. JE 2812, BH 822, MGH Epp. 6:593. The question concerned a "patriarch," but the pope seemed hesitant about the title, perhaps because it connoted autonomy. Thus he equated it to "archbishop," a title with stricter ties to Rome (ibid., 6:592).

116. Ibid.

117. Martí points out that these concepts followed the example of Gregory the Great's erection of the English hierarchy and represented the "juridical crystallization" of Augustine of Canterbury's pallium privilege (*Palio*, 113).

118. JE 2986, GP 7.1:34 no. 66, BU 96, MGH Epp. 7:314. See Lohrmann, *Register*, 249–50.

tion of office, this logic proposed that an archbishop lacking the vestment, being *imperfectus* in his own position, could not establish others in theirs. If the pallium represented the final step in the process of installation, a metropolitan without it was not yet truly a metropolitan and lacked the concomitant powers, including that of appointing others to offices. Two years later, John's Council of Rome (875) instituted the three-month deadline for the acquisition of the vestment as a response to the "danger" of lengthy delays in the consecration of suffragans. The council also provided for outside metropolitans to perform this function if the local metropolitan was uncooperative.[119] The canon assumed that unpalliated archbishops were simply unable to ordain bishops, and thus did not do so. But did this assumption correspond to reality? The revision of this canon at the Council of Ravenna (877) refrained from such assumptions and instead made the inability to ordain bishops, along with suspension of office, into a penalty for noncompliance with the three-month rule.[120]

Perhaps the papal program was far more theory than practice in the Latin church of the late ninth century. This possibility would explain John's surprise when he traveled to Francia and his vehemence in the letters he left there. Appointing Rostagnus of Arles as his vicar in Gaul in 878, he inserted special directives in a document that otherwise followed a pallium grant of Gregory the Great: "For grief's sake! When we were in the regions of Gaul, we found that one thing among the rest must be very much forbidden: metropolitans, before they receive the pallium from the apostolic see, presume to perform consecration, which our predecessors and we have forbidden to happen by canonical decree."[121] He then ordered the archbishop to assist the execution of that regulation. Similarly, in his notice to the bishops of Gaul concerning the revived vicariate, John, once again diverging from his Gregorian model, warned them of the task he had committed to Rostagnus: "We have also enjoined him to allow no archbishop in these regions to perform consecration without the pallium sent by the Roman pontiff, and by our authority to reprove

---

119. MGH Conc. 5:9–10.
120. MGH Conc. 5:68.
121. JE 3148, BU 353, MGH Epp. 7:110.

those doing so."[122] The pallium, in short, canonically conveyed the faculty to exercise certain episcopal powers, and to carry them out without it was considered a crime. It remained to be seen how successfully the papacy could impose this idea, but it was a bold venture in the evolution of an honorary sash into a juridical instrument.

Conclusion

Sharing the principal sign of papal authority with others demanded a delicate balancing act. Although the bishops who enjoyed such a great honor had submitted to Roman dominance in order to receive the pallium, how would they continue to be kept in place once they bore this prestigious insigne? And as metropolitans were expected to acquire the vestment and thereby subject themselves to papal influence, how would the pallium remain something they not only sought but even needed? The popes responded to these problems by imposing a series of canonical and liturgical limitations, meant to subordinate non-papal palligers to papal power. They balanced the increasingly common and customary conferral of the pallium with an insistence on their own discretion, applied to specific individuals *à titre personnel*. They balanced the right to wear this papal vestment with strictly regulated limits on how it could be worn. And, ingeniously, they balanced the authority over other bishops that the pallium came to signify with a dependence on the same vestment (and hence its donor) in order to exercise that authority. The imposition of rules, however, can only go so far in implementing a program. More effective is the exploration of ideas that justify its willing acceptance. The next chapter will probe the various understandings of the pallium that made it valued, meaningful, and still more useful in the pursuit of papal control over the church.

122. JE 3149, BU 354, MGH Epp. 7:93.

4

Interpreting the Pallium

When Alcuin learned the good news that his friend Arno had gained the pallium as the first archbishop of Salzburg in 798, he penned a congratulatory and hortatory letter. To the new palliger he offered some pious reflections and advice:

Think always, as you are vested with the pallium of holiness and see the sign of the holy cross affixed to it, whether in front or in back, that you ought to follow him who carried his own cross, on which he prepared the trophy of our redemption. As you see it, kiss it and venerate the holiness of this sign, as is fitting, and remember that you ought to follow him who said: "He who wishes to come after me should take up his cross and follow me" [Mt 16:24].[1]

Alcuin's words furnished instructions both liturgical and moral. When donning the pallium, the wearer should kiss its cross, the *sanctitas* of which matched that of the vestment itself. Crosses and relics were traditionally kissed as a sign of veneration, and so it was natural to kiss the pallium, which bore crosses and had the characteristics of a contact relic.[2] Furthermore, as he acknowledged the cross, the

---

1. In 799, MGH Epp. 4:287.
2. Around 876 John the Deacon witnessed that Gregory the Great's pallium, phylacteries, and belt were customarily kissed, but their status as relics once worn by the sainted pope was likely the reason (*Vita Gregorii Magni*, in PL 75:228). Still, even ordinary pallia were kissed. Twelfth-century sources reported that they were

wearer should remember to follow Christ crucified, who taught his followers to bear their own crosses. The vestment's symbolism thus spurred the recipient to virtue after the pattern of Christ.

As is clear from the preceding chapters, much was expected of the pallium. It was supposed to entice prospective recipients as a highly sought prize, to influence relationships through and after its bestowal, and to communicate canonical and liturgical consequences. For it to be able to bear such weight, the popes and others invested the vestment with value and meaning. It has long been recognized that gifts have immaterial meanings and can acquire "cultural biographies" and distinct "historical identities" that freight their donation with symbolic and ideological significance.[3] A gift may be imbued with the donor's characteristics and power, as displayed in various rituals; a gift may also be considered sacred in itself. Praising its value increases the prestige of both donor and recipient.[4] Labeling the gift thus becomes crucial, and official documents help to define it and to stabilize its meaning when in doubt.[5] In addition, because a variety of subtle, sometimes conflicting attitudes may be involved in the ritualized conventions of gift-giving, expressions of humility can be included in order to protect against latent pride, envy, and the social dangers of competition.[6] All these ideas found parallels in typical pallium practices.

A strip of wool of little worth in itself, the pallium was neverthe-

---

kissed when taken from the altar after being received in the palliger's cathedral (e.g., Eadmer of Canterbury, *Historia Novorum in Anglia*, in *Rerum Britannicarum Medii Aevi Scriptores* (Rolls Series) [London: Longman, etc., 1858–96], 81:73, 230 [hereafter "Rolls"], and Carlo Castiglioni, ed., *Landulphi Junioris sive de Sancto Paulo Historia Mediolanensis ab anno MXCV usque ad annum MCXXXVII*, Rerum Italicarum Scriptores 5.3 [Bologna: Zanichelli, 1934], 22). In the next century William Durandus instructed the palliger to kiss the pallium's posterior cross when vesting (Michel Andrieu, ed., *Le pontifical romain au moyen-âge*, vol. 3, *Le pontifical de Guillaume Durand*, Studi e testi 88 [Vatican City: Biblioteca Apostolica Vaticana, 1940], 642) and explained this act as an acknowledgement of what the vestment signified (*Rationale Divinorum Officiorum*, in CCCM 140:218-19).

3. See Bijsterveld, *Do ut des*, 18–19, 55.
4. See John-Henry Wilson Clay, "Gift-giving and Books in the Letters of St. Boniface and Lul," *Journal of Medieval History* 35 (2009): 315, 319, 324–25.
5. See Algazi, "Introduction," 18.
6. See Clay, "Gift-giving," 317–18, 321.

less the object of significant religious, intellectual, and moral exegesis. Those who conferred it, and those who reflected on its conferral, made it into a rare and precious boon. It was charged with sacredness and closely connected to the cult of the apostle Peter. It was explained through symbolism and allegories in order to justify its role in ecclesiastical affairs. And it was the occasion for admonitions that tried to control the behavior of its recipients. In these ways the ideas imposed on the pallium contributed to its impact in the service of papal programs.

Sacredness

The pallium was sacred or holy: texts of nearly every genre, time, and situation concurred in this evaluation. As a vestment intended for the liturgy, it was sacred, or set apart for religious use; and as a contact relic of Peter, it was also holy, or venerated for its association with the divine.[7] The sacral quality of the pallium appeared most often in descriptive epithets. In the poems of Theodulf of Orléans, it was called *pallia sancta*.[8] To the popes, it was a liturgical vestment, hallowed for ceremonial purposes: Leo III spoke of the *sacer usus pallii,* Hadrian II of the *sacratum munus,* John VIII of the *sacrum indumentum,* and both Leo IV and John VIII of the *sacrum pallium.*[9] Simi-

---

7. Willard G. Oxtoby defines these two (sometimes overlapping) senses, and suggests parallel distinctions in usage between the Latin words *sacrum* and *sanctum* and the English words "sacred" and "holy" ("Holy, Idea of the," in *The Encyclopedia of Religion,* ed. Mircea Eliade [New York: Macmillan, 1987], 6:434–35).

8. *Epitaphium Chrodegangi,* in MGH Poet. 1:108, and *De Suo Exilio,* in Schaller, "Philologische Untersuchungen," 45 (both using the poetic plural). The selection of *sanctum* over *sacrum* may have resulted from metrical demands. In the second text, *pace* Freeman and Meyvaert ("Meaning," 126), scansion of the elegiac couplet reveals that the terminal letter in *sancta* is short and so modifies *pallia* rather than *manu.*

9. Leo III to Aethelhard of Canterbury in 802, JE 2510, Haddan and Stubbs, *Councils,* 3:537; Hadrian II to Charles the Bald in 868, JE 2902, MGH Epp. 6:706; John VIII to Willibert of Cologne in 873, JE 2986, GP 7.1:34 no. 66, BU 96, MGH Epp. 7:314; Leo IV to Lothar I in 851, JE 2607, BH †?239, MGH Epp. 5:591; John VIII to the Dalmatian bishops in 879, JE 3262, BU 530, MGH Epp. 7:157 (twice); and John VIII to Basil I in 879, JE 3271, BU 551, MGH Epp. 7:174, where it was said to be used during the "sacred" liturgy, which explained its sacral character.

larly, Walafrid Strabo included the pallium among the *vestes sacrae* as he described the esoteric apparel that had developed from the originally ordinary clothing of the priest.[10] Secular rulers stressed the holiness of the vestment's source: to Louis the Pious, writing to Pope Eugene II in 824, it was the *pallium sanctae auctoritatis vestrae*, while an edict of Lothar I at the Council of Ingelheim (840) named it the *sanctae largitatis apostolicae pallium* and the *pallium sanctae et apostolicae auctoritatis*.[11] These designations connected the pallium with papal authority, itself holy. Finally, Alcuin indulged in more intricate turns of phrase, such as *sanctum palleum dignitatis, sacri pallei dignitas, sacri pallei auctoritas, superhumeralis sanctitas*, and *pallium sanctitatis*.[12] These interpretations invoked several complex concepts: *dignitas*, connoting not only worthiness and distinction, but also authority and rank; *auctoritas*, pointing to the influence that Alcuin imagined the papally backed palliger to wield; and *sanctitas*, recalling the piety and virtue he expected of one so adorned.

Indeed, recipients of the pallium—especially those who were given it, not because their sees customarily received it, but as a deliberate distinction, such as palliated suffragans and newly constituted archbishops—were often called holy themselves. The *Liber Pontificalis* recorded Pope Stephen II's grant to Chrodegang of Metz, "a most holy man."[13] Chrodegang's epitaph, probably composed by Theodulf, also associated the "holy pallium" with a bishop whose "actions were holy."[14] The forger of the acts of the bishops of Le Mans, perhaps patterning the alleged palliger Aiglibert after Chrodegang, mentioned,

---

10. *De Exordiis et Incrementis Quarundam in Observationibus Ecclesiasticis Rerum*, in Harting-Correa, *Libellus*, 150.

11. MGH Epp. 5:313, and MGH Conc. 2.2:792, 805. Though bearing Lothar's name, the latter document did not originate in the imperial chancery, but rather was taken from the protocol of the assembled bishops (E. Mühlbacher, "Die Datirung der Urkunden Lothar I," *Sitzungsberichte der philosophisch-historischen Klasse der kaiserlichen Akademie der Wissenschaften Wien* 85 [1877]: 507–10). The second of its two phrases, moreover, was found in the coda attached to Drogo of Metz's signature, which was probably forged later by Ebo of Reims.

12. *Vita Willibrordi*, in Reischmann, *Willibrord*, 58; to Leo III in 797, MGH Epp. 4:184; and to Arno of Salzburg in 799, MGH Epp. 4:286–87.

13. Duchesne, *Liber pontificalis*, 1:456 (JE *2314).

14. MGH Poet. 1:108.

just after his possession of the pallium, that "he was zealous to live in a noble and holy manner."[15] And Pope John VIII sent the imperial envoy Adalgar of Autun, whom he characterized as "most holy," back to Charles the Bald with the vestment.[16] As for new metropolitans, Pope Leo III notified the Bavarian bishops that he was palliating "holy Arno," the first archbishop of Salzburg, while he assured King Charlemagne that he had agreed to his demand to grant the "most reverend and most holy Bishop Arno the usage of wearing the pallium."[17] Likewise, Agnellus of Ravenna depicted John, the first archbishop of Ravenna, as holy enough to catch an emperor's attention. After finally meeting him, Valentinian III promptly made him a metropolitan and bestowed the pallium on him.[18] In all these cases the palliger's holiness was juxtaposed with his acquisition of the vestment, as if to say that the granted pallium recognized the recipient's holiness.

Hincmar of Reims took the opposite viewpoint. To Pope Nicholas I in 867 he confessed that he possessed the pallium simply because he was a metropolitan, not because of any merit on his part: "I do not suppose that the use of the pallium belongs to my own dignity.... Many bishops who do not have the use of the aforesaid pallium are holy."[19] It served Hincmar's agenda to separate the idea of holiness from the wearing of the pallium, for he wished to uphold it as the badge of a churchman made powerful and independent by virtue of his office, not his personal worth.[20] Nevertheless, his very protestation bore witness to the more common presumption in this period: holiness of life suited the wearer of this holy vestment. Indeed, sanctity was often a criterion sought in the candidate for the pallium.

15. Weidemann, *Geschichte*, 1:82.
16. In 876, JE 3063, BU 213, MGH Epp. 7:23.
17. JE 2495, GP 1:8–9 no. 8, Dopsch, "Papst Leo III. schreibt an die Bischöfe," 26; and JE 2496, GP 1:9 no. 9, Dopsch, "Papst Leo III. schreibt an König Karl," 23, both in 798.
18. *Liber Pontificalis Ecclesiae Ravennatis*, in Nauerth, *Bischofsbuch*, 204.
19. MGH Epp. 8.1:216. Here the use of *dignitas* is particularly confusing: its sense of "office" contradicted Hincmar's point, and so the archbishop must have meant "worthiness."
20. Cf. to Nicholas I in 867, MGH Epp. 8.1:222; and *De Iure Metropolitanorum*, in PL 126:191.

Testimony to the recipient's holiness paved the way for a number of grants, such as those to Tilpin of Reims and Egilo of Sens.[21] Also, several of the intercessory letters sent to Pope Hadrian II on behalf of Willibert of Cologne in 870 testified to the archbishop's holiness; for example, King Louis the German remarked that he had chosen Willibert for the see "due to the merit of his holiness," and now requested the pallium as a result.[22]

Although its use as a liturgical vestment rendered the pallium sacred in the sense of "set apart for religious purposes," it was further charged with holiness because of its close association with Peter, Christ's chief apostle. Later witnesses would make clear that pallia were customarily placed in the *confessio* of St. Peter's Basilica, over the tomb of the apostle, before being bestowed upon their recipients.[23] The *confessio* in the early Middle Ages consisted of a small arched recess under the church's high altar, richly decorated and closed by gates, all that remained of a second-century memorial raised upon the saint's traditional resting place in the Roman cemetery on the Vatican hill, next to the circus where legend said he had been crucified. In the floor of the niche was an opening (*fenestella*) that led down through a shaft to a subterranean hollow—the spot believed to be the location of Peter's body. In this niche contact relics, including pallia, were laid, and probably also lowered through the shaft into the grave.[24] Sources of this period, however, only hinted of the practice, although it seems

---

21. Hadrian I to Tilpin ca. 780, JE 2411, GP 4:61 no. 22, Lesne, "Lettre," 349; and Nicholas I to Egilo in 865/66, JE 2809, BH 766, MGH Epp. 6:644.

22. MGH Epp. 6:251. Cf. Liudbert of Mainz, MGH Epp. 6:244, and Louis the German, MGH Epp. 6:249.

23. The most important witnesses were a line of ritual texts concerning the consecration of a pope: *Ordo Romanus XL A*, the *Liber Diurnus*, *Ordo Romanus XXXVI* (including a significant eleventh-century variant), *Ordo Romanus XL B*, the Romano-Germanic Pontifical, and the Roman Pontifical of the Twelfth Century; certain twelfth-century liturgical writers (Peter Mallius, Romanus of St. Peter's, and Albinus of Albano); and statements in papal letters that the vestment was "taken from the body of blessed Peter," beginning with Paschal II after 1105, and taking standard form with Alexander III in 1161. See Sible de Blaauw, *Cultus et decor: liturgia e architettura nella Roma tardoantica e medievale: Basilica Salvatoris, Sanctae Mariae, Sancti Petri*, Studi e testi 356 (Vatican City: Biblioteca Apostolica Vaticana, 1994), 2:609, 710–12, and J. Wickham Legg, "The Blessing of the Episcopal Ornament called the Pall," *Record Series (Yorkshire Archaeological Society)* 15 (1899): 127–41.

24. A *confessio* was the part of a martyr's tomb where visitors came closest to the

to have been ancient.²⁵ The *Liber Diurnus* included a sixth-century liturgical *ordo* for the ordination of a pope that described his investiture with the pallium, the traditional insigne of the papal office: "The elect processes from the sacristy with seven candlesticks and comes to the *confessio*.... Then the bishop of Ostia consecrates him pontiff. After this the archdeacon puts the pallium on him. Next he ascends the seat and gives the sign of peace to all the priests."²⁶ The pope's episcopal consecration took place at the Vatican—not at the Lateran, Rome's cathedral—and there, at Peter's tomb, he was vested with the pallium; only then did he take his chair as pope.²⁷

The Pseudo-Isidorian decretals preserved two genuine letters of Gregory the Great that alluded to this connection between the pallium and Peter. To Leander of Seville the pope wrote: "We have sent you the pallium from the blessing of blessed Peter, prince of the apostles."²⁸ The phrase *ex benedictione* may have referred to its hal-

---

remains (Blaauw, *Cultus*, 2:474). Despite the erection of Constantine's basilica around the site and renovations over the centuries, the *locus sacer* was preserved inviolate. See Vittorio Lanzani, "'Gloriosa confessio': lo splendore del sepolcro di Pietro da Costantino al Rinascimento," in *La confessione nella basilica di San Pietro in Vaticano*, ed. Alfredo Maria Pergolizzi (Milan: Silvana, 1999), 11–41; Jocelyn Toynbee and John Ward Perkins, *The Shrine of St. Peter and the Vatican Excavations* (New York: Pantheon, 1957), 202–3, 220–25, and figs. 22–25; and Blaauw, *Cultus*, 2:472–73, 539–42, and figs. 21–22, 24. On the hollow beneath the tomb, see Hans Georg Thümmel, *Die Memorien für Petrus und Paulus in Rom: die archäologischen Denkmäler und die literarische Tradition*, Arbeiten zur Kirchengeschichte 76 (Berlin: de Gruyter, 1999), 52–59, and figs. 22–26, 28–34; and Blaauw, *Cultus*, 2:226–29. See also 159 below.

25. Blaauw admits that it seems impossible to establish when the practice began (*Cultus*, 2:710). Nevertheless, other vestments were incubated at Peter's tomb in this period. *Ordo Romanus XXXVI* around 897 testified that stoles (*orarii*) were taken from the *confessio*, where they had lain overnight, and given to newly ordained deacons and priests (Andrieu, *Ordines*, 4:198). *Ordo Romanus XXXVII A* around 800 said much the same, but spoke of the altar instead of the *confessio* (ibid., 4:237). If the sashes of office for lesser orders were treated thus, it seems likely that the bishop's pallium would also have been incubated.

26. V57, Foerster, *Liber Diurnus*, 111, with slight variants C56 on 209 and A51 on 315–16, based on *Ordo Romanus XL A* (Andrieu, *Ordines*, 4:297). The *Liber Diurnus* text lay behind the similar one in *Ordo Romanus XL B* around 950, which expanded it as an intermediate step towards the Romano-Germanic Pontifical (ibid., 4:308).

27. Blaauw views this practice as a tangible sign of the "personal transmission" of Peter's office to his successor (*Cultus*, 2:609).

28. Schon and Zechiel-Eckes, *Projekt Pseudoisidor*, at http://www.pseudoisidor.mgh.de/html/304.htm, quoting JE 1756.

lowing at Peter's tomb, by which the apostle could be said to have blessed it himself.[29] Gregory also wrote to King Reccared of the Visigoths: "We have sent a little key from the most sacred body of blessed Peter the apostle as his blessing, in which is enclosed iron from his chains.... Moreover, we sent the most reverend man, our father and fellow bishop Leander, the pallium from the see of blessed Peter the apostle."[30] The key containing a sliver of Peter's chains, first laid upon his tomb and then given *pro eius benedictione,* invites comparison with the pallium, which also came from Peter's see as Peter's blessing on its recipient.[31] The details are obscure, but clearly the vestment derived some of its value from its association with the presence of Peter's remains in Rome.

These glimmers from Gregory's time illuminate the expressions of a later era. Alcuin called the vestment "the pallium of sacred blessing," an ambiguous epithet.[32] It may have evoked the pallium's status as a sacred object laid on Peter's tomb, or its use when its wearer celebrated solemn rites of consecration, or its representation of the pope's blessing (in the sense of confirmation) of its wearer's office. Pope John VIII was clearer when writing to the Dalmatian bishops in 879. He exhorted their metropolitan to come to Rome for episcopal consecration and the pallium, "so that, having the grace and blessing of St. Peter and ours, free from all evils and filled with all good things, you may both rejoice here in the present age and, beyond a doubt, exult with the Lord in the future without end."[33] The invocation of Peter's blessing was certainly a commonplace to express papal favor, but it had further resonance when that blessing was depicted

---

29. John M. McCulloh's interpretation of *benedictio* as "wealth or property, i.e. those things with which St. Peter has been blessed" ("The Cult of Relics in the Letters and 'Dialogues' of Pope Gregory the Great: A Lexicographical Study," *Traditio* 32 [1976]: 170n97), seems less appropriate, for the pallium was a special kind of gift, distinct in meaning and use from standard assets.

30. Schon and Zechiel-Eckes, *Projekt Pseudoisidor,* at http://www.pseudoisidor.mgh.de/html/305.htm, quoting JE 1757.

31. McCulloh points out that *benedictio* was a term for this kind of container, holding objects that had been in contact with a saint ("Cult," 169–73). Nevertheless, the facts that the key was taken "from the most sacred body" and that it represented Peter's "blessing" strengthen the comparison with the pallium.

32. To Eanbald II of York in 796, MGH Epp. 4:168.

33. JE 3262, BU 530, MGH Epp. 7:157.

as an effect of gaining the pallium. Finally, Ado of Vienne's forged claim to his see's Roman ties paired the "venerable pallium," the "ancient gift of blessed Peter," with a relic of the apostle Paul.[34] Like the *brandea* of old, the vestment touched to the tomb of the apostle could be viewed as a contact relic, imbued with apostolic *virtus*.[35]

Given these associations, and considering that this gift was granted by the successor and vicar of the head apostle, it is no wonder how often Peter was invoked in the act of conferring and receiving the pallium. Arbeo's *vita* claimed that Corbinian had obtained the vestment "with the sanction of blessed Peter, prince of the apostles," that is, with his support.[36] Pope Leo IV allowed Hincmar of Reims to use the pallium "from the authority of blessed Peter the apostle and ours."[37] Pope John VIII sent the pallium to Willibert of Cologne "from the generosity of blessed Peter, prince of the apostles" and to Wala of Metz "by the authority of blessed Peter, prince of the apostles."[38] Even Hincmar, whose ambition sometimes competed with

34. JE †2146, GaP 3.1:85–86 no. †63b, MGH Epp. 3:92.
35. On *brandea* or *sanctuaria*—contact relics created from cloths laid on saints' tombs—see McCulloh, "Cult," 158–69; Lanzani, "Gloriosa confessio," 19–22; and Blaauw, *Cultus*, 2:209, 212–13. Cf. Acts 19:12. Sixth-century witnesses to the practice included Popes Hormisdas (JK 829, PL 63:477; cf. PL 63:474–75), Pelagius I (JK 979, Gassó and Batlle, *Epistulae*, 62–63), and Gregory the Great (JE 1302, CCSL 140:248–50). Gregory of Tours described the creation of *pignora* by lowering cloths through a *fenestella*, keeping vigil with fasting and prayer, and raising them out again (*Gloria Martyrum*, in *Monumenta Germaniae Historica: Scriptores Rerum Merovingicarum* [Hannover: Hahn, etc., 1885–], 1.2:54). Such *palliola* taken from the *confessiones* of the saints were also mentioned in the *Liber Diurnus*: in one formula, the pope allowed a bishop to dedicate a basilica in which apostolic *sanctuaria* had been placed (V22, Foerster, *Liber Diurnus*, 89, with slight variants C19 on 189 and A14 on 279–80). Before those who doubted their efficacy, Gregory the Great was said to have cut such a cloth, which thereupon bled (Bertram Colgrave, ed., *The Earliest Life of Gregory the Great, by an Anonymous Monk of Whitby* [Lawrence: University of Kansas Press, 1968], 108, 110). Since all that was needed to produce pallia was wool and access to the Petrine shrine, this effectively unlimited supply of contact relics neatly avoided a problem sometimes faced by lords, when distributing gifts to gain support sapped the very wealth required for a reputation of largesse (White, "Politics," 173–74).
36. MGH SSRG 13:197.
37. In 851, JE 2608, BH †?240, MGH Epp. 5:592.
38. In 874, JE 2988, GP 7.1:34–35 no. 67, BU 120, Wisplinghoff, *Rheinisches Urkundenbuch*, 2:158 (for the first quotation). When the clergy and people of that city had asked John's predecessor, Hadrian II, for Willibert's pallium, they professed great love for Peter (MGH Epp. 6:248). Since Cologne's cathedral was dedicated to

the Roman pontiff's, attributed the pope's competence to distribute pallia throughout the church to "the primacy of St. Peter."[39] These cases tied the prerogative closely to the papal office, and thus to the power of Peter, who was said to have ratified, authorized, or even given the pallium himself.

More abstractly, the *Liber Diurnus* formula *Pallii usum* portrayed the reception of the vestment as a manifestation of unity with Peter on the part of the sheep committed to him by Christ. The pope in return, according to the same formula, willingly granted it "by the tradition of the church founded by the same apostles," that is, by Peter and Paul, patrons of the Roman church.[40] Boniface similarly envisioned the pallium as an integral part of a close filial relationship to the chief apostle. As he told Cuthbert of Canterbury, his reform synod of 747 had endorsed the acquisition of pallia as an expression of submission to the apostolic see: the fathers had resolved "to be willing to be subjected to St. Peter and his vicar ... and (for metropolitans) to seek pallia from that see, and to desire to canonically follow the instructions of St. Peter in all things, so that we may be counted among the sheep commended to him. And all agreed to this confession and signed it and sent it to the body of St. Peter, prince of the apostles."[41] Receiving the pallium from the pope implied the flock's obedience to the successor of Peter, or really to Peter himself, and this synodal pledge of allegiance was fittingly delivered to the *confessio* of St. Peter's Basilica, that is, to the saint himself. In short, just as a Petrine pedigree provided the papacy with its own credentials and claims, the popes and their faithful adherents called upon the Petrine associations of the pallium to heighten the garment's sacredness and desirability, which enabled it to be employed effectively in the exercise of papal power.

Peter, they may have been emphasizing their status as Peter's clients and the common devotion that united them with Peter's successor in order to persuade the pope to consent. In 878, JE 3183, BU 427, PL 126:799 (for the second quotation).

39. *De Iure Metropolitanorum*, in PL 126:191.

40. V47, Foerster, *Liber Diurnus*, 106, with slight variants C46 on 204–5 and A41 on 307–8. Despite the words "the same," Paul had not been mentioned up to this point.

41. Rau, *Briefe*, 240.

Symbolism

Another way of ensuring the pallium's appeal, while also construing it in manners suited to its use, was the creative interpretation of the vestment, usually through symbolic expressions or allegorical expositions. The popes of this period themselves did not, on the whole, indulge in such fancies in their juridically oriented letters, but there were minor exceptions. Pope Hadrian II, bestowing the pallium on Actard of Nantes in 868 after invaders had driven him from his see, imagined the woolen band as a replacement for a metal one: the gift was given "so that he may have the decoration of the pallium instead of exile and chain.... Therefore, let him possess the adornment of such great honor, which is known to hold a special place among the festoons of priests."[42] A widely esteemed symbol of exaltation was to replace a symbol of degradation. Also, at the Councils of Rome (875) and Ravenna (877), Pope John VIII quoted Gregory the Great, who had chastised those who wore the pallium, "a heavy yoke and bond of the neck, not as an ecclesiastical, but as a certain secular dignity."[43] In other words, anyone who treated the pallium as if it were a worldly honor, to be worn around the city in order to procure respect, was guilty of misunderstanding and abusing it. Its weight was derived from its concomitant pastoral responsibility: it was not a necklace, but a yoke.[44] These popes limited themselves to an occasional image that underscored the reasons for which they conferred the pallium.

It was chiefly Carolingian liturgical commentators who contemplated how the pallium was being employed in their era, and incor-

---

42. To Charles the Bald, JE 2902, MGH Epp. 6:706. Cf. to Actard, JE 2904, MGH Epp. 6:709.

43. MGH Conc. 5:10, 68.

44. There was probably no allusion here to Jesus's yoke, which was not "heavy," but "pleasant" and "light" (Mt 11:29–30). Later sources, however, explicitly compared the pallium to Jesus's yoke. See Rutger of Cologne, *Vita Brunonis*, in *Monumenta Germaniae Historica: Scriptores Rerum Germanicarum, nova series* (Berlin: Weidmann, etc., 1922–), 10:27 [hereafter "MGH SSRG n.s."], and Marie A. Conn, ed., "The Dunstan and Brodie (Anderson) Pontificals: An Edition and Study" (PhD diss., University of Notre Dame, 1993), 104, 254.

porated it into theological frameworks that made sense of its role in the church. The religious reforms of Louis the Pious's Council of Aachen (816) may have provided the stimulus.[45] Shortly thereafter, in his *De Institutione Clericorum* of 819, Rabanus Maurus dwelled on the purple crosses found on both sides of the vestment:

This kind of apparel portrays the sign of the cross in purple color, so that, clothed with it, the pontiff may have the cross on his back and breast. And in his mind he should think piously and worthily about the passion of the Redeemer, and point out to the people, for whom he prays to God, the sign of his redemption. It is also quite fitting that this apostolic dignity should make an apostolic man, so that with full devotion, sound speech, and worthy work he can say with the apostle: "Far be it from me to boast, except in the cross of our Lord Jesus Christ, through whom the world has been crucified to me and I to the world" [Gal 6:14].[46]

The crosses served a dual purpose: to prompt the wearer to meditate on Christ's passion and to remind his flock of the mystery of salvation. Rabanus held that this *apostolica dignitas*—"apostolic" because it came from the pope—rendered the palliger an *apostolicus vir*. As such he should not only behave as an apostle, in accord with Paul's teaching, but he also became a "papal man," arguably exercising a kind of papal vicariate.[47] In this view the pallium was a medium for displaying and bearing the cross, which contributed to the spiritual edification of the recipient and those who saw him.

---

45. On the synod, see Hartmann, *Synoden,* 156–60. Gregory the Great's *Regula Pastoralis* and Bede's *De Tabernaculo* had interpreted the high priestly garb detailed in the Old Testament as representing the virtues that its wearer ought to exhibit, and the synod repeated some of the Gregorian material (MGH Conc. 2.1:346–47). Carolingian commentators then began to apply this method to Christian priestly vestments, seen as symbols of virtues and counterparts to ancient Jewish vestments (Miller, *Clothing the Clergy,* 53–58). They may also have been inspired by Pseudo-Germanus's *Expositio Antiquae Liturgiae Gallicanae* (CCCM 187:360–65).

46. Zimpel, *De Institutione,* 315. See Raymund Kottje and Harald Zimmermann, eds., *Hrabanus Maurus: Lehrer, Abt und Bischof,* Akademie der Wissenschaften und der Literatur, Abhandlungen der geistes- und sozialwissenschaftlichen Klasse 4 (Wiesbaden: Steiner, 1982); Barton Brown, "*Enigmata Figurarum*: A Study of the Third Book of the *Rationale Divinorum Officiorum* of William Durandus and its Allegorical Treatment of the Christian Liturgical Vestments" (PhD diss., New York University, 1983), 142–46; and Wallace-Hadrill, *Frankish Church,* 314–22.

47. See 85n46 above.

Interpreting the Pallium   163

In his *Liber Officialis*, finished in 835/36, Amalar of Metz offered a more comprehensive allegorical interpretation of the pallium at a time of liturgical ferment, as the Roman liturgy was being mixed with Gallican features and promoted by the Carolingian rulers.[48] In a chapter *de pallio quo utuntur archiepiscopi*, he first compared it to "the plate on the forehead of the pontiff alone," that is, the golden *lamina* worn only by the Aaronic high priest (Ex 28:36–38).[49] Both items were donned atop all other garments, and both were restricted to the highest priestly rank. Amalar then alluded to classical athletics to explain the pallium, which was a ring-shaped stole: "The pallium signifies the wreath that those legitimately competing were accustomed to receive; by this gift others are admonished to legitimate competition." Drawing on the Pauline image of the Christian life as a race, he related the vestment to the *torques* received by the winners of the games, a trophy that prompted observers to strive to win the race themselves.[50] But the competition was "legitimate," and worthy of a

---

48. See Brown, "Enigmata Figurarum," 127–42; Wallace-Hadrill, *Frankish Church*, 326–29; Wolfgang Steck, *Der Liturgiker Amalarius: eine quellenkritische Untersuchung zu Leben und Werk eines Theologen der Karolingerzeit*, Münchener theologische Studien, historische Abteilung 35 (St. Ottilien: EOS, 2000); and Celia Chazelle, "Amalarius's *Liber Officialis*: Spirit and Vision in Carolingian Liturgical Thought," in *Seeing the Invisible in Late Antiquity and the Early Middle Ages*, ed. Giselle de Nie, Karl F. Morrison, and Marco Mostert, Utrecht Studies in Medieval Literacy 14 (Turnhout: Brepols, 2005), 327–57. On this period's liturgical developments, see Rosamond McKitterick, *The Frankish Church and the Carolingian Reforms, 789–895* (London: Royal Historical Society, 1977), 115–54; Wallace-Hadrill, *Frankish Church*, 212–13; Cyrille Vogel, *Medieval Liturgy: An Introduction to the Sources*, trans. William G. Storey and Niels Krogh Rasmussen, with the assistance of John K. Brooks-Leonard (Washington, D.C.: Pastoral, 1986), 61; Riché, *Carolingians*, 76–77; Yitzhak Hen, *The Royal Patronage of Liturgy in Frankish Gaul to the Death of Charles the Bald (877)*, Henry Bradshaw Society Subsidia 3 (London: Boydell, 2001); and Claussen, *Reform*.

49. Hanssens, *Opera*, 2:248–49. Amalar's comparison of the pallium to an ancient Hebrew vestment may have been inspired by Germanus of Constantinople's liturgical commentary (Paul Meyendorff, ed. and trans., *St. Germanus of Constantinople: On the Divine Liturgy* [Crestwood, N.Y.: St. Vladimir's Seminary Press, 1984], 66), which he could have encountered during his trip to that city, attested by Florus of Lyon in 838 (MGH Epp. 5:270–71). The order of Amalar's treatment is somewhat rearranged here in order to organize his scattered comments on the pallium's strips.

50. E.g., 1 Cor 9:24–26, 2 Tm 4:7–8, Phil 3:12–14. The language here recalled 2 Tm 2:5: "He who competes in a contest is not crowned unless he competes legitimately." It also invoked Prv 1:9 ("That grace may be added to your head, and

crown, according to Paul (2 Tm 2:4–5), only when it avoided entanglement in secular affairs.

The learned liturgist then examined the various segments of the garment. The circular band upon the shoulders was linked to speech: "The circle around the neck is the discipline of the Lord around the word of the preacher, so that the word of preaching may not be one thing and the work another." The pallium's loop thus symbolized the responsibility of preaching (which came forth from the neck), specifically the consonance of preaching and practice.[51] The bands hanging in front and back, moreover, evoked God's precepts: "That it has two strips from top to bottom, behind and before, signifies indeed the adornment of the highest teaching through the pleasing discipline of the Lord's commandments.... Let the pontiff carry the commandments of the Old Testament, from the beginning of Genesis onward, on the shoulder strip by working and teaching, and on the breast [strip] those of the New [Testament], from the primitive church onward." Each represented the dictates of a covenant—the back or humeral band was the Old, and the front or pectoral band was the New—which the archbishop was obliged both to explain and to live out. In sum, the pallium in Amalar's eyes was a gift, a badge of office with Hebrew roots, which increased the wearer's prestige. Simultaneously it was a mystical symbol illustrating that the palliger was a teacher, a preacher, and a practitioner of virtue, embedded in biblical doctrine. Thus, by its very appearance, the pallium goaded the wearer to fulfill his pastoral duties.[52]

Other writers of the period likewise looked to the ancient Jewish scriptures for the prototypes of contemporary Christian vestments, since they assumed that the Christian priesthood was derived and took its pattern from, and replaced, the Israelite priesthood.[53] In his *De Exordiis et Incrementis* of 840/42, the monk Walafrid Strabo followed the example of Amalar both in finding parallels between

---

a wreath to your neck") and Bede's interpretation of that passage (*In Proverbia*, in CCSL 119B:26), which clearly inspired Amalar's subsequent reflection on preaching.

51. Amalar supported this principle by appealing to Paul (2 Cor 6:3) and Ambrose, *recte* Ambrosiaster (*In Epistolam Beati Pauli ad Corinthios Secundam*, in PL 17:299).

52. Cf. Amalar's summary of the pallium's meaning (Hanssens, *Opera*, 2:254).

53. See Chydenius, *Medieval Institutions*, esp. 58–59.

the sacred attires of the Old and New Covenants and in interpreting them symbolically.⁵⁴ Christian vestments were invented "either in imitation of those which ancient priests used, or as an expression of mystical significance." His project matched Hebrew and Christian garb in a one-to-one fashion: as Amalar did, Walafrid paired the pallium with the Aaronic *lamina*, because each was the proper insigne of the most exalted priests of its dispensation.⁵⁵

In the previous generation, Alcuin had chosen a different Old Testament parallel in his *vita* of Willibrord. He described how Pope Sergius I had ordained Willibrord archbishop: "He imposed on the ordained the name Clement, and clothed him with his own priestly vestments and the holy pallium of dignity, as if with the superhumeral of Aaron, and confirmed him with the glory of his garment."⁵⁶ To Alcuin, who was not attempting a comprehensive analysis of priestly vestments, it must have seemed obvious to liken the pallium, which rested upon the shoulders, not to the plate on the forehead but to the Aaronic superhumeral or ephod (Ex 28:6–14).⁵⁷ His point was simply to stress the antiquity, biblical foundation, and priestly eminence of the pallium, which signified the pope's approval of Willibrord's *dignitas* or office and bound him to Peter and the papacy.⁵⁸

Accompanying Admonitions

The practice of pious admonition, which embraced preaching but extended to any oral or written hortatory counsel, was highly valued in the Carolingian age. Regarded as the proper form of Christian

---

54. See Brown, "Enigmata Figurarum," 146–48, and Wallace-Hadrill, *Frankish Church*, 322–26.
55. Harting-Correa, *Libellus*, 152.
56. Reischmann, *Willibrord*, 58. The pope may have given Willibrord his own pallium.
57. The pallium was sometimes called *superhumerale* in this period (see 90n61 above). But only here was it specifically compared to Aaron's vestment, which would not recur until the twelfth century (Bruno of Segni, *De Sacramentis Ecclesiae*, in PL 165:1105–6).
58. The place of ordination (St. Peter's Basilica), the new name (Clement, traditionally the disciple and successor of Peter), and the possibility that the pope put his own vestment on him (a sign of special favor) also affirmed Willibrord's bond to Peter's successor.

speech and a concrete expression of love of neighbor, it permeated the letters of Alcuin and guided the composition of capitularies.[59] For the gift of the pallium to be accompanied by moral admonishment directed at its recipient became an accepted custom, one which prodded the palliger to behave in ways the popes thought appropriate for bishops. These repeated presentations of normative ideas about the episcopal office, moreover, helped to create the social consensus that delineated the range of a prelate's duties, and thus constructed his power.[60] This kind of instruction went back at least to Gregory the Great's *Regula Pastoralis,* a manual that shaped medieval thinking on the episcopal office, and it was natural for similar guidance to be offered directly to a bishop as he assumed his duties.[61] A genuine letter of Gregory found in the Pseudo-Isidorian decretals paid Leander of Seville an extraordinary compliment: "Having sent [the pallium], I very much should have admonished you on how you must live, but I stifle my speech because you anticipate my words with your behavior."[62] By dispensing with the usual exhortations, the pope witnessed to the bishop's virtue, but also to the more typical expectation of his time.

Indeed, it seems clear that this practice continued unabated. In a letter to Boniface in 744, Pope Zachary, having granted pallia to the archbishops of Rouen, Reims, and Sens, mentioned "the charters that, according to custom, are bestowed by our writing office for their confirmation and teaching."[63] Not only was it customary for a document (none extant in this case) to accompany the pallium, but

59. See Thomas Martin Buck, *Admonitio und Praedicatio: zur religiös-pastoralen Dimension von Kapitularien und kapitulariennahen Texten (507–814),* Freiburger Beiträge zur mittelalterlichen Geschichte 9 (Frankfurt: Lang, 1997), 67–156.

60. The reliance of social power on shared knowledge lies at the heart of Patzold's analysis of the Carolingian episcopate (*Episcopus*).

61. See Silke Floryszczak, *Die* Regula Pastoralis *Gregors des Großen: Studien zu Text, kirchenpolitischer Bedeutung und Rezeption in der Karolingerzeit,* Studien und Texte zu Antike und Christentum 26 (Tübingen: Mohr Siebeck, 2005). The *Regula Pastoralis* had the impact of a canon law manual and profoundly influenced the Carolingian reform (Buck, *Admonitio,* 144). The admonitions of the *Liber Diurnus* pallium formulas clearly contained many echoes (cf., e.g., Rommel et al., *Règle,* 1:160–64, 250).

62. Schon and Zechiel-Eckes, *Projekt Pseudoisidor,* at http://www.pseudoisidor.mgh.de/html/304.htm, quoting JE 1756.

63. JE 2271, GP 4:24 no. 58, Rau, *Briefe,* 172.

this document was meant to confirm the position of the recipient and to teach, in the sense of admonish, him. Likewise, Alcuin's life of Willibrord recounted that Pope Sergius I, having ordained and palliated Willibrord, sent him home "confirmed with his blessing and enriched with gifts, along with salvific instructions, for the work of the Gospel."[64] Moreover, in 868 Pope Hadrian II agreed to send the pallium to Wulfhad, archbishop of Bourges, "for the splendor and glory of the church entrusted to him and for his instruction."[65] These popes took their magisterial duties seriously.

During a squabble over the conduct of Hincmar of Reims in 866, Pope Nicholas I reminded him that the proper attitude of a palliger had already been communicated to him: "[The pallium] must not be used for empty glory, but must be worn for the decoration of all virtues. This was shown to you and well instructed in the usual manner by the text of a document at the time when you received the use of that pallium from the apostolic see."[66] In his reply of the following year, Hincmar admitted his awareness of such admonitions: "I am not ignorant that, if I use the pallium without the virtues that the pallium signifies, as blessed Gregory explains—even if, in the eyes of men, the use of the pallium demonstrates that the metropolitan see is more excellent than the rest of the sees of the province of Reims—nevertheless it does not make me greater in the eyes of the Lord."[67] The archbishop was recalling the exhortations that Gregory the Great had often incorporated into his pallium grants, in an effort to expound the moral implications of the vestment.[68] Perhaps Hincmar's own lost privilege contained such Gregorian axioms. It was generally accepted, then, that the popes had the right and responsibility to lecture recipients of the pallium on their demeanor. Put differently, the vestment carried expectations to which palligers had to live up.[69]

64. Reischmann, *Willibrord*, 58.
65. To the fathers of the Council of Troyes (867), JE 2894, MGH Epp. 6:699.
66. JE 2823, BH 838, MGH Epp. 6:430–31.
67. MGH Epp. 8.1:216.
68. E.g., to Maximus of Salona in 599, JE 1761, CCSL 140A:816–17.
69. For evidence that these expectations were actually read, even frequently, see 384 below.

The *Liber Diurnus* provided these exhortations in most pallium grants. The content was specific not to using the pallium, but to exercising the pastoral office. It was unusual for papal privileges to feature such personal material, but the pallium formulas were rare exceptions.[70] Each of the formulas available to the papal chancery gave ample room to admonitions, often much greater than that left for its legal core. The preamble (*arenga*) of *Si pastores ovium*, perhaps partly inspired by the pallium's woolen composition, compared the duties of prelates to those of shepherds. Although these "shepherds of souls" were at present "loftier in reverence of honor than the rest," they were reminded that they would have to answer to the "supreme Shepherd" for their "protection of the Lord's sheep."[71] (Pope Nicholas I may have had this preamble in mind when he instructed King Lothar II to hurry and send the new archbishops of Cologne and Trier to Rome for their pallia, lest their flocks be devoured by wolves.)[72] Later in the document, a lengthy exhortation declared that the "honor of this apparel" was maintained by proper conduct, and so the "decorations of [one's] behavior" should match it. The result would be a palliger "properly striking on both counts," that is, distinguished in garb and in deed. This logic proposed that what caused prominence in action should parallel what caused prominence in dress, and so the pallium was a sign of and stimulus to good works. Advice followed on how to govern wisely as a bishop, by living an exemplary life, making wise judgments, and following the path of virtue. It concluded: "Behold, dearest brother, among many other things, these things belong to the priesthood, these things belong to the pallium. If you keep them zealously, you have on the inside what you are shown to have received on the outside." Faith-

---

70. *Ermahnungsformeln* in the *Liber Diurnus* were characteristic of, and almost exclusive to, pallium privileges (Santifaller, *Liber Diurnus*, 9, 30). Buck distinguishes the personal purpose of letters from the legal purpose of documents (*Admonitio*, 101); in pallium grants, the two were combined.

71. V45, Foerster, *Liber Diurnus*, 101, with slight variants C44 on 200 and A39 on 299–300.

72. Nicholas's images, while biblical and traditional, showed linguistic similarity to *Si pastores ovium* (in 867, JE 2878, GP 7.1:27–28 no. 44, GP 10.1:34–35 no. 40, BH 855, MGH Epp. 6:334).

ful observance of the qualities befitting the episcopal office, and the vestment that was its symbol, led to the realization of a correspondence between internal disposition and external ornament.[73]

The formula *Officium sacerdotis* proceeded along similar lines. The long preamble treated the "office of the priest" and again invoked the imagery of shepherds and sheep. The "care of pastoral rule" was a duty, even a burden, and those with the *cura animarum* were encouraged to exercise "concern for others with pious foresight," through an urgently vigilant protection of the flock against the predations of the wolf, who was the devil.[74] A series of admonitions, as to a brother bishop, explained how to care for his charges and how to labor to win souls through his teaching and example.[75] Later in the document came a section discussing the trouble of the "simoniacal heresy," the practice of buying and selling holy orders, in the recipient's region. Such a crime continually spread its evil, for those so ordained were corrupted in their very promotion and corrupted those they tried to promote. The pope threatened to correct these abuses severely.[76] While simoniacal ordinations were a common problem, a formulary such as the *Liber Diurnus* might contain textual segments meant for optional use, as the occasion warranted. In fact, Pope Leo III's grant to Arno of Salzburg in 798 included the simony admonition, but his grant to Fortunatus of Grado five years later did not.[77]

---

73. V45, Foerster, *Liber Diurnus*, 101–3, with slight variants C44 on 201–2 and A39 on 300–302. The forged pallium grants of Gregory IV and Nicholas I for Ansgar, even if based on authentic models, made strange alterations to the admonitions of *Si pastores ovium* (JE 2574, GP 6:25–28 no. 11, Curschmann, *Ältere Papsturkunden*, 14–15; and JE 2759, GP 6:31–33 no. 21, BH 706, Curschmann, *Ältere Papsturkunden*, 23). Part of the preamble was replaced with a simple, vague directive: "We admonish that you should not involve the office you have received in earthly affairs to any extent." Also, the exhortation "let your defense come to the aid of the oppressed" was expanded with "widows and orphans unjustly oppressed" (perhaps witnessing to a lost version of the formula?). See Knibbs, *Ansgar*, 149–51.

74. V46, Foerster, *Liber Diurnus*, 103–4, with slight variants C45 on 202 and A40 on 303–4.

75. V46, ibid., 104, with slight variants C45 on 203 and A40 on 304–5.

76. V46, ibid., 105–6, with slight variants C45 on 203–4 and A40 on 305–7.

77. JE 2498, GP 1:8 no. 7, Dopsch, "Papst Leo III. verleiht," 20–21; and JE 2512, IP 7.2:40–41 no. 28, Cessi, *Documenti*, 1:57–58. Cessi notes that, in a codex containing two copies of this privilege, the simony passage was lacking in the first but

In fact, the pallium had a long and problematic relationship with simony. The "pallium fee," a more or less expected donation offered to the Roman church by the vestment's recipient, was first the object of regulation in 595, at a synod of Gregory the Great. John the Deacon later described that pope's efforts to combat this customary gift, euphemistically called the *pastellus* or *pastellaticum* (a word of uncertain meaning), and John's quotations from the synodal decree and Gregory's letter to John of Corinth in the same year were frequently repeated in the canonical tradition.[78] The issue came to the fore again in this period when Boniface requested pallia for the archbishops of Rouen, Reims, and Sens. He reported that certain Franks found the Roman custom to be simoniacal, and Zachary took great pains to defend his church from the charge.[79] Contentions surrounding the pallium fee, rarely discussed in the sources, would linger unresolved throughout the Middle Ages.[80]

The remaining two formulas were briefer, but did not fail to admonish their recipients. *Pallii usum* lacked a preamble. (Pope Paschal I's chancery tried to fill this gap in one instance, to Bernard of Vienne in 817, with additional scene-setting and a brief admonishment using pastoral imagery, not unlike those of other formulas.)[81] Immediately after the grant proper, this formula encouraged the palliger, "having acquired the dignity with whose office [he is] honored," to carry out his government suitably. Playing on the external and internal meanings of "adornment," it urged him to be "further decorated": his "integrity of faith" (already demonstrated through his

---

included in the second. Since the original is lost, it is unknown which was more accurate; the passage may have been added to the second copy after comparison with another letter following the same formula.

78. *Vita Gregorii Magni*, in PL 75:90, 132 (quoting c. 5 and JE 1378), 144. See 291–92nn44, 48 below.

79. In 744, JE 2271, GP 4:24 no. 58, Rau, *Briefe*, 170, 172; and in 751, JE 2291, GP 4:35–36 no. 88, Rau, *Briefe*, 294.

80. Rudolf Schieffer attributes the lack of evidence to the fact that the exaction was an accepted matter of course ("Die Romreise deutscher Bischöfe im Frühjahr 1070: Anno von Köln, Siegfried von Mainz und Hermann von Bamberg bei Alexander II," *Rheinische Vierteljahrsblätter* 35 [1971]: 160).

81. JE 2549, GaP 3.1:96–97 no. 81, MGH Epp. 3:97. The additions seemed to echo *Apostolicae sedis* and *Si pastores ovium*.

profession of faith) should be adorned with the virtue, vigor, and vigilance befitting the episcopal office. This admonition, as a standard part of a pallium privilege, was said to be offered "suitably and necessarily."[82] A preamble was also missing in the last formula, *Apostolicae sedis*. After the grant proper, it promised that the recipient would find joy in "the use of this ornament for the honor of the priestly office." Even so, it instructed the palliger to adorn the "priestly office [he has] undertaken" with virtuous deeds. Then he would stand out "by a complementary beauty, one to the other," through the harmony of the internal "goods of [his] mind" with the external "dress of [his] body."[83]

Occasionally the popes added particular exhortations, suited to the situation, that went beyond the concerns expressed in the formulas. Zachary told Boniface in 744 that he had written the three Frankish archbishops,

informing them that they should know ... how to preach to their subjects the way of salvation, and that ecclesiastical discipline should be kept unreduced in their churches and remain unshaken. And the priesthood in [those churches] should be able to be, not polluted as it was before, but clean and acceptable to God, as much as the human condition is able, such that no one can be found to deviate from the sacred canons, and a clean sacrifice may be offered by them.[84]

Here the pope's advice responded to the corrupt state of the Frankish church before the Bonifacian reform, and so addressed issues of canonical observance and ritual purity.[85] In 868 Pope Hadrian II directed the admonitions accompanying the pallium for Actard of Nantes

---

82. V47, Foerster, *Liber Diurnus*, 106, with slight variants C46 on 204–5 and A41 on 307–8. John VIII's chancery tacked a version of this clause onto a pallium grant that generally followed *Si pastores ovium* (to Wala of Metz in 878, JE 3183, BU 427, PL 126:799). Perhaps, having added special material necessitated by this grant to a suffragan, the notary looked to *Pallii usum* to conclude it gracefully.

83. V48, Foerster, *Liber Diurnus*, 107, with slight variants C47 on 205 and A42 on 308–9. A letter of Gregory the Great to John of Palermo (JE 1905), which offered quite similar admonitions, seems to have formed one of the textual bases for this formula.

84. JE 2270, GP 4:23 no. 55, Rau, *Briefe*, 166.

85. Zachary may have been reacting to the Frankish abuses reported by Boniface in 742 (Rau, *Briefe*, 142, 144).

to Charles the Bald instead: "Through this insigne may your excellent Industry be admonished, and may your pious heart be prodded more carefully and more wholesomely by reverence for this sacred gift. Through it such a great man [Actard] should also, by your favor, obtain the government of a vacant church."[86] Urging the king to find a see for this homeless palliger, the pope hoped that the vestment itself would prompt him to do so, since so honored a churchman should not be left unchurched.

Usually, however, the popes followed the lead of the traditional formulas. A theme that occurred in three of the four was the desired correspondence between the luster of the honorific decoration on the outside and the character of the wearer on the inside (made manifest in his actions).[87] This virtue, the opposite of hypocrisy, found its Christian roots in Jesus's condemnation of the Pharisees, outwardly refined but inwardly corrupt (Mt 23:27), and continued even to Dante, who dressed his hellish hypocrites in monastic habits golden without and leaden within.[88] In several instances Pope John VIII emphasized this expectation in his own words. For Willibert of Cologne in 874, he prayed that, "just as you will begin to shine on the outside, more splendid than others by the dignity of this [pallium], now, in the eyes of the heavenly Majesty, you may gleam more brightly all around, in life, behavior, and the word of preaching."[89] To King Carloman of Bavaria in 877, he expressed his hope that Thietmar I of Salzburg would "gleam on the inside, to the eyes of the inner Judge, by this ornament, by which he shines on the outside to human gazes."[90] And to the archbishop himself he insisted that the vestment implied virtuous behavior: "We were eager to adorn your Fraternity with the great ornament of the pallium, so that, with Christ's aid,

86. JE 2902, MGH Epp. 6:706. See the matter's resolution by the Council of Douzy in 871 (MGH Conc. 4:527–28).
87. On early Christian attention to this theme, see Miller, *Clothing the Clergy*, 16–20.
88. See Frederic Amory, "Whited Sepulchres: The Semantic History of Hypocrisy to the High Middle Ages," *Recherches de théologie ancienne et médiévale* 53 (1986): 5–39. Perhaps medieval people were sensitive to this sin because they did not readily distinguish outer sign from inner reality (Fichtenau, *Living*, 50).
89. JE 2988, GP 7.1:34–35 no. 67, BU 120, Wisplinghoff, *Rheinisches Urkundenbuch*, 2:158.
90. JE 3114, BU 289, MGH Epp. 7:58.

you may also be powerful before God's eyes in good and holy actions."⁹¹

Nor was this motif limited to popes, although their documents may have inspired it. In the early ninth century Alcuin wrote to several friends who sported the pallium. Encouraging Riculf of Mainz in the face of ecclesiastical tensions, Alcuin counseled him to act in a way worthy of his apparel: "I admonish only this, that the most upright works befit the name of the highest dignity, and the most holy behavior in all fairness embellish the superhumeral of priestly honor, so that what is seen by the eyes of many on the shoulder may be preached by the mouth of all and loved in your behavior."⁹² The goal, in keeping with the deeper meaning of his external distinctions (his title and pallium), was to edify others through deeds. Alcuin also congratulated Theodulf of Orléans on his reception of the vestment: "Know that the brightness of this honor demands persistence in preaching. The priestly pallium is a diadem: as the flash of gems decorates the royal diadem, so trustworthiness in preaching ought to decorate the honor of the pallium. For in this it has its own honor, if its bearer is a preacher of the truth."⁹³ His very attire bespoke a pastoral obligation to spread the Gospel, and doing so complemented its outer glory.

Indeed, Alcuin's letters continually suggested that preaching was the chief duty of the palliger, the source of whose honor was not so much his dress as his activity as a preacher, which his dress signified.⁹⁴ While urging Arno of Salzburg to exhort other bishops to the *praedicationis officium*, Alcuin reminded him of the expectation bound up with his vestment: "When you received the pallium from the apostolic see, you received a greater burden, and you are under obligation to preach the word of God trustworthily to every person and dignity. Do not, do not be silent, but cry out and do not cease. Raise your voice like a trumpet and show to all the way of eternal salvation!"⁹⁵ He also

91. JE 3115, GP 1:12–13 no. 24, BU 290, MGH Epp. 7:58.
92. In 800/801, MGH Epp. 4:353.
93. In 801, MGH Epp. 4:368.
94. Good preaching was often emphasized in the Carolingian church, perhaps because ineffective preaching was prevalent, or because preaching served as a potent instrument of reform. See Wallace-Hadrill, *Frankish Church*, 260, 320, and Buck, *Admonitio*, 157–238.
95. In 800, MGH Epp. 4:321.

admonished Aethelhard of Canterbury to fulfill the responsibilities of his office as archbishop and palliger: "Consider this highest and vicarious dignity of apostolic honor most diligently.... Preach the word of God with all the persistence of piety.... The highest work of the priest is to preach the word of God."[96] The origin of the pallium's association with preaching may have lain in the idea of palliated missionaries approved by Rome to preach to the nations.[97] This connection was carried over to metropolitans of the Carolingian reform, who began to receive the pallium regularly.[98] Eventually the duty to preach well became a commonplace applicable to any palliated archbishop.[99]

From within the context of comparing exterior and interior, distinctive vestment and virtuous behavior, arose a satirical poem by Theodulf of Orléans, "On hypocrites," probably in the late eighth century. As he contrasted the merits of the apostolic church with the vices of his own day, Theodulf castigated hypocrites (*simulatores*), with their fraudulent hearts and dishonest speech:

> Then pallia, given from the apostolic see, used to thrive,
> And the vestment was the right of power and order.
> Now a fake vestment has come, and a fake authority,
> Which fit each other well, both mind and dress.
> A loose cap covers the head, dark will the mind,
> Rough wool the limbs, sheep's clothing the wolf.
> A double cloak is on the outside, on the inside a double heart.
> Simplicity and honor is far from both.[100]

---

96. In 802/804, MGH Epp. 4:479–80. The precise meaning of *hanc altissimam vicariamque apostolici honoris dignitatem* is unclear. Perhaps it reflected the idea that a metropolitan was a papal vicar (cf. Rabanus Maurus, *De Institutione Clericorum*, in Zimpel, *De Institutione*, 315).

97. E.g., Corbinian (Arbeo of Freising, *Vita Prima Corbiniani*, in MGH SSRG 13:197) and Ansgar (Stephen V to Herman I of Cologne in 890, JL 3458, GP 7.1:37 no. 76, MGH Epp. 7:358–59).

98. E.g., the archbishops of Rouen, Reims, and Sens (Zachary to Boniface in 744, JE 2270, GP 4:23 no. 55, Rau, *Briefe*, 166) and Arno of Salzburg, both within his province (Leo III to Charlemagne in 798, JE 2496, GP 1:9 no. 9, Dopsch, "Papst Leo III. schreibt an König Karl," 24) and in missionary areas (*Conversio Bagoariorum et Carantanorum*, in Lošek, *Conversio*, 114, 116).

99. E.g., Willibert of Cologne (John VIII in 874, JE 2988, GP 7.1:34–35 no. 67, BU 120, Wisplinghoff, *Rheinisches Urkundenbuch*, 2:158).

100. MGH Poet. 1:472–73. *Camilla* was rare but seems to have indicated a head-covering among the Aaronic (and thus archiepiscopal) vestments (PL 121:559n).

In this passage Theodulf took his cue from the language and imagery of Gregory the Great, but his focus on hierarchical hypocrites cast those conventions in a new light.[101] The pallium, once representing *ius potestatis et ordo*, had become a hypocritical garment (*simulata vestis*) manifesting pretended authority. Hence there was a perverted kind of inner-outer equivalence between deceitful mind and deceptive dress. With the pallium in mind, the readers (probably a small, highly educated clerical audience) could not help but link its "rough wool" to the "sheep's clothing" hiding the wolf. Even the "double cloak," concealing a duplicitous heart, may have evoked the two layers of the vestment's left side.[102] In short, Theodulf combined the Gregorian exegetical tradition, the increasing prominence of the pallium in the Western church, and the theme of inner-outer correspondence popular in papal pronouncements to create a stinging reproach of the corrupt prelates of his era.[103]

The principal temptation of the palliger was pride. Instead of matching his outer splendor to inner virtue, bearing fruit in good works, the sinful bishop ignored papal admonitions and took his prestigious insigne as an outward sign of his own glory. As John the Deacon remembered, Gregory the Great had had harsh words for John of Ravenna, guilty of abusing the pallium through overuse: "I find that the honor of your episcopate is wholly on the outside, in

---

101. See Amory, "Whited Sepulchres," 25–30. Gregory defined a hypocrite (*Moralia in Iob*, in CCSL 143A:893), spoke of a wolf in sheep's clothing (CCSL 143B:1569), and, citing Dt 22:11, referred to a double-woven garment as a symbol of hypocrisy (CCSL 143:450–51).

102. The double layer of the part of the pallium that went over the left shoulder was a consequence of its original form and was retained even when that form changed (see 393n107 below). Later liturgical commentators, including Bruno of Segni (*De Sacramentis Ecclesiae*, in PL 165:1105–6), Sicard of Cremona (*Mitrale*, in PL 213:80–81), Lothar of Segni (*De Missarum Mysteriis*, in PL 217:797–98), and William Durandus (*Rationale Divinorum Officiorum*, in CCCM 140:219–20), interpreted this doubling to mean the duplicity of this world, as opposed to the simplicity of the world to come (the single layer on the right shoulder).

103. Cf. Amory, "Whited Sepulchres," 31. However, the last part of this passage probably did not concern the monastic life (Amory does not explain why he translates *camilla* as "hood"), and the allusions to the pallium discussed above indicate that Theodulf was doing more than producing "a poetic version of Gregory's gloss on *Deuteronomy*."

display, not in mind.... Do not seek to seem more than you are, so that you can be more than you seem."[104] The pope was concerned that the pallium not become the cause of vain pomp—merely for show, conducive to vanity, perhaps out of ambition to resemble the Roman pontiff—but instead reflect an inward integrity. In this spirit, Pope Leo III quoted (or rather misquoted) his predecessor Celestine I in order to discourage the bishops of London from aspiring to metropolitan rank—in effect, seeking the pallium out of pride.[105]

Similarly, in 799 Alcuin exhorted one of his palliated friends, Arno of Salzburg, to humility after he had been vested with the honor: "I rejoiced very much when I heard that your Beatitude was wearing the holiness of the superhumeral and standing in the most lofty stability of ecclesiastical honor.... By the steps of humility one reaches the height of the heavenly kingdom.... How much more ought we, elevated from the dung of poverty to the seat of glory, to lift up our dignity with the duty of humility!"[106] Finally, in 866, accusing Hincmar of Reims of wearing the pallium too frequently, Pope Nicholas I recommended modesty: "Fittingly admonished by these our allocutions, be zealous to use [the pallium] discreetly, such that neither pride of mind invade you, nor bragging puff you up, nor vainglory wound you, nor you surpass the measure of your own dignity, nor temperance (without which the rest of the virtues are incomplete) be handed over to oblivion."[107] Indignantly, Hincmar contended that he avoided any trace of pride: "Although I am fabricated as someone else by my friends across the Alps in the Roman regions (as many boast), I ought to ... think about things other than applauding or serving any pomp and display in any way—and hardly in ecclesiastical ministry from the use of the pallium."[108] For a pope to share his insigne was a risky affair that could generate self-important potentates with delusions of grandeur, even of equality with the donor himself. To this malady constant insistence on virtue, especially humility, was one antidote.

104. *Vita Gregorii Magni*, in PL 75:174.
105. To Cenwulf in 797/98, JE 2494, MGH Epp. 4:188, quoting JK 369.
106. MGH Epp. 4:286–87.
107. JE 2823, BH 838, MGH Epp. 6:431.
108. MGH Epp. 8.1:222.

Conclusion

The papacy used the pallium to exercise power in the church, but it was not power for the sake of power. In subtle ways the vestment could influence individual thought and action in the service of cultic, doctrinal, and ethical ends. The result was the reinforcement and justification of its own significance, as well as the accomplishment of papal goals for the welfare of the Christian people. As a sacred object from the tomb of Peter, the pallium was a treasured relic in an age of fervent Petrine devotion, and also a tangible link to Peter's successor, the pope, who alone could provide it. When Carolingian commentators tried to account for the vestment's importance, they created richly symbolic interpretations that increased the authority of its pedigree and reminded its wearer of Christian truths and morals. And the custom of coupling the pallium with admonitions heightened awareness of the gravity of the pastoral charge it signified, while giving the popes an opportunity to train its recipient in the conduct suited to their idea of the perfect pastor. In these respects, one can observe the pallium's effectiveness as a cultural artifact, a manmade material object associated with certain attitudes and behaviors, which lay at the intersection of ideas and human society: it incarnated the former, with ramifications for the life of the latter.

By 882, when Pope John VIII was allegedly poisoned and clubbed to death by his own followers, an empire had risen and fallen. Western Christendom, fragmenting and beset by invaders, seemed to be descending into the same chaos in which the period had begun. But much had changed. The popes were heirs to an old and rich theoretical tradition that justified their ecclesiastical primacy, but—apart from sporadic precedents—it was not until the Carolingian era that some of them attempted to implement that theory in a more universal, systematic manner. The protection, stability, and renewal provided by the Frankish realm afforded them the possibility, and the pallium, among other tools at their disposal, helped them to realize it, however partially and temporarily.

The pallium allowed the papacy to be something more than

a prestigious figurehead, the distant court of last appeal, and the guardian of prized Roman relics. It allowed popes to make their presence felt in far-flung lands and to make a difference in the ecclesiastical affairs of those lands. They, and those like Boniface, Alcuin, and Hincmar, who shared their program in varying degrees, found in the vestment a sign of sacred power essential to the proper functioning of the church. By sharing their own insigne, the popes took a special kind of relic, laden with cultural import, and made it an object of desire to other bishops. Yet the many conditions they placed upon its reception and use made it also a potent means of control over the hierarchs of the Latin church and strategically influenced relationships with lords spiritual and temporal, all in the service of papal interests.

Their interests in this period were still somewhat conservative: the canonical accession of worthy bishops, the maintenance of orthodoxy, the promotion of virtue, the orderly hierarchical organization of the church, and especially the recognition of papal preeminence. The last permitted the enforcement of the others. Grants of the pallium, though essentially favors, were also means of exercising authority and evoking submission; although they formed bonds between Rome and other churches, those bonds did not work the same in both directions. The very act of giving created dependence in the recipient—reliance on the donor's will (whom did he choose to receive the gift? when, where, and how did he give it? what conditions did he attach to its reception? what did he expect in return?), as well as the social attitudes and obligations concomitant with gratitude. In this respect the pallium was an instrument of papal power, a gift that may have seemed to more independent metropolitans like a Trojan horse.

The pattern had been woven. Although the Roman church became entangled in local, often internecine intrigues in the following years, this fundamental design from the Carolingian loom held fast and refused to be unraveled. Part 2 will study how this pattern fared in changing times, even as the papacy reached a nadir in its influence.

PART 2

A WELL-WORN GARMENT (882–1046)

The century and a half that lay between Carolingian ingenuity and Gregorian reform, a period notoriously branded as an "age of lead," was often a bleak time for the papacy. Most of the popes rose through the intrigues of powerful Roman families, whose playthings they threatened to become. Some were renowned for shocking misconduct, and a number, caught in political strife, met unhappy ends. Despite the local preoccupations of the papacy and the low ebb of its standing and influence, the sources of this era indicated that the popes continued to employ the pallium much as their predecessors had, as an attempt at control over the wider Latin church.

How did the popes stray from or build on the Carolingian tradition? For what reasons, and to what effect? Significant changes will be examined in the following chapters, but to a large extent the patterns inherited from the Carolingians were preserved. Continuity was thus the backdrop of this period. Even so, continuity did not mean uniformity: the old customs were manifested in new forms and contexts, and thus could take on fresh connotations. The previous period's heritage was articulated, to some degree systematized, and occasionally adjusted. One of the chief ways in which this process of integration happened was through canon law, and it is worthwhile briefly to survey the role of the pallium in ecclesiastical law at this time. Canonical collections incorporated the ancient paradigms of Pope Gregory the Great and the newer legislation of Pope John VIII in order to affirm the developments of the eighth and ninth centuries and promote their acceptance in the Western church.

The first canonical collection to treat the pallium as a legal object in its own right, rather than referring to it incidentally, was the *Collectio Anselmo Dedicata*.[1] It was compiled following a key moment in the vestment's history, between 882 and 896, soon after the crucial councils of John VIII. Indeed, it both arose from and extended the Carolingian renewal, including the bold efforts of the previous three popes.[2] The compiler drew six letters from the register of Gregory the Great and excerpted and inserted them in the collection's first part, which dealt not only with the primacy of the Roman see, but also with metropolitan archbishops, the vestment's ordinary recipients. He outfitted them with rubrics that drew attention to how the pallium could be gained, what it meant, what sort of status and behavior it implied, when it could be worn, and how important humility was for its wearer.[3]

The Johannine rules from the Councils of Rome (875) and Ravenna (877) themselves, however, did not enter the mainstream of the canonical tradition until Burchard of Worms incorporated them into his *Decretum* between about 1012 and 1022.[4] In Book I, which among other things discussed the papacy, metropolitans, honors, and the episcopal ministry, he inserted the canon *Quoniam quidam* from John VIII's Roman synod, along with its rubric.[5] It fell within

---

1. See Lotte Kéry, *Canonical Collections of the Early Middle Ages (ca. 400–1140): A Bibliographical Guide to the Manuscripts and Literature* (Washington, D.C.: The Catholic University of America Press, 1999), 124–28, and Fowler-Magerl, *Clavis Canonum*, 70–74.

2. See Paul Fournier and Gabriel Le Bras, *Histoire des collections canoniques en occident dépuis les Fausses Décrétales jusqu'au Décret de Gratien* (Paris: Sirey, 1931; reprinted in Aalen: Scientia, 1972), 1:234–35, 239–42, and Besse, "Liber Primus," 208. Its anonymous author, an Italian cleric devoted to the apostolic see and John VIII's ideals, offered his work to Archbishop Anselm II of Milan, who had been a close ally of that pope.

3. Canons 1.123–28, Besse, "Liber Primus," 287–93, quoting JE 1491, 1761, 1751, 1905, 1259, 1272.

4. See Kéry, *Canonical Collections*, 133–55; Fowler-Magerl, *Clavis Canonum*, 85–90; and Schrör, *Metropolitangewalt*, 87–95.

5. Canon 1.25, Gérard Fransen and Theo Kölzer, eds., *Burchard von Worms: Decre-*

A Well-Worn Garment (882–1046) 181

Figure 4. Archbishop Heribert of Cologne (with halo) about to receive the pallium from Pope Sylvester II (misidentified as "Pope John"), himself wearing a pallium, in 999 (lower half). The pope seems to be praying over the vestment as it lies upon the altar. The lower inscription reads: "The pope kindly gives the full insigne of a prelate." Heribertschrein (Dach der Petrusseite, 4. Medaillon), Cologne and Limoges, ca. 1150–75, Sankt Heribert (Neu), Köln-Deutz; photograph: © Rheinisches Bildarchiv Köln, RBA 094 352.

a series of texts dealing with the consecration of bishops, a function made canonically possible by the possession of the pallium. He attributed the canon, however, to Pope Damasus I—a falsified inscription that would leave a lasting imprint on the transmission of the

---

torum Libri XX (supplemented reprint of the *editio princeps* of 1548, Aalen: Scientia, 1992), fol. 3v.

text.[6] Although the pallium did not play a large role in Burchard's work, written for the practical needs of a non-metropolitan diocese, this canon ensured the timely ordination of the bishops of Worms by compelling the archbishop of Mainz to seek the pallium within three months of his consecration. By insisting on this submission to Rome, Burchard may have wanted to make known the limits of his metropolitan's power.[7] The general educational purpose of this collection, clearly asserted in its preface, must also not be forgotten.[8]

In the same book of the *Decretum*, Burchard reproduced the canon *Quicumque sane* of John VIII's Ravennese synod, with the corresponding rubric from the Roman synod.[9] As he did for *Quoniam quidam*, Burchard forged the inscription (or accepted a previously forged inscription) and attributed the canon to Pope Honorius I, which would influence its future transmission.[10] The context in which he placed it addressed episcopal discipline and bishops as shepherds—

---

6. See JK †250. The reason for the falsification is unknown, but various hypotheses can be offered. Burchard shied away from later legislation as lacking in prestige, and he did not include Italian councils among the authoritative sources listed in his preface (Fransen and Kölzer, *Decretorum Libri*, 49). Substituting the name of an early pope fixed these problems. See Greta Austin, *Shaping Church Law around the Year 1000: The* Decretum *of Burchard of Worms* (Farnham: Ashgate, 2009). Alternatively, Burchard may have gotten this text from a lost collection that had forged the inscription for its own reasons. In any case, the ancient pedigree must have increased respect for John VIII's regulation in the many ecclesiastical circles that came to use the *Decretum*.

7. See Schrör, *Metropolitangewalt*, 89–90.

8. See Robert Somerville and Bruce C. Brasington, *Prefaces to Canon Law Books in Latin Christianity: Selected Translations, 500–1245* (New Haven, Conn.: Yale University Press, 1998), 72–74.

9. Canon 1.211, Fransen and Kölzer, *Decretorum Libri*, fol. 29r. Despite the Roman rubric, the variants followed the Ravennese text, which is unlikely to have been coincidental. Either cc. 1.25 and 211 were taken from two different councils (but why were two different sources with nearly identical texts used?), or the relations between the Roman and Ravennese canons need to be reexamined (were they actually different versions of the same council, or was there a lost intermediate step between the ninth and eleventh centuries, or did the lost manuscript witness to the Ravennese council rely partially on Burchard?). Four canons in the *Decretum* unrelated to the pallium also came from these two councils (Canons 11.30, 47–49, ibid., fols. 149v–150v). They too were falsely attributed to ancient popes and presented a confusing hodgepodge of the two traditions. See 46n62 above.

10. See JE 2030. Possible reasons for the falsification are the same as for c. 1.25, and work equally well no matter which council was the source.

an appropriate setting, for the abuse of the pallium was considered a serious offense, and being a bad shepherd was the antithesis of what it stood for (as explained in the formulas of the *Liber Diurnus*). This canon may have seemed pertinent because it concerned the proper conduct of the archbishop of Mainz. Once again, a pallium regulation in the *Decretum* may have served to remind the local metropolitan of the bounds of his power. Also, this interest in behavior as the outward expression of virtue was typical in the schools of this era, and a student at Worms could himself become a palliger one day.[11]

Around 1022 the *Collectio XII Partium*, a canonical corpus created in Freising during a period of lively exchange between that city and Worms, drew on the two Johannine canons known to Burchard and added the first two pallium-related canons of the *Anselmo Dedicata*.[12] Most of these it placed in a section concerning metropolitans and their rights, for the vestment and the office were by now firmly associated.[13] But *Quoniam quidam*, in accord with its rubric, was located among canons concerning episcopal ordinations, since that text treated the vestment as a prerequisite for such acts.[14] Moreover, when the collection was augmented around 1039, a text serving to introduce the first three canons on the pallium was inserted.[15] It was

---

11. See C. Stephen Jaeger, *The Envy of Angels: Cathedral Schools and Social Ideals in Medieval Europe, 950–1200* (Philadelphia: University of Pennsylvania Press, 1994). Heribert, later archbishop of Cologne, was educated at the cathedral school of Worms in the late tenth century.

12. See Kéry, *Canonical Collections*, 155–57, and Fowler-Magerl, *Clavis Canonum*, 91–93. On the collection's relationships with Burchard and the *Anselmo Dedicata*, see Jörg Müller, *Untersuchungen zur Collectio Duodecim Partium*, Abhandlungen zur rechtswissenschaftlichen Grundlagenforschung 73 (Ebelsbach: Gremer, 1989), 261–76, 316–25. For a different view of its relationship with Burchard, see Hartmut Hoffmann and Rudolf Pokorny, *Das Dekret des Bischofs Burchard von Worms: Textstufen, frühe Verbreitung, Vorlagen*, Monumenta Germaniae Historica Hilfsmittel 12 (Munich: Monumenta Germaniae Historica, 1991), 87–107. See also Greta Austin, "Secular Law in the *Collectio Duodecim Partium* and Burchard's *Decretum*," in *Bishops, Texts and the Use of Canon Law around 1100: Essays in Honour of Martin Brett*, ed. Bruce C. Brasington and Kathleen G. Cushing (Aldershot: Ashgate, 2008), 29–32.

13. Canons 1.28–30, *Clavis* TX01.028–030; in the augmented version, Canons 1.31–34, *Clavis* TW01.031–034.

14. Canon 1.54, *Clavis* TX01.054; in the augmented version, Canon 1.61, *Clavis* TW01.061.

15. See Müller, *Untersuchungen*, 235–60, 350–64, and Austin, "Secular Law," 32n15.

reworded from Rabanus Maurus's commentary on the vestment.[16] The general rubric (*de pallio*) hinted that the augmenter wished to explain the character of the vestment, and the text he chose did so by focusing on the symbolism of the pallium's crosses.[17]

Canon law is one useful measure of how pallium traditions were preserved. The character of this period, and how it appropriated these traditions, can also be gathered from various episodes in which the vestment figured at critical moments in ecclesiastical relationships. In each of the three cases that follow, popes were contending with prelates, and the pallium was exploited as a weapon by one side or the other. It was typical of an era when the papacy was struggling to exert control over powerful metropolitans, especially imperial ones such as the archbishops of Cologne, Salzburg, and Mainz.

An Archbishop with Ambitions

Relationships among palligers and the proper use of the pallium were still contested areas over which the papacy had to remain vigilant. In these respects Archbishop Herman I of Cologne ran afoul of two popes during his long tenure (ca. 890–924). When he took office, he tried to reassert Cologne's power over the diocese of Bremen, which had been its suffragan. The successors of Ansgar, the famous missionary to the north, now held Bremen because they needed its resources in order to maintain their new archbishopric of Ham-

---

16. Canon 1.31, Bamberg, Staatsbibliothek, Can. 7, fol. 6v. Perhaps there was an intermediate source that had paraphrased Rabanus, or perhaps the augmenter himself felt free to paraphrase because the source was not as authoritative as a pope or a council. This canon recurred elsewhere only in an undated addition to a ninth-century pontifical from Sens (St. Petersburg, Rossiyskaya Natsional'naya Biblioteka, Ms. Q. v. I no. 35, fol. 94v; see Niels Krogh Rasmussen, with the assistance of Marcel Haverals, *Les pontificaux du haut moyen âge: genèse du livre de l'évêque*, Spicilegium Sacrum Lovaniense, études et documents 49 [Louvain: Spicilegium Sacrum Lovaniense, 1998], 89–135), and in a slightly shortened form in the *Collectio X Partium*, Gerland of Besançon's *Candela*, and the interpolations to the *Panormia* in Arch. S. Pietro G.19bis.

17. The canon may have lacked an inscription because Rabanus did not have papal or conciliar authority, or because the text was seen, not as a canon, but as an explanatory preface to the subsequent pallium-related canons.

burg.[18] Herman had written to Pope Stephen V in an attempt to reclaim Bremen, but the pope found his reasoning preposterous, as he scornfully replied in 890:

> On that account we laughed, when we read that you had written that the good will of Gunther [of Cologne] once merited the use of the pallium from the apostolic see, so that [Ansgar] should preach the word of God more honorably and obey his archbishop. And we were amazed that your Prudence thought that the use of the pallium was bestowed on anyone at his pleasure, not for the honor of most sacred ministry but for the honor of worldly dignity. In other words, if a province is missing, and suffragans of whom he is in charge, it is doubtful how he merited the use of the pallium.[19]

Apparently Cologne contended that its former Archbishop Gunther, in whose time Ansgar was bishop of Bremen while carrying out his mission to the north, had agreed to a pallium for his suffragan Ansgar. Its alleged purpose, in keeping with the tradition of palliated missionaries, was to increase Ansgar's honor, so as to make his preaching more effective; yet somehow it was also supposed to reinforce his submission to his metropolitan in Cologne.[20] Stephen ridiculed this thinking, for a pallium in Bremen weakened Cologne's case. The pope was surprised at Herman's belief that the pallium could be granted so casually, as a mere honor instead of a badge of ecclesiastical ministry. Indeed, it implied jurisdiction over suffragan sees, and if they were lacking, the vestment would not have been granted.[21] According to this pope, where there was a pallium, there was a full-fledged province. Thus the archbishop had foolishly provided proof of Bremen's independence from Cologne.

---

18. On the convoluted history of the relationship between Hamburg and Bremen (made murkier by layers of forgery), and the resultant strife with Bremen's former metropolis of Cologne, see Knibbs, *Ansgar,* 211–20.

19. JL 3458, GP 7.1:37 no. 76, MGH Epp. 7:358–59.

20. In 864 Nicholas I had asserted that it was not Gunther's to grant Bremen the status of an archbishopric (to Louis the German, JE 2758, GP 6:30 no. 20, BH 705, MGH Epp. 6:291–92). Since gift-giving put the donor in a position of power over the recipient, Nicholas may have been trying to prevent the claim to Bremen's submission that Herman was now advancing.

21. Stephen was ignoring the phenomena of palliated missionaries, such as Boniface, and palliated suffragans, which were becoming rare in this period.

Near the end of his life, between 922 and 924, Herman tried again to elevate Cologne over Hamburg-Bremen and other sees when he requested a more frequent use of the pallium from Pope John X.[22] Perhaps Hincmar of Reims's falsified privilege, which had supposedly granted him daily use of the vestment, offered the idea; certainly its memory lived on in this century.[23] To Herman's petition for a similar honor, John, while cushioning his answer with effusive expressions of esteem, steadfastly replied *non audemus*: "The use of the pallium, which your Fraternity begs us to grant on all feast days, we dare not grant, for on nobody was it bestowed by our predecessors ... except on predesignated solemnities." The lack of precedent cited by the pope (ignoring the fabricated case of Hincmar) presumed the desirability of treating all palligers equally. John further forbade the archbishop's ambition, "since in fact the most blessed Pope Gregory forbade it too with very great testimony, and under oath altogether prohibited using the pallium except on prenamed festivities."[24] As always in questions relating to the vestment, Gregory the Great's example was normative.[25] The deeper reasons for restricting the palli-

22. Herman's suffragan Richer of Liège's acquisition of the pallium may have prompted the metropolitan to seek to expand his own use of the vestment in order to maintain his prestige (Harald Zimmermann, "Der Streit um das Lütticher Bistum vom Jahre 920/921: Geschichte, Quellen und kirchenrechtshistorische Bedeutung," *Mitteilungen des Instituts für österreichische Geschichtsforschung* 65 [1957]: 35).

23. Flodoard of Reims, *De Triumphis Christi*, in PL 135:815, and his *Historia Remensis Ecclesiae*, in MGH SS 36:206. Whether people in Cologne knew of this tradition in Herman's time, however, is uncertain.

24. JL 3568, GP 7.1:46 no. 103, BZ 62, ZPUU 1:87. "Testimony" probably meant the witnesses gathered by Gregory the Great to determine the customary use of the pallium in Ravenna (John the Deacon, *Vita Gregorii Magni*, in PL 75:172–76), and "oath" may have recalled the one through which he had attempted to gather further evidence (JE 1411, reproduced in the *Collectio IX Librorum* in Vat. lat. 1349, Canon 7.161, *Clavis* FY07.161).

25. The rule being cited is difficult to pinpoint. Gregory had been deeply concerned about pallium abuse, as seen in his clash with Ravenna. Or John may have been thinking of a Gregorian letter, such as the one in the *Collectio Anselmo Dedicata* indicating that the vestment should be worn at specific, traditionally determined times (Canon 1.126, Besse, "Liber Primus," 291, quoting JE 1905). But perhaps most likely was an invocation of the canon *Quicumque sane* from John VIII's councils, which forbade the use of the pallium except "on special festivities and times published by the apostolic see" and cited Gregorian texts to support its threat of deprivation (MGH Conc. 5:10, 68).

um's use remained unspoken, but they were urgent enough that the pope refused to relent, even for a prelate he claimed to regard highly.²⁶ This incident casts into suspicion the claim, apparently found only in Rutger of Cologne's *vita* of 968/69, that Herman's successor Bruno was permitted to wear the pallium "beyond custom, as often as he wished"; but that royal duke-archbishop's position was exceptional in many respects.²⁷

A Renegade Palliger, and Other Depositions

At the Council of Ravenna (967) Pope John XIII fulminated against the deposed Harold of Salzburg, who had conspired in a rebellion against Emperor Otto the Great:

> Harold, formerly archbishop of the church of Salzburg, against canonical and apostolic authority, with heinous presumption, is seen to celebrate the holy mystery after the loss of his eyes, and (what is ridiculous) to wear the pallium solemnly. Indeed, this belongs to no small heretical insanity, and ought to be regarded as accursed by us and by the prudence of all orthodox brethren, especially since his eyes were put out due to his own fault and the rashness of his treachery.... Consequently, every priestly duty was frequently forbidden him by our predecessors.²⁸

It was not the first papal complaint. In 962 Pope John XII had instructed the new archbishop, Frederick, to forbid Harold (*ille caecus*) to chant the Mass under pain of anathema, but he had said nothing about the pallium.²⁹ John XIII, reacting to new information, went further. For the blinded Harold to use the vestment, the pope claimed, was not only a violation of canon law and papal prohibition, but even *ridiculum*—probably not due to his blindness *per se*, but because that blindness was a punishment inflicted, along with deposition, for heinous crimes.³⁰ Removed from his see, he could not

---

26. Cf. Nicholas I to Hincmar of Reims in 866, JE 2823, BH 838, MGH Epp. 6:430.
27. MGH SSRG n.s. 10:27.
28. JL 3717, GP 1:15 no. 33, BZ 420, ZPUU 1:352.
29. JL 3689, GP 1:14–15 no. 31, BZ 302, ZPUU 1:279.
30. Blind bishops could not read the prayers prescribed in the liturgical books—a particular problem for solemn consecrations whose validity depended on their

wear the pallium once granted to him as archbishop in that see. This consequence may have been assumed as self-evident when Harold was deposed in 955, but now it had become necessary to link deprivation of the vestment explicitly to loss of ecclesiastical office. Although the pallium was a personal privilege, it was also given in virtue of a particular office, and meant to be worn during the liturgy. As Harold was permitted neither to celebrate Mass nor to exercise his office, the privilege was effectively revoked.

The link between deprivation and deposition was well known in the Roman church. Pope Silverius had been stripped of his pallium when the Byzantine authorities deposed him in the sixth century.[31] At a Lateran synod in the eighth century, a subdeacon had ripped off the irregularly elected Antipope Constantine's pallium and cast it at his feet, along with his ceremonial slippers.[32] Thus a key moment in, and a chief sign of, the deposition of a pope or the rejection of an antipope was the ritual removal of the pallium. In the present period this tradition lived on, and was enacted with similar drama at least once, as Liutprand of Cremona described soon after the event in 964. The papal claimant Benedict V entered a Lateran synod "clothed in pontifical vestments," and the cardinal archdeacon accused him: "'By what authority or by what law, invader, have you usurped these pontifical clothes for yourself while this our lord, the venerable Pope Leo, here present, survives, whom you, with us, elected to the pinnacle of the papacy?'"[33] Prostrate before Leo VIII and Otto the Great, Benedict confessed his crime and (at least in Liutprand's version) abdicated his usurped office.[34]

---

words. After a blind bishop had laid hands upon ordinands but had a priest recite the consecratory prayer, the Second Council of Seville (619) ruled that the improperly ordained clerics should be degraded. This canon was preserved in various collections, including the tenth-century *Collectio IX Librorum* in Vat. lat. 1349 (Canon 1.180, *Clavis* FY01.180). Despite this tradition, John applied his disparaging comment not to Harold's celebration of the Mass, but to his wearing of the pallium.

31. Duchesne, *Liber pontificalis*, 1:293. Cf. Aimoin of Fleury, *Historia Francorum*, in PL 139:679.

32. Duchesne, *Liber pontificalis*, 1:472. Duchesne argues convincingly that this text's *orarium* was the papal pallium. The papal slippers (*campagi*) were another papal insigne (ibid., 1:481-82nn20-21).

33. *Historia Ottonis*, in CCCM 156:182.

34. Since some questioned the legitimacy of Leo VIII's own pontificate, which

A Well-Worn Garment (882–1046)   189

He removed the pallium from himself. This, along with the pontifical staff that he was carrying in his hand, he returned to the lord Pope Leo. The same pope broke this staff and showed it broken to the people. Then he commanded Benedict to sit on the ground, and he removed from him the chasuble ... together with the stole. And afterwards he said to all the bishops: "We deprive Benedict, invader of the holy Roman and apostolic see, of every honor of pontificate and priesthood."[35]

This account gave chief place to the papal vestments, among them the pallium. These insignia were intimately representative (usurping the office required usurping the clothes) and even constitutive (being divested of the pallium and staff meant yielding the office).[36]

A Palliger Stripped

Confusingly, the pallium's use could be withdrawn as a penalty in its own right, without accompanying deposition. Another rare instance of deprivation in this period was the case of Aribo of Mainz, to which three non-papal letters are the only witnesses.[37] Countess Irmingard of Hammerstein, whom the archbishop had excommunicated for her consanguineous marriage, had appealed to Rome. In

---

began after the emperor had deposed John XII, it was important to convince the Roman church that Benedict V, elected during Leo's tenure to succeed John, had voluntarily resigned in Leo's favor. However, Adalbert of Magdeburg made the divestiture not an act of Benedict, but of Leo, who "tore apart" the pallium (*Continuatio Reginonis*, in MGH SSRG 50:174).

35. CCCM 156:182.

36. On the role of vestments and insignia in clerical degradation and restoration, see Roger E. Reynolds, "Rites of Separation and Reconciliation in the Early Middle Ages," in *Segni e riti nella chiesa altomedievale occidentale*, Settimane di studio del Centro italiano di studi sull'alto medioevo 33 (Spoleto: Sede del Centro, 1987), 1:421–22, 428–30; Timothy Reuter, "*Pastorale pedum ante pedes apostolici posuit*: Dis- and Reinvestiture in the Era of the Investiture Contest," in *Belief and Culture in the Middle Ages*, ed. Richard Gameson and Henrietta Leyser (Oxford: Oxford University Press, 2001), 197–210; and Dyan Elliott, "Dressing and Undressing the Clergy: Rites of Ordination and Degradation," in *Medieval Fabrications: Dress, Textiles, Clothwork, and Other Cultural Imaginings*, ed. E. Jane Burns (New York: Palgrave Macmillan, 2004), 55–69.

37. Philippus Jaffé, ed., *Bibliotheca Rerum Germanicarum*, vol. 3, *Monumenta Moguntina* (Berlin: Weidmann, 1866; reprinted in Aalen: Scientia, 1964), 358–63. See Richard Müller, *Erzbischof Aribo von Mainz, 1021–1031*, Historische Studien 3 (Leipzig: Veit, 1881), 21–36.

response, the provincial Council of Seligenstadt (1023), led by Aribo, forbade such appeals without the local bishop's permission. Pope Benedict VIII was not amused at this infringement of papal rights, and punished Aribo by prohibiting him from using his pallium.[38] Early in 1024 Aribo wrote to Meinhard I of Würzburg about his plight: "Based on the denunciation of the anathematized Irmingard, the pope has forbidden me the primary decorations of my dignity. From this fact, truly, when I face my conscience, I feel the greatest comfort. But when I observe what can happen to others, if this so easily slips by without discussion, great mourning immediately arises in me."[39] The censure had left him without the chief insigne of his office. Although he did not directly challenge the pope's action, he worried about the implications of so tyrannical an exercise of papal authority.

Aribo sounded less serene in a contemporaneous letter to Empress Cunigund. He complained "how unreasonably the pope had ridiculed me," and that "the honor of the pallium was forbidden to me, though unjustly," which was a "bitter calamity of lost honor."[40] While he accused the pope of lacking reason and justice, he still did not deny his right to inflict this punishment. Later in the year, at the provincial Council of Höchst (1024), Aribo's suffragans wrote passionately in his defense: "The crown of our head has fallen—in other words, the dignities of our metropolitan have been taken away.... Who could restrain himself from tears when an innocent metropolitan loses even a bit of dignity based on the denunciation of one woman?" Twice in the letter the pallium's loss was compared to deposition, although Aribo himself was not said to have been deposed.[41] The nature of the penalty, at least from his own standpoint,

---

38. *Monumenta Germaniae Historica: Constitutiones et Acta Publica Imperatorum et Regum* (Hannover: Hahn, etc., 1893–), 1:638 (cc. 16, 18) [hereafter "MGH Const."]. See Klaus-Jürgen Herrmann, *Das Tuskulanerpapsttum (1012–1046): Benedikt VIII., Johannes XIX., Benedikt IX,* Päpste und Papsttum 4 (Stuttgart: Hiersemann, 1973), 74–79, and BZ 1266–67.

39. Jaffé, *Bibliotheca,* 3:359. Beumann sees in the plural *ornatus primos* not only the use of the pallium, but also Mainz's papal vicariate, preeminence, and right to crown the king (*Theutonum nova metropolis,* 26–27).

40. Jaffé, *Bibliotheca,* 3:361.

41. To Benedict VIII, Jaffé, *Bibliotheca,* 3:362–63. When the bishops speculated

was rather injury to his prestige as a prelate. In an age when representation was key to retaining and wielding authority, such a loss was serious indeed.[42]

Aribo also testified to the pallium's nature as a gift expressing a bond between donor and recipient. After his own pallium had been taken away, the archbishop spoke somewhat bitterly in 1024 about his nephew Pilgrim of Cologne's reception of the vestment. Despite Benedict VIII's mistreatment of Aribo (which Pilgrim may have helped bring about), Pilgrim "both received [the pope's] gifts as an intimate and loaded him down with his own gifts as a friend."[43] Similarly, Aribo's suffragans begged the pope to restore to their metropolitan, "a son most devoted to you, the gift of love."[44] In both letters, the exchange of gifts with the pope, including the reception of the pallium, signified a favorable relationship. For Aribo to regain it would mean the recovery of the pope's good graces. Unfortunately, it appears that he never did.[45]

These episodes demonstrate that the pallium was still a living concern in this period. The popes who dealt with Herman, Harold, and Aribo drew on traditions that served the papacy well. Yet other popes were not nearly as energetic. Sometimes past practices were neglected, and they came close to letting the pallium escape their

---

that they themselves might be deposed, they may have been offering to share their metropolitan's punishment, because they had shared in the offending decision at Seligenstadt. Alternatively, they were alluding to the consequences of the pallium's loss, viz., the possible endangerment of their own orders when their consecrator lost the constitutive sign of his power to consecrate bishops (Herrmann, *Tuskulanerpapsttum*, 78).

42. See Fichtenau, *Living*, 64–70. The repercussions may have gone beyond the representational. In 1025 Aribo complained that the king had appointed Azecho bishop of Worms (and suffragan of Mainz) "without our counsel and consent," although he declared himself willing to perform the consecration (to the clergy and people of Worms, in *Monumenta Germaniae Historica: Briefe der deutschen Kaiserzeit* [Weimar: Böhlau, etc., 1949–], 3:30 [hereafter "MGH Briefe"]).

43. To Cunigund, Jaffé, *Bibliotheca*, 3:361. See Herrmann, *Tuskulanerpapsttum*, 77, 83.

44. In 1024, Jaffé, *Bibliotheca*, 3:363.

45. Benedict VIII died in 1024, and his successor, John XIX, never seems to have answered the synodal plea or issued any privileges for Aribo. The archbishop finally made a penitential pilgrimage to Rome in 1031, but died suddenly on the way home (Herrmann, *Tuskulanerpapsttum*, 78–79).

management (chapter 5). In certain respects, nevertheless, they expanded upon traditional themes, in an effort to make the vestment a more effective instrument of power (chapter 6). These mixed messages—which reveal no coherent papal plan—advance the story of the pallium from the end of the Carolingian age to 1046, when King Henry III at the Council of Sutri instigated a decisive shift in the papacy's direction. Many histories skim swiftly over these years due to the scarcity of surviving sources or the blinders of a periodization fixed on ninth- and twelfth-century renaissances. Far from a stagnant interlude, however, this period, despite its imperfections, manifested a resilient continuity, coupled with occasional flashes of resourceful initiative.

5

Carelessness

Though a suffragan with no precedent in his favor, Peter, bishop of Girona, managed to win the pallium from Pope John XIX in 1030. He did so by proposing an unusual deal: he would engineer the release of Spanish captives, as a good deed done on the pontiff's behalf, and John in turn would confer the vestment, effectively for the profit of his own soul. Implicit here was a theory of vicarious merit, that one person could apply the fruits of his virtuous acts to the soul of another.[1] In his grant the pope claimed to have taken the initiative: "Because, as pastoral concern prodded ... we asked, when you came to the thresholds of the apostles, if we could redeem some Spanish captives, you answered that you were willing and able to redeem and set free thirty captives for the remedy of our soul, if we granted you the use of the pallium."[2] Peter must have planned to use his contacts and resources to liberate the captives, probably captured in ongoing skirmishes with the Muslims. Perhaps the idea was really his; he certainly showed some cheeky ingenuity. The terms of the barter were

    1. Such a principle was operative in gifts *pro anima* (Bijsterveld, *Do ut des*, 20–21).
    2. JL 4089, BF 129, ZPUU 2:1109. Since 1019 Peter had sought closer contact with Rome to increase the status of his bishopric (Herrmann, *Tuskulanerpapsttum*, 129). See P. Kehr, *Das Papsttum und der katalanische Prinzipat bis zur Vereinigung mit Aragon*, Abhandlungen der preussischen Akademie der Wissenschaften, philosophisch-historische Klasse 1926.1 (Berlin: de Gruyter, 1926), 21–22.

193

telling: the vestment was a highly sought prize, especially for a bishop with no hope for it otherwise, worth the bargaining chip of thirty ransoms. John's capitulation showed that the "papal tool" into which the pallium had evolved could be employed in reverse to influence the pope himself. It had become such a plum that this bishop extorted it from the papacy, in what almost amounted to a purchase.[3]

The incident raises questions. Was the pope still master of the pallium? To what extent was it still a gift? Was it still a means of exercising power over bishops, or had it degenerated from a tool to a bauble? This surprising story was an isolated case. But it reflected a pattern of behavior in this period: the popes were not always as careful as their predecessors in managing the vestment. This pattern can be seen in three trends. To some degree, a predictable simplification followed the innovations of the Carolingian era, as the pallium became a routine element of ecclesiastical practice, less suited to exceptional situations. Yet the often weak papacy of this age must also be blamed for a good deal of negligence, as popes ignored or confused the finer points of the tradition and its possibilities for strengthening their position. Eventually, problems arose that surfaced the possibility that the popes might no longer retain control of the vestment. These three areas—routinization, neglect, and loss of control—represented deviations from the main developments observed thus far.

Routinization

It was a tribute to the achievements of the Carolingian popes that the pallium was so firmly linked to metropoles—and so regularly given to archbishops, who generally submitted to the requirement to request it—that its role became a routine aspect of ecclesiastical affairs.[4] Consequently, certain features of the tradition grew superflu-

3. In this case, gift-giving took the "economic" form of a well-defined exchange specifying the benefits for each party (White, "Politics," 179–80).
4. Based on the paucity of the sources, Schrör theorizes that pallium grants in this period were exceptional, and efforts to attain the vestment a rarity (*Metropolitangewalt*, 78). Yet there was arguably much more extensive activity than indicated by extant grants. E.g., Falkenstein, "Verlorene päpstliche Privilegien," surveys the evidence for the use of the pallium in Reims. Despite persuasive indications

ous and more or less ceased during this period.⁵ Either they were no longer needed (as was true for precedents, vicariates, and secular intercession), or they failed to mesh with the usual paradigm (as was true for exceptional situations, such as denials and palliated suffragans). Although this routinization does not demonstrate carelessness *per se*, it sets the stage by accounting for an inattentive conventionality that began to creep into papal habits.

Now that the provincial structure of the Latin church, with its fixed metropolitan sees, had been restored in the wake of the Carolingian reforms, citing precedents was no longer necessary when seeking the pallium. Only occasionally did the mention of previous conferrals embellish pallium grants. In 1008 Meingaud of Trier requested the pallium "according to the authority of [his] ancient predecessors of the same holy church of Trier, who used the same [vestment]," and Pope John XVIII consented: "We too, considering it unworthy to change the pious deeds of our predecessors to any extent, or rather wishing to confirm and strengthen them in all things, grant to your Bountifulness the grace of the same apparel."⁶ Nevertheless, by the eleventh century there was no need to offer evidence of Trier's metropolitan standing, as might have been done earlier.

Only in doubtful cases would precedents have been required. The premier example was Pilgrim of Passau's attempt in 973/74 to win the pallium. On the basis of a series of false papal precedents, many of them pallium grants, for an alleged ancient archbishopric of Lorch, Pilgrim tried to position himself as heir to that see—and thereby raise Passau to a metropolis.⁷ In one of these forgeries, Pope Agapitus II

---

that many of the archbishops from the mid-eighth through the twelfth century possessed the vestment, only one genuine pallium privilege before the pontificate of Innocent III has been preserved: Urban II's privilege for Rainald of Reims in 1089 (JL 5415, PL 151:309–11). Sylvester II's letter to Arnulf of Reims in 999 (JL 3908, BZ 867, ZPUU 2:712–14), with its cursory confirmation of the right to use the pallium, is not counted by Falkenstein (198n96).

5. Such an assertion is admittedly arguing *ex silentio*, but it is based on the totality of extant pallium-related evidence from this period. While textual survival is often haphazard, findings that are fairly consistent during a long period throughout the West may well indicate broader trends.

6. JL 3957, GP 10.1:51 no. 82, BZ 1032, ZPUU 2:842.

7. See Hacke, *Palliumverleihungen*, 3–16; Waldemar Lehr, *Piligrim, Bischof von Passau, und die Lorcher Fälschungen* (Berlin: Schade, 1909), 7–29; Heinrich Fichtenau,

allegedly knew which sees were metropolitan and were "owed" the vestment by consulting ancient evidence, "as we read in the authentic privileges constantly sent to us by you, after certain papyrus documents, very worn with age, had also been found in the archive of St. Peter."[8] The documents culminated in a petition to Benedict VI, but since the pope made no known reply, it is argued that Pilgrim gave up his plan when he encountered the fierce opposition of his metropolitan, Archbishop Frederick of Salzburg. In the reply Pilgrim drafted for the pope's endorsement (never obtained), Benedict was supposed to restore Lorch based on "the very ancient witnesses of privileges," which testified that the pope "owed" Lorch the pallium, as "commended by ancient apostolic authority."[9] Pilgrim would not have gone to such trouble to invent so many papal letters if the force of precedent were not an effective factor in acquiring the pallium. Yet, apart from this kind of aberration, such appeals were no longer called for, because the Western church's structure had become settled.

In addition, the papacy of this period, at least until John XIX in the early eleventh century, stopped attaching apostolic vicariates to pallium grants.[10] Perhaps one reason was the tradition that every palli-

---

"Zu den Urkundenfälschungen Pilgrims von Passau," in his *Beiträge zur Mediävistik: ausgewählte Aufsätze* (Stuttgart: Hiersemann, 1977), 2:157–79; Gerhart Marckhgott, "Bischof Pilgrim (971–991): Realpolitik und 'Lorcher Legende,'" in *Kirche in Oberösterreich: 200 Jahre Bistum Linz*, ed. Helga Litschel (Linz: Land Oberösterreich, 1985), 51–62; and Beumann, *Theutonum nova metropolis*, 88–110.

8. JL †3644, GP 1:165 no. †17, BZ †217, ZPUU 1:204.

9. JL †3771, GP 1:166–67 no. †19, BZ †514, ZPUU 1:438–39. Pilgrim's petition asked Benedict to confirm the (forged) papal privileges that he was sending for consideration (Richard Marsina, ed., *Codex Diplomaticus et Epistolaris Slovaciae* [Bratislava: Academia Scientiarum Slovaca, 1971], 1:42), which must have included JK †767, GP 1:159–60 no. †1; JE †2566, GP 1:162 no. †10; JL †3602, GP 1:164 no. †15, BZ †120; and JL †3644, GP 1:165 no. †17, BZ †217.

10. Apparently under John XIX the custom was revived. In 1027 he exalted Aquileia as a "vicarious" second Rome (to Poppo, JL 4085, IP 7.1:29–30 no. 53, BF 101, ZPUU 2:1093). He also offered a sort of limited or emergency vicariate to Thietmar II of Salzburg in 1026 and Bardo of Mainz in 1032 (JL 4074, GP 1:17 no. 37, BF 66, ZPUU 2:1073; and JL 4098, GP 4:89 no. 110, BF 149, ZPUU 2:1122). Herrmann believes that the Mainz vicariate was an accommodation to Bardo's predecessor Aribo's resistance to appeals to Rome, as pronounced at the Council of Seligenstadt in 1023 (*Tuskulanerpapsttum*, 79), but he offers no account of the earlier Salzburg vicariate.

ated metropolitan was effectively a vicar of the pope.[11] The chancery of Archbishop Frederick of Salzburg, attempting to foil the forgeries of Pilgrim of Passau with its own forgery (or perhaps a draft that never received papal approval), articulated this tradition through the mouth of Pope Benedict VI: "As was needed and fitting, the holy successors of blessed Peter the apostle appointed archbishops throughout [various] locales, who would hold their place in the churches, for they could not rule all the churches themselves."[12] Since it was a non-Roman document, and one meant to sound genuine, it appears likely that contemporaries were not unfamiliar with the idea, and that it served the interests of, and was advanced by, churchmen beyond the popes.[13] Moreover, around 1039 the augmented version of the *Collectio XII Partium* from Freising used Rabanus Maurus's words to introduce its pallium-related canons: "The honor of the pallium is decreed for a supreme pontiff, that is, an archbishop, because of his apostolic vicariate."[14] This explanation viewed the *summus pontifex*, a bishop above other bishops, as a local representative of Roman authority, which justified his use of a papal vestment, once commonly given to papal vicars. Freising was a suffragan of Salzburg, and conceivably both Frederick's forgery and Freising's invocation of Rabanus reflected a Bavarian interest.

Yet it was not limited to Bavaria. Rutger of Cologne was also conscious that the pallium brought with it a share in the pope's own responsibility. According to the *vita* he wrote in 968/69, Bruno of Cologne had been endowed with the pallium, allowed to wear it whenever he desired (as the pope did), and put on par with the pope himself: "After everything that was asked for had been granted, he was admitted, due to the greatness of his virtue and wisdom, to partnership in [the pope's] work—and nearly to the common seat

---

11. See Schrör, *Metropolitangewalt*, 78–79.
12. JL 3767, GP 1:16 no. †35, BZ †515, ZPUU 1:441–42. It then granted a papal vicariate to Frederick and his successors, as his predecessors had allegedly also received. See Beumann, *Theutonum nova metropolis*, 90–91.
13. See Kempf, "Primatiale und episkopal-synodale Struktur," 55–56.
14. Canon 1.31, Bamberg, Staatsbibliothek, Can. 7, fol. 6v: "Summo pontifici, hoc est archiepiscopo, propter apostolicam uicem pallii honor decernitur." See 85n46 above.

[*consessus*] of such a great dignity."[15] Accepted as a papal collaborator in the oversight of the churches, as were all metropolitans, Bruno was imagined as sharing Peter's chair itself. When such ideas were accepted, there was no longer need for vicariates explicitly connected to the pallium.[16]

In contrast with earlier times, instances of secular intercession during this period were rare. The papacy may have been largely beholden to secular rulers, but those rulers' power meant that they did not need to submit to begging. The influence of lay lords seldom appeared in pallium grants; even when it did, the role it played was vague or limited. According to Flodoard of Reims in the mid-tenth century, Archbishop Fulk of Reims had written to Charles the Fat "for the sake of receiving the pallium from the Roman see."[17] It is not clear, however, what part the emperor was being asked to take. At least twice Otto the Great used his influence to increase the number of days on which German archbishops could wear the pallium. In 962, the year Otto was crowned emperor, Pope John XII increased the pallium days of Frederick of Salzburg "because of the petition of the most serene and unconquered Emperor Otto," and a few days later did the same for Henry of Trier, "out of love for the most pious King Otto, our spiritual son."[18] Both prelates had already received the pallium; these acts merely enhanced the original privileges.

---

15. MGH SSRG n.s. 10:27–28. See Henry Mayr-Harting, *Church and Cosmos in Early Ottonian Germany: The View from Cologne* (Oxford: Oxford University Press, 2007), 1–63, esp. 49, where he calls Bruno clearly "Rome-orientated," as also seen in his acquisition of Peter's staff and chains and his enlargement of St. Peter's cathedral in Cologne (MGH SSRG n.s. 10:31–32).

16. Occasionally a vicariate was granted separately from the vestment. Although, e.g., William of Mainz thanked Agapitus II in 955 for both gifts (Jaffé, *Bibliotheca*, 3:347), the letter in which the pope had appointed him vicar (JL 3668, GP 4:75 no. 65, BZ 246, ZPUU 1:237–38) did not mention the pallium, which must have come separately. Even if every pallium grant contained an implicit (though vague) vicariate, William's specially granted vicariate was not necessarily redundant, for it signified Mainz's preeminence, in a tradition reaching back to Boniface.

17. *Historia Remensis Ecclesiae*, in MGH SS 36:380.

18. JL 3689, GP 1:14–15 no. 31, BZ 302, ZPUU 1:279; and JL 3691, GP 10.1:43 no. 63, BZ 303, ZPUU 1:281. Helmut Beumann suggests that the emperor obtained the increase for all the German archbishops—except Cologne, where Bruno wore the pallium whenever he wished, and Magdeburg, still being erected—and so pos-

Later, in 998, Pope Gregory V renewed the right to use the pallium for Alfanus I of Benevento "through the intercession" of Otto III, although this privilege was probably meant simply to ensure the succession of the archbishop's nephew, Alfanus II.[19] And in 1014 Pope Benedict VIII confirmed the archiepiscopal rights of the same Alfanus II, including the pallium, "on account of the intercession and petition" of Henry II.[20] Yet here again it was a case of a second privilege, perhaps a renewal, rather than an original grant. Finally, around 1027 King Canute of England negotiated with the pope (apparently successfully) on behalf of his archbishops, who were dismayed at the costs and hardships of the long journey to Rome for the pallium.[21] But none of the above situations clearly followed the classic model of royal intervention, in which the ruler's petition secured the vestment for a subject prelate. Perhaps the distribution of the pallium had become so routine, at least for established metropolitans, that the good word of the local authorities was no longer needed.

The popes of this period seemed reluctant to withhold the pallium or impose conditions upon its reception. Forceful antecedents, such as the case of Syagrius of Autun, were known to contemporaries.[22] And a theoretical basis for depriving palligers of their gift was still in circulation, since the papal chancery continued to produce pallium grants modeled on Pope Gregory IV's revision of the *Si pastores ovium* formula, with its minatory clause.[23] The principle enunciated

---

its *deperdita* for Hamburg and Mainz ("Das Kaisertum Ottos des Grossen: ein Rückblick nach tausend Jahren," in his *Wissenschaft vom Mittelalter: ausgewählte Aufsätze* [Cologne: Böhlau, 1972], 435–38); but see Michael F. La Plante, "A Deperditum for Mainz in 962?," *Archiv für Diplomatik* 25 (1979): 33–36.

19. JL 3884, IP 9:56 no. 19, BZ 822, ZPUU 2:680. See ZPUU 2:679.
20. JL 4005, IP 9:57 no. 21, BZ 1135, ZPUU 2:923.
21. To the English bishops, Whitelock et al., *Councils*, 1:510.
22. Transmitted in the *Collectio Anselmo Dedicata*, Canons 1.123, 125, Besse, "Liber Primus," 287, 290, quoting JE 1491, 1751.
23. Stephen V to Herman I of Cologne in 890, JL 3457, GP 7.1:36 no. 72, Wisplinghoff, *Rheinisches Urkundenbuch*, 2:160; Anastasius III to Ragimbert of Vercelli in 912, JL 3550, IP 6.2:11–12 no. 15, BZ 7, ZPUU 1:60; John XII to Henry of Trier in 957, JL 3682, GP 10.1:42 no. 62, BZ 275, ZPUU 1:263–64; a Passau forgery attributed to Leo VII, JL †3602, GP 1:164 no. †15, BZ †120, ZPUU 1:117; Sergius IV to Alfanus II of Benevento in 1011, JL 3970, IP 9:56–57 no. 20, BZ 1054, ZPUU 2:856;

in that clause—that improper use of the vestment could result in its removal—effectively made all such grants conditional. Nevertheless, the popes seldom exercised their right to deny or remove the pallium. Only three examples, widely separated in time—a conditional grant to Theodosius of Split in 888, the condemnation of Harold of Salzburg in 967, and the punishment of Aribo of Mainz in 1023—can be cited.[24] An often weak papacy, sometimes unaware of provincial misbehavior, coupled with the expectation that metropolitans would gain the vestment as a matter of course (and retain it for life), may explain these facts.

The phenomenon of palliated suffragans also receded. These exceptional situations, when popes chose to decorate non-metropolitan bishops, did not fit the dominant paradigm. Some grants to suffragans in this age were made only in view of a connection to a metropolis. Theodosius, bishop of Nin, was promised the pallium in 888 after his election as metropolitan of Split, which he seems to have held simultaneously with his first see.[25] In 900 Argrim was permitted to keep the pallium he had once had as archbishop of Lyon when he returned to his former see of Langres.[26] Grants to suffragans in the strictest sense were just as scarce. The only extant authentic letter of Pope Anastasius III bestowed the pallium on Ragimbert, bishop of Vercelli, in 912.[27] Because it was an important city in Berengar I's Italian realm, this gesture may have been a favor to the king.[28] Also, at the end of a schism in Liège in 921, Richer had emerged (according to

---

and Benedict VIII to Vitalis of Dubrovnik in 1022, JL 4042, BZ 1252, ZPUU 2:1027. By John's time in JL 3682, this quotation from JE 1326 was no longer recognized as such, for his chancery generalized its attribution and substituted a newer term for "sacristy." In JL 3970 Sergius revised the quotation in form but not in gist, added "synods" to the phrase restricting the use of the pallium to the Mass, and reworded the threat of deprivation. In JL 4042 Benedict wove together the quotation with the original clause of *Si pastores ovium* that it had replaced.

24. Stephen V, JL 3448, MGH Epp. 7:351; John XIII, JL 3717, GP 1:15 no. 33, BZ 420, ZPUU 1:352; and letters of Aribo and the Council of Höchst (1024), Jaffé, *Bibliotheca*, 3:358–63.
25. Stephen V, JL 3448, MGH Epp. 7:351.
26. Benedict IV, JL 3527, ZPUU 1:25.
27. JL 3550, IP 6.2:11–12 no. 15, BZ 7, ZPUU 1:59–60.
28. See ZPUU 1:59 (*pace* Martí, *Palio*, 135–36).

Folcuin of Lobbes, writing sixty years later) as the papally approved claimant, "with the archiepiscopal pallium presented to him alone of all his predecessors."[29] The irony of calling the vestment *archiepiscopale*, though conferred on a suffragan, not only highlighted Richer's distinction but was also a slap in the face of his metropolitan, Herman I of Cologne, who had ordained his rival Hilduin and failed to appear when Pope John X judged the case.[30] The four instances just described took place in the first decades of this period; by its end, one is hard pressed to find any.[31]

Neglect

Some trends in this period went beyond routinization and can better be explained by papal negligence, at least in comparison with the tighter control exercised by many Carolingian popes. Opportunities for bolstering Roman involvement and oversight or subordinating bishops to the apostolic see seem to have been passed by without reason. Although the usual patterns of handling the pallium remained by and large in place, it must be admitted that the popes were sometimes careless. This carelessness can be seen in two notable respects: they relaxed their attention to certain traditional concerns, and they gave inconsistent signals about the nature of the privilege of pallium use.

Whither Orthodoxy and Equality?

First, these popes were not as fastidious as their predecessors when approving statements of faith. Most contemporary pallium grants followed one or more of the *Liber Diurnus* formulas, two of which (*Si pastores ovium* and *Officium sacerdotis*) contained a clause accepting the submitted profession of faith while also lamenting its in-

29. *Gesta Abbatum Lobiensium*, in MGH SS 4:63 (JL *3566).
30. See Zimmermann, "Streit," 34–35.
31. But cf. the extraordinary case of Peter of Girona (John XIX in 1030, JL 4089, BF 129, ZPUU 2:1109) and the probably misunderstood case of John the Lamb, bishop of Tongeren (J. Barbier, ed., "La vie de saint Monon," *Analectes pour servir à l'histoire ecclésiastique de la Belgique* 5 [1868]: 411, and "Passio S. Mononis," *Analecta Bollandiana* 5 [1886]: 199).

adequacy.³² Of the sixteen documents that drew on these two formulas in this period, however, only three included the profession clause.³³ The others omitted it, presumably because the profession was deemed satisfactory and required no comment.³⁴ The lack of evidence may hint that the maintenance of orthodoxy among the higher clergy was not as pressing a concern as it had once been.³⁵ Here-

32. V45–46, Foerster, *Liber Diurnus,* 103–5, with slight variants C44–45 on 202–3 and A39–40 on 302–3, 305.

33. John XII to Henry of Trier in 962, JL 3691, GP 10.1:43 no. 63, BZ 303, ZPUU 1:281; John XIII to Atto of Vic in 971, JL 3747, BZ 477, ZPUU 1:410; and John XIV to Alo of Benevento in 983, JL 3822, IP 9:56 no. 17, BZ 626, ZPUU 1:553. The first document described the profession as "full of reason," rather than the standard "correct," perhaps because it was unusually eloquent or thoughtful; however, the wording may have been chosen by the recipient (Egon Boshof, *Das Erzstift Trier und seine Stellung zu Königtum und Papsttum im ausgehenden 10. Jahrhundert: der Pontifikat des Theoderich* [Cologne: Böhlau, 1972], 48–49). Gregory IV's form of *Si pastores ovium* ordinarily lacked the profession clause, but a Passau forgery that followed this form included it, though slightly corrupted (attributed to Leo VII, JL †3602, GP 1:164 no. †15, BZ †120, ZPUU 1:118). Perhaps the forger hoped to make his work seem more authentic, but this violation of Gregory IV's pattern only confirmed its inauthenticity.

34. Seven clearly omitted the clause: John XII to Dunstan of Canterbury in 960, JL 3687, BZ 284; Leo VIII to Rodwald of Aquileia in 963, JL 3701, IP 7.1:27–28 no. 45, BZ 338; John XIII to Theoderic of Trier in 965, JL 3737, GP 10.1:45 no. 68, BZ 457; Benedict VIII to Vitalis of Dubrovnik in 1022, JL 4042, BZ 1252; John XIX to Peter of Girona in 1030, JL 4089, BF 129; John XIX to Bardo of Mainz in 1032, JL 4098, GP 4:89 no. 110, BF 149; and Benedict IX to Hugh I of Besançon in 1037, JL —, GaP 1:44–45 no. 21, BF 199. The other six used the formulas only partially, and so their omission of the clause may not have been intentional: Leo VII to Adaldag of Hamburg in 937/39, JL 3612, GP 6:45 no. 46, BZ 133; John XIII to Adalbert of Magdeburg in 968, JL 3728, GP 4:78 no. 74, BZ 450; Benedict VII to Willigis of Mainz in 975, JL 3784, GP 4:79 no. 77, BZ 542; John XV to Hartwig of Salzburg in 993, JL 3851, GP 1:16 no. 36, BZ 719; John XVIII to Meingaud of Trier in 1008, JL 3957, GP 10.1:51 no. 82, BZ 1032; and Benedict IX to Amatus III of Salerno in 1036, JL 4032, IP 8:348–49 no. 17, BF 190.

35. It is also conceivable that the profession clause was sometimes omitted because the petitioner had made the profession orally before the pope. In any event, petitions continued to include professions of faith, if Pilgrim of Passau's draft to Benedict VI was any indication (Marsina, *Codex,* 1:42–43). He introduced his profession as a way to persuade the pope that he would not lead into falsehood the flock he was charged with enlightening. He then incorporated an abridged version of the creed promulgated by the Eleventh Council of Toledo (675), which was highly regarded in the medieval church as an authentic expression of patristic doctrine (Joseph Madoz, *Le symbole du XIe concile de Tolède: ses sources, sa date, sa valeur,* Spicilegium Sacrum Lovaniense, études et documents 19 [Louvain: Spicilegium Sacrum

tics did not arise in significant numbers until after the millennium, and perhaps the tenth-century papacy, entangled in more worldly problems, relaxed its vigilance over doctrine, at least compared to the more intellectually inquisitive era of the Carolingians.[36]

Second, palliated metropolitans sometimes had to struggle, with or without papal support, to realize the "equal and distinct" status theoretically allotted to them. In 968 Pope John XIII allowed the newly created archbishop of Magdeburg to wear the pallium on the same occasions as two other German metropolitans, the archbishops of Mainz and Trier.[37] By no means an inconsequential liturgical rule, this parity in pallium days was a favor and sign of prestige, for it placed Magdeburg on the same level as the empire's older and more powerful metropoles. It is likely, however—to judge from Magdeburg's later efforts—that it encountered resistance to this envisioned equality. For evidence one must turn to forgeries, which offer an avenue not only into the forgers' concerns, but also into the historical situations that spurred those concerns. Probably working under Archbishop Tagino in 1011/12, the interpolator of Pope Benedict VII's 981 privilege added: "In the order of standing and sitting, and in handling all ecclesiastical business, [the archbishop of Magdeburg] should be equal in all things to the archbishops, namely of Mainz, Trier, and Cologne. Indeed, our apostolic judgment has decreed that the church of Magdeburg will be equal and just like these and the others."[38] Likewise, the

---

Lovaniense, 1938], 144–62). Finally, he added a sort of oath to assure the pope that he would keep this faith.

36. See Fichtenau, *Living*, 400–402, and Malcolm Lambert, *Medieval Heresy: Popular Movements from the Gregorian Reform to the Reformation*, 3rd ed. (Malden, Mass.: Blackwell, 2002), 14–40.

37. To Adalbert, JL 3728, GP 4:78 no. 74, BZ 450, ZPUU 1:375. Nevertheless, neither Theoderic of Trier's list of pallium days from 965 (John XIII, JL 3737, GP 10.1:45 no. 68, BZ 457, ZPUU 1:388) nor Willigis of Mainz's from 975 (Benedict VII, JL 3784, GP 4:79 no. 77, BZ 542, ZPUU 1:472)—the closest extant lists for the two sees—agreed with Adalbert of Magdeburg's. See Beumann, *Theutonum nova metropolis*, 35.

38. JL 3808, GP 5.2:214–15 no. 19, BZ 600, ZPUU 1:531. See Mogens Rathsack, *Die fuldaer Fälschungen: eine rechtshistorische Analyse der päpstlichen Privilegien des Klosters Fulda von 751 bis ca. 1158*, trans. Preben Kortnum Mogensen, with the assistance of Harald Zimmermann, Päpste und Papsttum 24 (Stuttgart: Hiersemann, 1989), 1:263–71, and Beumann, *Theutonum nova metropolis*, 177–82. "The others" probably meant Hamburg and Salzburg.

interpolator of Pope Benedict VIII's grant to Walthard of Magdeburg in 1012 inserted the right "to be equal in all things to the archbishops of Trier, Cologne, and Mainz."[39] Magdeburg's persistent declaration of parity can be explained by the other sees' tendency to differentiate themselves, based partly on antiquity of pedigree.[40]

Yet Magdeburg tried to reach too far, even to outshine its rivals. The failure of a draft privilege to gain acceptance in Rome in 1003 (if in fact it was ever presented to the pope, and not meant for a German audience) must have been due to its inflated claims.[41] Among them was its conferral on the archbishops of the right "to wear the pallium both in their own church and in others, as required by a journey."[42] A later interpolator drew on this language when he added a similar right to Pope Benedict VIII's 1012 grant.[43] Even prelates who traveled much, perhaps accompanying the royal court in an era when the exercise of power was itinerant, had never received permission to wear the vestment outside their own churches.[44] This ef-

39. JL 3989, GP 10.1:51 no. 83, BZ 1100, ZPUU 2:897. The phrase was taken from a draft privilege, locally produced in 1003, that Pope John XVIII had never endorsed (JL †3823, BZ †738 = †981a, ZPUU 2:785). See Rathsack, *Fuldaer Fälschungen*, 1:261–63, and Beumann, *Theutonum nova metropolis*, 1–6, 120–69, 198–202. The latter dates the draft to 1004.

40. See Zotz, "Pallium," 163–71. Zotz explains that Magdeburg's standing was defined as *cum primis prima et cum antiquis antiqua* and modeled on that of Mainz and Trier; the three Rhenish archbishoprics possessed a special place in the imperial church, but Cologne may have been omitted because Bruno's privilege of unlimited use made it incomparable. Zotz also shows that Trier may have reacted against Magdeburg's claims when it obtained special rights from the pope shortly after the new archbishopric's erection.

41. The most excessive was that the archbishops of Magdeburg were "to be enthroned only by a messenger of the Roman see" and were permitted "to have partnership among the cardinal bishops of our see" (JL †3823, BZ †738 = †981a, ZPUU 2:784–85). See Beumann, *Theutonum nova metropolis*, 192–97, 203–9.

42. JL †3823, BZ †738 = †981a, ZPUU 2:784.

43. To Walthard of Magdeburg, JL 3989, GP 10.1:51 no. 83, BZ 1100, ZPUU 2:897.

44. Hincmar of Reims had attested that he rarely had the chance to wear the pallium because he was rarely in his see, thanks to his travels on behalf of church and kingdom (to Nicholas I in 867, MGH Epp. 8.1:216). Beumann believes, however, that the right to anoint the king, mentioned in Benedict VII's 975 privilege for Willigis of Mainz (JL 3784, GP 4:79 no. 77, BZ 542, ZPUU 1:472)—in the exercise of which the archbishop would have used the pallium, as Urban II later made explicit (to Rainald of Reims in 1089, JL 5415, PL 151:311)—must have allowed him

fort to expand the use of the pallium, especially if meant to include places outside the archbishop's own province, would have violated the bounds traditionally set by the popes to mark a metropolitan's limited jurisdiction.[45]

Similarly, other archbishops tried to ignore or reinterpret the principle of equality among palligers. A twelfth-century interpolator added a confirmation of Canterbury's primacy over York to Pope John XII's 960 privilege for Archbishop Dunstan.[46] And a falsifier inserted a renewal of Aquileia's supposedly ancient primacy in Pope Leo VIII's 963 grant to Patriarch Rodwald, "that it should be held first after the Roman see among all the Italian sees of God's churches."[47] Against Hincmar's maxim that every metropolitan was a primate within his own province, these sees sought superiority over other provinces, and they considered pallium grants to be appropriate venues for such claims.

Eventually the popes themselves began coupling primatial prerogatives to pallium grants, despite the violation of the "equal and distinct" standard. When Pope Benedict VII bestowed the pallium on Willigis of Mainz in 975, he incorporated a personal preeminence: "By [the pallium] you should stand out more prominently (after the pinnacle of the supreme pontiff) than all the rest, both archbishops and bishops, in all ecclesiastical affairs in all Germany and Gaul,

---

to wear the vestment outside Mainz, e.g., when crowning Otto III in Aachen in 983 (*Theutonum nova metropolis*, 85–86).

45. Indications of the places in which the pallium could be worn were rare, usually presumed from the restriction to the Mass, which took place within church. In 989 John XV allowed Libentius I of Hamburg to don the vestment anywhere within his province, "in all places on both banks of the Elbe River" (JL 3835, GP 6:50–51 no. 61, BZ 677, ZPUU 1:585). The wording reflected the fact that Bremen (south of the Elbe) had been united to Hamburg (north of the Elbe). Perhaps the missionary status of the area spurred this broad permission; still, it cannot be supposed to have extended outside of churches. In 1036 Benedict IX clarified that Amatus III of Salerno could wear his pallium when celebrating Mass or ordinations in his cathedral (JL 4032, IP 8:348–49 no. 17, BF 190, ZPUU 2:1132–33). This reading was probably also the correct one in earlier, more garbled privileges for Salerno.

46. JL 3687, BZ 284, ZPUU 1:273. An apostolic vicariate was also included. See Levison, *England*, 201n4, and R. W. Southern, "The Canterbury Forgeries," *The English Historical Review* 73 (1958): 205–6, 211.

47. JL 3701, IP 7.1:27–28 no. 45, BZ 338, ZPUU 1:300.

that is, in consecrating the king and holding a synod, by apostolic authority."[48] By virtue of the vestment—literally, because it distinguished the wearer, but also because it represented papal authority—the archbishop would take the lead before all other imperial prelates. Pope John XIX went further in 1027 by acceding to imperial demands to prefer Poppo of Aquileia over his rival, the patriarch of Grado, and designating Aquileia "head and metropolis over all the churches of Italy."[49] Thus Aquileia finally attained its primacy, and the papacy modified, albeit under pressure, its traditional treatment of palliated metropolitans as equals.

Personal or Ecclesial?

The use of the pallium was still regarded as a prerogative granted to an individual, but its connection to metropolitan sees more and more clouded the distinction between the personal and the ecclesial. During the first half of this period, the phrase *diebus vitae tuae tantummodo*, limiting the privilege to the recipient's lifetime, continued to preface pallium grants, which regularly followed the formulas of the *Liber Diurnus*.[50] From the time of Pope John XIII, however, the papal

---

48. JL 3784, GP 4:79 no. 77, BZ 542, ZPUU 1:472. See Heinrich Büttner, "Erzbischof Willigis von Mainz (975–1011)," in *Zur frühmittelalterlichen Reichsgeschichte an Rhein, Main und Neckar*, ed. Alois Gerlich (Darmstadt: Wissenschaftliche Buchgesellschaft, 1975), 305–6; La Plante, "Deperditum," 35–36; Schrör, *Metropolitangewalt*, 77–78; and Beumann, *Theutonum nova metropolis*, 7–22, who interprets this status as a papal vicariate. By *Germania et Gallia* the pope meant the parts of the empire on both sides of the Rhine.

49. JL 4085, IP 7.1:29–30 no. 53, BF 101, ZPUU 2:1093.

50. Variants of the phrase occurred in the protocols of at least ten documents: Stephen V to Herman I of Cologne in 890, JL 3457, GP 7.1:36 no. 72, Wisplinghoff, *Rheinisches Urkundenbuch*, 2:159; Sergius III to Hoger of Hamburg in 911, JL †3549, GP 6:43 no. 42, ZPUU 1:56; Anastasius III to Ragimbert of Vercelli in 912, JL 3550, IP 6.2:11–12 no. 15, BZ 7, ZPUU 1:59; Leo VII to Adaldag of Hamburg in 937/39, JL 3612, GP 6:45 no. 46, BZ 133, ZPUU 1:130; John XII to Henry of Trier in 957, JL 3682, GP 10.1:42 no. 62, BZ 275, ZPUU 1:263; John XII to Dunstan of Canterbury in 960, JL 3687, BZ 284, ZPUU 1:273; John XII to Henry of Trier in 962, JL 3691, GP 10.1:43 no. 63, BZ 303, ZPUU 1:280; Leo VIII to Rodwald of Aquileia in 963, JL 3701, IP 7.1:27–28 no. 45, BZ 338, ZPUU 1:299; a Passau forgery attributed to Symmachus, JK †767, GP 1:159–60 no. †1, Lehr, *Piligrim*, 30; and a Passau forgery attributed to Leo VII, JL †3602, GP 1:164 no. †15, BZ †120, ZPUU 1:116. These followed *Si pastores ovium*, either the original or Gregory IV's revision; but JK †767 followed *Pallii usum*.

chancery omitted this proviso from both formulaic grants and newly emerging non-formulaic grants.[51] A few letters, moreover, incorporated precisely the opposite condition. The phrase *suisque successoribus in perpetuum*, a formula of perpetuity customarily attached to solemn privileges, turned up in pallium grants occasionally.[52] It was as if the lifelong, personal nature of this special kind of privilege was being forgotten. But suddenly, if only sporadically, the chancery seems to have realized the problem. The old phrase *diebus vitae tuae tantummo-*

51. The phrase was lacking in at least eleven formulaic grants: John XIII to Theoderic of Trier in 965, JL 3737, GP 10.1:45 no. 68, BZ 457; John XIII to Adalbert of Magdeburg in 968, JL 3728, GP 4:78 no. 74, BZ 450; John XIII to Atto of Vic in 971, JL 3747, BZ 477; Benedict VII to Willigis of Mainz in 975, JL 3784, GP 4:79 no. 77, BZ 542; John XIV to Alo of Benevento in 983, JL 3822, IP 9:56 no. 17, BZ 626; John XV to Hartwig of Salzburg in 993, JL 3851, GP 1:16 no. 36, BZ 719; Gregory V to Gerbert of Ravenna in 998, JL 3883, IP 5:52 no. 166, BZ 830; John XVIII to Meingaud of Trier in 1008, JL 3957, GP 10.1:51 no. 82, BZ 1032; Benedict VIII to Walthard of Magdeburg in 1012, JL 3989, GP 10.1:51 no. 83, BZ 1100; Benedict VIII to Gero of Magdeburg in 1012, JL 3990, BZ 1101; and Benedict IX to Hugh I of Besançon in 1037, JL —, GaP 1:44–45 no. 21, BF 199. These followed one or more of the *Liber Diurnus* pallium formulas. In addition, the phrase was lacking in at least eleven non-formulaic grants: John XIII to Landulf of Benevento in 969, JL 3738, IP 9:54–55 no. 15, BZ 459; a Passau forgery attributed to Agapitus II, JL †3644, GP 1:165 no. †17, BZ †217; John XV to Libentius I of Hamburg in 989, JL 3835, GP 6:50–51 no. 61, BZ 677; Gregory V to Alfanus I of Benevento in 998, JL 3884, IP 9:56 no. 19, BZ 822; Sergius IV to Alfanus II of Benevento in 1011, JL 3970, IP 9:56–57 no. 20, BZ 1054; Benedict VIII to Alfanus II of Benevento in 1014, JL 4005, IP 9:57 no. 21, BZ 1135; Benedict VIII to Poppo of Trier in 1016, JL 4010, GP 10.1:52 no. 85, BZ 1169; Benedict VIII to Humphrey of Magdeburg in 1024, JL 4058, GP 7.1:54 no. 134, BZ 1271; John XIX to Poppo of Aquileia in 1027, JL 4085, IP 7.1:29–30 no. 53, BF 101; John XIX to Peter of Girona in 1030, JL 4089, BF 129; and John XIX to Bardo of Mainz in 1032, JL 4098, GP 4:89 no. 110, BF 149. These were freely composed or drew on non-pallium-related formulas (although JL 4058, JL 4089, and JL 4098 drew on *Si pastores ovium* for their admonitions only). This list excludes privileges for archbishops of Salerno that assumed and regulated the use of the pallium without explicitly conferring it (e.g., John XV to Grimwald of Salerno in 994, JL 3852, IP 8:346 no. 12, BZ 720, ZPUU 1:626).

52. Variants of the phrase occurred in the protocols of at least five documents: John XIV to Alo of Benevento in 983, JL 3822, IP 9:56 no. 17, BZ 626, ZPUU 1:552; John XV to Libentius I of Hamburg in 989, JL 3835, GP 6:50–51 no. 61, BZ 677, ZPUU 1:584 (perhaps altered by a later interpolator); Gregory V to Gerbert of Ravenna in 998, JL 3883, IP 5:52 no. 166, BZ 830, ZPUU 2:691; Sergius IV to Alfanus II of Benevento in 1011, JL 3970, IP 9:56–57 no. 20, BZ 1054, ZPUU 2:855; and Benedict VIII to Alfanus II of Benevento in 1014, JL 4005, IP 9:57 no. 21, BZ 1135, ZPUU 2:923. See Rabikauskas, *Diplomatica*, 31–32.

do recurred in several grants in the 1020s; one of them, for the archbishop of Bari, hammered home the point by repeating variants of the phrase no fewer than four times.⁵³ In short, the papacy had become inconsistent in this matter. Perhaps John XIII, noted for his foundation of new archbishoprics, started an ambiguous trend when he began to merge personal pallium grants with ecclesial metropolitan privileges.⁵⁴

As a result, the old tension between the pallium as a distinction for chosen churchmen and the pallium as a prerogative "due" to certain churches persisted and worsened. In 914 Pope John X declared that he had conferred the vestment on Archbishop Agius of Narbonne, "for we deny to no church that which justly suits it."⁵⁵ This principle implied that the pallium befitted Narbonne because it was a metropolitan see, almost as if its incumbent had a right to the apparel. According to Rutger of Cologne in 968/69, Bruno, the new archbishop of Cologne, "in accord with the dignity of his see, also had to be distinguished with the privilege of the Roman see and of apostolic blessing," and so he sent an announcement of his election and a pallium request to Rome.⁵⁶ Because of the metropolitan rank of his city, it was expected that he would receive a papal privilege, together with the pallium. And between 1013 and 1018 Thietmar of Merseburg related that Henry of Würzburg had agreed to King Henry II's plan for the

---

53. Variants of the phrase occurred in various parts of at least three documents: Benedict VIII to Vitalis of Dubrovnik in 1022, JL 4042, BZ 1252, ZPUU 2:1027; John XIX to Bisantius of Bari in 1025, JL 4068, IP 9:317–18 no. 2, BF 65, ZPUU 2:1070–71 (four times); and John XIX to Thietmar II of Salzburg in 1026, JL 4074, GP 1:17 no. 37, BF 66, ZPUU 2:1072. A later privilege for Bari followed JL 4068 (Alexander II to Andrew in 1063, JL 4515, IP 9:318–19 no. 4, J. von Pflugk-Harttung, ed., *Acta Pontificum Romanorum Inedita* [Stuttgart: Kohlhammer, 1884; reprinted in Graz: Akademische Druck- und Verlagsanstalt, 1958], 2:97–98).

54. John XIII tied the conferral of the pallium to the erection of the archbishoprics of Magdeburg in 968 (to Adalbert, JL 3728, GP 4:78 no. 74, BZ 450, ZPUU 1:374–76), Benevento in 969 (to Landulf, JL 3738, IP 9:54–55 no. 15, BZ 459, ZPUU 1:389–92), and Vic (substitute for the desolate Tarragona) in 971 (to the Catalonian bishops, JL 3748, BZ 478, ZPUU 1:410–11; and to various Catalonian parties, JL 3749, BZ 479, ZPUU 1:412). The Vic documents were probably prepared by Roman notaries, but not approved when presented to the pope. As pieces meant for approval, however, they surely reflected attitudes and practices current in papal circles.

55. To the Narbonnese bishops, JL 3554, BZ 31, ZPUU 1:68.

56. *Vita Brunonis*, in MGH SSRG n.s. 10:26.

erection of the see of Bamberg in exchange for "allowing the pallium to his church," as if it would henceforth be a right of the church of Würzburg, rather than a privilege of this particular bishop.[57]

The regular pairing of the pallium with papal privileges for the recipient's church must have tended to confuse the matter further. In the early 950s Flodoard of Reims's history bore witness to this continual juxtaposition. Around the time he received the pallium, Fulk of Reims wrote to the pope "about granting the privilege due to the church of Reims," and to the emperor about "strengthening the privileges once given by the Roman pontiffs to the church of Reims," while his successor Seulf obtained the pallium "with a letter of the privilege of this see."[58] Since receiving the vestment was so closely bound to confirmation of the local church's *privilegia*, the archbishop's use of the pallium could be seen as one more ecclesial *privilegium*.

Furthermore, references to *successores* began to creep into pallium grants, which were thereby extended beyond the individual recipient and portrayed as pertaining to his church.[59] Pope Gregory V approved the petition of Alfanus I of Benevento in 998, "granting to you and your successors the use of the pallium," since the archbishop was keen to guarantee the succession of his nephew, Alfanus II.[60] Pope John XIX, admittedly under imperial pressure, did the same for Poppo of Aquileia in 1027.[61] And in 1036 Pope Benedict IX instructed Amatus III of Salerno on the proper use of the pallium, "which we confirm by apostolic authority for you and your successors."[62] It

57. Werner Trillmich, ed., based on the edition of Robert Holtzmann, *Thietmar von Merseburg: Chronik*, Ausgewählte Quellen zur deutschen Geschichte des Mittelalters 9 (Darmstadt: Wissenschaftliche Buchgesellschaft, 1974), 274.
58. MGH SS 36:363, 380, 410.
59. Cf. the evolution of the inheritance of fiefs when strong central power faltered.
60. JL 3884, IP 9:56 no. 19, BZ 822, ZPUU 2:680.
61. JL 4085, IP 7.1:29–30 no. 53, BF 101, ZPUU 2:1093.
62. JL 4032, IP 8:348–49 no. 17, BF 190, ZPUU 2:1133. See Valerie Ramseyer, *The Transformation of a Religious Landscape: Medieval Southern Italy, 850–1150* (Ithaca, N.Y.: Cornell University Press, 2006), 130. This reading is likely the correct one also for the similar passages in other Salerno privileges. When the popes demanded that southern Italian metropolitans routinely come to Rome for consecration and the pallium, they implicitly promised the vestment to the holders of those sees for the indefinite future, as long as each was acceptable to the papacy.

is little wonder that Pilgrim of Passau in the 970s depicted the pallium as a church's due, something the apostolic see owed it.[63] He went so far as to claim that Agapitus II had confirmed the pallium for Gerard of Lorch, "to be held by [his] successors unceasingly."[64] Such a pledge was crucial to Pilgrim's goal, to gain the pallium for the bishops of Passau as successors of the archbishops of "Lorch." But since he intended to send the forgery to Rome, this idea must also have been credible to contemporary churchmen. While wearing the pallium remained a personal privilege, requested by each recipient, it had become so habitual, at least for metropolitans, that one can speak of two "rights": the customary right of a see to have its incumbents (barring irregularities) receive it, and the personal right of a bishop to use it, as specifically granted by the pope.

All things considered, the messages being sent about the nature of the pallium privilege were conflicting and confusing. To some extent this confusion could be traced back centuries. A canon in the late ninth-century *Collectio Anselmo Dedicata* showed that Pope Gregory the Great had differentiated between the personal honor of the pallium and the ecclesial distinctions coupled with it ("the order of reason altogether admonishes us that we ought to bestow some privileges together with the use of the pallium") and yet regarded the gift of the pallium as a decoration for the whole diocese ("for the splendor and honor of your church").[65] This tension produced a muddled state of affairs by the pontificate of John XIII, and the same document could express opposing tendencies. In that pope's grant to Adalbert of Magdeburg in 968, the use of the vestment was pledged to future archbishops, even if each had to request it individually:

---

63. JL †3644, GP 1:165 no. †17, BZ †217, ZPUU 1:204; and JL †3771, GP 1:166–67 no. †19, BZ †514, ZPUU 1:438–39.

64. JL †3644, GP 1:165 no. †17, BZ †217, ZPUU 1:205. Some forged grants for Hamburg contained similar language; Knibbs concludes that later archbishops were troubled by the papally imposed limits, and that Agapitus II's 948 privilege for Adaldag (JL 3641, GP 6:45–46 no. 48, BZ 215, ZPUU 1:199–201) was interpolated (*Ansgar*, 148–49).

65. Canon 1.125, Besse, "Liber Primus," 290, quoting JE 1751. Here Gregory seemed not to regard the pallium's use itself as a "privilege," but later it was certainly so regarded; e.g., Folcuin of Lobbes called Richer of Liège's reception of the pallium "such and so great a privilege" (*Gesta Abbatum Lobiensium*, in MGH SS 4:63).

"By the present privilege we, from the authority of the apostolic see, grant and confirm it to your successors for the future, nevertheless such that each one who is there at the time should receive it from the apostolic see according to custom."[66]

Likewise, Pope Gregory V, freely adapting the seldom employed formula *Apostolicae sedis* in his grant to Gerbert of Ravenna thirty years later, retained that text's juxtaposition of personal favor and ecclesial tradition: "Since, stirred by the zeal of the good will of the apostolic see and the custom of an ancient see, we have put your Fraternity in charge of the church of Ravenna, we have considered it worthy for the insignia of the prelates of the same church to be conferred on you, along with the use of the pallium."[67] A decade later Pope John XVIII bestowed the vestment on Meingaud of Trier "because you have requested us to grant your Confraternity the use of the pallium, according to the authority of your ancient predecessors of the same holy church of Trier, who used the same, lest it seem to have come forth casually from our will."[68] On the one hand, precedents in Trier constituted *auctoritas,* as if previous grants of the pallium had created a right to the present grant. On the other hand, the pope did not give it at random or thoughtlessly (*temere de nostra voluntate*), but as a deliberate choice.

The self-contradictory emergence of the two competing currents in the same or similar texts continued nearly to the end of this period. In 1011, when Pope Sergius IV granted the pallium to Alfanus II of Benevento, he did so "to you and your successors." But when Pope Benedict VIII confirmed that privilege three years later, although he repeated it nearly word for word, he gave the vestment only "to you and your Fraternity."[69] This small change, however awkward, may have reflected a renewed awareness of the personal privilege and a desire to correct past grants' carelessness. Moreover, when Fulbert of

---

66. JL 3728, GP 4:78 no. 74, BZ 450, ZPUU 1:375.
67. JL 3883, IP 5:52 no. 166, BZ 830, ZPUU 2:691. The insignia were likely the staff and ring; cf. Sylvester II to Arnulf of Reims in 999, JL 3908, BZ 867, ZPUU 2:714.
68. JL 3957, GP 10.1:51 no. 82, BZ 1032, ZPUU 2:842.
69. JL 3970, IP 9:56–57 no. 20, BZ 1054, ZPUU 2:855; and JL 4005, IP 9:57 no. 21, BZ 1135, ZPUU 2:923.

Chartres counseled Arnulf of Tours about the absence of his pallium in 1024, he employed a curious double standard. The pope had to have a good reason to deny the vestment (the archbishop was almost entitled to it), yet Arnulf had to request it in order to avoid presuming a right to it (it was still the pope's free gift).[70] Fulbert was describing a delicate balance between papal good will and archiepiscopal claim, between gift and right, and between mutual obligations. Finally, when John XIX palliated Peter of Girona in 1030, even though the bishop had practically extracted the privilege from the pope in exchange for ransoming captives, John made sure that the preamble stressed the condescension of charity as his chief motive.[71] Was the vestment truly a gift, or did this traditional language conceal the reality that it could not only be expected, but even demanded? The answer was murky, and there was no clear-cut policy. But the ambiguity signaled that the papacy risked losing control of the pallium.

Loss of Control

Deterioration in the patterns bequeathed by the eighth- and ninth-century papacy could have serious consequences. The cessation or obfuscation of these traditional practices meant that the popes lost some sway over the ecclesiastical affairs of the provinces and over the use of the pallium itself. Then an opportunity was offered to other powers to control the vestment for their own ends. Resistance to, even rivalry with, Roman authority led to the seizure of its instruments of power, including the pallium, and the popes were forced to fight back. These struggles focused on who received the pallium, who gave it, and who could take it away, while rivals, both secular and ecclesiastical, competed with the popes for the disposition of the vestment.

---

70. Frederick Behrends, ed., *The Letters and Poems of Fulbert of Chartres*, Oxford Medieval Texts (Oxford: Clarendon, 1976), 160.
71. JL 4089, BF 129, ZPUU 2:1109.

Whose Pallium, and Who Decides?

Alarming portents that the pallium could escape papal control were seen throughout this period. The prominence of the pallium as a mark of prestige in the Western church inevitably elicited a yearning in the rank and file of the episcopate to acquire this distinction too. Between 952 and 954 Flodoard of Reims referred to a letter sent by Archbishop Fulk of Reims to Pope Formosus, in which he had complained

> about certain bishops of Gaul who were unduly demanding the pallium for themselves from the Roman see, and were scorning their metropolitans with such an intent. And he asserted that, unless precautions were taken with prudent concern, the same matter would generate no small confusion for the church and could inflict a great cost on charity. Thus he said that both he and all the church were praying that [the pope] would not quickly agree to the unreasonable petition of anyone without general assent and letters. Otherwise, the honor of ecclesiastical dignity would thereby start to become cheap, if an undue thing that is rashly grasped at be handed over indiscreetly.[72]

If the papacy did not show proper caution, a more widespread use of the vestment would blur the lines of the hierarchy and lead to strife between suffragans and metropolitans. Fulk proposed that the pope should not confer the pallium without general agreement among the bishops, expressed in letters of recommendation. Privileges had to be uncommon in order truly to be privileges, and it was the task of the pope, as distributor of the vestment, to make sure it remained prized but rare.

A similar concern must have troubled Liutprand of Cremona in 969 when he reported to Emperor Otto the Great on his legation to Constantinople. Liutprand blamed the Eastern emperor's bribery of Alberic II, patrician of Rome and puppeteer of the papacy of his time, for extorting a papal privilege for the patriarch of Constantinople. This supposed privilege had led to a Greek practice quite different from that observed in the Latin church: "From this disgraceful deal a blameworthy custom developed, that not only the patriarchs but

---

72. *Historia Remensis Ecclesiae*, in MGH SS 36:371.

also the bishops of all Greece use pallia. How absurd this is does not require a critic [to see]."[73] It was one (stridently partisan) Westerner's explanation for the manifestly "absurd" fact that all Eastern bishops wore the *omophorion* without special papal permission. Liutprand assumed it was not always so, found a situation in recent memory that provided an occasion for the "change," and leapt to a dubious conclusion that accounted for the contemporary practice.[74] The gulf between Latin and Greek custom pointed to a like gulf in conception: the Western pallium had become so entangled in the ecclesiastical power structure that a more casual role for the vestment, as in the East, was scarcely imaginable.

Connecting an office to a material object could backfire if the popes were not careful. Around 1045 Ralph Glaber recalled an episode in the succession of the archbishops of Lyon that may have resulted in a setback to papal power:

It was suggested to [Pope John XIX] by faithful men that he elect by his authority Father Odilo, abbot of the monastery of Cluny, to be consecrated as pontiff in [Lyon], for thus the wishful devotion of the whole clergy and people was acclaiming. Sending the pallium at once to the same father, along with the ring, he commanded him to become archbishop of the aforesaid city. But the religious man, heeding the resolution of his humility, utterly refused to become [archbishop]. Nevertheless, receiving the pallium and the ring, he reserved them for him who was worthy to God to be the future pontiff of the same see.[75]

When Odilo, due to his monastic vows, declined the office and saved the archiepiscopal insignia for the eventual archbishop, he effectively deprived the pope of his ability to refuse to confirm that prelate—and thus of his say about who sat in the see of Lyon.[76] In 1032 John

---

73. CCCM 156:215.

74. He asserted that the patriarchs of Constantinople had once worn the vestment only by the pope's leave, until Alberic's privilege let them forgo that permission. From the patriarch the practice supposedly spread to the entire Eastern episcopate. However, the *omophorion* appears to have always been a generally used episcopal badge of office in the East.

75. Guglielmo Cavallo and Giovanni Orlandi, eds., *Rodolfo il Glabro: cronache dell'anno mille (storie)* (Milan: Mondadori, 1996), 280, 282. See Herrmann, *Tuskulanerpapsttum*, 141.

76. Ralph's information is not always trustworthy, and it seems odd that the

responded furiously to the abbot's perceived disobedience.[77] There was probably nothing nefarious in Odilo's intent, but the pope had acted rashly in sending the vestment against the usual policy, without a preceding request from the recipient. Linking the pallium so closely to the making of metropolitans increased the papal role in the process, but simultaneously endangered that role if the vestment escaped papal management.[78]

It was no idle concern. While the popes of this period seemed reluctant to refuse or withdraw the pallium, other authorities had no such qualms. During his conflict with the counts of Vermandois, Archbishop Artold of Reims testified to the Council of Ingelheim (948) about his attempted deposition: "After they see that I am in their power, they begin to ask me to hand over to them the pallium granted to me by the Roman see and utterly deny myself priestly ministry. This I attest that I will by no means do, not even for love of this present life."[79] The vestment was more than a symbol of his office, for he could no longer exercise that office without it.[80] Also, when Frederick of Salzburg learned of Pilgrim of Passau's fraudulent attempt to gain the pallium, he concocted his own papal letter in Benedict VI's name and tried to restrict the vestment's acquisition: "We judge it to be illicit for any bishop to presume to obtain the pallium or any privilege of the archiepiscopate from the Roman

---

pope immediately sent Odilo the pallium (before his consecration) and included a ring (an insigne not customarily conferred by the pope). Still, Ralph knew Odilo, to whom this work was dedicated, and so it seems unlikely that he would invent the story.

77. JL 4095, ZPUU 2:1119–21.

78. According to Hugh of Flavigny's chronicle, the pallium had been kept at Cluny until his own day, about seventy years later (MGH SS 8:403). Had the monastery preserved it as an heirloom? Or was Hugh sarcastically commenting on the unworthiness of all the archbishops since then?

79. Flodoard of Reims, *Historia Remensis Ecclesiae*, in MGH SS 36:432.

80. For years Artold had competed with Hugh for the see, and at one time or another both had gained the pallium (ibid., 36:416, 421). It was thus a struggle between rival palligers, and one would have to give up the vestment. Falkenstein blames the papacy's careless grants for worsening the situation ("Verlorene päpstliche Privilegien," 192–96). Why the pallium was not wrested from Artold by force was not explained; presumably a voluntary abdication was necessary, for the counts lacked the canonical power to depose a bishop.

pontiff, without the agreement of his whole province and his suffragans."[81] Such a condition, meant to guard against backdoor tactics by involving the knowledge, and even approval, of the affected hierarchy—much as Fulk of Reims had urged decades before—nullified the claims of "Lorch" being foisted upon the province of Salzburg. Yet it was hardly likely that the pope would have tied his own hands in such a manner and made his gift dependent on the will of other bishops. In short, because of the pallium's intimate relation to the metropolitan office, both lay and ecclesiastical lords were trying to manipulate it for their own purposes.

The papacy tried to reassert its command of the pallium in the case of Arnulf, archbishop of Reims, whom the Council of St.-Basle (991) deposed after he had plotted against King Hugh Capet.[82] The synodal acts, composed by Arnulf's enemy and successor, Gerbert of Aurillac, detailed the deposition. Citing the Fourth Council of Toledo (633), which required the return of a cleric's insignia when he was restored to his office, the fathers inferred the procedure for the opposite situation: "Each ought to return those things at his deposition that he had received at his promotion. At his promotion Arnulf had received the ring and the staff and a certain kind of stole, which for the sake of differentiation is called the pallium. Therefore [it was decided] that he ought to return these things, and that prejudice is not inflicted on the Roman primate in this deed."[83] Gerbert downplayed the pallium's importance by speaking of it in simplistic, dismissive terms. Both the ordinary stole (*orarium*) and the pallium were bands of cloth draped around the shoulders, but while the former was ubiquitous and common to all priests, the latter was rare and specific to the highest churchmen.[84] The assumption was that,

---

81. JL 3767, GP 1:16 no. †35, BZ †515, ZPUU 1:442. Frederick's desire for the right to veto a suffragan's use of the pallium showed the real concern of metropolitans that palliated suffragans would diminish or even nullify their own authority.

82. See Jason Glenn, *Politics and History in the Tenth Century: The Work and World of Richer of Reims* (Cambridge: Cambridge University Press, 2004), 89–109, and Falkenstein, "Verlorene päpstliche Privilegien," 196–98.

83. MGH SS 3:682.

84. See Grisar, "Römisches Pallium," 101–5; Duchesne, *Origines*, 410–15; Schramm, "Trabea triumphalis," 1:28–30; and Berger, "Liturgische Gewänder," 324–25.

just as the insignia had made him an archbishop, so their loss deprived him of that state—with no need to involve the pope. Stripping Arnulf of his pallium with this glib assertion, the synod underestimated the bond between palliger and papal donor, which could not be written off so lightly.

In response, succeeding popes sought to restore Arnulf through a new pallium. In 996 Abbo of Fleury, acting as papal messenger, reported to Gregory V that he had achieved Arnulf's release from prison and given him the pallium he had brought from Rome.[85] Abbo's *vita*, written by Aimoin of Fleury between 1005 and 1022, left no doubt about the juridical result: "[Abbo] restored Arnulf of Reims, released from custody, to the pontificate: he returned to him the pallium sent by the lord pope."[86] And in 999 Pope Sylvester II confirmed Arnulf in the archbishopric and allowed him to use the pallium once more. The preamble of this privilege associated the badge with the restored office: "It belongs to the apostolic pinnacle not only to console sinners, but also to raise the fallen and to reform those deprived of their own ranks through the insignia of the recovered dignity."[87] There was no strong distinction between the office and the outward signs of the office.[88] Gregory and Sylvester (both non-Roman, imperially appointed popes) were by no means careless, but the opposition they faced showed that the vestment, once it had left Rome, entered contested territory. If the papacy, which distributed pallia from Peter's tomb to all the provinces, were unable to determine who kept the pallium and who did not, it would risk

---

85. Pierre Riché and Jean-Pierre Callu, eds., *Gerbert d'Aurillac: correspondance*, 2nd ed., Les classiques de l'histoire de France au moyen âge 45 (Paris: Belles Lettres, 2008), 660.

86. Robert-Henri Bautier and Gillette Labory, eds., *L'abbaye de Fleury en l'an mil*, Sources d'histoire médiévale 32 (Paris: Centre National de la Recherche Scientifique, 2004), 96. "Returned" did not necessarily mean that he gave back the same pallium that Arnulf had once had (taken away by the Council of St.-Basle in 991), but perhaps that he returned Arnulf's office or authority, manifested in a new pallium.

87. JL 3908, BZ 867, ZPUU 2:714. Sylvester had shown a much different attitude as Gerbert of Aurillac, Arnulf's enemy and, for a while, replacement as archbishop of Reims (Congar, *L'ecclesiologie*, 180–86).

88. See Fichtenau, *Living*, 50.

losing control over the composition of the Latin church's hierarchy.

Not everyone was willing to bend to Roman dominance. Indeed, many bishops in this period enjoyed an effectively independent position, with minimal obligations to the hierarchy outside their dioceses.[89] Replying to Arnulf of Tours in 1024 about that archbishop's failure to obtain the pallium, Fulbert of Chartres maintained that it did not necessarily mean much: "If you sought the pallium from the Roman pontiff, and he denied it to you without legitimate cause, there is no need to give up your ministry because of it."[90] On the one hand, Fulbert implied that a *legitimately* denied pallium should result in loss of office, probably because papal confirmation had been refused.[91] On the other hand, Fulbert entertained the possibility that the vestment could be denied *illegitimately*, and then the archbishop could appropriately ignore the implicit deposition. The reasons for the denial were key, not the denial itself. Unfortunately, the learned

---

89. Timothy Reuter argues that provinces were at most a means of collective regional leadership, archbishops possessed merely an honorific distinction and dispensed advice rather than orders, and popes were distant and verging on toothless ("A Europe of Bishops: The Age of Wulfstan of York and Burchard of Worms," in *Patterns of Episcopal Power: Bishops in Tenth and Eleventh Century Western Europe / Strukturen bischöflicher Herrschaftsgewalt im westlichen Europa des 10. und 11. Jahrhunderts*, ed. Ludger Körntgen and Dominik Waßenhoven, Prinz-Albert-Forschungen 6 [Berlin: de Gruyter, 2011], 33–36). Theo Riches links this argument to Patzold's Carolingian model by explaining that these bishops retained the strong roles imagined for them in the previous age, but having lost their ties to external institutions with the breakup of Carolingian authority, dioceses came to understand themselves as "freestanding, semi-autonomous units" ("The Changing Political Horizons of *gesta episcoporum* from the Ninth to Eleventh Centuries," in ibid., 51–62).

90. Behrends, *Letters*, 160.

91. The popes may have agreed with this statement in theory, but it was not clearly applied in practice. There was no indication that the denial of the pallium to Altheus of Autun and Festinian of Dol threatened their positions—but their rank as suffragans made their possession of the vestment unnecessary (Leo IV to Lothar I between 847 and 850, JE 2603, BH 116, MGH Epp. 5:604; and Nicholas I to Solomon of Brittany in 865, JE 2789, BH 764, MGH Epp. 6:640). As for metropolitans, Aribo of Mainz was stripped of his pallium without the loss of his office, and Mauger of Rouen lasted years without ever gaining the pallium before he was formally deposed (Aribo to Meinhard I of Würzburg in 1024, Jaffé, *Bibliotheca*, 3:359, and R. H. C. Davis and Marjorie Chibnall, eds., *The Gesta Guillelmi of William of Poitiers*, Oxford Medieval Texts [Oxford: Clarendon, 1998], 86, 88). However ambiguous the distinction between the personal and the ecclesial was in this period, the vestment was never wholly reducible to the office.

bishop of Chartres did not explain which reasons were legitimate, or who decided whether the pope was acting unjustly. Nevertheless, his attitude indicated that the powerful prelates of provinces distant from Rome might not forfeit their self-determination so easily.

A further sign of resistance can be glimpsed in a strange story by Thietmar of Merseburg, writing between 1013 and 1018, who described the short career of Walthard, archbishop of Magdeburg "for only seven weeks and two days." Thietmar recorded a reflection in retrospect, perhaps from Walthard's deathbed: "He complains about this one thing above all, that he did not bless churches and clergy; however, he was in no way sorry about the pallium."[92] The archbishop had not dedicated churches or ordained clerics, probably because he had not yet received the pallium (the grant from Pope Benedict VIII was dated six days after his death).[93] While he regretted those consequences, Walthard had no regrets about his lack of the pallium. He seemed not to value the vestment, except insofar as it would have allowed him to carry out his ministry. Perhaps it was a showy badge of honor that he spurned out of humility, or perhaps he resented the reliance on Rome it involved.[94] Nevertheless, his protest was a tacit acknowledgement of its importance: like it or not, the full exercise of his office was inseparably tied to this Roman garb, and he could not simply ignore it.

An extreme manifestation of resistance was the counterfeit pallium, which represented a direct attempt to wrest control of the insigne from the papacy. A later hand added a startling line after the

92. Trillmich, *Chronik*, 324. Thietmar himself inserted this sentence above a line in the manuscript.
93. In 1012, JL 3989, GP 10.1:51 no. 83, BZ 1100, ZPUU 2:896–98. Engels blames Walthard's inability to consecrate and ordain not on his lack of the pallium, but on the shortness of his tenure ("Pontifikatsantritt," 736). Since such acts were linked to possession of the vestment, however, it seems more than coincidental that Walthard specified them, and not other episcopal duties.
94. Sometimes a gift is rejected because the recipient does not wish to accept the moral debt or the social relationship implicated in it (Curta, "Merovingian and Carolingian Gift-giving," 696). Dietrich Claude simply observes that the pallium did not mean much to Walthard (*Geschichte des Erzbistums Magdeburg bis in das 12. Jahrhundert*, Mitteldeutsche Forschungen 67.1 [Cologne: Böhlau, 1972], 1:282). Zotz disagrees but offers no explanation, other than relying on the version in the twelfth-century *gesta* of the archbishops of Magdeburg ("Pallium," 168).

eschatocol (closing section) of Pope John XV's 989 privilege for Libentius I of Hamburg: "We send you the pallium, and in addition we grant you to be clothed with this one, or with another of dazzling whiteness, of whatever kind it pleases you. Amen!"[95] This clause, considered to be false given its diplomatically uncouth location as a postscript, allowed the archbishop to wear either a pallium sent from Rome or some other—in effect, a non-Roman pallium, perhaps of local manufacture, as long as it was white in color.[96] Since this permission could only have weakened the bond the pallium represented, no pope would have written such a thing. Did this forgery come from a period of schism between Hamburg and Rome, when Roman pallia were no longer available and Hamburg sought to separate itself from papal dominion?[97] Other originally papal prerogatives, such as the miter, were eventually shared with so many prelates that their use became general, and they were no longer specially granted by the popes.[98] They were thus transformed from properly papal insignia to archiepiscopal, episcopal, or abbatial insignia, after the papacy failed to retain control of them. Perhaps this forger, underestimating the status of the pallium as the papal insigne *par excellence*, was trying to hasten a similar devolution.

Rivals for Control

Although secular intercession for the pallium had become scarce, laymen had not yielded all their customary rights. When new arch-

95. JL 3835, GP 6:50–51 no. 61, BZ 677, ZPUU 1:586.
96. What was the different *genus* envisioned—a kind of pallium proper to Hamburg? Was the color white stressed because it made the wearer stand out, or because it symbolized something, or because it was necessary to distinguish the pallium from the chasuble beneath (cf. *Ordo Romanus VIII*, in Andrieu, *Ordines*, 2:321), or because the cleanliness of vestments was a traditional Frankish concern (Miller, *Clothing the Clergy*, 31–32)? Not taken from Peter's tomb, would it lack Petrine associations and status as a contact relic?
97. The period of the Investiture Contest springs to mind. Neither Humbert nor Frederick, early twelfth-century archbishops of Hamburg, ever received the pallium thanks to their adherence to the king (Bernhard Schmeidler, *Hamburg-Bremen und Nordost-Europa vom 9. bis 11. Jahrhundert: kritische Untersuchungen zur hamburgischen Kirchengeschichte des Adam von Bremen, zu Hamburger Urkunden und zur nordischen und wendischen Geschichte* [Leipzig: Dieterich, 1918], 189–91).
98. See Braun, *Liturgische Gewandung*, 424–98, esp. 448–52.

bishoprics were erected, the ruler's role came to prominence. In a vehement letter to Pope Agapitus II in 955, William of Mainz complained about the papacy's ready capitulation to the demands of King Otto the Great, his father. Abbot Hadamar of Fulda had been sent to Rome to obtain Bruno of Cologne's pallium and discuss the foundation of the see of Magdeburg, and William was not pleased with the results.[99]

One of the false prophets—coming to Rome in sheep's clothing, but on the inside a ravenous wolf [Mt 7:15], stuffed with gold and gems—boasts when he returns from there that he brings home, by someone's gift, as many pallia as he wishes, bought with a hundred pounds. It seems discordant to me that this can be done by your apostolic Majesty. He [also] brings apostolic letters saying that it will thus be permitted to the king by the apostolic Majesty to establish bishoprics wherever it please him.[100]

The abbot's claim to have purchased all the pallia he wanted was probably an offhand, hyperbolic reference to those of Cologne and the planned archbishopric of Magdeburg.[101] But the implication was

---

99. See Eduard Quiter, *Untersuchungen zur Entstehungsgeschichte der Kirchenprovinz Magdeburg: ein Beitrag zur Geschichte des kirchlichen Verfassungsrechtes im zehnten Jahrhundert* (Paderborn: Bonifacius, 1969), 52–53, and Claude, *Geschichte*, 1:66–67.

100. Jaffé, *Bibliotheca*, 3:349. See Beumann, *Theutonum nova metropolis*, 47–56. The irony of a messenger "in sheep's clothing" receiving the ill-gotten woolen vestments was probably intentional, as was the irony of having to buy a "gift."

101. On Cologne, see Mayr-Harting, *Church*, 27. As for Magdeburg, Hadamar may have brought a pallium to be reserved for the future archbishop, or he may have been promised a pallium once the see was erected. But since Otto intended to move the see of Halberstadt to Magdeburg, and Agapitus bestowed a rational on Bernard of Halberstadt (Hildeward of Halberstadt to Adalbero II of Metz between 984 and 996, Gustav Schmidt, ed., *Urkundenbuch des Hochstifts Halberstadt und seiner Bischöfe*, Publicationen aus den Königlichen Preussischen Staatsarchiven 17 [Leipzig: Hirzel, 1883], 1:42–43), the abbot may only have acquired this lesser vestment for the bishop as a pledge (Klemens Honselmann, *Das Rationale der Bischöfe* [Paderborn: Verein für Geschichte und Altertumskunde Westfalens, 1975], 26–27). See Beumann, "Rationale," and Helmut Beumann, "Zu den Pontifikalinsignien und zum Amtsverständnis der Bischöfe von Halberstadt im hohen Mittelalter," in *Kirche und Reich: Beiträge zur früh- und hochmittelalterlichen Kloster-, Bistums- und Missionsgeschichte*, ed. Irmgard Fees, Bibliotheca Eruditorum 33 (Goldbach: Keip, 2004), 345–49. Bernard's was the first Christian rational mentioned in medieval sources. If someone in Agapitus's circle had invented it to placate the bishop, it was a sign of tenth-century papal creativity—but also an example of papal neglect when it escaped papal control (Miller, *Clothing the Clergy*, 65–66).

that Hadamar, not Agapitus, had determined the shape of the transaction. Although William was politely reluctant to attribute the simoniacal deed to the pope, his words were an accusation as much of Rome's venality and mismanagement of the pallium as of Hadamar and his master Otto's corrupt machinations. William also took these acts as a personal affront, since he was papal vicar in Germany and had not been consulted. The king's license to order the German church as he wished meant that the pope had forfeited the influence he could have wielded through a bolder use of his vicar and of the pallium.[102]

Facing the opposition of powerful German prelates, the erection of Magdeburg dragged on for years, but the king retained his mastery *vis-à-vis* the Roman pontiff.[103] As Otto wrote to the nobles of his realm in 968, he himself chose the first archbishop of Magdeburg and then sent him to the pope for the pallium.[104] In Otto's view, this appointment, an exercise of imperial care for his people, lay within his own competence, and the subsequent acquisition of the pallium, while resting in papal hands, was something of an afterthought, to be presumed. As in other aspects of the Ottonian ecclesiastical reform, the initiative here was the emperor's. Pope John XIII admitted as much, although he preferred to speak of Otto's role as submitting a request: he granted the pallium "by the petition of our aforesaid spiritual son, the august Emperor Otto, who is the author and founder of the same church."[105] When the same pope established the

---

102. William feared that "the intercession of Hadamar's money may be stronger than the pious constitution of St. Boniface, our predecessor, and of your predecessors as well as our forerunners also, and there be as many pallia as bishops" (Jaffé, *Bibliotheca*, 3:349–50). The obscure final clause, if not simply William's alarmist fantasy, perhaps referred to Otto's plan to make the bishop of Halberstadt the archbishop of Magdeburg, and thus to palliate him. Honselmann speculates that all references to pallia in this letter—including the payment of a hundred pounds, the large number acquired by Hadamar, and their possession by every bishop—are better understood as rationals, made of expensive materials and worn by many prelates, even suffragans (*Rationale*, 26–29).

103. See Quiter, *Untersuchungen*, and Claude, *Geschichte*, 1:63–113.

104. *Monumenta Germaniae Historica: Diplomata Regum et Imperatorum Germaniae* (Hannover: Hahn, etc., 1879–), 1:502–3 (diplomas of Otto I).

105. To Adalbert, JL 3728, GP 4:78 no. 74, BZ 450, ZPUU 1:375.

archbishopric of Benevento in the following year, he mentioned not only the emperor's influence on the bestowal of the vestment, but also the local princes'.[106] Any shift in the standing of churchmen undoubtedly affected power relations within a realm, and it is not surprising that the agreement of lay lords was needed.

Otto's grandson, the third of that name, also acted as if the pallium was his to grant, even in the ordinary case of a long-established see. When Lambert of Deutz composed his life of Heribert in the mid-eleventh century, he included the salutation of the letter in which Otto III had appointed Heribert to the archbishopric of Cologne in 999: "He writes a letter to him in his own hand, promising Cologne with the pallium as a gift, in these words: 'Otto, emperor by the grace of God alone, to Heribert, archchancellor: grace and Cologne and one cubit of cloth [*pallium*].'"[107] The humorous figure of speech clearly referred to the vestment; its irony lay in the juxtaposition of its material insignificance with its immaterial significance.[108] This prize was at the emperor's casual disposal, as if it were an imperial *donum*, so certain he was of securing it from Pope Sylvester II (whose choice of name bespoke the collaboration both men expected).

If it was not the emperor, it was the local aristocracy. At the papacy's nadir during this period, the Roman bishop did nothing without the consent of the family controlling the city at the time. Such a plight explained a wry observation by Flodoard of Reims in the 950s: "Bishop Artold [of Reims], a year after his ordination, receives the

106. To Landulf, JL 3738, IP 9:54–55 no. 15, BZ 459, ZPUU 1:390.
107. MGH SSRG 73:152.
108. Scholars have offered many other interpretations. Gerd Althoff cites this letter as evidence of the casual, unconventional style of Otto III with his intimate friends. He also notes Schramm's opinion, that this phrase was not only a "parody of the pomposity of diplomatic style," but also a joke: "A pallium only a yard long would have been laughably short" (*Otto III*, trans. Phyllis G. Jestice [University Park: Pennsylvania State University Press, 2003], 144). Others suggest that a subsidy was included with the letter to cover Heribert's traveling expenses and pallium fee, as if he were given money to buy himself some cloth. Alternatively, the short pallium may have indicated Otto's plan to found a bishopric in Aachen, which would have lessened Cologne's territory, or shortened its pallium, so to speak. Finally, Lambert may have altered the letter's text to fit his rhyming prose or to make his listeners laugh (MGH SSRG 73:152–53n90).

pallium sent to him through legates of the church of Reims by Pope John, son of Mary, who was also called Marozia—or rather, by Alberic the patrician, brother of that pope, who was holding the same John, his brother, in his power and keeping their aforesaid mother shut up under guard."[109] John XI ostensibly sent the vestment, but really it came from his half-brother Alberic, who was running Rome and its church. It was a pallium grant by a layman, *de facto* if not *de iure*.

If limitations on the pallium's use emphasized the limited authority of palligers *vis-à-vis* the pope, its unrestricted use upset their proper subordination. Though false, the notion that Hincmar of Reims had received the extraordinary privilege of daily use endured in this age. Flodoard of Reims, relying no doubt both on Hincmar's authentic pallium grant and on the forgeries permitting him *cotidianus usus*, mistakenly concluded that the archbishop had gained two pallia.[110] In his mid-tenth-century history of the church of Reims, Flodoard spelled out the distinction between the two: Hincmar retained the right to his original pallium, "to be duly enjoyed on the solemnities defined for him," but supposedly Leo IV had sent him another, which, like the pontiff's own, could be worn every day.[111] The only later parallel to this exceptional situation was Rutger of Cologne's brief report in 968/69 that Bruno of Cologne had received "a privilege handed over by the authority of apostolic loftiness, by which the priest of the Lord was also allowed to be clothed with the same pallium beyond custom, as often as he wished."[112] The grant itself has not survived, and it is uncertain how much credence should be lent to this lone witness. If accurate, it was probably a unique prerogative

---

109. *Historia Remensis Ecclesiae*, in MGH SS 36:416.
110. Cf. Leo IV to Lothar I and to Hincmar in 851, JE 2607–8, BH †?239–†?240, MGH Epp. 5:591–92; and see Falkenstein, "Verlorene päpstliche Privilegien," 187–90. Perhaps Flodoard's erroneous inference came from a reference in one of Hincmar's forgeries to "the pallium, which we have allowed you for daily use," which he could have read as a restrictive, rather than nonrestrictive, clause.
111. MGH SS 36:206. Trying to explain Hincmar's second pallium, Flodoard claimed that it had been granted "out of reverence for his holiness and wisdom." That language was not found in the falsified letters, but must have seemed a likely reason for the extraordinary gift. Cf. Flodoard, *De Triumphis Christi*, in PL 135:815.
112. *Vita Brunonis*, in MGH SSRG n.s. 10:27 (JL *3658, GP 7:47 no. *108).

that set this archbishop, who was also brother of the emperor and duke of Lotharingia, apart from other palligers and made him like the pope himself.[113]

Regulating pallium use was by no means a trivial liturgical detail, but rather a political tool in the papacy's hands. Yet the same tool could also be wielded to achieve the ends of others. Something of this sort may have occurred at the Second Council of Limoges (1031). Ademar of Chabannes composed the acts of this synod, one of whose purposes was to defend the apostolicity of Martial, evangelizer and first bishop of Limoges.[114] According to the acts, the council met on the anniversary of the dedication of the abbey church in Limoges, where the saint was buried. After the session the archbishop of Bourges, president of this provincial synod, "having donned the sacred pallium," celebrated Mass in that church.[115] Why did he wear the pallium then? It was during the Mass, but what pallium day was it? Ademar's aim in this mostly concocted narrative provides a clue.[116] The archbishop offered first a collect for the Mass of the anniversary, *de solemnitate ecclesiae,* and then a collect for Martial, *de beati Martialis commemoratione,* which referred to him as an apostle.[117] As the council had decreed, Martial was truly an apostle, and so his feast was an apostolic feast, and thus a standard pallium day.[118] By

---

113. See Mayr-Harting, *Church,* 52. Evidence *ex silentio* in favor of Bruno's extraordinary privilege may be seen in John XIII's declaration that Magdeburg should enjoy the same pallium days as Mainz and Trier, without mention of Cologne (to Adalbert of Magdeburg in 968, JL 3728, GP 4:78 no. 74, BZ 450, ZPUU 1:375), and the lack of a 962 privilege increasing Cologne's pallium days, as John XII did for Salzburg and Trier in that year (to Frederick of Salzburg, JL 3689, GP 1:14–15 no. 31, BZ 302, ZPUU 1:279; and to Henry of Trier, JL 3691, GP 10.1:43 no. 63, BZ 303, ZPUU 1:281).

114. See Richard Landes, *Relics, Apocalypse, and the Deceits of History: Ademar of Chabannes, 989–1034,* Harvard Historical Studies 117 (Cambridge, Mass.: Harvard University Press, 1995), 195–281.

115. PL 142:1377.

116. See Daniel Callahan, "Adémar of Chabannes, Apocalypticism and the Peace Council of Limoges of 1031," *Revue bénédictine* 101 (1991): 32–49.

117. PL 142:1377–78.

118. Feasts of the apostles had been pallium days since the early ninth century (e.g., Gregory IV to Liudpram of Salzburg in 837, JE 2580, GP 1:10 no. 14, Hauthaler and Martin, *Salzburger Urkundenbuch,* 2:27), and still were during this period (e.g., John XII to Henry of Trier in 957, JL 3682, GP 10.1:42 no. 62, BZ 275, ZPUU 1:263).

emphasizing that the archbishop was wearing the pallium, Ademar reinforced and illustrated the conciliar decision. He also hijacked the vestment to serve his own agenda.

Conclusion

The pallium was, as it were, fraying around the edges. The clear vision and firm hand of many Carolingian popes had slipped into some degree of shortsighted carelessness, partly a result of success—laxity due to the accepted integration of the vestment into ecclesiastical practice—but partly too a result of failure—the inattention of lackluster popes with diminished power and capable rivals. Thus far the story falls into line with the stereotypical view of this period as a bleak interlude of decay between the preceding era of ingenuity and the following era of reform. But that narrative is too simplistic, and the same period could offer surprises. As the next chapter will reveal, the pallium's story was far from over. The same popes who fumbled in some ways while handling the vestment grasped the pallium's potential in other ways, and honed it into an ever more responsive instrument of papal power.

Perhaps the archbishop wore the vestment because he was presiding over the synod; yet his pallium had not been mentioned to this point, and now the fathers had been dismissed to join a popular throng for a festive Mass, which implied that the synod was no longer in session.

6

Creativity

After Archbishop Aribo of Mainz had been stripped of his pallium and died without regaining it, his successor Bardo acquired the vestment in 1032, apparently without a problem. But the preamble of John XIX's privilege was unlike that of any previous pallium grant. Departing from the usual formulas, the pope took the opportunity to express the nature of this gift:

> Although it is fitting for all Christians to follow the charity of Christ ... we especially who perform the priestly office ought to follow charity in all things, such that we show, according to the divine word, how to love our neighbor as ourselves [Mt 19:19, 22:39]. Following this, our most holy predecessors found it honorable to grant a most sacred ornament on certain festivities to other fellow bishops whom kindly works have made more famous than the rest. It was invented by divine providence particularly for prelates in the see of blessed Peter the apostle: the pallium, to be worn during the solemnities of the Mass, as the insigne of dignity and holiness and the cultivation of all honorable behavior.[1]

Here the pope offered an interpretation of the pallium firmly rooted in tradition. It was a *decus sacratissimum*, a liturgical vestment worn

---

1. JL 4098, GP 4:89 no. 110, BF 149, ZPUU 2:1121–22. "Cultivation" (*cultus*) could also mean "fancy outfit, fashion, style," bringing to mind the correspondence between outer dress and inner integrity that often appeared in the admonitions of pallium grants.

on specific occasions, yet also an emblem of office and a mark of holiness. It belonged to the exceptionally virtuous, for it represented or evoked the righteous life required of pastors. But John also offered a rationale for the papal practice of distributing it. Since bishops should provide an example of love of neighbor, the popes shared their own distinction with others. Though a papal insigne, created for Peter's successors according to God's plan, it was granted to fellow bishops out of charity.[2] Perhaps in reaction to the case of Aribo, the older concept of the pallium as an honor or reward for worthiness, freely given, here trumped the newer concept of it as the expected badge of metropolitan office.

In such subtle ways, the post-Carolingian popes sometimes displayed a creative inclination to consolidate their control of the pallium and advance its use in new directions. Given the deviations surveyed in the last chapter, the overall picture was not entirely coherent. Even as they relaxed some aspects of customary procedure, these pontiffs were not averse to tightening others and innovating. This tendency can be observed in three movements: they built upon the practices they had inherited; they used the pallium more energetically to tie its wearers to Rome; and they pioneered shrewd changes to increase its effectiveness as an instrument of control. These signs of inventiveness attest to a more complex reality than the typical narratives of the pre-reform papacy portray. It was by no means a wholly otiose age in papal history, but one with surprising moments of vision.

Expanding the Practice

Some popes of this period not only remained faithful to the legacy they had received, but even extended it. They accepted the principles behind the practices of the past and introduced new practices with the same purposes. This strategy was obvious, first, when they used the pallium to resolve problematic elevations to episcopal of-

---

2. A similar emphasis on charity as his motivation had emerged in the same pope's privilege for Peter of Girona two years before, but it rang rather hollow in that situation (JL 4089, BF 129, ZPUU 2:1109).

fice. They also tried to eliminate threats to their freedom to select the recipients of this personal gift. Finally, they reinforced the vestment's character as a relic intimately connected to Peter.

Irregular Successions

It was already accepted that the pallium represented the pope's consent to the choice of an important see's next occupant.[3] Now, in addition, the pallium served to patch up specific problems with an official seal of approval, offering not simply consent, but remedy. Such was the case in three irregular situations.

One was a bishop's translation from one see to another, traditionally considered a violation of canon law.[4] Flodoard of Reims in the mid-tenth century recorded that Archbishop Fulk of Reims had defended Frothar, formerly archbishop of Bordeaux, to Pope Hadrian III. Frothar had been charged with seizing a second see, Bourges: "[Fulk] showed that [Frothar] was requested and chosen by the bishops of [the province of Bourges] and all the clergy and people of the same city, and that [Hadrian's] predecessor Marinus [I] gave pious assent to their petition in this matter, and in addition presented him with the pallium and strengthened his promotion in the church of Bourges in writing."[5] This demonstration of legitimacy invoked the pallium as a symbol of papal confirmation, but now in the atypical case of a translation rather than a consecration.[6] Likewise, when Pope Benedict VII suppressed the see of Merseburg and translated its incumbent, Giselher, to Magdeburg in 981, he excused this unusual act partly by not-

3. E.g., Seulf of Reims requested the pallium to obtain papal backing of his position (Flodoard of Reims, *Historia Remensis Ecclesiae*, in MGH SS 36:410). Since this confirmation made an archbishop legitimate, one could say that the pope, through the pallium, gave a palliated prelate his very office (*Chronicon Gradense*, in Monticolo, *Cronache*, 1:41–42).
4. See Scholz, *Transmigration*, and Sommar, "Hincmar."
5. *Historia Remensis Ecclesiae*, in MGH SS 36:364–65. See Scholz, *Transmigration*, 147–57. John VIII had approved the translation, but perhaps Marinus I had also confirmed it.
6. Presumably Frothar already had a pallium as archbishop of Bordeaux, and so this one (unattested elsewhere) was his second. If so, it was the first time a translated palliger received a new pallium for his new see, which implied that this personal privilege was also connected to a specific office and place. Just as the pallium could not be passed to a successor, so too it could not be used if the recipient changed sees.

ing Giselher's due election: "Sons of [Magdeburg], standing in our sight, professed by word of mouth both that he was a son of that church and that they had certainly elected him.... We decree that the aforesaid Bishop Giselher, who had approached this desired honor not by greed, but by the election and petition of his sons ... is set over the holy church of Magdeburg as archbishop and presented with the pallium."[7] The stress on the bishop's election did double duty: it verified that the translation arose not from his ambition but from the church's desire, and it accounted for the pope's approval of his new position. The gift of the pallium, then, endorsed a state of affairs that should ordinarily have been disallowed.

Another extraordinary circumstance was a bishop's restoration after he had been removed, rightly or wrongly, from his see. After a Lateran synod in 900 under Pope Benedict IV ratified Argrim's restoration to the see of Langres, the pope permitted him the pallium, which he had previously worn during his short-lived tenure as archbishop of Lyon: "We granted him ecclesiastical rights, namely that, because he had been deprived of his church in an unjust procedure, it should also be returned by just supervision.... On this account we have ordered a privilege of our authority to be made for him, and in it we have granted him the use of the pallium ... which he had formerly received from our most holy predecessor, Pope Formosus."[8] After the back and forth of Argrim's career in Lyon and Langres, a definitive sign of papal confirmation was needed for the sure possession of his old bishopric. Although Langres was not a metropolis, the pallium provided a solution. In addition, in Abbo of Fleury's canonical collection around 995, the abbot discussed a higher principle, *necessitas*, by which ecclesiastical authority could override the

---

7. JL post 3807, GP 5.2:213–14 no. 18, BZ 599, ZPUU 1:528. Cf. Benedict to the Gallican and German bishops in 981, JL 3808, GP 5.2:214–15 no. 19, BZ 600, ZPUU 1:530–31. See Scholz, *Transmigration*, 177–87.

8. To the clergy and people of Gaul, JL 3527, ZPUU 1:25. The events involving Argrim are not easy to unravel. See Gerhard Schneider, *Erzbischof Fulco von Reims (883–900) und das Frankenreich*, Münchener Beiträge zur Mediävistik und Renaissance-Forschung 14 (Munich: Arbeo-Gesellschaft, 1973), 82–89, 139–40, 149–51, and Rudolf Pokorny, "Ein unerkanntes Brieffragment Argrims von Lyon-Langres aus den Jahren 894/95 und zwei umstrittene Bischofsweihen in der Kirchenprovinz Lyon, mit Textedition und Exkurs," *Francia* 13 (1985): 608–20.

canons for the good of the churches. As an example, he cited Pope Gregory the Great's restoration of Maximus of Salona: "Gregory too reformed those condemned by other bishops to their original ranks by the privilege of his authority.... Gregory excommunicated the bishop of the city of Salona, named Maximus, because, ordained for money, he had incurred the simoniacal heresy.... After seven years, when he had been led by penance, [Gregory] restored him to his see and presented him with the pallium."[9] The vestment was a means of validating the recipient's position, but even more a sign of regained papal favor, which undid not only the penalty of deposition, but also that of excommunication.[10]

Schism was another irregular situation, when two or more claimants to a see fought for recognition as its true bishop. After a struggle over the see of Narbonne between Agius and Gerard, Pope John X rejected the latter in 914 because of his uncanonical accession, as he told the province's bishops: "We wish and by apostolic authority command that ... you should not hold [Gerard] among the bishops, since he was neither demanded by the clerics or people of the city nor ordained by you, his comprovincials, in the usual manner. We have sent a privilege, the pallium, and the use of the pallium to your metropolitan Agius, as your Belovedness asked."[11] Presumably Agius, unlike Gerard, had been properly elected and consecrated, and now the reception of the pallium clinched his legitimate acquisition of the archbishopric. It was not merely seemly, but even necessary, since the bishops had requested this decisive gesture to resolve a lo-

---

9. Canon 8, PL 139:482. Gregory himself had addressed this episode in JE 1703, transmitted, through John the Deacon's *vita*, by the *Collectio V Librorum* (Canon 2.106.6 [2.89.3], CCCM 6:251–52).

10. Cf. Abbo to Gregory V in 996, Riché and Callu, *Correspondance*, 660, and Aimoin of Fleury, *Vita et Passio Abbonis*, in Bautier and Labory, *L'abbaye*, 96.

11. JL 3554, BZ 31, ZPUU 1:68. See Thomas Deswarte, "Rome et la spécificité catalane: la papauté et ses relations avec la Catalogne et Narbonne (850–1030)," *Revue historique* 294 (1995): 10–11. The phrase *pallium et usus pallii*, as if there were two gifts—one physical, the other legal—occurred only under Stephen V in 888 (to Theodosius of Split, JL 3448, MGH Epp. 7:351), John X in 914 (here), and Leo VI in 928 (to the Dalmatian bishops, JL 3579, BZ 93, ZPUU 1:100). *Usus pallii* may have meant the regulations for its usage, or simply the permission to use it, as distinct from possessing it.

cally insoluble division. Further, Folcuin of Lobbes around 980 described a contest over the see of Liège between Hilduin and Richer some decades before:

> When it is learned [that Hilduin evaded papal judgment], Richer is acclaimed, elected, brought forth, and ordained and consecrated pontiff by the supreme pontiff himself, with the archiepiscopal pallium presented to him alone of all his predecessors.... Therefore, having returned to Gaul with such and so great a privilege, he put an end to the quarrel of the contrary side and alone sat in the high office of the church of Liège.[12]

The pallium was again a mark of victory after a schism, a sign of papal support for the genuine bishop. It did not only approve the position he had won, but even allowed him to win it. Once clad in the authoritative vestment, Richer could end the rift and secure the bishopric for himself.

These cases showed that the conferral of the pallium was transcending its original function in regard to episcopal appointments. Rather than simply corroborating promotions that had already happened, or verifying that the rules had been followed, it now settled canonical and political conundrums. It was a stronger instrument of power when it could not only declare what was acceptable, but also make it so.

Between Donor and Recipient

As has been seen, various factors could erode the idea that the pallium was a personal gift from pope to chosen palliger. One factor was lay interference. The ambiguous role of secular authorities in the pallium's acquisition was nothing new, but occasionally the popes seemed willing, as some of their Carolingian predecessors had done, to defy their desires. When Pope Benedict IV restored Argrim to Langres in 900 and permitted him to use the pallium, he warned against secular meddling with the bishop's rule.[13] Perhaps this restitution, and the pallium grant that backed it up, displeased the local powers. Similarly, Andrew of Fleury, in his *vita* of Gauzlin of Bourges around 1042,

---

12. *Gesta Abbatum Lobiensium*, in MGH SS 4:63 (JL *3566). See Zimmermann, "Streit," 34, 51.

13. To the clergy and people of Gaul, JL 3527, ZPUU 1:25.

reported that Pope Benedict VIII had bolstered his pallium grant with sanctions against the noble who was preventing the archbishop's enthronement: in Rome, Gauzlin "was presented with the pallium of episcopal blessing and obtained that Geoffrey, viscount of Bourges, be struck with the censure of anathema in the very church of blessed Peter ... for [Geoffrey] was denying him access to the see of the aforesaid city."[14] Here the *pallium episcopalis benedictionis* indeed represented the pope's blessing, or confirmation, of a bishop's authority, no matter the hostility of lay lords.

A more striking example is found in Thietmar of Merseburg's chronicle, completed between 1013 and 1018. King Henry II, planning to make his favorite city of Bamberg a bishopric, asked Henry of Würzburg, in whose diocese the city lay, to give up that part of his territory in exchange for various properties. But the bishop's asking price was higher: "The prelate, receiving kindly the just petitions of his beloved lord, agreed under this condition, that, allowing the pallium to his church, [the king] would put the shepherd of Bamberg under him. And when his staff had been given to the king, and a certain estate had been handed over for the aforesaid exchange, he secretly confirmed it." The stipulation would have converted Würzburg to a metropolitan see, and the assumption on both sides was that the pallium was effectively the king's to give, rather than the pope's. Yet the exchange of collateral in token of the agreement was secret, as if they were afraid that this sort of backroom deal was illicit. Eventually, the bishop "felt that he could by no means attain the archiepiscopate," and backed out of the plan.[15] Pope John XVIII, who made Bamberg a suffragan of Mainz in 1007, was not so easily manipulated, and the king was not so omnipotent, even within the "imperial church system," as may be supposed.[16] By remaining a matter

---

14. Robert-Henri Bautier and Gillette Labory, eds., *André de Fleury: Vie de Gauzlin, abbé de Fleury*, Sources d'histoire médiévale 2 (Paris: Centre National de la Recherche Scientifique, 1969), 58 (JL *3994).

15. Trillmich, *Chronik*, 274. See Erich Freiherr von Guttenberg, *Die Regesten der Bischöfe und des Domkapitels von Bamberg*, Veröffentlichungen der Gesellschaft für fränkische Geschichte 6 (Würzburg: Schöningh, 1963), 14, 17.

16. To the Gallican and German bishops, JL 3954, GP 3:248–49 no. 1, BZ 1023, ZPUU 2:830–33. See Josef Fleckenstein, "Zum Begriff der ottonisch-salischen

between donor and recipient, the pallium could exclude other powers' involvement in ecclesiastical arrangements.

Another factor that threatened the personal nature of the gift was the possibility that the pallium could be passed from one palliger to another, and thus escape papal control. But the sources of this period revealed a custom that excluded this possibility: the burial of the vestment with its wearer. Around 900 Sigloard of Reims wrote an elegiac poem after the murder of Archbishop Fulk of Reims, and he described the funeral vividly: "Abbots and bishops, / Vested, hold [Fulk's body] up, / Transferred into the church, / Standing upright at the altars. / They clothe him with chasuble / And pallium and tunic; / The stole is placed on his neck, / And a candle is lit. / Nor is the staff lacking there, / But it is attached to his hands."[17] In preparation for his burial, Fulk was arrayed in his liturgical vestments and pontifical insignia, including pallium and staff. Also, around 963 Sigehard composed the *miracula* of his monastery's patron, Maximin, an early bishop of Trier, and included an eyewitness account of the opening of his tomb many decades before: "So whole were the vestments, so incorrupt was the entire body, [it was] as if they had been buried there on the same day.... Wishing also to convince those slower [to believe], lest they be stirred by some scruple of doubt concerning the discovery of the saint, [Archbishop Radbod of Trier] spread out the very stole and pallium for all to see."[18] The prelate conducting the *inventio*, to counter doubts that it was really Maximin, showed the people his pallium, still intact. It was unmistakable evidence, first, that they had discovered an archbishop and, second, that God had preserved his remains.

In his *vita* of the late 960s, Rutger of Cologne remarked that Archbishop Bruno of Cologne was buried in the same place he had once

---

Reichskirche," in *Geschichte, Wirtschaft, Gesellschaft,* ed. Erich Hassinger, J. Heinz Müller, and Hugo Ott (Berlin: Duncker and Humblot, 1974), 61–71, and Timothy Reuter, "The 'Imperial Church System' of the Ottonian and Salian Rulers: A Reconsideration," *Journal of Ecclesiastical History* 33 (1982): 347–74.

17. *Rhythmus de Morte Fulconis,* in PL 129:1145–46.

18. *Acta Sanctorum* (Antwerp/Brussels: Société des Bollandistes, 1643–1940), Mai 7 (die 29): 32–33 [hereafter "AASS"]. See John Nightingale, *Monasteries and Patrons in the Gorze Reform: Lotharingia c. 850–1000* (Oxford: Clarendon, 2001), 174–84.

received the envoy bringing his pallium from Rome: "This venerable garment was received there first, there last, once with happy song, once with doleful. For the body of the religious, God-worthy priest, to be buried in the same place, did not lose the insignia of his office, which nevertheless his soul carried with it, spiritually and so happily, as we believe."[19] While Bruno's corpse kept the badges of his archiepiscopate, including the pallium, it was piously believed that *spiritualiter* his soul had brought them along to heaven. Such a belief had been corroborated around 944 by an anonymous *translatio* in which the ghost of Bernard of Vienne ordered a priest to have his remains moved: "While he was resting in his bed in the deep silence of the night, there appeared to him a certain man of great authority, clothed in a priestly stole, wearing the archiepiscopal pallium, who called to him."[20] The vestment served as a distinctive means of identifying the phantom and lending authority to the vision. It was intimately bound to its recipient from the time he had received it from Pope Paschal I in 817 even into the afterlife.[21] Through burial customs and ghost stories, the notion that the pallium was restricted to a single recipient penetrated popular consciousness.

The Gift of Peter

Vague hints tying the pallium to Peter's tomb became clearer in this period. Around 897 *Ordo Romanus XXXVI* depicted a new pope's ordination at the site of Peter's remains: "Coming to the *confessio* of St. Peter, he prostrates himself in prayer.... Afterwards he is lifted up by the bishops and set between the seat and the altar, [where he is consecrated].... And the archdeacon places the pallium upon him. And then he is raised on the seat between the archdeacon and a deacon."[22] Entrance into the papal office naturally included assuming that office's insigne. At Peter's tomb, immediately after consecration,

---

19. MGH SSRG n.s. 10:28.
20. PL 123:449–50.
21. JE 2549, GaP 3.1:96–97 no. 81, MGH Epp. 3:97–98.
22. Andrieu, *Ordines*, 4:203. This ordo was later incorporated into the Romano-Germanic Pontifical (Cyrille Vogel and Reinhard Elze, eds., *Le pontifical romano-germanique du dixième siècle*, Studi e testi 227 [Vatican City: Biblioteca Apostolica Vaticana, 1963], 2:151).

the pope was vested with the pallium as the first ritual action upon becoming bishop of Rome. Two late eleventh-century manuscripts offered a variant reading of the last two sentences of this text: "And the archdeacon, having taken the pallium from the *confessio*, places it upon him. Then he is raised on the seat by the archdeacon and the archpriest."[23] Apparently the pallium was kept within the *confessio*, the niche above Peter's grave, until the pope was vested with it.[24] This evidence seems to be the earliest direct connection of the pallium to the *confessio* of St. Peter's Basilica, and it throws new light on the prostration before that holy place at the beginning of the liturgy.

The manner of receiving the pallium could also connect it to Peter. The late tenth-century Pontifical of St. Dunstan (Sherborne Pontifical) included the authentic (uninterpolated) form of Pope John XII's 960 privilege for that archbishop of Canterbury. It was an appropriate addition to a metropolitan's book, since it affirmed the authority of the one who performed the rites therein.[25] A narrative setting the scene preceded the privilege: "Here begins the letter of privilege that, at the order of Pope John, having received a blessing from him, Archbishop Dunstan received from his hands. But he did not receive the pallium from his hands, but rather at his order from the altar of St. Peter the apostle."[26] This seems to be the earliest mention of the so-called Roman manner of bestowing the pallium:

---

23. Andrieu, *Ordines*, 4:203n46.1. The manuscripts with this variant, which contain the canonical collections of Deusdedit and Anselm of Lucca, provide a shorter, more precise recension of this *ordo*. Andrieu demonstrates that Deusdedit and Anselm drew upon the work of a Roman canonist, who took a Roman copy of the Romano-Germanic Pontifical (which included this *ordo*) and made revisions, including this variant (ibid., 4:117–18).

24. See 156–57 above.

25. See Jane Rosenthal, "The Pontifical of St. Dunstan," in *St. Dunstan: His Life, Times and Cult*, ed. Nigel Ramsay, Margaret Sparks, and Tim Tatton-Brown (Woodbridge: Boydell, 1992), 143–63, esp. 154n59, 157; Rasmussen, *Pontificaux*, 258–317; and Francesca Tinti, "The Archiepiscopal Pallium in Late Anglo-Saxon England," in *England and Rome in the Early Middle Ages: Pilgrimage, Art, and Politics*, ed. Francesca Tinti, Studies in the Early Middle Ages 40 (Turnhout: Brepols, 2014), 320.

26. D. Whitelock, M. Brett, and C. N. L. Brooke, eds., *Councils and Synods with Other Documents Relating to the English Church* (Oxford: Clarendon, 1981), 1:90. The pontifical (Paris, Bibliothèque Nationale de France, lat. 943) ironically also contained a note that defended the possibility of not receiving the pallium in Rome (Conn, "Dunstan," 103).

it was taken from Peter's altar, as if given by the hand of Peter himself.[27] Thus, while the conferral occurred at the pope's behest, the pallium was ultimately not his gift, but Peter's. Another archbishop of Canterbury, Aethelnoth, was also said to have taken the pallium from Peter's altar in 1022, although the account in a version of the *Anglo-Saxon Chronicle* is problematic.[28] Even when the pope handed over the vestment himself, as when Pope Gregory V entrusted Arnulf of Reims's pallium to Abbo of Fleury, it was envisioned as a sacred token from Peter's vicar. Thus Abbo wrote to Gregory in 996 that he had received it "from your holy hands," and then acknowledged the pope "as if [you are] blessed Peter, prince of the apostles, whose place on earth you now bear."[29] Clearly, a large part of the

27. Ordinarily, as implied by the ceremony of investiture that developed, the pope vested churchmen with the garment when they came to him in person. But according to later evidence, the "Roman manner" was practiced at their own consecration by the popes themselves, who received their office in succession from Peter—and thus took the pallium from his altar through the hands of the archdeacon (e.g., Landulf the Younger, in Castiglioni, *Historia Mediolanensis*, 33). It is unclear which altar in St. Peter's Basilica was meant: the high altar above the *confessio*, or the crypt altar behind it. The axial gallery of the crypt, which approached the *confessio* from the west and ended in the crypt altar, was called *ad corpus* (Blaauw, *Cultus*, 2:535–37)—which may shed light on the description of the pallium as *de corpore beati Petri sumptum*. The presence of a *fenestella* and a reliquary-recess in the crypt altar suggests that pallia could have been incubated there as easily as in the niche of the *confessio* (Toynbee and Perkins, *Shrine*, 217, and Blaauw, *Cultus*, 2:538–39).

28. G. P. Cubbin, ed., *The Anglo-Saxon Chronicle: A Collaborative Edition* (Cambridge: Brewer, 1996), 6:63–64. In this "D" version two statements conflicted: that the pope vested Aethelnoth, and that Aethelnoth himself took the vestment from the altar. The later "E" and "F" versions lacked the second statement (Susan Irvine, ed., *The Anglo-Saxon Chronicle: A Collaborative Edition* [Cambridge: Brewer, 2004], 7:75, and Peter S. Baker, ed., *The Anglo-Saxon Chronicle: A Collaborative Edition* [Cambridge: Brewer, 2000], 8:111). Oddly, "D" also said that Benedict VIII consecrated Aethelnoth archbishop *after* bestowing the pallium, though Wulfstan II of York had already consecrated him in England. Rather than episcopal ordination, this passage (also in "E," but not in "F") probably referred to the investiture ceremony, in which the final prayer was labeled *consecratio* in certain pontificals (e.g., Nicholas Orchard, ed., *The Sacramentary of Ratoldus* (Paris, Bibliothèque nationale de France, lat. 12052), Henry Bradshaw Society 116 [London: Boydell, 2005], 46). Through this blessing, it was imagined, a bishop became an archbishop; "D" and "E" called Aethelnoth a bishop when he set out for Rome, but an archbishop afterwards. Indeed, the Old English word *arce, ærce, erce* meant the pallium (Baker, *Anglo-Saxon Chronicle*, 8:91, 95): for the English, the pallium put the "arch" in "archbishop."

29. Riché and Callu, *Correspondance*, 660, and PL 139:419–20.

pallium's mystique arose from its relation to Peter, which ensured that it was firmly tied to Rome, Peter's resting place, and hence to the papacy, his tomb's guardian.

Although the pallium was a contact relic of Peter, it could also become a more immediate sort of relic if the palliger was himself a saint. This phenomenon was illustrated in Sigehard's compilation of the miracles of Maximin around 963. The *inventio* of the saint's remains yielded his pallium, with which he had been buried: "After his clothes and body had been found whole, the venerable bishop [Radbod of Trier], removing the stole and pallium as relics, immediately placed others around [the body's] holy shoulders.... [The stole and pallium] are the most sacred relics of the body of blessed Maximin, ever venerable and dearer than all treasure to the people of Trier, and today they are kept in this monastery undefiled."[30] Was this *pallium* the pontifical pallium? The fact that it encircled the shoulders made it likely.[31] Further, in a sixteenth-century Trier inventory, under the title "Relics of the patrons of our church," "a large part of the pallium sent to blessed Maximin from Rome" was listed.[32] The recovered garments manifested the *virtus* of true relics, for Sigehard described the wonders God worked through them. For example, after a priest of the abbey was stricken with fever while celebrating Mass, the abbot ran to his aid with Maximin's relics: "When he had taken the stole and pallium of the saint and placed them upon the head of the priest, after all the pain was forced into his chest, his senses returned.... Thus the sacred relics by divine power chased the harmful suffering from the chest into the belly, from the belly into the hips, and also from there into the legs, so that they finally drove it out from the feet."[33] A sacred object in its own right, the pallium was so intimately associated with its wearer that it could also reflect his holiness and, through his

---

30. AASS Mai 7 (die 29):33. With what garb did Radbod replace the pallium on Maximin's body? Perhaps a copy was made, since the pope would not have provided a second pallium, especially for a dead man.

31. At least, it was interpreted as such. Since Maximin lived in the fourth century, before the popes are known to have sent the pallium to other bishops, it may have been some other vestment.

32. Ibid., 34.

33. Ibid., 30.

presence in heaven, become an instrument of God's might—a relic twice over.

Tightening the Bond

An important way of developing pallium usages was to broaden those which fostered tighter ties to Rome. Strengthening the personal association with the pope that the vestment signified would relate key bishops more clearly and closely to the Roman bishop as their theoretical head. In this period it took two chief forms: encouraging the reception of the pallium in Rome, and adding further papal prerogatives to the grant of the pallium.

Personal Reception

Embassies, pilgrimages, special missions, and problematic situations continued to afford opportunities for the pallium to be obtained in person, but they were sporadic.[34] Nevertheless, personal reception of the vestment escalated in the present era: in particular cases it became habitual rather than exceptional.[35] These cases fell into three categories: newly established metropolitans, southern Italian metropolitans, and English metropolitans.

First, the archbishop of a metropolitan see in the process of being erected often went to Rome to receive his pallium. Adalbert did so upon the foundation of the see of Magdeburg for the newly evangelized territory of the Slavs, as Pope John XIII made specific note in his privilege of 968: "Because you yourself have come to the apostolic see to do this ... and because we know that it is effective for the progress of the Christian religion and the salvation of a countless

---

34. Four examples from this period can be cited: Richer of Liège (Folcuin of Lobbes, *Gesta Abbatum Lobiensium*, in MGH SS 4:63), Heribert of Cologne (Lambert of Deutz, *Vita Heriberti*, in MGH SSRG 73:156), Bruno of Querfurt (Thietmar of Merseburg, in Trillmich, *Chronik*, 342), and Peter of Girona (John XIX in 1030, JL 4089, BF 129, ZPUU 2:1109).

35. In this regard Reuter may have too quickly dismissed the pallium as an instrument of papal influence ("Europe," 34). Indeed, the efforts surveyed in this chapter may have indicated, at least on the part of some popes, a worried reaction to the trend toward independent bishoprics noted by Reuter.

people, we ourselves give you the pallium ... we ourselves, moved by excessive love, place it around you."[36] The archbishop's personal presence permitted John himself, in a clear sign of favor and support, to vest him with the pallium. Indeed, the wording conjured the scene of an emotional pope draping the vestment around Adalbert's shoulders. Such a scene conveyed something of the bond established by a face-to-face encounter between pope and palliger. A gift's impact was felt more strongly when handed over personally, for the recipient had to display his gratitude immediately and convincingly. When the same pope was pressed to unite the metropolis of Tarragona, long abandoned due to Muslim occupation, to the see of Vic and raise Vic's bishop, Atto, to archbishop in 971, the document prepared for the occasion implied that Atto had come to Rome by changing the formulaic "we have sent the pallium" to "we give the pallium."[37] Atto and Count Borrell II of Barcelona had indeed journeyed to the Eternal City to erect Vic as a substitute for Tarragona and free Catalonia from the metropolitan jurisdiction of Narbonne, although it is doubtful whether John approved this scheme and issued the privilege.[38]

Even Pilgrim of Passau's forgeries, which sought a retroactively justified erection of that see as an archbishopric, adhered to this pattern. According to one falsified letter, a ninth-century prelate, "coming to the thresholds of the apostles for the sake of prayer," regained the metropolitan rights that Lorch had possessed of old, along with the pallium.[39] But Pilgrim's own pallium petition to Pope Benedict VI in 973/74 (probably never sent) excused his absence in Rome by invoking the magnitude of his missionary efforts: "Behold, most loving

36. JL 3728, GP 4:78 no. 74, BZ 450, ZPUU 1:375.
37. JL 3747, BZ 477, ZPUU 1:409.
38. See Kehr, *Papsttum,* 12–14; Lawrence J. McCrank, "Restoration and Reconquest in Medieval Catalonia: The Church and Principality of Tarragona, 971–1177" (PhD diss., University of Virginia, 1974), 94–101; and Deswarte, "Rome," 14–15. Because the papyrus original of JL 3747 has been preserved, most scholars assume its authenticity; Jonathan A. Jarrett, however, argues compellingly that it was prepared by a Roman notary at the Catalonians' initiative but failed to win papal approval and was never officially issued ("Archbishop Ató of Osona: False Metropolitans on the Marca Hispanica," *Archiv für Diplomatik* 56 [2010]: 29–33).
39. JE †2566, GP 1:162 no. †10, Marsina, *Codex,* 1:5. The forger duly changed the formulaic "we have sent" to "we have given" (ibid., 1:6).

of lords, I am held back, delivered to ecclesiastical duties of this sort. And lest I had delayed the conversion [of the Hungarians and Slavs], I put off going and throwing myself at your most holy feet."[40] Since he could not personally pay his respects to the pope, as may have been expected for the effective elevation of Passau to an archbishopric, he sent envoys with his request. To judge from these cases, perhaps because precedent was lacking to a newly created archdiocese, attaining the vestment at this crucial moment of ecclesiastical reorganization required more serious negotiations than a mere letter could accomplish.

Second, the popes usually required the archbishops of southern Italy, which had once lain within the ecclesiastical province of Rome, to come to the apostolic see for both episcopal consecration and the pallium. In order to counter Byzantine expansion, Latin archbishoprics were erected in this period south of Rome, and the popes hoped to retain sway over them.[41] When Pope John XIII raised Benevento to archiepiscopal status in 969, he laid a special obligation on future holders of the see, as he wrote to Archbishop Landulf: Benevento's rights were guaranteed in perpetuity only if "your successors do not delay to receive consecration and the use of the pallium by decree from the holy Roman and apostolic see."[42] To be ordained in Rome, the archbishops had to travel there, where they would also be given the pallium. Certainly this practice reflected a tighter rein on southern Italian prelates than that exercised over others in the contemporary Western church.[43] Later popes remembered it. Its clearest expression occurred in privileges for the archbishops of Salerno, as in Pope John XV's letter to Archbishop Amatus I in 989: "After your death your successors should come to the apostolic see and receive the use of the pallium and consecration by decree."[44] Consecration

---

40. Marsina, *Codex*, 1:42.

41. See Ramseyer, *Transformation*, esp. 127–29, 135, and G. A. Loud, *The Latin Church in Norman Italy* (Cambridge: Cambridge University Press, 2007), esp. 32–46, 118. For a later period, see Claudia Alraum, "Pallienprivilegien für Apulien zwischen 1063 und 1122," *Specimina Nova Pars Prima Sectio Mediaevalis* 6 (2011): 11–32.

42. JL 3738, IP 9:54–55 no. 15, BZ 459, ZPUU 1:391.

43. It revived the ancient relations between the area and its metropolis of Rome (Ramseyer, *Transformation*, 40–41).

44. JL 3833, IP 8:346 no. 11, BZ 674, ZPUU 1:581. Practically the same clause

by the pope himself and personal reception of the pallium were remnants of previous subjection to the pope as Roman metropolitan, as well as signs of current subjection to the pope as Italian primate.

Aspects of the southern Italian model could be applied more broadly. The popes attempted to do so in Istria and Dalmatia, where encroaching Aquileian and Byzantine claims threatened to undermine Rome's traditional influence. In 888 Pope Stephen V promised the pallium to Theodosius, bishop of Nin and recently elected archbishop of Split, but only if he appeared in person: "The pallium and its use, which you keep asking for, will be more prudently given when, with God's mercy cooperating, you yourself come to the thresholds of the apostles."[45] The pope may have wished to reinforce the connection of Dalmatia to the Roman church, or to scold Theodosius for his pluralism or his consecration by the patriarch of Aquileia rather than the pope.[46] The early patriarchs of Grado, though consecrated at home, had been instructed to "hasten" to the pope to receive the pallium, according to the early eleventh-century *Chronicon Gradense*.[47] Pope Benedict VIII palliated Vitalis of Dubrovnik in 1022 in terms that expected personal presence: "We grant you [the pallium], while reserving the consecration of your successors to us and our successors forever."[48] The alteration of the formulaic "we

---

occurred in succeeding letters to archbishops of Salerno: John XV to Grimwald in 994, JL 3852, IP 8:346 no. 12, BZ 720, ZPUU 1:626; Sergius IV to Michael in 1011, JL 3988, IP 8:346–47 no. 13, BZ 1073, ZPUU 2:862; Benedict VIII to Benedict in 1016, JL 4011, IP 8:347 no. 14, BZ 1170, ZPUU 2:953–54; Benedict VIII to Amatus II in 1019, JL 4027, IP 8:348 no. 16, BZ 1207, ZPUU 2:999–1000; and Benedict IX to Amatus III in 1036, JL 4032, IP 8:348–49 no. 17, BF 190, ZPUU 2:1133.

45. JL 3448, MGH Epp. 7:351.

46. See Vlasto, *Entry*, 189–97. Two years before, Stephen had charged Theodosius with presiding over both sees at once and having gone to Aquileia instead of Rome for his consecration (JL 3416, MGH Epp. 7:338). The latter point seems to have resurfaced in the present letter. Perhaps the pluralism had been resolved, and the pope was offering him the pallium for his new see, Split; because an episcopal translation was involved, the pope wanted him to appear personally and justify it. The problem of pluralism was often connected to translation (Scholz, *Transmigration*, 159, 173). It may have seemed more important to tie Split more closely to Rome than to worry about the status of its current occupant; after all, the pallium was described as "more prudently given."

47. Monticolo, *Cronache*, 1:40.

48. JL 4042, BZ 1252, ZPUU 2:1027. See Heinrich Schmidinger, "Die Pallium-

have sent" to "we grant," and the requirement to come to Rome for ordination, implied that Vitalis and later archbishops would receive the vestment directly from the pope. As in southern Italy, the papacy desired to hold on to its ecclesiastical territories in the northeast. One way to strengthen its bonds with that area was to use the pallium to form relationships of personal dependence.

Third and last, it became customary, even compulsory, for English archbishops to procure the pallium personally in Rome. With few exceptions, archbishops of Canterbury made the trip from the early tenth century on, and those of York from the late tenth or early eleventh century on.[49] The long, hard journey from England to Italy was a momentous event that could exact a heavy toll on these churchmen.[50] Aelfsige of Canterbury froze to death in an Alpine blizzard *en route*, as the priest "B." described around 1000: "When he strove, according to the custom of supreme pontiffs, to hasten to the Romulan city for the princely festoon of the pallium, a very great hardship opposed him in the Alpine mountains because of snow. It had immobilized him with such great numbness of cold that he expired, dying under these circumstances."[51] Here the practice of going to Rome

---

verleihung Benedikts VIII. für Ragusa," *Mitteilungen des Instituts für österreichische Geschichtsforschung* 58 (1950): 31–49. Schmidinger speculates that this grant was the first to Dubrovnik and that the pope was erecting the see as an archbishopric (ibid., 42–46). The absence of the clause leaving the church's status unchanged and the reservation of the archbishops' consecration to the pope support this notion. But the instruction to wear the pallium as his predecessors had, unless ignored as "rein formelhaft," militates against it.

49. See R. R. Darlington, "Ecclesiastical Reform in the Late Old English Period," *The English Historical Review* 51 (1936): 417–18; Levison, *England*, 242; Whitelock et al., *Councils*, 1:442–43; Brooks, *Early History*; Veronica Ortenberg, "The Anglo-Saxon Church and the Papacy," in *The English Church and the Papacy in the Middle Ages*, ed. C. H. Lawrence, rev. ed. (Phoenix Mill: Sutton, 1999), 49, 52; and Tinti, "Archiepiscopal Pallium," 311–19. There may have been earlier instances, e.g., Bertwald of Canterbury in 693 (Levison, *England*, 242n1) and Egbert of York in 735 (according to an entry in the *Anglo-Saxon Chronicle* that Levison claims to be mistaken, ibid., 243).

50. See Stephen Matthews, *The Road to Rome: Travel and Travellers between England and Italy in the Anglo-Saxon Centuries*, BAR International Series 1680 (Oxford: Archaeopress, 2007).

51. *Vita Dunstani*, in Rolls 63:38. See Michael Lapidge, "B. and the *Vita S. Dunstani*," in *St. Dunstan: His Life, Times and Cult*, ed. Nigel Ramsay, Margaret Sparks, and

for the pallium was characterized as the *consuetudo* of English metropolitans. The same hagiographer portrayed Dunstan of Canterbury's journey in much rosier hues:

> Soon after he had received the episcopate, he made the long march to the Roman city, which is customary for high priests, by a successful route. And the Lord was the companion of his journey and did not abandon the one who held on to him with a pure faith.... Finally, with the Lord leading, he reached the desired church of the Roman see, where he gloriously received the princely pallium with the privilege of the prelacy, together with the apostolic blessing. And having surveyed the burial places of the saints and relieved Christ's poor, he returned again to his country by roads of peace.[52]

Dunstan's fortunate travel was evidence of his sanctity: the stories told about him on the road and in Rome illustrated his virtue and God's guidance. His presence in the Eternal City was corroborated in 960 by Pope John XII's grant, which substituted "we commend the pallium" for the formulaic "we have sent the pallium."[53] It is unclear why it came to be expected that English metropolitans had to obtain the pallium in person. Perhaps the fact that the archbishops of Canterbury and York had increasingly been translated from other sees made it necessary to seek explicit papal permission for their canonically dubious promotions. Even then, what started the practice may not have been the popes' insistence, but rather English desire for these metropolitans' authority to be seen as incontestable.[54] The English church's history of close association with the papacy, and the prominence the pallium had always held in its ecclesiastical organization, help to explain the extra efforts expended by its prelates to acquire the vestment.

Nevertheless, some English bishops came to complain vociferously about the practice. Clearly they felt bound to it, and resented it.

Tim Tatton-Brown (Woodbridge: Boydell, 1992), 247–59. *Pallium principalis infulae* must be interpreted in reverse as "the princely festoon of the pallium," a strip of cloth marking him who held first place among the bishops. Cf. Aribo of Mainz's phrase "the primary decorations of my dignity" (to Meinhard I of Würzburg in 1024, Jaffé, *Bibliotheca*, 3:359).

52. Rolls 63:38, 40.
53. JL 3687, BZ 284, ZPUU 1:273.
54. See Brooks, *Early History*, 216–17.

Creativity   245

In the early eleventh century one of them, probably Wulfstan II of York, drafted a protest to the pope revealing awareness of an older tradition and lamenting the present predicament: "We want it to be known to your Bountifulness, just as we read in the histories of the English written by Bede, our historian and praiseworthy teacher, that so huge a labor, namely to take the pains of traveling to Rome continually for the sake of the pallium, did not press upon our ancestors as the custom afterwards developed."[55] Citing Bede, Popes Boniface V and Honorius I, and Alcuin, the English episcopate struggled to throw off a yoke unknown to previous centuries, a burdensome innovation, as they saw it.[56] Shortly thereafter, King Canute of

55. Whitelock et al., *Councils*, 1:445. Levison proves that the letter belonged to a much later period than its traditional date of 805 (*England*, 241–48). The abrupt beginning and ending, and the address *venerabili pape illi*, suggest that it was a draft (perhaps never sent) or formula (perhaps a recurring grievance) or generalized argument. Whitelock dates it to around 1020, but Brooks believes that it originated earlier, perhaps in the late tenth or early eleventh century (*Early History*, 386n104). Dorothy Bethurum argues persuasively that its author was Wulfstan, who may have been pressured to go to Rome and composed this letter when another archbishop, perhaps Lyfing or Aethelnoth of Canterbury, was likewise being pressured ("A Letter of Protest from the English Bishops to the Pope," in *Philologica: The Malone Anniversary Studies*, ed. Thomas A. Kirby and Henry Bosley Woolf [Baltimore: Johns Hopkins University Press, 1949], 97–104). Gareth Mann ("The Development of Wulfstan's Alcuin Manuscript," in *Wulfstan, Archbishop of York: The Proceedings of the Second Alcuin Conference*, ed. Matthew Townend, Studies in the Early Middle Ages 10 [Turnhout: Brepols, 2004], 261–65) and Tinti ("Archiepiscopal Pallium," 332) examine how Wulfstan developed his thoughts on the matter. Wulfstan's intimate relationship with Canute may explain that king's efforts in a similar cause.

56. Bede's history showed that the popes had established the English hierarchy to be self-propagating, with the pallium sent from Rome (Michael Lapidge, André Crépin, Pierre Monat, and Philippe Robin, eds., *Bède le Vénérable: histoire ecclésiastique du peuple anglais (Historia ecclesiastica gentis Anglorum)*, Sources chrétiennes 489 [Paris: Cerf, 2005], 1:192–96, 206–40, 302–8, 322–38, 380–88). Boniface V had sent the pallium to Justus of Canterbury in 624, along with the authority to consecrate bishops (JE 2006, Haddan and Stubbs, *Councils*, 3:72–73). In Honorius I's letter to Honorius of Canterbury in 634, the two archbishops were meant to consecrate each other and thus were sent pallia, an arrangement spurred by the great distance between England and Rome (JE 2020, Haddan and Stubbs, *Councils*, 3:84–85). According to Alcuin, *two* archbishoprics had been erected precisely so that their incumbents could avoid the long journey to Rome for consecration and the pallium, an intention at times hampered "on account of the disagreements of kings" (to Offa of Mercia in 792/93, Lehmann, *Holländische Reisefrüchte*, 33–34). Wulfstan concluded his letter with anti-simoniacal sentiments, perhaps an oblique protest against the pallium

England, returning from a pilgrimage to Rome in 1027, reported to the English clergy his advocacy to the pope on their behalf: "I complained again before the lord pope, and I pleaded that it displeased me very much that my archbishops were being compelled so much by the immensity of the moneys that were exacted from them as they headed for the apostolic see to receive the pallium according to custom. And it was decreed that it should not happen henceforth." His grievance was directed against the expenses of the pallium trip, but the obligation to trek to Rome itself was assumed without comment as *mos* (custom). The *pecuniae* may have been travel expenses, tolls, the pallium fee, or some combination of these. The involvement not only of the pope, but also of the emperor and the king of Burgundy and "the other princes through whose lands we have passage to Rome," hinted that bothersome tolls were a major issue.[57] Despite these indications of reluctance, English archbishops continued to make the arduous journey. Indeed, a mid-eleventh-century Canterbury pontifical detailed a ceremony for enthroning an archbishop upon his return from Rome with the pallium, which he laid on the altar before solemnly putting it on.[58]

Whether archbishops of newly erected metropoles, prelates of southern Italy, metropolitans of England, or others in more exceptional cases, those receiving the pallium in person were numerous enough that a ceremony of investiture developed during this period. An early pontifical, the so-called Leofric Missal, originally compiled

---

fee. Whitelock points out that the letter addressed not only the obligation to go to Rome, but also the consecration of one archbishop by the other—a rare occurrence in England, where translations were the norm (*Councils*, 1:443–45). She proposes a connection to the similarly argued *additamentum* in certain English pontificals (e.g., the Pontifical of Dunstan, in Conn, "Dunstan," 103).

57. Whitelock et al., *Councils*, 1:510. Although the original Old English text (now lost) dated from Canute's journey, it was not translated into Latin until after the Norman Conquest. "Again" implied a similar, earlier complaint, either a lost one by the king or the English bishops' protest drafted by Wulfstan. It is unknown what improvements, if any, were effected. Some scholars (e.g., Levison, *England*, 248, and Ortenberg, "Anglo-Saxon Church," 48–49), perhaps influenced by Wulfstan's complaint, assume that the king meant the pallium fee, which is possible, though not certain from the text itself.

58. On this rite, found in Cambridge, Corpus Christi College, 44, see Tinti, "Archiepiscopal Pallium," 326–28.

around 900 for the church of Canterbury, is the oldest extant attestation of a set of three prayers to be said over an archbishop, two before and one after he received the pallium.[59] These texts may have been old Roman prayers, transmitted to England early because of that land's long-established reception of the vestment.[60] A number of later pontificals carried the same prayers, in two slightly varying recensions, English and continental.[61] The continental family, represented by certain copies of the Romano-Germanic Pontifical (originally composed in Mainz between 950 and 962), was destined to have the greater impact.[62] The oldest copies that contained the pallium prayers, though made in the mid-eleventh century, were likely based on a book used in Rome around 1000.[63] They prefaced the prayers with a special rubric: "These prayers are to be said by the lord pope over an archbishop before [giving] the pallium."[64] It was presumed that an archbishop was the usual recipient, and that the pope himself performed the rite of conferral, with the archbishop present. The rubric was likely tenth-century, since it was also present in the Sacramentary of Ratold, which outfitted the prayers of an English pontifical with continental features between 972 and 986.[65]

---

59. Nicholas Orchard, ed., *The Leofric Missal*, Henry Bradshaw Society 114 (London: Boydell, 2002), 2:432–33. These texts belonged to the original layer of the book, before tenth- and eleventh-century supplementation. At this time English archbishops did not yet regularly go to Rome for the pallium, and unlike the rubrics of the later Romano-Germanic Pontifical, these made no mention of the pope; the investiture was a local rite that occurred upon receipt of the vestment sent from Rome.

60. See ibid., 1:108.

61. See ibid., 1:106–7.

62. See Vogel, *Medieval Liturgy*, 230–39, and Vogel and Elze, *Pontifical*.

63. On the earliest manuscripts (Monte Cassino, Biblioteca della Abbazia, 451, and Rome, Biblioteca Vallicelliana, D.5), see Vogel and Elze, *Pontifical*, 3:16–18, and Tinti, "Archiepiscopal Pallium," 323. Tinti connects the Cassinese provenance of these manuscripts with the custom that southern Italian archbishops had to come to Rome for the pallium, which encouraged the rite's spread to the south.

64. Vogel and Elze, *Pontifical*, 1:229.

65. Orchard, *Sacramentary*, 46. The so-called Sacramentary of Ratold contained an English pontifical adjusted for use on the Continent, and its section on episcopal consecration and the conferral of the pallium may be called a hybrid (ibid., xcvi–xcvii, cxxiv, cxxviii). Its last rubric indicated that the pallium was conferred just before the final prayer, called a "consecration"—not a prayer of episcopal consecration, which had already taken place, but rather a solemn blessing.

The papacy would come to rely on this procedure as metropolitans came more often to Rome, especially during the reform period.

Again, evidence of English discontent may be seen, now in their liturgical books. In place of the rubric preceding the pallium prayers, the Pontifical of St. Dunstan included a note that Oda of Canterbury may have composed: "There should be this addition if the archbishop of Christ Church [Canterbury] or St. Peter's Church [York] wishes to ordain an archbishop on one side or the other, according to the decree of Pope Honorius to Archbishop Honorius, as is read in the eighteenth chapter of the second book of the history of the English."[66] The prayers were presented as an *additamentum* to the rite of episcopal consecration in a particular case: when one English archbishop ordained the other, in accord with Honorius I's instructions. Then, presumably, the pallium would have been sent from Rome, to be received after the consecration. Thus the ordaining archbishop would substitute for the pope and say these prayers over the new archbishop. Whether this case ever happened in this era, when English archbishops were ordinarily translated from other sees (thus not needing consecration) and then traveled to Rome for the pallium, seems doubtful. Instead, the note may have been meant to remind the English of their ancient rights, and was spurred perhaps by the same forces that would later produce the English bishops' letter of complaint.[67]

Additional Prerogatives

Sometimes a routine gift had to be enhanced for its meaning to be appreciated. If the bestowal of the pallium derived its appeal and

---

66. Conn, "Dunstan," 103; cf. 253. The reference was to JE 2020, as reproduced in Bede's history (Lapidge et al., *Histoire*, 1:386, 388). Story, "Bede," believes that Bede and Willibrord similarly used Honorius's privilege as a precedent for ensuring the continuity of archbishoprics. Orchard proposes as the note's author not Dunstan, who went to Rome for his pallium, but one of his predecessors, probably Oda, reacting as the successor of Wulfhelm, "the first archbishop of Canterbury in centuries to have collected the pall in person from the pope" (*Leofric Missal*, 1:107–8). However, the note may have been included in view of Dunstan's potential role as consecrator of an archbishop of York (Tinti, "Archiepiscopal Pallium," 326n62).

67. Michael Richter's list of seven liturgical books that contained the note seems inaccurate (*Canterbury Professions*, Canterbury and York Society 67 [Torquay: Devonshire, 1973], lxiii n2); Orchard counts only four (*Leofric Missal*, 1:108).

relevance from sharing a papal insigne, its significance was heightened when it was the pope's own vestment that was removed from his shoulders and given to a petitioner. Gregory V may have invented this extraordinary practice. Abbo of Fleury informed that pope in 996 that the see of Reims was once more occupied by Arnulf, "to whom I offered *your* pallium, with that tenor with which I had received it from your holy hands."[68] As a special sign of papal favor, perhaps intended to comfort Arnulf, who had lost his own pallium, the gift would surely have shored up the authority of an archbishop who had been deposed and imprisoned for the last six years. The same pope around the same time, according to a twelfth-century version of the *Anglo-Saxon Chronicle,* endowed Aelfric of Canterbury with a similar honor: "Archbishop Aelfric came to Rome, and the pope received him with great honor and ordered him to celebrate Mass in the morning at the altar of St. Peter, and the pope himself put his own pallium on [him] and greatly honored him."[69] At the time a struggle for the see of Canterbury was raging between secular and regular clergy. Gregory vested Aelfric, the regular candidate, with *his agene pallium* as a mark of approbation, which buttressed the archbishop's questioned authority.[70]

In 1006 the saintly Alphege of Canterbury enjoyed the same favor, as recorded in Osbern's late eleventh-century *vita*: "Reaching Rome, he appeared before the Roman pontiff and sought conversation [with him]. When [the pope] had offered him every opportunity to speak, they were allied to each other, while speaking with such great love that the same pope surrounded him with his own stole of his apostolate, and honored him before all the Roman senate, in memory of the heavenly keybearer."[71] Expressing an intimate bond with the archbishop, Pope John XVIII made this remarkable gesture, which brought Alphege public honor and connected him

---

68. Riché and Callu, *Correspondance,* 660; emphasis added. Cf. Alcuin, *Vita Willibrordi,* in Reischmann, *Willibrord,* 58.

69. Baker, *Anglo-Saxon Chronicle,* 8:91; cf. 95.

70. Brooks judges much of this story "as fictitious as 'F's other insertions on the same theme," i.e., regarding the contest between seculars and regulars, but he does not provide detail (*Early History,* 259).

71. AASS Apr 2 (die 19): 635.

more closely to Peter. Finally, Aethelnoth of Canterbury received the pope's own pallium in 1022, as two twelfth-century versions of the *Anglo-Saxon Chronicle* asserted: "Archbishop Aethelnoth traveled to Rome, and was received there with great honor by Pope Benedict [VIII], and [he] put *his* pallium on him with his own hands. Afterwards [Aethelnoth] celebrated Mass there with the same pallium, and after Mass feasted with the pope. With the pope's blessing he returned to his archiepiscopal see."[72] The honorable welcome, the carefully worded manner of receiving the vestment, the permission to celebrate Mass there (presumably at the *confessio* of Peter) while wearing it, and the banquet afterwards all hinted of special treatment. The several English examples suggest that the papacy, at a time when complaints were forming around pallium practices, intended to reinforce its relationship with England and sweeten the prospect of the onerous trip to Rome.[73]

A similar intent to fortify relations with Rome must have lain behind a new custom in the eleventh century: coupling the conferral of the pallium with the bestowal of other prerogatives originally created for and restricted to the papacy. The first indication of this practice arose in the tenth century, according to Folcuin of Lobbes. In 980 he testified that Richer, the winner of a schismatic clash over the bishopric of Liège, had been not only given the pallium, unlike any of his predecessors, but even presented with "the horse covered for processing in the apostolic manner."[74] Along with the pallium, this *nac-*

72. Baker, *Anglo-Saxon Chronicle*, 8:111; emphasis added. The "E" version said the same (Irvine, *Anglo-Saxon Chronicle*, 7:75), but the Latin version of "F" omitted "his" before "pallium" (Baker, *Anglo-Saxon Chronicle*, 8:112).

73. Brooks suggests that Aethelnoth's election as the first English archbishop in a century to need consecration (and thus not to have to approach the pope for permission for his translation), the two-year delay in his journey to Rome for the pallium, and the contemporaneous preparation of the English bishops' letter of complaint (Whitelock et al., *Councils*, 1:445) all contributed to Benedict's extravagant response: the pope sought to entice English archbishops to continue to come to Rome, since the custom reinforced papal authority so clearly (*Early History*, 291). Stressing Aethelnoth's special honors, Brooks accepts the dubious "D" version of the *Anglo-Saxon Chronicle* (Cubbin, *Anglo-Saxon Chronicle*, 6:63–64) as evidence of the bestowal of *two* pallia, as Lanfranc later received (Janet M. Bately, ed., *The Anglo-Saxon Chronicle: A Collaborative Edition* [Cambridge: Brewer, 1986], 3:85), and of the pope's reconsecration of Aethelnoth.

74. *Gesta Abbatum Lobiensium*, in MGH SS 4:63.

cus, a ceremonial saddlecloth used by the popes during processions, must have increased the user's prestige due to its papal associations (at least for those who were aware of them).[75] Pope John XIX provided this right in pallium grants to Thietmar II of Salzburg in 1026 and Bardo of Mainz in 1032, in almost the same words: "We give permission to ride upon a caparison in festive stational processions."[76] Just as the pope mounted a specially clad horse for processions to Roman churches on feast days, so now these palligers could do the same in their own cities. The pallium could not be worn outside of church, but through this privilege the use of other papal trappings penetrated the sphere of civic life.

The other shared prerogative of this period was the *crux gestatoria* or processional cross, a crucifix raised on a long staff and carried before the pope during processions.[77] In 1012 Pope Benedict VIII gave this right to Walthard of Magdeburg ("You may have the banner of the cross carried before you") and, with an interpretive admonition, to his successor Gero ("We grant your Fraternity to have the banner of the cross carried before you, and you should always remember to follow that which goes before you by denying both the vices and the desires of the world").[78] In 1016 the same pope gave it to Poppo of Trier, and in 1024 to Humphrey of Magdeburg.[79] In 1026 Pope John XIX continued the tradition by permitting the cross to Thietmar II of Salzburg, and in 1032 to Bardo of Mainz.[80] As with the *naccus,* these

---

75. See Hacke, *Palliumverleihungen,* 125; Braun, *Liturgische Gewandung,* 526–27; Pierre Salmon, *Étude sur les insignes du pontife dans le rit romain: histoire et liturgie* (Rome: Officium Libri Catholici, 1955), 40–41; and Rathsack, *Fuldaer Fälschungen,* 1:301–2.

76. JL 4074, GP 1:17 no. 37, BF 66, ZPUU 2:1072–73. The later grant replaced the possibly unfamiliar "caparison" (*naccus*) with "horse," but the intended meaning was the same (JL 4098, GP 4:89 no. 110, BF 149, ZPUU 2:1122).

77. See Hacke, *Palliumverleihungen,* 125; Salmon, *Étude,* 40–41; and Rathsack, *Fuldaer Fälschungen,* 1:302–4.

78. JL 3989, GP 10.1:51 no. 83, BZ 1100, ZPUU 2:897; and JL 3990, BZ 1101, ZPUU 2:899.

79. JL 4010, GP 10.1:52 no. 85, BZ 1169, ZPUU 2:952; and JL 4058, GP 7.1:54 no. 134, BZ 1271, ZPUU 2:1039. Dagmar Jank argues that the former was likely altered fifty years later, but he does not specifically question its content ("Bemerkungen zu einigen Trierer Palliumurkunden des 11. Jahrhunderts (JL 4010, JL 4151, JL 4646)," *Kurtrierisches Jahrbuch* 22 [1982]: 13–22).

80. JL 4074, GP 1:17 no. 37, BF 66, ZPUU 2:1072; and JL 4098, GP 4:89 no. 110,

prelates were exalted in the civic arena when the *vexillum crucis* was borne before them, as occurred in Rome. Perhaps all these beneficiaries were Germans because, like the pope, they were prince-archbishops, with accoutrements both spiritual and secular. Or perhaps the pope singled out imperial prelates to stress the Roman character of the empire. The German metropolitans, ever striving for further distinctions, certainly did not object.

As other papal prerogatives joined the pallium in distinguishing favored bishops, it was only natural that envy arose and falsification followed. The see of Magdeburg, only recently founded and elevated to a place among the older German archbishoprics, was especially eager to accumulate such rights. An interpolator, probably from the circle of Archbishop Tagino around 1011/12, inserted perquisites next to the use of the pallium in Pope Benedict VII's confirmation of Magdeburg's privileges for Archbishop Giselher in 981: "Whoever is ordained archbishop in the church of Magdeburg should bear before himself the standard of the cross.... He should have the power to ordain cardinal priests, deacons, and subdeacons, who should wear dalmatics, *lisinae*, and sandals in the Roman manner for celebrating Mass at the altar of St. Maurice the martyr."[81] The key phrase was *more Romano*: the processional cross and the specially vested cardinals made Magdeburg into a little Rome.[82] A related interpolator added similar prerogatives to Pope Benedict VIII's 1012 pallium grant to Archbishop Walthard: "You may ordain cardinal priests in your church, whose number is complete at twelve. Those who minister at the high altar may be clothed every day with dalmatics, and on feast days with sandals. Similarly I have also granted [you] seven cardinal deacons, who use dalmatics every day (except for a fast), and sandals on feasts. In

---

BF 149, ZPUU 2:1122. In the latter, clauses from *Si pastores ovium* were modified to group the *naccus* and the cross with the pallium as *dignitates*.

81. JL 3808, GP 5.2:214–15 no. 19, BZ 600, ZPUU 1:531. *Lisinae* was perhaps a Latinized Old High German word for a type of garment, which betrayed the interpolation's origin. Alternatively, it referred to the maniple (*mappula*) or *pallium linostinum*, a vestment worn by Roman deacons, and thus another sign of Magdeburg's connection with the Roman church (MGH Conc. 6.2:375n79).

82. On local cardinalates outside Rome, see Carl Gerold Fürst, *Cardinalis: Prolegomena zu einer Rechtsgeschichte des römischen Kardinalskollegiums* (Munich: Fink, 1967), 74–86, 146–51.

addition, I also allow [you] to have partnership among the cardinal bishops of our see."[83] These words may well have been drawn from a draft privilege composed by the church of Magdeburg around 1003 but never accepted by Rome. In it were included not only the pallium, the processional cross, the cardinal priests and deacons, and the archbishop's status as a cardinal, but also his right "to be enthroned only by a messenger of the Roman see."[84] The extravagant privileges claimed by Magdeburg were never achieved, probably because the papacy wished to uphold a balance among the powerful German archbishops. But the fact that such ties to Rome were highly sought illustrated that they were not viewed as constricting, but uplifting.

Bestowal of the pallium had now become one among a number of papal gestures of favor.[85] Such gestures seem to have mattered to prelates, and could cause competitive instincts to surface. To the chagrin of Aribo of Mainz, whose own use of the pallium had been removed, that of his nephew Pilgrim of Cologne was embellished with further honors. Aribo grumbled to Empress Cunigund in 1024: "Whereas the honor of the pallium was forbidden to me, though unjustly, the honor of [Pilgrim's] pallium was not only improved, but in a certain way, as they say, gilded, as if his dignity were thus increased, and his solemnity doubled."[86] Perhaps Aribo was referring to Pilgrim's appointment as librarian of the Roman church, a second cause for Cologne's celebration, but its conjunction with the pallium prompted Aribo to bemoan his own sorry lack.[87] As papal preroga-

83. JL 3989, GP 10.1:51 no. 83, BZ 1100, ZPUU 2:897.
84. JL †3823, BZ †738 = †981a, ZPUU 2:783–85. The preamble also alluded to the special relationship between Magdeburg and Rome.
85. When John XIX palliated Poppo of Aquileia in 1027, he also instructed him to wear the rational, an episcopal vestment sometimes seen as a counterpart to the pallium, only on certain festivities, just as the pallium itself (JL 4085, IP 7.1:29–30 no. 53, BF 101, ZPUU 2:1094; *ceteris* was probably an error for *certis*). The pope did not grant him the rational, nor was it a papal prerogative, but he attempted to bring it under his control by regulating its use. On the rational, possibly descended from an early non-Roman pallium common in Gaul, or created in the tenth century as an equivalent to the ancient Jewish high priestly rational, see Braun, *Liturgische Gewandung*, 676–700; Honselmann, *Rationale*; Gamber, "Superhumerale"; and Miller, *Clothing the Clergy*, 64–76.
86. Jaffé, *Bibliotheca*, 3:361.
87. See BZ 1267. Alternatively, Aribo was referring to a greater number of pal-

tives proliferated among palligers, such "gilded pallia" became less and less exceptional.[88]

Adapting the Use

The tenth- and early eleventh-century papacy could be creative when fine-tuning the use of the pallium and the ideas surrounding it. The limitations on its use and the admonitions accompanying it were now often adapted to its recipient. In addition, writers of this period deepened the symbolic interpretations that imbued it with significance and value. In these ways the pallium retained its freshness as a meaningful gift, more complex and more highly prized than the other prerogatives with which it was sometimes joined.

Pallium Days

The occasions on which the pallium was permitted to be worn were at first hardly different from those of the Carolingian age. The language of customary usage—that a palliger should wear the vestment as his predecessors had worn it, or as previous popes had dictated—continued to pepper pallium grants.[89] But only in a handful of cases was this language the sole regulation governing its use.[90]

---

lium days than that allowed to the archbishops of Mainz. Some scholars even theorize that the privilege of crowning the king had been stripped from Aribo and given to Pilgrim (Beumann, *Theutonum nova metropolis*, 24–25). Given the expressions "as they say" and "in a certain way," the improved or "gilded" pallium was not meant materially.

88. Hacke concludes that the pallium alone was no longer sufficient to express the archiepiscopal dignity (*Palliumverleihungen*, 126).

89. The clause from *Si pastores ovium* might be retained (Benedict VIII to Vitalis of Dubrovnik in 1022, JL 4042, BZ 1252, ZPUU 2:1027). Or, instead of relying on the recipient's knowledge of past regulations, the written prescriptions of previous grants (John XII to Dunstan of Canterbury in 960, JL 3687, BZ 284, ZPUU 1:273) or the pope's own knowledge of a see's tradition (John XII to Henry of Trier in 962, JL 3691, GP 10.1:43 no. 63, BZ 303, ZPUU 1:281) might be invoked. Lacking palliated predecessors, a newly elevated archbishop had to use the vestment as other archbishops did (John XIII to Atto of Vic in 971, JL 3747, BZ 477, ZPUU 1:409). New cautions to cling to precedent might be raised (John XIX to Thietmar II of Salzburg in 1026, JL 4074, GP 1:17 no. 37, BF 66, ZPUU 2:1073; and to Bardo of Mainz in 1032, JL 4098, GP 4:89 no. 110, BF 149, ZPUU 2:1122).

90. Seven grants in this period lacked lists of pallium days. The form of one was

Usually it was supplemented by a more explicit list of pallium days. During the first half of this period, such lists were entirely traditional: grants following Gregory IV's version of *Si pastores ovium* continued to name Christmas and Easter; the feasts of the apostles, St. John the Baptist, and the Virgin Mary's assumption; and the anniversaries of the dedication of the recipient's cathedral and of the recipient's consecration.[91]

But in 957 innovations began that greatly altered the shape of these lists, fit them better to their recipients, and allowed them to be employed in a more subtle exercise of influence. The credit belonged to John XII, often maligned for his youth and debauchery. In his grant that year to Henry of Trier, this pope (or his chancery) gave the old list of pallium days a major overhaul. The series was increased from seven to sixteen, with the additions of the octave of Christmas (January 1), the Epiphany (January 6), Maundy Thursday (more specifically, "at the consecration of the sacred chrism," three days before Easter), the Ascension (forty days after Easter), Pentecost (fifty days after Easter), the feasts of the purification (February 2) and birth (September 8) of the Virgin Mary, particular feasts observed in the province,

---

unusual and possibly inauthentic (John XV to Libentius I of Hamburg in 989, JL 3835, GP 6:50–51 no. 61, BZ 677, ZPUU 1:585). Four others relied on the appeal to local custom found in their respective *Liber Diurnus* formulas (Leo VIII to Rodwald of Aquileia in 963, JL 3701, IP 7.1:27–28 no. 45, BZ 338, ZPUU 1:299; a Passau forgery, JK †767, GP 1:159–60 no. †1, Lehr, *Piligrim*, 31; Gregory V to Gerbert of Ravenna in 998, JL 3883, IP 5:52 no. 166, BZ 830, ZPUU 2:691; and Benedict IX to Hugh I of Besançon in 1037, JL —, GaP 1:44–45 no. 21, BF 199, ZPUU 2:1138). Two more were directed to Salerno, but extant grants to these archbishops often have corrupt texts (Benedict VIII to Amatus II in 1019, JL 4027, IP 8:348 no. 16, BZ 1207, ZPUU 2:999; and Benedict IX to Amatus III in 1036, JL 4032, IP 8:348–49 no. 17, BF 190, ZPUU 2:1133).

91. E.g., Stephen V to Herman I of Cologne in 890, JL 3457, GP 7.1:36 no. 72, Wisplinghoff, *Rheinisches Urkundenbuch*, 2:159–60; and Anastasius III to Ragimbert of Vercelli in 912, JL 3550, IP 6.2:11–12 no. 15, BZ 7, ZPUU 1:59. A Hamburg privilege had this list, but added another occasion, "when the relics of saints are deposited by you" (Sergius III to Hoger in 911, JL †3549, GP 6:43 no. 42, ZPUU 1:56)—perhaps reflecting concern for relic translations in an area that had to import relics, and for church dedications in an area still being evangelized. (For an isolated precedent, see Gregory the Great to John II of Ravenna in 594, JE 1330, IP 5:25–26 no. 32, CCSL 140:280–81.) The list in one Hamburg privilege broke off after the first four feasts (Leo VII to Adaldag in 937/39, JL 3612, GP 6:45 no. 46, BZ 133, ZPUU 1:130).

and the celebration of episcopal ordinations.[92] The anniversary of the cathedral's dedication was replaced with the broader expression "at the dedications of churches," and thus the local feasts, while still celebrating times of importance to the regional church, now included acts of consecration (of churches and of bishops) not permitted before receiving the pallium. Through these changes the pallium's visibility was significantly augmented. It was also linked more closely to its wearer's power, as manifested in consecratory rites.

By no means did this list for Trier become standard, even in the privileges of John XII himself. From now on the only rule was variety, along with a certain degree of confusion.[93] Yet meaningful trends can be noticed.[94] Liturgical feasts considered important enough for

---

92. JL 3682, GP 10.1:42 no. 62, BZ 275, ZPUU 1:263. As the *missa chrismalis* was celebrated on Maundy Thursday, its inclusion may have belatedly adhered to Nicholas I's decree that allowed the pallium's use on that day (to Ralph of Bourges in 864, JE 2765, BH 711, MGH Epp. 6:636); cf. a Passau forgery, JL †3602, GP 1:164 no. †15, BZ †120, ZPUU 1:116, and Benedict VIII to Gero of Magdeburg in 1012, JL 3990, BZ 1101, ZPUU 2:899. It is unclear whether all Maundy Thursday ceremonies or the Chrism Mass alone was intended, but Nicholas's decree and the frequent appearance elsewhere of the entry *in cena Domini* implied the former. Consecrating the chrism was occasionally emphasized perhaps because it was one of the archiepiscopal functions forbidden before reception of the pallium (*Invectiva in Romam*, in Ernst Dümmler, ed., *Gesta Berengarii Imperatoris: Beiträge zur Geschichte Italiens im Anfänge des zehnten Jahrhunderts* [Halle: Waisenhaus, 1871], 149).

93. Privileges that cited lists in other privileges sometimes got them wrong, as if no clear records were being kept. Some grants, without explanation or apparent reason, dropped otherwise traditional pallium days, even days that had consistently been conceded to a prelate's predecessors. Ambiguity plagues some entries, e.g., in the difference between the anniversary of a cathedral's dedication and the dedication of a new church, or between all the feasts of the apostles and the feast of *the* apostles (Peter and Paul). Some lists were inexplicably vague. Finally, long lists were particularly subject to corruption during transmission (and few originals have been preserved); moreover, lists affecting one's standing or power were prone to tampering. Thus the trends described here must be accepted cautiously, even if the quantity and distribution of evidence are broad enough to lend them credence. These sorts of problems echo those encountered in diplomatic studies of the *enumeratio bonorum* (Dietrich Lohrmann, "Formen der Enumeratio bonorum in Bischofs-, Papst- und Herrscherurkunden (9.–12. Jahrhundert)," *Archiv für Diplomatik* 26 [1980]: 281–311, and Giles Constable, "Les listes de propriétés dans les privilèges pour Baume-les-Messiers aux XIe et XIIe siècles," *Journal des savants* [1986]: 97–131).

94. One of Pilgrim of Passau's forgeries (JL †3602, GP 1:164 no. †15, BZ †120, ZPUU 1:116–17) is included in this analysis because it seems to have been based on authentic privileges.

the use of the pallium multiplied at this time. After John XII added two Marian celebrations to the traditional one, John XIII added yet another (the Virgin's annunciation, March 25) in a privilege of 969.[95] Now all four of the major Marian feasts authorized by Pope Sergius I in the late seventh century were pallium days.[96] Other notable saints' feasts, including Stephen (December 26) and All Saints (November 1), as well as significant days from the temporal cycle, such as Holy Saturday (that is, the Easter Vigil, since the day before Easter was otherwise aliturgical) and Easter Monday (the day after Easter), began to crop up in this period.[97] Increased exposure to the pallium among the faithful would have amplified its associations with its wearer and his prelatial role, but its continuing limitation to the most solemn days kept it from being regarded as just another vestment.

In addition, palligers were increasingly allowed to wear the vestment on saints' days of particular significance to their churches. Frederick of Salzburg could don the pallium on the feast of St. Rupert, the see's founder (usually March 27, but in Salzburg September 24, when his relics had been translated to the cathedral), and his successor Hartwig could do so also on the feasts of St. Michael the Archangel (September 29) and St. Martin of Tours (November 11), the patrons of early churches in Salzburg.[98] Successive archbishops

95. To Landulf of Benevento, JL 3738, IP 9:54–55 no. 15, BZ 459, ZPUU 1:391.

96. See Vogel, *Medieval Liturgy*, 69, 128n241. Some or all of these must have been meant by the phrase *in festivitatibus Mariae* (e.g., a Passau forgery, JL †3602, GP 1:164 no. †15, BZ †120, ZPUU 1:117; and Benedict VIII to Gero of Magdeburg in 1012, JL 3990, BZ 1101, ZPUU 2:899), but they were sometimes expressly numbered as four (e.g., John XIX to Poppo of Aquileia in 1027, JL 4085, IP 7.1:29–30 no. 53, BF 101, ZPUU 2:1093–94). When the phrase was singular and non-specific ("the festivity of Mary"), her principal feast, the Assumption, was probably implied (e.g., John XIII to Adalbert of Magdeburg in 968, JL 3728, GP 4:78 no. 74, BZ 450, ZPUU 1:375, where that feast fit chronologically in the list according to the liturgical year).

97. St. Stephen first occurred in 973/74 (a Passau forgery, JL †3602, GP 1:164 no. †15, BZ †120, ZPUU 1:117), All Saints in 993 (John XV to Hartwig of Salzburg, JL 3851, GP 1:16 no. 36, BZ 719, ZPUU 1:624), Holy Saturday in 1026 (John XIX to Thietmar II of Salzburg, JL 4074, GP 1:17 no. 37, BF 66, ZPUU 2:1072), and Easter Monday in 1030 (John XIX to Peter of Girona, JL 4089, BF 129, ZPUU 2:1110).

98. John XII to Frederick in 962, JL 3689, GP 1:14–15 no. 31, BZ 302, ZPUU

of Benevento were granted the pallium for the feasts of St. Michael, whose nearby shrine on Monte Gargano was a renowned pilgrimage goal, and the translation of St. Bartholomew (June 13), whose relics were preserved in Benevento.[99] To Willigis of Mainz the use of the vestment was given on the feasts of St. Victor (October 10), in whose honor the archbishop had founded a collegiate church; St. Alban (June 21), an early martyr of the city, on whose burial site a famous monastery had grown up; and Sts. Sergius and Bacchus (October 7), whose relics had been translated to the nearby town of Heiligenstadt.[100] To his successor Bardo it was granted also on the feasts of St. Martin of Tours, the patron of the recently constructed cathedral; St. Lambert (September 17), the patron of an important church in the city; and Sts. Aureus and Justina (June 16), an early martyred bishop of Mainz and his sister, to whom a new foundation in Heiligenstadt was dedicated.[101] Peter of Girona was allowed to wear the pallium on the feast of St. Saturninus (November 29), who had preached in northern Spain near the city.[102]

Sometimes more summary expressions were proffered, which could indicate locally venerated saints ("each festivity of the church entrusted to you"), patron saints ("those saints whose bodies or

---

1:279; and John XV to Hartwig in 993, JL 3851, GP 1:16 no. 36, BZ 719, ZPUU 1:624. See GP 1:4, 46–47.

99. John XIII to Landulf in 969, JL 3738, IP 9:54–55 no. 15, BZ 459, ZPUU 1:391; John XIV to Alo in 983, JL 3822, IP 9:56 no. 17, BZ 626, ZPUU 1:552; and Sergius IV to Alfanus II in 1011, JL 3970, IP 9:56–57 no. 20, BZ 1054, ZPUU 2:856. See IP 9:46, 71. St. Michael's on Monte Gargano was confirmed among the archbishopric's possessions.

100. Benedict VII in 975, JL 3784, GP 4:79 no. 77, BZ 542, ZPUU 1:472. On St. Victor's, see GP 4:52–53, 207–8, and Georg May, "Die Organisation der Erzdiözese Mainz unter Erzbischof Willigis," in *Willigis und sein Dom: Festschrift zur Jahrtausendfeier des Mainzer Domes, 975–1975*, ed. Anton Ph. Brück (Mainz: Gesellschaft für Mittelrheinische Kirchengeschichte, 1975), 62; on St. Alban's, see GP 4:52, 199–202, and May, "Organisation," 64; and generally, see Büttner, "Erzbischof Willigis," 306.

101. John XIX in 1032, JL 4098, GP 4:89 no. 110, BF 149, ZPUU 2:1122. On the cathedral, see GP 4:195–97 and May, "Organisation," 62; on St. Lambert's, see GP 4:52; and on Sts. Aureus and Justina's, see GP 4:52 and May, "Organisation," 63. Bardo retained the feasts of St. Alban and of Sts. Sergius and Bacchus, but not that of St. Victor. Either it had been intended only for the house's founder (the previous archbishop), or it accidentally dropped out during transmission.

102. John XIX in 1030, JL 4089, BF 129, ZPUU 2:1110.

memories especially seem to serve as patrons for your bishopric," or "that saint in whose name your church seems to be dedicated"), or saints whose relics were located in the diocese ("those saints whose bodies and relics are in your bishopric," or "your lords, whose bodies you have").[103] The differences suggest that there was no formula, but the similarities imply that a pattern had developed in the papal chancery. Whatever the turn of phrase, the popes tailored the rules governing the use of the pallium to the recipient's church, so that the vestment accentuated the honor of the see and its pastor on the most solemn days in the local calendar. This adaptation made the pallium more desirable to prelates, which is why pallium days were treated as favors that supplemented the central gift. By distributing them judiciously, the popes could reward certain bishops, renew interest in the routine practice of receiving the vestment, and retain an ongoing say in how it was worn.

Honoring bishops was not the only purpose of proliferating pallium days; it could also please lay rulers. Shortly after he crowned Otto the Great emperor in 962, Pope John XII increased Frederick of Salzburg's pallium days: "We grant your Fraternity the pallium, to be used on four festivities on which we did not grant it to you in the other privilege. But now, because of the petition of the most serene and unconquered Emperor Otto, we grant permission, namely on the festivity of St. Lawrence, on the festivity of St. Maurice, on the festivity of St. Rupert, and on the day of your anniversary."[104] The

---

103. John XV to Libentius I of Hamburg in 989, JL 3835, GP 6:50–51 no. 61, BZ 677, ZPUU 1:585; John XIII to Theoderic of Trier in 965, JL 3737, GP 10.1:45 no. 68, BZ 457, ZPUU 1:388; Benedict VII to Willigis of Mainz in 975, JL 3784, GP 4:79 no. 77, BZ 542, ZPUU 1:472 (the celebrations of the cathedral's patron and its dedication assumed special significance here because Willigis was constructing a new cathedral for Mainz)—repeated nearly verbatim in Benedict VIII to Walthard of Magdeburg, JL 3989, GP 10.1:51 no. 83, BZ 1100, ZPUU 2:897, and to Gero of Magdeburg, JL 3990, BZ 1101, ZPUU 2:899, both in 1012; a Passau forgery, JL †3602, GP 1:164 no. †15, BZ †120, ZPUU 1:117; John XVIII to Meingaud of Trier in 1008, JL 3957, GP 10.1:51 no. 82, BZ 1032, ZPUU 2:842; Benedict VIII to Poppo of Trier in 1016, JL 4010, GP 10.1:52 no. 85, BZ 1169, ZPUU 2:952; and John XIX to Thietmar II of Salzburg in 1026, JL 4074, GP 1:17 no. 37, BF 66, ZPUU 2:1072.

104. JL 3689, GP 1:14–15 no. 31, BZ 302, ZPUU 1:279. Frederick's original grant is lost.

new feasts were those of Otto's two favorite patrons, Lawrence and Maurice, and two occasions of significance for Salzburg, the feast of St. Rupert and the anniversary of the archbishop's consecration. A few days later the pope acted similarly for Henry of Trier: "Out of love for the most pious King [sic] Otto, our spiritual son, we grant you the pallium, to be used on St. Lawrence's [day] and on St. Maurice's [day], and on all the festivities on which they are celebrated in your bishopric."[105] On the feast of St. Lawrence (August 10), Otto had won the Battle of Lechfeld (955), and following a vow, he had later founded the bishopric of Merseburg in the saint's honor. Maurice (September 22) was a soldier-saint, the martyred leader of the legendary Theban Legion, to whom Otto had dedicated a monastery in Magdeburg and in whose honor he had later founded an archiepiscopal see there.[106]

Pope John XIII offered a rationale for these extra pallium days when he conferred the vestment on Henry's successor, Theoderic of Trier, in 965: "Out of inestimable love for our most beloved son, Lord Otto, the ever blessed emperor, we bestow [the pallium] in addition on the anniversary of the most blessed Lawrence, on which the same glorious emperor deserved to be the conqueror of his enemies in battle, and the solemnity of blessed Maurice, which he himself, along with the faithful of his kingdom, is said to venerate quite readily."[107] When the same pope palliated Adalbert as the first archbishop of Magdeburg in 968, he included only Lawrence in the list of feasts, but he admitted that the grant arose "out of love for blessed Maurice and Innocent, martyrs, and of those saints who rest in Magdeburg"— and so Maurice must have been assumed under the entry concern-

---

105. JL 3691, GP 10.1:43 no. 63, BZ 303, ZPUU 1:281. The last clause may have referred to lesser commemorations of the same two saints.

106. The Theban Legion was allegedly a Roman military unit composed entirely of Christians, martyred *en masse* in the late third or early fourth century; they were popular saints in the Middle Ages, especially among warriors. On royally fostered devotion to Lawrence and Maurice in the Ottonian era, see Beumann, "Kaisertum," 435–43, and Weinrich, "Laurentius-Verehrung," esp. 58–60.

107. JL 3737, GP 10.1:45 no. 68, BZ 457, ZPUU 1:388. Boshof believes that John's explicit rationale showed that distance from the events was prompting articulation of their meaning (*Erzstift*, 48).

ing saints with relics in that city.[108] Other imperial archbishoprics also enjoyed the addition of these Ottonian feasts, which continued to be mentioned during the next two reigns. To Willigis of Mainz in 975, Pope Benedict VII permitted the pallium "particularly" on these days and on several occasions of importance to Mainz, "out of love" for Otto II.[109] To Libentius I of Hamburg in 989, Pope John XV conceded the vestment on the usual feasts of Sts. Lawrence and Maurice, but rather than acting on an imperial request, he did so "at the wish of [Libentius's] most worthy petition."[110] Probably the archbishop wanted to keep up with the other German metropoles. But in 1012, when Pope Benedict VIII bestowed the pallium on Walthard of Magdeburg in a document based on Willigis of Mainz's, the Ottonian days were omitted: by this time the Ottos were no more.[111]

Other occasions were also deemed to demand the pallium. Through this distinction Pope Benedict VII wished Willigis of Mainz to assume a position of imperial prominence at synods and royal anointings.[112] Although these occasions were not included in the list of pallium days proper, the implication was that he would stand out

---

108. JL 3728, GP 4:78 no. 74, BZ 450, ZPUU 1:375. (Innocent was another martyr of the Theban Legion.) See Beumann, *Theutonum nova metropolis*, 35, 39.
109. JL 3784, GP 4:79 no. 77, BZ 542, ZPUU 1:472.
110. JL 3835, GP 6:50–51 no. 61, BZ 677, ZPUU 1:585.
111. JL 3989, GP 10.1:51 no. 83, BZ 1100, ZPUU 2:897. The Lawrence-Maurice pairing recurred in 1047 (Clement II to Adalbert of Hamburg, JL 4146, GP 6:55–56 no. 78, BF 370, Curschmann, *Ältere Papsturkunden*, 48), 1053 (Leo IX to Adalbert of Hamburg, JL 4290, GP 6:56–57 no. 81, BF 1026, Curschmann, *Ältere Papsturkunden*, 50), and 1068 (Alexander II to Udo of Trier, JL 4646, GP 10.1:66–67 no. 121, Jank, "Bemerkungen," 21). These Ottonian pallium days in Salian times may indicate that the lists had been based on earlier ones in these sees and then submitted by the petitioner to the papal chancery. In addition, a grant to Ralph I of Tours in 1073 included Lawrence and Maurice, but not paired (Alexander II, JL —, Johannes Ramackers, ed., *Papsturkunden in Frankreich: neue Folge*, Abhandlungen der Akademie der Wissenschaften in Göttingen, philologisch-historische Klasse, 3. Folge, 35 [Göttingen: Vandenhoeck and Ruprecht, 1956], 5:70); Maurice was the patron of Tours's cathedral at the time, and Lawrence followed Stephen as the two most important martyrs in the calendar. Finally, a grant to Baldric of Dol in 1109 contained the pairing (Paschal II, JL 6224, PL 163:252), but the document may have been forged.
112. In 975, JL 3784, GP 4:79 no. 77, BZ 542, ZPUU 1:472. Willigis presided at the installation of King Henry II in 1002 (Wolfherr of Hildesheim, *Vita Godehardi Prior*, in MGH SS 11:185).

(*praeminere*) not only as the papally approved principal celebrant, but also by virtue of the distinguishing garment that he wore. Other lists similarly included the celebration of synods, provincial councils at which the palliger presided over his suffragans.[113] Furthermore, the pallium now appeared not only at episcopal consecrations but at other ordinations as well: those of *presbyteri* or *clerici* were added in several lists, or the generic phrase "whenever you fittingly decide to make sacred orders" appeared. Ember Saturdays, a traditional time for ordaining priests and deacons, and those Sundays when bishops were to be consecrated were sometimes specified as pallium days.[114] In sum, like episcopal consecrations, synodal celebrations were acts of provincial jurisdiction; and like church dedications, clerical ordinations were acts of solemn blessing. Both sorts of acts came to be seen as dependent (at least for metropolitans) on possessing the pallium, and so it was natural for it to be worn during them.[115]

---

113. A Passau forgery, JL †3602, GP 1:164 no. †15, BZ †120, ZPUU 1:117; and Sergius IV to Alfanus II of Benevento in 1011, JL 3970, IP 9:56–57 no. 20, BZ 1054, ZPUU 2:856. The latter phrase was taken from a similar one in another Beneventan privilege (John XIV to Alo in 983, JL 3822, IP 9:56 no. 17, BZ 626, ZPUU 1:552), and reinforced by the addition "or at holy synods" to the customary phrase from JE 1326 restricting the pallium's use to the Mass. There is no evidence for southern Italian councils between the ninth and mid-eleventh centuries, but these privileges served as statements of papal intent and blueprints for the development of the new southern Italian archbishoprics (Loud, *Latin Church*, 34–38, 118). For other variations, cf. John XIX to Peter of Girona in 1030, JL 4089, BF 129, ZPUU 2:1110; and Benedict VIII to Alfanus II of Benevento in 1014, JL 4005, IP 9:57 no. 21, BZ 1135, ZPUU 2:924.

114. A Passau forgery, JL †3602, GP 1:164 no. †15, BZ †120, ZPUU 1:117; John XIX to Thietmar II of Salzburg in 1026, JL 4074, GP 1:17 no. 37, BF 66, ZPUU 2:1072; John XIX to Bardo of Mainz in 1032, JL 4098, GP 4:89 no. 110, BF 149, ZPUU 2:1122; John XV to Hartwig of Salzburg in 993, JL 3851, GP 1:16 no. 36, BZ 719, ZPUU 1:624; and Benedict VIII to Poppo of Trier in 1016, JL 4010, GP 10.1:52 no. 85, BZ 1169, ZPUU 2:952. See Vogel, *Medieval Liturgy*, 312–13.

115. All the functions proper to an archbishop and depending on the pallium were never definitively listed in this period; but see Robert L. Benson, *The Bishop-Elect: A Study in Medieval Ecclesiastical Office* (Princeton, N.J.: Princeton University Press, 1968), 168–69, and Sergius IV to Alfanus II of Benevento in 1011, JL 3970, IP 9:56–57 no. 20, BZ 1054, ZPUU 2:856. A unique occasion occurred in a forgery of Pilgrim of Passau: the pallium was permitted "if by chance there is an assembly of neophytes who must be led to the faith of Christ by your exhortation" (JL †3602, GP 1:164 no. †15, BZ †120, ZPUU 1:117). The lack of parallel in authentic documents suggests that the clause was fabricated. It certainly suited the agenda of the

The quantity of pallium days in a list, which generally ranged from ten to nineteen, could be significant.[116] The fact that the pope sometimes increased that number by adding feasts in a second privilege hinted that a greater quantity meant a higher honor.[117] The German metropolitans, for instance, put great weight on this seemingly small matter, which measured their comparative standing and could spark competition.[118] Pope John XIX's 1030 privilege for Peter of Girona was a revealing case. When the bishop agreed to arrange the release of captives on the pope's behalf if the pope palliated him, a mere suffragan, Peter insisted on "at least twelve times a year," a moderate number that would perhaps make him comparable in prestige to his metropolitan in Narbonne.[119] The frequency of wearing the pallium measured the palliger's stature, especially since it determined how often he could be *seen* as a palliger. John consented to this request, but granted Peter the minimal return, "twelve times a year only." The opposition between the bishop's hopeful *vel* ("at least") and the pope's restrictive *solummodo* ("only") is noteworthy. In the subsequent list of pallium days, moreover, John showed himself a stingy donor. Rather than including all apostolic feasts, as was typical, he mentioned only the feast of St. Peter, probably the bare minimum thanks to the vestment's close association with his body. In addition, the pope specified that the bishop could wear the pal-

---

would-be archdiocese of Passau-Lorch, hoping to control a wide swath of missionary territory, to stress its pastor's preaching to the newly converted.

116. In this period the briefest (excluding clear anomalies) were those of Canterbury (John XII to Dunstan in 960, JL 3687, BZ 284, ZPUU 1:273) and Vic (John XIII to Atto in 971, JL 3747, BZ 477, ZPUU 1:410), and the longest were those of Salzburg (John XV to Hartwig in 993, JL 3851, GP 1:16 no. 36, BZ 719, ZPUU 1:624) and Benevento (Sergius IV to Alfanus II in 1011, JL 3970, IP 9:56–57 no. 20, BZ 1054, ZPUU 2:855–56). Counting pallium days involves ambiguity: sometimes it is debatable whether certain occasions were meant to be grouped together.

117. E.g., John XII to Frederick of Salzburg in 962, JL 3689, GP 1:14–15 no. 31, BZ 302, ZPUU 1:279; John XII to Henry of Trier in 962, JL 3691, GP 10.1:43 no. 63, BZ 303, ZPUU 1:281; and possibly John XV to Libentius I of Hamburg in 989, JL 3835, GP 6:50–51 no. 61, BZ 677, ZPUU 1:585.

118. See Zotz, "Pallium," esp. 158–63, 171–75.

119. Only one pallium grant from Narbonne (dated 1097) is known, and its probably corrupt list (lacking Christmas) contained fifteen occasions (Urban II to Bertrand, JL 5688, PL 151:495–96).

lium "in *one* council of your province," that is, at only one synod a year, again to restrict the occasions as much as possible.[120] John's strategy bore all the signs of a reluctant capitulator: coerced, he gave in to pressure, but to preserve some semblance of independent authority, he yielded only what he had to.

Fresh Ideas

New attention was now given to interpreting the pallium. As with the other phenomena discussed in this chapter, these interpretations were rooted in the past, but there were clear signs of a creative engagement with the tradition. The liturgical commentary *De Divinis Officiis*, probably composed in southern Gaul in the early tenth century but falsely attributed to Alcuin, quoted Amalar of Metz's interpretation of the vestment, which compared it to the *lamina* or golden plate on the Jewish high priest's forehead.[121] But the writer expanded this comparison by noting that the plate was likewise worn only on certain occasions and, as a sacred object, was consecrated and bore the "holy," God's very name. Pseudo-Alcuin's understanding of the letters engraved on the plate (Ex 28:36) resonated with Rabanus Maurus's analysis of the pallium's crosses as a reminder of Christ's passion and humanity's redemption.[122] To the later liturgist, the letters stood for "He is the beginning of the passion of life," and he observed: "Many suffered before Christ, but none of them brought life to men through his passion. But Christ, whose blood was poured out on the cross for the redemption of the whole world, brought life to the human race."[123] The choice of images suggests that he was applying the significance of both plate and inscription to the medieval vestment: the crosses were the "inscription" on the new "plate," the pallium.

In another chapter, Pseudo-Alcuin took a different tack. Describing the vestments peculiar to the *summus pontifex* (the Jewish high priest), he strayed from his Carolingian sources in seeking the pallium's antecedent: "Now, instead of the breastplate, the supreme

---

120. JL 4089, BF 129, ZPUU 2:1109–10; emphasis added. According to the Council of Nicaea (325), c. 5, provincial synods should be held twice a year, a rule that circulated widely in medieval Europe.
121. See Brown, "Enigmata Figurarum," 149–51.
122. Zimpel, *De Institutione*, 315.   123. PL 101:1243.

pontiffs, whom we call archbishops, use the pallium, which they receive from the holy Roman see by gift of the pope."[124] He gave no reasons for his selection of the *rationale* (breastplate), but its position on the breast and its connection to the *superhumerale* (ephod) on the shoulders must have called to mind the pallium. This correspondence between the breastplate and the pallium was juxtaposed with the more traditional correspondence between the *lamina* and the pallium, without resolution of the discrepancy. Since Pseudo-Alcuin borrowed the latter from Amalar, perhaps he himself preferred the breastplate as the true prototype.[125] His choice would compete with Amalar's in future works.[126]

Archbishop Oda of Canterbury, a local ecclesiastical reformer of the mid-tenth century, is thought to have elaborated the final prayer traditionally recited at the conferral of the pallium by adding passages with symbolic import.[127] The late tenth-century Pontifical of St. Dunstan preserved these additions. One prayed for humility for the palliger:

Just as, on the outside, he is seen to carry the yoke of sheep's clothing ahead of other priests as the highest of vestments, so, on the inside, may he bear a meek heart before Christ. Thus he may appear to be the producer and bearer of the Lord's word, in which he says: "Take my yoke upon you and learn from me, for I am meek and humble of heart" [Mt 11:29].[128]

---

124. PL 101:1239.
125. See Chydenius, *Medieval Institutions*, 60–61.
126. Cf. Bonizo of Sutri (Ernst Perels, ed., *Bonizo: Liber de Vita Christiana* [Hildesheim: Weidmann, 1998], 108), Bruno of Segni (*De Sacramentis Ecclesiae*, in PL 165:1105–6)—where the pallium succeeded both the rational and the superhumeral combined, a view later followed by William Durandus (*Rationale Divinorum Officiorum*, in CCCM 140:218)—and Lothar of Segni (*De Missarum Mysteriis*, in PL 217:782). Although Boniface IV had mentioned the rational in his pallium grant to Florian of Arles in 613, he did not directly connect the two vestments (JE 2001, MGH Epp. 3:454, quoting JE 1092). However, Pseudo-Alcuin may have drawn upon Pseudo-Germanus's seventh- or eighth-century *Expositio Antiquae Liturgiae Gallicanae*, which compared the *palleum* (perhaps in this case a Gallican vestment, rather than the Roman pallium) to the Jewish rational (CCCM 187:361).
127. See Orchard, *Leofric Missal*, 1:108.
128. Conn, "Dunstan," 104; cf. 254. The hypocritical overtones of "sheep's clothing" seem to have gone unnoticed (cf. Theodulf of Orléans, *De Hypocritis*, in MGH Poet. 1:473).

In this manner symbolism and admonition worked together. Another interpolation had similar characteristics: "Just as the fringes of the fleecy garment reach the feet, this way and that, so, almighty God, may you grant your servant to persevere to the end of life prudent and innocent before your gaze, in things contemplative and active."[129] Besides witnessing that the pallium was woolen and fringed and stretched nearly to the ground, this allegorization of the vestment paralleled its two strips with the active and contemplative lives, and its ample length with final perseverance.[130] The prayer for prudence and innocence alluded to the Gospel episode in which Christ sent his disciples as sheep in the midst of wolves and told them to be both clever and simple (Mt 10:16). Viewed through this imaginative lens, the very fabric of the pallium reminded its wearer how to live a good Christian life.

One of Pilgrim of Passau's forgeries in 973/74 incorporated a reflection on the import of the pallium's crosses: "This clothing, with which you are decorated at the solemnities of the Mass, presents the sign of the cross. Through it, know that you ought both to have compassion for your brothers and to be crucified in your heart to worldly allurements."[131] Pilgrim's sense that such symbolic musing would be appropriate in a papal document was ahead of its time. Forty years later Benedict VIII became the first pope to consider the pallium's allegorical potential in a grant. To Poppo of Trier in 1016 he offered a word of guidance that pointed to the vestment's crosses: "You will appear striking to all if ... you decide to bear in your inner mind the cross of Christ, which you wear on your body under the appearance of the pallium. Then you cry out with the apostle: 'The world has been crucified to me, and I to the world' [Gal 6:14], and with longing also add the prophet's saying: 'Pierce my flesh with nails by your fear' [Ps 118:120]."[132] The palliger was supposed to act

129. Conn, "Dunstan," 105; cf. 255.
130. In the 1190s Lothar of Segni revived this interpretation of the two strips (*De Missarum Mysteriis*, in PL 217:798).
131. JK †767, GP 1:159–60 no. †1, Lehr, *Piligrim*, 31. It is unclear whether the "sign of the cross" referred to the crosses embroidered on the vestment or the T-shape which the vestment assumed in this period.
132. JL 4010, GP 10.1:52 no. 85, BZ 1169, ZPUU 2:951. *Sub pallii specie* may in-

as a Christ-like cross-bearer, while the appended verse from the psalter may have referred to the pallium pins, recalling the nails of Jesus's cross and representing the fear of God.

Thinkers such as Oda, Pilgrim, and Benedict inherited the concept and style of symbolically interpreting the pallium from Carolingian liturgists, but they did something new by aiming it at the wearers of the garb. It was not so much what was said, but where it was said: what had previously been the pious musings of commentators were now inserted into the rites and documents through which the vestment was conferred. The examples were limited, but they paved the way for future changes. In both Pilgrim's forged document and Benedict's authentic one, the significance was tropological—to spur the wearer to moral betterment—and thus served the goal of admonition, a traditional element in pallium grants. Nevertheless, it was innovative for a pope (false or true) to take a page from the liturgical commentaries, and the experiment was not without issue. Interest in pallium symbolism seems to have been largely a Bavarian phenomenon: Pilgrim (in Passau) labored in that land, as did the augmenter of the *Collectio XII Partium* (in Freising), who had inserted Rabanus's remarks into that collection.[133] Even Benedict VIII was exposed to Bavarian influence through his friendship with Emperor Henry II.[134] These facts shed light on the striking allegorical penchant of two later Bavarian popes, Suidger of Bamberg (Clement II) and Gebhard of Eichstätt (Victor II).[135]

---

stead have referred to the crosslike T-shape of the vestment, but the gist was the same.

133. Canon 1.31, Bamberg, Staatsbibliothek, Can. 7, fol. 6v.

134. When Henry, formerly duke of Bavaria, went to Rome to be crowned emperor in 1014, he brought the southern German bishops Egilbert of Freising, Eberhard of Bamberg, and probably Bruno of Augsburg, each of whom had served as his chancellor (Stefan Weinfurter, *Heinrich II. (1002–1024): Herrscher am Ende der Zeiten* [Regensburg: Pustet, 1999], 112–16, 235). Perhaps Benedict's grant to Poppo of Trier was drafted by the recipient, formerly provost of Bamberg's cathedral (ibid., 122). See Kortüm, *Päpstliche Urkundensprache*. This hypothesis may explain the unusual eschatocol, in which the *datarius*, Benedict of Porto, was called a papal legate, as if he had brought the pallium from Rome (JL 4010, GP 10.1:52 no. 85, BZ 1169, ZPUU 2:951–52). See Jank, "Bemerkungen." The early twelfth-century *Gesta Treverorum*, however, reported that Poppo had gone to Rome to receive the pallium (MGH SS 8:175).

135. In 2005 another Bavarian pope, Benedict XVI, spent nearly a third of his

Even without symbolism, the popes continued to admonish palligers. During the first half of this period, customary admonitions were routinely copied in pallium grants, but in the second half, minor alterations were occasionally introduced. It is often difficult to gauge the significance of these changes. For example, Pope John XII's privilege for Dunstan of Canterbury in 960, which followed the formula *Si pastores ovium*, added a directive "not to flee as if terrified when the wolf comes" to the pastoral imagery of the preamble.[136] Was it simply a rhetorical flourish (based on Jn 10:12), or did it urge the archbishop not to abandon his flock during the Viking assaults on England? Similar uncertainty attends other changes in the grant, which variously stressed the archbishop's fellowship with his charges, his discretion, his concern for the good of souls, and his rights.[137] One change reflects wordplay relying on a knowledge of Old English, which suggests that the recipient had influenced the document's wording.[138] Examples of altered exhortations in other privileges can be multiplied; the admonitions of each *Liber Diurnus* formula were tweaked at one time or another.[139] The variety of treatments revealed a papacy convinced of the suitability of admonitions in pallium grants, beholden to the rich deposit found in the traditional formulas, but unafraid to adjust this material (or to accept others' adjustments) when it seemed appropriate.

The aim of these admonitions was nothing less than forming a bishop who was a good shepherd like his Lord—who took his pastoral responsibility humbly but seriously, governed his flock with

---

inaugural homily discussing the pallium's symbolism ("Sollemne Initium Ministerii Summi Ecclesiae Pastoris," *Acta Apostolicae Sedis* 97 [2005]: 705–12).

136. JL 3687, BZ 284, ZPUU 1:273. See Rosenthal, "Pontifical," 157–58.

137. JL 3687, BZ 284, ZPUU 1:273–74.

138. This privilege changed the formula's phrase "loftier (*sublimiores*) among the rest" to "on a loftier pinnacle (*in sublimiori arce*) than the rest" (ibid., 1:273). Although *arce* meant "height" or "pinnacle" in Latin, it was also an Old English word for the pallium (Baker, *Anglo-Saxon Chronicle*, 8:91, 95).

139. See, e.g., a Passau forgery, JK †767, GP 1:159–60 no. †1, Lehr, *Piligrim*, 31; Gregory V to Gerbert of Ravenna in 998, JL 3883, IP 5:52 no. 166, BZ 830, ZPUU 2:691; Sergius IV to Alfanus II of Benevento in 1011, JL 3970, IP 9:56–57 no. 20, BZ 1054, ZPUU 2:856; and John XIX to Bisantius of Bari in 1025, JL 4068, IP 9:317–18 no. 2, BF 65, ZPUU 2:1071 (cf. Alexander II to Andrew of Bari in 1063, JL 4515, IP 9:318–19 no. 4, Pflugk-Harttung, *Acta*, 2:98).

tireless zeal and love, and served as a model of integrity in thought and action. In his pallium grant to Gero of Magdeburg in 1012, Pope Benedict VIII supplied a new preamble that expounded these ideas, containing language reminiscent of *Si pastores ovium* and *Officium sacerdotis*, but also agricultural imagery not found in the traditional formulas. The pope admonished the archbishop, as one who shared the duty "to be vigilant every day for the stewardship of the Lord's sheep, which has been entrusted to us by the supreme Shepherd," to be humble, to follow charity as his guide, to labor and not to rest, and to work hard cutting back thorns, plowing the field, sowing the seed, and storing the fruit.[140] This material did not occur in the privilege of Gero's short-lived predecessor, Walthard, issued only two months before.[141] Rather than repeating that document, Benedict chose to alter it slightly by creating this exhortation. While there may have been a pragmatic reason for distinguishing the two letters, perhaps he also wanted Gero's to be noticed and read, not dismissed as a carbon copy of Walthard's. This suggestion may explain the notable variety of admonitions in the second half of this period. Forming a good shepherd was nothing new, and the *Liber Diurnus* formulas were time-honored ways of approaching that task. But formulas become stale. Tweaking and supplementing them was one way of catching the recipient's attention.[142] Walthard's privilege itself, in fact, had been a modified form of Willigis of Mainz's, which was a patchwork of snippets from three different formulas.[143]

There were indications that the connection between the vestment and the behavior of a good shepherd did indeed sink in. The Saxon priest "B.," writing the life of Dunstan of Canterbury around 1000, testified that when the archbishop returned from Rome bedecked

---

140. JL 3990, BZ 1101, ZPUU 2:898. The letter carried an additional admonition based on the privilege of bearing the processional cross (ibid., 2:899).

141. JL 3989, GP 10.1:51 no. 83, BZ 1100, ZPUU 2:896–98.

142. The *Liber Diurnus* formulas provided a rich lode of language and themes that were selectively mined to fashion personal messages for recipients (H. E. J. Cowdrey, "Archbishop Thomas I of York and the *Pallium*," *Haskins Society Journal* 11 [1998]: 34–35). For evidence that recipients took documentary admonitions seriously, see 384 below.

143. Benedict VII in 975, JL 3784, GP 4:79 no. 77, BZ 542, ZPUU 1:471–73.

with the pallium, he began "to fulfill the name of a true shepherd in all things."[144] Dunstan's predecessor, Oda of Canterbury, prefaced his *Constitutiones*, a canonical collection compiled between 941 and 946, by citing the same pastoral authority, symbolized by his pallium: "The people of God are discreetly granted to the care of shepherds to be multiplied in faith and number. Therefore, I, the humble and least Oda, enriched, as divine clemency bestowed, with the honor of a bountiful prelate and of the pallium, have decided to unite in this document certain teachings not unworthy (unless I am mistaken) of any worshipper of Christ."[145] The archbishop composed this work because he had been endowed with the pallium, a sign of the *pastorum cura* to which Christians were entrusted.[146] Thus, he argued, he had the right and duty to offer guidance to Christ's flock.

Finally, when Archbishop Hugh I of Besançon received the pallium from Benedict IX in 1037, his privilege followed *Si pastores ovium* closely. But the pope added one sentence to the formulaic admonitions, a sentence which had not occurred in previous grants: "Let no intrusion of venality defile the work of your sacred blessing and just judgment."[147] This clause, which would not recur for another quarter-century, introduced a primary point in the agenda of the eleventh-century reform popes, the eradication of simony, despite the early date (a decade before the generally considered advent of the reform papacy).[148] Interestingly, in the same year Benedict re-

144. Rolls 63:40.
145. Whitelock et al., *Councils*, 1:69. *Almi presulis* may have referred to the pope as giver of the honor. Perhaps it echoed *Si pastores ovium*, as revised under Gregory IV, which called Gregory the Great *huius alme sedis presul* (e.g., Gregory IV to Liudpram of Salzburg in 837, JE 2580, GP 1:10 no. 14, Hauthaler and Martin, *Salzburger Urkundenbuch*, 2:27). Although Oda's privilege is lost and its formula unknown, Augustine of Canterbury's successor would have noticed this reference to the "apostle of the English."
146. Oda may have been alluding to the pallium in his images of the shepherd (a commonplace in the traditional formulas) and the race (Amalar's interpretation of the vestment; see *Liber Officialis*, in Hanssens, *Opera*, 2:248–49).
147. JL —, GaP 1:44–45 no. 21, BF 199, ZPUU 2:1138.
148. The next extant pallium grant with the clause was that of Alexander II to Bisantius of Trani in 1063 (JL 4514, IP 9:291 no. 3, Arcangelo di Gioacchino Prologo, ed., *Le carte che si conservano nello archivio del capitolo metropolitano della città di Trani (dal IX secolo fino all'anno 1266)* [Barletta: Vecchi, 1877], 55–57).

structured the papal chancery, which culminated in the appointment of the chancellor, Peter of Silva Candida, as librarian of the Roman church—thus uniting the *sacrum palatium* (the papal administration) with the *scrinium* (the office of document production and preservation).[149] It is tempting to imagine that early currents of ecclesiastical reform, present in the reorganized chancery, inspired the inserted sentence.[150] Even if it lay dormant until the pontificate of Alexander II, the simony clause was a foretaste of a new trend: putting the pallium to work in the cause of the papacy's new preoccupation, church-wide reform.

Conclusion

The innovations of the pre-reform papacy were neither momentous nor systematically carried out, but they put to rest any notion that the period was merely a lull without substantial contributions. In fact, the various kinds of creativity surveyed above were not forgotten during the subsequent era. Thus the portrait of the time between Popes John VIII and Clement II is a strikingly contradictory one. While some aspects of pallium practice settled into routinization, some popes also enriched the tradition with multiplied pallium days and added papal prerogatives. While there was ample evidence of papal neglect, some popes also showed initiative in encouraging personal reception and employing fresh forms of interpretation and

---

149. See Herrmann, *Tuskulanerpapsttum*, 23–24, and Uta-Renate Blumenthal, "The Papacy, 1024–1122," in *The New Cambridge Medieval History*, ed. David Luscombe and Jonathan Riley-Smith (Cambridge: Cambridge University Press, 2004), 4.2:17–20. Herrmann puts Peter's appointment in November 1037, but already in this grant, dated April 15, the *datarius* was "Peter, bishop of Santa Rufina, chancellor and librarian of the sacred Lateran palace" (JL —, GaP 1:44–45 no. 21, BF 199, ZPUU 2:1138).

150. Alternatively, the document may have been forged. In 1049 Hugh was involved in a struggle over his see, which was aired at Leo IX's Council of Mainz, convoked to root out simony (JL 4188, GaP 1:46 no. 27, BF 658, MGH Const. 1:97–100). Perhaps a partisan of Hugh's drew upon a reform-era privilege to produce the present text as support for his beleaguered master. Or the original document (now lost) had deteriorated, and a copyist replaced illegible portions with passages borrowed from a later privilege. See Bernard de Vregille, *Hugues de Salins: archevêque de Besançon, 1031–1066* (Besançon: Cêtre, 1981), 27–28, 60–62, 143–48.

admonition. And while effective control of the vestment sometimes threatened to dissipate, some popes also took steps to enhance key principles behind the use of the pallium, as a sign of confirmation, a papal gift, and an apostolic relic. What accounted for such conflicting currents? A lack of creativity cannot be blamed, but perhaps a lack of focus can. The political vicissitudes that the papacy underwent in this age, and the frequent absence of strong personalities with clearly defined goals, meant that the full potential of the pallium was yet to be harnessed. But with the emergence of the papal reform movement, focus aplenty was soon supplied.

At the Councils of Sutri and Rome in 1046, eager to restore order to a corrupt papacy and thus to gain the imperial crown indisputably, King Henry III engineered the deposition or abdication of three rival claimants to the apostolic see. His nominee for the chair of Peter, Bishop Suidger of Bamberg, took a name—Clement II—that hearkened back to the early church and inaugurated a series of popes dedicated to ecclesiastical reform.[151]

It was a turning point in papal history, but a deeper continuity underlay the activity of the Roman bishops. They had inherited a tool, the papally conferred pallium, that kept taut the ties that bound the provincial churches to Rome. The sweeping vision of some Carolingian popes had become obscured by the more limited scope of their successors in the tenth and early eleventh centuries. But the persistence of the customary use of the pallium in ecclesiastical relationships had ensured that the pontiffs never descended to purely local lords. Continually involved, through the pallium, in affairs throughout the Western church, they had at their disposal a pretext for the more intensive intervention demanded by the coming reform.

The theme of continuity in this period, however, should not veil the real changes introduced by various popes. Some changes reflected the mere conventionality of pallium practice (the scarce demand for precedent, the decline in attached vicariates, the reluctance to withhold the gift, the rarity of royal intercession and palliated suffra-

---

151. See Gresser, *Clemens*, 65–80.

gans) or even the negligence of a papacy not in its prime (less concern for orthodoxy, laxness in treating metropolitan palligers equally, confusion surrounding the personal nature of the privilege). At times these signs of deterioration endangered the pope's hold on the vestment, or at least offered opportunities to other powers to use it for their own ends. Still, these problems were not the whole story. Innovation flared even in the *saeculum obscurum*. Embellishments to traditional practices strengthened the bond between pope and palliger and made past formulas and ideas more relevant. Such improvements proved to be the greatest contribution of this age, as they were maintained and expanded with focused rigor in the next period.

The fabric knit in the Carolingian era, though threadbare in spots, had lasted. The well-worn garment was now patched in places and embroidered with frills, as it were, which enhanced its attractiveness and effectiveness. As the papacy began to exert its headship of the church in unparalleled ways, it would naturally turn, in part, to the pallium to accomplish its goals.

PART 3

THE REFORMER'S BADGE (1046–1119)

The reform papacy and its supporters contributed to a time of great ferment in the Western church's history. To eradicate what were deemed the most flagrant abuses of the age, including simony, clerical unchastity, and lay interference in ecclesiastical affairs, reformers put their hopes in a newly invigorated papacy. The so-called Gregorian Reform was underway. Now asserting and exercising primacy as never before, the popes assumed a role of more active leadership and control, and with little hesitation intervened regularly in nearly every region and aspect of the Latin church. When forces devoted to an earlier model of ecclesiastical organization resisted these innovations, the ensuing conflict, customarily called the Investiture Contest, consumed the attention and divided the loyalties of Christendom for nearly half a century. The paradigm shift involved in this by and large victorious ecclesiastical revolution paved the way for the papal monarchy of the high Middle Ages.

Aspects of this narrative have come under question in recent decades. The reform movement's program was certainly not monolithic. Many laypeople, such as Emperor Henry III, were sincere reformers, although they had no misgivings about intervening in ecclesiastical affairs.[1] Even among the more radically reform-minded,

---

1. See, e.g., John Howe, "The Nobility's Reform of the Medieval Church," *American Historical Review* 93 (1988): 317–39.

275

Figure 5. Henry V receiving the imperial insignia from Pope Paschal II, wearing the pallium, in 1111. From a German copy of Ekkehard of Aura's *Chronicle*, ca. 1114–25. Cambridge, Corpus Christi College, Ms. 373, fol. 83r. Used with permission of the Master and Fellows of Corpus Christi College, Cambridge.

The Reformer's Badge (1046–1119) 277

differing emphases and strategies were present, although the currents largely overlapped and cohered, particularly after the papacy came to dominate the enterprise. Even so, historians have often focused too much on Pope Gregory VII. He did not originate the "Gregorian Reform," and it is dubious how much of a lasting impact his eventful pontificate had.[2]

The "Investiture Contest," moreover, had little to do with lay investiture of bishops, at least at first.[3] Although traditional interpretations of this period are contested, many agree that one of its most significant results was a papacy with a substantially augmented profile and portfolio. This historical turning point invites further attention to *how* the papacy exercised its increased influence in the Western church and world, that is, to "the technologies of power, the cultural and administrative practices" that it used.[4] In this vein, scholars have explored papal legislative, judicial, and financial activity and papal management of synods, legates, and cardinals.[5] But there were other mechanisms as well.

Among the traditional tools at the disposal of the reform papacy, now wielded in robust, inventive ways in the pursuit of reshaping Christian society, was the pallium.[6] The following chapters examine the vestment as a powerful weapon in the hands of the reformers. The ends to which it was put (chapter 7), the manners in which it was employed (chapter 8), and the ways in which it was construed (chapter 9) were adapted to the demands of this era. Accepted ideas and practices surrounding the pallium were resourcefully exploited to serve reform principles and the vision of a Rome-centered

---

2. See, e.g., John T. Gilchrist, "Was There a Gregorian Reform Movement in the Eleventh Century?," in his *Canon Law in the Age of Reform, 11th–12th Centuries*, part 7 (Aldershot: Ashgate Variorum, 1993).

3. See Rudolf Schieffer, *Die Entstehung des päpstlichen Investiturverbots für den deutschen König*, Monumenta Germaniae Historica Schriften 28 (Stuttgart: Hiersemann, 1981).

4. Maureen C. Miller, "The Crisis in the Investiture Crisis Narrative," *History Compass* 7 (2009): 1574.

5. See, e.g., I. S. Robinson, *The Papacy, 1073–1198: Continuity and Innovation* (Cambridge: Cambridge University Press, 1990).

6. On the role of vestments in the reform generally, see Miller, *Clothing the Clergy*, 177–206, 240–41.

church. This climactic movement brings the pallium's story to 1119, the death of Pope Gelasius II, who, as the papal chancellor Cardinal John of Gaeta, had revamped the form and content of pallium grants, and who then served as the last pontiff before the Investiture Contest was settled under his successor. The focus here is on the vestment's part in the dynamics and mechanics of reform; unless noted otherwise, earlier trends can be assumed to have continued more or less intact. These trends had already fashioned an effective instrument of papal influence, but now that instrument would be honed to achieve a passionately pursued purpose.

7

A Tool of the Reform: The Ends

That something new was happening in the Western church became apparent in the first pallium grants issued by the reform popes. Gone, for the most part, were the stale old formulas, and new styles of speaking revealed a shift in attitude. When Pope Clement II bestowed the pallium on Eberhard of Trier in 1047, the document began with a unique preamble that highlighted the vestment as a papal insigne:

> That we keep watch over the sheep of our God and Lord Jesus Christ to banish the plots of diabolical deceit, the name that we have [*episcopus*] indicates. Nevertheless, because we are seen to be greater than the other bishops appointed under us, there is a certain insigne on us, which alleges that we are truly shepherds, not only of sheep, but also of other shepherds—namely, the festoon that is also called the pallium.[1]

Although the pope shared the garment with certain bishops, it was a badge that first distinguished him from bishops, as their bishop, the *pastor pastorum*. Clement's words also applied derivatively to palliated metropolitans, who looked after their suffragans. But fundamentally, as he prefaced the grant to Eberhard, he was engaging in self-

---

1. JL 4151, GP 10.1:56 no. 94, BF 382, Jank, "Bemerkungen," 19. See Gresser, *Clemens*. The "name that we have" probably referred to "bishop," since it had just occurred in the protocol (*Clemens episcopus*), and since Greek *episkopos* meant "overseer."

definition. The reformers' vision of the peculiar role of the papacy was already present: more than simply the highest among bishops, the Roman pontiff exercised a distinct universal responsibility.[2]

As the papacy assumed the leadership of the eleventh-century ecclesiastical reform movement and began to implement its program throughout the Latin church, it sought tools that could extend its influence and enforce compliance with its principles. In its store was the pallium, which had already proven its usefulness for realizing the theoretical reach of papal primacy and creating relationships of subordination and dependence between the popes and the most important churchmen in the West. Thus, as soon as the German king sat reformers on Peter's chair, it was not surprising that use of the vestment took on a new energy and purposefulness. This chapter will attend to the twin goals that the reform papacy hoped to achieve through adroit management of the pallium. First, it was put to work in the struggle against the abuses especially repugnant to the reformers. Second, it provided a means for the popes to attain their desired position as supervisors of the entire church, with the ability to arrange its structures as they saw fit.

The Struggle Against Abuses

It would be simplistic to reduce the reform program to opposition to a handful of abuses, however systemic. Nevertheless, the reformers' concerns followed a general pattern, handily summarized as *puritas et libertas ecclesiae*: the restoration of the church's unsullied integrity, free of undue worldly influences.[3] In this effort to cleanse the church, pallium grants could be occasions for admonishment to correct offenses against the patristic and canonical standards held dear

---

2. Contrast John XIX's preamble for Bardo of Mainz in 1032 (JL 4098, GP 4:89 no. 110, BF 149, ZPUU 2:1121–22), which also mentioned the pallium and its papal origin, but proposed that popes shared it with "other fellow bishops" out of charity—a more horizontal vision of its ecclesiological significance.

3. See Szabó-Bechstein, *Libertas ecclesiae*; Uta-Renate Blumenthal, *The Investiture Controversy: Church and Monarchy from the Ninth to the Twelfth Century* (Philadelphia: University of Pennsylvania Press, 1988); and Kathleen G. Cushing, *Reform and Papacy in the Eleventh Century: Spirituality and Social Change* (Manchester: Manchester University Press, 2005).

by the reform-minded.[4] More specifically, the popes targeted certain widespread problems that compromised ecclesiastical liberty. Positively, they promoted episcopal elections performed freely and according to canon law. Negatively, they challenged lay interference in the making of bishops, as well as the pervasive contagion of simony.

Free Canonical Elections

Leo IX refused to become pope without a free canonical election, that is, uncoerced acceptance by the clergy and people of Rome.[5] Indeed, the early reformers prized this concept, which they interpreted as the local church's voluntary acclamation of a candidate designated for the episcopacy.[6] Since traditionally the pallium was bestowed only after proof of legitimate accession, as a sign of papal confirmation of a bishop's promotion, it was natural in this period to emphasize proper election when the pallium was at stake. Pope Clement II did so in 1047 to justify the translation of John to the see of Salerno and his concomitant reception of the pallium, and Pope Victor II did so a decade later to explain his consecration of Winiman, whom he then palliated and sent to the see of Embrun.[7] Furthermore, intercessory letters sent to the pope to support an archbishop's request for the pallium were often careful to mention the candidate's canonical election. Anselm of Canterbury did so to Pope Paschal II in 1101 on behalf of Gerard of York, and the community of the Canterbury cathedral priory did likewise to the same pope in 1114 for the sake of their newly elected archbishop, Ralph.[8]

The reform popes sometimes went further to ensure that this

4. E.g., Leo IX to Ulric of Benevento in 1053, JL 4299, IP 9:58 no. 23, BF 1107, PL 143:732; Stephen IX to Ulric of Benevento in 1058, JL 4383, IP 9:58–59 no. 24, BF 1370, Paul Fridolin Kehr, ed., *Papsturkunden in Italien: Reiseberichte zur Italia Pontificia*, Acta Romanorum Pontificum 1 (Vatican City: Biblioteca Apostolica Vaticana, 1977), 1:236; and Stephen IX to Alfanus I of Salerno in 1058, JL 4386, IP 8:350 no. 21, BF 1390, Pflugk-Harttung, *Acta*, 2:83.
  5. *Vita Leonis IX*, in MGH SSRG 70:184.
  6. See Paul Schmid, *Der Begriff der kanonischen Wahl in den Anfängen des Investiturstreits* (Stuttgart: Kohlhammer, 1926).
  7. JL 4143, IP 8:349 no. 18, BF 363, PL 142:586; and JL 4369, BF 1306, PL 143:835. See Gresser, *Clemens*, 99–102.
  8. Franciscus Salesius Schmitt, ed., *S. Anselmi Cantuariensis Archiepiscopi Opera Omnia*, 2nd ed. (Stuttgart: Frommann, 1984), 2.4:113, and Rolls 81:227.

principle was consistently followed. Pope Stephen IX palliated Alfanus I of Salerno in 1058, which allowed the archbishop to consecrate his suffragan bishops—but only "with the clergy and people, according to the statutes of the holy canons."[9] When Pope Urban II elevated Daimbert of Pisa as metropolitan over the bishoprics of Corsica and palliated him in 1092, he promised the same right and honor to his successors forever—as long as they entered the see "by the legitimate election of the clergy and people."[10] Pope Leo IX made perhaps the most forceful statement. To his pallium grant to Stephen of Le Puy in 1051, he attached a condition: although the consecration of this bishop of an exempt see was reserved to the pope, he still had to take office through the choice of the clergy and people of Le Puy, or else, presumably, the privilege was void.[11]

Lay Investiture

Despite the notoriety of lay investiture as the defining issue of the reform—the antithesis of *libertas ecclesiae*, and the *cause célèbre* that pitted pope against king—it was seldom mentioned in connection to the pallium.[12] One reason for the silence was that, from the time of Pope Gregory VII, those prelates who had received ring and staff from secular rulers in violation of the reform edict were usually ineligible for papal confirmation through the pallium. Kings apparently never attempted to invest bishops with the pallium themselves, probably because of its long association with the papacy and firm connection to Peter's tomb in Rome. The voices of powerful laity, moreover, tended to disappear from this period's pallium-related evidence; as the reformers tried to demarcate the spiritual and the secular ever more clearly, lay competence to influence any aspect of a

---

9. JL 4386, IP 8:350 no. 21, BF 1390, Pflugk-Harttung, *Acta*, 2:83.

10. JL 5464, IP 3:321 no. 9, PL 151:345. The pope reserved the archbishop of Pisa's consecration to himself, thus subordinating him in the same manner as the metropolitans of southern Italy.

11. JL 4265, BF 897, PL 143:681. Exemption gave the pope consecratory, but not electoral, rights (Vehse, "Bistumsexemtionen," 158–59).

12. See Schieffer, *Entstehung*; Johannes Laudage, *Priesterbild und Reformpapsttum im 11. Jahrhundert*, Beihefte zum Archiv für Kulturgeschichte 22 (Cologne: Böhlau, 1984); and Stefan Beulertz, *Das Verbot der Laieninvestitur im Investiturstreit*, Monumenta Germaniae Historica Studien und Texte 2 (Hannover: Hahn, 1991).

bishop's installation, not only investiture but also palliation, was no longer recognized.

Certainly, not everyone objected to lay investiture. Adam of Bremen, writing in a royalist stronghold between 1074 and 1076, under Archbishop Liemar, one of Henry IV's fiercest supporters, reflected those sympathies. His history of the archbishops of Hamburg repeatedly used the formula "received the staff from King (or Emperor) N. and the pallium from Pope N." to describe the installation of past prelates.[13] Investiture by the secular ruler was thus put on par with the pope's conferral of the pallium, and both acts were necessary, with the two powers harmoniously cooperating, for the elevation of a metropolitan. Wenric of Trier, in a polemical letter to Gregory VII in 1080/81, pointed out an inconsistency in the pope's attitude. He accused him of pursuing a vendetta against Henry IV, whose candidates for the episcopate were persecuted, while pallia were not refused "to persons not introduced but slipped in through the sacred right hand of Rudolf," as he sarcastically put it.[14] The reformers had no problem with lay interference, he implied, if the antiking was involved, and they allowed to him the quasi-sacramental power they had denied to the true king.

Lay investiture came up more often in relation to the pallium when the vestment was bestowed in spite of this abuse. In 1089 Pope Urban II reminded Anselm III of Milan of problems with his accession, including his investiture by the king, "which you yourself know is altogether forbidden in the Roman church."[15] Still, in view of the church's need and the advantage that the archbishop could offer, the pope had reinstated him after his deposition and grant-

---

13. MGH SSRG 2:38, 47, 52, 55, 61, 89, 107, 123, 127–28, 130, 142. The terminology for the insignia and the order in which they occurred seem random. Cf. *Chronicon Breve Bremense*, in MGH SS 7:390–92.

14. *Monumenta Germaniae Historica: Libelli de Lite Imperatorum et Pontificum* (Hannover: Hahn, etc., 1891–), 1:297 [hereafter "MGH LdL"]. See I. S. Robinson, *Authority and Resistance in the Investiture Contest: The Polemical Literature of the Late Eleventh Century* (Manchester: Manchester University Press, 1978), 153–56.

15. JL 5386, IP 6.1:53 no. 124, Robert Somerville, ed., in collaboration with Stephan Kuttner, *Pope Urban II, the* Collectio Britannica, *and the Council of Melfi (1089)* (Oxford: Clarendon, 1996), 120. This letter was preserved only in the *Collectio Britannica*, which also provided a note summarizing Anselm's situation (ibid., 58).

ed him the pallium. Similarly, according to the twelfth-century *Gesta Treverorum*, Pope Paschal II and the Council of Guastalla (1106) deposed Bruno of Trier because he had received the *episcopalia* from a layman. But after three days of penance he was restored and endowed with the pallium, because a person of his "discretion and prudence" was judged necessary for the contemporary church.[16] In the following year the same pope chastised Adalgot of Magdeburg: "We took it hard that you received investiture from the hand of the king, against the prohibition of the apostolic see. Because of this, the pallium should not be sent to your Belovedness at present."[17] Despite the punitive response, Paschal left the door open for a solution in which the archbishop would offer restitution and receive the pallium. In all these cases, the conferral of the vestment could be a gesture of clemency and dispensation, typical of the later reform popes, who strove to coax the reluctant, to avoid full-blown confrontations, and to salvage a battered movement through politically realistic accommodations.[18]

The pallium, moreover, could serve as a reward for those who renounced lay investiture. Since the ninth century, Brittany had longed to win ecclesiastical independence from Tours through the elevation of the see of Dol as a metropolis, which would require the pallium for its bishop. When the Breton leaders embraced the reform program, a gleeful Pope Gregory VII could not refrain from bowing to their request, as he explained in 1077: "When we heard that the princes of that land, against the ancient and very bad custom, out of reverence for almighty God and apostolic authority, wished neither to hold the control of investiture nor to seek the payment of money

---

16. MGH SS 8:192. On the synod, see Georg Gresser, *Die Synoden und Konzilien in der Zeit des Reformpapsttums in Deutschland und Italien von Leo IX. bis Calixt II., 1049–1123* (Paderborn: Schöningh, 2006), 368–78.

17. JL —, Martin Brett, ed., "Some New Letters of Popes Urban II and Paschal II," *Journal of Ecclesiastical History* 58 (2007): 84. The hitherto unknown letters that Brett discovered were probably derived ultimately from the papal registers (ibid., 77–79).

18. See Blumenthal, *Investiture Controversy*, 137–41, 167–70, and Robert Somerville, "Mercy and Justice in the Early Months of Urban II's Pontificate," in his *Papacy, Councils and Canon Law in the 11th–12th Centuries*, part 4 (Aldershot: Ashgate Variorum, 1990), 140–42.

in ordaining bishops anymore ... we considered it worthy to rejoice very much at their devotion and to assent to their petitions."[19] The pope did not free Dol from Tours's metropolitan authority, but this concession was a first step in that direction. Desperate for allies, he used the gift of the pallium in a *quid pro quo* exchange that gained a victory for the reformers.

Simony

Simony was the *bête noire* of the early reform. Named after Simon Magus, who had attempted to purchase the Holy Spirit from Peter (Acts 8:9–24), and long condemned as a heresy (*simoniaca haeresis*), the buying and selling of sacramental grace or ecclesiastical office through customary payments or gifts was nevertheless endemic to the culture. Since it so clearly showcased the church's entanglement in the world, the reform papacy planted it firmly in its crosshairs.[20] In fighting this abuse, the pallium often came into play. As they did when faced with other problems, the popes might justify their bestowal of the vestment by citing the recipient's freedom from simony—as Clement II did regarding John of Salerno—or might reward those who had forsworn the vice with the gift of the pallium— as Gregory VII did for Dol.[21] In the same vein, four canonical collections of this period repeated a notice taken from Pope Gregory the Great's register concerning his treatment of Maximus of Salona.[22] Af-

---

19. To Ralph I of Tours, JL 5021, Santifaller, *Quellen*, 1:136.

20. See E. Hirsch, "Der Symoniebegriff und eine angebliche Erweiterung desselben im elften Jahrhundert," *Archiv für katholisches Kirchenrecht* 86 (1906): 3–19; Jean Leclercq, "Simoniaca Haeresis," *Studi Gregoriani* 1 (1947): 523–30; N. M. Häring, "The Augustinian Maxim: *Nulli Sacramento Injuria Facienda Est*," *Mediaeval Studies* 16 (1954): 87–117; John T. Gilchrist, "'Simoniaca heresis' and the Problem of Orders from Leo IX to Gratian," in *Proceedings of the Second International Congress of Medieval Canon Law*, ed. Stephan Kuttner and J. Joseph Ryan, Monumenta Iuris Canonici, ser. C, Subsidia 1 (Vatican City: Sacra Congregatio de Seminariis et Studiorum Universitatibus, 1965), 209–35; and Reuter, "Gifts."

21. Clement to John in 1047, JL 4143, IP 8:349 no. 18, BF 363, PL 142:586–87; and Gregory to Ralph I of Tours in 1077, JL 5021, Santifaller, *Quellen*, 1:136.

22. These included (in roughly chronological order) the *Collectio Sinemuriensis (Remensis)*, Gregory of San Grisogono's *Polycarpus*, the *Collectio VII Librorum* in Vienna 2186, and possibly the collection in Vallicelliana B.89, as well as a paraphrase in Abbo of Fleury's collection.

ter the bishop "swore that he was not mixed up in all the things that had been said against him about women or simoniacal schism," the pope, "moved to mercy ... sent the pallium for the confirmation of the same bishop."[23] These words caught the attention of reformers, and in the early twelfth century Cardinal Gregory of San Grisogono's *Polycarpus*, and another collection based on it, inserted the text among canons on simoniacal episcopal installations.[24]

Conversely, the popes denied the pallium to those guilty of having purchased their offices. Pope Leo IX in 1050, long before Gregory VII's decision, called the bishop of Dol "a simoniac and an outlaw" and excommunicated him and the other Breton bishops "because of the simoniacal heresy with which they have been polluted and are seen to contaminate those ordained by them." Of course, he said, Dol's bishop could not have the pallium or be an archbishop.[25] Also, the zealous reformer Bonizo of Sutri narrated in 1085/86 that Bishop Herman of Bamberg went to Rome for the pallium, was found to have received his see "through money," and was deposed and replaced.[26] Bonizo seems to have conflated two incidents, Herman's trip to Rome to obtain the vestment from Pope Alexander II in 1070, which was successful, and his deposition by Pope Gregory VII in 1075 after his failure to answer complaints of simony.[27]

Pope Alexander II was particularly energetic in combating simony by managing the pallium in new ways. In his grants, among the formulaic admonitions, he began to insert an anti-simony clause, perhaps revived from an isolated occurrence under Benedict IX in 1037.[28] Occurring in his privileges for Bisantius of Trani in 1063, Pe-

23. CCSL 140A:1097.
24. Canon 2.37.9, Horst Fuhrmann and Uwe Horst, eds., *Die Sammlung "Policarpus" des Kardinals Gregor von S. Grisogono*, at http://www.mgh.de/fileadmin/Downloads/pdf/polycarp.pdf, 140; and, in the *Collectio VII Librorum* in Vienna, Österreichische Nationalbibliothek, lat. 2186, also compiled in Rome a few years later, Canon 1.78.12, *Clavis* SV01.078.12. On the collections, see Kéry, *Canonical Collections*, 266–69, and Fowler-Magerl, *Clavis Canonum*, 229–34.
25. To the Breton princes, JL 4225, BF 775, PL 143:648–49.
26. *Liber ad Amicum*, in MGH LdL 1:602. See Robinson, *Authority*, 119–20. Bamberg's bishops were often palliated.
27. See Guttenberg, *Regesten*, 206, 233–40.
28. To Hugh I of Besançon, JL —, GaP 1:44–45 no. 21, BF 199, ZPUU 2:1138.

ter of Bar in 1067, Udo of Trier in 1068, and Arnold of Acerenza in the same year, the clause cautioned the recipient to avoid the taint of lucre: "Let no intrusion of venality defile the work of your sacred blessing and just judgment."[29] Protests against interference and pollution were typical of reform attitudes, which sought the freedom and purity of the church in its functions both sacramental ("sacred blessing") and juridical ("just judgment").[30] In addition, Alexander began to enforce regularly the dictate that petitioners for the pallium had to appear in person to receive the vestment, first formulated under his predecessor. To Ravenger of Aquileia in 1063 he explained one of the reasons for this practice: it was "a precaution especially against the simoniacal heresy, which we know now prevails in certain areas."[31] A face-to-face encounter, presumably, would allow intensive questioning that could uncover a promotion achieved through payment. In fact, indirect evidence shows that Alexander required applicants appearing in person to affirm by oath that they had not taken office through simony.[32] A journey to Rome could also reveal a candidate's unsuitability in unexpected ways. Three hagiographies of this period recalled the tragic death of Aelfsige of Canterbury in the Alpine snow on his way to Rome for the pallium in 959. Each work remarked on his simoniacal acquisition of the see, and two depicted his freezing to death as an act of divine vengeance for his faults.[33]

---

29. JL 4514, IP 9:291 no. 3, Prologo, *Carte*, 56–57; JL 4628, Fr. Rački, ed., *Documenta Historiae Chroaticae Periodum Antiquam Illustrantia*, Monumenta Spectantia Historiam Slavorum Meridionalium 7 (Zagreb: Academia Scientiarum et Artium, 1877), 202; JL 4646, GP 10.1:66–67 no. 121, Jank, "Bemerkungen," 21; and JL 4647, IP 9:456–57 no. 6, PL 146:1344. The Bar document's authenticity has been questioned as an anticipation of later events (Vlasto, *Entry*, 379n159), but its typical Alexandrine characteristics are reassuring. The appearance of the anti-simony clause in 1063 may have coincided with Alexander's synodal restatement of his predecessor Nicholas's decrees against simony (Schieffer, *Entstehung*, 84–95, with edition of JL 4501 on 213–25, col. 4).

30. See Cushing, *Reform*, 111–38.

31. JL 4504, IP 7.1:31 no. 62, S. Loewenfeld, ed., *Epistolae Pontificum Romanorum Ineditae* (Leipzig: Veit, 1885; reprinted in Graz: Akademische Druck- und Verlagsanstalt, 1959), 41.

32. Schieffer discusses the cases of Ralph I of Tours, Udo of Trier, and Herman of Bamberg ("Romreise," 168–69).

33. Osbern of Canterbury, *Vita Dunstani*, in Rolls 63:107; Eadmer of Canterbury,

But the pallium was not just a tool for resisting simoniacal trends in the church. The story was more complicated, for the garb itself had often been an occasion for simoniacal exchanges. As an ecclesiastical favor closely bound to the assumption of high office, the vestment had always been open to treatment as a commodity, if not directly through sale, at least indirectly through more or less compulsory donations. From the age of Gregory the Great, some popes had legislated against the pallium fee, although the problem seems to have never fully disappeared, and many pontiffs of lesser caliber probably accepted such countergifts.[34] That was the secular clergy's assumption in the dispute over the see of Canterbury in 995, according to a version of the *Anglo-Saxon Chronicle*. Their envoys approached the pope and "offered him much treasure and silver, provided that he give them the pallium," but he refused and dismissed them.[35] This blatant attempt to buy the pallium, and thus confirmation, for an archiepiscopal claimant could not have been unique, especially in contested situations.

Even the stalwart reformer Pope Alexander II was the object of simoniacal accusations. In 1066 Anno II of Cologne warned Alexander against the bribes that his enemy, Udo of Trier, was bringing to Rome in expectation of obtaining the pallium:

They come to you laden with gifts, by which they desire to bait you.... You will keep, O my lord, the first sentence of the Apostle [Peter] concerning a matter of this sort—for "their own money to remain with them to their destruction" [Acts 8:20]—for through [money] they say that the successor of Peter can be separated from patristic tradition.... I beseech that they make no settlement with you about the pallium by this exchange.[36]

Vita Odonis, in Andrew J. Turner and Bernard J. Muir, eds., *Eadmer of Canterbury: Lives and Miracles of Saints Oda, Dunstan, and Oswald,* Oxford Medieval Texts (Oxford: Clarendon, 2006), 30, 32, 34; and, without reference to divine vengeance, Eadmer of Canterbury, *Vita Dunstani,* in Turner and Muir, *Lives,* 110, 112.

34. See John the Deacon, *Vita Gregorii Magni,* in PL 75:90, 132 (quoting c. 5 and JE 1378), 144; Zachary to Boniface in 744, JE 2271, GP 4:24 no. 58, Rau, *Briefe,* 170, 172, and in 751, JE 2291, GP 4:35–36 no. 88, Rau, *Briefe,* 294; and the British bishops' complaint, Whitelock et al., *Councils,* 1:445–47.

35. Baker, *Anglo-Saxon Chronicle,* 8:91. The Latin version of this "F" report was similar, but implied that messengers from the regular clergy had forewarned the pope (ibid., 8:94).

36. Wilhelm von Giesebrecht, ed., *Geschichte der deutschen Kaiserzeit,* 5th ed.

Anno invoked the episode of Simon Magus and the tradition of the fathers to exhort the pope to reject the bribes and refuse the pallium; nevertheless, Udo was eventually successful in his quest.[37] Further, in 1077/78 Lambert of Hersfeld included the story of Herman of Bamberg in his annals, but it differed significantly from Bonizo's:

> The bishop of Bamberg, accused of giving money and invading the bishopric through simoniacal heresy, gave [Alexander] many and precious gifts. Through them he swayed his mind, savage against him, to such great meekness that he who (it was thought) would not escape without danger to his honor and rank not only gained impunity for the crime that had been charged, but also received the pallium and certain other insignia of the archiepiscopate from the apostolic see as a blessing.[38]

Lambert was hostile to Herman, and so this account was no more trustworthy than Bonizo's confused rendition.[39] But the notion that bribery could secure papal grace, and the pallium could be bought, was apparently easy to believe.

These perceptions died hard, and repugnance against simony in this period was so fierce that reforming ire was sometimes turned against the reform papacy itself. A satirical poem, probably written in Normandy in the time of Pope Urban II, bemoaned the state of the church: "Spiritual things are now gotten as if cheap gifts, / And holy things are not bestowed for free by the wicked. / ... The things that are particular to [Rome], pallia and money, / Would be lacking and would not suffice to put an end [to her insatiable maw]. / England, Scotland, and bountiful France have given many things, /

(Leipzig: Duncker and Humblot, 1890), 3:1260. See Georg Jenal, *Erzbischof Anno II. von Köln (1056–75) und sein politisches Wirken: ein Beitrag zur Geschichte der Reichs- und Territorialpolitik im 11. Jahrhundert*, Monographien zur Geschichte des Mittelalters 8.1–2 (Stuttgart: Hiersemann, 1974–75), 1:48–52, 2:314–15.

37. At a Roman synod in 1068, Udo was cleared of simony by oath, recognized as archbishop of Trier, honored by the assembly, and soon after given the pallium (Jenal, *Erzbischof Anno*, 1:52, 2:326–27); see Alexander to Udo, JL 4646, GP 10.1:66–67 no. 121, Jank, "Bemerkungen," 21–22.

38. MGH SSRG 38:111–12. If accurately reported, the "other insignia" may have included the processional cross, the *naccus*, and the miter, which Alexander also bestowed on Burchard of Halberstadt (ibid., 38:82).

39. Schieffer does not doubt that Herman gained the pallium, but judges Lambert's version not credible—perhaps he misunderstood the customary pallium fee as bribery ("Romreise," 160).

And they have put together red, scarlet, white fleeces."⁴⁰ The author was lamenting the greedy, simoniacal workings of the papal curia. Characteristic of the Roman church, in his view, were two things: money, the goal of its unquenchable avarice, and the pallium, a constant source of such profit. The countries nearest to the author's heart had tendered considerable amounts, and in return were merely given pallia, described unflatteringly (by their material, their color, and the color of their crosses) as simple textiles. Rome was swindling the Western church by perpetrating a massive, unholy fraud.

However well or ill the Roman church lived up to its ideals, it is unfair to portray reformers as tough on simony but simultaneously willing to sell the pallium.⁴¹ Reform thinkers used a revived interest in canon law to hammer home the impropriety of selling the pallium. Numerous reform collections included canons, often clarified by rubrics, that condemned simony in general and simoniacal handling of the pallium in particular.⁴² The most popular text was *Antiquam patrum*, canon 5 of Gregory the Great's Roman synod of 595:

> Following the ancient rule of the fathers, I decide that nothing is ever to be received from ordinations—neither from the giving of the pallium, nor from the handing over of documents, nor from that which a new pretense has founded through ambition, by the name of *pastellus*.... I altogether forbid the one who is to be ordained or the one who has been ordained to give anything for the ordination or the pallium or the documents or the *pastellus*. As a result, if perhaps anyone presumes to demand or seek anything in the name of payment, he will be subject to guilt at the strict examination of almighty God. However, if the one who has been ordained wishes to offer something to any of the clergy only for the sake of

---

40. *Versus de Romana Avaritia*, in MGH LdL 3:702.

41. In this period many traditional gift-giving practices, which often involved forms of reciprocation, fell under suspicion as sales, especially when the transactions touched on the attainment of office and the conduct of churchmen (Reuter, "Gifts," 161–63). While the popes may have felt this way about gifts between secular rulers and bishops, they continued to draw upon gift-giving models, including the expectation of reciprocity—as long as money was not involved—when conferring the pallium.

42. E.g., the *Collectio Britannica* excerpted Zachary's repudiation of simony in his exchange with Boniface concerning the three pallia (Canon 7[V].9, Paul Ewald, ed., "Die Papstbriefe der brittischen Sammlung," *Neues Archiv der Gesellschaft für ältere deutsche Geschichtskunde* 5 [1880]: 286, quoting JE 2271).

Reform: The Ends   291

thanks—not from an agreement, and not demanded or sought, after the documents and the pallium have been received—we by no means forbid it to be received. For his offering, which has not proceeded from the recipient's ambition, causes no stain of fault.[43]

No fewer than twenty-nine collections in this period contained this prohibition against giving or receiving anything in exchange for any part of episcopal installation, including the grant of the pallium.[44] The final sentence's loophole, allowing a thanks-offering under certain conditions, obviously lay open to abuse. Some collections drew attention to this loophole in their rubrics; one, from northern France in the third quarter of the eleventh century, must have worried some reformers, because it allowed a licit form of donation for the pallium: "In what way to accept that it is a crime, in what way not."[45] Other collections, beginning with those assembled in Italy in the 1050s,

---

43. JE post 1365, MGH Epp. 1:364–65. The *pastellus* may have been a celebratory banquet after the ordination, or a wax seal that gave its name to the documents to which it was affixed and the fee charged for their production (ibid., 1:364n7). The *cartae* must have attested to the grant of the pallium. In response to the suspicions of simony relayed by Boniface, Zachary was perhaps referring to this canon when he protested that no payment had been demanded for the vestments or the documents (in 744, JE 2271, GP 4:24 no. 58, Rau, *Briefe*, 172).

44. These included (in roughly chronological order) the collection in BNF lat. 3858C, the collection in Vat. lat. 3830, the *Collectio Lanfranci*, the *Collectio S. Hilarii Pictaviensis (XVII Librorum)*, the *Collectio CLXXXIII Titulorum (S. Mariae Novellae)*, the collection in BNF n.a.l. 326, the *Collectio LXXIV Titulorum*, Atto of San Marco's *Breviarium Canonum*, the *Collectio IV Librorum*, the *Collectio Burdegalensis*, the *Collectio Tarraconensis* (version 1), Anselm of Lucca's collection, the *Collectio Ashburnhamensis*, the *Collectio XIII Librorum* in Savigny 3, the *Collectio II Librorum vel VIII Partium*, the *Collectio Atrebatensis*, the *Collectio Tripartita A*, the *Collectio IX Voluminum (Sangermanensis)*, Ivo of Chartres's *Decretum*, the *Collectio Tarraconensis* (version 2), the collection in Celle C.8, the *Collectio VII Librorum* in Turin D.IV.33, the *Collectio Brugensis*, the collection in BNF lat. 13368, the *Collectio X Partium* in Cologne 199, Gregory of San Grisogono's *Polycarpus*, the *Collectio III Librorum*, the *Collectio VII Librorum* in Vienna 2186, and the collection in Vat. lat. 3829. In addition, Humbert of Silva Candida included it in his *Adversus Simoniacos* of 1058 (MGH LdL 1:122), and Pseudo-Liutprand paraphrased it (with the threat of anathema) between 1077 and 1085 in his lives of the popes (PL 129:1229–30). The latter added a note, taken from the *Liber Pontificalis* (Duchesne, *Liber pontificalis*, 1:360) but generalized, about Leo II's ruling that archbishops should not have to pay a *consuetudo* for the use of the pallium or any ecclesiastical office (PL 129:1236).

45. Canon 1.183, *Clavis* MY01.183, found in Paris, Bibliothèque Nationale de France, lat. 3858C. On the collection, see Fowler-Magerl, *Clavis Canonum*, 148–50.

chose to lop the sentence off. Humbert of Silva Candida, the dogged enemy of simoniacs, may well have been responsible for this branch of the transmission.[46]

The other prevalent anti-simony text that pertained to the pallium was *Novit fraternitas*, taken from a letter of Gregory the Great to John of Corinth in 595:

> Your Fraternity knows that previously the pallium was not given except after a payment had been given. Since this was unsuitable, having called a council before the body of blessed Peter, prince of the apostles, we forbade anything to be received, either for it or for ordinations, under strict prohibition. Therefore, it is necessary that you do not agree or allow anyone to be led to sacred orders either through payment or favor or the supplication of certain men.[47]

Seventeen collections in this period contained this Gregorian precedent.[48] The three forms of simony listed in the final sentence had also found their way into the admonitions of the *Liber Diurnus* formula *Officium sacerdotis*, and so this train of thought was already associated with the pallium in ecclesiastical tradition.[49] Around 1083 Anselm of Lucca clarified the three forms of simony in the rubric he attached to this canon in his collection, compiled at the request of Pope Gregory VII to defend the reform: "Just as sacred orders, so also

---

46. The earliest witnesses were the collection in Vatican City, Biblioteca Apostolica Vaticana, Vat. lat. 3830, compiled in north-central Italy after 1054 (Canon 7, *Clavis* XC007), and Humbert's *Adversus Simoniacos*, composed in Florence in 1058 (MGH LdL 1:122). Perhaps the former was an intermediate collection from which Humbert drew canonical material for his treatise. On the collection, see Kéry, *Canonical Collections*, 198–99, and Fowler-Magerl, *Clavis Canonum*, 98–99, who labels it "Humbertinish."

47. JE 1378, CCSL 140:366.

48. These included (in roughly chronological order) the collection in BNF lat. 3858C, the collection in Vat. lat. 3830, the collection in BNF n.a.l. 326, the *Collectio LXXIV Titulorum*, the *Collectio IV Librorum*, the *Collectio Tarraconensis* (version 1), Anselm of Lucca's collection, the *Collectio Ashburnhamensis*, the *Collectio XIII Librorum* in Savigny 3, the *Collectio II Librorum vel VIII Partium*, the *Collectio Tarraconensis* (version 2), the collection in Celle C.8, the *Collectio VII Librorum* in Turin D.IV.33, Gregory of San Grisogono's *Polycarpus*, the *Collectio III Librorum*, the collection in Vat. lat. 3829, and possibly the collection in BNF lat. 13658. In addition, Humbert of Silva Candida included it in his *Adversus Simoniacos* (MGH LdL 1:122).

49. V46, Foerster, *Liber Diurnus*, 105–6, with slight variants C45 on 203–4 and A40 on 305–7.

the pallium ought to be given neither for a price nor through favor or petitions."⁵⁰ In 1118/19 a northern Italian collection employed a rubric that was blunt, more so than the text itself: "That the pope should not sell the pallium."⁵¹ It was aimed directly at the Roman pontiff and called the pallium fee a sale; perhaps the redactor had special reason to be vehement in opposing this practice.

The Exaltation of the Papacy

Since the abuses against which the reformers strove were systemic to the Latin church of their day, they sought an equally systemic solution to restore its pristine integrity in head and members. Opting for a top-down approach, they looked to the only authority that spanned the church and, ideally, could carry out a program whose scope transcended regional differences and local interests: the Roman papacy. They achieved a crucial first step, with the help of the German king, by securing the apostolic see for the forces of reform in 1046. From that time forward, the popes took the lead in transforming the Western church according to reform ideals, with or without secular cooperation. Vesting the hopes of the reform in the office of the papacy meant that papal primacy, long acknowledged but seldom fully exploited, had to be reaffirmed, strengthened, and applied on a level heretofore unimagined. As a result, a major aim of the movement, alongside its moral endeavors, was to support and defend both Roman supremacy in Christendom and papal control of ecclesiastical affairs.⁵² Intimately connected to the papacy, yet simul-

---

50. Canon 6.78, Friedrich Thaner, ed., *Anselmi Episcopi Lucensis Collectio Canonum una cum Collectione Minore* (Innsbruck: Wagner, 1915), 2:308. The *Collectio XIII Librorum* in Berlin, Staatsbibliothek Preußischer Kulturbesitz, Savigny 3, compiled around 1089 possibly in Poitiers, borrowed and refined this rubric (Canon 5.54, *Clavis* SA05.054). On Anselm's collection, see 324n7 below; on the other collection, see Kéry, *Canonical Collections*, 226–27, and Fowler-Magerl, *Clavis Canonum*, 155–56.

51. Canon 63.108, *Clavis* PG63.108. On the collection, found in Vatican City, Biblioteca Apostolica Vaticana, Vat. lat. 3829, see Kéry, *Canonical Collections*, 288, and Fowler-Magerl, *Clavis Canonum*, 216–18.

52. See Michele Maccarrone, "La teologia del primato romano del secolo XI," in *Le istituzioni ecclesiastiche della 'societas christiana' dei secoli XI–XII: papato, cardinalato ed episcopato*, Miscellanea del Centro di studi medioevali 7 (Milan: Vita e Pensiero, 1974), 21–122.

taneously reaching out to key prelates throughout the church, the pallium was one means of accomplishing this campaign. The reform popes and their supporters used the pallium to highlight the unique authority of the papacy, to justify papal intervention in and disposition of the local churches, and to modify traditional hierarchical structures to achieve their own ends.

The Pope at the Pinnacle of the Church

The reform popes took advantage of their privileges, particularly the preambles, to emphasize the singular and supreme character of their office.[53] Because this portion of a document spoke in general principles, the pallium was rarely discussed directly.[54] Nevertheless, several preambles were clearly applicable to the vestment that was the subject of their documents. In one, Pope Gregory VII declared: "We are advised by the consideration of the supreme apostolic see ... that we [should] gladly assent ... to the rulers [of churches] seeking the insignia of their honors that they are known to have acquired from of old."[55] Although this preamble implied that the pallium would not be refused if there was legitimate precedent, it also made clear from where it had to be obtained. In two others, Pope Paschal II began: "The kindness of the apostolic see has been accustomed to reserve for each person his own rights, and to guard the privilege of the honor bestowed by the Lord, such that it does not deny to worthy brothers the partnership of dignity [*consortium dig-*

---

53. On the "primacy arengae," see Maria Kopczynski, *Die Arengen der Papsturkunden nach ihrer Bedeutung und Verwendung bis zu Gregor VII* (Bottrop: Postberg, 1936), 61–66, for the popes up to Gregory VII. On the preamble *Potestatem ligandi*, developed under Urban II and often used in pallium grants, see Alfons Becker and Dietrich Lohrmann, "Ein erschlichenes Privileg Papst Urbans II. für Erzbischof Guido von Vienne (Calixt II.)," *Deutsches Archiv für Erforschung des Mittelalters* 38 (1982): 95. On trends in preambles from Clement II to Celestine III, see Heinrich Fichtenau, *Arenga: Spätantike und Mittelalter im Spiegel von Urkundenformeln*, Mitteilungen des Instituts für österreichische Geschichtsforschung, Ergänzungsband 18 (Graz: Böhlau, 1957), 101–12.

54. See, however, Clement II to Eberhard of Trier in 1047, JL 4151, GP 10.1:56 no. 94, BF 382, Jank, "Bemerkungen," 19.

55. To Alcherius of Palermo in 1083, JL 5258, IP 10:229 no. 20, Santifaller, *Quellen*, 1:252–53.

nitatis]."⁵⁶ Here receiving the pallium was portrayed as partaking in honor or authority alongside the pontiff and with his consent. The same pope in three other privileges favored this clause: "We are invited by the debt of charity and compelled by the authority of the apostolic see to show due honor to brothers, and to impart the dignity of the holy Roman church to the rest of the churches, to each in its own measure."⁵⁷ The vestment, in short, was a Roman prerogative graciously given to other bishops as a way of sharing papal prestige with the provinces in varying degrees. Despite the benevolent tone of these privileges, they reminded the recipients of an old principle sometimes obscured: the papacy was the source of the prize, distributed solely at its discretion.⁵⁸

This principle governed some choices made in compiling collections of canon law in this period. Four reform-oriented collections, all from the late eleventh or early twelfth century, appeared conscious of the pallium's role in demonstrating papal primacy when they ordered their canons, wrote their rubrics, or dug up new canonical material. Both the *Decretum* attributed to Ivo of Chartres and the *Collectio Tripartita B* partly derived from it reproduced Pope Nicholas I's ninth-century allowance to wear the pallium on Maundy Thursday.⁵⁹ The first work placed it near canons concerning instruments of papal power (appeals to Rome, papal vicars, synods, and the like); the other work made it the second canon in a book devoted to papal primacy. These prominent places for what seems a liturgical detail must have pointed

---

56. To Crescentius of Split in 1102, JL 5914, PL 163:96. Cf. to Peter of Aix in 1102, JL 5904, PL 163:108, which spoke of a partnership of "honor" rather than "dignity."

57. To Risus of Bari in 1112, JL 6314, IP 9:320 no. 9, Pflugk-Harttung, *Acta*, 2:202. Cf. to Pontius of Besançon in 1105, JL 6056, GaP 1:52 no. 46, Hacke, *Palliumverleihungen*, 153; and to Otto of Bamberg in 1111, JL 6291, GP 3:264 no. 46, PL 173:1323.

58. See Friedrich Kempf, "Die Eingliederung der überdiözesanen Hierarchie in das Papalsystem des kanonischen Rechts von der gregorianischen Reform bis zu Innocenz III," *Archivum Historiae Pontificiae* 18 (1980): 65–68.

59. Canon 5.20, PL 161:329; and Canon 3.8.2, Martin Brett, ed., *Tripartita*, at https://ivo-of-chartres.github.io/tripartita/trip_b_a.pdf, 69, date / revision stamp 2015-09-23 / 898fb. See Nicholas to Ralph of Bourges in 864, JE 2765, BH 711, MGH Epp. 6:636. On the collections, see 326nn17–18 below.

to the pope's unique authority over the pallium's use. Further, pallium-related canons in the two-part Italian *Collectio II Librorum vel VIII Partium* were given such rubrics as "That the custom of any church is either from the privilege of the Roman church or from usurpation," "That no bishop or deacon should use dalmatics without the permission of the apostolic see," and, with the threat of sanctions, "On those who do not ask for the pallium from the pope."[60] These texts gave the impression that all ecclesiastical faculties and practices had to stem from Rome. Finally, among many otherwise lost papal letters preserved in the northern French *Collectio Britannica,* one was Leo IV's ninth-century letter to Ignatius of Constantinople, in which the pope declined a pallium from the patriarch because the Roman church's custom was not to receive pallia, but to distribute them to those of its choosing.[61] By guarding this prerogative, the pope maintained his singular position of power as donor (and avoided a position of dependence as recipient). Indeed, when Pope Alexander II bestowed the vestment on Ralph I of Tours in 1073, he said that the gift redounded "to the glory of Christ, and ours in him."[62]

Papal uniqueness was also highlighted when canon law looked at

---

60. Canon 1.59 [1.60], *Clavis* VA01.059, which drew on JE 1259 but conveniently omitted a third option found there, "general custom"; Canon 1.68 [1.69], *Clavis* VA01.068, which drew on JE 1748 and went on to discuss a similarly granted vestment, the pallium; and Canon 2.228 [5.27], Jean Bernhard, ed., "La collection en deux livres (Cod. Vat. lat. 3832): la forme primitive de la collection en deux livres, source de la collection en 74 titres et de la collection d'Anselme de Lucques," *Revue de droit canonique* 12 (1962): 441, which drew on the canon *Quoniam quidam* from the Council of Rome (875). On the collection, see Kéry, *Canonical Collections,* 227–28, and Fowler-Magerl, *Clavis Canonum,* 150–55.

61. Canon 10(VIII).42, Ewald, "Papstbriefe," 392, quoting JE 2647, edited at MGH Epp. 5:607. On the collection, see Somerville, *Pope Urban,* 3–21; Kéry, *Canonical Collections,* 237–38; Fowler-Magerl, *Clavis Canonum,* 184–87; and Christof Rolker, "History and Canon Law in the *Collectio Britannica*: A New Date for London, BL Add. 8873," in *Bishops, Texts and the Use of Canon Law,* ed. Brasington and Cushing, 141–52.

62. JL —, Ramackers, *Papsturkunden,* 5:69. This phrase was similar to one in another Alexandrine document a decade before: "ad gloriam in xristo et curam," the last word perhaps an editorial misreading of "n[ost]ram" (to Bisantius of Trani in 1063, JL 4514, IP 9:291 no. 3, Prologo, *Carte,* 56)—which may have expanded on the formula *Apostolicae sedis*: "ad gloriam in christo" (V48, Foerster, *Liber Diurnus,* 107, with slight variants C47 on 205 and A42 on 308).

the pope's own pallium. Between 1075 and 1085, a series of titles or theses, perhaps meant to provide the backbone of a canonical collection justifying Gregorian politics, were assembled in Rome to delineate the papacy's prerogatives. These *Propriae Auctoritates Apostolicae Sedis* may have been meant to clarify and expand the more famous *Dictatus Papae*.[63] The thirty-third *auctoritas* said of the pope: "He alone from ancient custom uses the pallium in every Mass or procession."[64] Other palligers wore it only within church, during the Mass on specified feasts, as the popes had customarily restricted it. The Roman bishop, however, was free to use his own badge every time he celebrated Mass, and even outside church, during processions such as litanies.[65] The pope thus enjoyed a right distinctive in quality as well as quantity. In contrast, as Clement II reminded Eberhard of Trier in 1047, non-popes could wear the pallium only on certain occasions, "nor further, unless you wish to incur offense against the authority of our apostolic see."[66]

Whether primacy resided in the person of the bishop of Rome or in the Roman church as a collective was not always clear.[67] Occasionally the cardinal bishops of the Roman suburbicarian sees, whose role as collaborators in the leadership of the church blossomed under the reform popes, came to the fore when the pallium was involved. In

---

63. See Hubert Mordek, "Proprie auctoritates apostolice sedis: ein zweiter Dictatus Papae Gregors VII.?," *Deutsches Archiv für Erforschung des Mittelalters* 28 (1972): 105–32, and Fowler-Magerl, *Clavis Canonum*, 158–59.

64. Mordek, "Proprie auctoritates," 132, occurring among theses pertaining to papal insignia. It was taken into the *Collectio Casinensis*, compiled at Monte Cassino after 1110, within material concerning the primacy of the Roman church (Canon 299.4, Roger E. Reynolds, ed., *The* Collectio Canonum Casinensis Duodecimi Seculi (Codex Terscriptus), *a Derivative of the South-Italian Collection in Five Books: An Implicit Edition with Introductory Study*, Monumenta Liturgica Beneventana III, Studies and Texts 137 [Toronto: Pontifical Institute of Mediaeval Studies, 2001], 93, *Clavis* RO299.04yk).

65. He was able to violate the regulations found in traditional pallium grants (e.g., Gregory IV to Liudpram of Salzburg in 837, JE 2580, GP 1:10 no. 14, Hauthaler and Martin, *Salzburger Urkundenbuch*, 2:27–28) and to ignore the canon *Quicumque sane* from John VIII's councils (MGH Conc. 5:10, 68).

66. JL 4151, GP 10.1:56 no. 94, BF 382, Jank, "Bemerkungen," 20.

67. See Uta-Renate Blumenthal, "Rom in der Kanonistik," in her *Papal Reform and Canon Law in the 11th and 12th Centuries* (Aldershot: Ashgate Variorum, 1998).

1060 Peter Damian, on behalf of the other cardinal bishops, replied to Empress Agnes's request for the pallium for Siegfried of Mainz. Since Pope Nicholas II was in Florence at the time, the cardinals must have stepped in to handle routine ecclesiastical business, which was carried out in their own names.[68] Similarly, Pope Urban II reminded Rainald of Reims in 1089: "You received the pallium from our confreres, the suffragan cardinal bishops of the Roman church, as there was no supreme pontiff at that time."[69] The archbishop had made his request during a vacancy in the apostolic see, either 1085–86, between Gregory VII and Victor III, or 1087–88, between Victor III and Urban II, and the cardinals had assumed the prerogative of palliating him.[70] Perhaps there had been no hope of a speedy papal election, which would better fit the first vacancy.

One cardinal bishop had a special claim to the pallium. Based on an act of the fourth-century Pope Mark mentioned in the *Liber Pontificalis*, the right of the bishop of Ostia was described in Bernold of Constance's chronicle: "This is the privilege of the church of Ostia, that by perpetual right its bishop (and archpriest if the bishop is not present) ought to take part in the ordination of the Roman pontiff. And if the bishop is present, from then on he will have the privilege of wearing the pallium, which will be allowed to no other cardinal bishop."[71] Whatever spurred Bernold's digression—perhaps the other cardinals were coveting the bishop of Ostia's pallium—it affirmed that the vestment was allowed in virtue of a task closely associat-

---

68. See 328–30 below. Nicholas's documents datable to January 1060 were issued in Florence (JL 4425–30).

69. JL 5385, Somerville, *Pope Urban*, 117.

70. At this time Cardinal Deusdedit, a proponent of the Roman clergy's rights, dedicated his canonical collection to Victor III, and in its preface defended the authority of the Roman church "even while it lacked a pontiff" (Glanvell, *Kanonessammlung*, 1–5). Yet Urban insisted that Rainald return to Rome now that there was a pope, perhaps because he did not support such power for the cardinals during a vacancy (Falkenstein, "Verlorene päpstliche Privilegien," 205).

71. MGH SS 5:413. It is unclear whether the bishop wore it only when consecrating the pope or habitually on solemn occasions; "from then on" suggests the latter. John of Salisbury later agreed, as long as it was during the Mass (Marjorie Chibnall, ed., *The Historia Pontificalis of John of Salisbury*, rev. ed., Oxford Medieval Texts [Oxford: Clarendon, 1986], 68).

ed with the papacy.[72] It was not permitted to mere priests, not even an archpriest, nor to other bishops, even the cardinals, without that special association. In sum, except in special cases, the cardinals had no power over the pallium themselves, and it remained essentially a papal thing.

The Pope as Ecclesiastical Impresario

An enhanced and emboldened papal primacy implied more pervasive Roman interventions in the affairs of local churches, even to the extent that the entire church was subject to the pope's disposition. The gift of the pallium had always provided an opportunity for involvement. When Count Conrad of Luxembourg captured Archbishop Eberhard of Trier and "his pallium was torn apart," according to the *Gesta Treverorum*, the citizens of Trier turned to Rome. The pope excommunicated Conrad, entrusted his absolution to Eberhard, and sent the archbishop a new pallium.[73] Even a forgery recognized that the vestment gave the pope a say in otherwise exclusive relationships. A letter attributed to Pope Stephen V but fabricated in the circle of Dalmatius of Narbonne in 1090 attempted to place the restored province of Tarragona under the primatial thumb of Narbonne.[74] Its archbishop would have the right to consecrate the arch-

---

72. Not everyone in the past had interpreted the Ostian right in this way. While the *Liber Pontificalis* said that the bishop of Ostia had the pallium because he ordained *episcopum, the* bishop, i.e., the pope, as clarified in the following clause (Duchesne, *Liber pontificalis,* 1:202), the second recension of Ado of Vienne's martyrology changed it to *episcopos urbis,* the bishops of *the* city, i.e., Rome, whose suffragan Ostia was (PL 123:431). Then in 896 Notker the Stammerer's martyrology, revising Ado's text for the abbey of St. Gall, changed it to *episcopos,* bishops in general (PL 131:1157). Notker's version, applicable beyond the Roman province, mirrored the traditional presumption that possession of the pallium was required for episcopal consecrations. See Jacques Dubois, *Les martyrologes du moyen âge latin,* Typologie des sources du moyen âge occidental 26 (Turnhout: Brepols, 1978), 42–45, 57, and Henri Quentin, *Les martyrologes historiques du moyen âge: étude sur la formation du martyrologe romain* (Paris: Lecoffre/Gabalda, 1908; reprinted in Aalen: Scientia, 1969), 470–73, 672–81.

73. MGH SS 8:174, 182. The pallium was not the only casualty among the archbishop's possessions, but it was mentioned alongside other sacred objects of the highest import, and surely the destruction of his badge of office was a challenge to his authority.

74. See McCrank, "Restoration," 194–203.

bishop of Tarragona, who "should yield always in everything to due obedience to the church of Narbonne—all but to receive the pallium, with the authority of a privilege, from the Roman pontiff."[75] Even the most stringent subjection of one church to another had to allow for the rights of the Roman church, expressed here by the grant of the pallium, the one thing Narbonne could not itself provide.

The pallium could offer an opportunity to judge between bishops. In 1078 Pope Gregory VII deferred a request from King Michael of Zeta for the pallium for the archbishop of Dubrovnik until the pope could investigate the dispute between that prelate and the neighboring archbishop of Split.[76] The king's plan for the consolidation of his kingdom and its church would have to wait, for whenever the vestment was concerned, the pope had the right to place conditions on its reception. The pallium could also permit the papal imposition of a bishop upon a church. In 1079 Gregory chastised the clergy and people of Arles because of the long vacancy of that see after their previous pastor's deposition. He sent a legate to advise them in their election of an archbishop, but if no suitable candidate could be found (which the pope regarded as likely), they were to promise to "receive him as shepherd whom we send you from the side of St. Peter, consecrated and distinguished with the honor of the pallium."[77] The new pastor would be invested with papal authority, symbolized by the vestment, which assisted—and perhaps served as pretext for—such active interference.

Arising from these sorts of acts, and serving to justify them, the theoretical role imagined for the pallium in the church was further developed in this period. In his *passio* of Alban in the early 1060s, Goswin of Mainz said that the papacy used the pallium to reorder the Western church after the barbarian invasions and heretical incursions of late antiquity: "The authority of the apostolic see resolved to transfer from certain places both the summit of the archiepiscopate and the reverence of the pallium, and from certain ones the dig-

---

75. JL †3462, PL 129:819.
76. JL 5061, MGH Epp. sel. 2.2:365. See Vlasto, *Entry*, 210–12, and H. E. J. Cowdrey, *Pope Gregory VII, 1073–1085* (Oxford: Clarendon, 1998), 442–43.
77. JL 5112, MGH Epp. sel. 2.2:433.

nity of the primacy." He then applied that pattern to his city: "The apostolic pontiff Gregory, then Zachary, awarded the great Boniface and the see entrusted to him to be perpetually distinguished with the dignity of the primacy and the honor of the pallium, and to exercise the apostolic vicariate through all Gaul and Germany in all councils and ecclesiastical assemblies."[78] Goswin painted his history with overly broad strokes, but his perception of the pallium's utility for organizing the churches according to papal determinations was accurate. An example from the reform period was Leo IX's arrangement of the African church, described in a letter of 1053. Although the pope was aware of the ancient tradition that the most senior bishop in Africa, regardless of his see, was considered the metropolitan, he decreed that the archbishop of Carthage had this status by papal privilege. It was he "who alone in Africa is accustomed to have the pallium from the apostolic see; therefore, he also retains the chief and ancient right to consecrate bishops."[79] The grant of the pallium, in effect, altered the African ecclesiastical structure in accord with Leo's resolution.

During the Investiture Contest the reformers attempted to rule out the participation of laymen in the disposition of the church and focused on papal responsibility for all things ecclesiastical. They accordingly highlighted the pallium's role in the exercise of this responsibility. Around 1085 Manegold of Lautenbach, arguing against the imperialist viewpoint, cited Pope Gregory the Great in support of an extraordinary claim:

> Gregory ... shows that pontificates and priesthoods, which they try to claim must be distributed at the choice of the royal dignity, properly belong, and have belonged from of old, to the rights of the apostolic see.... Thus also, when John, bishop of the church of Ravenna, died, the same father ... consecrated Marinian, a monk and his intimate, as bishop for the Ravennese, to whom he also sent the pallium. Behold where it appears openly that even those churches whose commendation wicked princes are now known to have usurped belonged to the apostolic see from of old![80]

---

78. MGH SS 15.2:989.
79. To Bishops Peter and John, JL 4305, BF 1123, PL 143:729–30.
80. *Liber ad Gebehardum*, in MGH LdL 1:413. See Robinson, *Authority*, 124–31.

This precedent gave the popes a strong hand in episcopal appointments. Although Manegold did not distinguish between palligers and non-palligers, the unique bestowal of the vestment by the pope strengthened his assertion that making bishops belonged by right to the papacy.

A liturgical commentator, Rupert of Deutz, spun an elaborate justification of the pallium as the centerpiece of a papally oriented ecclesiastical constitution.[81] His *De Divinis Officiis,* finished in 1111/12 and reflecting the ecclesiological controversies of his day, presented a historically based *ratio* for this archiepiscopal privilege. The original apostles, Rupert said, were dispersed through the world and set up seats in various places, from which they and their successors sent preachers into the neighboring provinces. These preachers were consecrated bishops, so that they in turn could consecrate comprovincial bishops in the various cities. The successors of these three tiers were, for the apostles, the patriarchs (except for Peter's successor, called *apostolicus* because of the eminence of the prince of the apostles); for the preachers sent to the provinces, the archbishops; and for the pastors appointed in the provincial cities, the suffragan bishops. From this pattern he deduced a rule: since a metropolitan church had once received its faith from the apostolic see, it should only have a pontiff sent from where its first evangelizer had come. "That sending is the bestowal of the aforesaid pallium, which, hanging down from the neck, as was said, signifies the humility of the Lord, who said: 'As the Father has sent me, I too send you' [Jn 20:21]."[82] Papal confirmation, expressed through the vestment, was equivalent to the apostolic provision of a successor to a metropolis's first preacher. The biblical quotation used Christ's humility—having derived his own mission from above, he similarly passed it on—to express the idea that his mission was continued in the apostles he commissioned. Rupert con-

---

81. See John H. Van Engen, *Rupert of Deutz* (Berkeley: University of California Press, 1983), and Maria Lodovica Arduini, *Rupert von Deutz (1076–1129) und der "Status Christianitatis" seiner Zeit: symbolisch-prophetische Deutung der Geschichte,* Beihefte zum Archiv für Kulturgeschichte 25 (Cologne: Böhlau, 1987). According to Schrör, the reception of the pallium was by this time interpreted as a "participation in the papacy's universal primacy" (*Metropolitangewalt,* 240).

82. CCCM 7:22.

cluded with examples of archbishoprics near his city of Liège, which had a claim to (and need of) the pallium due to their subapostolic origins, each tied to Rome by succession from Peter or Paul.[83]

Another milestone in ecclesiological thinking about the pallium evoked the dyad "share of the responsibility" and "fullness of power." First formulated by Pope Leo the Great to characterize the partial, delegated authority of a papal vicar, the expression *in partem sollicitudinis, non in plenitudinem potestatis* came in the course of the canonical tradition to be applied to the limited jurisdiction of legates, metropolitans, and bishops in general, as distinguished from the papacy's universal oversight.[84] After Pope Urban II palliated Peter of Grado in 1093, he also appointed him papal vicar in his patriarchate, but reminded him of the limits of his calling by using this venerable phrase.[85] Curiously, he had just called the vestment that he was giving to Peter *plenitudo pontificalis officii*; the "fullness of the pontifical office" possessed by the palliger was clearly something distinct from the "fullness of power" possessed by the pope alone.[86]

Around the same time, the reformer Bonizo of Sutri compiled his church handbook, the *Liber de Vita Christiana*, in which he commented on priestly vestments. When he came to the pallium, he observed that not every prelate wore it: "The dignity of the pallium is

---

83. The six examples, drawn from histories and legends, were Reims, evangelized by Remigius, sent by Pope Hormisdas; Trier, evangelized by Maternus, sent by Peter; Mainz, evangelized by Crescens, sent by Paul; Utrecht, evangelized by Willibrord, sent by Sergius I; Cologne, also evangelized by Crescens, sent by Paul; and Canterbury, evangelized by Augustine, sent by Gregory the Great (CCCM 7:22–23). Neither Mainz nor Utrecht was originally a metropolis, but the see of Utrecht was founded by a palliger, and Mainz became an archbishopric after the palliger Boniface occupied the see.

84. See Robert L. Benson, "Plenitudo Potestatis: Evolution of a Formula from Gregory IV to Gratian," *Studia Gratiana* 14 (1967): 193–217, and Kenneth Pennington, *Pope and Bishops: The Papal Monarchy in the Twelfth and Thirteenth Centuries* (Philadelphia: University of Pennsylvania Press, 1984), 43–74.

85. JL —, IP 7.2:59 no. 103, Kehr, *Papsturkunden*, 3:214.

86. See Benson, *Bishop-Elect*, 172–73. In the thirteenth century the canonist Hostiensis would attempt to combine the traditional epithet for the pallium with the terms of the Leonine dyad (*Lectura sive Apparatus Domini Hostiensis super Quinque Libris Decretalium* [Strasbourg, 1512], ad X 1.8.4 s.v. *potestatis* [1:89v] [hereafter "*HostLect*"]).

not granted to other bishops, except to those to whom the rights of superintendence are handed over by dispensation from the Roman pontiffs, at any rate such that they are called to a share of the responsibility, not to the fullness of power."[87] Metropolitans received their rights from the pope *dispensatorie*—providentially, managerially, as from a steward or dispenser. It was a vision of the papacy as administrator of the whole church, with subsidiary ecclesiastical offices existing only by its leave and on its behalf.[88] This view of the pallium had been implicit in aspects of previous ages' behavior, but only now was articulated in a sophisticated fashion.[89] It also appeared to take root. In 1107 Ruthard of Mainz admitted that, when he had been "confirmed in the episcopal dignity and advanced in the holy church with the honor of the pallium," Pope Paschal II had called him "to a share of [his] responsibility."[90] Through the vestment Ruthard participated in, and accepted a local portion of, the pope's comprehensive supervision.

The Pope as Meddler in the Hierarchy

The pallium helped the popes to arrange ecclesiastical structures as they deemed appropriate. One manner of doing so was to fine-tune relationships among bishops by adjusting the hierarchy, even in non-traditional ways. Through the conferral of the pallium, prelates of lesser rank could be fortified *vis-à-vis* their superiors, and new distinctions within the hierarchy could be created or resisted—all by papal choice and for reasons that served papal policies. The church's

---

87. Perels, *Liber de Vita*, 108.

88. Cf. *Liber ad Amicum*, in MGH LdL 1:602, where Bonizo reinterpreted Leo the Great to mean that every archbishop was a papal vicar in this limited sense. Reform theorists improvised on the terms *plenitudo potestatis* and *pars sollicitudinis* and exploited them in the service of papal power; to Bonizo, metropolitan power was derivative, bestowed by the papacy and subject to its oversight (Benson, "Plenitudo Potestatis," 209–11, and Schrör, *Metropolitangewalt*, 233–34).

89. For earlier expressions, see Rabanus Maurus, *De Institutione Clericorum*, in Zimpel, *De institutione*, 315; a Salzburg forgery, JL 3767, GP 1:16 no. †35, BZ †515, ZPUU 1:441–42; and, in the augmented version of the *Collectio XII Partium*, Canon 1.31, Bamberg, Staatsbibliothek, Can. 7, fol. 6v. On the reformers' conceptions of metropolitan authority in the church, see Schrör, *Metropolitangewalt*, 148–237.

90. To Paschal, Georg Christian Joannis, ed., *Rerum Moguntiacarum* (Frankfurt: Sande, 1722), 1:531.

rigid organization was thus made more flexible, and those on lower rungs might be rewarded, while those on higher rungs were punished.

The reform papacy seems to have understood this prospect, since pallium grants to suffragans—already exceptional in the ninth century, and ever rarer in the following years—experienced a notable uptick in this period. Of course, suffragan bishops were interested in acquiring this sign of prestige, which had become so well known in the church. When the *Gesta Pontificum Autissiodorensium* in the late 1050s described a precious set of vestments donated by Emperor Otto III to Bishop Hugh of Auxerre, it mentioned a chasuble with orphreys (decorative bands stitched onto the outside) "in the manner of an archiepiscopal pallium."[91] The wearer visually evoked an archbishop using his pallium—the only way for a bishop to attain a semblance of the distinction without being granted it. The popes took advantage of such eagerness by allowing palliated suffragans to multiply, but this meddling had conflicting consequences. Each of the eight examples that follow is illustrative in its own way.[92]

Two suffragans in northern Italy managed to gain the pallium, though in starkly different manners. In 1105 Pope Paschal II answered the petition of Guy of Pavia and confirmed "every dignity of your church granted through the privileges or authentic writings of our predecessors," including the pallium, the *naccus* or caparison, and the processional cross, all comparable to an archbishop's honors.[93] But what precedents was he citing? A suspicious document attribut-

91. Sot et al., *Gestes*, 257.
92. To these instances may be added that of Lausanne, although contemporary testimony is slight. A Besançon pontifical from just after 1050, now lost, detailed the seating order of the archbishop and his suffragans at a banquet following an episcopal consecration: "To the right of the lord archbishop [sits the bishop] of Lausanne, because he uses the pallium, and by his hands the archbishop is consecrated." See Vregille, *Hugues de Salins*, 277–78, 349, and Bernard de Vregille, "Besançon et Lausanne: métropolitains et suffragants des origines au XIe siècle," *Zeitschrift für schweizerische Kirchengeschichte* 82 (1988): 86–87. Remarkably, the archbishop of Besançon did not appear threatened by his palliated suffragan and provided him a place of honor. As with Ostia, Lausanne's pallium may have been connected to the bishop's duty to ordain his metropolitan; cf. John of Salisbury, *Historia Pontificalis*, in Chibnall, *Historia*, 68.
93. JL 6013, IP 6.1:179 no. 26, PL 163:151.

ed to Pope John VIII and addressed to John II of Pavia had anachronistically granted the same three distinctions in the ninth century.[94] The twelfth-century bishop may well have forged or doctored this document to prove his church's invented rights to Paschal.[95] In this case the papacy was taken advantage of. It was the opposite, however, in another case. When Bruno of Verona requested the pallium in 1073, Pope Gregory VII demurred, asking him to come to Rome and bring his see's former privileges.[96] No previous pallium grants to Verona are known, and as a non-metropolis it probably had none. Nevertheless, a note in Gregory's register from the first year of his pontificate recorded that he bestowed both the pallium and the *naccus* on Bruno.[97] Since it is unknown what transpired in Rome after the bishop obeyed the papal summons, it cannot be assumed that he was able to produce the desired precedents to verify his claim. As the German occupant of a strategically important Italian see, however, Bruno may have succeeded in his quest because Gregory treated the matter as a political expedient in papal-royal relations.[98]

Sometimes the pallium was given to a non-metropolitan to illustrate and reinforce a special relationship with the apostolic see, always a goal of the reformers. Pope Leo IX's grant to Stephen of Le Puy in 1051 was ostensibly motivated by veneration for the Virgin Mary, who was supposedly revered more in that city than anywhere in Gaul. Yet he also decreed that "the ordination of the bishops of this see pertains to the Roman pontiff."[99] It was an exempt diocese, and

94. In 877, JE 3111, IP 6.1:174–75 no. 5, BU 278, PL 126:740. The grant was oddly buried within a rambling privilege. The cross and *naccus* would not be attached to the pallium for a century or more after John VIII.
95. See BZ †4. However, Vehse ("Bistumsexemtionen," 97–101) and Erwin Hoff (*Pavia und seine Bischöfe im Mittelalter: Beiträge zur Geschichte der Bischöfe von Pavia unter besonderer Berücksichtigung ihrer politischen Stellung* [Pavia: Fusi, 1943], 348–76) maintain that the Pavian bishops received the pallium in the past because they were consecrated in Rome as a result of their exemption.
96. JL 4795, IP 7.1:222–23 no. 20, MGH Epp. sel. 2.1:41.
97. MGH Epp. sel. 2.1:123.
98. Cowdrey points out Gregory's need of friends and his efforts to appease them (*Pope Gregory*, 291).
99. JL 4265, BF 897, PL 143:681. See Vehse, "Bistumsexemtionen," 101–6, and Pierre Cubizolles, "Les évêques du Puy honorés jadis du *pallium*," *Cahiers de la Haute-Loire* (1999): 23–38, esp. 37.

the popes continued to recognize this unusual condition by palliating its pastors. In 1105 Pontius of Le Puy acquired the pallium from Pope Paschal II, who declared that the city was "known to cling to the apostolic see more particularly, as a member to its head. Thus deservedly, from the generosity of the same see, it merited to be distinguished by our predecessors with the ornament of the pallium." And, as he renewed that privilege, he ordered that its bishops "should be subject to no metropolitan except the Roman, and all who will succeed you in the same see should be consecrated by the hand of the Roman pontiff, as particular suffragans of the Roman see."[100] It was fitting that a church with such direct ties to Rome should have a bishop adorned in a papal manner. Similarly, in the previous year Paschal conferred the vestment on Diego of Compostela out of respect for the apostle James, believed to be buried in that city. But as he did so, he mentioned the see's exempt status, which he called "freedom, so that it might become a particular member of the apostolic see."[101] A mark of esteem for this church's relics, the pallium also showcased the fact that the pope alone was its metropolitan.[102]

The origin of the custom that Bamberg's bishops received the pallium was bound up with the papal reform. To Hartwig of Bamberg in 1053 Pope Leo IX offered the vestment, "which, never before granted to your predecessors, now for the first time we grant to you, at the request of our most beloved son, Emperor Henry [III], and out of veneration for your predecessor, the lord Pope Clement [II]." It was a gesture of regard for the first of the reform popes, who had been

---

100. JL 6016, PL 163:155–56.

101. JL 5986, PL 163:133. See Vehse, "Bistumsexemtionen," 132–34. A supposed pallium grant to Diego in 1109 (JL *6249) does not fit these facts and may be mistaken. Gregory of San Grisogono dedicated his canonical collection, the *Polycarpus*, to Diego sometime after the latter received the pallium in 1104. The preface began: "To the beloved lord D. of the church of Santiago, worthily adorned with the pontifical festoon" (Fuhrmann and Horst, *Sammlung "Policarpus,"* at http://www.mgh.de/fileadmin/Downloads/pdf/polycarp.pdf, 1). *Infula* was commonly used to describe the pallium, and Gregory may have wanted to highlight this milestone in Diego's campaign to advance his standing.

102. However, the pallium was not a necessary component of exemption, but rather signified a relationship with Rome that sometimes accompanied, resulted from, or led to exempt status (Vehse, "Bistumsexemtionen," 156–57).

bishop of Bamberg and was buried in its cathedral. Leo instructed that the pallium should be worn "on the solemnity of St. Dionysius, because the anniversary day of the lord Pope Clement, mentioned above, is celebrated at that time; and by apostolic authority we establish this holy day to be solemn throughout the whole bishopric."[103] The anniversary of Clement's death (October 9) was now observed in the diocese of Bamberg as if the feast of a saint of the reform, and thus a suitable time to display the vestment. It could be worn on only two other days each year: Easter, and the feast of Sts. Peter and Paul, which accentuated the garb's Petrine associations. The number of pallium days was thereby restricted to the most essential, probably to differentiate this suffragan palliger from his metropolitan.[104] In fact, the pope conditioned the pallium's use on preserving "the authority of the lady metropolitan church of Mainz," to which the bishop, though palliated, was still subject.[105] It was an attempt to defuse any pretensions from Bamberg or worries from Mainz. Even so, this phrase's erasure in one manuscript indicated that the proviso chafed against the ambitions of some in Bamberg.[106]

Indeed, papal interference resulting in pallium grants to suffragans could raise serious tensions with their metropolitans. A later bishop of Bamberg, Gunther, received the pallium in the early 1060s and

---

103. JL 4287, GP 3:254 no. 13, BF 1023, MGH SSRG 69:263–64. This copy of the letter was found in Adalbert of Bamberg's life of Henry; the original is unedited, but Johann Georg von Eckhart edits another copy (*Corpus Historicum Medii Aevi* [Leipzig: Gleditsch, 1723], 2:90–91). See Gresser, *Clemens*, 121–25.

104. The same was not always true for other palliated suffragans. Burchard II of Halberstadt received a generous list of twenty-two days (in 1063, JL 4498, GP 5.2:220–21 no. 36, Joachim Dahlhaus, ed., "Zum Privileg Alexanders II. für Burchard II. von Halberstadt," in *Von Sacerdotium und Regnum: geistliche und weltliche Gewalt im frühen und hohen Mittelalter*, ed. Franz-Reiner Erkens and Harmut Wolff, Passauer historische Forschungen 12 [Cologne: Böhlau, 2002], 672; on the days, see ibid., 656), which reflected Alexander II's exuberant gratitude. Stephen of Le Puy received ten days (Leo IX in 1051, JL 4265, BF 897, PL 143:681), Pontius of Le Puy sixteen (Paschal II in 1105, JL 6016, PL 163:156), and Diego of Compostela nineteen (Paschal II in 1104, JL 5986, PL 163:133); but these exempt bishops had no metropolitans whom such privileges might have threatened.

105. JL 4287, GP 3:254 no. 13, BF 1023, Eckhart, *Corpus*, 2:90; cf. Adalbert's version (MGH SSRG 69:263).

106. The erasure, in a twelfth-century manuscript used at Bamberg's cathedral, is noted at MGH SS 4:801.

felt the need to write a preemptive letter to Siegfried of Mainz. In it he explained, lest the archbishop be disturbed, that the rationale for this custom lay in the special protection into which Rome had taken Bamberg:

The Roman pontiff, in order to make this unique subjection of ours more solemn and distinguished, granted to all the prelates of our church the use of the pallium by a general privilege. And from then on, other popes, admonished and invoked, solemnly granted the same to our predecessors. By their example and authority, this one too, N., having been called upon, has sent the pallium to our Humility according to the tenor of the ancient privilege. For this reason, lest anyone can interpret it as pride or an insult to you (such are the temperaments of men!), I have taken care for the sequence and manner of the matter to be made known to you—certain, of course, that your Charity sincerely congratulates whatever is done for the stability of the churches.[107]

Gunther exaggerated his position. Instead of a personal privilege for his predecessor Hartwig, he claimed a general privilege for all bishops of Bamberg. And instead of respect for Clement II as its motive, he asserted a special relationship with the Roman church. Because his pallium could become a pretext to inflame rivalry between metropolitan and suffragan, Gunther wished to set the record straight and avoid an affront to Siegfried. But whatever the archbishops of Mainz thought, subsequent bishops of Bamberg continued to receive the pallium. According to conflicting accounts, Herman either was summoned to Rome and won it through bribery (said Lambert of Hersfeld), or traveled to Rome to obtain it, but was refused, deposed, and replaced by another, who gained it (said Bonizo of Sutri).[108] And in 1111 Pope Paschal II gave Otto the vestment, with a list of pallium days only slightly larger than Hartwig's, along with the use of the processional cross—again, without prejudice to the rights of Mainz.[109]

---

107. MGH Briefe 5:201. The stricken papal name may have been that of Antipope Honorius II, but no consensus has been achieved (Dahlhaus, "Privileg," 661–66). In the protocol Gunther addressed Siegfried submissively, as "his most dedicated suffragan" offering "the perpetual devotion of respect" (MGH Briefe 5:200).

108. For Lambert's account, see *Annales*, in MGH SSRG 38:111–12; for Bonizo's, see *Liber ad Amicum*, in MGH LdL 1:602. See Schieffer, "Romreise," 159–61.

109. JL 6291, GP 3:264 no. 46, PL 173:1323–24. In addition to Hartwig's pallium days, Otto gained two feasts crucial to the liturgical year, Pentecost and Christmas,

The case of another subject of Mainz, Halberstadt, illustrated the simultaneously privileged and contested position of a palliated suffragan. After Burchard II of Halberstadt was sent to Rome to adjudicate the papal schism between Alexander II and Honorius II, which he decided in Alexander's favor, the grateful pope awarded him the pallium in 1063 as a sign of friendship and esteem. Calling him a "spiritual son," and his church a "daughter of the Roman church," he decorated him with the vestment—"nevertheless, save the authority and superintendence of the holy metropolitan church of Mainz, save also both the order and the place of your brother bishops."[110] The careful stipulations hinted that disorder could easily ensue, but this gift to a non-metropolitan was not meant to disrupt relations among the German bishops. Rather, it was an honorary and ceremonial distinction, as were the other perquisites included in the privilege (the processional cross, the *naccus*, and the miter). Lambert of Hersfeld's acknowledgement of Burchard's reward as "the insignia of the archiepiscopate" highlighted the incongruity to show the height of the honor.[111] Burchard's metropolitan, Siegfried of Mainz, was not pleased. In the following year he complained to Alexander and laid out the destructive consequences of this hierarchical befuddlement:

> Not content with the honor of his predecessors (illustrious men, to be sure), he has usurped for himself a new "papacy." And having cast off the superhumeral and rational that he used to wear during the sacred solemnities of the Mass there, he boasts in church to dumbstruck walls about a new pallium.... If each observes his own right and proper order in secular things, how much more is it necessary that no confusion be introduced in

---

and two occasions important to a bishop, the anniversary of his ordination and the dedication of churches.

110. JL 4498, GP 5.2:220–21 no. 36, Dahlhaus, "Privileg," 672. On the language of spiritual kinship, which equated Burchard with one consecrated by the pope, see ibid., 641–42. Burchard may have brought this document, already composed, to the pope for approval (Jenal, *Erzbischof Anno*, 2:238n167). See Lutz Fenske, *Adelsopposition und kirchliche Reformbewegung im östlichen Sachsen: Entstehung und Wirkung des sächsischen Widerstandes gegen das salische Königtum während des Investiturstreits*, Veröffentlichungen des Max-Planck-Instituts für Geschichte 47 (Göttingen: Vandenhoeck and Ruprecht, 1977), 100–133, esp. 101–2, 123–24. Beumann notes the role of Burchard's uncle, Anno of Cologne, in this affair, and thus its repercussions on the rivalry between Cologne and Mainz ("Pontifikalinsignien," 329–45).

111. *Annales*, in MGH SSRG 38:82.

ecclesiastical arrangements! For it is not right for discord to have a place where peace and harmony ought to reign, especially among the priests of Christ.... Let this scandal of novelty be removed from the church, and let the unanimity of the brethren, which has been gravely shattered by this presumptuous pride (rather than honor), be recalled to its peace. For this is not my cause, but that of my brothers in general.[112]

Instead of the rational, an episcopal vestment patterned after the ancient Jewish high priestly breastplate and granted to the bishops of Halberstadt in the tenth century, Burchard now donned a *novum pallium* that elevated him to a *novus papatus*.[113] Siegfried claimed that this grievance came from the whole hierarchy, although his own role was obviously most threatened. The severity of his reaction demonstrated the importance of the pallium and its ramifications for episcopal power-relationships.[114] The popes had to tread carefully when engaging in this kind of meddling. But Alexander apparently did not back down.[115]

The see of Metz had boasted a number of palliated bishops in earlier centuries.[116] There were none in this period (although Pope Ca-

---

112. Manfred Stimming, ed., *Mainzer Urkundenbuch* (Darmstadt: Historischer Verein für Hessen, 1932; reprinted in Darmstadt: Hessische Historische Kommission, 1972), 1:200. *Papatus* meant not the office of the papacy, but honors granted by the pope from among his own prerogatives, which exalted the recipient to pope-like status.

113. Cf. Hildeward of Halberstadt to Adalbero II of Metz between 984 and 996, Schmidt, *Urkundenbuch*, 1:42–43, and Sigebert of Gembloux, *Vita Deoderici*, in MGH SS 4:468. See Beumann, "Rationale" and "Pontifikalinsignien."

114. Lambert of Hersfeld offered a laconic account: "The archbishop of Mainz, having interpreted the deed as obscuring the summit of his own priority, bore this most unworthily. But through the intervention of the archbishop of Cologne, after satisfaction had been received, his indignation was stilled" (*Annales*, in MGH SSRG 38:82). Mainz seems to have worried that Halberstadt would challenge, or at least ignore, its authority. Siegfried may also have been upset because he had not yet received his own pallium (Peter Damian to Agnes of Poitou in 1060, N. D'Acunto and L. Saraceno, eds., based on the edition of Kurt Reindel, *Petri Damiani Epistulae / Pier Damiani lettere*, Opere di Pier Damiani 1 [Rome: Città Nuova, 2005], 4:94), and Anno's "intervention" with the pope may have led to the "satisfaction" of a pallium for Mainz (Jenal, *Erzbischof Anno*, 2:238).

115. Dahlhaus critiques Beumann's hypothesis that the pope had promised Siegfried to revoke Burchard's privilege and that Burchard eventually relinquished his pallium ("Privileg," 643).

116. See Abel, "Étude," 75–97, and Heydenreich, *Metropolitangewalt*, 31–36.

lixtus II would soon revive the tradition), but contemporary writers dwelled on the historical situation, which revealed the pallium as a treasured but confusing favor.[117] In the 1050s Sigebert of Gembloux praised Metz's pastors in his *vita* of Bishop Theoderic I: "Certain of the pontiffs of Metz, honored beyond the ordinary measure of prelates, frequently attained such a privilege from the apostolic see, whether due to the grace of holiness or due to the glory of nobility, that they performed the office and honor of archbishop, save subjection to the metropolitan."[118] Here the title of archbishop was honorary, without the functions of a metropolitan. But it had appeared so frequently in Metz that Sigebert felt he had to make excuses for some bishops' lack of the vestment.[119] In contrast, when Hugh of Flavigny around 1102 told the story of Chrodegang, that "he merited the pallium with the name of archbishop," he clarified that it was "due to the manifold devastation of the mother church of Trier." Thus, "when [Trier] was vacant, the prelates of Metz were performing the office and dignity of metropolitan."[120] Because "archbishop"

117. Hugh of Flavigny claimed that Herman of Metz had been buried with the insignia of "cross, miter, and pallium" (*Chronicon*, in MGH SS 8:472). All were papally granted privileges, and certainly Gregory VII could have thus decorated his loyal supporter, but neither the *Gesta Episcoporum Mettensium* nor the *Gesta Treverorum* mentioned Herman's pallium when one would expect them to do so. Calixtus II palliated his nephew, Stephen of Metz, which caused several conflicts with Trier (*Gesta Treverorum*, in MGH SS 8:196–97, 201).

118. MGH SS 4:469. Sigebert listed Urbicius, Chrodegang, Angilram, Drogo, Wala, and Robert, but specifically mentioned the pallium only for the last two. Corroborating evidence exists for Chrodegang, Drogo, and Wala (Duchesne, *Liber pontificalis*, 1:456; *Epitaphium Chrodegangi*, in MGH Poet. 1:108–9; Charles the Bald to Nicholas I in 864, MGH Epp. 6:223; Hincmar of Reims in 863, MGH Epp. 8.1:128; and John VIII to Wala of Metz in 878, JE 3183, BU 427, PL 126:799). Later evidence of questionable trustworthiness also exists for Urbicius and Robert (John of Gorze, *Vita Chrodegangi*, in MGH SS 10:568, and *Gesta Episcoporum Mettensium*, in MGH SS 10:541). Abel's evidence for Urbicius is vague and undocumented, and his evidence for Angilram rests on a transcription error ("Étude," 76, 80, 86).

119. MGH SS 4:469. Abel's interpretation, that a perpetual privilege was obtained for all Metz bishops to wear the pallium ("Étude," 93–94), conflicts with later sources, from both Trier and Metz, that depicted the honor as occasional and personal, as in the case of Stephen (*Gesta Treverorum*, in MGH SS 8:196, and *Gesta Episcoporum Mettensium*, in MGH SS 10:544). Abel's sigillographical evidence cannot be treated here.

120. *Chronicon*, in MGH SS 8:341. See Patrick Healy, *The Chronicle of Hugh of*

and "metropolitan" had become synonyms, Hugh felt the need to offer this explanation. But it was not accurate, since in the eighth century the pallium was not yet linked to metropolitan rank, and Chrodegang's was only a mark of honor and preeminence in the Frankish episcopate. By the twelfth century, it seems, suffragans with pallia were viewed as anomalies requiring justification in light of special circumstances.

Around the same time as Hugh's chronicle, the *Gesta Treverorum*, a local history of Metz's metropolis, provided a vivid lesson of the hierarchical upset caused by pallium grants to suffragans. It recounted that Pope John VIII had palliated Wala of Metz, and the archbishop of Trier reacted as if threatened:

Bertulf, the metropolitan, hearing that Wala was walking in procession with the pallium on the holy day of Easter, sent a letter and summoned him to Trier.... In the ears of all who were present, Wala read the privilege on the use of the pallium that was sent to him by the pope, and claimed that he was not the first but the fifth [in Metz] whom the apostolic see deigned to elevate with this honor—nevertheless, save subjection to the metropolitan in all things.... Bertulf, not satisfied by these assertions ... forbade him, through the holy obedience that he owed him in all ecclesiastical affairs, to use the pallium anymore, except with permission sought from and granted by him. And when Wala offered apostolic authority as an excuse, and the archbishop defended the privileges of metropolitans, an intense enmity was kindled on both sides.... This Bertulf was very fierce and impatient with such presumptions of his suffragans, and did not suffer his church's privilege to be violated in any way.[121]

Wala had replaced Bertulf's relative, Adventius of Metz, who had obtained the archbishopric for Bertulf, but who was apparently not palliated himself.[122] Beyond this personal grudge, Bertulf pitted *metro-*

Flavigny: Reform and the Investiture Contest in the Late Eleventh Century (Aldershot: Ashgate, 2006).

121. MGH SS 8:165–66. Cf. Flodoard of Reims, *Historia Remensis Ecclesiae*, in MGH SS 36:316. This conflict occurred in the context of other quarrels (Heydenreich, *Metropolitangewalt*, 32–34). Heydenreich asserts that Wala relinquished his pallium, but does not specify his evidence, besides a letter of Hincmar advising Wala to obey his metropolitan.

122. *Gesta Treverorum*, in MGH SS 8:165, and Flodoard of Reims, *Historia Remensis Ecclesiae*, in MGH SS 36:304.

politanorum privilegia against *apostolica auctoritas* by boldly questioning the pope's explicit privilege and later refusing to accept papal letters on Wala's behalf. The relevance for the reform papacy was clear: for every friendship fostered by such a gift to a suffragan, enmity was liable to ensue.

Finally, there were the twists and turns of the case of Dol. As previously shown, the Breton king, in an effort to achieve ecclesiastical independence for his land paralleling its political autonomy from Francia, had unsuccessfully attempted in the ninth century to win Dol's bishop the pallium, and thus freedom from the metropolitan jurisdiction of Tours. The Bretons stirred up these pretensions again in the eleventh century. In 1050 Leo IX disqualified Bishop Juthael as an archbishop because he lacked "the see of a city" (Dol was originally an abbey) and "the archiepiscopal pallium"—a circular rationale, in that he could not be an archbishop without the pallium, but he could not receive it unless he was an archbishop.[123] Still, if Dol could somehow secure it, the recognized badge of archiepiscopal office, the tide would be turned. The stage was set for an interminable dispute, described in Gregory VII's register as "between the archbishop of Tours and the bishop of Dol concerning the pallium," as if the entire quarrel was encapsulated in the vestment.[124] Different popes wrestling with contradictory pressures generated a profusion of decisions, and the result was a mess not fully resolved until Innocent III's time.[125]

Despite Leo IX's resolve, there was an about-face in papal policy towards Dol in 1076.[126] Gregory VII consecrated and palliated Bishop Evan, though without prejudice to the outcome of the dispute with Tours. Even if the case were decided in Tours's favor, Gregory guaranteed the pallium for Evan and his successors, as long as they were virtuous and licitly installed. The vestment would be a conso-

---

123. To the Breton princes, JL 4225, BF 775, PL 143:648.
124. MGH Epp. sel. 2.2:488.
125. Innocent decided definitively in favor of Tours in 1199 (Smith, "Archbishopric," 60).
126. See Paula de Fougerolles, "Pope Gregory VII, the Archbishopric of Dol and the Normans," *Anglo-Norman Studies* 21 (1998): 47–66. She believes that Gregory retained all parties' good will by offering small concessions, while substituting promises for a proper resolution (ibid., 65).

lation prize to lessen the bitterness of Dol's fate; it would also ensure suitable bishops, for through it the pope could effectively veto a bishop-elect. In the meantime, the Breton bishops were to show Evan the obedience due to an archbishop, whereby Gregory recognized "the sovereignty of the whole province."[127] Predictably, Archbishop Ralph I of Tours was enraged, but the pope defended his decision as a reward to Brittany for its eradication of simony and lay investiture.[128] In 1080 a Roman synod committed the case between Tours and Dol to legates. But whatever happened, Gregory added, Evan would retain the pallium, although none of his successors could aspire to it—thus backtracking from his position in 1076.[129] In preparation for the legatine synod, Dol composed a misleading chronicle and forged at least one papal privilege witnessing to its supposed tradition of receiving the pallium.[130] Nevertheless, the Council of Saintes (1081) finally decided in Tours's favor.[131]

When Bishop Roland came to Urban II and requested the pallium in 1093, he cunningly presented Gregory's 1076 grant as evidence of his right to receive it. Determining that the document was authentic, Urban conferred on him "the gift of the pallium under the same condition"—that is, without prejudice to the dispute with Tours.[132] This surprising statement revealed that he was unaware both of Gregory's 1080 letter and of the resolution at Saintes. By the following year Tours had supplied for this gap in the papal memory, especially regarding the ruling that Evan's successors could not be palligers. Having been duped when Roland came to him "as if archbishop of the Bretons," Urban now ruled that never again after Roland's death should Dol aspire to the pallium.[133] He notified the bishops of Brit-

---

127. JL 5004, MGH Epp. sel. 2.1:302.
128. In 1077, JL 5021, Santifaller, *Quellen*, 1:136.
129. JL 5155, MGH Epp. sel. 2.2:489.
130. F. Duine, ed., *La métropole de Bretagne: chronique de Dol composée au XIe siècle et catalogues des dignitaires jusqu'à la révolution*, La Bretagne et les pays celtiques 12 (Paris: Champion, 1916), 44–45, 47, 52, and JE †2950, MGH Epp. 6:764–65, version B.
131. On the 1080 Roman synod and the 1081 synod at Saintes, see Gresser, *Synoden*, 193–202, and Fougerolles, "Pope Gregory," 61–62.
132. To the Breton bishops, JL 5475, PL 151:359.
133. To Ralph II of Tours, JL 5519, PL 151:385–86.

tany of his decision, with specific mention of the Council of Saintes and the *"twofold* letters" of Gregory VII.[134]

Against this background, the common supposition that Paschal II gave Bishop Baldric the pallium in 1109 comes as a shock. Indeed, there is reason to question the authenticity of the grant.[135] First, the *Si pastores ovium* formula had been abandoned since the time of Pope Alexander II, and it is hard to see why it would suddenly have been resurrected in a wholly isolated case. Second, the recipient was addressed as *Dolensis archiepiscopus,* a title never willingly used by the popes before, and Paschal took no notice of the foregoing controversy or the rights of Tours. Third, the Bretons had shown themselves obsessed with erecting a province and capable of underhanded methods. If forged, it was modeled on an authentic pallium grant from Alexander's pontificate, since it bore all the features of the format in use then.[136] A notice from Paschal to the suffragans, clergy, and people of Dol, supposedly issued at the same time, also called Baldric "archbishop of Dol" and made no mention of the controversy with Tours; further, a line of instruction about how to wear the pallium was more typical of a grant than a notice.[137] Perhaps a genuine papal letter from another situation had been altered. In short, Baldric may never have received a legitimate pallium.[138]

The reform popes' inclination to bestow the pallium on suffragans was a form of direct papal intervention in the ecclesiastical hierar-

134. JL 5520, PL 151:387; emphasis added.

135. JL 6224, PL 163:251–52. A number of sources called Baldric "archbishop," but this discussion focuses only on the evidence concerning his supposed reception of the pallium.

136. The list of pallium days was almost identical to that in Alexander's 1068 grant to Udo of Trier, which contained typically German feasts of a bygone era, such as those of Lawrence and Maurice, ill suited to twelfth-century Dol (JL 4646, GP 10.1:66–67 no. 121, Jank, "Bemerkungen," 21). Alexander's 1073 grant to Ralph I of Tours also had a list somewhat similar to Baldric's; perhaps the forger's model came from Dol's rival (JL —, Ramackers, *Papsturkunden,* 5:70).

137. JL 6225, PL 163:253.

138. Two other texts (a letter of Baldric to the monks of Fécamp, and a confirmation of the monastery of St.-Florent's property) brought up both the vestment and the archiepiscopal title (PL 166:1173, 1213). But Baldric himself may have been behind the falsification project, and the monk of St.-Florent may have been proceeding on hearsay.

chy, which could be useful to papal ends, though not without its perils. It could secure needed allies (Verona), but was open to exploitation (Pavia). It symbolized strong, even immediate ties to the Roman church (Compostela and Le Puy). It might honor a see connected to the reform (Bamberg) or reward a see for promoting the reform (Halberstadt), but it ran the risk of infuriating metropolitans or engendering controversial customs. Contemporaries did not always know what to make of it (Metz), and the popes themselves changed their minds, or were deceived, about its propriety (Dol). As a weapon for pursuing the reform and controlling the episcopate, the vestment, when applied to suffragans, had become too connected with metropolitan status to be anything more than a two-edged sword.

A final form of hierarchical meddling by the reform papacy was the use of the pallium to promote or resist primacies. A primate, in the more than honorary sense, was a metropolitan with authority over other metropolitans.[139] Primacy, a middle rank between papacy and province, thus spread supraprovincial authority beyond the apostolic see and violated the "equal and distinct" status of palligers upheld by Hincmar of Reims and the Carolingian papacy. However, it could also be a step towards centralizing the church, a way to reduce the number of prelates requiring direct control by the papacy, and a means of diluting the power of problematic metropolitans. Pope Gregory VII had no objection to primatial authority, as long as it was founded on authentic tradition and subordinated to Rome; nevertheless, he often had to "feel his way" through the complications of how pope, primates, metropolitans, papal vicars, and papal legates related to one another.[140]

Pope Urban II handled a number of these situations and used the pallium to enforce his approaches. In Spain, by ancient right, Toledo held the primacy. Urban reminded Berengar of Tarragona in 1092

139. See Horst Fuhrmann, "Studien zur Geschichte mittelalterlicher Patriarchate," *Zeitschrift der Savigny-Stiftung für Rechtsgeschichte, kanonistische Abteilung* 39 (1953): 112–76; 40 (1954): 1–84; 41 (1955): 95–183, and Fabrice Delivré, "The Foundations of Primatial Claims in the Western Church (Eleventh–Thirteenth Centuries)," *Journal of Ecclesiastical History* 59 (2008): 383–406. Cf. Hincmar's use of the term (*De Iure Metropolitanorum*, in PL 126:191).

140. See Cowdrey, *Pope Gregory*, 602–4.

that he had granted him the pallium, but it did not subject him directly to Rome: "You have been instituted archbishop such that both you and all the bishops of the province of Tarragona ought to be subject to Toledo as your primate."[141] It was strikingly different from the pallium's meaning for Compostela and Le Puy. In 1098 the same pope declared that Salerno was primate over Cosenza and Acerenza, which had once been subject to it but, "for what reason we do not know, deserved both the dignity of the pallium and the authority of privileges from the apostolic see in past times."[142] They could continue to receive the vestment, but rather than gaining autonomy through it, they were to promise obedience to Salerno. In addition, the pallium could be employed as a threat. After Gregory VII had affirmed Lyon's primacy over Sens, Rouen, and Tours, Urban at the Council of Clermont (1095) punished the sees unwilling to capitulate to this arrangement: "With the agreement of the whole council, we forbade the archbishop of Sens the use of the pallium and the obedience of his suffragans until he obeys; we also promulgate the same sentence against Rouen."[143] In these examples the pope supported primates by finessing the traditional significance of the pallium.

In England, despite Canterbury's ambitions, the primacy was a thorny question because Pope Gregory the Great, long before any political unity was achieved, had set up two equal metropoles, distinguished only by seniority.[144] After the Norman Conquest, Lanfranc of Canterbury compelled Thomas I of York to profess obedience to him as head of the English church. Yet the pallium was a sign of direct subjection to Rome, as Urban implied when he rebuked Thomas in 1094: "After you received the pallium from the apostol-

---

141. JL 5465, Demetrio Mansilla, ed., *La documentación pontificia hasta Inocencio III (965–1216)*, Monumenta Hispaniae Vaticana, registros 1 (Rome: Instituto Español de Estudios Eclesiasticos, 1955), 53.
142. To Alfanus II of Salerno, JL 5707, IP 8:354–55 no. 35, PL 151:508.
143. To Hugh of Lyon, JL 5600, PL 151:439. The absent archbishop of Rouen was allowed three months from his receipt of the decree to proffer his submission in person or in writing. On the synod, see Gresser, *Synoden*, 303–9.
144. Cf. John the Deacon, *Vita Gregorii Magni*, in PL 75:100, and a Passau forgery, JL †3771, GP 1:166–67 no. †19, BZ †514, ZPUU 1:439, both referring to JE 1829.

ic see ... without consulting the Roman pontiff, you unduly subjected your church to the bishop of Canterbury ... against the decree of blessed Gregory. How seriously it behooves us to take this cannot be hidden from your Prudence."[145] The pro-York Norman Anonymous followed a complementary line of thought in a treatise on the English hierarchy, written around 1101: "What is the reason that an archbishop should be subject to an archbishop, since both were elevated by equal, or rather by the same, sacraments? For both were distinguished by the same sacrament of the pallium, by the same sacrament of anointing and consecration and blessing, not by different and unequal sacraments, of which one is more outstanding, the other inferior."[146] Finally, Anselm of Canterbury, a proponent of his see's primacy, was understandably nervous in 1108 when Thomas II of York sought the pallium. He complained to Pope Paschal II: "This is the greatest of my prayers in this matter, that he should not receive the pallium from your Excellency before he is consecrated and professes the obedience due me.... I do not say this because I envy him the pallium, but because certain men assert and even contrive that, if it is granted by you, he may be confident that he can deny the profession due me."[147] As was true with palliated suffragans, so also with primates, the pallium could cut both ways: to show independence or dependence. The popes had to handle it carefully, depending on the political context and whom they wished to favor, if they were to achieve their aims.

145. JL —, Charles Johnson, ed., revised by M. Brett, C. N. L. Brooke, and M. Winterbottom, *Hugh the Chanter: The History of the Church of York, 1066–1127*, Oxford Medieval Texts (Oxford: Clarendon, 1990), 10. The pope then summoned Thomas to Rome to make satisfaction. This letter's authenticity is debated, but Johnson argues convincingly in its favor (ibid., xl–xli). The discovery of a letter of Urban closely similar in wording, despite differences in content, provides further support (Brett, "Some New Letters," 85).

146. J29b, James R. Ginther and Tomás O'Sullivan, eds., *Electronic Norman Anonymous Project*, at http://normananonymous.org/ENAP/index.jsp?view=edition&p=301, 303. Depicting the pallium as a "sacrament" likened its reception to ordination, both components of an archbishop's installation. Indeed, it could be seen as a conduit of sacred power, i.e., the grace of ecclesiastical ministry. Goscelin of St.-Bertin, close in time and place to the Anonymous, used the same metaphor (*Vita Augustini*, in PL 150:753).

147. Schmitt, *Opera*, 2.5:399.

Conclusion

For centuries the popes had been using the pallium to ensure the legitimate promotion of virtuous prelates and to involve themselves, as chief overseers, in the affairs of local churches. When seen in such general terms, the reform papacy's goals were not essentially different. But the boldness of vision and the breadth of execution signaled a new era, especially in contrast to the preceding period's occasional negligence. Now the reformers used the pallium to target specific problems in the church and to advance papal intervention in startling ways. Their endeavor was programmatic, systematic, and universal in scope, and they harnessed canon law on an unprecedented scale. They had other tools at their disposal, but the pallium helped to create a free, pure church watched over by a single, supreme earthly head. This chapter has focused on what they hoped to accomplish. The next chapter will analyze how the traditional patterns of manipulating the pallium were modified to make it more effective in its task.

8

A Tool of the Reform: The Means

As English metropolitans customarily did, Ealdred, the newly elected archbishop of York, traveled to Rome in 1061 to ask the pope for the pallium.[1] He had no particular reason to expect any difficulty with his confirmation: his translation from Worcester to York and his retention of the former see while possessing the latter were hardly unprecedented.[2] But it was a new era, and the papacy was applying a program of reform to the church. There were even rumors that Ealdred's accession had been marred by simony and deceit.[3] Arriving in Rome during a synod "against the simoniacs," Ealdred may have unwittingly condemned himself by his own statements. Pope Nich-

---

1. Nicholas II to Ealdred, JL 4463, Rolls 71.3:5–7; Cubbin, *Anglo-Saxon Chronicle*, 6:76; Frank Barlow, ed., *The Life of King Edward Who Rests at Westminster, Attributed to a Monk of Saint-Bertin*, 2nd ed. (Oxford: Clarendon, 1992), 52, 54, 56; M. Winterbottom, ed., with the assistance of R. M. Thomson, *William of Malmesbury: Gesta Pontificum Anglorum, the History of the English Bishops*, Oxford Medieval Texts (Oxford: Clarendon, 2007), 1:380, 382; *Chronica Pontificum Ecclesiae Eboracensis*, in Rolls 71.2:346–47; *Vita Wulfstani*, in M. Winterbottom and R. M. Thomson, eds., *William of Malmesbury, Saints' Lives: Lives of SS. Wulfstan, Dunstan, Patrick, Benignus and Indract*, Oxford Medieval Texts (Oxford: Clarendon, 2002), 40, 42; Simeon of Durham, *Historia Regum*, in Rolls 75.2:174; and R. R. Darlington and P. McGurk, eds., *The Chronicle of John of Worcester*, Oxford Medieval Texts (Oxford: Clarendon, 1995), 2:586.
2. See Darlington, "Ecclesiastical Reform," 399.
3. The Roman synod's purpose may have given rise to the possibly mistaken notion that simony was involved (ibid., 401).

olas II denied him the pallium and deposed him from the archbishopric, leaving him Worcester alone. On the return journey, brigands assaulted Ealdred's party and robbed them of everything but their clothing. When he turned back to Rome, pity for his plight—along with the earl of Northumbria's threats to withhold the tribute of Peter's pence—moved the pope to relent. Provided that Ealdred give up the see of Worcester, Nicholas restored him to the see of York and granted him the pallium. Papal legates were sent to England to make certain that the archbishop followed the pope's wishes.

This episode, which happened just as the papacy was undertaking to compel all petitioners to come to Rome personally to receive the vestment, must have reinforced the notion that such a policy would be useful to papal goals. Clearly, the reformers did more than channel old practices to new ends. Innovative ways of using the pallium also sharpened its effectiveness and made it a tool better suited to carrying out the reform. This chapter turns from *why* it was used to *how*. It shifts the focus to the changes introduced by the reform popes in the customary techniques of handling the pallium. First, its old role as a mechanism of control was intensified through new requirements exacted from those who received it. Second, its use was manipulated to reward, to punish, and to bond palligers more tightly than ever to the apostolic see.

Stricter Control of the Episcopate

Traditionally the pallium offered an opportunity to control prelates. In addition to more specifically reform-oriented purposes, such as combating abuses and exalting the papacy, popes in this period pursued such control with unmatched vigor. The seeming goal was to place the episcopate (usually through its local leaders, the metropolitans) firmly under the thumb of the apostolic see, so that the hierarchy's adherence to the reform program could be assured. Many patterns in the pallium's treatment from previous centuries continued to contribute to papal control, but there were several noteworthy developments. The reformers reiterated and enforced the Johannine legislation of the 870s as never before. They also instituted a new policy that made personal reception of the vestment the norm. Finally, they began to require an oath of fidelity from those on whom it was bestowed.

Enforced Obligation

In 875 and 877 Pope John VIII had ruled that every metropolitan should submit a profession of faith and request the pallium from the apostolic see within three months of his consecration. This ruling was not mentioned again in existing sources until Burchard of Worms's *Decretum* in the early eleventh century, and it is doubtful, under the often weak tenth-century papacy, to what extent the deadline was known and observed in the century and a half after its formulation.[4] However, the reform popes and their supporters, who particularly valued the retrieval and implementation of old canon law, understood this obligation's value and expended significant efforts to enforce it. In 1081 Pope Gregory VII reprimanded William, archbishop of Rouen, essentially for having ignored the Johannine law:

> So far you have put off obtaining from the apostolic see, according to custom, the very splendid insigne of your dignity, namely the pallium. For indeed we think that you yourself are not ignorant of how strictly it must be judged, as the censure of the holy fathers has established, against those who are indifferent about acquiring the pallium, which belongs to their office, for three months in a row after their consecration.[5]

The pope was trying to rein in a distant province verging on autonomy at a time when the Roman church was weakened by German opposition and a recently elected antipope, and he strove to reforge bonds of communion with and dependence on Rome through the pallium. The Norman archbishopric continued to be a thorn in the papal side: Paschal II had a similar problem with William's successor Geoffrey in 1112, and blamed him for not seeking the vestment

---

4. Canon 1.25, Fransen and Kölzer, *Decretorum Libri*, fol. 3v. A prelate who delayed for more than three months was Hugh I of Besançon, who became archbishop in 1031 but did not receive the pallium until 1037. Vregille suspects he had no reason to communicate with Rome at first, but eventually needed the vestment to consecrate a new bishop of Lausanne (*Hugues de Salins*, 60–61).

5. JL 5204, Santifaller, *Quellen*, 1:223. For possible reasons for William's negligence, see Schrör, *Metropolitangewalt*, 201.

"within the time set by the fathers."[6] Both popes' invocation of the "fathers" probably referred to John's canon *Quoniam quidam*, even if Burchard's misattribution may have caused them to believe that it went back to the ancient Pope Damasus I.

This papal attitude was supported by numerous canonical collections that sprang up in this period to support reform ideas. Only the most important will be treated here. In an Italian collection around 1083, Anselm of Lucca compiled the largest cache of pallium-related canons since the late ninth-century *Collectio Anselmo Dedicata*.[7] The reproduction of two well-known anti-simony texts, both mentioning the pallium, must have seemed an appropriate juncture to insert other pieces of pallium legislation that he had gathered, some new to the canonical tradition.[8] The first of them was *Quoniam quidam*, canon 2 of the Council of Rome (875); its misattribution to Damasus bespoke dependence on Burchard (or a source also used by Burchard).[9] In all, twelve texts in a row mentioned the pallium, and the topics included the obligation to acquire it, the requirements for obtaining it, its use as a reward for cooperating with the pope, and its effect of confirming the recipient in office. Anselm was obviously interested in a more careful regulation of the pallium's use, perhaps because of his emphasis on papal primacy (of which the pallium was a tool), or at least out of a desire to be comprehensive.

Soon afterwards, another reformer, Cardinal Deusdedit, assembled an extensive canonical collection that drew on some of the same sources and treated the pallium at length.[10] The texts—including pallium-related precedents from Pope Gregory the Great's letters, along with a nearly forgotten letter of Pope Honorius I—were scattered throughout his work, but bore rubrics that explicitly ad-

6. JL —, Brett, "Some New Letters," 82.
7. On Anselm's collection, see Kéry, *Canonical Collections*, 218–26, and Fowler-Magerl, *Clavis Canonum*, 139–45. It had many versions, whose relationships are not always clear. Thaner's edition presents the texts of the "A" version, considered the original, but his rubrics are taken from different versions.
8. Canons 6.78–89, Thaner, *Collectio*, 2:308–13. Outside this sequence was another pallium-related text, Canon 7.65, ibid., 2:391–92.
9. Canon 6.80, ibid., 2:309.
10. On the collection, see Kéry, *Canonical Collections*, 228–33, and Fowler-Magerl, *Clavis Canonum*, 160–63.

dressed the vestment's role.[11] Among them was a brief excerpt from *Quoniam quidam* focusing on the obligation imposed on metropolitans—again related to the Burchardian tradition, and here placed among prerogatives setting the pope over other bishops.[12] Later in the same section, under the same rubric, was a trimmed version of canon 1 of the Council of Ravenna (877), attributed (correctly) to Pope John VIII and showing no trace of the Burchardian tradition.[13] The juxtaposition of these two closely similar texts must be wrapped up in the confusing history of the transmission of the Johannine councils.[14] In any event, the pallium's function of controlling the behavior of metropolitans was pronounced. From Deusdedit both canons found their way a few years later into Bonizo of Sutri's *Liber de Vita Christiana* and into the northern French *Collectio Britannica*, where the second canon was for the first time specifically associated with Ravenna.[15] Around the same time, the northern Italian *Collectio Ambrosiana I* dealt with the double tradition differently. Probably confused by the identical incipits, the compiler kept only the first canon, with its attribution to Damasus, while tacking on John VIII's name from the second canon.[16]

This transmission was further complicated in the canonical works

11. Canons 1.79 (1.97), 1.135 (1.166), 1.160.1 (1.203), 1.165.2 (1.210), 1.166 (1.211), 1.167 (1.212), 1.168.1 (1.213), 1.169a (1.214a), 1.188 (1.235), 1.191 (1.238), 2.95 (2.111), 4.162.1 (4.423), Glanvell, *Kanonessammlung*, 79, 106, 119–20, 123–25, 137, 139, 237–39, 599.
12. Canon 1.79 (1.97), ibid., 79—beginning *Quisquis metropolitanus* and ending *subvenire*.
13. Canon 1.135 (1.166), ibid., 106—beginning *Quisquis metropolitanus* and ending *contempserit*.
14. See 46n62, 182n9 above.
15. In Bonizo's work, see cc. 3.10, 3.13, Perels, *Liber de Vita*, 74–75—found among eight consecutive canons on the pallium (cc. 3.10–17, ibid., 74–76); on that collection, see Kéry, *Canonical Collections*, 234–37, and Fowler-Magerl, *Clavis Canonum*, 174–76. In the *Britannica*, see cc. 11(IX).23, 11(IX).38, Ewald, "Papstbriefe," 585–86. The *Britannica* sometimes erred in its inscriptions, which casts some doubt on the latter text's connection to the Council of Ravenna.
16. Canon 18, Giorgio Picasso, ed., *Collezioni canoniche milanesi del secolo XII* (Milan: Vita e Pensiero, 1969), 40. On the collection, see Kéry, *Canonical Collections*, 285, and Fowler-Magerl, *Clavis Canonum*, 176–78. Fowler-Magerl believes that the inscription was unique and demonstrated reliance on Deusdedit, although she mistakenly considers the two *Quisquis metropolitanus* texts to be the same.

attributed to Ivo of Chartres from the end of the eleventh century. The *Collectio Tripartita A*, a source for the Ivonian *Decretum*, retained the Ravennese canon but discarded the Roman.[17] The Ivonian *Decretum* itself, however, included both texts, the Ravennese from the *Tripartita* and the Roman, apparently from Burchard.[18] But the *Panormia*, a revised abbreviation of the *Decretum*, included only one of the latter's six pallium-related canons: the Roman-Burchardian *Quoniam quidam*.[19] For the purposes of this compact canon law manual, it was the only text important enough to be carried over; furthermore, the Roman version—more expansive and strict—was chosen in preference to the more focused and lenient Ravennese version.[20] Several factors may have been at play: respect for its purportedly ancient pedigree, interest in its larger legal content, or desire for its more stringent response to naysayers. In any case, the metropolitan obligation to obtain the pallium was clearly valued, whether as a papal instrument for the sake of reform, or more narrowly as a traditional prerequisite for metropolitan authority.[21] After 1111, the Italian *Collectio III Librorum* also reproduced *Quoniam quidam*, but inexplicably attributed it not to Damasus but to a Pope Pelagius.[22] It was placed under the title "On the measure of metropolitans"—*mensura* in the

17. Canon 1.65.1 (1.63.1), Brett, *Tripartita*, at https://ivo-of-chartres.github.io/tripartita/trip_a_1.pdf, 326. On the collection, see Kéry, *Canonical Collections*, 244–50, and Fowler-Magerl, *Clavis Canonum*, 187–90.

18. Canons 5.136, 5.354, PL 161:369, 431. On the collection, see Kéry, *Canonical Collections*, 250–53, and Fowler-Magerl, *Clavis Canonum*, 193–98.

19. Canon 3.11, Martin Brett and Bruce Brasington, eds., *Panormia*, at https://ivo-of-chartres.github.io/panormia/pan_3.pdf, 13, date / revision stamp 2015-09-23 / 898fb. On the collection, see Kéry, *Canonical Collections*, 253–60; Fowler-Magerl, *Clavis Canonum*, 198–202; and Christof Rolker, *Canon Law and the Letters of Ivo of Chartres* (Cambridge: Cambridge University Press, 2010), 265–89.

20. Cf. MGH Conc. 5:9–10, 68.

21. A longer rubric than in the *Decretum* (Martin Brett, ed., *Ivo, Decretum*, at https://ivo-of-chartres.github.io/decretum/ivodec_5.pdf, 60, date / revision stamp 2015-09-23 / 898fb) was supplied in the *Panormia* (Brett and Brasington, *Panormia*, at https://ivo-of-chartres.github.io/panormia/pan_3.pdf, 13). It changed the focus from expeditious episcopal consecrations to the pallium's role in an archbishop's installation.

22. Canon 2.6.4, Joseph Motta, ed., *Collectio Canonum Trium Librorum, Pars Prior (Liber I et II)*, Monumenta Iuris Canonici, ser. B, Corpus Collectionum 8 (Vatican City: Biblioteca Apostolica Vaticana, 2005), 143–44. See JK †1064. On the collection, see Kéry, *Canonical Collections*, 269–71, and Fowler-Magerl, *Clavis Canonum*, 234–35.

sense of capacity, but also of limit, as in control of the higher clergy.[23] From that collection *Quoniam quidam*, with its Pelagian attribution, passed into the earlier recension of Gratian's *Decretum* and joined the main body of the church's canonical inheritance.[24]

The rule articulated in canon law and enforced by the reform papacy seems to have sunk into the hierarchy's consciousness. One indication was a letter from Anselm of Canterbury to the papal intimate Hugh of Lyon in 1094. There Anselm vented his frustrations with King William Rufus, who had not recognized Urban II as legitimate pope: "I spoke about the pallium; [the king] did not wish me to ask for it, nor even to make known to the lord pope an excuse for this delay, as long as he himself accepted no pope.... If I, a metropolitan, having been consecrated a bishop, for the whole first year seek neither the pope, when he is alive, nor the pallium, when I am able, I must justly be removed from that honor."[25] The perceived obligation displayed awareness of the Johannine legislation—probably the softer Ravennese version, in light of the mention of an excuse. If an archbishop did not obey it for well beyond the three-month deadline, he should lose his office, as established by the law. Urban, however, would show himself quite flexible in Anselm's case, perhaps to win over the English king.[26]

23. This title may have been borrowed from Gregory of San Grisogono's *Polycarpus* (Title 2.24, Fuhrmann and Horst, *Sammlung "Policarpus,"* at http://www.mgh.de/fileadmin/Downloads/pdf/polycarp.pdf, 107). In that collection, however, *Quoniam quidam* occurred not there, but as the first canon under a new title, perhaps indicating its importance (Title 2.10, ibid., 94). Elsewhere, the *Polycarpus* invented a title wholly devoted to the vestment: "On the use and authority of the pallium" (Title 2.20, ibid., 102). This title was adopted by the *Collectio VII Librorum* in Vienna, Österreichische Nationalbibliothek, lat. 2186 (Title 1.41, *Clavis* SV01.041), which supplemented the canons from *Polycarpus* 2.20 with two further texts, including *Quoniam quidam*.
24. D.100 c.1, Emil Friedberg, ed., *Corpus Iuris Canonici* (Leipzig: Tauchnitz, 1879; reprinted in Graz: Akademische Druck- und Verlagsanstalt, 1959), 1:352.
25. Schmitt, *Opera*, 2.4:58, 60. Anselm's desire to approach the pope personally accorded with both English custom and reform policy, but the condition *vivens* questioned its necessity during a papal vacancy (cf. Urban II to Rainald of Reims in 1089, JL 5385, Somerville, *Pope Urban*, 117).
26. Eadmer of Canterbury indicated that the pope had finally sent the pallium to the king in order to gain his recognition during the schism (*Historia Novorum in Anglia*, in Rolls 81:68–69).

Personal Reception as a Rule

When Empress Agnes, regent during the German King Henry IV's minority, appointed Siegfried as archbishop of Mainz at the beginning of 1060, she sent an intercessory letter to Rome asking for the pallium to be sent to him. In bygone days it would have been unremarkable, but the reformers were beginning to execute new policies in the Latin church. Apparently Pope Nicholas II was in Florence at the time, and so the cardinal bishops (newly prominent in ecclesiastical affairs, thanks to the decree of the previous year entrusting them with papal elections) responded. The names of Humbert of Silva Candida and Boniface of Albano headed the letter, but Peter Damian is commonly credited with its composition. It must have come as a shock: the petition was refused as "opposed to canonical rules" and "contrary to the sanctions of the holy fathers." The cardinals then enunciated a new principle: "From the usage of ancient tradition, the pontiffs themselves ought to hurry to the thresholds of the apostles and receive that without which they cannot be metropolitans, the sign of completing their dignity."[27] Since his dignity was as yet incomplete, they never called Siegfried *archiepiscopus* or *metropolitanus* in the text, but only *electus*. His very office was placed in doubt, at least until he complied.

Maybe the cardinals anticipated resistance, for they immediately added a historical justification for what was really a change in customary practice:

> But if perhaps it is objected to this claim that the pallium has often been sent by the Roman pontiffs to very many places through messengers, a distinction must be made in this business for the reason that, at that time, legates of the Roman church, appointed throughout the provinces, discharged the place of the pope. Therefore, they used to examine those who were promoted to the summit of the episcopate, and so they used to obtain the pallium from the apostolic see through messengers.[28]

---

27. Siegfried may have sent a personal request in addition to Agnes's; the cardinals did not bring up that requirement.

28. D'Acunto and Saraceno, *Epistulae*, 4:94.

In the present, they implied, the pope himself would perform that examination, probably to determine compliance with the reform platform. The cardinals' goals can be guessed: careful control over powerful hierarchs, respect for legates, and in general the extension of papal power.

Perhaps too earnestly, but in keeping with the reform's emphasis on old law, they proceeded to provide backing for their rule by citing three cases from the canonical tradition.[29] First, another powerful woman, Queen Brunhild of the Franks, secured the pallium for her brother, Syagrius of Autun, only after he had gone to Candidus, *defensor* and papal *apocrisiarius*, for examination, no matter the bishop's eminent virtue. By so doing he showed "worthy reverence to the Roman pontiff in his legate." But Syagrius was not Brunhild's brother, Candidus did not hold those offices, and no examination beyond submitting a petition (perhaps containing a profession of faith) was required.[30] Second, Emperor Maurice gained the pallium for Maximus of Salona only after the latter had gone to papal representatives in Ravenna and cleared himself of various charges. But Maurice was not involved, except perhaps through an exarch; and in the cases of both Syagrius and Maximus, there were extenuating circumstances, rather than a papal intent never to send pallia.[31] Third, Damasus I (*recte* John VIII) ruled that metropolitans who delayed the pallium request and the profession of faith for more than three months after consecration should be deposed. But the canon was paraphrased and altered to remove the possibility that envoys could be sent for the vestment. Even as altered, the text did not discuss whether a metropolitan had to come to Rome personally.[32] Yet the cardinals' implication was clear: Siegfried had to come by the deadline, or face depo-

---

29. Ibid., 4:96.
30. Gregory the Great to Brunhild in 597, JE 1491, CCSL 140A:519.
31. A notice in Gregory the Great's register, CCSL 140A:1097. At this time the pope showed no hesitation to send pallia (e.g., JE 1164, 1374, 1378, 1387, 1756, 1829).
32. The most important alterations were three: "the Roman pontiff" replaced "the apostolic see"; "beseech" replaced "receive," perhaps to stress that reception was not guaranteed; and "delays" replaced "does not send," which suppressed the idea of sending envoys for the pallium.

sition. The new rule was defended as canonical and traditional, but on grounds at best ignorant of circumstances, at worst deliberately deceptive.

Nicholas probably agreed with the cardinals' move, for he could see the advantage of personal examination in the case of Ealdred of York a year later.[33] The next pope, Alexander II, began to enforce the new rule vigorously throughout the Western church. Three fragments of his letters, dating from around 1063 and preserved only in the *Collectio Britannica*, witnessed to his efforts.[34] Following Peter Damian's train of thought, Alexander declared to Ravenger of Aquileia: "Although in ancient times pallia were sometimes granted to absent metropolitans, because their promotions were discussed in a diligent inquiry by representatives of the holy Roman church, nevertheless, after this authority fell idle, our predecessors decided by wholesome counsel for [pallia] to be given only to those present."[35] He vastly underestimated the older practice as occasional and long ago, and misleadingly invoked more than one predecessor for support. Because the old system had broken down, he claimed, the new system would prevent the approval of unsuitable prelates. Writing to Anno II of Cologne, however, he modified his approach: "Recently it was instituted by the Roman pontiffs altogether discreetly, out of foresight for various matters, for the pallium, namely the sum of the whole priesthood, to be sent to no absent person."[36] Here he gave up an appeal to tradition and admitted that the popes had lately, though wisely, established the practice. Had he been facing opposition from archbishops aware of the true tradition? Finally, he mentioned to Abbot Hugh of Cluny: "Our brother Richer, archbishop of Sens, sent

---

33. JL 4463, Rolls 71.3:5–7. Siegfried, however, may have eventually obtained the pallium without having to go to Rome (see Schieffer, "Romreise," 162n57, and Jenal, *Erzbischof Anno*, 2:238).

34. See Dahlhaus, "Privileg," 662–63.

35. JL 4504, IP 7.1:31 no. 62, Loewenfeld, *Epistolae*, 41. The rubric in the *Britannica*'s index enunciated the principle clearly: "On giving pallia to metropolitans only when present" (Canon 2(II).48, *Clavis* LO02.048).

36. JL 4507, GP 7.1:62 no. 167, Ewald, "Papstbriefe," 338. Here the *Britannica* rubric put the principle negatively: "On not giving the pallium to an absent person" (Canon 2(II).51, *Clavis* LO02.051).

to us to grant him the pallium. This, of course, we ought not to give lightly and without the greatest consideration, especially since it is clear that it should not be sent to an absent person."[37] Richer's act had ample precedent, but Alexander's reluctance heightened perception of the vestment's importance, and his assertion that the rule was obvious was likely a bid to gain support.

Gregory VII also insisted on the policy. When Bruno of Verona asked for the pallium to be sent to him in 1073, the pope refused: "The authority of our predecessors has decreed that the pallium must not be granted except to a present person.... At that time we also wish to show your Presence with how sincere a love we love the royal welfare, and how much we desire to look out for his honor."[38] The pope found the required journey politically useful, for, once he could talk with this German bishop, he hoped to smooth over tensions with the German king. Bruno apparently complied.[39] Urban II too lent support to the effort.[40] In 1089 he told Rainald of Reims of his many complaints against him, but one was egregious. When the archbishop had received the pallium from the cardinals during a vacancy in the apostolic see, it was under the condition "that, as soon as a supreme pontiff had been ordained in the Roman church, as the Lord arranged, you would show yourself present to his sight." The demand to approach the pope was retained, even if deferred. However, Rainald had delayed "for such a long time now."[41] Urban had good reason to want to see him, since the king of France had probably invested him.[42] The archbishop soon complied, and the grateful pope showered him with privileges.[43] Similarly motivated, Paschal II

---

37. JL 4529, Loewenfeld, *Epistolae*, 43. The rubric was the same as the last (Canon 2(II).57, *Clavis* LO02.057).

38. JL 4795, IP 7.1:222–23 no. 20, MGH Epp. sel. 2.1:41.

39. A notice in Gregory's register, MGH Epp. sel. 2.1:123.

40. He even tried to impose the practice, which he called an "ancient and canonical" custom of the Roman church, on those seeking any kind of privilege from the papacy (to William of St. Benedict in 1088, JL 5352, IP 7.1:330 no. 7, Somerville, *Pope Urban*, 47).

41. JL 5385, Somerville, *Pope Urban*, 117.

42. See ibid., 118.

43. In 1089, JL 5415, PL 151:309–11. See Falkenstein, "Verlorene päpstliche Privilegien," 214–16. It was Rainald's second pallium-related journey over the Alps,

was concerned that "the fullness of the pontifical office ought not to be entrusted to a man whose lifestyle, election, and learning are unknown," and so he wished to see Geoffrey of Rouen in 1112 in order to "know [his] person more surely."[44]

Did metropolitans, obeying the new dictate, regularly go to receive the pallium in person during this period? It is difficult to find genuine evidence of a case that could qualify as typical. Some instances are known only from the accounts of enemies, and these stories, not to mention the motives of the players, are obscure.[45] Other prelates who went to Rome appeared eager to establish themselves as legitimate archbishops in new or contested situations.[46] And several testimonies may have been falsified.[47] Even when a trip to Rome

---

but the pope did not hesitate to impose such a burden when control of the vestment was involved (ibid., 204–5).

44. JL —, Brett, "Some New Letters," 82.

45. Udo of Trier was journeying to Rome to bribe the pope, according to his enemy, Anno II of Cologne (to Alexander II in 1066, Giesebrecht, *Geschichte*, 3:1260). Herman of Bamberg made the trip in 1070, and in Bonizo of Sutri's confused account was deposed for simony (*Liber ad Amicum*, in MGH LdL 1:602); in Lambert of Hersfeld's account, the papal summons to Rome may have resulted from the new policy (Schieffer, "Romreise," 160–61).

46. Bernard of Toledo paid his personal respects in 1088, as the first archbishop after the see's restoration (in the *Collectio Britannica*, Canon 8[VI].17, Ewald, "Papstbriefe," 357, edited at Somerville, *Pope Urban*, 72). Roland of Dol made the journey in 1093 in order to prove his right to receive the vestment (Urban II to the Breton bishops, JL 5475, PL 151:359). In 1099 Gerald of Braga requested the metropolitan rank and the pallium from the pope in person (Bernard of Braga, *Vita Geraldi*, in Academia das Ciências de Lisboa, *Portugaliae Monumenta Historica: Scriptores* [Lisbon: Typis Academicis, 1856], 1.1:54). Ebremar of Jerusalem came to Rome in 1107, probably because his position was questioned and his opponents were also coming to make their case to the pope (Paschal II to the clergy and people of Jerusalem, JL 6175, Rudolf Hiestand, ed., *Papsturkunden für Kirchen im Heiligen Lande: Vorarbeiten zum Oriens Pontificius III*, Abhandlungen der Akademie der Wissenschaften in Göttingen, philologisch-historische Klasse, ser. 3, 136 [Göttingen: Vandenhoeck and Ruprecht, 1985], 106).

47. Interpolations made in 1095 to Odorannus of Sens's chronicle claimed that two archbishops of Sens, the late tenth-century Seguin and the early eleventh-century Leoderic, had received the pallium from the pope's hand, but these statements during the struggle for primacy between Sens and Lyon are not necessarily trustworthy (Robert-Henri Bautier and Monique Gilles, eds., *Odorannus de Sens: Opera Omnia*, Sources d'histoire médiévale 4 [Paris: Centre National de la Recherche Scientifique, 1972], 96, 110, 112). Baldric of Dol's trip to Rome in 1109 may never have happened (see 316 above). A letter probably forged in the late eleventh or

really happened, it is hard to tell whether circumstances other than the reform policy may have warranted the journey.

Still, the expectation that the pallium should be personally received continued to be expressed. In the late eleventh or early twelfth century, the *Collectio Britannica* devoted substantial attention to providing canonical backing for this policy. No fewer than seven (over a quarter) of its twenty-five pallium-related canons—all seven appearing only in this collection—dealt with the principle that archbishops should visit the pope in person. In one canon, the mid-sixth-century Pope Pelagius I forbade the use of the pallium to Secundus of Taormina, who had lost touch with the apostolic see for almost three years, and summoned him to Rome.[48] Yet the rubric attached to the canon made a telling mistake: it focused not on the charges Pelagius actually made, but on the bishop's supposed refusal to "go to Rome"—which was not the offense, but rather part of the pope's disciplinary solution. The compiler also included Stephen V's letter calling Theodosius of Split to Rome before he could obtain the pallium.[49] To these the *Britannica* added the three Alexandrine texts analyzed above and two letters of Urban II, one to Anselm III of Milan, treated below, and the other to Rainald of Reims, discussed above.[50] This collection had gathered a formidable arsenal of prece-

early twelfth century and attributed to Abbot Caesarius of Santa Cecília de Montserrat, who had unsuccessfully claimed the desolate archbishopric of Tarragona in the mid-tenth century, contained a plea for the pallium and a promise to come soon to Rome (Ramon Ordeig i Mata, ed., *Catalunya carolíngia*, vol. 4, *Els comtats d'Osona i Manresa*, part 2, Memòries de la secció històrico-arqueològica 53 [Barcelona: Institut d'Estudis Catalans, 1999], 786). On this garbled forgery, see Ramon d'Abadal i de Vinyals, *Dels visigots als catalans*, vol. 2, *La formació de la Catalunya independent*, ed. Jaume Sobrequés i Callicó, 2nd ed., Col·lecció estudis i documents 14 (Barcelona: Edicions 62, 1974), 25–55, and McCrank, "Restoration," 80–91; but Jarrett maintains the possibility of genuineness ("Archbishop Ató," 13–16). See Deswarte, "Rome," 13–14.

48. Canon 1(I).93 (28 of Pelagius), Ewald, "Papstbriefe," 548, quoting JK 1000, edited at Gassó and Batlle, *Epistulae*, 114–15, with rubric ("On the archbishop of Taormina being unwilling to go to Rome") at *Clavis* LO01.093. The rubric made the bishop into an archbishop, the usual palliger in the Middle Ages.

49. Canon 9(VII).29a, Ewald, "Papstbriefe," 407, quoting JL 3448, edited at MGH Epp. 7:351.

50. Canons 2(II).48, 2(II).51, 2(II).57, Ewald, "Papstbriefe," 337–38, quoting JL 4504, 4507, 4529; canon 8(VI).12, Ewald, "Papstbriefe," 356, quoting JL 5359; and canon 8(VI).32, Ewald, "Papstbriefe," 361–62, quoting JL 5385.

dents for denying the pallium to prelates unwilling to make the journey to see the pope.

However zealously pursued, the new rule was not always well received. Adam of Bremen sounded obstinate in the mid-1070s when he described the accession of his hero, Adalbert of Hamburg, some decades before: "As did his predecessors, he received the archiepiscopal pallium through legates."[51] Were Adam and his current archbishop, the ardent royalist Liemar, resentful at papal reluctance to dispatch the vestment through messengers? In 1080/81 the anti-reform writer Wenric of Trier complained that the antiking Rudolf's candidates for bishoprics were favored over Henry IV's, without regard to the new policy: to the former bishops, he said, "blessings are not denied, and pallia are sent home." He implied that the pope insisted that the king's candidates come to Rome for the pallium. This selective enforcement of the reform agenda arose, he claimed, "not from zeal for religion, but from hatred of the prince."[52]

In addition, the early twelfth-century anti-papal writer known as the Norman Anonymous composed two tracts against forced trips to Rome. One, a defense of the archbishop of Rouen, may have been reacting to Gregory VII's reprimand of William of Rouen two decades before (or some similar rebuke).[53] It did not explicitly mention the pallium, and its reasoning could apply as well to regular *ad limina* visits as to journeys to receive the vestment.[54] But the demand to see the pope and the reception of the pallium were likely linked in the author's mind. His chief grievance was that the long road presented hazards to body and soul. The other treatise, a complaint against pa-

---

51. *Gesta Hammaburgensis Ecclesiae Pontificum*, in MGH SSRG 2:142.
52. To Gregory VII, MGH LdL 1:297.
53. J4, Ginther and O'Sullivan, *Electronic Norman Anonymous Project*, at http://normananonymous.org/ENAP/index.jsp?view=edition&p=39, 43–44. Cf. Gregory to William in 1081, JL 5204, Santifaller, *Quellen*, 1:223. Perhaps William himself was the Anonymous (George Huntston Williams, *The Norman Anonymous of 1100 A.D.: Toward the Identification and Evaluation of the so-called Anonymous of York*, Harvard Theological Studies 18 [Cambridge, Mass.: Harvard University Press, 1951], 102–27). But the author, while familiar with the suspension, did not seem to know Gregory's letter (Karl Pellens, *Die Texte des normannischen Anonymus*, Veröffentlichungen des Instituts für europäische Geschichte Mainz 42 [Wiesbaden: Steiner, 1966], 35n1, 40n3).
54. See Pater, *Bischöfliche visitatio liminum*.

pally imposed burdens, contained another version of the same argument.[55] It did not refer to the pallium either, but probably reflected local reaction to *ad limina* visits, of which the pallium trip was a special case. The pope's demand, the author said, was based on whim and desire for domination, and it should be disobeyed for many reasons: it caused prelates to abandon their flocks; it subjected them to dangers, persecutions, sickness, and great labor; it forced them to disguise themselves as laymen for protection; it prevented them from celebrating Mass while on the road; and the papal curia's exactions compelled them to sell their churches' goods and neglect the poor. All this, he maintained, "bishops who are forced to go to Rome for any affairs most certainly experience."[56]

As the debate raged on, it became clear that canon law could be harnessed by either side. Around the same time as the *Collectio Britannica* sought to defend the policy, Bonizo of Sutri, though a reformer, offered an opposing viewpoint in his *Liber de Vita Christiana*. Among his pallium-related canons he inserted three under the rubric, "That the pope can send the pallium to a metropolitan through a messenger."[57] Instead of the bland rubrics provided for these texts in other collections, Bonizo drew forth a principle only vaguely contained in them and appeared deliberately to pose an alternative to the new rule. Clearly, not all reformers agreed on every plank of the reform papacy's platform.

Even those supportive of papal goals and willing in theory to adhere to this demand presented excuses for their lack of cooperation. The papal legate Hugh of Die wrote to Pope Gregory VII in 1078 and asked for the pallium to be sent to Gebuin of Lyon: "He himself, having set aside all inconveniences and dangers of want and the journey, would most devotedly present himself to the sight of your Holiness,

---

55. J28, Ginther and O'Sullivan, *Electronic Norman Anonymous Project*, at http://normananonymous.org/ENAP/index.jsp?view=edition&p=285, 286–88. See Williams, *Norman Anonymous*, 33.
56. J28, Ginther and O'Sullivan, *Electronic Norman Anonymous Project*, at http://normananonymous.org/ENAP/index.jsp?view=edition&p=285, 287.
57. Canons 3.14–16, Perels, *Liber de Vita*, 75–76—unremarkable excerpts from letters in which Gregory the Great sent the pallium to Prima Justiniana (JE 1164), Nicopolis (JE 1387), and Corinth (JE 1378).

if the church entrusted to him, for so long weary and robbed of a shepherd's comfort, could somehow suffer his absence without great loss."[58] Thus the staunchly pro-Gregorian legate acknowledged the truth of some of the objections raised by critics such as the Norman Anonymous. Another papal supporter, Anselm of Canterbury, ran into King William Rufus's opposition when he "humbly asked him to give him permission to go to Rome to Pope Urban for the stole of his archiepiscopate," according to Eadmer of Canterbury's *vita* between 1112 and 1114. The king had not yet decided between the rivals Urban II and Clement III. But after further negotiations he "received Urban as pope through Walter, bishop of Albano, who brought the pallium from Rome to Canterbury for Anselm," a concession likely made to secure English loyalty to Urban's cause.[59] Shortly afterwards the archbishop felt bound to write the pope an apology:

I admit, of course, that it concerned our order and office both to visit your presence, according to custom, and to honor it with worthy reverence.... That I have not done this, I ask your holy Eminence not to resent, nor to attribute it to my neglect or arrogance.... But because we are battered by wars on all sides and unceasingly fear hostile attacks and the plots of opponents, our lord the king has so far not allowed me to proceed ... outside the kingdom. Furthermore, even if no other causes coincided that would forbid me to see your face at this time—and I am very annoyed that I cannot—it suffices that age, sickness, and the weakness of my body make me unable to endure both the long journey and the immeasurable roughness of the roads. But amidst these things, burdened by this labor and this anxiety, I would try to make the journey, if almighty God ... bestowed that peace on the kingdoms and provinces of the kingdoms through which one must travel to you. Thus it might be permitted to fulfill that journey, as would be necessary and fitting.[60]

In Anselm's eyes, personally appearing before the pope was a way to establish a right relationship, to show adherence to the true pope during the schism, and to render him due honor.

58. PL 148:744.
59. R. W. Southern, ed., *The Life of St. Anselm, Archbishop of Canterbury, by Eadmer*, Oxford Medieval Texts (Oxford: Clarendon, 1979), 85, 87. Cf. Irvine, *Anglo-Saxon Chronicle*, 7:106, where the phrase *hider to lande* hinted that such was not the usual practice.
60. In 1095, Schmitt, *Opera*, 2.4:82–83.

The custom for English archbishops to go to Rome for the pallium, which predated the reform policy by more than a century, did not seem to make it easier for them to comply. Anselm attested to Paschal II in 1101 that Gerard, the newly elected archbishop of York, wanted to present himself to the pope, but was kept back by King Henry I.[61] Within a year, however, he wrote the pope again to intercede for Gerard, who was making the journey for the pallium.[62] The about-face was the king's doing, who told Paschal: "Both the love that I very much have for you and the kindness that much adorns your actions were giving me the confidence, upon holding back Archbishop Gerard of York with me, to seek the pallium for him from your Holiness. But because he himself was wholly gripped by the desire to be able to be presented to your sight and to ask for it from you himself, I have sent him to you."[63] Despite the sugary language, Henry had probably lifted his prohibition of the trip because he commissioned the archbishop to relay to the pope his position (against Anselm's) concerning lay investiture.[64]

Some years later, Anselm's successor Ralph of Canterbury wished to be excused from the obligation to go to Rome. The canonist Ivo of Chartres wrote Paschal in 1114 on Ralph's behalf and explained that the archbishop desired to visit the apostolic see "according to the instructions of the forefathers," but was deterred by physical frailty and the hazards of travel. Given the long, politically manipulated vacancy that had preceded Ralph's election, Ivo advised the pope to "come to the aid of the languishing church with some dispensation and, because of the need of the church, and for the advantage and integrity of the person, mercifully bend your ear to the entreaties of the petitioners." He argued that teachers "can temper the rigor of the laws because of ecclesiastical needs, when that remission of the laws contains nothing against the truth of the faith or the integrity of behavior."[65] It was typical of Ivo to defend the possibility of dispensa-

---

61. Ibid., 2.4:113–14.   62. Ibid., 2.4:122.
63. In 1101/02, ibid., 2.4:123.
64. Eadmer of Canterbury, *Historia Novorum in Anglia*, in Rolls 81:132; William of Malmesbury, *Gesta Pontificum Anglorum*, in Winterbottom, *Gesta Pontificum*, 1:172; and Hugh the Chanter, *Historia Ecclesiae Eboracensis*, in Johnson, *History*, 22.
65. PL 162:256–57.

tion based on circumstantial necessity, ecclesiastical usefulness, and personal merit.[66] The community of the Canterbury cathedral priory likewise begged the pope to send Ralph the pallium and explained why his receiving it in person was impracticable.[67] In its reasoning and terminology this testimonial showed similarity to Ivo's, and may have been part of a coordinated campaign to secure the pallium despite the deviation from papal expectations.[68]

In the face of resistance and excuses from metropolitans and alternative views from reformers such as Bonizo and Ivo, the papacy seems to have backpedaled somewhat from its policy. Pope Urban II, whose realistic temperament sought to rebuild a reform papacy in disarray after Gregory VII's death and to reclaim Peter's mantle from Antipope Clement III, was willing to relax the rule in certain cases. In 1088 he allowed Anselm III of Milan, deposed for his irregular accession, to return to office: "Beseeched by your letter, we send the pallium to your Fraternity with the blessing of the apostolic see, beyond the custom of the Roman church, which grants this kind of dignity to no one unless present."[69] Given the fragile situation in Milan, the pope broke "Roman custom"—and was sure to point it out, so that the archbishop would realize the favor being conceded. The next year Urban was in Bari for the translation of the relics of Nicholas of Myra. There he installed Elijah as archbishop, as he narrated in the pallium grant: "Against the custom of our Roman and apostolic church, won over by reverence for blessed Nicholas and love for your people, we consecrated you, most beloved brother, in your own see."[70] Southern Italian metropolitans ordinarily came to Rome for both consecration and palliation, but here the pope made an exception as a special grace—and for practical reasons, since his hold on the city against the antipope was still tenuous.[71]

A year later Urban rewarded his legate, Altmann of Passau, by

---

66. See Somerville and Brasington, *Prefaces*, 114–15.
67. Rolls 81:227.
68. The campaign succeeded (Irvine, *Anglo-Saxon Chronicle*, 7:118 [JL *6482]).
69. JL 5359, IP 6.1:52–53 no. 121, Somerville, *Pope Urban*, 60.
70. JL 5412, IP 9:319–20 no. 7, PL 151:308.
71. See Alraum, "Pallienprivilegien," 23–24.

permitting him to bring the pallium to Tiemo of Salzburg: "Hearing of your vigor in the things of God and the labors of the church, we rejoice in the Lord, and so we have heard your petitions in those things which seem against the custom of our church."[72] Altmann had helped to settle Tiemo's contested election, and as recompense for his fidelity to the reform cause as papal legate in Germany, the pope consented to his unusual request. In 1093 Urban also agreed to send Peter of Grado the pallium, "what our holy apostolic church would by no means bestow on another person at another time," and let him receive consecration from his own suffragans.[73] It was abnormal for the patriarch to gain the vestment without coming to the pope—and even before being ordained a bishop—but his personal worthiness was the deciding factor. Finally, in 1095 Urban complained that Guy of Vienne was ignoring papal instructions, despite leniency shown him in the past: "Providing for the need and advantage of the church, we tolerated in your promotion what was lacking in your age. Against the custom of our church, we bestowed the pallium on you when absent and also granted you a privilege."[74] If the pope, with a shrewd grasp of political advantage, were thus indulgent to a prelate, he had a right to require a return for his favor.

Although Pope Paschal II did not tend to emphasize that he was acting "against the custom of the Roman church," he followed his predecessor's footsteps in offering occasional accommodations by sending the pallium through legates. At first, sometime after 1105, he faulted Lawrence of Esztergom's manner of seeking the vest-

---

72. JL 5440, GP 1:170 no. 35, MGH SS 12:239. Josef Oswald interprets the violation of custom as the fact that Altmann, rather than Tiemo himself, requested the pallium ("St. Altmanns Leben und Wirken nach der Göttweiger Überlieferung: 'Vita Altmanni,'" in *Der heilige Altmann, Bischof von Passau: sein Leben und sein Werk* [Göttweig: Abtei Göttweig, 1965], 165). But the phrase *contra morem nostrae ecclesiae* was similar to Urban's words on other occasions when he dispensed with the policy of personal reception.

73. JL —, IP 7.2:59 no. 103, Kehr, *Papsturkunden*, 3:214. An attached condition warned future patriarchs not to expect such indulgent treatment. Apparently the pope himself would consecrate them; the reform papacy may have hoped to extend the southern Italian custom to the entire peninsula.

74. JL 5548, GaP 3.1:141 no. 195, PL 151:406. See Schilling, *Guido von Vienne*, 62–64.

ment: "It befit you yourself to have come and explained your faith, as was instituted by the sanctions of the holy fathers. Indeed, your messenger performed the business enjoined on him prudently and quite insistently. But the clerics of your church or, if there is a dearth of clerics, better laymen should have been designated for this matter."[75] Paschal preferred a personal appearance, but was willing to accept (respectable) envoys. Lawrence must have sent the latter, for eventually the pallium was delivered to Hungary by papal *apocrisiarii*.[76] Similar concessions permeated this pontificate. In 1107 Paschal permitted Adalgot of Magdeburg to make up for problems with his pallium request "either yourself or through suitable persons," and even implied that this option was "according to the custom of our church."[77] In 1108 Thomas II of York, at the urging of King Henry I, sent envoys to Rome to ask for the vestment.[78] And in 1117 Cardinal Conon of Palestrina was on his way to Mainz to bring Archbishop Adalbert his pallium.[79]

A compromise between reform ideals and practical difficulties had at last been reached. It was not officially articulated, but in 1111 Gilbert of Limerick expressed his own understanding: "Both an archbishop and a primate ought to be ordained by the pope in Rome; or the pallium ought to be brought to them from Rome from the pope, and he ought to be elevated by his fellow bishops. This permission is given only if sickness or war or some other necessary cause perchance intervenes."[80] Gilbert was following a strict version of the reform program: *all* archbishops had to go to Rome personally for consecration and the pallium, as did the southern Italian metropolitans; but in problematic circumstances the pallium might be sent, and or-

---

75. JL —, Brett, "Some New Letters," 82–83.
76. Paschal to Lawrence, JL 6570, PL 163:428–29.
77. JL —, Brett, "Some New Letters," 84.
78. Thomas to Anselm of Canterbury, Schmitt, *Opera*, 2.5:391. Thomas claimed that he was having trouble raising the necessary funds (whether for traveling expenses or the pallium fee was unclear). Anselm replied that the embassy would be fruitless, not because Thomas did not go himself, but because he had not yet been consecrated (ibid., 2.5:393).
79. Conon to Theoger of St. George, Jaffé, *Bibliotheca*, 3:387.
80. *De Statu Ecclesiae*, in John Fleming, ed., *Gille of Limerick (c. 1070–1145): Architect of a Medieval Church* (Dublin: Four Courts, 2001), 162.

dination conferred locally. In sum, this item of the reform agenda met with only partial success, and the popes were forced to lower their expectations. There were limits to papal power, which always had to be negotiated. The hardships of travel in this era were at least as decisive as any theoretical opposition to the papacy's attempt to control the episcopate.[81]

Oath of Fidelity

Past popes had tested the orthodoxy of those who wished to wear the pallium by requiring the submission of a profession. But the reform popes desired more than adherence to correct faith: they demanded adherence to the person of the Roman pontiff to an unprecedented extent. Thus developed the oath of fidelity or loyalty, through which the petitioner was required to swear fealty to the pope and his successors before he could acquire the vestment. The evidence concerning this new prerequisite is not plentiful, and only those cases conjoined to the grant of the pallium will be examined here.[82] Even if it was only fitfully enforced at first, the popes seem to have tried to impose this obligation on archbishops across the Latin church.

As far back as the Carolingian era, the profession of faith had sometimes been accompanied by an oath of fidelity to the Roman church (as for Lull of Mainz) or obedience to papal decrees (as for the missionary Ansgar).[83] Some such pledge may have continued through the years as part of the process of obtaining the pallium.

---

81. Only in 1983, under John Paul II, was the reform policy fully realized, and for the next three decades the world's newest metropolitans journeyed to Rome each year to be vested with the pallium by the pope on St. Peter's day (June 29). In 2015, however, Pope Francis reversed the practice and decreed that a country's papal nuncio would impose the vestment on a metropolitan in his cathedral, in the presence of his suffragans, clergy, and people, in order better to highlight his relationship to the local church—and presumably to save the costs of travel.

82. Not all oathtaking to the pope was linked to the pallium. See Gottlob, *Kirchlicher Amtseid*, 42–74, and Pater, *Bischöfliche visitatio liminum*, 31–48.

83. Levison, *England*, 240, and Nicholas I to Ansgar in 864, JE 2759, GP 6:31–32 no. 21, BH 706, Curschmann, *Ältere Papsturkunden*, 23. Sometimes such oaths may have been associated primarily with being a papal legate, and only incidentally with receiving the pallium.

Pope Leo IX was perhaps referring to it in 1053 when he promised to endow Adalbert of Hamburg and his successors with honors "if, by the example of the martyr Boniface, they be ever ready by oath and due subjection to obey us and our successors in the apostolic see"—and then confirmed Adalbert's use of the pallium and increased the days on which he could wear it.[84] Boniface had sworn to his faith and obedience, in the manner of a Roman suffragan, when Pope Gregory II consecrated him in 722.[85]

Something different was afoot in 1078, when Hugh of Die asked Pope Gregory VII to send the pallium through a legate "to confirm the ordination of the most religious archbishop [Gebuin] of the church of Lyon.... Instruct the [legate], and receive his promise in your hand."[86] The pope was to convey the usual admonitions to the messenger and receive a pledge of fealty from him, as a proxy for the archbishop. The phrase *in manu vestra* brings to mind the feudal act of homage. Albeit vicarious in this case, this description provided further insight into what the papacy hoped to gain from personal presence: personally vowed faithfulness, and the opportunity to advise and instruct the petitioner.

In the next decade Cardinal Deusdedit included two oaths in his canonical collection. The first was taken from the *Liber Diurnus*, though heavily revised and supplemented, and given two rubrics: "The guarantee of a bishop before consecration and of him who seeks the pallium," and "On the consecration and guarantees of the archbishop of Ravenna."[87] It was thus meant (at least originally) for Italian metropolitans supposed to come to Rome for ordination and palliation. Ravenna may have simply been an exemplary case among Italian metropolitans, or may have been included as a reminder of

---

84. JL 4290, GP 6:56–57 no. 81, BF 1026, Curschmann, *Ältere Papsturkunden*, 50.

85. See Gottlob, *Kirchlicher Amtseid*, 27–29. Leo must have hoped to create the same kind of relationship with the archbishops of Hamburg.

86. PL 148:744. *Securitas* could be a "*promise of fealty* in the negative sense of abstention from acts prejudicial to the person receiving the promise," or more generally a "solemn promise" or "oath" (Niermeyer, *Mediae Latinitatis Lexicon*, 951–52).

87. Canon 2.95 (2.111), Glanvell, *Kanonessammlung*, 237–39, *Clavis* DU02.095. Cf. the formulas V73–74, Foerster, *Liber Diurnus*, 128–36, with parallels C67–68 on 238–46 and A62–63 on 363–74.

its subordinate status to the Roman church during a time when its archbishop was schismatic. The promise was useful for enforcing the reform agenda: the oathtaker pledged to the pope (and Peter and Paul and the Roman church) not only to hold and defend the apostolic faith, including papal decrees, but also—in additions reflecting current ideas—to avoid simony, to urge the clergy to chastity and the common life, to make *ad limina* visits, to attend synods when called, and to treat papal legates honorably.

Deusdedit's second oath was taken from Pope Alexander II's register and given two rubrics: "The oath of bishops who are consecrated in the Roman church and receive the pallium from her," and, once more, "On the consecration and guarantees of the archbishop of Ravenna."[88] Unlike the foregoing formula, this text kept the name of the oathtaker, Guibert of Ravenna. It was thus the oath he had sworn to Alexander at his consecration in 1073, and its inclusion here may have served to accuse Guibert—now Antipope Clement III—of breaking his oath. He had promised to be faithful to Peter, the Roman church, and the popes, not to plot against them, not to betray their confidence, to help them retain the *papatus Romanus et regalia sancti Petri*, and to pay heed to papal legates, synods, and *ad limina* visits. It resembled a feudal oath, with additions based on reform principles and suited to the needs of the age.[89] There was some overlap with the first text, and the relationship between the two is unclear. Possibly they were meant to model the oaths that the popes began to exact from all archbishops. Since all were now required to come to Rome personally for the pallium, as the Italians did, they

---

88. Canon 4.162.1 (4.423), Glanvell, *Kanonessammlung*, 599, *Clavis* DU04.162.01. Around 1192 the *Liber Censuum* made this oath into a formula, under the title "The oath of bishops receiving pallia" (P. Fabre and L. Duchesne, eds., *Le Liber censuum de l'église romaine*, Bibliothèque des écoles françaises d'Athènes et de Rome, ser. 2, 6 [Paris: Fontemoing, 1889–1910], 1.3:417).

89. Gottlob sees it as a papal attempt to win aid in enforcing the papal election decree of 1059 and enlist allies against German influence (*Kirchlicher Amtseid*, 44). For very similar oaths, see Robert Guiscard's in 1059 (in Deusdedit's collection, Canon 3.285, Glanvell, *Kanonessammlung*, 393–94); Henry of Aquileia's in 1079 (in Gregory VII's register, MGH Epp. sel. 2.2:428–29); and Diego of Compostela's in 1104 (according to the *Historia Compostellana*, in CCCM 70:43). Professions of faith must have been rendered separately.

were also required to swear fealty to the Roman church in the Italian manner.

Whether with these or other formulas, metropolitans from many Western sees took oaths during the subsequent pontificates. Two historical notices in the *Collectio Britannica* bore witness to this fact. One recorded that Anselm III of Milan, having been deposed, "was instructed and compelled by the lord Pope Urban [II] to return to the bishopric, as the need of the church forced, and swore an oath to him and the Roman church according to the custom of bishops. To him, suppliantly asking for it afterwards, the pallium was sent by the same lord Urban."[90] The phrase *pro more episcoporum* indicated that the practice went beyond Anselm, but since he was an Italian archbishop, it was unsurprising in light of Deusdedit's material. In the second note, however, something similar was said of Bernard of Toledo: "At this time Bernard, archbishop of Toledo, coming to Rome to the lord pope [Urban II], swore to him according to the custom of bishops, received the pallium and a privilege, and was instituted primate for the kingdoms of Spain."[91] The same phrase used of this Spanish prelate proved that the oath was a universal expectation, at least in theory.[92]

Indeed, Urban rebuked William of Rouen in 1094, for although he had apparently heeded Gregory VII's call to meet his obligation to request the pallium, he had never supplied the oath of fidelity: "When [the Roman church] adorned you with the pallium, confirmed it with a privilege, pardoned very many things, and put up with many things from you, nevertheless, as if ungrateful for her favors, you refused to do fealty to her, as is the custom for all metropolitans." As a result, William had been suspended from office and the use of the vestment. Now, since he had ignored these measures,

---

90. Canon 8(VI).11, Ewald, "Papstbriefe," 355, edited at Somerville, *Pope Urban*, 58.

91. Canon 8(VI).17, Ewald, "Papstbriefe," 357, edited at Somerville, *Pope Urban*, 72. Honorius III specified that this notice had come from Urban's register (Somerville, *Pope Urban*, 73–74).

92. The note cited the custom of "bishops" in general, rather than "archbishops," perhaps because some suffragans were also required to take the oath (Gottlob, *Kirchlicher Amtseid*, 47–48).

the pope reiterated the pallium's deprivation and commanded him to appear before him.[93] In the same year Urban chastised Thomas I of York for subjecting his church to Canterbury "after you received the pallium from the apostolic see, after you swore fidelity, as is the custom for metropolitans."[94] The pope saw Thomas's act as contradicting an English metropolitan's direct subjection to the papacy, partly expressed by the pallium oath.

In 1107 Pope Paschal II complained that Adalgot of Magdeburg's pallium petition contained neither a profession of faith nor "the promise of obedience due to us."[95] He denied him the vestment until he supplied for this defect. And in 1118, after Archbishop Maurice of Braga had usurped the apostolic see as Gregory VIII, Pope Gelasius II wrote a series of letters informing his allies and asking for support. To the clergy and people of Rome he exposed the heinousness of Maurice's disloyalty: "He once received from us, according to custom, confirmation, consecration, and the pallium, and we received from him, according to the statutes, the canonical oath of fidelity and obedience, etc. Therefore, we ask ... that you refrain from him as from an excommunicate, perjurer, invader, and rapist of holy mother church and the catholic faith, etc."[96] The oath, portrayed as legally prescribed, showed that Maurice was subordinate to the pope, by whose authority he had any office to begin with. To the clergy and people of Gaul and the papal legate Cardinal Conon of Palestrina he stressed the same: "When he had once received the pallium through our hands, he swore fidelity to our same lord [Paschal II] and his catholic successors, of whom I am the first."[97] Apparently Gelasius, as Cardinal John of Gaeta, was the deacon who had

---

93. JL —, Brett, "Some New Letters," 84. Cf. Gregory VII to William in 1081, JL 5204, Santifaller, *Quellen*, 1:223. Urban spoke of his suspension *ab officio episcopali* and then *postmodum ... ab usu pallei*, which meant that the two were separable. Perhaps the former was administrative and jurisdictional, while the latter was liturgical and sacramental.

94. JL —, Johnson, *History*, 10.

95. JL —, Brett, "Some New Letters," 83–84.

96. JL 6632, IP 1:13 no. 21, PL 163:488. Mansi notes that the passage is corrupt, and has apparently abbreviated it.

97. JL 6635, PL 163:489. Cf. JL 6642, PL 163:493.

vested Maurice with the pallium in Rome; at that time the archbishop had given Paschal an oath of fealty, which he had broken by his rebellion against Paschal's successor. Gelasius wanted to impugn the antipope's integrity and demonstrate the bond that subjected him, through pallium and oath, to the papacy.

The most significant testimony to the oath and its understanding by the reform papacy was Paschal II's canonically important and rhetorically elegant letter *Significasti frater,* probably written after 1105 to Lawrence, archbishop of Esztergom.[98] According to the archbishop's report, the king and nobles of Hungary had been outraged, the pope said, "because the pallium was offered to you by our emissaries under the condition that you swore the oath they had brought, written by us." The oath was thus a prerequisite for receiving the vestment. Paschal then engaged in a lengthy defense of swearing in general and the pallium oath in particular. For one thing, he simply did not know the recipient: "With what concern, with what precaution, ought we to impose such a great prelacy of the church, such a great care for Christ's sheep, on our brothers, whose consciences we do not see, especially those whom we know by no familiarity, of whose love we are thoroughly ignorant?" For another thing, the oath would prevent certain evils, such as the tendency "to recoil from the unity of the church, from the obedience of the apostolic see," or "to burst forth against the statutes of the sacred canons." Therefore, the popes required this guarantee "for fidelity, for obedience, for unity."[99]

Having established its practical utility, the letter went on to justify the oath on ecclesiological grounds. The gift of the pallium and the subjection it incurred were a concrete way of representing and effecting the unity of the church through her head, the pope: "When you demand the insignia of your dignity from the apostolic see, which are taken up only from the body of blessed Peter, it is just

---

98. The date and addressee are debated, but Brett's discovery of a version of the letter with the inscription *Strigonie episcopo* suggests Lawrence as the recipient ("Some New Letters," 89–94). For evidence in support of this identification, see X 5.3.18, Friedberg, *Corpus,* 2:754–55.

99. JL 6570, PL 163:428–29.

that you also pay due signs of subjection to the apostolic see, which make clear that you cling to blessed Peter as if limb from limb, and keep the unity of the catholic head."[100] Paschal was also not above employing peer pressure. The oath's content, he said, was acceptable to all bishops "who have decided to persist under the obedience and unity of Peter and Paul, princes of the apostles. Are not the Saxons and Danes far away from you? And yet their metropolitans also affirm the same oath, and treat legates of the apostolic see honorably, and help in their needs, and visit the thresholds of the apostles through their legates, not merely every three years but every year."[101] Perhaps the pope was overstating the observance of these practices. But he was surely reflecting the reformers' vision of a centralized church with an episcopate firmly subsidiary and accountable to its head.[102]

Stronger Inducement to Loyalty

The oath attached to the pallium's reception was one way of ensuring the loyalty of the higher clergy, but the pallium itself could also be manipulated to that end. Because its bestowal created an alliance with the donor, the act of giving or withholding the vestment reflected the recipient's standing in the reform papacy's eyes. Refusing to grant the pallium or suspending its use was common in this period, especially as a means of disciplining bishops uncooperative with the reform. Conversely, those who had aided papal efforts were

---

100. This seems to be the earliest occurrence in an authentic papal letter (excluding a probably later forgery, JL †4119a, BF †307, ZPUU 2:1169–71) of the comment that the pallium was "taken from the body of blessed Peter." The addition of "only" implied that the pope alone could bestow it, because only the Roman church possessed Peter's body, and the only genuine pallium was one taken from his tomb.
101. JL 6570, PL 163:429–30. Cf. Guibert's oath in Deusdedit's collection (Canon 4.162.1 [4.423], Glanvell, *Kanonessammlung*, 599).
102. The letter also had an obscure passage: "By them [Peter's keys?], nevertheless, in the decrees of four councils [in four conciliar decrees?] a manner of giving the pallium was prescribed, and an order of profession and obedience was sanctioned" (JL 6570, PL 163:429). A way of bestowing the vestment, with formulas for the profession of faith and the oath of fidelity, had been established, but what was it and where was it found?

often rewarded with the vestment, and those whose allegiance was sought might be enticed with it. In times of schism, however, the woolen bond could work as well for antipopes as for popes, and "antipallia" were distributed to cement the fidelity of bishops opposed to the Gregorian take on reform.

Denial and Punishment

Regarding the pallium, Pope Gregory VII declared to Henry of Aquileia in 1079: "The excellence of this ecclesiastical honor, just as it is justly denied to the wicked and disobedient, so sometimes seems to have to be paid by apostolic direction to the good and those endowed with integrity of behavior due to their merits."[103] His carefully qualified statement reinforced the fact that the gift could always be withheld. Indeed, several cases in which the popes denied the pallium, at least initially, in order to punish misconduct or to increase their influence in a conflicted situation have already been discussed. Nicholas II refused it to Ealdred of York in 1061 because of his illicit translation and pluralism, although he relented because of a robbery the archbishop suffered on his way home.[104] Gregory VII declined King Michael of Zeta's request for the pallium for the archbishop of Dubrovnik in 1078, so that he could first decide a dispute between Dubrovnik and Split.[105] Urban II, using punishment to compel compliance, confirmed in 1094 that William of Rouen was forbidden to wear the vestment after failing to swear fidelity to the pope.[106] Paschal II turned down Bruno of Trier's petition in 1106 because of his lay investiture, although the pallium was conferred after suitable penance.[107] The next year the same pope withheld the vestment from Adalgot of Magdeburg because of problems with his petition and promotion, although this penalty would be lifted if he remedied the problems.[108] Anselm of Canterbury begged Paschal to

103. JL 5131, IP 7.1:33 no. 70, Santifaller, *Quellen*, 1:198.
104. JL 4463, Rolls 71.3:7. Avoiding the appearance of supporting uncanonical behavior, however, the pope added that the grant could not be used as a precedent.
105. JL 5061, MGH Epp. sel. 2.2:365.
106. JL —, Brett, "Some New Letters," 85.
107. *Gesta Treverorum*, in MGH SS 8:192.
108. JL —, Brett, "Some New Letters," 84.

deny Thomas II of York in 1108, because the latter had not yet professed obedience to Canterbury; shortly after Anselm's death, however, Thomas made the promise and gained the pallium.[109] Finally, Paschal refused the vestment to Geoffrey of Rouen in 1112 until he submitted the requisite request and came to Rome.[110] It was accepted, then, that the pope could, and occasionally did, refuse those who sought this privilege.

In the 1070s William of Poitiers described the notorious career of Mauger of Rouen from several decades before: "He was never distinguished with the pallium, which is the principal and mystical insigne of the archiepiscopate. The hand of the Roman pontiff refused to send it to him as usual, as to someone less than suitable."[111] Not only did he waste the resources of his church, but he "harmed with no light injury the universal church, whose only primate, the supreme bishop in the whole world, he did not venerate with the obedience that was fitting. For, summoned quite often by the pope's command to a Roman council, he refused to go."[112] In effect, the pope failed to confirm his position, although it did not result in deposition until a synod of Norman bishops, along with the papal legate, passed sentence. Rouen's pallium was threatened again in 1095, when Pope Urban II forbade the vestment's use to the archbishops of Sens and Rouen until they recognized the primacy of the archbishop of Lyon.[113] What effect this penalty had was implied by Ivo of Chartres, writing in the pope's name to Richer of Sens in the following year. A new bishop of Paris had been elected, and Ivo instructed Richer, Paris's metropolitan, "to lay hands on him before the feast of St. Remigius, according to the authority and custom of your church, and by

---

109. Schmitt, *Opera*, 2.5:399. Anselm also asked the pope not to palliate the bishop of London, who had never had the vestment before, for this too would undermine Canterbury's primacy.

110. JL —, Brett, "Some New Letters," 82.

111. Which pope was meant? Mauger took office around 1037, during Benedict IX's pontificate, and was not deposed until 1054/55, just after Leo IX's pontificate.

112. Davis and Chibnall, *Gesta Guillelmi*, 86, 88. This charge was probably made at the synod that deposed Mauger, in which the papal legate Ermenfrid of Sion participated.

113. To Hugh of Lyon, JL 5600, PL 151:439.

no means to be afraid to use the honor of the pallium, temporarily forbidden to you, at his ordination and consecration."[114] An arrangement between the pope and the French king may have prompted this exception to the suspension. If not for it, this stripped palliger would have been unable to consecrate a bishop.

As usual, canonical support was sought for the reform papacy's actions. In Gregory VII's later years, Bernold of Constance wrote the *Apologeticus* to defend the pope's strict measures as congruent with tradition. One chapter justified the lack of *induciae* (stays) accompanying papal condemnations. It called Gregory the Great to witness, who had not hesitated to inflict ecclesiastical penalties, even automatically. Bernold cited the case of Natalis of Salona, whom the pope had sentenced to be deprived of "the pallium and communion" if he did not obey his orders. Thus later popes also condemned those "who rashly usurped anything forbidden, under [pain of] excommunication or suspension of office."[115] Reference to the letter in which Gregory had inflicted this punishment occurred in five subsequent canonical collections of this period.[116] One, compiled in northern Italy around 1118/19, added a rubric, "That a disobedient bishop should be deprived of honor," which focused not on Natalis's crime (as had been typical) but on the penalty imposed on the palliger to pressure him to comply with the pope's wishes.[117] A version of Anselm of Lucca's collection made in Paschal II's early years included not only the Natalis text, as Anselm had originally designed, but also an excerpt of another Gregorian letter, addressed to Maximus of Salona.[118] This text treated the pallium as a sign of communion, to be

---

114. Jean Leclercq, ed., *Yves de Chartres: correspondance*, Les classiques de l'histoire de France au moyen âge 22 (Paris: Belles Lettres, 1949), 1:204.

115. MGH LdL 2:86. Here "communion" corresponded to "excommunication," and "pallium" to "suspension of office"—the effect, in Bernold's eyes, of the pallium's loss. See Robinson, *Authority*, 165–66.

116. These included (in roughly chronological order) Anselm of Lucca's collection, Deusdedit's collection, the *Collectio Ambrosiana I*, the collection in Turin E.V.44, and the collection in Vat. lat. 3829, to which may be added the earlier recension of Gratian's *Decretum*, all quoting JE 1175.

117. Found in Vatican City, Biblioteca Apostolica Vaticana, Vat. lat. 3829, Canon 63.123, *Clavis* PG63.123.

118. On this version of Anselm's collection, called "Bb" and found in Vatican

Reform: The Means 351

granted to those who submitted to the pope. But the rubric stretched the logic: "That the pallium is to be given according to custom, but not to those persevering in fault"—a principle only implied in the canon, but apparently important to the redactor.[119]

The northern French *Collectio Britannica*, from the late eleventh or early twelfth century, is considered to reflect the spirit of the reform, and is also an important source for the study of the pallium. This is true not only because it preserved a number of otherwise unknown papal letters, but also because an unmistakable interest in the vestment can be deduced from its texts. As an "intermediate collection," it may appear as a hodgepodge, without a clearly expressed program.[120] Nevertheless, its pallium-related canons fell mostly into distinct categories, and twelve (almost half) of the twenty-five concerned putting conditions on or withholding the vestment. All but one of these twelve also seem to have been the results of contemporary research, often claimed to be derived from the papal registers themselves.[121] Nine were transmitted exclusively through the *Britannica*.[122] One first appeared there, before recurring in two Ivonian works, and one was excerpted in an unusual fashion that hinted of original treatment.[123] The emphasis on pallium denials and the sig-

---

City, Biblioteca Apostolica Vaticana, Barb. lat. 535, see Kéry, *Canonical Collections*, 219; Fowler-Magerl, *Clavis Canonum*, 157–58; and Kathleen G. Cushing, "Polemic or Handbook? Recension Bb of Anselm of Lucca's *Collectio Canonum*," in *Bishops, Texts and the Use of Canon Law*, ed. Brasington and Cushing, 69–77.

119. Canon 6.89, *Clavis* AG06.089, quoting JE 1703.

120. An intermediate collection was a preliminary gathering of canonical material, frequently from archives, for later organization into systematic compilations (Somerville, *Pope Urban*, 5–6).

121. Despite the *ex registro* assertions, doubts have been raised about some texts. See Peter Landau, "Gefälschtes Recht in den Rechtssammlungen bis Gratian," in *Fälschungen im Mittelalter*, part 2, *Gefälschte Rechtstexte; der bestrafte Fälscher*, Monumenta Germaniae Historica Schriften 33.2 (Hannover: Hahn, 1988), 40–42; Somerville, "Mercy," 148–49; and Herbers, *Leo*, 344–48.

122. Canons 1(I).93 (28 of Pelagius), 2(II).48, 2(II).51, 2(II).57, 6(IV).25, 8(VI).12b, 8(VI).32a, 8(VI).33a, 9(VII).29a, Ewald, "Papstbriefe," 548, 337–38, 305, 356, 361–62, 407, quoting JK 1000, JL 4504, 4507, 4529, JE 2982, JL 5359, 5385, 5386, 3448.

123. The former text was c. 10(VIII).36a–b, ibid., 390, quoting JE 2603, which recurred in the Ivonian *Decretum* (Canon 4.210a–b, PL 161:311) and the collection in Paris, Bibliothèque de l'Arsenal, 713 (Canon 545a–b, *Clavis* LP0545a–b). On the

nificant amount of new material suggest that the anonymous compiler was preoccupied with the vestment as a means of papal control over the hierarchy, to be held back as papal goals dictated.

Seven of these canons made the pallium's reception dependent on a personal appearance before the pope, as examined above.[124] The other five established the pope's traditional right to refuse the pallium and to examine vigilantly the faith and promotion of the petitioner. One text recalled that Leo IV had denied Emperor Lothar I's petition to palliate Altheus of Autun in the mid-ninth century, arguably because the bishop had not requested it himself.[125] Another attested that John VIII, upon Bertulf of Trier's pallium request, had summoned him to Rome in 873 to testify more precisely to his "rule of faith" and to satisfy the pope about his possibly uncanonical consecration.[126] Two more texts were drawn from the same pope's letter to Willibert of Cologne, also called to Rome in the same year. One focused on the inadequacy of his profession of faith.[127] The other expounded more theoretically on the reasons for and effects of denying the pallium.[128] Similar, although the pallium was conceded by way of exception, was Urban II's letter to Anselm III of Milan in 1089. That archbishop's lay investiture, irregular consecration, and possible simony should have barred his confirmation, but the pope palliated him for the church's good—while threatening to reverse his decision if Anselm proved problematic.[129]

Arsenal collection, see Fowler-Magerl, *Clavis Canonum,* 192–93. The latter text was c. 6(IV).29, Ewald, "Papstbriefe," 306–7, quoting JE 2986—beginning *Non perfectus est cui tantum pallii* and ending *miseris penitus indicaveris*. The twelfth canon about withholding the pallium (Canon 11[IX].49, ibid., 587, also quoting JE 2986) was apparently borrowed from Deusdedit (Canon 1.191 [1.238], Glanvell, *Kanonessammlung,* 139).

124. See 333–34 above. Even if the mistaken rubric of the Pelagian canon is ignored, its text still involved the suspension of the vestment's use as a punishment.

125. Canon 10(VIII).36a–b, Ewald, "Papstbriefe," 390, quoting JE 2603.

126. Canon 6(IV).25, ibid., 305, quoting JE 2982, edited at MGH Epp. 7:288.

127. Canon 11(IX).49, Ewald, "Papstbriefe," 587, quoting JE 2986.

128. Canon 6(IV).29, ibid., 306–7, quoting JE 2986.

129. Canon 8(VI).33a, ibid., 362, quoting JL 5386, edited at Somerville, *Pope Urban,* 120–21.

Rewards and Reciprocity

The pallium could function not only as a stick, but also as a carrot. Several times when its grant figured as an act of grateful recompense for a deed pleasing to the donor have already been surveyed. Alexander II endowed Burchard II of Halberstadt with the vestment in 1063 because, as royal mediator, he had sided with the pope during the recent schism.[130] As Lambert of Hersfeld put it in 1077/78: "To him, upon his return, [Alexander] gave the pallium and certain other insignia of the archiepiscopate, as a reward for a well cared-for legation."[131] It was essentially a gesture of thanks for services rendered in the victorious pope's cause. Gregory VII broke precedent and gave Evan of Dol the pallium in 1076 when the princes of Brittany renounced simony and lay investiture and embraced the reform movement.[132] And Urban II allowed his legate, Altmann of Passau, to bring the pallium to Tiemo of Salzburg in 1090, even though it violated the dictate of personal reception, because of Altmann's diligent service to the church.[133] The prestige associated with the pallium made it an ideal way to reinforce behavior in line with papal objectives.

Thrice in this period the popes took a cue from their tenth-century predecessors and increased the number of days on which the vestment could be worn, as a sign of approval and gratitude. In 1052 Pope Leo IX palliated Leopold of Mainz, and after listing his pallium days, added: "Because we love you in place of a son, we charitably grant you these two days which your predecessors did not have, namely the octave of the Lord [January 1] and the festivity of All Saints [November 1]."[134] The next year the same pope confirmed the pallium's use for Adalbert of Hamburg, with a list of occasions nearly identical to Clement II's original privilege of 1047.[135] Howev-

---

130. JL 4498, GP 5.2:220–21 no. 36, Dahlhaus, "Privileg," 672.
131. *Annales*, in MGH SSRG 38:82. Lambert mistakenly thought that Antipope Honorius II had palliated Burchard in exchange for helping to settle him in Rome.
132. To Ralph I of Tours in 1077, JL 5021, Santifaller, *Quellen*, 1:136.
133. JL 5440, GP 1:170 no. 35, MGH SS 12:239.
134. JL 4281, GP 4:90 no. 114, BF 1007, Stimming, *Mainzer Urkundenbuch*, 1:184.
135. JL 4290, GP 6:56–57 no. 81, BF 1026, Curschmann, *Ältere Papsturkunden*, 50. Cf. JL 4146, GP 6:55–56 no. 78, BF 370, ibid., 48. See Gresser, *Clemens*, 88–93.

er, the pope added: "Because we learn of your devotion, by which you desire to evangelize the nations, from our munificence we add to your aforesaid honor the use of the pallium also on the Holy Saturday of Easter [the Easter Vigil], on the invention of the Holy Cross [May 3], and on the festivity of Stephen the protomartyr [December 26]."[136] The archbishop's evangelical zeal had earned him three more feasts, the latter two occurring here for the first time in a genuine pallium grant. Finally, in 1079 Henry of Aquileia was bold enough to ask Gregory VII to increase his pallium days, and the pope responded favorably:

> Because we are confident that you have the affection of sincere love toward us; because you are known to have treated our legates ... kindly and to have helped them faithfully, as you ought; and finally because you are proven to have sweated much for the sake of arranging peace, we received your petition gladly. Therefore ... we grant you to have permission to use the pallium in the celebration of the Mass on the observances of blessed Ulric the confessor and pontiff [July 4] and blessed Afra the martyr [August 5/7]. Nevertheless, know that this has been granted to you for your lifetime, and not to your place.[137]

The reasons for this special allowance were political, reflecting Henry's assistance in negotiations with the German king during the thick of the Investiture Contest. The two additional feasts commemorated saints of Augsburg, where Henry had been a cathedral canon before his appointment to Aquileia. The concluding caveat clarified that the honor was personal, not meant to become part of his see's tradition. But a personal gesture was precisely the point: Henry found this liturgical distinction important enough to request, and Gregory, who needed allies who had the royal ear, did not hesitate to grant it.

Rewards were favors given for past conduct; but the pallium could also be granted in view of hoped-for future conduct. This notion, that one good turn deserved another, lay at the heart of gift-giving (*do ut des*). Often the expectation of reciprocal benevolence and beneficence went without saying. But in this period the popes, pressed by political struggles and sometimes in a weakened position, had

---

136. JL 4290, GP 6:56–57 no. 81, BF 1026, Curschmann, *Ältere Papsturkunden*, 50.
137. JL 5131, IP 7.1:33 no. 70, Santifaller, *Quellen*, 1:198–99.

to rely more heavily on friends, and so they articulated anticipated countergifts more explicitly. In 1092 Pope Urban II raised the see of Pisa to an archbishopric and subjected the bishops of Corsica to its metropolitan authority. In doing so, he palliated its new archbishop, Daimbert, with this rationale: because Pisa had rendered so many services to the Roman church during schisms, and Daimbert had labored for its freedom, the pope wished to respond to these kindnesses, "so that, just as we are mindful of past things, so also, themselves presented with the favor of such great grace, they may be more faithful and devoted to the holy Roman church in future times, and respond to their very kind mother by assisting, helping, and complying always."[138] It was political *quid pro quo* taken to an extreme: the help of one party merited the help of the other, offered in turn so that the first would continue to help the second.

In the following year Urban conferred the pallium on Peter of Grado, even though he failed to make a personal appearance for consecration and palliation: "Let your Fraternity, perpetually mindful of such great kindness and generosity, be eager to respond with gratitude to your catholic mother ... and pursue the hostile with the effort of all your might, and fervently comfort friends and sons according to the ability given you by God ... so that, in the present distress of tribulations, you may offer great relief to the church."[139] But this obligation of reciprocal regard was not always observed. Even though he was below the canonical age for ordination and did not come to see the pope as the reform policy required, Guy of Vienne had been confirmed in office and granted the pallium. Nevertheless, he proved unresponsive to Urban's instructions during a dispute with the bishop of Grenoble, which caused the pope to rebuke him as "unmindful of such great favors."[140] Guy was ignoring the duties of the bond created by the vestment, to the pope's dismay. In short, he was ungrateful for the gift.

---

138. JL 5464, IP 3:321 no. 9, PL 151:344–45. Cf. Bernold of Constance, *Chronicon*, in MGH SSRG n.s. 14:517.
139. JL —, IP 7.2:59 no. 103, Kehr, *Papsturkunden*, 3:214–15.
140. In 1095, JL 5548, GaP 3.1:141 no. 195, PL 151:407. See Schilling, *Guido von Vienne*, 128–29.

Pope Paschal II followed Urban in this regard. When he decorated Diego of Compostela with the pallium in 1104, it was done in honor of the apostle James, but he also had a more practical motive: "To you, Diego ... we grant the dignity of the pallium from the generosity of the apostolic see, so that you may learn that you and your church always ought to comply further with the same apostolic see."[141] The vestment was a reminder of the close bond between the two churches, and it incurred subjection as a countergift. Shortly afterwards, during negotiations with Lawrence of Esztergom, the same pope complained that the archbishop had not allowed Hungarian bishops to visit the pope or papal legates to hold reform synods in Hungary.[142] These practices were fixtures of the reform period, and if Lawrence wanted the gift of the pallium, he would have to cooperate. Indeed, Paschal instructed him, it was *iustum* for "due signs of subjection" to be offered in exchange for the pallium.[143] Finally, in 1111 Paschal furnished Otto of Bamberg with the pallium and the processional cross "so that, endowed with the particular dignity of the holy Roman church, you may be particularly zealous to sweat over obedience and services to her."[144] The more exceptional the gift, the more exceptional the dependence to be tendered in return.

Schisms and Antipopes

If the pallium could create loyalty, it could also express loyalty. After Archbishop Ruthard of Mainz had abandoned Emperor Henry IV and his antipope and thrown his support behind Henry V's rebellion, Pope Paschal II granted him the pallium in 1105—but only after he had ascertained where his loyalty truly lay. Writing to the bishop of Constance, the pope affirmed that he had "received the oath of competent persons as a result of [Ruthard's] infamy" and had acted only "at the request of good men of your regions, both clerical and lay."[145] Even so, Ruthard ran afoul of Paschal two years later, and so the arch-

---

141. JL 5986, PL 163:133. Cf. *Historia Compostellana*, in CCCM 70:41.
142. JL —, Brett, "Some New Letters," 83.
143. JL 6570, PL 163:430.
144. JL 6291, GP 3:264 no. 46, PL 173:285.
145. To Gebhard, JL 6057, GP 4:117–18 no. 202, Stimming, *Mainzer Urkundenbuch*, 1:327.

bishop desperately reminded the pope that, having merited the pallium, he had ever since "labored zealously, according to my ability, to obey your commands and to keep your decrees solicitously."[146] In both men's eyes, the vestment displayed that Ruthard was now an adherent of the Gregorian party, faithful to Paschal, from whom he had received it.

From whom an archbishop received the pallium mattered, for it was with the donor that he formed a bond and reciprocated by his obedience and service. Such concepts lay behind the confrontation between Anselm of Canterbury and King William Rufus of England in the mid-1090s, when Urban II and Clement III were vying for the papacy. When Anselm asked leave to approach the former for the pallium, according to Eadmer of Canterbury, the king balked: "Upset at the name of Urban, he said that he did not hold him as pope, nor was it his custom that it should be permitted to anyone in his kingdom to name the pope without his own choice." A *gravis dissensio* developed, requiring the attention of a national synod (Rockingham, 1095). The bishops who supported William asserted "that Anselm could by no means hold Urban, bishop of the apostolic see, as pope in his kingdom, without violating the fidelity that he owed the king."[147] Since the question of receiving the pallium had sparked the conflict, that act was clearly seen as equivalent to the endorsement of the one who gave it. Anselm's position was made plain in a letter to Hugh of Lyon: if he were not permitted to seek the pallium from Urban, "it is better for me to reject the archbishopric than to renounce the pope."[148] The controversy was settled when William accepted Urban and Anselm received the pallium from Urban's legate. Even then, rumors flew that the archbishop had embraced schism by siding with the king. Anselm retorted that the pope was fully aware of the circumstances, and "nevertheless, not as one reproving but as one approving, he sent the pallium, which the archbishop of Canterbury is accustomed to have, to me, not as a schismatic but as one ac-

---

146. Joannis, *Rerum*, 1:531.
147. *Vita et Conversatio Anselmi*, in Southern, *Life*, 85–86.
148. In 1094, Schmitt, *Opera*, 2.4:60.

cepted."¹⁴⁹ The vestment marked a prelate in communion with the church and with the pope who had presented it.

Implied in this story was the possibility that Anselm could have gotten his pallium from Urban's rival, Clement III. That the antipopes of this period wore the vestment and bestowed it on others loyal to them seems certain. The *Annales Romani* described the fall of Antipope Adalbert, one of Clement's successors, in 1101: "Those who were on the side of the pontiff [Paschal II] immediately arrested [Adalbert] and took the pallium from his neck, and shamefully dragged him out of church."¹⁵⁰ The Clementine faction had made a pallium for their candidate (although it had not been laid on Peter's tomb, since they did not have control of the basilica), and removing it stripped him of his papal pretensions and bolstered Paschal's legitimacy.

Since both parties in a papal schism wore the pallium, both must have also tried to recruit and confirm adherents by sharing their insigne, as popes had done for centuries. At least six "antipallia" can be cited in this period. After Robert of Jumièges had been deposed and exiled in 1052, Stigand received the archbishopric of Canterbury, while keeping the see of Winchester. Condemned by the reform popes on that account, he was never able to obtain the pallium from them. At first he usurped Robert's, left behind in the latter's hasty flight.¹⁵¹ Eventually, in 1058, he found a willing donor in Antipope Benedict X, who noteworthily *sent* the pallium to Stigand, against both English custom and reform policy.¹⁵² William of Malmesbury later wrote that Benedict had been overjoyed that Stigand "had called pope him whom other archbishops were considering a sham." But after Stigand's deposition "it was decreed by a wholesome council that he who had not justly had the papacy could not have legitimately given the pallium."¹⁵³

149. To Walter of Albano in 1095, Schmitt, *Opera*, 2.4:80.
150. Duchesne, *Liber pontificalis*, 2:345.
151. Remigius of Dorchester's profession to Lanfranc of Canterbury, in Richter, *Canterbury Professions*, 27.
152. Irvine, *Anglo-Saxon Chronicle*, 7:85 (JL *4389). Cf. Cubbin, *Anglo-Saxon Chronicle*, 6:76, and Baker, *Anglo-Saxon Chronicle*, 8:126–27.
153. Winterbottom, *Gesta Pontificum*, 1:46.

A few years later, a new antipope, Honorius II, conferred the pallium on Gunther of Bamberg—if that is the correct explanation for the removal of the papal name in the extant text of the bishop's letter to Siegfried of Mainz.[154] The fact that Honorius had *sent* the pallium, as Gunther mentioned in his letter, must have galled Siegfried, whom the reformers were forcing to fetch his pallium in person.[155] The *Gesta Treverorum* reported that, toward the end of Gregory VII's pontificate, Archbishop Egilbert of Trier, a supporter of the German king, dispatched an envoy to Antipope Clement III to ask for the pallium: "That Clement, I say, having rejoiced that someone was looking to him to receive a blessing, sent what he sought, with a letter teaching at what times he would use it. Because the author does not strengthen it, but rather weakens it—for no faithful person receives the decrees of heretics and excommunicates—on that account we have not taken care to commend it to memory."[156] Once again, the vestment was sent, rather than accepted in person. The sarcastic commentary indicated that the papal claimant gladly fulfilled this request, for it cemented his claim if he could act as a pope by bestowing the pallium and forging his own network of relationships. Further, the annals compiled by the cathedral canons of Augsburg recorded Emperor Henry IV's appointment in 1084 of Wezilo as archbishop of Mainz, who was promptly consecrated and then "palliated by a legate of Guibert," that is, Clement III.[157] Yet again, a personal appearance was not demanded; the antipope sent the pallium to Mainz through his representative.

In 1091 Clement also bestowed the vestment on Peter of Braga and elevated his see to its ancient status as an archbishopric. Since Peter's reception of such a gift showed disloyalty to Urban II, the response from that side was severe: "Because he received the pallium and a privilege from Pope Clement, he was deposed by the archbish-

---

154. MGH Briefe 5:201.
155. Peter Damian to Agnes of Poitou in 1060, D'Acunto and Saraceno, *Epistulae*, 4:94.
156. MGH SS 8:187–88. The antipapal privilege is not extant (JL *5321, GP 10.1:77 no. *149).
157. MGH SS 3:131.

op of Toledo and the legate of the holy Roman church.... On this account, Braga, which of old had been a metropolis, was in modern times deprived of its proper dignity." Peter's successor Gerald, in contrast, threw in his lot with the reform papacy, as his *vita* attested. He traveled to Rome to petition Paschal II for the restoration of Braga's metropolitan rank, and "carried away from there the pallium and a privilege and the authority of his church."[158] The pope likely had little choice in this grant, lest he once more lose the allegiance of the Portuguese church.

Finally, in 1112 Paschal updated Guy of Chur about recent events, among which he announced: "Aquileia is using a Guibertine pallium, apart from our grant."[159] Ulric of Aquileia had received the vestment from Clement, and Paschal's words essentially declared that the patriarch was schismatic. In effect, Ulric possessed relations with and exhibited dependence on a rival to the church's legitimate head. The garment was thus an emblem of partisan adherence. Even if it looked no different from a pallium bestowed by Paschal, this antipallium lacked authority, and by its origin made manifest the wearer's true loyalties.

One reform polemicist saw the danger inherent in this instrument of antipapal power. When Bernard of Hildesheim compiled his *Liber Canonum contra Henricum IV* in 1085, at a low point in the Gregorian party's fortunes and a high point in Clement III's, he attacked the efficacy of anything stemming from the antipope. He argued "that those who were deceived into receiving the archiepiscopal pallium from a usurping pope, or any divine thing from him—or from an archbishop of his (or anyone ordained by such an archbishop)—had

---

158. Bernard of Braga, in Academia das Ciências, *Monumenta*, 1.1:54. In 1103 Paschal notified Count Raymond of Galicia of this event (JL —, Carl Erdmann, ed., *Papsturkunden in Portugal*, Abhandlungen der Gesellschaft der Wissenschaften zu Göttingen, philologisch-historische Klasse, neue Folge, 20.3 [Berlin: Weidmann, 1927; reprinted in Göttingen: Vandenhoeck and Ruprecht, 1970], 157). See Demetrio Mansilla, "Formación de la provincia bracarense después de la invasión árabe," *Hispania Sacra* 14 (1961): 8–11.

159. JL 6626, GP 2.2:90 no. 14, Paul Ewald, ed., "Reise nach Italien im Winter von 1876 auf 1877," *Neues Archiv der Gesellschaft für ältere deutsche Geschichtskunde* 3 (1878): 172.

received only execration instead of consecration, as from those who did not have anything they could give."¹⁶⁰ Just as their blessing was a curse, so was their curse a blessing: the anathema of an antipope or "of anyone presented by him with the archiepiscopal pallium" should be regarded instead as "a salvific, hoped-for, and, so to speak, most blessed blessing."¹⁶¹ In short, he maintained that an antipalliger was not truly an archbishop, and his acts were void: "He who received or will receive the archiepiscopal pallium from [Clement] neither was nor can become an archbishop. And he is not a bishop who is ordained by these pseudo-archbishops. And ecclesiastical ranks cannot be given [to anyone] by the same most corrupt pope, or by any of those who are archbishops from his pallium, or by a bishop promoted by archbishops of that sort."¹⁶² Facing a false pope who was erecting a parallel church in part through pallium conferrals, Bernard contended that an antipallium could not do the things a real pallium could, whether confirming its recipient in office or empowering him to consecrate. In this respect, Bernard shared the view of a defender of Pope Formosus, who had observed around 914 that invalidating a pope invalidated the entire stream of sacramental consequences flowing from him through his pallium grants.¹⁶³

160. MGH LdL 1:475; cf. 1:500. See Robinson, *Authority*, 107–9.
161. MGH LdL 1:476–77; cf. 1:512.
162. Ibid., 1:515.
163. *Invectiva in Romam*, in Dümmler, *Gesta*, 149. During a dispute over the status of Formosus and the validity of his ordinations, this anonymous cleric attempted a *reductio ad absurdum*. To say that Formosus's ordinations were void because his episcopacy had been void would call into question the power of his own consecrators. This domino effect would implicate several past popes, and a segment of the apostolic succession would have been without standing for many years. Metropolitans throughout the church needed the pallium from Rome in order to carry out their tasks. If there was no valid *apostolica potestas*, there was no pallium (assuming that it could only be gotten from the pope, indeed from a valid pope). Without pallia, new bishops could not be consecrated; without bishops, churches could not be blessed, chrism made, or priests ordained. In this vision of ecclesiastical order, the pallium, by making episcopal consecrations possible, was the linchpin of the entire sacramental system. See Ernst Dümmler, *Auxilius und Vulgarius: Quellen und Forschungen zur Geschichte des Papsttums im Anfange des zehnten Jahrhunderts* (Leipzig: Hirzel, 1866), 1–46.

Conclusion

Attempting some of the most ambitious enterprises in their history—and confronting some of the most virulent opposition—the popes reached a level of ingenuity in their use of the pallium that rivaled their efforts during the Carolingian age. Insisting on the requirements imposed by Pope John VIII in that era, they supplemented them with new requirements, such as personal appearance and the oath of fidelity. They also employed the pallium, far more energetically than in the past, in meting out both reward and penalty, in both encouraging loyalty and punishing disloyalty. The lofty goals examined in the last chapter demanded these stringent measures in a divided church. But contemporary creativity did not end with the spheres of law and politics. Just as use and understanding had always worked together, the pallium's augmented role found echo in the rhetorical and theological realms. The next chapter will investigate new ways of imagining and describing the vestment in the reform period, ways which heightened its significance to match its broadened use.

9

New Meanings for a New Age

At the end of the eleventh century, the monk Goscelin of St.-Bertin composed two lives of Augustine of Canterbury, one for the monks of St. Augustine's abbey, and a simpler version for the general public. In the latter, when he came to Pope Gregory the Great's bestowal of the pallium on Augustine, perhaps because his audience was unfamiliar with it, Goscelin included an explanation of—almost a paean to—the vestment: "He sends Augustine the apostolic pallium, namely the great sacrament of Christ and the church, as the apparel of all virtues, which is the bond of the love of God and brothers, so that the vicar of Christ may be an intervening mediator between God and men and, girded about with the sash of fatherly justice, may ally angels and men, earth and heaven."[1] Condensed in this sentence was a rich array of meanings attached to the garment. The pallium was apostolic because it came from the pope and from Peter's tomb. It was sacramental, perhaps because it was a symbol that communicated and effected a spiritual reality. As the admonitory portions of pallium grants had always maintained, it signified the virtues, especially charity. Ideally, Goscelin asserted, it made the

---

1. PL 150:753. Gregory the Great had similarly called it a *vinculum* (to John of Ravenna in 593, JE 1259, IP 5:25 no. 29, CCSL 140:201).

wearer, who represented Christ by virtue of his pontificate, into a bridge between the human and the divine.[2] All this was much to ask of any object, but much had come to be expected of this one.

Throughout the pallium's history, conceptual development went hand-in-hand with juridical and political application. The larger the role the vestment assumed in ecclesiastical relationships and the exercise of power, the richer the significance imposed on this simple band of wool. These meanings helped to justify its increasingly important functions and to influence the conduct of those who wore it. In this period, as the pallium shouldered the weightiest task ever asked of it—assisting church-wide reform and the creation of a papal monarchy—there was an unparalleled efflorescence in the ideas supporting its use. New ways of thinking and talking about the vestment arose both in Rome and in the provinces. They can be studied, first, in the substantial changes in form that pallium documents underwent. In addition, symbolic interpretation of the garb took off in new directions and with new intensity.

The Language of Documents

The changes occurring in the Western church and the papacy during this period were accompanied by experimentation and transformation in the realm of papal diplomatics. For two and a half centuries the formulas of the *Liber Diurnus* had dominated pallium privileges, although exceptions and variations had emerged on occasion. With the advent of the reform papacy, however, more fundamental modifications began.[3] The last pallium grant to follow a *Liber Diurnus* formula for the most part (even while making significant alter-

---

2. The description of the pallium as a "sacrament" may have been a northern French idea (cf. the Norman Anonymous, J29b, Ginther and O'Sullivan, *Electronic Norman Anonymous Project*, at http://normananonymous.org/ENAP/index.jsp?view=edition&p=301, 303). On the bishop's role as a bridge-builder, cf. Leo IX in 1049, JL 4188, GaP 1:46 no. 27, BF 658, MGH Const. 1:98–99.

3. See Reginald L. Poole, *Lectures on the History of the Papal Chancery down to the Time of Innocent III* (Cambridge: Cambridge University Press, 1915; reprinted in Clark, N.J.: Lawbook Exchange, 2005), 98–122, and Rabikauskas, *Diplomatica*, 44–87. Santifaller calls it an era of "Neubildungen und Umbildungen" (*Liber Diurnus*, 32).

ations) was Leo IX's privilege for Hartwig of Bamberg in 1053, which followed *Si pastores ovium*.[4] Thereafter, attempts to produce new formulas—an organized innovation, rather than a total liberty of style without formulas—can be perceived. They seem to have started under Pope Alexander II. His privilege for Bisantius of Trani in 1063 represented an early stage: perhaps a chancery official was reworking *Si pastores ovium* by making judicious cuts, rewording a few passages, and adding material of contemporary concern (namely, the simony clause).[5]

This Alexandrine form came to fruition in 1067 and 1068 in the quite similar privileges for Peter of Bar, Udo of Trier, and Arnold of Acerenza.[6] Three years later, a newly revised and streamlined form of *Si pastores ovium* was introduced in Alexander's privilege for Thomas I of York.[7] It retained the shepherd imagery of the preamble and a few lines from the admonitions, but it avoided the verbosity and occasional obscurity of the old formula. In the final months of his pontificate, Alexander's privilege for Ralph I of Tours in 1073 began with a modified line from *Apostolicae sedis* and continued with snippets of *Si pastores ovium* and shortened, ad-libbed admonitions similar to the York document's.[8] Like-minded simplifications, involving the abbreviation and paraphrase of passages from *Si pastores ovium*, were attempted in Gregory VII's privilege for Alcherius of Palermo in 1083 and Urban II's privilege for Elijah of Bari in 1089.[9] During these decades in the mid-eleventh century, the *Liber Diurnus* gradually fell

---

4. JL 4287, GP 3:254 no. 13, BF 1023, MGH SSRG 69:263–65.
5. JL 4514, IP 9:291 no. 3, Prologo, *Carte*, 55–57.
6. JL 4628, Rački, *Documenta*, 201–3; JL 4646, GP 10.1:66–67 no. 121, Jank, "Bemerkungen," 21–22; and JL 4647, IP 9:456–57 no. 6, PL 146:1343–44. Cf. Urban II to Bisantius of Trani in 1089, JL 5414, IP 9:291 no. 4, Prologo, *Carte*, 65–67, despite possible tampering. Baldric of Dol's 1109 privilege was thoroughly Alexandrine—another reason to suspect its inauthenticity (Paschal II, JL 6224, PL 163:251–52).
7. JL 4693, Cowdrey, "Archbishop Thomas," 33–34. Despite its variations from the formula, Cowdrey regards it as the last to follow a *Liber Diurnus* formula so fully (ibid., 34–35).
8. JL —, Ramackers, *Papsturkunden*, 5:69–70.
9. JL 5258, IP 10:229 no. 20, Santifaller, *Quellen*, 1:252–54; and JL 5412, IP 9:319–20 no. 7, PL 151:307–9. In the former, the pope seemed to admit that he was imitating and shortening an old formula.

out of use as the formulary of the papal chancery, and the appointment of John of Gaeta (the future Pope Gelasius II) as chancellor in 1089 brought a profound revision in documentary practice.[10]

Among these formal changes, three were most meaningful to the pallium's understanding in this era. First, the popes began to summarize the vestment's significance in an epithet that evoked the fullness of pastoral power attached to it. With renewed ardor they also emphasized the generosity that motivated the gift's bestowal. Finally, while preserving the traditional role of admonitions in pallium grants, they allowed for variety and completely new turns of phrase.

The Fullness of the Pontifical Office

At the Council of Mainz (1049), one of the reform synods conducted by Pope Leo IX while traveling through Europe, he issued a document to fortify Hugh I as archbishop of Besançon against the claims of his rival Bertald.[11] In it the pope confirmed, "together with the episcopal office, also the archiepiscopal insignia," including the pallium, so that Hugh "may also be powerful in the beauty of his decorations, in all the fullness of the archiepiscopal pinnacle."[12] The final phrase's flourish seems to have meant that Hugh was fully an archbishop when thus attired. This idea, though not fully developed, would continually recur. When Peter Damian replied to the empress's request for the pallium for Siegfried of Mainz in 1060 and demanded that archbishops come to Rome for it themselves, he called it "that without which they cannot be metropolitans, the sign of completing their dignity."[13] As an essential prerequisite for office, its reception indicated that the process of installation was consummat-

---

10. See Poole, *Lectures,* esp. 83–86; Richard Krohn, *Der päpstliche Kanzler Johannes von Gaëta (Gelasius II.)* (Berlin: Ebering, 1918); Leo Santifaller, "Saggio di un elenco dei funzionari, impiegati e scrittori della Cancelleria Pontificia dall'inizio all'anno 1099," *Bullettino dell'Istituto storico italiano per il medio avo e archivio muratoriano* 56 (1940): 208–14; and Lohrmann, *Register,* 87–94. Although these changes are commonly attributed to John's leadership, it is unknown what influence other officials and the popes themselves had on the shape of documents.
11. On the synod, see Gresser, *Synoden,* 17–22.
12. JL 4188, GaP 1:46 no. 27, BF 658, MGH Const. 1:98–99.
13. To Agnes of Poitou, D'Acunto and Saraceno, *Epistulae,* 4:94.

ed, sealed by papal confirmation. Both Leo and Peter, then, saw the pallium as the symbol of an archbishop firmly established in office, in full possession of his authority.

From 1063 to 1091, a multitude of similar epithets were proposed, as if the popes were casting about for the perfect summation of the pallium's significance as an emblem of priestly plenitude. All of them conveyed the same message, but varied in connotation. When Alexander II stressed the importance of coming personally for the vestment, it was "the sum of the whole priesthood."[14] When Gregory VII chastised an archbishop for failing to seek the pallium, it was "the supplement of your honor."[15] In a Gregorian pallium grant (apparently the only one preserved) it was "the supplement of the whole priestly order."[16] When Urban II restored an archbishop to office, it was "the fullness of the pontificate"; in his pallium grants it was "the fullness of all priestly dignity" and "the fullness of the whole priestly dignity."[17] These phrases portrayed the pallium as the sign of complete priestly power, the mark of one who was fully a bishop, without which he was deficient in his office.[18] It was not yet clear if this *dignitas* or *sacerdotium* was chiefly cultic (for instance, performing the sacraments), juridical (for instance, governing a part of the church), ethical (for instance, representing the good shepherd through teaching and example), or some combination of these or other aspects.

From 1092 on, probably under the influence of the papal chancellor, John of Gaeta, the phrase settled into a fairly stable formulation

---

14. To Anno II of Cologne in 1063, JL 4507, GP 7.1:62 no. 167, Ewald, "Papstbriefe," 338.

15. To William of Rouen in 1081, JL 5204, Santifaller, *Quellen*, 1:223.

16. To Alcherius of Palermo in 1083, JL 5258, IP 10:229 no. 20, Santifaller, *Quellen*, 1:254. Since Gregory's register preserved no pallium grants—perhaps considered too routine—this *epistola vagans* is the only taste of his style.

17. To Anselm III of Milan in 1089, JL 5386, IP 6.1:53 no. 124, Somerville, *Pope Urban*, 121; to Bernard of Toledo in 1088, JL 5366, Mansilla, *Documentación*, 44; and to Berengar of Vic in 1091, JL 5450, Mansilla, *Documentación*, 51.

18. Such epithets were not yet considered more properly due to the papacy alone; cf. Rabanus Maurus's characterization of an archbishop as a "supreme pontiff" (Zimpel, *De Institutione*, 315). Still, the pallium was chiefly the pope's insigne, and others used it in a limited, derivative manner; perhaps the same applied to these ideas.

and became a routine part of pallium grants. This standard epithet for the pallium was "the fullness of the pontifical office" (*plenitudo pontificalis officii*). It first appeared in Urban II's privilege for Daimbert of Pisa in 1092, and again the following year in his privilege for Peter of Grado.[19] In 1095 a variation, "the fullness of the whole pontifical dignity," occurred in his privilege for Hugh III of Besançon—apparently an anomalous deviation.[20]

By Paschal II's pontificate, "the fullness of the pontifical office" had become the typical way in which the popes described the vestment. At least nine letters of Paschal, ranging from 1102 to 1112, used it.[21] In a notice to Gebhard of Constance in 1105, the pope said that he had conferred "the fullness of the pontifical office" on Ruthard of Mainz, recently returned to the Gregorian allegiance—but did not mention the pallium explicitly.[22] By then the epithet was so standard that it seems obvious what Paschal had done: he had bestowed the pallium (presumably a new one, to replace a previous one from the antipope) on Ruthard. Another letter from Paschal concerning Arnulf of Jerusalem in 1116 adapted the phrase to the high rank of that prelate: "What he was yet lacking in his dignity, namely the apparel of the pallium, we have granted from the kindness of the apostolic see. Now, therefore, [we send] him back to you with the wholeness of the patriarchal dignity and the fullness of our grace."[23] Even a patriarch's grasp on his office was incomplete without the woolen band.

In three Paschalian pallium grants, where one might expect to see

---

19. JL 5464, IP 3:321 no. 9, PL 151:345; and JL —, IP 7.2:59 no. 103, Kehr, *Papsturkunden*, 3:214.

20. JL 5569, GaP 1:51 no. 44, PL 151:421.

21. To Peter of Aix in 1102, JL 5904, PL 163:108; to Gerard of York in 1102, JL 5886, Rolls 71.3:27; to Crescentius of Split in 1102, JL 5914, PL 163:97; to Peter of Acerenza in 1102, JL 6088, IP 9:458 no. 9, PL 163:194; to Gerald of Mt. Tabor in 1103, JL 5948, Hiestand, *Papsturkunden*, 98 (on this hybrid document's authenticity, see ibid., 93–96); to Pontius of Le Puy in 1105, JL 6016, PL 163:156; to Pontius of Besançon in 1105, JL 6056, GaP 1:52 no. 46, Hacke, *Palliumverleihungen*, 153; to Lawrence of Esztergom after 1105, JL 6570, PL 163:428; and to Risus of Bari in 1112, JL 6314, IP 9:320 no. 9, Pflugk-Harttung, *Acta*, 2:202.

22. JL 6057, GP 4:117–18 no. 202, Stimming, *Mainzer Urkundenbuch*, 1:327.

23. To the clergy and people of Jerusalem, JL 6528, Hiestand, *Papsturkunden*, 126.

the epithet, it was missing. None of the three recipients—Diego of Compostela in 1104, Guy of Pavia in 1105, and Otto of Bamberg in 1111—were metropolitans, which suggests that "the fullness of the pontifical office" belonged only to archbishops.[24] Further, the untrustworthy evidence surrounding Baldric of Dol presented conflicting impressions. The pallium grant itself, dated to 1109, did not use the phrase, since it followed the Alexandrine form from forty years before. But the notice to the suffragans, clergy, and people of Dol had a version of it, "the fullness of the pontificate," and the monastic confirmation for St.-Florent had an unusual equivalent, "the perfection of his order."[25] The lack of the standard epithet in any of these texts adds to their dubiousness.

The brief pontificate of Gelasius II produced only two extant pallium grants, both in 1118. One, for Walter of Ravenna, contained the phrase; the other, to Oleguer of Barcelona—a suffragan, though promised the archbishopric of Tarragona upon its restoration—did not.[26] The pattern was thus preserved, and unsurprisingly the former chancellor ensured that his chancery employed the epithet correctly.

The precise interpretation of "the fullness of the pontifical office" is not easy, because the phrase was usually included formulaically, without elucidation, outside of a broader discussion. Three letters, however, offered important clues. When Pope Gregory VII reprimanded William of Rouen in 1081 for failing to seek the pallium, he announced a punishment while invoking a forerunner of the standard epithet: "We instruct you by apostolic authority, because you have thought

24. JL 5986, PL 163:132–34; JL 6013, IP 6.1:179 no. 26, PL 163:151–52; and JL 6291, GP 3:264 no. 46, PL 173:1323–24. The epithet was absent in a grant to an archbishop, William of Brindisi, in 1104 (JL —, IP 9:390 no. 19, Kehr, *Papsturkunden*, 1:306); however, the document nowhere referred to him as an archbishop (it called him *antistes* and subjected his suffragans to him "by episcopal right"), so his standing may have been in question (see Alraum, "Pallienprivilegien," 26–27). Conversely, the epithet was present in a grant to a mere bishop, Pontius of Le Puy, in 1105; however, the text is corrupt at that point, and a substitute chancellor, not John of Gaeta, issued the document (JL 6016, PL 163:156).
25. JL 6225, PL 163:253; and PL 166:1213. See 316 above.
26. JL 6647, IP 5:57 no. 189, PL 163:496; and JL 6636, Josep M. Martí i Bonet, ed., with the collaboration of Anna Rich i Abad and Joan Bellés i Sallent, *Oleguer, servent de les esglésies de Barcelona i Tarragona: comentaris als documents de sant Oleguer* (Barcelona: Claret, 2003), 390.

little of the statutes of the holy fathers, to presume henceforth to ordain no bishop or priest and to consecrate [no] churches, until you procure from this see the supplement of your honor, namely the use of the pallium."[27] The pope prohibited him from acts of consecration as long as he lacked the vestment. Was it an inflicted penalty, or was Gregory simply stating the automatic canonical effects of the archbishop's lack? Since Nicholas I in the ninth century, at least, popes had attached the power to consecrate to the possession of the pallium.[28] Was that power the *supplementum* the archbishop still required? In 1088 Pope Urban II reinstated Anselm III of Milan in his archbishopric with these words: "We restore to you the entirety of the whole episcopal office, namely in the consecrations of bishops and the ordinations of churches, insofar as it pertains to episcopal right and duty. Specifically, to accomplish this vigorously and carry it out more fully, we, beseeched by your letter, send the pallium to your Fraternity, with the blessing of the apostolic see."[29] Again, acts of consecration traditionally requiring the pallium were mentioned near to a phrase much like the standard epithet, which thus seems primarily liturgical in meaning. To execute these acts *strenue* and *plenius*—as if they would be weak or partial without it—the pallium was sent.

These hints were corroborated by Pope Paschal II's letter *Significasti frater* from after 1105. In it he sought to convince Lawrence of Esztergom that the oath of fidelity was a prudent requirement, given the weightiness of the gift being proffered: "In the pallium, brother, the fullness of the pontifical office is granted, for, according to the custom of the apostolic see and the whole church, it is not permitted to metropolitans before receiving the pallium either to consecrate bishops or to celebrate a synod."[30] The fullness Paschal spoke of

---

27. JL 5204, Santifaller, *Quellen*, 1:223–24.
28. To the Bulgarians in 866, JE 2812, BH 822, MGH Epp. 6:593.
29. JL 5359, IP 6.1:52–53 no. 121, Somerville, *Pope Urban*, 60. "Ordinations of churches" was odd; perhaps intervening words, e.g., "of priests and dedications," had fallen out during transmission.
30. JL 6570, PL 163:428. One version had "Europe" instead of "church" (Brett, "Some New Letters," 89). See Benson, *Bishop-Elect*, 169–72. A formula in William Durandus's pontifical joined the epithet to mention of celebrating councils and consecrating bishops (Andrieu, *Pontifical*, 3:393).

New Meanings   371

included not only acts of consecration, such as the making of other bishops, but also the celebration of councils of bishops. These liturgical phenomena may be considered manifestations of a juridical reality: a preeminence of authority above ordinary bishops that allowed a metropolitan to act outside his own diocese. When he ordained suffragans for other churches or gathered his suffragans in a provincial synod, he was performing functions that went beyond episcopal jurisdiction strictly conceived. It was this superior authority which the vestment represented or conveyed—or rather, which the pope granted or conceded to metropolitans through the vestment.[31]

Several sources from the turn of the twelfth century supported this interpretation. Hugh of Flavigny narrated an incident from two centuries before: "Argrim, deposed by Pope Stephen [V] from the bishopric of Langres, but restored by Formosus in Lyon, ordained [Wala of Autun], although he did not have the pallium or the restored dignity by which he could consecrate a bishop.... As a result, Formosus deposed Argrim without possibility of recovery and excommunicated Wala."[32] Without the pallium, regarded as necessary for a metropolitan to perform his prerogative of ordaining his suffragans, both ordainer and ordained were severely punished. When the *Gesta Treverorum* described Bruno of Trier's deposition by Pope Paschal II at the Council of Guastalla (1106), it blamed not only his lay investiture, but also the fact that, "not yet having attained the pallium, he had dedicated churches and promoted clerics."[33] Again, carrying out acts of consecration before receiving the pallium was an of-

---

31. See Schrör, *Metropolitangewalt*, 218.
32. *Chronicon*, in Eduard Hlawitschka, ed., "Textkritisches zur Series abbatum Flaviniacensium," in *Landschaft und Geschichte: Festschrift für Franz Petri zu seinem 65. Geburtstag*, ed. Georg Droege et al. (Bonn: Röhrscheid, 1970), 253–54 col. 4. Cf. MGH SS 8:356. "Restored dignity" is confusing, because Argrim had already been restored to episcopal office when he was translated to Lyon after his deposition from Langres. Probably Hugh meant that, in light of Argrim's new archiepiscopal office, his restoration was not complete until he had attained the pallium, which conveyed the faculty to ordain bishops. Hugh's version of events seems irreconcilable with Benedict IV's letter in 900 (to the clergy and people of Gaul, JL 3527, ZPUU 1:25), which stated that Formosus had palliated Argrim, presumably as archbishop of Lyon (JL *3508). See Pokorny, "Unerkanntes Brieffragment."
33. MGH SS 8:192.

fense resulting in removal from office. The same history recounted the dilemma of the royalist Egilbert of Trier, who, after the king appointed him to the archbishopric in 1079, met with opposition when he tried to ordain clergy: "They said, 'Because you have not yet acquired the pallium, which is owed to our metropolis by the Roman church, we do not wish to receive the imposition of hands from you, especially since it is decreed in the canons: "If any metropolitan bishop presumes to consecrate without the pallium, both the consecrator and the consecrated will be subject to the serious risk of their order."'"[34] In all these cases, the validity of such illicit consecrations was not questioned. But they endangered the pallium's role, articulated since the ninth century, and the control exercised over metropolitans through it, and so harsh discipline was applied.

To what canon were the reformers of Trier referring? The answer may lie in a canonical collection associated with nearby Cologne. This *Collectio X Partium* borrowed the three pallium-related canons of the *Collectio Tripartita A*.[35] For one, the compiler invented a new *distinctio*, "On the pallium, to be sought by metropolitans within three months, and on its virtue," within a *pars* on clerical ordinations.[36] To this distinction he then added three unusual texts.[37] The last two decried ordinations *sine pallio*; as the distinction's title did not fit them well, they may have been appended at a later stage.[38] One, with the

34. Ibid., 8:187. They then taunted Egilbert: "'If you ought to obtain [the pallium], at any rate, you have need of the pope whom you so despise, for Gregory to humble you, so that you may deserve to receive it.'"

35. Canons 4.2.19, 5.3.1, 5.7.5, *Clavis* KO04.02.19, KO05.03.01, KO05.07.05. On the collection (not to be confused with the later *Collectio X Partium* attributed to Walter of Thérouanne), see Kéry, *Canonical Collections*, 287, and Fowler-Magerl, *Clavis Canonum*, 191–92. To the copy in Cologne, Historisches Archiv, W 199, may be added another in Leipzig, Universitätsbibliothek, Haenel 16, which unfortunately is missing the pallium distinction.

36. Distinction 5.3, Cologne, Historisches Archiv, W 199, fol. 60r: "De pallio a metropolitanis intra tres menses repetendo et de uirtute ipsius."

37. The first of the three was John VIII's 873 letter to Willibert of Cologne (JE 2986), atypically excerpted to focus on the effects of the pallium's conferral and denial (Canon 5.3.2, *Clavis* KO05.03.02).

38. The copy kept today in Cologne was made east of the Rhine several decades after the collection's composition, possibly in the Premonstratensian house of Knechtsteden, founded in 1130. Perhaps at this time conciliar decrees from the 1130s were added to the end of the manuscript (Fowler-Magerl, *Clavis Canonum*, 192).

inscription "Pope Gregory to Bishop Victor," stated: "Whatever metropolitan presumes to ordain anyone without the pallium (which we hardly believe), both the ordainer and he who is ordained and their collaborators should be deposed from every order, without possibility of recovery."[39] The other, with the inscription "Pope Innocent to Victricius, bishop of Rouen," read: "If any archbishop presumes to ordain any of his suffragans without the pallium, let him know that he himself is the destroyer of his order, and he who is ordained should be deposed from episcopal office, and all his collaborators likewise."[40]

These two canons are mysterious. The inscriptions seem spurious; no such texts were found in Gregory the Great's register or Innocent I's famous letter to Victricius of Rouen. Their content appears to belong to a later age, for the principle was reminiscent of ninth-century developments.[41] These canons meshed well with Hugh of Flavigny's discussion of Argrim of Lyon (the first even used the word *irrecuperabiliter*); did they arise from that event or originate in the province of Lyon? And the law cited by the reformers of Trier bore a striking similarity to the first canon; was it coincidence that that part of the *Gesta Treverorum* was composed very close in time and place to the extant copies of the *Collectio X Partium*? In any case, the two texts were rare. The first canon occurred elsewhere in only two sources, both connected to twelfth-century Passau.[42] The second canon has

39. Canon 5.3.3, Cologne, Historisches Archiv, W 199, fol. 60r: "*Gregorius papa Victori episcopo.* Quisquis metropolitanorum, quod minime credimus, sine pallio aliquem ordinare praesumpserit, et ordinator et is qui ordinatur et cooperatores inrecuperabiliter ab omni ordine deponantur."

40. Canon 5.3.4, ibid., fols. 60r–60v: "*Innocentius papa Victorico episcopo Rothomagensi.* Si quis archiepiscopus aliquem suffraganeorum suorum sine pallio ordinare praesumpserit, sciat se ipsum destructorem ordinis sui esse, et is qui ordinatur ab episcopali officio deponatur, et omnes cooperatores eius similiter."

41. See John VIII to Rostagnus of Arles, JE 3148, BU 353, MGH Epp. 7:110; and to the bishops of Gaul, JE 3149, BU 354, MGH Epp. 7:93, both in 878.

42. It appeared in a copy, from the second half of the twelfth century, of a pontifical composed in Passau in 1002/03; see Vienna, Österreichische Nationalbibliothek, lat. 1817, fol. 134v, printed at PL 138:1010. The copyist made some suppressions and additions (including various canons), and so may well have inserted this uncommon text. See Andrieu, *Ordines*, 1:388–97. It also appeared in the appendices to a canonical collection related to Passau and created in the twelfth century; see Göttweig, Stiftsbibliothek, Ms. 53 (56), printed in Max Sdralek, ed., *Die Streitschriften Altmanns von Passau und Wezilos von Mainz* (Paderborn: Schöningh, 1890), 176. See

been found nowhere else. The texts were possibly forgeries, but they reflected the mindset that had emerged from the late reform papacy.

A final witness to the pallium's primary association with the ability to consecrate was Gilbert of Limerick. When he described an archbishop's characteristics in 1111, he directly connected the vestment with the faculty: "He is clothed with the pallium of honor, for he himself, though helped by all the bishops of his province, ordains a bishop. For if he cannot be present at their ordination, excusing himself, he confirms by his letter and legates that he gives his assent for them to be ordained."[43] The addition of the need for consent exhibited another element in this thinking: the pallium not only conferred the power to consecrate suffragans, but also placed suffragans under their metropolitan's power. Once again, the liturgical phenomenon also created a juridical reality.

From the Generosity of the Apostolic See

When the popes did someone a favor, they wanted him to know it. In this period language expressing that a privilege arose from papal munificence was commonly included in pallium grants—to the extent that another standard phrase became attached to the mention of the vestment. This phrase's origin lay in exceptional grants in the early years of the reform papacy. When Nicholas II gave Ealdred of York the pallium in 1061 despite his uncanonical translation and pluralism, he warned him to behave well, "so that you may never cause us to repent of the mercy and kindness that we have had towards you."[44] In 1063 Alexander II conveyed his gratitude to Burchard II of Halberstadt for his work in ending the papal schism: "We decide to decorate you with the pallium with pious and fatherly affection."[45] And when Gregory VII palliated Evan of Dol in 1076, despite two centuries of papal refusals to elevate that bishopric, he

---

J. Friedrich Schulte, "Die Rechtshandschriften der Stiftsbibliotheken von Göttweig Ord. S. Bened., Heiligenkreuz Ord. Cisterc., Klosterneuburg Can. Regul. Lateran., Melk Ord. S. Ben., Schotten in Wien Ord. S. Ben," *Sitzungsberichte der kaiserlichen Akademie der Wissenschaften, philosophisch-historische Classe* 57 (1867): 560–69.

43. *De Statu Ecclesiae*, in Fleming, *Gille*, 162.
44. JL 4463, Rolls 71.3:7.
45. JL 4498, GP 5.2:220–21 no. 36, Dahlhaus, "Privileg," 672.

informed the Breton hierarchy: "We granted him the honor and use of the pallium out of love for you and the whole province."[46] *Misericordia, benignitas, affectus, dilectio*: such sentiments helped create the intimate relationship that the donor desired.

During Urban II's formative pontificate the shape of these expressions was solidified, and started to be used in routine as well as exceptional situations. As he bestowed the pallium on Bernard of Toledo in 1088, Urban said that he was prompted "by the usual good will of the Roman church."[47] A year later he confirmed the pallium that Rainald of Reims had received during a papal vacancy "by the authority and good will of the apostolic see."[48] And in 1091 he acknowledged the restoration of the see of Tarragona, which was being recaptured from the Muslims. To it he assigned Berengar, bishop of Vic, vested with the pallium "from the grace of the generosity of the Roman [church]."[49] Under Chancellor John of Gaeta, in the same year as the standard epithet for the pallium was introduced, the phrase assumed the contour it would keep for many years: "from the generosity of the apostolic see" (*ex apostolicae sedis liberalitate*). From now on it was frequently inserted in pallium grants, often alongside the standard epithet. It first occurred in connection to the vestment in Urban's privilege for Daimbert of Pisa in 1092, and next in his notice to the Breton bishops concerning Roland of Dol's pallium in 1093.[50] An anomalous deviation again appeared in his privilege for Hugh III of Besançon in 1095, which preferred to say "from the kindness and grace of the apostolic see."[51]

Unlike the standard epithet, the generosity phrase was not unique to pallium-related documents. Even within such documents, it was not always attached to the vestment itself. In 1088—four years before the chancellor first applied it in this form to the conferral of the pallium—it referred to the confirmation of Toledo's ancient privileg-

---

46. JL 5004, MGH Epp. sel. 2.1:302.
47. JL 5366, Mansilla, *Documentación*, 44.
48. JL 5415, PL 151:310.
49. JL 5450, Mansilla, *Documentación*, 51.
50. JL 5464, IP 3:321 no. 9, PL 151:345; and JL 5475, PL 151:359.
51. JL 5569, GaP 1:51 no. 44, PL 151:421.

es, and in 1098 it accompanied the bestowal on Salerno of primacy over Cosenza and Acerenza.⁵² Stressing papal liberality was thus a wide-ranging effort, suitable to many kinds of privileges. In relation to the pallium, the phrase meant that the vestment was a sign of papal favor, given freely by papal right. That idea seems to have been a fertile one, for under succeeding popes its use flourished. The generosity phrase was found in ten letters of Paschal II and one of the short-lived Gelasius II.⁵³ Slight deviations were uncommon but possible: to Crescentius of Split in 1102 Paschal granted the pallium "by apostolic generosity," and to the church of Jerusalem in 1116 he said that he had palliated Patriarch Arnulf "from the kindness of the apostolic see."⁵⁴ Even when John of Gaeta was pope, shorthand was used in Walter of Ravenna's privilege in 1118, when Gelasius gave him the pallium *liberaliter.*⁵⁵

What was the purpose of the generosity phrase? The grant of the pallium had long ago become a routine part of ecclesiastical affairs, and perhaps the reform papacy wished to refocus attention on its character as a gift. By emphasizing that its motivation was the free choice and good will of the donor, that the transaction was a gesture of kindness and favor, and that its goal was to honor and support the recipient, the popes may have hoped to gain allies, strengthen friendships, and kindle regard for the papacy and zeal for its cause. It was a smart move at a tense time, and seems to have been effective. After Anselm of Canterbury received the pallium in 1095, he wrote Pope Urban II in effusive terms:

52. Urban II to Alfonso VI, JL 5367, Somerville, *Pope Urban,* 75; and to Alfanus II of Salerno, JL 5707, IP 8:354–55 no. 35, PL 151:508.

53. Paschal to Peter of Aix in 1102, JL 5904, PL 163:108; to Gerard of York in 1102, JL 5886, Rolls 71.3:27; to the Scottish bishops in 1102, JL 5885, Rolls 71.3:22; to Peter of Acerenza in 1102, JL 6088, IP 9:458 no. 9, PL 163:194; to Gerald of Mt. Tabor in 1103, JL 5948, Hiestand, *Papsturkunden,* 98; to William of Brindisi in 1104, JL —, IP 9:390 no. 19, Kehr, *Papsturkunden,* 1:307; to Diego of Compostela in 1104, JL 5986, PL 163:133; to Pontius of Le Puy in 1105, JL 6016, PL 163:156 (twice); to Pontius of Besançon in 1105, JL 6056, GaP 1:52 no. 46, Hacke, *Palliumverleihungen,* 153; and to Risus of Bari in 1112, JL 6314, IP 9:320 no. 9, Pflugk-Harttung, *Acta,* 2:202; as well as Gelasius to Oleguer of Barcelona in 1118, JL 6636, Martí, *Oleguer,* 390.

54. JL 5914, PL 163:97; and JL 6528, Hiestand, *Papsturkunden,* 126.

55. JL 6647, IP 5:57 no. 189, PL 163:496.

I thank your holy Munificence that you sent worthy legates of the apostolic see to us, and that you instructed the favor of the pallium to be presented to me, solely by the bounty of your grace.... For my conscience is my witness that, after I learned that you had been exalted at the peak of holy church, I rejoiced, and I reverently loved (and love) you, and I wished (and wish) for you to make daily progress; and hearing it made, I exult.[56]

This fervor, moreover, could be harnessed to the benefit of the reform, for a liberal donor put the recipient in his debt. Generosity evoked gratitude, which found expression in countergifts and services. As already observed, the reform popes put great stock in reciprocation. Finally, as bishops throughout the church became accustomed to looking to the Roman pontiff for personal boons, the process of centralization accelerated. Rome became a fountain of favors, which, through privileges and dispensations and the like, could cause the rise or fall of a prelate and spark competition within the hierarchy.

A problem with heightening the impression of largesse in ordinary circumstances was that it was more difficult to demonstrate extraordinary favor. To this end the popes employed practices invented in the previous period, such as coupling the gift with additional prerogatives or increasing the number and quality of pallium days. But, as the case of Lanfranc of Canterbury illustrated, extreme measures sometimes proved necessary. When this archbishop approached Alexander II for the pallium in 1071, as he wrote to the pope two years later, he had been honored in unparalleled fashion:

Nothing will ever be able by any pretext to cast out from the treasury of my heart that unheard-of humility which you displayed in Rome to me, least of men, unworthy of such great honors, and the fact that you paid me two pallia, one from the altar according to custom, and another with which your Holiness had been accustomed to celebrate Mass, in order to show your good will towards me.[57]

Alexander had been a student of Lanfranc's at his school in Bec and probably wished to pay his respects to his former master. The

---

56. Schmitt, *Opera*, 2.4:82.
57. Helen Clover and Margaret Gibson, eds., *The Letters of Lanfranc, Archbishop of Canterbury*, Oxford Medieval Texts (Oxford: Clarendon, 1979), 54, 56.

"unheard-of humility" was clarified by an entry in the *Anglo-Saxon Chronicle* called the *Acta Lanfranci*: "Pope Alexander honored him so much that he rose for him, against custom, and he bestowed two pallia as a sign of special love: one of which he received from the altar in the Roman manner, but the other, with which he had been accustomed to celebrate Mass, the pope himself presented with his own hand."[58] Standing in Lanfranc's presence and granting him two pallia were astonishing enough, but the pope also combined two gestures occasionally allowed in past times: taking the vestment from Peter's altar *Romano more,* and receiving the pope's own pallium. In an age when the papacy claimed to treat all its beneficiaries with special favor, this accumulation of tokens of esteem was needed to demonstrate a truly exceptional intimacy.

New Styles of Exhortation

Although the reform popes abandoned the traditional formulas, they did not forgo the idea that the pallium's conferral was an appropriate opportunity to admonish its recipient. Thus they were sure to place hortatory words in their grants. Until John of Gaeta's time, these clauses, perhaps devised separately for each occasion, showed considerable variety. Still, they drew on the rich body of themes present in the customary admonitions of centuries of pallium privileges. For example, Clement II advised Eberhard of Trier in 1047 to act virtuously so that he would please both God and men, and men would find God in him and him in God. It availed nothing "to become glorious with outer decorations" and yet "lack inner decoration," for the pallium could not be "evidence of religiosity" if its wearer lacked the "good of truth itself." Having earlier declared that the title *episcopus* meant keeping watch over Christ's sheep, the pope hoped that "the archiepiscopal name may not become empty in you."[59] These three themes—setting a good example, matching interior to exterior honor, and laboring as an effective pastor—also occurred two years later in Leo IX's privilege for Hugh I of Besançon.

---

58. Bately, *Anglo-Saxon Chronicle*, 3:85. Cf. Lanfranc in 1073/75, Clover and Gibson, *Letters*, 42.

59. JL 4151, GP 10.1:56 no. 94, BF 382, Jank, "Bemerkungen," 20.

The pallium and its accompanying prerogatives were granted so that one who was meritorious in thought and action would also flourish "in the beauty of decorations," with the distinguishing symbols of glory reflecting his personal excellence. His insignia were meant to remind him "in his outer ornamentation" to foster his "inner ornamentation," for they represented and promoted integrity. Then he would become a "a model for the Lord's flock" who provided "an example of good work in himself for his own people." He would have "the virtue of the pontificate together with its name": since pontiff meant "bridge-builder," he would allow his people to reach God.[60]

Over the next four decades the popes instructed palligers along similar lines. The desired correspondence between inside and outside was a prevalent theme. In 1061 Nicholas II charged Ealdred of York "that what you wear in appearance you may present in behavior, and what shines forth in dress you may show to the flocks subject to you, in the deeds as well as the words of religious life and salvific teaching."[61] Alexander II likewise encouraged Burchard II of Halberstadt in 1063: "As it is yours on the outside (as it is for us), so may you decorate yourself on the inside, that you can be striking in front and back by teaching and doing whatever things are just, whatever honorable."[62] Not only did the pope refer to the inner-outer correspondence, but he also played on a phrase from *Si pastores ovium* evoking the vestment's two-sidedness (*ante ac retro*).[63] And in 1083 Gregory VII reworked admonitions from *Si pastores ovium*: he exhorted Alcherius of Palermo to harmonize his actions with his apparel and to use the pallium to adorn "not only your outer, but also your inner man" (Rom 7:22, Eph 3:16). The vestment demanded love of God and neighbor (Mt 22:37–39); although "the decorations of all virtues are necessary for the use of the pallium," charity surpassed the rest and had to characterize the wearer. The archbishop should set a good example for his subjects through his "holy lifestyle," cor-

---

60. JL 4188, GaP 1:46 no. 27, BF 658, MGH Const. 1:98–99.
61. JL 4463, Rolls 71.3:6.
62. JL 4498, GP 5.2:220–21 no. 36, Dahlhaus, "Privileg," 672.
63. V45, Foerster, *Liber Diurnus*, 101–3, with slight variants C44 on 201–2 and A39 on 300–302.

rect them with zeal but also with moderation, and—as the reformers were wont to stress—follow "whatever you discover in the sayings of the holy fathers" for the edification and salvation of both himself and his flock.[64]

Despite the traditional content of these early reform admonitions, the broad variations and occasional innovations in their form bespoke a papacy in a time of flux, filled with a spirit of creativity. The new look of pallium grants reflected experimentation, attempts to simplify and refine the wordy formulas of yesteryear and to catch the attention of recipients with something fresh. But after John of Gaeta became chancellor in 1089, he seems to have tried to bring uniformity to the situation. As did many reformers, he looked back to Pope Gregory the Great for inspiration, and in a letter to Dominic of Carthage in 596, he found a fitting series of admonitions for a bishop. He trimmed them and first inserted them (after a single line from *Si pastores ovium*) in Urban II's privilege for Rainald of Reims in 1089. They addressed the recipient as "dearest brother, whom the office of pastoral care binds fast," and followed with a pastiche of biblical quotations exhorting him to various virtues. Perhaps John chose this Gregorian letter, originally unrelated to the pallium, because of a passage about two high priestly vestments from the Old Testament, the rational (breastplate) and the superhumeral (ephod): "Let the rational of judgment, joined with the action of the superhumeral, shine on your breast: walk in procession thus in the sight of God and all Israel [Ex 28:27–30]. Furnish examples of this sort to the flock entrusted to you."[65] As Bruno of Segni, Urban's trusted counsellor, later wrote, such garments were types of Christian vestments, and those two in particular called to mind the pallium.[66] The words conjured the image of a bishop in a procession, wearing his pallium before the assembly of the faithful. John, however, did not seem sat-

---

64. JL 5258, IP 10:229 no. 20, Santifaller, *Quellen*, 1:254.
65. JL 5415, PL 151:311, based on JE 1444 (*pace* Martí, *Palio*, 207).
66. *De Sacramentis Ecclesiae*, in PL 165:1105–6. In Bruno's interpretation, the rational symbolized reason, wisdom, and truth (thus its biblical description as "the rational of judgment"), while the superhumeral evoked the wearer's duty to carry his people's burdens—perhaps the "action" mentioned here.

New Meanings 381

isfied with this venture. He used it only twice more—in Paschal II's privileges for Diego of Compostela in 1104 and Pontius of Besançon in 1105—although it would be resurrected from time to time later in the century.[67]

John's much more successful endeavor involved another passage by Gregory the Great, this time from a pallium grant to Maximus of Salona in 599.[68] It was first inserted in Urban II's privilege for Daimbert of Pisa in 1092 and used in no fewer than seventeen more documents between 1094 and 1118, and on further occasions later in the century.[69] Perhaps because of its wide-ranging use, as well as defects

---

67. JL 5986, PL 163:133–34; and JL 6056, GaP 1:52 no. 46, Hacke, *Palliumverleihungen*, 154. Both changed "Israel" in Gregory's original letter and Rainald's privilege to "church." The copy of Diego's privilege in the *Historia Compostellana*, however, had "Jerusalem" (CCCM 70:42).

68. In the late ninth-century *Collectio Anselmo Dedicata* this passage appeared in c. 1.124, where "never receiving the appearance of anyone against the truth" was omitted (probably by a skip of the eye to the next phrase, beginning with the same words) and *ratio* was dropped from "this, dearest brother, is the rationale of the pallium you have received" (Besse, "Liber Primus," 289). During John of Gaeta's first years as chancellor, Bonizo of Sutri compiled his *Liber de Vita Christiana*, in which this passage appeared in c. 3.12; it repeated the first variant from the *Anselmo Dedicata*, and for the missing "rationale" of the second it supplied "dignity" (Perels, *Liber de Vita*, 75). Perhaps Bonizo drew on the *Anselmo Dedicata* (or a derivative) and inserted *dignitas*, a term often connected to the pallium. Since papal letters used "dignity" instead of "rationale," and at least five omitted the "never receiving ..." phrase, there was likely some relationship between Bonizo's work and the papal chancery.

69. Urban II to Daimbert of Pisa in 1092, JL 5464, IP 3:321 no. 9, PL 151:346; to Guy of Vienne in 1094, JL —, GaP 3.1:138–39 no. 187, Becker and Lohrmann, "Erschlichenes Privileg," 111; to Ralph II of Tours in 1094, JL 5519, PL 151:386–87; to Hugh III of Besançon in 1095, JL 5569, GaP 1:51 no. 44, PL 151:421–22; to Raymond of Auch in 1097, JL —, Wilhelm Wiederhold, ed., *Papsturkunden in Frankreich: Reiseberichte zur Gallia Pontificia*, Acta Romanorum Pontificum 8 (Vatican City: Biblioteca Apostolica Vaticana, 1985), 2:750; and to Bertrand of Narbonne in 1097, JL 5688, PL 151:496; Paschal II to Guy of Vienne between 1099 and 1103, JL 6596, GaP 3.1:147–48 no. 219, MGH Epp. 3:107; to Peter of Aix in 1102, JL 5904, PL 163:109; to Gerard of York in 1102, JL 5886, Rolls 71.3:27; to Crescentius of Split in 1102, JL 5914, PL 163:97; to Peter of Acerenza in 1102, JL 6088, IP 9:458 no. 9, PL 163:195; to Gerald of Mt. Tabor in 1103, JL 5948, Hiestand, *Papsturkunden*, 98; to William of Brindisi in 1104, JL —, IP 9:390 no. 19, Kehr, *Papsturkunden*, 1:307; to Pontius of Le Puy in 1105, JL 6016, PL 163:156; to Otto of Bamberg in 1111, JL 6291, GP 3:264 no. 46, PL 173:1324; and to Risus of Bari in 1112, JL 6314, IP 9:320 no. 9, Pflugk-Harttung, *Acta*, 2:202–3; Gelasius II to Oleguer of Barcelona in 1118, JL 6636, Martí, *Oleguer*, 390; and to Walter of Ravenna in 1118, JL 6647, IP 5:57 no.

in textual transmission, these witnesses varied in many details.[70] Paschal II's privilege for Crescentius of Split in 1102 presented a typical rendition:

> Certainly we wish you to lay claim to the splendor of this pallium in every way. Indeed, the honor of this apparel is humility and justice. Therefore, your Fraternity should hasten with his whole mind to show himself humble in successes, upright with justice in misfortunes (if they ever occur), friendly to the good, opposed to the wicked, never receiving the appearance of anyone against the truth, never oppressing the appearance of anyone who speaks for the truth, persisting in the works of mercy according to the means of your wealth, and yet desiring to press on even beyond your means, compassionate to the weak, rejoicing with people of good will, reckoning another's losses as your own, exulting over another's joys as if over your own, piously fierce in correcting vices, persuading the mind of your hearers in fostering virtues, in wrath keeping judgment without wrath, but in tranquillity not deserting the censure of just severity. This, dearest brother, is the dignity of the pallium you have received. If you keep it solicitously, you will have on the inside what you are shown to have received on the outside.[71]

The true meaning of the vestment—its splendor or honor or dignity—lay in its wearer's virtue. He was urged to appropriate this ideal by practicing virtue in manifold ways; then his inward and outward selves would exist in harmony. The late reform popes settled on this new formula as an adequate expression of their expectations for a palliger.

There were infrequent exceptions. In 1091 Urban II granted the pallium to Berengar of Vic in view of the coming restoration of the see of Tarragona, and his admonitions were adapted to the Spanish situation:

189, PL 163:496. On the two letters to Vienne, see Schilling, *Guido von Vienne*, 118–21, 344–45.

70. The most significant deviation occurred in Urban II's letter to Ralph II of Tours in 1094—not a pallium grant, but a declaration of the papal decision that Dol was subject to Tours (JL 5519, PL 151:386–87). This reaffirmation of Tours's metropolitan authority may have seemed an appropriate time to remind the archbishop of the behavior his pallium demanded, so that the authority he had fought to keep would not be used to excuse boasting or domination.

71. JL 5914, PL 163:97, based on JE 1761. The final clause concerning the inner-outer correspondence, similar to the words of *Si pastores ovium*, was present in Gregory's original letter, probably a source for that formula.

We encourage you with the deepest affection always to show yourself worthy of the honor of such great pontifical authority, taking care to be without offense to Christians and Saracens, and to be zealous to seek infidels for the faith by your words and examples, as God bestows. Excel in the eyes of men by the dignity of the pallium on the outside, such that on the inside you are powerful in the excellence of your virtues before the eyes of the heavenly Majesty.[72]

Closely similar admonitions were used in another Spanish setting, Paschal II's confirmation of Bernard of Toledo's primacy and pallium in 1101.[73] Finally, Urban II's privilege for Peter of Grado in 1093 contained a brief exhortation that could better be called a plea for reciprocation.[74]

Were these admonitions merely garnishes, pious sentiments to lend gravity to documents, routine and largely ignored? The evidence suggests that they were not confined to stale texts. The *Gesta Treverorum* related that, when Poppo of Trier had gone to Rome for his pallium in the early eleventh century, Pope Benedict VIII first instructed orally what he later put in writing: "He cleverly admonished him with the utmost effort about the preservation of that faith which is in God, and about the education of those subject to him, and about the chastisement (not frenzied, but fatherly) of sins, but also about purity of soul and body. And so that these very commands of his might not slip out of his memory, he gave him a document."[75] The same history described Bruno of Trier's treatment by Paschal II at the Council of Guastalla (1106): "Having received the blessing both of the pope and of the whole synod, presented with the honor of the pallium, and firmly instructed about observing the rule of faith, and diligently admonished about the instruction of the flock entrusted to him, he returned home with joy."[76] If these reports were correct, it may have been the papal custom either to advise the recipient before issuing the privilege or to read the privilege aloud to him.

The inculcation of such teachings, however, was not one-

72. JL 5450, Mansilla, *Documentación*, 52.
73. JL 5858, ibid., 65–66.
74. JL —, IP 7.2:59 no. 103, Kehr, *Papsturkunden*, 3:214–15.
75. MGH SS 8:175.
76. Ibid., 8:192.

sided. An invaluable witness from the palliger's side was provided by a collection of *ordines* compiled for the cathedral chapter of Besançon around 1050. The *ordo* for Christmas depicted a local liturgical custom:

The lord pontiff ascends the tribunal of the cathedra.... Then the chancellor reverently approaches before the seat and says, "Lord, give the blessing," and the prelate answers, "May the grace of the Holy Spirit fill our hearts." And [the chancellor] reads the pallium privilege, so that [the archbishop] may commend to memory how much carefulness he must apply to the protection of the flock. Having read through the privilege, the chancellor receives a gold coin, or twelve silver ones, from the archbishop. And so it happens whenever the archbishop, girded with the pallium, ascends the cathedra.[77]

On major feasts celebrated in the cathedral—as the archbishop, vested in his pallium, sat upon his chair, as a sign of his authority as pastor of his church—the archdiocesan chancellor reread the pallium grant before the congregation. He first received a blessing, as if about to read a sacred text, as a deacon did before proclaiming the Gospel at Mass. This ritual occurred at least half a dozen times a year, perhaps as many as a dozen.[78] In this way the prelate was periodically, solemnly, and publicly reminded of the ideals set forth by the pope and prompted by the vestment he displayed. It would be uncomfortably obvious to the assembled clergy and people if his life were not congruent with those ideals.

---

77. M. Richard, ed., *Histoire des diocèses de Besançon et de Saint-Claude* (Besançon: Cornu, 1847), 1:572–73. The description of the reading's purpose echoed *Si pastores ovium*, the formula used for the privilege of Hugh I, archbishop at this time (Benedict IX in 1037, JL —, GaP 1:44–45 no. 21, BF 199, ZPUU 2:1137–38).

78. The *ordines* specified that the privilege was recited on Christmas; the feast of St. Vincent, whose relics Besançon possessed; the feast of St. John at the Latin Gate, patron of the cathedral; Pentecost; the anniversary of the cathedral's dedication; and All Saints' day (Richard, *Histoire*, 1:573, 581, 610, 612, 619, 621). It can probably be assumed on other days when the archbishop ascended the cathedra, such as St. Stephen's day and Easter Monday, Tuesday, and Wednesday (ibid., 1:576, 605–6). It can further be presumed on other solemn occasions without specific indications, such as Easter Sunday. It would be illuminating to compare these days with the pallium days delineated in Hugh's privileges, but neither contained such a list (Benedict IX in 1037, JL —, GaP 1:44–45 no. 21, BF 199, ZPUU 2:1138; and Leo IX in 1049, JL 4188, GaP 1:46 no. 27, BF 658, MGH Const. 1:98–99).

"The Principal and Mystical Insigne of the Archiepiscopate"

When William of Poitiers applied the description *principale ac mysticum archipraesulatus insigne* to the pallium in the 1070s, it intimated both the importance and the symbolic depth of meaning carried by this badge of office.[79] This period beheld a renewal not only of admonitions related to the vestment, but also of its symbolism. As with the admonitions, the symbolic forays were rooted in traditional thought, while also showing creativity and variety.[80] These ideas reflected the increasing weight that the papacy was giving the pallium, but simultaneously helped to support that weight by justifying it. The reform popes themselves revived this kind of thinking, which had lain relatively dormant in the previous period. The endeavor then blossomed under a series of reform-minded liturgists and theologians, as interpretations of the pallium proliferated.

Allegories from the Popes

Almost as soon as the German king set a reformer on Peter's chair, changes began to appear in the style of pallium grants. Even beyond its diplomatic features, Pope Clement II's privilege for John of Salerno in 1047 (less than two months into his pontificate) made clear that something new was already afoot. The pope chose to incorporate a richly symbolic interpretation of the vestment, relying on its physical form, images from *Si pastores ovium*, and Gospel parables of the good shepherd.[81] Since it was made of sheep's wool, he said, the wearer should see himself as a shepherd. Since it was wrapped around him, he should look around, so that no sheep would wander away and fall among wolves. Since it was worn on the shoulders, he

---

79. Davis and Chibnall, *Gesta Guillelmi*, 86.
80. Roger E. Reynolds observes liturgical interest unrivaled since the Carolingians, and notes that the same reformers who wrote polemical treatises were frequently liturgical commentators ("Liturgical Scholarship at the Time of the Investiture Controversy: Past Research and Future Opportunities," *The Harvard Theological Review* 71 [1978]: 109).
81. JL 4143, IP 8:349 no. 18, BF 363, PL 142:587, corrected according to Vatican City, Biblioteca Apostolica Vaticana, Vat. lat. 5638, fols. 366r–368r.

should put any lost sheep on his shoulders and carry it back to the sheepfold. And since it had crosses on front and back, it should remind him of Paul's teaching about being crucified to this world.[82] This exhortation worked from the composition, placement, and ornamentation of the pallium to generate advice on a bishop's duties, without explaining much of the imagery—*topoi* readily understandable to their audience.[83]

Clement developed these themes in his privilege for Eberhard of Trier later the same year. The pallium was created, he said, to decorate not so much bodies as souls, and so the wearer should consider carefully what he wore.[84] Its composition "of white sheep's wool" should recall not only the sheep entrusted to him, but also his responsibility to be unstained in the chief Shepherd's sight. Its placement "around the shoulders" should indicate not only the pastoral duty of carrying home the lost sheep, but also the great love of Christ, who took human flesh on himself and bore it all the way to the cross. And its ornamentation with crosses—for on it "the banner of the holy cross has been imprinted"—should remind him not only to boast in the cross (Gal 6:14), but also to hand himself over to death for his sheep's sake, after Christ's example (1 Pt 2:21). This analysis was clearly the product of additional meditation. Clement built upon the explanations offered in the previous document by supplementing its pastoral points with Christocentric elements. This reform pope's comprehensive, methodical approach, based on a close description of the pallium, set a new trend in explaining it.

Pope Victor II was of a similar mind, though of a less lucid and systematic bent, when he palliated Winiman of Embrun in 1057. He

---

82. Another pope with Bavarian connections, Benedict VIII, had used the same biblical quotation in a pallium grant (to Poppo of Trier in 1016, JL 4010, GP 10.1:52 no. 85, BZ 1169, ZPUU 2:951).

83. Clement was in Salerno for John's installation and personally vested him with the pallium: "In the name of [God,] the Father and the Son and the Holy Spirit, we have distinguished your Belovedness with the archiepiscopal pallium by our apostolic hand." The Trinitarian invocation suggests that this document (or part thereof) was meant to be read aloud, perhaps during the ceremony of investiture—or that it subsequently incorporated such a rite. Its symbolic reflections were possibly also read aloud.

84. JL 4151, GP 10.1:56 no. 94, BF 382, Jank, "Bemerkungen," 19–20.

advised the archbishop to understand what behavior the vestment implied, and then he strung together three biblical quotations.[85] The first two (Gal 5:24, 6:17)—"by crucifying your flesh with its vices and desires, you should bear the marks of Jesus Christ in your body"—may have referred to the crosslike shape of the vestment in this period and to the three pins, seen as the nails of Christ's crucifixion.[86] The third (2 Cor 4:10)—"always carry around his mortification"—added "on the chest and shoulders," where the pallium was worn, instead of the biblical words, "in the body." The pallium thus assimilated the wearer to the crucified Christ. Yet this interpretation did not give cause for ostentatious pride. Rather, it should show "to the sheep entrusted to you the venerable sign of our Savior," the cross, as a reminder and an invitation to imitate Christ. For just as the archbishop placed the pallium on his shoulders, Christ carried home the lost sheep on his shoulders—surely an allusion to the pallium's woolen composition. In Victor's eyes, the vestment produced an *alter Christus*, which must have heightened appreciation for archiepiscopal authority, even if tempered by encouragement to humility and pastoral service.

Interpreters beyond the Popes

Whether or not the reform popes directly stimulated new efforts, non-papal commentators, usually proponents of reform, continued and expanded such allegorical understandings. In this period at least seven discussed the pallium. The reformer Peter Damian addressed certain liturgical questions in his treatise *Dominus Vobiscum* (be-

85. JL 4369, BF 1306, PL 143:837.
86. An obscure passage in Lambert of Deutz's life of Heribert of Cologne, written between 1046 and 1056, depicted the consecration of the archbishop, who had brought the pallium with him from Rome: "He is anointed by his suffragans with the chrism of the chief oil; he is wreathed with ecclesiastical wedding gifts as a dowry of the catholic faith; all 'the marks of Jesus' are canonically completed 'in his body'" (MGH SSRG 73:157). "Wreathing" was sometimes used of the pallium: perhaps at this point he was vested with it. If so, it was described as a "wedding gift" and associated with the faith (perhaps because of the required profession). As in Victor's privilege, the biblical quotation may have indicated the pins, viz., their insertion during the investiture. In the twelfth century Honorius Augustodunensis also associated the pins with the nails (*Gemma Animae*, in PL 172:611).

tween 1048 and 1055). At the archbishop of Rouen's request, John of Avranches wrote his liturgical commentary, *De Officiis Ecclesiasticis* (between 1060 and 1067), to help restore ecclesiastical discipline in that province. Guibert of Nogent produced a biblical commentary with a moralistic orientation called *Moralia in Genesim* (between 1067 and 1084). Perhaps from the school of Anselm of Laon, the *Liber Quare* (late eleventh century) emerged as a textbook for clerical education, with information digested from a variety of sources. In the *Liber de Vita Christiana* (between 1089 and 1095), the reformer Bonizo of Sutri prefaced his juridical take on the pallium with a symbolic interpretation focusing on virtue. Rupert of Deutz preceded his ecclesiological interpretation of the pallium in his liturgical commentary, *De Divinis Officiis* (1111/12), with symbolic reflections on the vestment. Most thoroughly of all, the reformer Bruno of Segni, once a confidant of several popes but fallen out of favor, wrote his liturgical commentary, *De Sacramentis Ecclesiae* (between 1116 and 1123), after discussing with a friend the priestly objects in the book of Exodus, their mystical significance, and their parallels with the church's implements.

Common to all these writers was a confidence in symbolism. Peter Damian maintained that ecclesiastical observances, when probed beneath the surface, were of "great virtue"; even vestments hinted of other things *figuraliter.* Nearly everything in the liturgy, whether in the Old or New Testament, was done "through mystical figures and enigmas," in which the "virtue of spiritual understanding" had to be sought. Indeed, "mystery [*misterium*] lies hidden in ministry [*ministerium*], when through the exercise of outer worship the secret sacrament of allegorical speculation is grasped."[87] His strong voice in favor of the use of allegory helped to legitimize the explosion of interest in it at this time.

Sometimes the commentators struck out in unprecedented directions. Rupert of Deutz was interested in applying his symbolic interpretation of the pallium to the hierarchy: "Hanging down from

---

87. G. I. Gargano and N. D'Acunto, eds., based on the edition of Kurt Reindel, *Petri Damiani Epistulae / Pier Damiani lettere*, Opere di Pier Damiani 1 (Rome: Città Nuova, 2001), 2:138, 140. See Brown, "Enigmata Figurarum," 151.

the neck around the breast, it openly points out by its location that wreath of humility or wisdom which very much befits the role of bishops and the prince of their council."[88] Those virtues suited episcopal ministry in general, and an archbishop's chief position over his suffragans (or even the pope's over all bishops) in particular. Guibert of Nogent, commenting on Genesis 2:13 and trying to interpret the name of the river Gehon, translated the word as *pectus*: "By 'breast' can be understood fortitude.... For what we cannot [handle] with our arms, we are accustomed either to dash against or to drag with our breasts. Thus also certain animals have greater force in [the breast]. And for archbishops, under this type, the pallium rests there, so that they may forcefully drag others by going before them."[89] His ethical exegesis took him from the body part to the virtue of fortitude, and his use of typology associated strong-chested animals, such as oxen, with archbishops, who also bore a yoke upon their chests. For him, the pallium represented a prelate's role as model for his flock, one who led the way and drew the rest after him. It was an inventive path of explanation, but seems to have remained unique.[90]

Other liturgists drew liberally on past commentaries, though seldom without tweaking them. John of Avranches's treatment of the pallium was taken mostly from Amalar of Metz, although he showed no interest in paralleling the vestment to ancient Jewish high priestly garb.[91] Rupert of Deutz offered a brief rendition of Amalar's analysis; then, perhaps following Pseudo-Alcuin, he stressed that the pallium was a papal gift.[92] Of the five passages in the *Liber Quare* concerning the pallium, one was borrowed from Amalar, another from Pseudo-Alcuin, and another from John of Avranches, each with only

88. CCCM 7:22. See Brown, "Enigmata Figurarum," 167–73.
89. PL 156:66.
90. The rest of the passage did not concern the pallium directly, but the language was strongly reminiscent of *Si pastores ovium*. Perhaps Guibert had a copy of a pallium grant, which had suggested the topic to him; or maybe he was recalling another text, the very source of the formula's admonitions.
91. R. Delamare, ed., *Le De Officiis Ecclesiasticis de Jean d'Avranches, archevêque de Rouen (1067–1079): étude liturgique et publication du texte inédit* (Paris: Picard, 1923), 51. See Amalar, *Liber Officialis*, in Hanssens, *Opera*, 2:248–49, and Brown, "Enigmata Figurarum," 152–53.
92. CCCM 7:22.

slight revisions. The fourth passage was a potpourri formed from the insights of Amalar, Pseudo-Alcuin, and Rabanus Maurus. The remaining passage, though mostly taken from Amalar, showed fresh thinking.[93] It reinterpreted Amalar's metaphor of the "competition" from the Christian life of virtue to the ecclesiastical *cursus honorum*: "Just as a wreath was not given except to one legitimately competing, so nobody will ascend to the honor of the pallium except the one who first legitimately sweats in each rank of honors." That is, to become an archbishop, one first had to serve in each of the lower orders. Also, in Pauline fashion, it glossed the Old Law as carried out "by work only," while the New was done "in heart and mind." As a result, one could not presume to wear this vestment unless he both taught the commandments and put them into practice.[94] Both these comments resembled the content of the final prayer recited at the pallium's conferral, as found in the Romano-Germanic Pontifical and other liturgical books.[95] Perhaps the writer was inspired by that text. As for his extensive borrowings, they proved that pallium commentaries old and new continued to garner interest.[96]

The desire to match the church's vestments to those of the Old Testament remained strong. For Peter Damian, the pallium was pontifical attire similar to the *lamina* or plate of the Aaronic priesthood (Ex 28:36–38), worn "for adornment and glory." Relying on Pseudo-Alcuin, he noted that the plate was engraved with the tetragrammaton, God's own name, containing profound meaning under its letters.[97] Bonizo of Sutri used the term *rationale* as a synonym for the pallium. It referred to the Jewish rational (breastplate), as if to imply that the later vestment was the successor or parallel of the earlier, as Pseudo-Alcuin had proposed. But he supplemented that writ-

---

93. CCCM 60:100–101, 131, 154, 175. Not all the passages occurred in all the manuscripts of this work.
94. CCCM 60:101.
95. Vogel and Elze, *Pontifical*, 1:229–30.
96. Reynolds positions the *Liber Quare* among the "conservative" liturgical productions of the reform period, which preferred the Carolingian expositions to the new trends in commentary ("Liturgical Scholarship," 116).
97. Gargano and D'Acunto, *Epistulae*, 2:138. Cf. Pseudo-Alcuin, *De Divinis Officiis*, in PL 101:1243.

er by explaining the rational's meaning: "One wears the rational on his breast when he distinguishes between good and evil things, and thinks about what is suited to each, and arranges them by the discipline of his care. In the mind of the Lord, all priests use this apparel when, by the judgment of reason, they both look for the things that are to be sought and despise the things that are to be scorned; but not all are clothed with it materially on the body."[98] Based on the biblical description of the *rationale iudicii* (Ex 28:15, 29–30) and the very sense of the words, he correlated the vestment with the virtue of discretion. It was thus a spiritual reality, within anyone's grasp, even if only certain bishops could use the physical version (the pallium).

Bruno of Segni equated the pallium with two Jewish vestments simultaneously, the superhumeral (ephod) and the rational (breastplate): the former because it lay "upon both the pontiff's shoulders," the latter because it reached down "on the pontiff's very breast." Also, in ancient Judaism both garments formed a single piece, and belonged to the high priest alone.[99] Bruno was not the first to draw this connection. A description of the orphrey on a chasuble from the late 1050s compared it to the two high priestly vestments and to the pallium.[100] And the papal chancery had begun using a passage that mentioned the superhumeral and rational in its pallium grants; Bruno had been a member of the papal entourage in those days, and may have influenced, or been influenced by, this selection.[101] Now he fleshed out these allusions with a lengthy symbolic treatment, for the pallium, he said, had the same *significatio*, if not the same *compositio*, as the older vestments. The superhumeral, weighing upon the bishop's shoulders, represented the "burden of the episcopal dignity," realized when the bishop carried "the burdens of the whole church

---

98. Perels, *Liber de Vita*, 108.
99. PL 165:1105–6. See Réginald Grégoire, *Bruno de Segni: exégète médiéval et théologien monastique*, Centro italiano di studi sull'alto medioevo 3 (Spoleto: Panetto and Petrelli, 1965); Brown, "Enigmata Figurarum," 160–62; and Louis I. Hamilton, *A Sacred City: Consecrating Churches and Reforming Society in Eleventh-Century Italy* (Manchester: Manchester University Press, 2010), 162–226.
100. *Gesta Pontificum Autissiodorensium*, in Sot et al., *Gestes*, 257.
101. E.g., Urban II to Rainald of Reims in 1089, JL 5415, PL 151:311.

and the weary sheep and the sins of the people." He pointed out that Jesus, "that supreme pontiff of ours," showed himself adorned with the superhumeral when he portrayed himself as the good shepherd, who sought out the lost sheep, set it on his shoulders, and carried it home.[102] The rational, as both its name and its location on the breast implied, protected "the treasury of the heart and the secret place of wisdom," where religiously enlightened understanding resided. The vestment should not decorate a heart without this virtue, lest it be "useless, and like a seal guarding nothing." In scripture it was also named the "rational of judgment," which meant that the palliger had to judge wisely, truly, and carefully.[103] In these reflections Bruno spoke of "rational" and "superhumeral" on three levels: as the Aaronic vestments, as the pallium, and as certain virtues. Together they showed palligers how to be prudent and caring pastors.

As Amalar did in the early ninth century, commentators in this period might subject every segment of the pallium to symbolic analysis.[104] John of Avranches made two small additions to Amalar's interpretation. The "circle around the shoulders" symbolized not only discipline, but also fear of the Lord, by which an archbishop should "rule his whole self and his fellow bishops subject to him." In addition, the two strips meant not only preaching in accord with both Testaments, but also love of God and love of neighbor.[105] More boldly, Bruno of Segni examined every aspect of the pallium, since each revealed hidden depths of meaning.[106] Its double thickness on the left side (a consequence of its original form) stood for the ups and downs and conflicting desires (*duplicitas*) of this world. Its single layer on the right side, in contrast, represented the singular, unblem-

---

102. Cf. Gregory the Great, *Regula Pastoralis*, in Rommel et al., *Règle*, 182, 184, 186. Perhaps due to his tense relationship with Paschal II, Bruno applied "our supreme pontiff" to Jesus rather than the pope.

103. Cf. ibid., 176, 178.

104. Miller finds this emphasis on the physical aspects of vestments characteristic of the period, and an effective pedagogical tool for inculcating doctrine and morals (*Clothing the Clergy*, 59–60).

105. Delamare, *De Officiis Ecclesiasticis*, 51. A twelfth-century revision repeated this passage nearly verbatim (*Expositio Divinorum Officiorum*, in PL 147:211).

106. PL 165:1106–7.

ished happiness of the next world.[107] The pallium's strips, located "before and behind," pulled the garment to the ground (*ad inferiora*). They symbolized the "cares and concerns of this life," which so burdened the pontiff emotionally and physically that he was diverted "from his own condition"—from his dignity as a bishop, or as a child of God called to higher things. They forced him to deal with "vain and transitory things," yet also reminded him to be free of such "harmful weight." The vestment's doctrinal and moral admonishments thus warned the wearer of the hardships of pastoral service, necessarily enmeshed in the struggles of earthly life, while calling him to a heavenly existence—a tension recognized since Gregory the Great's *Regula Pastoralis*.[108]

In addition, Bruno noted, the pallium was woven of wool, which was "cheap material," to show that its value came not from itself but from "that which is signified in it." Hence those who saw it should use their mind more than their eyes, and treat it as a symbol, not a mere adornment. In this way it achieved a sort of intellectual transparency: it was important only for what it represented. He concluded his analysis by considering the pallium's pins. Surprisingly, he rejected an allegorical interpretation—that they were meant to represent the "prickings of this life, as certain men think"—in favor of a pragmatic one: that they were meant to connect the pallium to the chasuble. Indeed, he remarked that eyelets were attached to the chasuble in olden times to hold the pins, by which the vestments were kept in place. He could not resist some symbolic musing, however. The number three indicated the theological virtues: faith, hope, and charity. He also returned to the motif of "attachment" by observing that a bishop could not keep the pallium without such virtues. A palliger had to have the pins, that is the virtues, by which he fastened, that is

---

107. The left side of the pallium's loop was double-layered because the vestment had originally been a single long band encircling the shoulders, its ends hanging down in front and back, which overlapped on the left shoulder. As the pallium's form changed over the centuries—when the hanging strips were sewn to the lowest (central) point of the loop in front and back, and the vestment was fashioned as one piece—the double layer was retained, though no longer needed.

108. E.g., Rommel et al., *Règle*, 1:218–30.

retained, the pallium. Bruno thus stood within the long tradition that demanded ethical worthiness from those who would wear it.

These writers produced often original, detailed interpretations of the pallium, rich in the evocation of its alleged Jewish heritage and its relevance for pastoral ministry, rife with multiple meanings centered on the wearer's attitude and behavior. None of these thoughts pertained to the charged issues typically associated with the reform. But the reform was about more than fighting simony or lay investiture. It sought a purified episcopate, free of worldly entanglements and fit to lead a holy church. It strove to ensure the sacred status of bishops, as well as their correct behavior.[109] In these respects, the commentators' take on the pallium worked very well.

Conclusion

Previous chapters have treated the pallium during the reform period as a tool, with certain techniques of operation aimed at certain desired outcomes. The vestment, however, should not be reduced to its instrumentality. It derived much of its effectiveness not from how or why it was used, but from what it was, a culturally constructed artifact. This chapter has shown that reformers, both inside and outside the papacy, built upon the pallium's traditional meaning in significant ways. What seemed a band of wool was really the summation of episcopal office and power. What was routinely requested and conferred in accord with canon law was really an expression of papal munificence, demanding favors in return. What was worn as a decoration really required one to act in a manner worthy of it. These tendencies culminated in a proliferation of interpretations in which the garment's most mundane details displayed to its wearer—and his flock, who saw him wear it—the way to be a good shepherd. As a symbol, then, the pallium embodied and served the idea of Rome-centered ecclesiastical renewal.

---

109. Indeed, this kind of liturgical commentary shaped clerical culture and created a spirituality centered on vestments (Miller, *Clothing the Clergy*, 53, 63–64).

New Meanings 395

After a yearlong pontificate full of troubles—at odds with the emperor, in competition with an antipope, in flight from a hostile Roman faction—the elderly Pope Gelasius II, the former Chancellor John of Gaeta, died at Cluny. It had been a momentous era of change for the Latin church, but a new age would dawn under his successor, Pope Calixtus II, the former Archbishop Guy of Vienne, who was able to achieve the peace with the empire that had eluded the popes of the Investiture Contest. The reform period had forever altered the Western view of the church, its relation to the world, and the role of the papacy in it. This fact speaks not only to the transformative power of reform ideas, but equally to the effectiveness of their reception and implementation. In the latter endeavor the pallium played no small part. The Roman pontiffs took advantage of its accepted place in ecclesiastical affairs and fashioned a reformer's badge, a tool uniquely suited to directing bishops to conform to a program of church-wide renewal.

A change in vision was the root. The reform movement sharpened the popes' focus in using the pallium and provided the passion with which they set it to the task of taking charge of, and reshaping, Christendom. A measure of audacity and shrewdness helped these efforts to blossom: what the Carolingians had begun to realize in halting and limited ways was now carried out regularly, across the board, with a sense of divine mission and a willingness to improve old practices. Though appealing to tradition, the reformers acted as innovators. Transactions involving the vestment became occasions to uncover and eliminate abuses and give teeth to papal primacy—excuses for repeated interventions and rearrangements by a formerly distant patriarch. Strict new rules attached to the pallium made its recipients more accountable and loyal to the donor, and the popes did not hesitate to wield it as a lure, a goad, a plum, or a club, as circumstances demanded. This highly sought gift, freely donated or denied by the popes, thus contributed to the Roman church's oversight. The pallium deserves to be recognized alongside the rest of the machinery of Roman centralization, such as legates, synods, canon law, *ad limina* visits, and curial bureaucracy. Employed with them, this simple textile helped to produce the papal monarchy that claimed, and to some extent attained, such far-reaching control over the Western church.

By the high Middle Ages the pope had become, in effect, the bishop of the entire church, in which subordinate prelates were tied to him with bonds of wool. The expression is deliberately chosen: these "bonds" both constrained and connected. On the one hand, they subjected and restricted their wearers, and on the other, they fostered an intimate relationship with their source. This paradoxical combination of devotion and dependence formed the strands that knit the reformed church—or so the papacy hoped—into a stainless, seamless garment.

EPILOGUE: The Pallium in Classical Medieval Jurisprudence (ca. 1140–ca. 1271)

During the classical period of medieval canonical jurisprudence, which stretched from Gratian, known as the "father of the science of canon law," through the great jurists of the twelfth and thirteenth centuries, Huguccio and Hostiensis were two of the brightest stars. Their attitudes toward the pallium were mixed. Huguccio, in his *summa* on Gratian's *Decretum* in the late 1180s, theorized that a metropolitan had to be forced to obtain the pallium because by it "he would be burdened not a little, and would experience little or no advantage or honor."[1] Henry of Susa (called Hostiensis because of his position as cardinal bishop of Ostia), in his *Lectura* or gloss apparatus on Gregory IX's *Decretals,* finished at the end of his life in 1271, scoffed at one archbishop's embarrassment over not being allowed to wear his pallium outside his own province: after all, it was only "a little thing, for there is little value in dress." He followed this comment with a castigation of contemporary standards, which prized "adorn-

---

1. Lons-Le-Saunier, Archive Dép., Ms. 12 F.16 ad D.100 c.1 s.v. *ac per hoc* (119r: "non modicum gravaretur, et emolumentum vel honorem modicum vel nullum sentiret").

Figure 6. An emperor investing an archbishop, wearing the pallium, with the *regalia* through the scepter. From a Cologne copy of Gratian's *Decretum*, ca. 1170–80. Cologne, Erzbischöfliche Diözesan- und Dombibliothek, Cod. 127, fol. 9r. Used with permission.

ment and honor" over pastoral "care, burden, and labor."[2] The two learned canonists' disparagement of the pallium belied the weight they gave it in their works. Both men expounded at great length the canonical principles underlying the acquisition, effects, proper use, and meaning of this "little thing." Indeed, ever since Gratian chose

2. *HostLect* ad X 1.8.5 s.v. *verecundum* (1:89v).

to include the pallium in the earlier recension of his canon law textbook, subsequent scholars had erected a sizeable legal edifice on his foundation and had accumulated an impressive body of interpretation and commentary on the subject. Like it or not, the pallium became firmly embedded in the mainstream of the medieval church's canonical tradition.

This juridical process distilled the developments in thought and practice traced throughout this book. By the time Pope Gelasius II died in 1119, urban schools were growing, and the study of Roman law had been revived, especially in Septimania, Provence, Lombardy, and Tuscany. The recovery and application of Justinianic sources and the methods employed in the new schools were revolutionizing legal learning. In this context, the systematic study of canon law was arising in Bologna, and Gratian was beginning, or about to begin, his scholarly career there. The collection of precedents that characterized canonistic inquiry was maturing into a rational legal science, a true jurisprudence.[3] The main lines of the medieval pallium's story, which had begun in the Carolingian age and reached a climax in the reform period, had by now been set. It was Gratian and his successors in the burgeoning law schools of the high Middle Ages who drew forth specific rules from this rich tradition, clarified the assumptions behind them, and integrated them into the broader corpus of the church's law. Often this effort involved the reconciliation of conflicting ideas and values into a coherent system. Thus it was more than a mere summarizing and smoothing out; it also shaped the use and understanding of the pallium for the future. The jurisprudence that evolved out of the background of the preceding chapters can be appreciated by examining the contributions of two

3. On this period in the history of medieval canon law, see Stephan Kuttner, *Harmony from Dissonance: An Interpretation of Medieval Canon Law* (Latrobe, Pa.: Archabbey Press, 1960; reprinted in his *The History of Ideas and Doctrines of Canon Law in the Middle Ages*, part 1 [London: Variorum, 1980]); Stephan Kuttner, "The Revival of Jurisprudence," in *Renaissance and Renewal in the Twelfth Century*, ed. Robert L. Benson and Giles Constable with Carol D. Lanham, Medieval Academy Reprints for Teaching 26 (Toronto: University of Toronto Press, 1991), 299–323; and Wilfried Hartmann and Kenneth Pennington, eds., *The History of Medieval Canon Law in the Classical Period, 1140–1234: From Gratian to the Decretals of Pope Gregory IX* (Washington, D.C.: The Catholic University of America Press, 2008).

phases of canonical thought: first, Gratian (or the several individuals to whom that name may apply) and those who commented on his textbook, called decretists (chapter 1 of the epilogue); and next, those who collected the *ius novum* of papal decretals, especially Raymond of Penyafort, editor of the *Decretals of Gregory IX*, and those who commented on these compilations, called decretalists (chapter 2 of the epilogue).[4]

4. Bernard d'Alteroche, "Le statut du pallium dans le droit canonique classique de Gratien à Hostiensis (vers 1140–1270)," *Revue historique de droit français et étranger* 83 (2005): 553–85, surveys some of this material.

Epilogue Chapter 1: *Decretum* and Decretists

Gratian

Around 1140 a teacher in Bologna named Gratian, about whom very little is known, produced the *Concordia Discordantium Canonum*, more commonly known as the *Decretum*, which has long been recognized as the standard textbook of scholastic canon law and the cornerstone of high medieval jurisprudence.[1] The research of Anders Winroth has uncovered an earlier recension of this work and thus demonstrated at least two stages of composition.[2] The earlier recen-

---

1. See John T. Noonan, "Gratian Slept Here: The Changing Identity of the Father of the Systematic Study of Canon Law," *Traditio* 35 (1979): 145–72; Peter Landau, "Gratian and the *Decretum Gratiani*," in *Canon Law, 1140–1234*, ed. Hartmann and Pennington, 22–54; Anders Winroth, "Where Gratian Slept: The Life and Death of the Father of Canon Law," *Zeitschrift der Savigny-Stiftung für Rechtsgeschichte, kanonistische Abteilung* 99 (2013): 105–28; and Kenneth Pennington, "The Biography of Gratian, the Father of Canon Law," *Villanova Law Review* 59 (2014): 679–706.

2. See Anders Winroth, *The Making of Gratian's* Decretum (Cambridge: Cambridge University Press, 2000). Some scholars disagree with certain details of Winroth's arguments, and recent work posits a more gradual evolution (e.g., Carlos Larrainzar, "La formazione del Decreto di Graziano per tappe," in *Proceedings of the Eleventh International Congress of Medieval Canon Law*, ed. Manlio Bellomo and Orazio Condorelli, Monumenta Iuris Canonici, ser. C, Subsidia 12 [Vatican City: Biblioteca Apostolica Vaticana, 2006], 103–18). But clearly there were two chief stages in the development of the *Decretum*, corresponding to the two stable versions of the text that achieved circulation. On the debates about the recensions, with a proposed new nomenclature, see Atria A. Larson, "Gratian's *De penitentia* in Twelfth-Century Manuscripts," *Bulletin of Medieval Canon Law* 31 (2014): 57–110.

401

sion was composed in the 1130s and chiefly intended for teaching purposes. It rationally organized many important themes in the canonical tradition, presented case studies or *causae* that probed knotty juridical quandaries, and (particularly through its comments or *dicta*) tried to resolve contradictions among the canons through dialectical reasoning. The later recension, developed over the next decade or so, may be attributed to Gratian himself at a later point in his career or to one or more of his students. It added a wealth of new texts that made it one of the most comprehensive of systematic canonical collections, and it included a section on sacramental law, citations of Roman law, and comments that had been accumulating in the intervening years. In short, it updated the work with the fruits of the quickly advancing science of canon law as it was unfolding in twelfth-century Bologna. For ease of reference, while allowing that they may have been the same man, or even many scholars working together, these two authors can be identified as Gratian 1 and Gratian 2.[3]

Gratian 1

In the earlier recension of the *Decretum*, the pallium was mentioned in only three canons and one *dictum*. A *distinctio* about the impermissibility of promoting clergy against their will included an excerpt from Pope Gregory the Great's letter threatening to deprive Natalis of Salona of the use of the pallium because of the forced promotion of his archdeacon Honoratus.[4] Gregory's legate was ordered to impose this penalty "from the authority of the apostolic see" if Natalis remained obstinate, for the privilege "had been granted to him by this see." If papal authority was the source of the privilege, the same authority could withdraw it. It was a serious punishment, for if, "even having lost the pallium, he still perseveres in the same stubbornness," then excommunication would follow. Nevertheless, the pallium was raised here only as a means of pressuring a bishop to comply with the pope's will. Later, in a question on a *causa* concern-

---

3. The texts of the earlier recension are here separated from the later according to Winroth's appendix (*Making*, 197–227).
4. D.74 c.8 (from JE 1175), Friedberg, *Corpus*, 1:264.

ing simony, Gregory's legislation from the Council of Rome (595) was quoted.[5] Here the pallium was one part of the process of installing a bishop that must be concluded before a voluntary donation might licitly change hands. Even so, the rubric attached to this canon seemed to favor that voluntary thanks-offering—a sort of loophole in Gregory's prohibition of simony—which made Gratian appear somewhat soft on the crime.

Besides these incidental references to the pallium, Gratian 1 devoted his hundredth *distinctio* to the pallium itself, although he treated the topic cursorily. Here he cited Pope John VIII's classic statement *Quoniam quidam,* which he probably took from the *Collectio III Librorum,* given its false attribution to a Pope Pelagius.[6] In the rubric he explained that every metropolitan was expected within three months to profess his faith and request the pallium "from the Roman church," not "from the apostolic see," as in the canon—perhaps acknowledging the role of the cardinals in bestowing the pallium during a papal vacancy or absence. Introducing this text was a short *dictum* that enunciated a principle implied in the canon: "It is permitted neither to an archbishop nor to a primate nor to a patriarch to ordain bishops before receiving the pallium."[7] Thus Gratian made explicit the link between refusal to seek the pallium and delay in consecrating bishops, which could be deduced from the original text, "though less obviously," as he said. The *dictum* went further, however, perhaps reflecting the practice of his own time: it applied the rule not just to metropolitans, as in the text itself, but also to all archbishops, primates, and patriarchs—all of whom were bishops with jurisdiction over other bishops, and thus with responsibility for episcopal consecrations.

In sum, Gratian 1 evinced only a very mild interest in the pallium. As in earlier canonical collections such as the *Panormia,* the *Collectio V Librorum* in Vat. lat. 1348, and the compilation in Arsenal 721, *Quoniam quidam* was the only canon directly concerning the

---

5. C.1 q.2 c.4 (from the Council of Rome of 595, c. 5), ibid., 1:409.
6. D.100 c.1 (from the Council of Rome of 875, c. 2), ibid., 1:352. Cf. Canon 2.6.4, Motta, *Collectio,* 143–44.
7. D.100 d.a.c.1, Friedberg, *Corpus,* 1:351–52.

vestment that was considered worthy of inclusion.[8] Nor did the great canonist do much with it, apart from explaining its underlying reasoning and extending its application to all the upper echelons of the ecclesiastical hierarchy.

Gratian 2

The *Decretum* changed significantly with the development of the later recension, as over time the number of references to the pallium more than quadrupled. Indeed, Gratian 2 showed more interest in the pallium than his predecessor had, for he expanded Gratian 1's D.100 to create a coherent body of pallium law. The original *distinctio* was augmented with eight canons and two *dicta* and organized into five parts. The first part (c. 1) was the core already established by Gratian 1, the requirement to obtain the pallium. The second part (c. 2) followed logically by specifying the conditions under which the pallium was granted. This excerpt from Gregory the Great's letter to Queen Brunhild focused on the prerequisites of sufficient merit and a request made vigorously (*fortiter*).[9] The third part (cc. 4–5) developed that topic by discussing preliminary professions and promises. John VIII's letter to Willibert of Cologne was trimmed to focus on the "customary profession of faith" (as the rubric called it) demanded before receipt of the pallium.[10] Gregory the Great's letter to Bishop Aregius received a rubric that reinterpreted the text: instead of promising to remove abuses from the church (as in the actual letter), the recipient was to promise to rid himself of illicit things.[11] Perhaps this point was meant to supplement the preceding canons' views on how to deserve the pallium. The fourth part (cc. 6, 8) added restrictions on the use of the pallium. Both Gregory the Great's letter to Virgilius of Arles and the same pope's letter to John of Ravenna discussed when it was licit to wear the vestment.[12] The rubric common to both stressed that

---

8. Canon 3.11, Brett and Brasington, *Panormia*, at https://ivo-of-chartres.github.io/panormia/pan_3.pdf, 13; Canon 1.3.6, *Clavis* NP01.03.06; and Canon 1.28, *Clavis* AS01.028. On the latter two collections, see Kéry, *Canonical Collections*, 217–18, 288, and Fowler-Magerl, *Clavis Canonum*, 102–4, 237–38.

9. D.100 c.2 (from JE 1491), Friedberg, *Corpus*, 1:352.

10. D.100 c.4 (from JE 2986), ibid., 1:353.

11. D.100 c.5 (from JE 1748), ibid., 1:353.

12. D.100 cc.6 (from JE 1374), 8 (from JE 1259), ibid., 1:353–54.

it was liturgical apparel, meant for the Mass alone, in accord—as the second text put it—with the "custom of the universal church." The final part (cc. 9–11) touched on privileges intended to accompany the pallium. Three more Gregorian letters—to Syagrius of Autun, John of Prima Justiniana, and the bishops of Epirus—maintained that a pallium grant ought to result in the renewal of privileges and responsibilities.[13] These might take the form of rights already bestowed on the recipient's predecessors, such as a papal vicariate, or simply of more attentive pastoral care for the recipient's charges.

Gratian 1 had introduced his canon with a *dictum* (d.a.c.1), and Gratian 2 went on to the second part without comment, perhaps because it was meant to follow directly from the first. The later author then inserted a *dictum* (d.p.c.3) to conclude the second part and introduce the third and fourth parts.[14] This comment interpreted the "merits of cases" mentioned by Gregory (c. 2) to require a deserving recipient, rather than an appropriate situation—so that "he who requests [the pallium] may deserve to receive it." The idea of personal merit provided the opportunity to draw out further implications: the recipient must first swear to uphold his profession of faith and pledge to comply with papal and conciliar legislation, and he must observe due restrictions on the vestment's use—namely, by wearing it only during the Mass, in church, on specified days. Another *dictum* (d.p.c.8) briefly introduced the fifth part by declaring the necessity for *privilegia* to complement the pallium.[15] Gregory may have meant "special rights," but by the twelfth century the term also commonly referred to documents, which had long been given to recipients alongside the vestment itself. Such documents, of course, listed the permitted pallium days and admonished the palliger to act in a manner worthy of his honor.

The vestment came up beyond D.100 only in passing. In a question on a *causa* about competing privileges, the compiler introduced Gregory the Great's letter to Augustine of Canterbury forbidding his interference in Gaul because of the bishop of Arles's pallium.[16] The

13. D.100 cc.9–11 (from JE 1751, 1164, 1387), ibid., 1:354–55.
14. D.100 d.p.c.3, ibid., 1:353.
15. D.100 d.p.c.8, ibid., 1:354.
16. C.25 q.2 c.3 (from JE 1843), ibid., 1:1013.

attached rubric declared that "no one ought to strip a church of the privilege of its dignity," which in this case was manifested in the vestment, characterized in the canon as "the authority he has received" and the result of "the ancient institution of the fathers." Also, in the first *distinctio* of the sacramental treatise (*De consecratione*, hereafter "De cons.") that became the third division of the compilation, Pope Nicholas I's permission to wear the pallium on Maundy Thursday was inserted, though only as an appendix to a related question about the singing of the *Gloria*.[17] Both pallium and *Gloria* were treated here as Roman liturgical customs regulated by the pope.

Finally, three passages related to the pallium (two in D.100 and one beyond) were labeled *paleae* or "chaff," supplemental matter probably added later by the earliest glossators. Often such addenda provided portions of texts that had originally been omitted, or they interpolated relevant texts that may have originally been overlooked.[18] Besides offering further context, these particular *paleae* had little impact on the thrust of Gratian's arguments.

In sum, Gratian 2's most important contribution was to enhance D.100 by gathering a group of canons that was fairly small but touched on many of the most salient legal principles concerning the pallium. The more comprehensive work that the *Decretum* had become now addressed not only an archbishop's obligation to procure the pallium, but also the prerequisites he must meet to get it, the rules he must observe in using it, and the legal and pastoral ramifications of possessing it. The only conceptual innovation, however, was to interpret the old phrase *causarum merita* in terms of the recipient's personal worthiness, particularly as manifested in his orthodoxy and obedience.

---

17. De cons. D.1 c.56 (from JE 2765), ibid., 1:1310.

18. The *palea* D.100 c.3 (from JE 1378; ibid., 1:352–53) introduced Gregory the Great's letter to John of Corinth on avoiding simony in the conferral of ordination and the pallium, perhaps in the spirit of the preceding canon's treatment of merit and petitioning. The *palea* D.100 c.7 (from JE 1259; ibid., 1:353–54) supplemented D.100 c.8, but did not itself mention the pallium. The *palea* C.1 q.2 c.3 (from the Council of Melfi of 1089, c. 7, and the Council of Rome of 595, c. 5; ibid., 1:408–9) is complex, containing an unrelated canon juxtaposed with a supplement to C.1 q.2 c.4.

The Decretists

The significance of Gratian's treatment of the pallium lay not in the breadth of its coverage of the topic, nor in the depth of its commentary on the pertinent canons, but in the fact that the matter had made it into the *Decretum* in several places, especially in its own *distinctio*. This fact ensured that, as the work became the manual of the developing field of canonical jurisprudence, teachers and students in the law schools would continually study, discuss, gloss, and further probe a received body of pallium-related texts considered normative for the Latin church.[19] The commentators whose glosses were either collected into apparatuses copied into the margins of Gratian's textbook (culminating in a standard apparatus or *Glossa Ordinaria*), or systematized into independent scholastic treatises called *summae*, were known as decretists.[20] Their writings reveal the increasing legal sophistication of the high Middle Ages, and their lines of thought influenced the understanding and implementation of the church's law until modern times. The following analysis examines the works of twelve of the leading decretists from the mid-twelfth to the mid-thirteenth century.[21] These are: Paucapalea's *summa* (ca. 1144–50), Roland's *Stroma* (ca. 1150), Rufinus's *summa* (ca. 1164), Stephen of Tournai's *summa* (1165–66), the *Summa Coloniensis* or *"Elegantius in iure divino"* (ca. 1169), the *Summa Parisiensis* or *"Magister G. in hoc opere"* (ca. 1170), Simon of Bisignano's *summa* (ca. 1177–79), the *Summa Lipsiensis* or *"Omnis qui iuste iudicat"* (ca. 1186), Honorius of Kent's *summa* or *"De iure canonico tractaturus"* (ca. 1188), Huguccio's *summa* (ca. 1188–90), the *Summa Bambergensis* or *"Animal est substantia"* (ca. 1206–10), and the *Glossa Ordinaria* on the *Decretum*, composed by

19. See James A. Brundage, "The Teaching and Study of Canon Law in the Law Schools," in *Canon Law, 1140–1234*, ed. Hartmann and Pennington, 98–120.
20. See Rudolf Weigand, "The Development of the *Glossa ordinaria* to Gratian's *Decretum*," in *Canon Law, 1140–1234*, ed. Hartmann and Pennington, 55–97; Kenneth Pennington and Wolfgang P. Müller, "The Decretists: The Italian School," in ibid., 121–73; and Rudolf Weigand, "The Transmontane Decretists," in ibid., 174–210.
21. Omnibonus's *Abbreviatio* (ca. 1156) chose to reproduce only the fifth part (d.p.c.8 and cc.9–11) of Gratian's D.100, and provided no commentary thereon (Cologne, Stadtarchiv, Ms. W folio 248, fol. 31r). The *Distinctiones Monacenses* or *Summa "Si mulier eadem hora"* (early 1170s) did not address the pallium at all.

Johannes Teutonicus (ca. 1215) and revised by Bartholomew of Brescia (ca. 1240–45).[22] In order to assess their collective impact on the points of pallium law found in Gratian, the discussion will approach these works not sequentially, but thematically.

---

22. Full citation information for these sources is as follows: Johann Friedrich von Schulte, ed., *Die Summa [des Paucapalea] über das Decretum Gratiani* (Giessen: Roth, 1890; reprinted in Aalen: Scientia, 1965) [hereafter "Paucapalea"]; Friedrich Thaner, ed., *Summa Magistri Rolandi* (Innsbruck: Wagner, 1874; reprinted in Aalen: Scientia, 1973) [hereafter "Roland"]; Heinrich Singer, ed., *Summa Decretorum* (Paderborn: Schöningh, 1902; reprinted in Aalen: Scientia, 1963) [hereafter "Rufinus"]; Johann Friedrich von Schulte, ed., *Stephan von Doornick (Étienne de Tournai, Stephanus Tornacensis): Die Summa über das Decretum Gratiani* (Giessen: Roth, 1891; reprinted in Aalen: Scientia, 1965) [hereafter "StephTourn"]; Gérard Fransen and Stephan Kuttner, eds., *Summa "Elegantius in iure divino" seu Coloniensis*, Monumenta Iuris Canonici, ser. A, Corpus Glossatorum 1 (Vatican City: Biblioteca Apostolica Vaticana, 1969–90) [hereafter *"Elegantius"*]; Terence P. McLaughlin, ed., *The Summa Parisiensis on the Decretum Gratiani* (Toronto: Pontifical Institute of Mediaeval Studies, 1952) [hereafter *"Magister"*]; Petrus V. Aimone, ed., *Summa in Decretum Simonis Bisinianensis* (Fribourg: University of Fribourg, 2007), http://www.unifr.ch/cdc/fr/document [hereafter "SimonBis"]; Rudolf Weigand, Peter Landau, and Waltraud Kozur, eds., *Summa "Omnis qui iuste iudicat" sive Lipsiensis*, Monumenta Iuris Canonici, ser. A, Corpus Glossatorum 7 (Vatican City: Biblioteca Apostolica Vaticana, 2007–12) [hereafter *"Omnis"*]; Rudolf Weigand, Peter Landau, and Waltraud Kozur, eds., *Magistri Honorii Summa "De iure canonico tractaturus,"* Monumenta Iuris Canonici, ser. A, Corpus Glossatorum 5 (Vatican City: Biblioteca Apostolica Vaticana, 2004–10) [hereafter "Honorius"]; Lons-Le-Saunier, Archive Dép., Ms. 12 F.16 [hereafter "Huguccio"]; E. C. Coppens, ed., *Animal est substantia*, http://medcanonlaw.nl/Animal_est_substantia/Introduction.html [hereafter *"Animal"*]; and *Corpus Iuris Canonici [Editio Romana]*, vol. 1, *Decretum Gratiani* (Rome: Aedes Populi Romani, 1582) [hereafter *"Glossa Ordinaria"*]. In the following discussion, the passage of the *Decretum* being commented on will be given after "ad," then (when applicable) the word or phrase within the passage after "s.v." (*sub verbo*), then the page, column, or folio number of the edition or manuscript source in parentheses. For example, *"Omnis* ad D.100 c.4 s.v. *iureiurando* (1:408)" means the part of the *Summa "Omnis qui iuste iudicat"* that comments on the word *iureiurando* within D.100 c.4 of Gratian's *Decretum*, as found in volume 1, page 408, of the edition cited above. Peter Landau, *Die Kölner Kanonistik des 12. Jahrhunderts: ein Höhepunkt der europäischen Rechtswissenschaft*, Kölner rechtsgeschichtliche Vorträge 1 (Badenweiler: Bachmann, 2008), proposes that the author of *Elegantius* was Berthold (Bertram) of Metz. In "Rodoicus Modicipassus: Verfasser der Summa Lipsiensis?," *Zeitschrift der Savigny-Stiftung für Rechtsgeschichte, kanonistische Abteilung* 92 (2006): 340–54, he proposes that the author of *Omnis* was the English master Rodoicus Modicipassus.

Who could receive the pallium?

For these commentators, the typical palliger was a metropolitan archbishop. Huguccio acknowledged the possibility of "a simple bishop [who] had been adorned with the honor of the pallium."[23] But palliated suffragans were so extraordinary that most decretists, often interested more in rules than in exceptions, paid them little heed. Instead, possession of the pallium indicated a higher rank. When Gregory the Great spoke of "Bishop" Natalis of Salona, Simon, *Omnis*, and *Animal* deduced from the canon in which the pope threatened to strip him of his pallium that Natalis must have been a metropolitan archbishop.[24] Their puzzlement was understandable, because metropolitans were usually called "bishops" before the ninth century; but their assumption was anachronistic, for metropolitans were not universally obliged to receive the pallium until the same century. In the eyes of these canonists, the vestment was at least a declarative sign, a badge of office. Twice Huguccio inferred from the mere mention of the pallium that the canons in question regarded archbishops.[25]

Simon, however, went further. Speculating why James the Just, "brother of the Lord," needed to be ordained bishop of Jerusalem—since he was regarded as an apostle (often conflated with James the Less), and thus a bishop already—the canonist proposed that he was "ordained not as bishop, but as archbishop through the giving of the pallium."[26] In other words, the pallium made an archbishop, and entrance into that *ordo* could be termed "ordination."[27] Simon's historical accuracy left much to be desired, but his view of the vestment

23. Huguccio ad D.74 c.8 s.v. *usum pallii* (94r: "simplex episcopus et erat decoratus honore pallii").

24. SimonBis ad D.63 c.24 (57), *Omnis* ad D.74 c.8 s.v. *usum pallii* (1:323), *Animal* ad D.63 c.24 (1088).

25. Huguccio ad C.1 q.2 c.4 s.v. *pallium* (135v) et ad C.25 q.2 c.3 s.v. *pallium* (323v).

26. SimonBis ad D.66 c.2 s.v. *ordinatus est* (61).

27. The *Liber Pontificalis* said that Chrodegang, already a bishop, was "ordained archbishop" at his palliation (Duchesne, *Liber pontificalis*, 1:456). Somewhat similarly, the *Anglo-Saxon Chronicle* described an elect as having been "consecrated" archbishop when he received the pallium (Cubbin, *Anglo-Saxon Chronicle*, 6:63–64, and Irvine, *Anglo-Saxon Chronicle*, 7:75).

as a constitutive sign had ample precedent. *Animal,* moreover, specified the nature of the office bestowed through the pallium. After discussing metropolitans in the preceding *distinctio,* Gratian in D.100 had shown "in what they preside over bishops." That medium or expression of authority was the pallium, "which is conferred on metropolitans as a sign that they preside over bishops."[28] Certainly, the idea that the vestment marked a bishop set over other bishops was a traditional one, and already three centuries earlier Pseudo-Alcuin had named it as the very thing that set an archbishop apart from his suffragans.[29] Huguccio must have been aware of this strain of thought when he maintained: "It is the particular insigne of his dignity; therefore, because he is distinguished from bishops by it, he ought not to be found negligent in seeking it."[30]

What was required in order to receive the pallium?

The decretists agreed that the one who sought the pallium had to make a formal request. *Animal* posited that the reason John VIII had called the pallium "desired" was that it had been asked for, and in fact rightly ought to have been asked for.[31] Huguccio explained that the same pope had complained that metropolitans "neither seek nor receive" the vestment because reception was conditioned upon a request: "It is not given except to one seeking it."[32] In making this point, he ignored the fact that popes had sometimes bestowed the pallium *motu proprio,* as an unexpected gift. *Omnis* likewise failed to acknowledge a grant at the pope's own initiative. It cited the need for a petition as an illustration of the principle that "a bishop [including the pope] ought not to do certain things unless asked."[33] The

---

28. *Animal* ad D.100 d.a.c.1 (1272).

29. *De Divinis Officiis,* in PL 101:1243. Pseudo-Alcuin had slightly revised a remark of Amalar of Metz.

30. Huguccio ad D.100 c.2 s.v. *postulanti* (119r–v: "cum hoc sit speciale insigne suae dignitatis, quia hoc ergo discernitur ab episcopis non debet inveniri negligens in eo petendo").

31. *Animal* ad D.100 c.4 s.v. *optatum* (1277) et ad D.100 c.1 s.v. *neque expetunt* (1273).

32. Huguccio ad D.100 c.1 s.v. *neque competunt et ideo neque percipiunt* (119r: "cum non detur nisi petenti").

33. *Omnis* ad D.100 c.2 s.v. *fortiter postulanti* (1:407–8).

reluctance of Huguccio and *Omnis* to conceive of an unrequested pallium seemed to lessen the freedom of the papal donor, but they may have been thinking of the vestment as routinely due to certain churchmen. Thus they were trying to explain why a request was necessary at all.

Both *Omnis* and Honorius emphasized that the petition, presented in the form of a written document, had to follow certain formalities (*debitae sollemnitates*) in order to be valid.[34] The *Glossa Ordinaria* was more thorough: "A whole contract or rescript or document is invalid and to be voided if it lacks some necessary things in it ... [but] superfluous things do not vitiate it."[35] One component of a pallium request that became embedded in the law was the manner in which it was to be made. Gregory the Great had asserted that it must be made "vigorously [*fortiter*]," and, beginning with *Magister* and stretching to the *Glossa Ordinaria*, this word was frequently equated with "insistently [*instanter*]."[36] Huguccio followed suit, and clarified that such insistence involved "offering many entreaties."[37] *Animal* compared it to the insistence necessary in seeking dimissorial letters from a bishop, and even claimed that the vehemence resulted from the fact that the pallium was "owed" to the recipient.[38] Once again a canonist glossed over the fact that the vestment was a gift—even though he later specifically called it "the gift of the pallium"—and as a gift should have been governed by the donor's discretion.[39] In any case, this explicit earnestness or perseverance, perhaps showing the seriousness of the request and the importance of its object, passed into the wording of

---

34. *Omnis* ad D.100 c.4 s.v. *minus quam oporteat* (1:408), Honorius ad D.100 c.4 s.v. *minus* (1:265).

35. *Glossa Ordinaria* ad D.100 c.4 s.v. *minus* (640). Cf. Huguccio ad D.100 c.4 s.v. *minus continere* (119v).

36. *Magister* ad D.100 c.2 (77), *Glossa Ordinaria* ad D.100 (637).

37. Huguccio ad D.100 c.2 s.v. *fortiter* et *postulanti* (119r–v: "multas preces porrigenti").

38. *Animal* ad D.72 d.a.c.1 s.v. *dimissorias* (ms. L, 1151) et ad C.2 q.6 c.31 s.v. *petentis* vel *instantiam* (1794–95; ms. K, 1796) et ad D.100 c.2 s.v. *et fortiter* (1277). The first of these passages contained the comment, "PP. dicit quod pallium debet peti de consensu ecclesie metropolitane." "PP" could refer to Paucapalea, but no such comment can be found in his *summa*.

39. *Animal* ad D.100 c.6 s.v. *missarum sollempnia* (1279–80).

a standard pallium petition, in which the candidate made his case *instanter, instantius, instantissime*.[40]

It was long recognized that a profession of faith had to accompany the petition, but precisely what did this profession entail? Stephen specified that it meant adherence to "the sacred scriptures, and the four universal councils, and the decretals of the Roman pontiffs," and he was followed by *Omnis* and Huguccio.[41] *Magister* differed by naming the first eight ecumenical councils, rather than only four, as well as the creed (*symbolum fidei*).[42] This allusion to a formulaic statement of faith may also have influenced Huguccio, who added that the candidate must profess "the articles of the faith"; yet this profession seemed more personal than a rote recitation, for he had to mention "how and what he thinks about the articles of the faith."[43] According to this approach, the occasion essentially became a test of personal orthodoxy.

As the twelfth century waned, and thanks to the influence of the *ius novum* and its inclusion of a more recent custom in the pallium's reception, the new oath of fidelity and the traditional profession of faith sat somewhat awkwardly side by side. After mentioning the oath by which the candidate affirmed his beliefs, Huguccio peered into another realm: "Perhaps," he said, "he will add to the oath" elements of a feudal promise.[44] *Animal* mentioned both things as possibilities, "the fidelity that the metropolitan swears to the pope" and "a confession concerning the articles of the faith," which it also described as a pledge to observe the canons, especially those containing the creed.[45] Nevertheless, allusions later in this work betrayed that an oath "to be faithful to the Roman church," offered "for the

---

40. See Braun, *Liturgische Gewandung*, 622.
41. StephTourn ad D.100 c.4 (119), *Omnis* ad D.100 c.4 s.v. *fidei tuae* (1:408), Huguccio ad D.100 c.4 pr. et s.v. *constitutorum* (119v). Huguccio preferred to call papal decretals "decreta" or "constitutiones" here.
42. *Magister* ad D.100 d.a.c.1 (77).
43. Huguccio ad D.100 c.4 pr. et s.v. *tuae fidei* (119v: "articulos fidei"; "qualiter et quid sentiat de articulis fidei").
44. Huguccio ad D.100 c.4 (119v: "forte addet iuramento"), referring to the decretal *Ego Petrus* (which became X 2.24.4) and D.23 c.6.
45. *Animal* ad D.100 c.1 s.v. *quidam fidem* (1273) et ad D.100 c.4 s.v. *minus* (1277).

sake of reverence" for the donor, the pope, was primarily in mind when considering the conferral of the pallium.⁴⁶ The *Glossa Ordinaria* too combined the customs by citing "fidelity, or also the creed"—the conjunction *vel etiam* may have meant that both were necessary.⁴⁷ Later it quoted John of Faenza to the effect that a candidate "ought to swear obedience, and that he should keep the canons," but then it resolved the bifurcated tradition by proposing that the object of the obedience was "apostolic decrees and synodal statutes" rather than the apostolic see itself.⁴⁸

A comment in *Omnis* cast a fascinating light on its time (ca. 1186). As this decretist discussed the profession of faith, he observed: "This must be referred to ancient times, when there were many heretics. For today it is not demanded, because it is not necessary."⁴⁹ In other words, requiring a metropolitan to profess his faith had resulted from the many doctrinal controversies of the ancient church, when determining orthodoxy was crucial. Whether or not he was correct in his esteem for twelfth-century orthodoxy, his words may have indicated that the old profession of faith had fallen away and in practice been replaced by the oath of fidelity. This possibility would also account for the shift in decretist discussions from the profession of faith to the oath of fidelity. If accurate, this significant change in the tradition marked one triumph in the reform papacy's transformation of the pallium into an instrument of loyalty and centralization.

The profession was not only an examination of a prelate's religious beliefs, as Huguccio intimated, but also a guarantee that he would keep his allegiance to the faith, as Honorius maintained.⁵⁰ As such it had to be confirmed in a solemn manner. *Magister* declared that the profession must be rendered to the pope in writing, although *Animal* added that, if the candidate was present in Rome, he could be more

---

46. *Animal* ad C.1 (1287) et ad C.2 q.5 c.1 s.v. *pro recta* [*fide*] (1667–68; ms. K, 1668). *Omnis* ad C.2 q.5 c.1 s.v. *sacramentum* (2:142) similarly testified to swearing "pro obedientia prestanda," with a cross-reference to D.100 c.4.
47. *Glossa Ordinaria* ad D.100 c.1 s.v. *fidem* (638).
48. *Glossa Ordinaria* ad D.100 d.p.c.3 (639–40).
49. *Omnis* ad D.100 c.1 s.v. *episcoporum consecratio protelatur* (1:406–7).
50. Huguccio ad D.100 c.4 pr. et s.v. *tuae fidei* (119v), Honorius ad D.100 c.4 s.v. *sinodorum* et *decretalium* (1:265).

thoroughly examined, as was supposed to happen whenever a prelate was installed; presumably it had an oral interrogation in mind.[51] If submitted in writing, the profession was to be signed. *Omnis* noted that "through a signature someone is seen to agree to the deed done."[52] According to Huguccio, the document was likely invalid without a signature, and *Animal* and the *Glossa Ordinaria* followed this opinion.[53] Further, the profession was to be corroborated by an oath. Stephen, followed by *Omnis* and Huguccio, allowed the oath to be taken either by the candidate himself or through a representative, just as the candidate could receive the pallium in person or through an envoy.[54]

The idea of absentee oathtaking through a messenger—who would swear on a prelate's behalf (*pro eo*), as the *Glossa Ordinaria* put it—raised complex legal questions.[55] Huguccio defended it in principle, insofar as it called to mind the case of a representative who swore on behalf of a mute or sick person who had previously indicated his will by gestures.[56] In an ambiguous passage, *Omnis* provided a procedure for this oath by proxy: before the messenger set out, the sender put his hands on the messenger's head and instructed him to swear on the sender's soul; then, when the messenger arrived, he swore that the sender had ordered him to swear in this way.[57] *Omnis* and Honorius both pointed out that the messenger swore on the sender's soul, but they disagreed about the consequence if the oath were broken. For *Omnis*, the sender, not the messenger, would be "guilty and infamous," while Honorius, citing Roman law, held that the sender had not perjured himself.[58] Later, *Animal* tried a different tack. The messenger actually swore on his own soul, it said, because the oath was based on his own belief about the sender's belief, as if

---

51. *Magister* ad D.100 d.a.c.1 (77), *Animal* ad D.100 c.1 s.v. *quidam fidem* (1273).
52. *Omnis* ad D.100 c.4 s.v. *propria subscriptione* (1:408).
53. Huguccio ad D.100 c.4 s.v. *subscriptionem* (119v), *Animal* ad D.100 c.4 s.v. *subscriptione* (1277), *Glossa Ordinaria* ad D.100 c.4 s.v. *subscriptione* (640).
54. StephTourn ad D.100 c.4 (119), *Omnis* ad D.100 c.4 s.v. *fidei tuae* (1:408), Huguccio ad D.100 c.4 (119v).
55. *Glossa Ordinaria* ad D.100 c.4 (640).
56. Huguccio ad D.100 c.4 s.v. *nec aliquem* (119v).
57. *Omnis* ad D.100 c.4 s.v. *iureiurando* (1:408).
58. *Omnis* ad D.100 c.4 s.v. *iureiurando* (1:408), Honorius ad D.100 c.4 s.v. *iureiurando firmaret miseras* (1:265).

he were to say, "'I swear that he believes that he has a just case.'" Otherwise, if he were to swear calumniously on the sender's soul, he could maliciously "conceive words against his person and bind his soul."[59] Ultimately, Huguccio suggested that an oath was not really necessary. But he admitted that the matter lay in the choice of the one who demanded it (the pope), according to what he found more advantageous, and in view of how much he trusted the candidate.[60]

The decretists accepted Gratian 2's interpretation of Gregory the Great's clause "as the merits of cases demand" to refer to personal worth rather than circumstantial suitability. Indeed, *Animal* reversed Gregory's words by glossing "merits of cases [*causarum meritis*]" with "that is, the causes of merits [*causis meritorum*]."[61] This interpretation allowed them to insist that the candidate should be a man whose good qualities made him eligible for the honor of the pallium. *Magister* said that he must be "worthy," while the *Glossa Ordinaria* required that he be "well deserving."[62] The pope's original concern for prudence was retained, but was given an emphasis that fit well with papal practice since the early Middle Ages.

Finally, the pallium continued to be recognized for its role in the proper accession of an archbishop. Honorius paralleled the three-month maximum period between a metropolitan's consecration and pallium request with the three-month maximum period between a bishop's election and consecration. He seemed to be implying that they were the same because palliation, like consecration, was a major moment in the prelate's installation.[63] Traditionally the pallium had been a sign of papal approval of the regularity of an archbishop's promotion, but it was sought as a final step, after his consecration. Since the middle of the twelfth century, however, decretist jurisprudence had introduced electoral confirmation as a necessary step between

---

59. *Animal* ad D.100 c.4 s.v. *nec aliquem* (1277–78).
60. Huguccio ad D.100 c.4 s.v. *nec aliquem* (119v).
61. *Animal* ad D.100 c.2 s.v. *causarum meritis* (1277).
62. *Magister* ad D.100 c.2 s.v. *et exigentibus meritis causarum* (77), *Glossa Ordinaria* ad D.100 (637) et ad D.100 d.a.c.1 (637–38) et ad D.100 c.2 (639). *Magister* called the candidate "qui est ordinandus," perhaps in the sense of entrance into the *ordo* of the archiepiscopate.
63. Honorius ad D.50 c.11 s.v. *ultra iii* (1:153).

election and consecration; for metropolitans who had no superior short of Rome, some believed that this confirmation pertained to the pope.[64] But how did reception of the pallium after consecration fit into this new system? Huguccio suggested that a metropolitan immediately under the pope should be confirmed by him after election—"unless perhaps it may be said that every archbishop is understood to be confirmed by the pope by the very fact that each receives the pallium from him."[65] This latter possibility explained why a metropolitan might be consecrated without the pope's knowledge, since his contact with Rome to request the pallium (and thus confirmation) would only come afterwards. Yet Huguccio held that such was the case only by custom or special privilege, or if there was a primate above the metropolitan who would have provided confirmation earlier.[66]

What usually happened in this period varied widely from the theories of the canonists, who struggled to account for it. *Animal* proposed that a metropolitan was confirmed either by his primate (if there was one) or by the very fact of his election (if there was not), and this confirmation explained his power to administer certain affairs before receiving the pallium. The later arrival of the vestment completed his power of administration, and so could be seen as a second stage of confirmation.[67] The same work later made a distinction based on distance from Rome: a metropolitan without a primate whose see lay in Italy or nearby provinces was bound to seek papal confirmation, but those in Gaul, England, and Germany, as well as the *transmarini et remoti*, were not. Even so, "all metropolitans, however far off they be, ought to seek the pallium," even if that meant a double act of papal confirmation for Italians.[68] By the time of the *Glossa Ordinaria*, the popes were trying to consolidate their claim on

64. See Benson, *Bishop-elect*, 173–89.
65. Huguccio ad D.63 c.9 s.v. *consentimus* (84r: "nisi forte dicatur quod quilibet archiepiscopus hoc ipso intelligitur confirmari a papa, quia quilibet ab eo accipit pallium").
66. Huguccio ad D.100 c.11 s.v. *ordinatum* (120r).
67. *Animal* ad D.23 c.1 s.v. *sicut papa* (451–53).
68. *Animal* ad D.63 c.9 s.v. *consentimus* (1065–66) et ad D.63 c.24 (1088) et ad D.100 c.11 s.v. *ordinant* (1282–83). Italian bishops had always been treated more strictly in regard to their installation, since they lay within the pope's immediate sphere of influence.

confirmation by means of the pallium. This apparatus recognized that, according to custom, it seemed that the only say the pope had in a metropolitan's installation was the conferral of the vestment; "today, nevertheless, the pope wishes that confirmation be sought from him along with the pallium."[69] Once more the papacy called upon the woolen band to cement its power. The popes wanted an earlier, more formal role in approving metropolitan elections, and this effort was naturally coupled with the pallium grant, which had for centuries provided confirmation as a final step.

By fulfilling these prerequisites, could the recipient incur the guilt of ambition or simony?

Especially because so many prerequisites were customary in obtaining the pallium, it had often been an occasion for simony or the appearance of simony. *Magister* toed the Gregorian line when it maintained that the would-be palliger "owes nothing, even to the writer" of the accompanying privilege.[70] Occasionally a decretist seemed to verge on laxity in this area. *Elegantius*, for example, did not prohibit an *honorarium* or gifts (*euxenia*) "offered in the name of good will"; furthermore, a scribe without a fixed salary was permitted to demand "the price of labor and parchment."[71] While condemning a simoniacal intention preceding ordination, Honorius felt that an intention to offer something following ordination might be acceptable when rendering a "sign of subjection," as when a benefice or the pallium was bestowed.[72] For the most part, however, the canonists sought to distance traditional pallium practice from any implication of simony. Huguccio denounced the pallium fee as an *antiqua consuetudo et pessima* that was simoniacal, at least in appearance, and had long (and rightly) been forbidden, and the *Glossa Ordinaria* said much the same.[73] The mention of the appearance of simony acknowledged

69. *Glossa Ordinaria* ad D.100 c.11 s.v. *ordinatum* (644).
70. *Magister* ad C.1 q.2 c.4 (92).
71. *Elegantius* 4.30 (2:11–12).
72. Honorius ad C.1 q.1 c.21§2 s.v. *sive ante sive post* (1:281).
73. Huguccio ad D.100 c.3 (119v) et ad C.1 q.2 c.4 s.v. *pallium* (135v), *Glossa Ordinaria* ad D.100 c.3 (639).

that some offerings might be simple expressions of thanks, which Gregory the Great had allowed, but concern to avoid scandal and to uproot every trace of the sin was paramount in the post-reform medieval church. *Animal* gave the most theologically reasoned account: "Sometimes something can be given for that which is due.... But it is different in the pallium because the metropolitan obtains a spiritual thing in the conferral of the pallium, for then he has the power to consecrate bishops."[74] Purchasing spiritual things, of course, was the very definition of simony.

Closely related to simony, and frequently lying at its root, was the vice of ambition. In the canons assembled in the *Decretum*, John VIII called the pallium "desired," and Gregory the Great urged that it be asked for "vigorously." How could requesting the vestment—often labeled an "honor"—not be construed as ambitious? Simon proposed (rather unconvincingly) that John VIII's *optatum pallium* referred to the pope's desire to bestow the pallium, not the archbishop's to receive it. Alternatively, if the archbishop desired it, his intent was not to lord it over his subjects, but to be of service to them out of charity.[75] *Omnis* and Huguccio repeated these two possibilities, with the second memorably phrased as *non ut praeesses, sed ut prodesses*.[76] As for the required vigor of the request, *Omnis* and Honorius excused it because it occurred after consecration; the archbishop was already in place, and acquiring the pallium was expected of him. Ambition was no longer at issue.[77] To Huguccio, seeking the vestment was simply an "accessory" or "consequence" of a metropolitan's consecration, and therefore reflected no ambition or simoniacal intent. Still, to be safe, "each person should consult his own conscience and beware of committing simony in it."[78] The *Glossa Ordinaria* tried a different route to the same answer: insistence was allowed, and even

---

74. *Animal* ad D.100 c.2 s.v. *et fortiter* (1277).

75. SimonBis ad D.100 c.4 s.v. *optatum* (88–89).

76. *Omnis* ad D.100 c.4 s.v. *optatum* (1:408), Huguccio ad D.100 c.4 s.v. *optatum* (119v).

77. *Omnis* ad D.100 c.2 s.v. *fortiter postulanti* (1:407–8), Honorius ad D.100 c.2 s.v. *fortiter postulanti* (1:265).

78. Huguccio ad D.100 c.2 s.v. *postulanti* (119r–v: "accessoria et sequelam suae consecrationis"; "unusquisque suam consulat conscientiam et caveat ne in ipsa symoniam committat").

advantageous, when one exercised a right.[79] Although one could not claim in an absolute sense to have a right to the gift of the pallium, since so many conditions had to be met, nevertheless an archbishop was required by law to secure its possession.

Simony could come in many forms, and making a pact, imposing a condition, or exacting a promise or guarantee before conferring a spiritual good qualified as simoniacal. Nevertheless, Gregory himself had placed a condition on his pallium grant to Syagrius of Autun, and the decretists discussed at length how this was possible. *Omnis* and Honorius permitted a pact if it was made after a prelate's election (and, for *Omnis*, after his confirmation as well).[80] Huguccio was subtler: the pact had to be licit (of which he provided several examples), and it could occur before or after the gift (if imposed by a superior) or only after the gift (if imposed by an inferior).[81] In the eyes of *Animal*, the pact had to be honorable and *de substantia rei*—that is, not extrinsically connected, but involved in the very nature of the gift. Such a proviso in the pallium's bestowal was not really a condition, but instead the manner of its reception.[82] In the *Glossa Ordinaria* Johannes Teutonicus listed three factors that made a pact licit: it had to occur after the election, to concern ecclesiastical property, custom, or doctrine, and to be required by a superior. As to whether it was really a condition, Johannes posed arguments both *pro* and *contra*, without resolution. His editor, Bartholomew of Brescia, more decisively embraced the permissibility of "an honorable and licit condition."[83]

Among these pacts or conditions, the requirement of an oath of fidelity especially interested *Animal*, perhaps because it was sometimes questioned in this period.[84] In a number of different ways, the author strove to justify this obligation. Only an oath required by old custom, not a newly invented, *ad hoc* promise, he said, was acceptable—one to which the candidate was bound by the very fact of taking office. A

79. *Glossa Ordinaria* ad D.100 c.2 s.v. *et fortiter* (639).
80. *Omnis* ad D.100 c.5 s.v. *si prius se promiserit* (1:408) et ad C.1 q.2 c.2 s.v. *absit pactio* (2:76), Honorius ad D.100 c.5 s.v. *si prius* (1:265).
81. Huguccio ad D.100 c.5 s.v. *si prius* (119v).
82. *Animal* ad D.100 c.5 s.v. *si prius* (1278–79).
83. *Glossa Ordinaria* ad D.100 c.5 s.v. *quod transmisimus* (641).
84. See 442–43 below.

person commanded to do something in order to gain something that he was already obliged to seek, such as the pallium, did not commit simony. His oath was not for the purpose of obtaining the vestment, but rather he was already going to obtain it and was consequently made to swear. In effect, "the pallium is not given because he swears, but he swears because it is given." The condition was not causal (as if the oath resulted in the pallium), but consequential (the anticipated pallium resulted in the oath). In this practice lay no wicked or dishonorable purpose. The pact—better called a "display of the law," an explication of what one was expected to do in one's office—was connected (*annexum*) to the office, part of the responsibility being assumed.[85] Despite the author's zeal in trying to reconcile the prerequisites of the pallium with the church's strict rules against simony, his arguments were not wholly convincing. If a candidate refused to take the oath, he would not receive the pallium, and so it was no mere consequence, as if the gift would happen no matter what.

How was the Johannine law to be applied?

By choosing *Quoniam quidam*, John VIII's pallium regulation from 875, as the core of the only *distinctio* dedicated to the pallium, Gratian 1 had assured its observance for the future. But it was not always clear how to interpret its provisions. Into this situation stepped the decretists, who attempted to resolve the concomitant problems raised by this law. For example, although the *Decretum* used the Roman version of the canon, *Magister* must have also been familiar with the Ravennese version, for it followed the latter in mentioning an exception to the obligation—"unless he is hindered by need"—and instructing what to do in such a case—he should "explain the reason why [he] cannot."[86] Huguccio provided insight into the motives of those who shirked the obligation (cited at the beginning of the text) by glossing "refusing [*detractantes*]" as "evading [*subterfugientes*] and

---

85. *Animal* ad D.61 c.18 s.v. *subdiaconus* (1054) et ad D.63 c.28 s.v. *iuramenta* (1095–96) et ad D.79 c.2 s.v. *remuneratione* (ms. L, 1190) et ad C.1 (1287) et ad C.1 q.2 c.2 s.v. *omnis pactio* (1424–25).

86. *Magister* ad D.100 d.a.c.1 (77) et ad D.100 c.1 s.v. *ultra* (77). The first phrase seems garbled; probably the "et" should be read as "aut."

putting off [*differentes*]."⁸⁷ Possibly his words indicated common excuses in his own time, as some archbishops tried to dodge the obligation or continually postponed its fulfillment. Since translations of bishops to archiepiscopal sees were becoming more common in this period, *Animal* noted that the law did not discuss such a case, when the candidate had already been consecrated to the episcopal order. It hinted, moreover, that the law's obligation was then unnecessary, because the pope must approve every translation, and so presumably would include the pallium with the appointment that he had authorized.⁸⁸

A number of canonists addressed the three-month deadline for requesting the pallium. According to Huguccio, one should begin counting from the day of the archbishop's consecration—or, with a nod to the growing practice of translation, his confirmation "if he was a bishop before."⁸⁹ The later suggestion of *Animal*, just discussed, questioned this theory, but the *Glossa Ordinaria* accepted it.⁹⁰ (Surprisingly, however, the latter work defined the three months as "within what time [the pallium] ought to be sought *and given*," even though the canon imposed no deadline on the pope's side, and it would have been difficult for emissaries from distant lands not only to set out for Rome but also to achieve their quest within the set period.)⁹¹ *Omnis* provided a rationale for the deadline by comparing it to the similar period of three months allowed both for a bishop's election and for his consecration.⁹² Still, many scholars noted that, later in *Quoniam quidam*, a bishop elected to a see was given five months to be consecrated before he lost the office. Why the disparity between the obligation incumbent upon a bishop to be consecrated and the one incumbent upon an archbishop to be palliated? Simon found it "amazing," perhaps because it made the sacrament of orders seem less important than the custom of palliation. But he justified it by ob-

---

87. Huguccio ad D.100 c.1 s.v. *detractantes* (119r).
88. *Animal* ad D.100 c.1 s.v. *ut quisquis metropolitanus* (1275).
89. Huguccio ad D.100 c.1 s.v. *ultra tres menses consecrationis* (119r: "si ante erat episcopus").
90. *Glossa Ordinaria* ad D.100 c.1 s.v. *consecrationis* (638).
91. *Glossa Ordinaria* ad D.100 d.a.c.1 (637–38); emphasis added.
92. *Omnis* ad D.50 c.11 s.v. *postquam* (1:210–11) et ad D.63 c.35 s.v. *infra tres menses* (1:299).

serving that an archbishop's negligence hurt the church more than a bishop's did.[93] *Omnis* agreed, for "a greater danger is feared from the delay of an archbishop," and Honorius thought the same.[94] Huguccio and *Animal* demonstrated why archbishops should be treated "more severely" and bishops "more mildly": a metropolitan "ought to provide for many," but a simple bishop "for one church alone," and "a province needs the promotion of a metropolitan more than a cathedral church the promotion of a bishop."[95] The higher up the hierarchy one went, the greater the consequences for the church, and the greater the harm if those offices were neglected.

The Johannine law also referred to three warnings to be proffered to a negligent metropolitan. This was odd, according to *Animal*; why were warnings needed when a deadline had already been imposed? Its solution was that warnings were not necessary for a self-imposed deadline, but were necessary when dealing with a general rule.[96] Both Honorius and Huguccio believed that the warnings had to be given during the three-month period, since afterwards the penalty of deposition would be inflicted. Huguccio further laid this responsibility on the archbishop's suffragans; if they failed to warn him, he could not use this excuse to avoid the law's penalty, but the negligent suffragans themselves lost the right to accuse him.[97] The *Glossa Ordinaria*, in contrast, cited an opinion that appended two months to the three-month grace period. The warnings were to be given during those two months, and if they were heeded, "the delay can be purged"—that is, the violation of the law could be remedied be-

93. SimonBis ad D.100 c.1 s.v. *quod si ultra v menses* (88).
94. *Omnis* ad D.100 c.1 s.v. *quod si ultra quinque menses* (1:407), Honorius ad D.100 c.1 s.v. *ultra v* (1:264).
95. Huguccio ad D.100 c.1 s.v. *quod si ultra v menses* (119r: "ille multis, iste uni soli ecclesiae providere debet ... et ideo severius cum archiepiscopo et mitius agitur cum episcopo"), *Animal* ad D.100 c.1 s.v. *quod si ultra quinque menses* (1276). *Animal* added that a parish church could remain vacant for six months, since the danger posed by vacancy was less than those on the diocesan or provincial level. Huguccio alluded to an opinion that applied the five-month deadline in the second part of the canon to the first part concerning the pallium, but he did not develop this stance.
96. *Animal* ad D.100 c.1 s.v. *post secundam et tertiam* (1275). In order to make sense of this passage, an extra "non" must be removed.
97. Honorius ad D.100 c.1 s.v. *tertiam commonitionem* (1:264), Huguccio ad D.100 c.1 s.v. *post secundam et tertiam* (119r).

fore punishment loomed.⁹⁸ As for the exaction of that penalty, both Huguccio and the *Glossa Ordinaria* did not make it an automatic consequence of noncompliance. It occurred not by the power of the law (*ipso iure*), but through a judicial proceeding (*per sententiam coram iudice*) after an accusation, so that the pope (or his delegate) might explore the circumstances of the case. Huguccio went on to extrapolate, based on the second part of the canon, that the one found guilty could never again be a bishop or archbishop there or elsewhere.⁹⁹

What happened if use of the pallium was refused or withdrawn?

Gregory the Great's threat to forbid Natalis of Salona the use of the pallium provided canonists with an opportunity to consider the effects of such an action. Stephen set the stage by directly equating the *usus pallii* with the *dignitas archiepiscopi*, the very rank and office of an archbishop.¹⁰⁰ Removing the former would result in disabling the latter. However, both Simon and Honorius remarked that further contumacy would have brought about Natalis's deposition, which intimated that the withdrawal of the pallium's use was not as severe a punishment as the complete loss of the archiepiscopate.¹⁰¹ It was *Omnis* and Huguccio who drew the final conclusion, which also made it into the *Glossa Ordinaria*: the prohibition to wear the pallium was tantamount to suspension from the archiepiscopal office. Huguccio in particular definitively ruled out deposition; instead, it was a loss of the *honor archiepiscopalis*, which was incarnated in the pallium.¹⁰²

---

98. *Glossa Ordinaria* ad D.100 c.1 s.v. *post secundam* (639). Cf. Huguccio ad D.100 c.1 s.v. *quod si ultra v menses* (119r).

99. Huguccio ad D.100 c.1 s.v. *caret dignitate sibi* (119r), *Glossa Ordinaria* ad D.100 c.1 s.v. *tres menses* (638). *Omnis* ad D.100 c.1 s.v. *commissa sibi careat dignitate* (1:407) earlier brought up the question of whether the penalty was automatic or imposed, but did not answer it.

100. StephTourn ad D.74 c.8 s.v. *usum pallii* (98–99).

101. SimonBis ad D.74 c.8 s.v. *quem si etiam amisso pallio in eadem pertinacia adhuc perseverare perspexeris Dominici quoque corporis* (66), Honorius ad D.74 c.8 s.v. *contradices privabis* (1:215).

102. *Omnis* ad D.74 c.8 s.v. *participatione privabis* (1:323–24), Huguccio ad D.74 c.8 s.v. *usum pallii et privabis* (94r), *Glossa Ordinaria* ad D.74 c.8 s.v. *adhuc* (476). A palliated suffragan, according to Huguccio, would simply be stripped of the "honor pallii," apparently without impact on his episcopal office.

This interpretation went back at least to Bernold of Constance in the later years of Gregory VII's pontificate.[103] Presumably it implied that the archbishop's later cooperation would cause the suspension to be lifted and the use of the vestment to be restored.

Some decretists seemed to hope that the pope would employ the pallium more often in penalizing prelates. For the sake of avoiding the appearance of simony, *Omnis* held that it would be "safer" for the pallium to be granted without strings attached. Then, if the palliger later disobeyed in some way, the pope could forbid the vestment's use.[104] In theory this approach made sense, but papal control was more easily exercised in the giving of the gift; once a palliger in a remote church possessed it, he might ignore the pope's interventions if he thought he could. Commenting on John VIII's denial of the pallium to Willibert of Cologne, Huguccio asserted that the matter had not actually been up to the pope's discretion. "By law" he should not have granted Willibert's petition, for there could be no allowance to do illegal things.[105] It is doubtful that the papacy would have readily embraced this legal obligation to withhold the pallium, which restricted the freedom of the donor.

How should the pallium be received?

Considering how forcefully the reform papacy had pushed for candidates to come to Rome to receive the pallium in person, it is startling to note the absence of such a principle in the decretist works. This silence must have reflected the fact that the policy of personal reception had met with significant obstacles and had more or less fallen away in practice. A rare, albeit ambiguous, trace of the policy may be glimpsed in *Magister* when it analyzed why Pope Zachary had instructed the eighth-century missionary Boniface to send his chosen successor to Rome for ordination. Probably the writer was unaware that such missionaries were regarded as Roman suffragans. His explanation was that, having succeeded Boniface the palliated archbishop, this new bishop had to go and fetch his own pallium,

---

103. *Apologeticus*, in MGH LdL 2:86.
104. *Omnis* ad D.100 c.5 s.v. *si prius se promiserit* (1:408).
105. Huguccio ad D.100 c.4 s.v. *nequivimus* (119v: "de iure").

apparently in person.[106] Still, this evidence was exceptional. When the canonists of this period mentioned the mode of reception at all, approaching the pope personally was usually presented merely as an option. Thus *Animal*, discussing the profession of faith, noted the difference between a papal examination of a metropolitan's faith in person "at the reception of the pallium, if he is present"—that is, at the papal court—and, "if absent," the submission of a written confession of faith, which he sent to the pope.[107] To Huguccio, it was also conceivable that the pope could designate an intermediary to deliver the vestment. As a rule, he said, "every archbishop receives the pallium from the pope"—whether in person or through the archbishop's emissaries—"unless the pope, wishing to defer to his primate, sends the pallium, and the archbishop receives it from him."[108] In effect, this procedure bolstered the position of the local primate by appointing him a papal stand-in.

Although obtaining the pallium in person was not seen as necessary, it happened anyway if the candidate went to Rome for consecration. *Magister* seemed to entertain that possibility. Commenting on the traditional obligation in *Quoniam quidam*, it added a condition so ordinary that, in former times, it would have gone without saying: "If perhaps they are ordained by their suffragans, they ought to seek the pallium within three months."[109] An alternative that the writer may have had in mind—one that did not require the usual approach to the apostolic see—was ordination by the pope himself, in which case the pallium would be granted immediately thereafter and the Johannine law would be unnecessary.[110] Otherwise, he stipulated that metropolitans should request the vestment "themselves or through a messenger." *Magister* thus acknowledged a mounting re-

106. *Magister* ad C.7 q.1 c.17 s.v. *ut huc veniat ordinandus* (136). Possibly "ordination" in this case actually referred to entrance into the *ordo* of the archiepiscopate.

107. *Animal* ad D.100 c.1 s.v. *quidam fidem* (1273).

108. Huguccio ad D.63 c.9 s.v. *consentimus* (84r: "quilibet archiepiscopus accipit pallium a papa, nisi papa volens deferre primati eius mittat pallium et ab eo accipiat archiepiscopus").

109. *Magister* ad D.100 d.a.c.1 (77).

110. Another possibility was ordination by a primate, but the Johannine obligation would still have applied. A third possibility was translation from another see, for which the pallium may have routinely accompanied papal approval.

ality in the twelfth-century Western church. Archbishops immediately under the pope (that is, lacking an intervening primate) were increasingly being consecrated by him, and by 1257 the pope was insisting upon this practice.[111] To the extent that prelates obeyed, it appeared that the reform policy of personal reception was regaining ground, if not as such, at least as a concomitant to a new policy of papal consecration.

What relationship did the pallium establish between donor and recipient?

For the decretists, the papal prerogative of bestowing the pallium set the pope apart from all other bishops. *Animal* listed *pallii largitio* among "those things that the supreme pontiff has reserved to himself," which "no bishop should dare to presume."[112] Because of the papal origin and control of the pallium, it was called "apostolic," according to Huguccio and the *Glossa Ordinaria*, and no one could wear it without the pope's leave.[113] Furthermore, because the archbishop of Ravenna in Gregory the Great's era had been found to be misusing the vestment, *Animal* held that an appeal to local custom could not be used as an excuse to injure another (here, the Roman) church's rights. Since "it belonged to the pope to give the pallium," the archbishop could not wear it "to the prejudice of the pope."[114] In short, the vestment came from the pope, which justified his continued say over its use and his control over its wearer. Only the pope could grant the pallium, and only he determined who wore it and how it was worn.

Presuming that the palliger submitted to papal authority in these respects, his standing in the church changed as he was now, in some sense, a papal agent. Simon, followed by *Omnis*, interpreted Gregory the Great's coupling of John of Prima Justiniana's pallium grant with

---

111. See Benson, *Bishop-elect*, 184–85.
112. *Animal* ad D.17 c.3 s.v. *huic sedi concessa* (mss. K/K2, 305–6) et ad C.2 q.6 c.10 s.v. *ideo huic sedi* (ms. K2, 1735). This claim had been advanced at least since Leo IV rebuked Patriarch Ignatius of Constantinople between 847 and 853 (JE 2647, BH 113, MGH Epp. 5:607).
113. Huguccio ad De cons. D.1 c.56 s.v. *apostolico* (434v: "apostolico"), *Glossa Ordinaria* ad De cons. D.1 c.56 s.v. *apostolico* (2496).
114. *Animal* ad D.100 c.8 s.v. *consuetudine generali* (1281–82).

an apostolic vicariate in one of two ways. Either the pope was simply appointing him legate, or the pope presumed that all such churchmen were papal vicars insofar as they were called "to a share of the responsibility," though not to the papal "fullness of power."[115] Again that ancient dyad was employed to illustrate the derivative responsibility and limited jurisdiction of a lesser prelate, as compared to and based on the pope's universal sway. Huguccio added a few thoughts to this tradition. The first interpretation, he said, would have meant the renewal of a legatine privilege, as John's predecessor had received before him. Huguccio also extended the second interpretation to "all bishops"—but since not all bishops sported the pallium, this approach failed to explain the connection between the vestment and the vicariate.[116] Later the *Glossa Ordinaria* added a third option opposed to the second: perhaps John had formerly been a papal legate, but ceased to be one when he became an archbishop, and so now the pope restored his position.[117] These canonistic attempts to make sense of Gregory's letter did not address the pallium's role explicitly. But apparently a palliger's bond with Rome at least made him suitable to represent Roman authority, if not also implicitly a papal legate.

How was the use of the pallium limited to its recipient?

Among matters that "need greater investigation," Honorius posed the question: "If an archbishop has to minister in another's church and does not have his own pallium [with him], will he be able [to minister] with another's [pallium]?"[118] At his time this question, which touched on the pallium's nature as a privilege, had not yet been definitively settled. However, *Omnis* had already offered an opinion. Responding to queries about the necessity for each succeeding archbishop to acquire a new pallium, rather than using his predecessor's, and about the permissibility of lending his pallium to a visiting archbishop, this work declared: "He can neither use the old

---

115. SimonBis ad D.100 c.10 s.v. *et vices suas sedis apostolice agere* (89); *Omnis* ad D.100 c.10 s.v. *vices sedis apostolicae* (1:410).
116. Huguccio ad D.100 c.10 s.v. *vices apostolicae sedis* (120r: "omnes episcopi"). The first option, he noted, was "de iure communi."
117. *Glossa Ordinaria* ad D.100 c.10 s.v. *vices* (644).
118. Honorius ad D.100 c.6 s.v. *ad sola* (1:265).

one nor lend his new one to another, for the privilege is personal; thus it does not transcend the person."[119] Anticipating the doctrine of the decretalists on this topic, *Omnis* may have been aware of a decretal of Alexander III that would eventually be taken into the *Liber Extra*.[120] *Animal* and the *Glossa Ordinaria* both reflected this tradition, which maintained that the pallium's nature as a personal gift meant that it could not be lent or borrowed, and that it must be buried with its recipient.[121] Even so, the *Glossa Ordinaria* betrayed some ambivalence: "These privileges were personal and passed away with the person.... Yet they ought to be granted to his successor when he asks, and injury is done to him unless it is granted to him; still, it is a favor if it is granted to him.... But nevertheless a judge can and ought to do many things to which he cannot be compelled."[122] This paradoxical attitude, that the pallium was a gift freely bestowed upon a person, but somehow also a debt routinely expected for a see—that the pope was not forced to grant this *beneficium*, but somehow also bound by custom and expectation—was nothing new in the vestment's history, but rarely had the conflicting currents been so clearly juxtaposed.

How was the recipient limited in his use of the pallium?

A *dictum* of Gratian 2 had emphasized that the pallium should be worn only in church, on certain days, during the Mass. That the use of the pallium was subject to restrictions could not be doubted, but some decretists did not understand why. *Omnis* shrugged, "The reason is hidden."[123] Honorius called for further inquiry and asked, "Why not outside, or not on other days?"[124] Although they found no solution, *Animal* provided fodder for an answer when it noted, among other prerogatives unique to the pope, that "he wears pallia always."[125] The

---

119. Omnis ad D.100 c.6 s.v. *ad sola missarum sollemnia* (1:408–9).
120. X 1.8.2; see 447–48 below.
121. *Animal* ad D.100 c.6 s.v. *missarum sollempnia* (1279–80), *Glossa Ordinaria* ad D.100 c.6 s.v. *intra tuam ecclesiam* (641).
122. *Glossa Ordinaria* ad D.100 c.11 s.v. *atque privilegia* (645).
123. Omnis ad D.100 c.6 s.v. *ad sola missarum sollemnia* (1:408–9).
124. Honorius ad D.100 c.6 s.v. *ad sola* (1:265).
125. *Animal* ad C.2 q.6 c.10 s.v. *ideo huic sedi* (ms. K2, 1735).

lack of restrictions enjoyed by the Roman bishop could be compared to the lesser palliger's imposed limitations; the difference was that between pope and bishop, between donor and recipient.

None of these decretists offered a definitive list of the "certain days" mentioned by Gratian, probably because they varied from palliger to palliger. *Omnis* described them as "feast days," and cited Maundy Thursday as an example from later in the *Decretum*; similarly, Honorius called them "special days," with the same cross-reference.[126] As for the restriction to the Mass, *Animal* specified that it had to be a solemn Mass, not a low Mass (*missa privata*), which may have been suggested by the fact that pallium days were always major festivals and occasions.[127] Huguccio added that the palliger himself had to be celebrating Mass; otherwise—when he himself was not presiding at the liturgy, perhaps during the visit of some dignitary—he should not wear the pallium.[128] At liturgical events outside the Mass, the pallium was not allowed. They included the Divine Office (which *Magister* mistakenly proposed as John of Ravenna's abuse when he had fallen afoul of Gregory the Great), as well as processions outside church, as *Omnis*, *Animal*, and the *Glossa Ordinaria* all declared.[129] *Omnis* anticipated a later decretal of Celestine III, which was recognized by the latter two works and eventually made it into the *Liber Extra*.[130] The *Glossa Ordinaria*, however, went on to mention an exception to the rule: a palliger could wear the vestment at a synod, presumably a provincial synod over which he was presiding.[131]

The case of the Ravennese pallium abuse, as enshrined by Gratian 2, fascinated the decretists. Perhaps they shared Gregory the Great's fear that, if a single palliger's "usurpation" were left unchallenged, "others may presume such things," as *Magister* put it.[132] Neverthe-

---

126. *Omnis* ad D.100 c.6 s.v. *ad sola missarum sollemnia* (1:408–9), Honorius ad D.100 c.6 s.v. *ad sola* (1:265), both referring to De cons. D.1 c.56.

127. *Animal* ad D.100 c.6 s.v. *missarum sollempnia* (1279–80).

128. Huguccio ad D.100 c.6 s.v. *ad sola* (119v).

129. *Magister* ad D.100 c.8 (77), *Omnis* ad D.100 c.6 s.v. *ad sola missarum sollemnia* (1:408–9), *Animal* ad D.100 c.6 s.v. *missarum sollempnia* (1279–80), *Glossa Ordinaria* ad D.100 c.6 s.v. *missarum* (641–42).

130. X 1.8.1; see 447–48 below.

131. *Glossa Ordinaria* ad D.100 c.6 s.v. *missarum* (641–42).

132. *Magister* ad D.100 c.8 s.v. *quod si* (78).

less, because Gregory had allowed the possibility that the archbishop of Ravenna might have had a special privilege permitting him to wear the pallium outside the Mass or outside church, *Magister* held that a metropolitan could have the right to do so *ex privilegio*.[133] This point seemed crucial to Huguccio: no less than four times in his work he hammered home that such a *privilegium speciale* might expand the permissible use of the vestment, and the *Glossa Ordinaria* followed this opinion.[134]

Even so, the canonists debated whether there were other justifications for contravening the general restrictions on the pallium's use. Stephen admitted "special custom" in addition to a "special privilege," and the *Glossa Ordinaria* entertained the idea that "the custom of other churches does not repeal the custom of this one."[135] However, *Omnis*, followed by Honorius, felt that "special" or "particular custom" was not mentioned in Gregory's letter because it applied only to "performing the offices of the church," not to "discussing cases."[136] Apparently this approach saw the Ravennese situation as a juridical, not a liturgical, matter. For *Animal*, "special custom" could only govern things belonging to a local church, while the use of the pallium touched on something belonging to the pope and thus might injure his rights.[137] In addition, Simon ruled out "prescription" (a longstanding custom that obtains force through the passage of time), because the pallium's use was not a general right, able to be modified by local usage, and prescription could not create such a right.[138] As a privilege, not a right, wearing the vestment was not subject to local variations, but reliant entirely on papal dictate. Although Honorius, Huguccio, and the *Glos-*

133. *Magister* ad D.100 c.8 s.v. *paene* (77).
134. Huguccio ad D.100 d.a.c.1 (119r) et ad D.100 d.p.c.3 s.v. *paene* (119v) et ad D.100 c.6 s.v. *ad sola* (119v) et ad D.100 c.8 s.v. *prope* (119v), *Glossa Ordinaria* ad D.100 d.a.c.1 (637–38).
135. StephTourn ad D.100 c.8 s.v. *si hoc non ostenditur* (119), *Glossa Ordinaria* ad D.100 c.8 s.v. *omnium* (643).
136. *Omnis* ad D.100 c.8 s.v. *si hoc non ostenderit* (1:409), Honorius ad D.100 c.8 s.v. *nec consuetudine generali nec privilegio* (1:266). For Huguccio and the *Glossa Ordinaria*, see 438 below.
137. *Animal* ad D.100 c.8 s.v. *generalis ecclesie consuetudinem* et *consuetudine generali* (1280–82).
138. SimonBis ad D.100 c.8 s.v. *usurpasse te comprobes quod fecisti* (89).

sa Ordinaria seemed to agree with Simon, *Animal* disagreed.[139] Many of these questions involved subtle points of law, but they shed light on the implications of the use of the pallium as a papal privilege.

How was the authority of the recipient dependent on the pallium?
Full exercise of the office of an archbishop, primate, or patriarch required the acquisition of the pallium from the pope.[140] Rufinus conceived a pithy way of expressing this fact when he stated that their *dignitas* was not only "less adorned [*minus decorata*]" without the vestment, but even "incomplete [*imperfecta*]."[141] Huguccio and the *Glossa Ordinaria* also posited an incompleteness, and the latter invoked the pallium's by now common epithet when it added that it was the "fullness of the pontifical office."[142] Honorius put it his own way: "Their authority is small or none without the pallium."[143] This deficiency in an unpalliated archbishop's position prevented him from performing his most essential functions, the foremost of which was ordaining bishops. Although Gratian 1 had not found the logic of *Quoniam quidam*—which connected possession of the pallium to the right to consecrate suffragan bishops—to be clear enough, *Magister* and Huguccio dismissed his concern and accepted the Johannine law's implicit rationale.[144] While some decretists summarized

139. Honorius ad D.100 c.8 s.v. *nec consuetudine generali nec privilegio* (1:266), Huguccio ad D.100 c.8 s.v. *restat ut postquam* (119v–120r), *Glossa Ordinaria* ad D.100 c.8 s.v. *te comprobes* (643), *Animal* ad D.100 c.8 s.v. *consuetudine generali* (1281–82).

140. Because Gratian had equated primates and patriarchs, some decretists omitted one or the other term: Rufinus ad D.100 (194), Honorius ad D.100 d.a.c.1 (1:264), Huguccio ad D.100 d.a.c.1 (119r), *Glossa Ordinaria* ad D.100 (637) et ad D.100 d.a.c.1 (637–38). Some even omitted both terms, perhaps because palligers were most commonly archbishops, or because primates and patriarchs were essentially higher kinds of archbishops: Roland ad D.100 (12), StephTourn ad D.100 (119).

141. Rufinus ad D.100 (194). The word choice recalled John VIII's 873 letter to Willibert of Cologne (JE 2986, GP 7.1:34 no. 66, BU 96, MGH Epp. 7:314).

142. Huguccio ad D.100 d.a.c.1 (119r), *Glossa Ordinaria* ad D.100 (637) et ad D.100 d.a.c.1 (637–38).

143. Honorius ad D.100 d.a.c.1 (1:264).

144. *Magister* ad D.100 d.a.c.1 s.v. *minus evidenter* (77), Huguccio ad D.100 d.a.c.1 s.v. *licet minus evidenter* (119r) et ad D.100 c.1 s.v. *ac per hoc* (119r). In defense of the canon's logic, Huguccio juxtaposed it with the three-month deadline for consecrating bishops promulgated by the Council of Chalcedon, c. 25.

this law in absolute terms—unpalliated archbishops were forbidden "to ordain," or "to celebrate ordinations," or "to consecrate"—it may be assumed that they had bishops in mind, given that *Quoniam quidam* immediately followed.[145]

But did the prohibition extend to further functions? Honorius, *Animal*, and the *Glossa Ordinaria* included convoking provincial synods; the last, moreover, went so far as to encompass all episcopal duties or services (*officia*).[146] This development moved beyond a metropolitan's role as a bishop over other bishops, as the head of a province, and affected even his duties as a bishop in his own diocese. In a similar vein, Huguccio listed ordaining lesser clergy, dedicating churches and altars, veiling virgins, and consecrating chrism among the deeds prohibited to an unpalliated archbishop, though he did not clarify his reasoning; perhaps he considered them all consecratory acts. However, he excluded juridical acts of administration, such as hearing cases, rendering verdicts, and accepting appeals.[147] The *Glossa Ordinaria* listed consecrating virgins, ordaining clerics, and participating in synods as *episcopalia iura*: "Even though the elect himself is consecrated, he cannot exercise episcopal rights before receiving the pallium."[148] *Animal*, furthermore, extended the law's reach even to certain acts of administration or jurisdiction: some the archbishop could do before the pallium, but others, such as calling synods, depended on the vestment.[149] Honorius may have agreed, for he claimed that an unpalliated metropolitan could not receive his suffragans' oaths of obedience—another act of jurisdiction—until he had obtained the vestment.[150]

If an archbishop broke the law and performed a forbidden function, the canonists generally acknowledged its validity, which indi-

---

145. Paucapalea ad D.100 (50), Roland ad D.100 (12, understanding "ordinari" as "ordinare"), StephTourn ad D.100 (119), *Glossa Ordinaria* ad D.100 (637).

146. Honorius ad D.100 d.a.c.1 (1:264), *Animal* ad D.100 c.1 s.v. *protelatur* (1273–75), *Glossa Ordinaria* ad D.100 c.6 s.v. *missarum* (641–42) et ad D.100 d.a.c.1 (637–38).

147. Huguccio ad D.100 c.1 s.v. *ac per hoc* (119r).

148. *Glossa Ordinaria* ad D.100 c.1 s.v. *episcoporum* (638).

149. *Animal* ad D.23 c.1 s.v. *sicut papa* (451–53). Celebrating synods (a liturgical action) was probably seen in earlier times as an act of order, but this canonist considered it an act of jurisdiction, which may have caused this bifurcated approach to an archbishop's administrative powers.

150. Honorius ad D.100 c.1 s.v. *ac per hoc* (1:264).

cated that his need for the pallium was a manmade rule, not a fundamental facet of his power. Although Rufinus used the word *valeat*, hinting that consecrations without the pallium were null and void, Paucapalea preferred *licet*, and Honorius similarly characterized the effect of acquiring the vestment as "permission [*licentia*] to consecrate bishops and gather comprovincial councils."[151] In the latter view, a metropolitan needed papal license to carry out the duties of his office, but his ability to do so, even when not permitted, was derived from his election and ordination. Accordingly, Simon hypothesized that, after an unpalliated archbishop had illicitly consecrated a suffragan, the new bishop "would be no less a bishop, even if both [he and his consecrator] were to be deposed on this account."[152] *Omnis*, Huguccio, and *Animal* all held this tenet that a missing pallium affected liceity, but not validity.[153]

Since a metropolitan's dependence on the pallium was a human regulation, not something relating to his order, why had it been imposed? The decretists agreed that its purpose was practical and disciplinary, not theological: it was simply meant to compel archbishops to seek the pallium. In Simon's blunt estimation, which was shared by *Omnis*, "they would not do it, if [consecrating bishops] were permitted to them before the reception of the pallium."[154] Huguccio had a similarly dim view of an archbishop's desire for the vestment: "If it were permitted to him by the lord [pope] to exercise his power fully before [receiving the pallium], he would be negligent, such that he would never seek the pallium, since from its petition and reception he would be not a little burdened, and would experience little or no advantage or honor."[155] This cynical appraisal may have reflected the opinions of

151. Rufinus ad D.100 (194), Paucapalea ad D.100 (50), Honorius ad D.100 d.a.c.1 (1:264).
152. SimonBis ad D.100 d.a.c.1 s.v. *ante pallium acceptum* (87–88).
153. *Omnis* ad D.100 c.1 s.v. *episcoporum consecratio protelatur* (1:406–7), Huguccio ad D.100 c.1 s.v. *ac per hoc* (119r), *Animal* ad D.100 c.1 s.v. *protelatur* (1273–75).
154. SimonBis ad D.100 d.a.c.1 s.v. *ante pallium acceptum* (87–88), *Omnis* ad D.100 c.1 s.v. *episcoporum consecratio protelatur* (1:406–7).
155. Huguccio ad D.100 c.1 s.v. *ac per hoc* (119r: "si ante liceret ei plenarie potestatem suam exercere a domino negligens esset quod numquam peteret pallium cum ex eius petitione et acceptione non modicum gravaretur, et emolumentum vel honorem modicum vel nullum sentiret").

some contemporary archbishops, even though it was hardly consistent with other observations by Huguccio that stressed the honor that the vestment conveyed.[156] *Animal* too blamed metropolitans' indifference *in petendo pallio*: the legal obligation was punishment for their negligence, and served to prevent future negligence.[157] The assumptions made by these canonists are noteworthy. They did not specify the reason for the negligence—which could have ranged from apathetic procrastination to resentful resistance in the face of Roman interference—but clearly they recognized the Johannine requirement as an imposition on archbishops, who had to be forced to observe it.

Some also saw coercion when the law summoned a neighboring metropolitan (rather than the province's suffragans) to consecrate a bishop whom the disobedient metropolitan could not consecrate. Simon, *Omnis*, Honorius, and Huguccio suggested that the canon envisioned a case in which the suffragans were too few, as yet unconsecrated, or even dead.[158] However, this provision too may have had a disciplinary purpose, as Honorius proposed: "Or it was introduced in hatred of metropolitans-elect who neglected their right [of the pallium]. To them injury is done, which would not happen if their suffragans should consecrate [a fellow suffragan] by their own authority."[159] In other words, the other bishops in the province could not step in to supply for the unpalliated archbishop's lack of power, for he would suffer no real harm thereby, and the law would lose its force. Likewise, Simon, *Omnis*, Huguccio, and the *Glossa Ordinaria* saw a means to embarrass and shame the noncompliant prelate when the law permitted outsiders to intervene on his turf. Otherwise, said the *Glossa Ordinaria*, "he would not care much if [a bishop] were consecrated by his own [comprovincial bishops]," and the law would not be obeyed.[160]

---

156. E.g., Huguccio ad D.74 c.8 s.v. *usum pallii* (94r) et ad D.100 c.8 s.v. *restat ut postquam* (119v–120r).

157. *Animal* ad D.23 c.1 s.v. *sicut papa* (451–53) et ad D.100 c.1 s.v. *protelatur* (1273–75).

158. SimonBis ad D.100 c.1 s.v. *sitque metropolitan[i]s licentia aliis* (88), *Omnis* ad D.100 c.1 s.v. *metropolitanis aliis* (1:407), Honorius ad D.100 c.1 s.v. *cum consilio* (1:264), Huguccio ad D.100 c.1 s.v. *aliis metropolitanis* (119r).

159. Honorius ad D.100 c.1 s.v. *cum consilio* (1:264).

160. SimonBis ad D.100 c.1 s.v. *sitque metropolitan[i]s licentia aliis* (88), *Omnis* ad

This line of commentary brought up possible ways of circumventing the law. *Omnis* posed two questions that later decretists took up: could an unpalliated archbishop, acting "not as an archbishop, but as a simple bishop," ordain a bishop? And could he "give permission to his suffragan bishops to ordain" a bishop?[161] Simon was aware of the first possibility, but took no stand, and the question remained dormant until the decretalists.[162] In regard to the second question, Huguccio was stern: an archbishop who delegated in this way would "cheat the law, which is forbidden ... for he would never seek the pallium, but would always enjoin on others the consecration of bishops, if this were permitted to him."[163] Honorius, however, seemed to allow the unpalliated archbishop to give *auctoritas* to his suffragans to carry out a consecration. But his other comments implied that this delegated ordination was only possible within the three-month grace period.[164] This hypothesis was clarified in later years. For *Animal*, the stricture against furnishing suffragans with the *potestas consecrandi* applied only when the metropolitan was negligent in seeking the pallium. If he had not yet violated the canon—that is, during the three months—he could delegate the consecration.[165] While such a delegation seemed to contradict Justinian's *Digest*, which held that "what he cannot do himself, neither can he do through another," *Animal* believed that the archbishop in fact possessed the power to consecrate, and was forbidden by law only as a penalty designed to prevent negligence. And because *Animal* cited a decretal of Alexander III, later included in the *Liber Extra*, which permitted such a delegation, it argued "more subtly" that the decretal had force only when the archbishop was not negligent in observing the deadline.[166] The *Glossa Ordina-*

D.100 c.1 s.v. *metropolitanis aliis* (1:407), Huguccio ad D.100 c.1 s.v. *aliis metropolitanis* (119r), *Glossa Ordinaria* ad D.100 c.1 s.v. *episcoporum* (638).

161. *Omnis* ad D.100 c.1 s.v. *episcoporum consecratio protelatur* (1:406–7).
162. SimonBis ad D.100 d.a.c.1 s.v. *ante pallium acceptum* (87–88). See 471–72 below.
163. Huguccio ad D.100 c.1 s.v. *protelatur* (119r: "faciet fraudem iuri quod prohibetur ... numquam enim peteret pallium sed semper aliis iniungeret consecrationem episcoporum si hoc liceret ei").
164. Honorius ad D.100 c.1 s.v. *ac per hoc* et *ultra iii consecrationis* (1:264).
165. *Animal* ad D.64 c.1 s.v. *potestas* (1110).
166. *Animal* ad D.100 c.1 s.v. *protelatur* (1273–75), X 1.6.11; see 447–48 below.

ria canonized this view when it allowed suffragans to supply for the archbishop's missing *episcopalia iura,* including consecrating bishops, as long as he was not "in delay of seeking the pallium."[167]

The decretists raised further questions as they continued to test the limits of *Quoniam quidam.* When a bishop was translated to an archiepiscopal see, why did his condition after the promotion seem, surprisingly, to become worse, "since first he could [consecrate bishops, but] now he cannot"? If he received the pallium but was later translated to a primatial see, could he immediately consecrate bishops, or did he fall again under the Johannine obligation and have to seek a new pallium?[168] If he lost his pallium, would he have to get a new one, and until then would the restriction on consecrating bishops temporarily resurface?[169] These questions were not immediately answered, but some would later receive attention in decretals and in the works of the decretalists.[170]

What other rights and duties accompanied the pallium?

The fifth part of Gratian's D.100 had dwelled on the Gregorian principle that the pallium should not be bestowed without the communication of accompanying privileges and responsibilities. To some decretists, this apparently auxiliary issue was important; for example, in his treatment of the *distinctio,* Omnibonus focused solely on this topic.[171] Rufinus, *Magister,* Huguccio, and the *Glossa Ordinaria* all clarified that the pertinent canons implied either the grant of new privileges or the renewal of old ones.[172] The latter were sometimes

---

167. *Glossa Ordinaria* ad D.100 c.1 s.v. *episcoporum* (638). But s.v. *post secundam* (639) this apparatus entertained an opinion that "translata est potestas" from a negligent metropolitan to his suffragans, who, after canonically warning the metropolitan, could themselves provide for the vacant sees.

168. *Omnis* ad D.100 c.1 s.v. *episcoporum consecratio protelatur* (1:406–7).

169. Honorius ad D.100 c.6 s.v. *ad sola* (1:265).

170. See 444–46, 471–72 below.

171. Omnibonus ad D.100 (31r).

172. Rufinus ad D.100 (194), *Magister* ad D.100 d.p.c.8 (78), Huguccio ad D.100 c.9 s.v. *aliqua privilegia* et *largiri* (120r), *Glossa Ordinaria* ad D.100 (637) et ad D.100 d.a.c.1 (637–38). This expression may well have been an attempt to reconcile D.100 c.9, which talks about privileges in general, with cc.10–11, which seem to regard renewed privileges.

also called "confirmations" of things previously granted.[173] When *Magister* described these privileges as "dictated" by a "scribe," it attested to the age-old papal practice of sending a written document along with the vestment.[174] In fact, whereas Gratian and the Gregorian texts he employed had always spoken of *privilegia* in the plural, the use of the singular by some canonists hinted that the document, rather than rights, was foremost in their minds.[175]

Probably because pallium privileges customarily included admonitions addressed to their recipients, the decretists often took this opportunity to expound upon the behavior expected of palligers. After all, Huguccio proclaimed, "Good works [can be] pointed out through vestments," and *Animal* stressed, "Decorations mean something!" Both cited a canon taken from Gregory the Great's *Regula Pastoralis*, which affirmed (albeit metaphorically) that priests should be clothed with righteousness.[176] In the same vein, *Animal*, reminiscent of previous writers such as Nicholas I and Goscelin of St.-Bertin, portrayed the pallium as "the fullness of virtues."[177] Thus, when Gregory said to John of Ravenna, "We, perhaps unadorned in behavior, want to be adorned with the pallium, while nothing shines more splendidly on the episcopal neck than humility," two scholars saw an implicit rebuke of the archbishop. "Clearly he accuses him by associating him with these words," *Magister* asserted, and Huguccio said, "In a way, he brands him with haughtiness and vain boasting."[178] Pride had ever been the temptation of the palliger.

173. Honorius ad D.100 c.9 s.v. *largiri* (1:266) et ad D.100 c.11 s.v. *privilegia concessisse* (1:266), Huguccio ad D.100 c.11 s.v. *concessisse* (120r), *Animal* ad D.100 c.11 s.v. *concessisse* (1283). Huguccio added that a personal privilege that had expired with its recipient would have to be granted anew to his successor, while a more "general" privilege would simply have to be confirmed.

174. *Magister* ad C.1 q.2 c.4 (92).

175. Rufinus ad D.100 (194), *Magister* ad D.100 d.p.c.8 (78), *Glossa Ordinaria* ad D.100 d.a.c.1 (637–38).

176. Huguccio ad D.100 c.9 s.v. *ornamenta actionis* (120r: "bona opera quae per vestimenta designantur"), *Animal* ad D.100 c.9 s.v. *conveniant* (1282). They referred to D.43 c.1, which drew upon *Regula Pastoralis* 2.4, which had in turn quoted Ps 132:9.

177. *Animal* ad D.100 d.a.c.1 (1272) et ad D.100 c.9 s.v. *conveniant* (1282). Cf. Nicholas to Hincmar of Reims in 866, JE 2823, BH 838, MGH Epp. 6:430–31; and Goscelin, *Vita Augustini*, in PL 150:753.

178. *Magister* ad D.100 c.8 s.v. *moribus* (78), Huguccio ad D.100 c.8 s.v. *decorari* (120r: "aliquantulum notat eundem de extollentia et vana gloria").

A favorite theme of the decretists was the wordplay between "honor" (root *honor-*) and "burden" (root *[h]oner-*) and the differing perspectives they produced. Huguccio recognized that, as a churchman's dignity grew, so did his burden and responsibility.[179] As *Animal* contended, "To him to whom honor belongs, burden does too"; in effect, the higher the honor, the greater the responsibility.[180] The *Glossa Ordinaria* agreed, and added that an increase in usefulness or benefit (*utilitas*)—for a pastor, solicitous care for his subjects—must come with *dignitas*.[181] The vestment was thus a spur to greater pastoral concern, rather than a decorative bauble or a reason to boast. Moreover, the archbishop of Ravenna could not have appealed to local custom to justify his misuse of the pallium, Huguccio (followed by the *Glossa Ordinaria*) stated, because such custom could only confer or legitimate a burden, but not an honor, such as using the pallium. A local church thus could not seize an honor for itself, but only oblige itself to follow a stricter usage.[182] In these ways, by urging palligers not to become puffed up by their apparel, the decretists reinforced a motif that dated back to the *Liber Diurnus*: the pallium marked a good shepherd who looked out for his sheep.

Conclusion

The contours of the decretists' discussions, of course, were shaped by the text on which they were commenting. Gratian 1 and 2 had chosen to focus on the general obligation for archbishops to acquire the pallium, the conditions they had to fulfill to get it, and the consequences of noncompliance for the performance of their office. As a result, the decretists poured most of their energy into interpreting the details of *Quoniam quidam*, examining the prerequisites for gaining the pallium, and analyzing how archbishops relied on it to car-

---

179. Huguccio ad D.100 c.9 s.v. *sicut enim excrescere* (120r).
180. *Animal* ad D.100 c.9 s.v. *oportet ut enixius* (1282).
181. *Glossa Ordinaria* ad D.100 c.9 pr. et s.v. *cura* (643–44).
182. Huguccio ad D.100 c.8 s.v. *restat ut postquam* (119v–120r; this reading should be supplemented by the one found in Vatican City, Biblioteca Apostolica Vaticana, Vat. lat. 2280, fol. 89r), *Glossa Ordinaria* ad D.100 c.8 s.v. *tueri* (643).

ry out their duties. These scholars were taking part in an intellectual enterprise of systematization. Thus points of pallium law sometimes provided opportunities to plunge into tangled thickets of legal questions on matters ranging from the nature of privileges to the force of custom. Sometimes, too, certain principles in canon law—such as the impropriety of putting conditions on spiritual transactions, of appearing to desire an honor, or of swearing on another's soul—had to be reconciled with traditional practices. This systematizing effort occasionally contradicted the original conception of pallium grants as gifts freely given at papal initiative, an unruly idea less conducive to codification, or less relevant to contemporary practice.

Decretist commentaries were also witnesses to their historical context and the impact it was having on pallium practice. The profession of faith seemed to lose importance, while the oath of fidelity became more and more accepted. Personal reception of the pallium as a reform policy may have failed, but a new policy of consecration by the pope began to take its place. Increasingly commonplace procedures, such as episcopal translations, and new canonical concepts, such as electoral confirmation, required adjustments to the pallium's role in ecclesiastical discipline. Perhaps most valuable were the canonists' hints about attitudes toward the pallium among the prelates of their time. Indifference, or even resistance, indicated a reaction by some against the papacy's use of the pallium in its relationships with archbishops, and the Johannine law was seen as a necessary means of forcing them to participate in the papal program. Law often responds to problems, and its normative nature suggests the deviations from the norm that give rise to it. Although much of the evidence in this book has traced the effectiveness of the pallium as a papal tool, these canonical sources sometimes revealed that this tool, like all tools, had its limits.

Epilogue Chapter 2: Decretals and Decretalists

The *Liber Extra*

Even as Gratian and the decretists were canonizing and synthesizing the *ius antiquum* (the body of excerpts from papal letters, conciliar canons, and other sources that had been collected since the early church), the twelfth-century papacy was replying to new questions being posed to it. Thanks to the papal reform movement and the enhanced prominence of the papacy that resulted, the popes and their court were beginning to exercise authority over the Western church more broadly and effectively than ever. Local churches increasingly sought out and paid heed to this authority, and indeed their initiative helped to form it; the Roman church responded by accepting appeals, hearing cases, and issuing instructions on a scale unprecedented in its history. From the flurry of papal decretal letters emanating from the judicial and consultative activity of the papal curia, it was inevitable that legal experts, including masters in the expanding schools, began to make selections.[1] They saw these decretals as new

---

1. On the formation of the *ius novum*, see Anne J. Duggan, "Making Law or Not? The Function of Papal Decretals in the Twelfth Century," in *Proceedings of the Thirteenth International Congress of Medieval Canon Law*, ed. Peter Erdö and Sz. Anzelm

juridical sources, called *extravagantes* because they wandered outside Gratian's established work. Cases settled and consultations issued by the popes were trimmed of circumstantial details to reveal the canonical principles at their cores, and these excerpts were gathered into new canonical collections, forming a new phase in canon law's history: the *ius novum*. Chief among them were the five "Old Compilations" (*Compilationes Antiquae*), composed from ca. 1190 to 1226, which the great editor Raymond of Penyafort, at the command of Pope Gregory IX, combined and streamlined in 1234 to make the exclusively authoritative *Decretals of Gregory IX*, more commonly known as the *Liber Extra*.[2] The following discussion will analyze the pallium canons in the *Liber Extra*, grouped according to the *Compilationes Antiquae* from which they were taken.[3]

From Bernard of Pavia's 'Compilatio Prima'

Between 1189 and 1191 Bernard of Pavia assembled twelfth-century papal decretals (mostly from Alexander III), as well as earlier canonical texts omitted by Gratian, into his *Breviarium Extravagantium*, later considered the first of the *Compilationes Antiquae*, al-

---

Szuromi, *Monumenta Iuris Canonici*, ser. C, Subsidia 14 (Vatican City: Biblioteca Apostolica Vaticana, 2010), 41–70, and her "Master of the Decretals: A Reassessment of Alexander III's Contribution to Canon Law," in *Pope Alexander III (1159–81): The Art of Survival*, ed. Peter D. Clarke and Anne J. Duggan (Farnham: Ashgate, 2012), 366–87.

2. See Stephan Kuttner, "Raymond of Peñafort as Editor: The 'Decretales' and 'Constitutiones' of Gregory IX," *Bulletin of Medieval Canon Law* 12 (1982): 65–80, reprinted in his *Studies in the History of Medieval Canon Law*, part 12 (Aldershot: Ashgate Variorum, 1990); Martin Bertram, "Die Dekretalen Gregors IX.: Kompilation oder Kodifikation?," in *Magister Raimundus*, ed. Carlo Longo, Dissertationes Historicae 28 (Rome: Istituto Storico Domenicano, 2002), 61–86; and Edward A. Reno, "Gregory IX and the *Liber Extra*," in *Pope Gregory IX (1227–41)*, ed. Christoph Egger and Damian J. Smith (New York: Routledge, forthcoming).

3. Although Raymond frequently trimmed these canons, his editorial work was not intended to change their legal substance. Gregory IX's letter *Rex pacificus* explained the editing process (Friedberg, *Corpus*, 2:1–4). This discussion will focus predominantly on the sections of the texts that made it into the *Liber Extra* (and thus into the mainstream of the canonical tradition), not the omitted portions or *partes decisae* (restored to the text in Friedberg's edition). In four canons (X 1.6.23, 1.15.1, 1.33.1, 2.9.2) the pallium was mentioned only in the *partes decisae*, usually as part of the background of the case at hand.

though it was partly based on previous decretal collections.[4] He set a decisive organizational precedent when he divided the collection into five books, subdivided into titles, but he was not particularly interested in the pallium and assigned no title to it. Nor did he have anything to say about the vestment in his *Summa de Electione* or in his *Summa Titulorum Decretalium*.[5] References to the pallium occurred only incidentally in Bernard's *Breviarium*. To judge by the titles under which they appeared, it was seen as the occasion of an oath of fidelity to the pope—here Bernard drew on Paschal II's important letter to Lawrence of Esztergom (*Significasti*, after 1105)—or as the potential occasion of simony: here he used part of a canon from Gregory the Great's Council of Rome (*In ordinando*, 595) and a letter of Alexander III to the archbishop of Esztergom (*Etsi quaestiones*, 1167/68).[6]

Raymond of Penyafort accepted these three canons into the *Liber Extra*. The rubric later attached to *Significasti* indicated his interest: "The apostolic see will not hand over the pallium to one elected as archbishop unless he first takes an oath of fidelity and obedience." Raymond's editing left out explanations of the vestment's meaning and effects. The legal content he chose to isolate justified three things: taking the oath as a condition placed on the pallium's reception; swearing in order to prevent evil and ensure faith, obedience, and unity; and rendering subjection to and showing unity with Rome in exchange for Roman insignia.[7] The short excerpt from the oft-repeated Gregorian anti-simony law of 595 overlapped with,

---

4. See Kenneth Pennington, "Decretal Collections 1190–1234," in *Canon Law, 1140–1234*, ed. Hartmann and Pennington, 295–300.

5. Ern. Ad. Theod. Laspeyres, ed., *Bernardi Papiensis Faventini Episcopi Summa Decretalium* (Regensburg: Manz, 1860; reprinted in Graz: Akademische Druck- und Verlagsanstalt, 1956).

6. 1Comp 1.4.21 [the *Compilationes Antiquae* (*Prima, Secunda*, etc.) are hereafter referred to as "1Comp," "2Comp," etc.] (from JL 6570), 5.2.1 (from the Council of Rome of 595, c. 5), 5.2.20 (from JL 11308): Emil Friedberg, ed., *Quinque Compilationes Antiquae nec non Collectio Canonum Lipsiensis* (Leipzig: Tauchnitz, 1882; reprinted in Graz: Akademische Druck- und Verlagsanstalt, 1956), 3, 54. Bernard included a further text that mentioned the pallium (1Comp 1.25.1, from JE 1829, ibid., 10), but when Raymond trimmed it for the *Liber Extra* (X 1.33.1, Friedberg, *Corpus*, 2:195), he left out most of this pallium grant because he was chiefly interested in what it said about precedence among bishops.

7. X 1.6.4, Friedberg, *Corpus*, 2:49–50.

but did not completely duplicate, the excerpt already used by Gratian 1. Indeed, it sounded stricter than Gratian's text: the pope forbade an ordinand to pay or offer anything for his ordination, or for the *usus pallii* (a refinement from the original text, which mentioned the pallium itself, as an object), or for the attesting documents.[8] Finally, according to the Alexandrine letter, a cardinal had been on his way to Esztergom to examine the accession of its new archbishop and give him the pallium sent by the pope. When the candidate's brother sent the legate a horse for the second leg of the trip, the candidate worried—overly scrupulously, according to Alexander—that the gift would appear simoniacal. The pope dismissed the concern and explained at some length why this transaction was guiltless.[9] He also dismissed an excessively tender conscience that might similarly question oathtaking—as a previous archbishop of Esztergom had done in connection with the pallium, resulting in *Significasti*.[10]

From Peter of Benevento's 'Compilatio Tertia'

In 1209 or 1210 Peter of Benevento compiled a supplement to Bernard's *Breviarium*, containing decretals chiefly from the first dozen years of Innocent III's pontificate. Copied from the papal registers and, for the first time, authenticated by the pope himself, these *Decretales Domini Innocentii Papae* became known as the third *Compilatio Antiqua* (the second came later, so named because it contained pre-Innocentian material).[11] Peter devised a title "on the authority and use of the pallium," closely similar to a title first used in Greg-

---

8. X 5.3.1, ibid., 2:749. Cf. C.1 q.2 c.4, ibid., 1:409.
9. X 5.3.18, ibid., 2:754–55.
10. Alexander brought up the hesitation to take a necessary, legitimate oath (*sacramentum*) as an example of *tenuis religio*; this topic seems unrelated to his discussion later in the letter of a promise (*indemnitas, promissio, securitas*) that the archbishop's brother made on his behalf to the king (see the *Appendix ad Concilium Lateranense*, Canon 50.1, Mansi, *Sacrorum Conciliorum Collectio*, 22:426–27). While there was no direct allusion to the oath of fidelity taken at the reception of the pallium, the mention of oathtaking in this context seems more than a coincidence, and may have been intended to forestall scruples on that account. It also lends support to Brett's opinion that the recipient of *Significasti* was an archbishop of Esztergom ("Some New Letters," 89–94).
11. See Pennington, "Decretal Collections," 309–11.

ory of San Grisogono's *Polycarpus* a century earlier, and the remaining *Compilationes Antiquae* followed this example, as did the *Liber Extra*.[12] Peter then populated his pallium title with three important precedents from Innocent III: to the cardinal legate Cinthius on the meaning of the vestment (*Nisi specialis*, 1200), to the Bulgarian archbishops of Tarnovo and Valebud (Kyustendil) on its proper use (*Ad honorem Dei*, 1204), and to the archbishop of Compostela on where it could be worn (*Ex litterarum tuarum (Ex tuarum tenore)*, 1209).[13] Furthermore, the vestment occurred in four canons outside the title: Innocentian letters to the chapter of Esztergom about translation to an archiepiscopal see (*Bonae memoriae V. (G.)*, 1205), to the cardinal legate John about the functions made possible by the pallium (*Quod sicut ex*, 1202), to the archbishop of York about an archbishop residing in another's province (*Ad supplicationem*, 1203), and to the Hungarian bishop of Csanád and the abbot of Cikedor about a palliger accused of immorality (*Cum in iuventute*, 1206).[14]

Raymond of Penyafort then included these seven canons in the *Liber Extra*, with the three from Peter's pallium title likewise placed in his own pallium title. Innocent III's letter to Cardinal Cinthius (c. 3) asserted that through the conferral of the pallium came not only the *plenitudo pontificalis officii*, but also the "title of the archiepiscopal name." In short, a metropolitan could not fully carry out his office or even call himself "archbishop" until he was palliated.[15] Per-

12. 3Comp 1.7 ("de auctoritate et usu pallii"), 2Comp 1.4 ("de usu pallii"), 4Comp 1.4 ("de usu et auctoritate pallii"), 5Comp 1.6 ("de auctoritate et usu pallii"): Friedberg, *Quinque Compilationes*, 107, 67, 137, 155. X 1.8 ("de auctoritate et usu pallii"), Friedberg, *Corpus*, 2:100. Cf. Title 2.20, Fuhrmann and Horst, *Sammlung "Policarpus,"* at http://www.mgh.de/fileadmin/Downloads/pdf/polycarp.pdf, 102.

13. 3Comp 1.7.1 (from Augustus Potthast, *Regesta Pontificum Romanorum inde ab Anno post Christum Natum MCXCVIII ad Annum MCCCIV*, vol. 1 [Berlin: Decker, 1874], no. 1112 [hereafter "Potthast"]), 1.7.2 (from Potthast 2145), 1.7.3 (from Potthast 3692): Friedberg, *Quinque Compilationes*, 107.

14. 3Comp 1.4.4 (from Potthast 2588), 1.6.13 (from Potthast 1735), 1.8.2 (from Potthast 1902), 2.14.2 (from Potthast 2837): Friedberg, *Quinque Compilationes*, 106–7, 114. Peter included two further texts that mentioned the pallium (3Comp 1.6.8, 1.11.1, from Potthast 1647, 2138, ibid., 107–8), but when Raymond trimmed them for the *Liber Extra* (X 1.6.23, 1.15.1, Friedberg, *Corpus*, 2:66–68, 131–34), he left out some of the background of these cases as superfluous.

15. X 1.8.3, Friedberg, *Corpus*, 2:101.

haps the pope's thinking was a vestige from the early Middle Ages, when "archbishop" and "metropolitan" were not equivalent terms, and metropolitans began to be called "archbishops" because they routinely received the vestment. As late as the *Anglo-Saxon Chronicle* the archbishops of Canterbury were not called such until they had acquired the pallium.[16] In the letter to the Bulgarian archbishops (c. 4), Innocent drew a distinction between papal use of the pallium and the practice of lesser palligers. The pope "alone uses the pallium always and everywhere," without restrictions of time or place. The only absolute requirement was that he must wear it during the Mass—apparently not in outside processions, despite the claim in the *Propriae Auctoritates Apostolicae Sedis* and the evidence of twelfth-century papal *ordines*.[17] Others, in contrast, could wear it only "on certain days, in their own church in which they have received ecclesiastical jurisdiction." The reason for the difference was the pope's "fullness of ecclesiastical power," which the pallium symbolized (not the "fullness of the pontifical office," which every palliated archbishop enjoyed), on the one hand, and on the other, the lesser bishop's "share of the responsibility [*pars sollicitudinis*]" vis-à-vis the papal *plenitudo potestatis*. Thus the restrictions on the pallium's use made manifest the metropolitan's partial authority, derivative from the pope's.[18] Lastly, when the archbishop of Compostela complained (c. 5) that he was obediently wearing his pallium only within his own province, while other Spanish palligers observed no such restriction, Innocent grumbled that the Spanish practice was not "custom," but rather "corruption." Yet he granted—"by special favor," against the

16. Cubbin, *Anglo-Saxon Chronicle*, 6:63–64, and Irvine, *Anglo-Saxon Chronicle*, 7:75. See 109n135 above.
17. Cf. Mordek, "Proprie auctoritates," 132. Benedict of St. Peter's *Liber Politicus* (Fabre and Duchesne, *Liber censuum*, 2.7:148, 152, 156), the Basel Ordo (Bernhard Schimmelpfennig, ed., "Ein bisher unbekannter Text zur Wahl, Konsekration und Krönung des Papstes im 12. Jahrhundert," *Archivum Historiae Pontificiae* 6 [1968]: 67), Albinus of Albano's *Digesta Pauperis Scholaris* (Fabre and Duchesne, *Liber censuum*, 2.6:131), and Cencius's *Liber Censuum* (Fabre and Duchesne, *Liber censuum*, 1.3:293, 296–98) described processions in which the pope wore the pallium on his coronation day, Candlemas, Good Friday, Easter, and the feast of St. Mark (for the Greater Litanies).
18. X 1.8.4, Friedberg, *Corpus*, 2:101. See Kempf, "Eingliederung," 90–91.

usual prohibition—that this archbishop, under certain conditions, had the "free faculty" to use the vestment outside his province. Perhaps the broader point was that the pope could dispense from the law in light of particular circumstances and subject to careful regulations. But the rubric later assigned to this canon simply stressed that an archbishop could not wear his pallium outside his own province, "even if custom holds this."[19]

The four canons distributed in other titles similarly contained considerable legal substance. When Innocent translated the archbishop of Kalocsa to the archbishopric of Esztergom and promised to send him a new pallium "for the name and use" of the latter church, he implied that every pallium was associated with a specific church and intended for use there. Thus he showed, first, that the pallium signified papal approval of a translation and, second, that even if an archbishop already had the vestment, he must secure a new one if he took a new metropolitan see.[20] In Innocent's letter to Cardinal John, he enumerated among the acts forbidden to an unpalliated archbishop: summoning synods, ordaining clergy, and consecrating chrism, churches, and bishops. What one could do "as a simple bishop" could not be done by such an archbishop: though episcopally ordained, he could not perform such functions because, in doing them, he would be seen "as an archbishop," and thus infringe upon the Johannine law (though not cited here).[21] In another case, the pope allowed the exiled archbishop of Dubrovnik to give up his see and become bishop of Carlisle in the province of York. The ex-archbishop would perform episcopal ministry there, but "without the use of the pallium," and had to obey the archbishop of York as his metropolitan. The deprivation of the vestment in this instance recognized that this prelate was living outside the province for which he had been granted it. By excluding the pallium's use, Innocent forestalled competition with the local metropolitan's authority.[22] Finally, the letter to the Hungarians cast doubt upon the charge that the palliated bishop of Pécs was guilty of incest. In fact, he had long ago proven that he was "mature, honorable, and prudent," and those merits had al-

19. X 1.8.5, Friedberg, *Corpus*, 2:101–2.
21. X 1.6.28, ibid., 2:71–73.
20. X 1.5.4, ibid., 2:45–47.
22. X 1.9.9, ibid., 2:107.

lowed him to be decorated with the vestment. For Innocent, the personal worthiness traditionally required in order to receive the pallium meant that accusations against its recipient must be approached with skepticism—even though the pope had not hesitated to investigate the charges.[23]

From John of Wales's 'Compilatio Secunda'

A few years after Peter of Benevento's work, John of Wales collected decretals primarily from Clement III and Celestine III to fill the gap between *Compilationes Prima* and *Tertia*; the result was thus called the second *Compilatio Antiqua*.[24] His title on the pallium contained only two letters: one of Celestine III—misattributed to Clement III—to the archbishop of Ravenna concerning the place where the pallium could be worn (*Cum super aliqua*, 1193), and an excerpt from a response of Alexander III—misattributed to Celestine III—to the archbishop of Rouen concerning the personal nature of the pallium privilege (*Ad haec (hoc) quia*, 1174).[25] A different extract from Alexander's letter, treating the possibility that an unpalliated archbishop could delegate the consecration of bishops to his suffragans in certain circumstances, had been inserted in the preceding title (*Suffraganeis autem (alicuius)*, 1174).[26]

Raymond of Penyafort adopted these three canons into the *Liber Extra*, and placed the two from John's pallium title into his own pallium title. The letter to Ravenna (c. 1) clarified the meaning of the words "within your church," a restriction on the vestment's use pronounced when a papal legate handed over the pallium to its recipient.[27] Celestine defined the phrase broadly, to mean "within any church of the province entrusted to you," as long as it was inside a

---

23. X 2.23.15, ibid., 2:358.
24. See Pennington, "Decretal Collections," 312–13.
25. 2Comp 1.4.1 (from JL 17049), 1.4.2 (from JL 17657): Friedberg, *Quinque Compilationes*, 67.
26. 2Comp 1.3.1 (from JL 14198), Friedberg, *Quinque Compilationes*, 67. Despite the differing attributions, JL 14198 and JL 17657 were both excerpts of a longer letter of Alexander III to Rothrud of Rouen in 1174 (JL 12377, PL 200:943–45); see Walther Holtzmann, *Walther-Holtzmann-Kartei*, 2012, at http://www.kuttner-institute.jura.uni-muenchen.de/holtzmann_formular.htm, no. 386 [hereafter "WH"].
27. Cf. Host*Aurea* ad X 1.8 s.v. *cui concedendum sit* (123–24).

church building—but not during processions, when one went outside wearing other ecclesiastical vestments.[28] This last comment would hardly have surprised any canonist who had studied Gregory the Great's quarrel with another archbishop of Ravenna six centuries before.[29] One part of the letter to Rouen (c. 2) declared that the pallium could not be lent to anyone. Alexander—who in the *pars decisa* explained that he had not found a canon (presumably in Gratian) to address the situation—believed that the use of the vestment was a personal privilege (*personam non transeat*), as witnessed by the custom of burying it with its recipient.[30] The other part of the Alexandrine letter seemed to contradict the spirit of the Johannine law when it allowed that a metropolitan, confirmed but lacking the pallium, could licitly order his suffragans to consecrate a bishop in his province. A clue to interpreting this text, however, lay in the rubric that was eventually added: "A confirmed metropolitan, although he has *not yet* received the pallium, can cause his suffragan to be consecrated."[31] If the archbishop was not resisting the obligation of *Quoniam quidam*—perhaps it was still within the three-month grace period, or perhaps the vestment had been sent for before the deadline and was now on its way—then the law's consequences would not come into play.

Raymond, however, left out some unusual material concerning the pallium from a canon he received from John of Wales, part of a letter from Alexander III to the archbishop of Trondheim (misidentified as Tortona) (*Quoniam in parte*, 1164/81).[32] In the sentence Raymond omitted from the *Liber Extra*, the pope responded to an inquiry whether the vestment could be worn on the feast of the Trinity, a solemn occasion not usually mentioned in pallium privileges.[33] Alex-

---

28. X 1.8.1, Friedberg, *Corpus*, 2:100.
29. John the Deacon, *Vita Gregorii Magni*, in PL 75:172–76.
30. X 1.8.2, Friedberg, *Corpus*, 2:100–101.
31. X 1.6.11, ibid., 2:53; emphasis added.
32. 2Comp 2.5.2 (from JL 14109), Friedberg, *Quinque Compilationes*, 72. On the see's identification, see WH 833.
33. Exceptions up to Alexander's time included privileges of Anastasius IV to John of Trondheim in 1154 (JL 9941, PL 188:1082) and of Alexander III himself to Richard of Syracuse in 1169 (JL 11619, PL 200:584), neither of which seems to have entered the canonical tradition. That a previous archbishop of Trondheim had

ander noted that customs surrounding that feast varied from place to place, and in fact the Roman church did not celebrate it at all; therefore, he could not provide a "certain answer about the use of the pallium on that day."[34] The pope seemed unwilling to issue a ruling on this matter, which left the door open for the archbishop to make his own decision. Raymond must have excised this line because it was not germane to the legal topic of this section (the proper observance of feast days) and offered no precedent for future cases. He may also have realized that Alexander's lack of a decision deprived the papacy of a means of control over the pallium and its wearer.

From Johannes Teutonicus's 'Compilatio Quarta'

Although he was denied the official papal authentication granted to Peter of Benevento's collection, Johannes Teutonicus composed the fourth of the *Compilationes Antiquae* in 1216 when he gathered decretals from the later years of Innocent III, as well as the canons of the Fourth Lateran Council (1215).[35] He too provided a title on the pallium, although it contained only a single canon: a letter from Innocent to an archbishop, perhaps of Uppsala, on how he should use the pallium (*Cum sis in partibus*, 1198/1215).[36] Johannes elsewhere inserted the fifth constitution of Lateran IV, which defined the privileges due to the ancient patriarchal sees (*Antiqua patriarchalium*, 1215).[37]

Raymond of Penyafort dutifully put both canons into the *Liber Extra*, keeping the one from Johannes's pallium title for his own pallium title. That canon (c. 6), however, did not appear to mesh well with settled law on the vestment: "Wherever you are placed at the celebrations of the Mass, you will be able to exercise quite freely on solemn days the use of the pallium, through which the fullness of

---

received this feast as a pallium day supports the identification of the recipient of JL 14109. The cathedral of Trondheim was dedicated to the Trinity, which explained the archbishop's interest.

34. X 2.9.2, Friedberg, *Corpus*, 2:271.
35. See Pennington, "Decretal Collections," 314–15.
36. 4Comp 1.4.1 (from Potthast 5034), Friedberg, *Quinque Compilationes*, 137.
37. 4Comp 5.12.6 (from the Lateran Council of 1215, c. 5), Friedberg, *Quinque Compilationes*, 149.

pontifical authority is represented." One had to supply some important restrictions missing from this text: that the archbishop must be in a church of his province, and that it must be a pallium day permitted in his privilege. These details were mentioned in the rubric, which thus clarified the meaning of the canon.[38] Maybe the looseness of the text, including the expression *liberius,* indicated a special privilege for a missionary archbishop; indeed, the original letter acknowledged that the recipient ministered *in partibus remotissimis.*[39] In any case, the canon added nothing to previous law about the pallium, and one must wonder if Raymond preserved it only out of a desire for completeness as he sifted through the *Compilationes Antiquae.*

Lateran IV's fifth constitution endeavored to incorporate the ancient patriarchs of Constantinople, Alexandria, Antioch, and Jerusalem into the church of the high medieval papal monarchy. It gave them powers similar to those of metropolitans, but broader—though firmly subordinate to papal power. Accordingly, each would receive the pallium, "the insigne of the fullness of the pontifical office," from the pope after proffering him an "oath of fidelity and obedience." But then each in turn would grant the vestment to his own suffragans—metropolitans, but perhaps also simple bishops, if the Eastern custom prevailed—after he had received a "canonical profession" for himself and a "pledge of obedience" to the Roman church. In this way, the *dignitas* of each patriarch would be preserved.[40] The patriarchs thus enjoyed an intermediate position: having been palliated, they could palliate the prelates in their patriarchates. But the Roman character of the practice was maintained by the demand for a double oath, to the patriarch and to the pope.

---

38. X 1.8.6, Friedberg, *Corpus,* 2:102.

39. Alternatively, the text may have been forged. Compared to traditional papal letters concerning the pallium, its language was unusual in several respects: "in missarum celebrationibus" instead of "in missarum sollemnibus," "usum pallii ... exercere" instead of "pallio uti," and "plenitudo pontificii" instead of "plenitudo pontificalis officii."

40. X 5.33.23, ibid., 2:866.

From Tancred of Bologna's 'Compilatio Quinta'

The fifth and last of the *Compilationes Antiquae* was the work of Tancred of Bologna, who in 1226, commissioned, assisted, and authorized by Honorius III, amassed decretals of that pope taken exclusively from the papal registers.[41] Tancred made use of the (by now customary) title on the pallium, even though he had only one canon to place there: a letter of Honorius to the archbishop of Lund (misidentified as the archbishop of Lyon) concerning two questions about the pallium's use (*Tua (Quia) nos*, 1225).[42] Raymond of Penyafort added this text (c. 7) to the other canons in his pallium title. In reply to one question, the pope directed that the archbishop could celebrate the Mass without wearing the pallium, in his province or elsewhere, but could not wear it anyway except in his province on the days listed in his privilege.[43] This reference to papally allowed pallium days answered the other question: whether an archbishop could wear the pallium while celebrating a Mass for the dead. Honorius implied that he could do so only if that occasion was mentioned in his privilege.[44]

The Decretalists

From Alexander III to Honorius III, the popes continually issued clarifications, qualifications, and additional precedents that illuminated and supplemented canon law regarding the pallium. By adding excerpts of these letters to their decretal collections, along with a few older texts that had escaped Gratian's notice, the authors of the *Compilationes Antiquae*—and especially Raymond of Penyafort, their editor in producing the *Liber Extra*—encouraged the juridical conver-

---

41. See Pennington, "Decretal Collections," 316–17.
42. 5Comp 1.6.1 (from Potthast 7455), Friedberg, *Quinque Compilationes*, 155.
43. Honorius used the word "dioecesi," which sometimes meant "province." He also spoke of "ecclesiae tuae privilegiis" in the plural, which may have indicated that lists of pallium days could build on each other and accumulate from palliger to palliger in a see; cf. *HostAurea* ad X 1.8 s.v. *et quibus diebus utendum sit pallio* (124–25).
44. X 1.8.7, Friedberg, *Corpus*, 2:102. Oddly, Raymond's inscription read: "Honorius III. Archiepiscopo Tri."

sation on the vestment to continue. Indeed, the fact that a title dedicated to the pallium became a standard part of the decretal inheritance ensured that the conversation would continue. Commentators in the law schools turned their attention to this *ius novum* in order to probe its implications for the church's functioning and to integrate it within the body of canonical thought that had been growing up around Gratian's *Decretum*. Known as decretalists, these scholars, in the tradition of their forebears, composed glosses that were gathered into apparatuses (culminating in a *Glossa Ordinaria* on the *Liber Extra*) or were systematized into *summae*.[45] The jurisprudence that they developed built upon that of the decretists and shaped the interpretation of ecclesiastical law for the rest of the Middle Ages and beyond. The following analysis examines seven important works of decretalists of the thirteenth century: Johannes Teutonicus's *Apparatus Glossarum in Compilationem Tertiam* (1216–18), the *Casus Parisienses* (possibly the work of Vincentius Hispanus) and the *Casus Fuldenses* on the Fourth Lateran Council (1215–20), the *Apparatus in Quinque Libros Decretalium* of Sinibaldo Fieschi, who became Pope Innocent IV shortly before completing his work (ca. 1245), the *Summa Aurea* of Henry of Susa, who became cardinal bishop of Ostia and is thus known as Hostiensis (ca. 1253), Bernard of Parma's *Glossa Ordinaria in Decretales* (reaching final form ca. 1266), and Hostiensis's *Lectura* or *Commentum super Decretalibus* (ca. 1271).[46] The discussion will

45. See Kenneth Pennington, "The Decretalists 1190–1234," in *Canon Law, 1140–1234*, ed. Hartmann and Pennington, 211–45.
46. Full citation information for these sources is as follows: Kenneth Pennington, ed., *Johannis Teutonici Apparatus Glossarum in Compilationem Tertiam*, vol. 1, Monumenta Iuris Canonici, ser. A, Corpus Glossatorum 3 (Vatican City: Biblioteca Apostolica Vaticana, 1981) [hereafter "JohTeut"]; Antonio García y García, ed., *Constitutiones Concilii Quarti Lateranensis una cum Commentariis Glossatorum*, Monumenta Iuris Canonici, ser. A, Corpus Glossatorum 2 (Vatican City: Biblioteca Apostolica Vaticana, 1981) [hereafter "*Casus Fuldenses*" and "*Casus Parisienses*"]; *Commentaria Innocentii Quarti Pontificis Maximi super Libros Quinque Decretalium* (Frankfurt, 1570) [hereafter "Sinibaldo"]; *Henrici de Segusio Cardinalis Hostiensis Summa Aurea* (Basel: Guarini, 1573) [hereafter "*HostAurea*"]; *Corpus Iuris Canonici* [*Editio Romana*], vol. 2, *Decretales Domini Gregorii Papae IX* (Rome: Aedes Populi Romani, 1582) [hereafter "BernParm"]; and *Lectura sive Apparatus Domini Hostiensis super Quinque Libris Decretalium* (Strasbourg, 1512) [hereafter "*HostLect*"]. In the following discussion, the passage of the decretal collection will be given after "ad," then (when applicable) the

treat these works thematically, using headings similar to those found in the previous chapter.

Who could receive the pallium?

Influenced by Innocent III's letter to Cardinal Cinthius, both Bernard of Parma and Hostiensis in his *Lectura* stressed the pallium's connection to the archiepiscopate. For Bernard, "the authority and power of the archiepiscopal dignity is completed in the pallium." Moreover, an archbishop-elect, even if already consecrated as a bishop, could not be called *archiepiscopus* before receiving the pallium; the title came not from his ordination, but from his palliation.[47] For Hostiensis, the title and the *plenitudo pontificalis officii* were acquired through the vestment—not through the object *per se*, but through its *traditio* and *susceptio*, the transaction between donor and recipient. What then should a consecrated but unpalliated archbishop be called? Hostiensis suggested, as an example, "bishop of Lyon," until reception of the pallium made him "archbishop of Lyon."[48]

The archiepiscopal association of the vestment affected the understanding of other legal points. When Innocent III required the archbishop of Compostela to procure the local bishop's permission before taking advantage of his special grant to use the pallium outside his own province, Sinibaldo, followed by Hostiensis's *Lectura*, cited an opinion that this permission should come instead from the local metropolitan, "since it is a matter of his own insignia."[49] It was he who might feel threatened by someone wearing the pallium—and so looking like an archbishop—on his own turf. Thus the reason for needing permission, Hostiensis went on, was that the privilege prejudiced the rights of this metropolitan. "Other insignia," such as

---

word or phrase within the passage after "s.v." (*sub verbo*), then the page or column number of the edition in parentheses. For example, "BernParm ad X 1.6.4 s.v. *oblatum* (111)" means the part of Bernard of Parma's *Glossa Ordinaria* that comments on the word *oblatum* within 1.6.4 of Gregory IX's *Liber Extra*, as found on col. 111 of the edition cited above.

47. BernParm ad X 1.8.3 pr. et s.v. *nominis* (220–21).
48. *HostLect* ad X 1.8.3 s.v. *in quo* et *archiepiscopalis nominis* (1:88v).
49. Sinibaldo ad X 1.8.5 s.v. *dummodo is* (88v), *HostLect* ad X 1.8.5 s.v. *id permittat* (1:89v–90r).

sandals, rings, and the remaining pontifical vestments, which bishops used "indifferently," posed no such threat, but the pallium did.[50] Sinibaldo, followed again by Hostiensis, further posited that the pallium was a "sign of prelacy [*signum praelationis*]," the badge of a superior, and so no suffragan, "even if he were a palliated bishop," suitably had a say over it—unless perhaps he were an exempt bishop (with no superior under the pope). In short, no lower bishop could ordinarily give permission to a higher one to wear this vestment.[51] Nevertheless, since the case at hand involved a special privilege from the pope, these commentators recognized that the usual rules did not necessarily apply.

Another situation that bent the usual rules was that of palliated suffragans, and Hostiensis took care to allow for their exceptional status. In his *Summa Aurea* he defined the pallium as "the distinctive decoration [*insigne ornamentum*] of *a bishop* or archbishop," a badge that set him apart from others.[52] He further noted that its proper recipients were "all archbishops and those higher ... but also certain bishops from long custom," among whom he listed the bishops of Pavia, Le Puy, Messina, and Ostia, whose churches had this customary privilege.[53] Hostiensis similarly remarked that the only ones who wore this insigne were either those "to whom it is fitting from the

---

50. *HostLect* ad X 1.8.5 s.v. *id permittat* (1:89v–90r) et ad X 1.8.7 s.v. *sandaliis* (90r). In the former passage Hostiensis referred to D.21 c.1, in which it was said that the pagan *flamines* "ubique pallio utebantur," but his logic suggested that "pallio" here was a later corruption of "pileo."

51. Sinibaldo ad X 1.8.5 s.v. *permittat* (88v), *HostLect* ad X 1.8.5 s.v. *id permittat* (1:89v–90r).

52. *HostAurea* ad X 1.8 s.v. *quid sit pallium* (122–23); emphasis added. Even so, the next comment adhered to Innocent III by attaching the archiepiscopal title to the vestment and implying that without it one was not truly an archbishop.

53. *HostAurea* ad X 1.8 s.v. *cui concedendum sit* (123–24). This passage's "Armicensis" was likely corrupted from "Aniciensis." On Messina, see Gregory the Great to Donus of Messina in 595, JE 1388, IP 10:335 no. 8, CCSL 140:377; but also JL —, IP 10:340 no. 26. According to John of Salisbury in his *Historia Pontificalis*, Eugene III proposed three reasons why a simple bishop might merit the pallium: his was the see of a nation's evangelist, e.g., Pavia; or he had the right to consecrate his metropolitan, as did the bishops of Autun, Lausanne (later mistakenly emended to Laon), and Ostia; or his see was a region's chief city, with the accompanying right to crown the king (Chibnall, *Historia*, 68). This pope's observations, however, seem not to have influenced the canonical tradition.

office of dignity" (churchmen of the rank that the insigne designated) or those who obtained it by "special privilege" (palliated suffragans).[54] In his *Lectura* he also held that the pope in one case used an indefinite pronoun, rather than specifying a rank, precisely because the pallium "is sometimes also granted to a bishop."[55] Not all decretalists were as careful as Hostiensis. Both the *Casus Parisienses* and the *Casus Fuldenses*, commenting on the fifth constitution of Lateran IV, assumed that the patriarchs' suffragans, mentioned in the text as recipients of the pallium, were archbishops.[56] Perhaps the authors did not know that all Eastern bishops traditionally received the *omophorion*, or perhaps the Latin churches of the East followed the Western custom and rarely permitted it to simple bishops.

What was required in order to receive the pallium?

Unlike the decretists, the decretalists did not dwell extensively on prerequisites for the reception of the pallium. Both Bernard of Parma and Hostiensis (in both his works considered here) repeated the necessity of a petition offered *fortiter* or *instanter*, but both also took account of a grant *motu proprio*, by which the pope "wished to do them a favor without any request," for "sometimes too it is offered by grace to one who does not ask."[57] The profession of faith, perhaps by now altogether replaced by the oath of fidelity, was rarely alluded to. The oath itself, which Hostiensis called an "oath of obedience," came up chiefly in relation to the Lateran IV constitution.[58] The *Casus Fuldenses* glossed both the oaths described in this canon, the *professio canonica* to the patriarch and the *sponsio oboedientiae* to the Roman church, as "fidelity," that is, an oath of fidelity, similar to the "oath of fidelity and obedience" offered by the patriarch himself to

---

54. *HostAurea* ad X 1.8 s.v. *et quibus diebus utendum sit pallio* (124–25). As an example of the former churchmen, he cited D.21 c.1, "pallium imponebant pro sacerdotii eminentia," in which a later scribe or editor mistook "pileum" for "pallium." Cf. *HostAurea* ad X 1.8 s.v. *et quo loco* (125–26).

55. *HostLect* ad X 1.8.2 s.v. *sed quisque* (1:88v).

56. *Casus Parisienses* ad c.5 (467), *Casus Fuldenses* ad c.5 (484).

57. BernParm ad X 1.6.4 s.v. *oblatum* (111), *HostAurea* ad X 1.8 s.v. *et a quo* (124), *HostLect* ad X 1.8.4 (1:89r).

58. *HostAurea* ad X 1.8 s.v. *et a quo* (124).

the pope.⁵⁹ Bernard of Parma used slightly different terms. Suffragans must swear "obedience and reverence" to their metropolitan or patriarch, while those immediately under the pope must swear "fidelity and obedience," perhaps a stronger obligation, to Peter's successor. Bernard never varied those two phrases in relation to their respective recipients, but in fact he hinted that they were essentially the same thing.⁶⁰ In effect, this practice fostered ties of alliance and dependence within the ecclesiastical hierarchy.

Innocent III's defense of the bishop of Pécs provided an occasion to discuss the traditional requirement of personal worthiness. Johannes Teutonicus, followed by Bernard of Parma, enunciated the pope's logic: "From the fact that he attained such a great dignity, it is presumed that he attained it by reason of his virtue."⁶¹ Bernard added that the bishop's privilege of using the pallium had been granted "because of merit," and consequently "from his past life it is presumed about the present."⁶² Such a presumption may sound dubious, but the argument was not unlike that of John VIII, who had held that receiving the pallium purged one of any suspicion of guilt from previous crimes.⁶³ In this case, the rationale was extended to behavior *after* the vestment's reception. Admittedly, Innocent had other reasons to doubt the bishop's guilt, but from the pope's viewpoint, the gift of the pallium was at least a *prima facie* judgment in favor of the recipient's good character.

By fulfilling these prerequisites, could the recipient incur the guilt of ambition or simony?

The decretalists were also not as preoccupied as the decretists with the simoniacal dangers of qualifying for the pallium. Sinibaldo admitted that the fee that had prevailed *in donatione pallii* was an "evil cus-

---

59. *Casus Fuldenses* ad c.5 (484).
60. BernParm ad X 5.33.23 pr. et s.v. *fidelitatis et oboedientiae* et *professionem* (1825–26).
61. JohTeut ad 3Comp 2.14.2 s.v. *ornamento pallii* (1:275–76), BernParm ad X 2.23.15 s.v. *honestum* (795).
62. BernParm ad X 2.23.15 (794–95).
63. JE 2986, GP 7.1:34 no. 66, BU 96, MGH Epp. 7:314.

tom" that Gregory the Great had tried to eradicate.[64] Bernard of Parma addressed the old concern about attaching conditions to "spiritual things," and offered many reasons why the grant of the pallium after an oath of fidelity was not simoniacal but wholly acceptable—in fact, the vestment "is not to be handed over otherwise." As he explained, the condition was honorable; it was applied by a superior; it was applied before the gift, as was allowed to a superior; it was connected (*annexum*) to the office being assumed; the "burden of the matter" was expressly stated; it belonged to *ius commune*; and it was applied "by the law itself." All seven of these things precluded simony.[65]

How was the Johannine law to be applied?

Because the obligation imposed by John VIII on all metropolitans had been the centerpiece of Gratian 1's treatment of the pallium, its importance was still acknowledged, even if there was little left to say about it. When Hostiensis began his treatise *de auctoritate et usu pallii* in his *Summa Aurea*, he contrived to do so with the words *quoniam quidam*, probably as a homage to that classic text.[66] In his *Lectura*, furthermore, he touched on a number of points that neatly summarized much of the decretists' work on the matter.[67] The three-month deadline should be counted from the day on which the candidate was consecrated. Within that time he should at least send a messenger, who would not necessarily reach Rome before the deadline passed; after all, some churches were so distant that it took more than three months to get to Rome, and of course there could not be a separate policy for each church. A "just cause" could excuse him from the deadline, in which case a year or even more might be permitted. Hostiensis adduced two opinions about when the penalty should be imposed: either immediately after the three months (a brief period that reflected the great danger presented by a metropolitan see improperly filled), or after five months (a longer period allowing time

64. Sinibaldo ad X 5.3.1 s.v. *notarius* (498r).
65. BernParm ad X 1.6.4 pr. et s.v. *conditione* (110–11).
66. *HostAurea* ad X 1.8 (122).
67. *HostLect* ad X 1.8.4 (1:89r). The following two paragraphs are also based on this passage.

for the three warnings alluded to in the canon). To suffer the penalty of deposition, the noncompliant archbishop must be accused *coram papa*, since nobody else could inflict such a sentence.

Hostiensis also took special interest in the messenger (*nuntius*) sent to the pope to request the pallium. He had to be "sufficient," which for this decretalist meant that he was suitable to the task, was sent from the candidate within three months from the latter's consecration, and was given an adequate *procuratorium*. This "mandate of proxy" required a number of things: an acknowledgement of papal decrees and the first four ecumenical councils; a signature by the sender's own hand; power given to the messenger to confirm all this by swearing on the sender's soul that he "firmly and simply" believed what he claimed to believe; power also to make a vigorous request for the pallium; and power lastly to swear on the sender's soul "fidelity and obedience" to the Roman church. If these things were not fulfilled, the pallium would be denied, and in the law's eyes the Johannine obligation would not have been met—as if the candidate had not sent to the apostolic see at all. In addition, Hostiensis made allowance for a messenger who acted "unfaithfully" or ran into trouble, or even died, on the way to Rome. In these cases the obligation was not yet met, and as soon as possible—within three more months, counted from the time when the candidate was notified of the problem—he had to send another messenger. In fact, he had to keep doing so until the law was fulfilled.

Hostiensis's most surprising comment was an aside he made during this discussion. "Although this rigor is so written," he said, "nevertheless we have not seen that it is kept. Thus it can be said that this solemn matter has fallen into desuetude, since not even the Roman church keeps it to a tee." He had just been treating the deadline, the requisite warnings, and the penalty of the Johannine law, and now admitted that archbishops did not always observe it, and that Rome did not always enforce it. Despite the frequency with which *Quoniam quidam* was repeated, it is difficult to conclude what success it actually enjoyed; indeed, the frequent repetition may have indicated negligence or even resistance by some metropolitans. Hostiensis also defended the law from a specific objection: the custom of the Roman curia ordinarily forbade an elect from presenting a petition, and so one might argue that *ubi nulla petitio, ibi nulla mora,* and no penalty should be suffered for such a delay. To this he replied that a written law was a different case, and custom could not stand if it robbed the law of its effect. As a result, the law still stood—even if, Hostiensis grumbled, it was "extremely harsh." Perhaps he had encountered this objection before. And perhaps he himself—a palliger, as archbishop of Embrun and later also as cardinal bishop of Ostia— had reservations about John VIII's law.

What happened if use of the pallium was refused or withdrawn?

Innocent III's prohibition of the pallium's use by the archbishop of Dubrovnik when he was translated to the bishopric of Carlisle gave canonists an opportunity to investigate the legal implications of this unusual case. In his *Summa Aurea* Hostiensis believed that the pope's commission to the ex-archbishop to perform episcopal ministry in another archbishop's province implied that he could keep wearing the vestment, and so Innocent had to deny that faculty specifically and command his obedience to the local metropolitan, lest there seem to be two metropolitans in the same province.[68] Somewhat differently, Bernard of Parma held that an archbishop in another archbishop's territory could not ordinarily wear the pallium anyway. Even so, he expressed a reservation about the case, since by both canon and Roman law "it is not permitted for those having discharged greater honors to descend to lesser ones."[69] He seemed to recognize that this metropolitan had essentially been demoted to the status of a suffragan bishop, and the withdrawal of the vestment was meant not simply to avoid upsetting the local hierarchy, but also to point out the churchman's new rank.

How should the pallium be received?

With his usual thoroughness Hostiensis, in his *Summa Aurea,* delineated three manners in which the pallium could be obtained.

68. *HostAurea* ad X 1.8 s.v. *et quo loco* (125–26).
69. BernParm ad X 1.9.9 pr. et s.v. *usu pallii* (231).

Sometimes it was granted to a recipient personally present before the pope (*existens in curia*); sometimes it was granted through the recipient's messenger, sent from the local church and described as "certain ... and particularly assigned for this purpose," that is, one whose specific aim was to fetch it; and sometimes it was granted through emissaries (*apocrisiarii*) of the papal curia, that is, legates who brought it to the local church.[70] In these words he nodded first to the policy that the reform papacy had attempted to enforce, then to the more traditional method of reception, and finally to the increasingly common use of papal legates in this transaction. Bernard of Parma added that, if the recipient was present in Rome, he took the pallium from the altar of Peter, or if he was not, another did so "on his behalf."[71] Bernard did not clarify what had happened in the case on which he was commenting, when papal legates carried the vestment to the archbishop of Esztergom. Perhaps the Hungarian messengers had received it from the altar and accompanied the legates back to Esztergom, or perhaps the legates themselves had so received it before setting out. Maybe too the pallium was later placed on the altar of the cathedral of Esztergom, to be taken up from there by the archbishop.[72]

The decretalists seemed to regret Raymond of Penyafort's decision to remove the *forma traditionis pallii*, the formula to be recited as the vestment was given to its recipient, from c. 4 of his pallium title. At times their comments on this canon included such a formula, though not Innocent III's original.[73] Hostiensis, for example, cited the

70. *HostAurea* ad X 1.8 s.v. *et a quo* (124).
71. BernParm ad X 1.6.4 s.v. *corpore assumuntur* (112).
72. Such a procedure was followed in the eleventh and twelfth centuries in places as disparate as Milan (Landulf the Younger, in Castiglioni, *Historia Mediolanensis*, 22), Antioch (William of Tyre, *Historia Rerum in Partibus Transmarinis Gestarum*, in CCCM 63A:642), and Canterbury (Eadmer of Canterbury, *Historia Novorum in Anglia*, in Rolls 81:72–73, 230; William of Malmesbury, *Gesta Pontificum Anglorum*, in Winterbottom, *Gesta Pontificum*, 1:142; John of Worcester, in Darlington and McGurk, *Chronicle*, 3:74, 76; and Ralph de Diceto, *Imagines Historiarum*, in Rolls 68.1:307). Cf. also the archbishop of Canterbury's enthronement ceremony in Cambridge, Corpus Christi College, 44 (Tinti, "Archiepiscopal Pallium," 326–28).
73. For the formula in Innocent's text, see X 1.8.4, Friedberg, *Corpus*, 2:101. This formula was unlike the ones provided by the decretalists in four minor ways: it gave

pars decisa of that canon, but apparently supplied the formula used at his own reception of the pallium as archbishop of Embrun:

> To the honor of almighty God, and the blessed Virgin Mary, and the blessed apostles Peter and Paul, and the lord Pope Innocent IV, and the Roman church, and the church of Embrun entrusted to you, we hand over to you the pallium, taken from the body of blessed Peter, for the fullness of the pontifical dignity, so that you may use it within your church, on the days that are expressed in the privileges granted to your church by the Roman church.[74]

It is not clear whether these words were spoken by an official in the papal court, or a papal legate or his own returning envoy in the cathedral of Embrun; all that seems certain is that the pope himself did not use them, since he was mentioned in the third person. This formula differed from the typical text of a traditional pallium privilege: not only was there a series of honorific invocations at the beginning, but the more tangible verb *tradimus* replaced the more abstract or legal *concedimus*. Also, the standard epithet for the pallium, "the fullness of the pontifical office," usually equated with the vestment, was now prefaced with the preposition *in*, as if to indicate that the garb conveyed that fullness, without itself being the fullness; also, *dignitas* was substituted for *officium*.[75] Finally, the list of pallium days was replaced with a general expression, which hinted that there was no single list in an accompanying document, but that the recipient must look at the past privileges of the pastors of his church to find precedents (as similarly indicated, Hostiensis noted, in c. 7).

When Bernard of Parma likewise inserted a *forma traditionis*, his version mentioned "the lord Pope Gregory [IX]," a clue to its date (1227–41), but left the name of the recipient's church generic.[76] He followed it with a list of pallium days that he took from elsewhere.[77] Hostiensis returned to the matter of a formula in his *Lectura*, where

---

the pallium the epithet "insigne plenitudinis pontificalis officii"; it specified the restriction "ad missarum solennia"; it detailed the place of use as "infra ecclesias tibi subiectas"; and its list of pallium days was somewhat stingier.

74. *HostAurea* ad X 1.8 s.v. *cui concedendum sit* (123–24).
75. Cf. *HostLect* ad X 1.8.4 (1:89r), BernParm ad X 5.33.23 (1825–26).
76. BernParm ad X 1.8.4 s.v. *ad honorem* (221).
77. Cf. *HostAurea* ad X 1.8 s.v. *et quibus diebus utendum sit pallio* (124–25).

he reproduced one that he attributed to Vincentius Hispanus—with both the pope and the recipient's church unnamed—and appended a list of pallium days from elsewhere.[78] Apart from minor variations, these three formulas were the same. Celestine III had quoted a brief part of the formula in the letter that became c. 1 of the *Liber Extra*'s pallium title, a line which Bernard of Parma repeated in his summary of that canon.[79] Nevertheless, in his background to c. 5 of the same title, Bernard gave a different rendition of the line: "It was said to the archbishop of Compostela at the giving of his pallium, 'Receive the pallium, [so that] you may use it within your church.'"[80] This imperative form, *accipe pallium*, was used when the pope himself was vested with the pallium at his installation, as twelfth-century *ordines* witnessed.[81] Yet Canon Peter Mallius of St. Peter's Basilica testified around the same time that Roman legates used the imperative when delivering the pallium, and in the late thirteenth century the great liturgist William Durandus said that the archpriest of the Roman church used it when handing over the vestment to an archbishop who was present in Rome.[82] The evidence from this period was inconsistent, but the imperative form was not dominant in the canonical tradition.

---

78. *HostLect* ad X 1.8.4 (1:89r). Hostiensis added "sive officii" after "dignitatis" in the epithet, as if bringing the formula into line with the traditional wording. Cf. *HostAurea* ad X 1.8 s.v. *et quibus diebus utendum sit pallio* (124–25).

79. X 1.8.1, Friedberg, *Corpus*, 2:100, and BernParm ad X 1.8.1 (220). Cencius's *Liber Censuum* from Celestine's time contained a formula, however, that differed slightly (Fabre and Duchesne, *Liber censuum*, 1.3:417). Its rubric specified that the pallium was given "upon the altar by the cardinal deacons and subdeacons of the Roman church."

80. BernParm ad X 1.8.5 (222).

81. Albinus (*Digesta Pauperis Scholaris*, in Fabre and Duchesne, *Liber censuum*, 2.6:124) and Cencius (*Liber Censuum*, in ibid., 1.3:312) testified to the imperative form.

82. Peter Mallius, *Descriptio Basilicae Vaticanae*, in Roberto Valentini and Giuseppe Zucchetti, eds., *Codice topografico della città di Roma*, Fonti per la storia d'Italia 90 (Rome: Tipografia del Senato, 1946), 3:385, and William Durandus's pontifical, in Andrieu, *Pontifical*, 3:393.

What relationship did the pallium establish between donor and recipient?

In the tradition of their predecessors, the decretalists insisted that bestowing the pallium was a papal prerogative. Nor did c. 5 of Lateran IV contradict this tenet when it allowed patriarchs to confer the vestment on their suffragans. After noting that the pallium was taken "only" from the body of Peter, Sinibaldo observed, "No one gives this insigne, namely the pallium, except the pope," while the patriarchs "give it not by their own authority, but by the pope's."[83] Hostiensis took a different approach in his *Summa Aurea*: the patriarchs could grant it within their respective jurisdictions, but only the pope could grant it "universally."[84] In his *Lectura*, commenting on c. 3 of the pallium title, the same canonist underscored the influence that the vestment allowed the pope to wield. It was questionable enough in this canon that a cardinal legate had translated a bishop to an archbishopric without papal approval, but the prelate began calling himself an archbishop before receiving the pallium from the pope, "who alone can grant it." This papal faculty guaranteed the pope's personal involvement, which provided an opportunity to check the legate's misbehavior.[85]

More generally, the pallium, as a papal insigne shared with others by the pope himself, ensured the wearer's acknowledgement of papal overlordship. Sinibaldo interpreted the pallium's Petrine associations as facilitating the incorporation of the wearer under Peter's vicar: archbishops received the vestment *a beati Petri corpore* because they "belong to the body of blessed Peter, that is, the church, whose head is Christ, and his vicar is Peter and his successors."[86] The pallium was thus a visible sign of their communion with the pope and the universal church. Moreover, Bernard of Parma construed the phrase "signs of due subjection," which Paschal II had called the oath

---

83. Sinibaldo ad X 1.6.4 s.v. *corpor[e]* (41v).
84. *HostAurea* ad X 1.8 s.v. *et a quo* (124).
85. *HostLect* ad X 1.8.3 s.v. *appellare* et *a nobis* (1:88v). See also *HostLect* ad X 1.8.1 s.v. *debes* (1:88v).
86. Sinibaldo ad X 1.6.4 s.v. *corpor[e]* (41v).

of fidelity attached to the pallium, as "insignia of subjection, which, having been shown, make clear that you keep the unity of the catholic head."[87] This subtle change to the pope's words and the use of the term *insignia* suggested that the vestment itself brought to mind the submission to papal authority that prompted the oath preceding it.

This differentiation between donor and recipient came to the fore when Hostiensis discussed the epithet that had commonly been applied to the pallium for over a century: *plenitudo pontificalis officii*. He found it necessary in his *Summa Aurea* to introduce variants of the epithet for the various types of palliger. The pallium on the pope meant "the fullest fullness of power" and "of office." On patriarchs it meant "the fullest power of office"; on archbishops it meant "the fuller power of office"; and on bishops it meant "the full power of office." The implications of the terminology were unclear, and the argument seemed strained for the sake of categorical neatness. Hostiensis himself admitted that the discussion was speculative: it had "no great force," but was made "academically, for subtlety rather than for usefulness." Nevertheless, he made a point about papal authority: since the pope had "fullness of power," he had "fullness of office" as well. By virtue of the latter he "renders justice according to the laws," but by virtue of the former he "transcends the laws." For the others, however, "power" and "office" were combined, and the gradations seemed to indicate that Hostiensis was talking about jurisdiction, which lessened as one went down the hierarchy.[88] In any event, the old epithet, enjoyed equally by every palliger from pope to metropolitan, was no longer comfortably seen as such. Later, in his *Lectura*, Hostiensis took the not wholly surprising step of conflating the standard epithet with the first term of the ancient dyad *plenitudo potestatis/pars sollicitudinis*. That is, he distinguished the pallium's meaning when worn by the pope—"the fullness of power"—from its meaning when worn by a lesser prelate—"the fullness of office," which he equated with "a share of the responsibility."[89] Of course,

87. BernParm ad X 1.6.4 (110).
88. *HostAurea* ad X 1.8 s.v. *quid sit pallium* (122–23).
89. *HostLect* ad X 1.8.4 s.v. *potestatis* (1:89v).

this development directly conflicted with several twelfth-century *ordines* in which the traditional epithet was recited at the pope's own investiture.[90]

Decretalists found such distinctions important. They often remarked, when speaking of the processional cross, that the reason patriarchs were forbidden to use it in Rome was that a lesser *iudex* could not exercise his *iurisdictio* when a greater one was present.[91] Hostiensis in his *Summa Aurea* applied this rule as well to the use of the pallium. A palliger should not wear it in the pope's presence, or in the presence of a papal legate with apostolic insignia when he was using those insignia. This principle would explain why, according to Eadmer of Canterbury and William of Malmesbury, no one at the Council of Bari (1098) wore the pallium—presumably not even the archbishop of Bari—except Pope Urban II.[92] At the same time, Hostiensis pointed out a piece of circumstantial counter-evidence from his own experience: why did the archbishop of Canterbury wear his pallium in Lyon, while the pope was residing there (1244–51)? "Perhaps he was not paying attention," he shrugged, "but neither must what is done be considered, but rather what *ought* to be done."[93] One suspects that the actual practice of individual palligers often deviated from the canonists' norms.

How was the use of the pallium limited to its recipient?

The first two canons of the *Liber Extra*'s pallium title clarified two restrictions on the vestment's use: a palliated archbishop could not wear it outside his province, nor could he lend it to another archbishop. These regulations spurred the decretalists to explore the na-

---

90. The *Basel Ordo* (Schimmelpfennig, "Bisher unbekannter Text," 64), the *London Ordo* (Bernhard Schimmelpfennig, ed., "Ein Fragment zur Wahl, Konsekration und Krönung des Papstes im 12. Jahrhundert," *Archivum Historiae Pontificiae* 8 [1970]: 329), Albinus (*Digesta Pauperis Scholaris*, in Fabre and Duchesne, *Liber censuum*, 2.6:124), and Cencius (*Liber Censuum*, in Fabre and Duchesne, *Liber censuum*, 1.3:312) testified to the epithet.

91. E.g., BernParm ad X 5.33.23 pr. et s.v. *nisi in urbe* (1825–26).

92. Eadmer, *Historia Novorum in Anglia*, in Rolls 81:107; and William, *Gesta Pontificum Anglorum*, in Winterbottom, *Gesta Pontificum*, 1:154.

93. HostAurea ad X 1.8 s.v. *cui concedendum sit* (123–24); emphasis added.

ture of the privilege more deeply. To begin with, they emphasized that the privilege was personal. As Hostiensis's *Lectura* declared, "Personal things are extinguished with the persons, nor are they extended to others.... Only in respect to the person of the archbishop is the pallium that has been handed over personal." Moreover, it was meant for the person *as a specific archbishop,* and therefore could not be used outside his province or if he was translated to a new church.[94] Bernard of Parma said much the same; in addition, just as lending was forbidden, borrowing a local metropolitan's pallium while one was visiting was likewise out of the question.[95] Hostiensis admitted that the local prelate might offer his pallium simply out of courtesy (*curialitas*). If he could invite an archiepiscopal visitor to celebrate Mass in his church, lending him his pallium would appear to be a natural consequence—but the law said no.[96]

As Alexander III had highlighted, the custom of burying the pallium with its recipient bore forceful witness to the personal character of the privilege. Parts of canon and Roman law that seemed to militate against such a practice, Bernard of Parma hastened to add, were meant to apply to the laity, not the clergy, or concerned costly decorations and jewelry rather than priestly vestments and *spiritualia*.[97] Sinibaldo wondered what happened if a deceased man had possessed two pallia, perhaps because he had been an archbishop and was later translated to a different archiepiscopal see. He believed that both pallia were to be buried with him. The first was considered already "buried"—that is, unusable—from the time when he had given up the first church. Thus the second pallium took precedence and should be placed on top of the body (*desuper*). Indeed, one opinion held that the corpse should wear only this second vestment, while the first should be placed (perhaps folded or rolled) upon him (*super eo*) or under his head. Sinibaldo found this a good rule of thumb.[98] In his *Lectura* Hostiensis agreed, and extended the application of this

---

94. *HostLect* ad X 1.8.2 s.v. *personam* (1:88v).
95. BernParm ad X 1.8.2 s.v. *commodes* (220) et ad X 1.8.5 s.v. *pallio* (222).
96. *HostLect* ad X 1.8.2 s.v. *commodare* (1:88v).
97. BernParm ad X 1.8.2 s.v. *sepeliri* (220).
98. Sinibaldo ad X 1.8.2 s.v. *sepeliri* (88r).

reasoning. If an archbishop was translated to a simple bishopric, he must guard his pallium, "not so that he may use it in life, but so that it may be buried with him."[99] Also, "if he received three or more pallia in his life," the same procedure outlined by Sinibaldo should be followed. Finally, as did Bernard, Hostiensis defended this custom against certain legal objections because "something special is long alleged by custom in the pallium and priestly vestments ... that the dead ought to be buried with them."[100]

A personal privilege should not be enjoyed, of course, without the favor that prompted it and the special grant that bestowed it. Just as it was permitted "to some by grace [*de gratia*]," so others should not usurp it, Hostiensis asserted in his *Summa Aurea*.[101] Yet some decretalists seemed to blur this principle when they spoke about the pallium. Hostiensis himself, in the same work, alluded to translated bishops who could gain the vestment "if the dignity of the pallium is due to the churches to which they are translated," as if to say that it was owed to sees, rather than freely conferred on individuals.[102] He also referred to simple bishops to whom the vestment was due "by the privileges of their churches," as if custom had created an ecclesial right, even though such an attitude opposed the pope's freedom of choice and the pallium's status as a personal privilege. Other simple bishops, however, received the vestment "by personal privilege," for instance the bishop of Pécs, "but this is extinguished with the person."[103] It seems unlikely that Hostiensis was denying that all pallium privileges were, in a sense, personal; probably he meant that some set a precedent for a see, while others did not. Still, the idea of a papal gift freely given at the donor's discretion did not seem paramount in his thought. This ambiguity was not unknown in the pallium's history, ever since the gift had become routinized. Even the *forma traditionis* recited at the pallium's bestowal made reference to the days listed previously "in the privileges granted to your church by

---

99. Hostiensis attributed this opinion to members of the papal curia.
100. *HostLect* ad X 1.8.2 s.v. *cum eo* et *sepeliri* (1:88v).
101. *HostAurea* ad X 1.8 s.v. *et quibus diebus utendum sit pallio* (124–25).
102. *HostAurea* ad X 1.8 (122).
103. *HostAurea* ad X 1.8 s.v. *cui concedendum sit* (123–24).

the Roman church," rather than in a particular privilege now granted to the palliger himself.[104]

In the same vein, Johannes Teutonicus maintained that, if the pope allowed it, an archbishop's pallium could be worn by his successor. Strictly speaking, his point was accurate: the authority that imposed the restriction could also dispense from it. But this possibility conflicted with the long custom of a lingering personal attachment all the way to the grave. Johannes's concern was to avoid injury to the successor, as if the pallium was owed him, and was expected in order to preserve his rights; here he called to witness Roman law. Nevertheless, he also recognized that it was a *beneficium* requiring a papal *concessio*.[105] He had examined the same tension between gift and right in his *Glossa Ordinaria* on Gratian's *Decretum*.[106] Bernard of Parma, in contrast, seemed hesitant. If an archbishop was translated to a different archiepiscopal see, although he should not use his previous pallium, could he use the one worn by his predecessor in the new see? After all, given his approved translation, he was confirmed in his new archbishopric and may not have needed the further confirmation of a new pallium. But Bernard decided he should not, except with special papal permission. Even so, the pope should not deny to the new archbishop whatever privilege the old one had possessed, lest he do him an injury.[107] Once again, a canonist appeared willing to limit the pope's freedom as donor.

The decretalists searched for a way to describe the odd nature of the privilege of wearing the pallium, which seemed bound to a specific recipient, yet also bound to an office in a church in a particular place. The archbishop of Kalocsa's need for a new pallium when he was translated to the archbishopric of Esztergom, despite the fact that his old one was still attached to him until burial, offered an opportunity to think through the problem. Each of the scholars under consideration here had his own formulation, but all agreed that the privilege was both personal and local. For Johannes Teutonicus, the

104. Ibid.
105. JohTeut ad 3Comp 1.4.4 s.v. *pallium* (1:39–40).
106. *Glossa Ordinaria* ad D.100 c.11 s.v. *atque privilegia* (645).
107. BernParm ad X 1.5.4 s.v. *pallium* (107).

pallium "follows the person" even to burial, and yet "is given in respect to a place [*respectu loci*]." That place indicated not only a local church, but also an office within that church, for an archbishop who "renounces the place of his archbishopric"—that is, resigns—"loses the use of the pallium."[108] Sinibaldo adopted the same argument, but worded the privilege as given "not only in view [*in contemplatione*] of a person, but also of a place."[109] In his *Summa Aurea* Hostiensis characterized the pallium as "partly real, partly personal." As a result, a palliger had to request a new one if he was translated to another metropolis, but even within his own church he could not lend it to another, and it had to be buried with him.[110] Only the papal donor could grant special permission for an *extensio* beyond the usual restrictions, and in such cases the real and the personal went hand-in-hand.[111] Finally, in Bernard of Parma's eyes, the pallium was a favor in part personal, in part local (*beneficium pro parte personale, pro parte locale*).[112] Or, as he put it in another place, it was "given to a person, but in view of a place [*contemplatione loci*]"—in other words, it was personal as long as the person held a particular position in a particular place.[113]

In order to define that place ("within your church"), Celestine III's decretal had specified "within any church of the province entrusted to you."[114] Bernard of Parma called this a "broad" interpretation, unlike an unrelated canon in which the term "church" signified the

---

108. JohTeut ad 3Comp 1.4.4 s.v. *pallium* (1:39–40).

109. Sinibaldo ad X 1.5.4 s.v. *ad nomen* (40r).

110. It was buried with him, Hostiensis added (based on the testimony of members of the papal curia), even if he became a cardinal—perhaps, that is, ceasing to function as a metropolitan.

111. *HostAurea* ad X 1.8 s.v. *et quo loco* (125–26). Cf. *HostLect* ad X 1.8.5 s.v. *indulgemus* (1:89v): "nec personam egreditur ... neque locum, nisi indulgeatur." According to *HostAurea*, in X 1.8.2 Alexander III refused a personal extension, which thus included the refusal of a real extension, while in X 1.8.5 Innocent III granted a real extension, which thus included the grant of a personal extension. Did this logic permit the palliger in the latter case to lend his pallium?

112. BernParm ad X 1.8.5 s.v. *consuetudo* (222).

113. BernParm ad X 1.5.4 s.v. *pallium* (107).

114. X 1.8.1, Friedberg, *Corpus*, 2:100. The decretist works *Animal* ad D.100 c.6 s.v. *missarum sollempnia* and *Glossa Ordinaria* ad D.100 c.6 s.v. *intra tuam ecclesiam* were aware of this decretal.

cathedral only. Narrowness was avoided here so that "there would be prejudice to no one."[115] In his *Lectura* Hostiensis called those who would restrict "church" to a cathedral "stingy interpreters," and believed that Innocent III had chosen looser words in his letter to Uppsala in order to remove such doubts.[116] Elsewhere in the same work, Hostiensis noted that "province" could mean both the metropolis and its territory as a whole. More exactly, it should comprise "all the churches of his city, diocese, and province," including not just cathedrals, but parish churches and chapels as well.[117] Indeed, arguing against an alleged Spanish custom by which archbishops wore their pallia outside their own provinces, this canonist contended that such a practice would cause prejudice to others. "Such things give a sign," that is, the pallium symbolized something important, namely that the place where "insignia of this sort" were worn was subject to the wearer's jurisdiction.[118] The pallium's status as a badge of office provided the legal rationale for the restriction to the palliger's province and the local nature of the privilege.

Unsurprisingly, the decretalists felt compelled to explain the strangely lax prescriptions on where to use the pallium that were found in c. 6 of the *Liber Extra*'s pallium title. Some entertained reasons that seemed to support a more universal use of the pallium, even though Innocent III had called it a *corruptela* in c. 5. Johannes Teutonicus, followed at first by Bernard of Parma, called to witness the rational and the miter, two episcopal insignia that could be worn "everywhere," even though his references to Gratian were not entirely relevant.[119] He also chose to justify the universal language of c. 6 by applying a criterion from c. 5: wearing the pallium outside one's province was permitted, though conditional upon the local bishop's

115. BernParm ad X 1.8.1 s.v. *quamlibet* (220).
116. *HostLect* ad X 1.8.6 s.v. *liberius* (1:90r).
117. *HostLect* ad X 1.8.1 s.v. *provinciae* (1:88v). Hostiensis added that the province included the "ambitus" of the church where the palliger celebrated Mass, but his meaning was unclear.
118. *HostLect* ad X 1.8.5 s.v. *utantur* (1:89v).
119. Johannes cited D.36 d.p.c.2, although Gratian meant the ancient Hebrew priestly rational, and D.21 c.1, although Gratian meant the pagan *pileum* or *filum*; moreover, neither passage said that the vestment in question could be worn "ubique."

permission, since the pope did not want such a practice to prejudice another prelate.[120] Nevertheless, this approach did not win the day. To c. 6's expression "wherever you are placed," Sinibaldo added the unstated but expected restriction to "within your province" (as in c. 1)—unless some "special privilege" allowed the palliger to wear the vestment elsewhere (as in c. 5).[121] Hostiensis in his *Summa Aurea* agreed, and supposed that "wherever" must have implied "in a suitable or fitting place," that is, within the palliger's province.[122] (In his *Lectura* he proffered a comparable expression, "Never let the psalter fall from your hand," in which "never" must have implied "at the fitting hours," that is, during the Divine Office.)[123] Bernard of Parma surrendered to this interpretive trend and counseled that one had to "restrict" the canon's apparent meaning in order to harmonize it with the rest of the law; "and so," he concluded rather glibly, "it is obvious."[124]

Hostiensis showed particular interest in the situation of a palliger who was invited to ordain outside his own province. Since he had to wear the pallium in order to perform such an act, but he could not wear it outside his province, it seemed that he could not accept the invitation without a special papal privilege. As a result, as the decretist work *Omnis* had already observed in another context, the condition of the palliger seemed to be worse than that of a non-palliger, who could carry out an ordination even as a retired bishop (*nullius loci episcopus*). However, Hostiensis argued that a prelate could only be seen to do a sacred act *tamquam archiepiscopus* if he was within his own province, where he was *archos*. Thus he could perform the act *tamquam simplex episcopus* outside his province, where he could at least use the other episcopal insignia, even if not the pallium. Just as he could celebrate Mass there, so he should be able to ordain there.

---

120. JohTeut ad 3Comp 1.7.3 s.v. *corruptela* et *permittat* (1:88), BernParm ad X 1.8.5 s.v. *pallio* (222). Bernard played on the "ratio" inherent in the "rationale" to propose that a palliger might have a "rationabilis causa" to transgress the usual restriction to his province.
121. Sinibaldo ad X 1.8.6 s.v. *ubicumque* (88v).
122. *HostAurea* ad X 1.8 s.v. *et quo loco* (125–26).
123. *HostLect* ad X 1.8.5 s.v. *indulgemus* (1:89v).
124. BernParm ad X 1.8.6 s.v. *ubicumque* (223).

After all, the pallium was not by its nature "of the substance of the conferral of orders"; rather, it was a privilege that could not be extended beyond a prelate's own province.[125] Therefore, when Innocent III gave the archbishop of Compostela a special privilege that also required the local bishop's permission, the latter should be understood as permission to ordain there (outside the province of Compostela), while the former applied to using the pallium outside the province, once the aforesaid permission had been acquired. In short, three things were necessary: a papal privilege, local permission, and an appropriate case that required the palliger to ordain. Without all three he could not wear the vestment in this situation.[126] In concluding thus, Hostiensis opposed the opinion of his teacher, James of Albenga, who held that an archbishop could wear his pallium in another's province with the permission of that local metropolitan, as long as the pope had not specifically forbidden it; the special privilege in the Compostela case pertained not to using the vestment, but to ordaining outside his province. "I think the contrary," Hostiensis averred, "even though I am palliated!"[127]

How was the recipient limited in his use of the pallium?

Just as the provincial limitation of the pallium's use showed the bounds of the wearer's jurisdiction, so the decretalists explored the other restrictions that had traditionally indicated his subordination. On the similar topic of the vestment's appropriate venue, they stressed that it should never be worn outside church, not even in liturgical processions.[128] In his *Lectura* Hostiensis allowed a possible exception—"from special indulgence"—but otherwise it should be worn "as a rule [*regulariter*]" during the Mass, which did not take place out of doors.[129] He later clarified that, even if Mass were celebrated "under a tent or in a camp or in some private house outside

---

125. *HostAurea* ad X 1.8 s.v. *et quo loco* (125–26), *HostLect* ad X 1.8.5 s.v. *ordinandis* (1:89v) et ad X 1.8.7 s.v. *sandaliis* (90r).
126. *HostLect* ad X 1.8.5 s.v. *id permittat* et *in iam dictis casibus* (1:89v–90r).
127. *HostAurea* ad X 1.8 s.v. *et quo loco* (125–26).
128. JohTeut ad 3Comp 1.7.2 s.v. *ecclesia sua* (1:88), Sinibaldo ad X 1.8.5 s.v. *permittat* (88v), *HostAurea* ad X 1.8 s.v. *et quo loco* (125–26).
129. *HostLect* ad X 1.8.1 s.v. *debes* (1:88v).

a church, although within the province," still the vestment was forbidden. He summarized the restrictions on the use of the pallium as four: "to the province, to church, to the solemnities of the Mass, and to certain days."[130] Such limits, of course, were applied only to the *granted* pallium. Uniquely, the pope used the vestment "always and everywhere," for "all Christendom [*christianitas*] is understood as his province," as Hostiensis declared in his *Summa Aurea*.[131] This right, he went on in his *Lectura*, was "one of the privileges of the pope," but it was "otherwise for others, who use it only on certain days," and they included not only archbishops but even patriarchs.[132] Thus the Spanish custom of ignoring provincial boundaries was tantamount to usurping a papal privilege.[133]

As for the days when the pallium was permitted, Hostiensis's *Summa Aurea* attempted to provide a general rationale. First, as suggested by the *forma traditionis*, there were occasions mentioned in "the privileges granted to a church"—apparently not only those listed in the document accompanying an archbishop's pallium, but also those given to previous archbishops of that church in their privileges, which may have been assumed to accumulate. Second, there were "special festivities," called "solemn days" in c. 6 of the pallium title of the *Liber Extra*. Hostiensis connected the first and second points with "but also"; apparently he was suggesting that they could be combined. Third, the pallium should be worn during the sacred episcopal acts permitted by its possession, such as the consecration of bishops.[134] A test case was Mass for the dead. Bernard of Parma followed Honorius III, who had simply appealed to whatever was listed in a palliger's privileges.[135] But Sinibaldo was unwilling to stop there. For him, a Mass for the dead was not a solemnity, and thus would never be found in a list of "privileged solemnities" to which use of the pallium was restricted.[136] Although he failed to define "solemnity," he

130. *HostLect* ad X 1.8.6 s.v. *ubicumque* (1:90r).
131. *HostAurea* ad X 1.8 s.v. *et quo loco* (125–26).
132. *HostLect* ad X 1.8.4 s.v. *semper* et *alii autem* (1:89r–v).
133. *HostLect* ad X 1.8.5 s.v. *utantur* (1:89v).
134. *HostAurea* ad X 1.8 s.v. *et quibus diebus utendum sit pallio* (124–25).
135. BernParm ad X 1.8.7 s.v. *quarta* (223).
136. Sinibaldo ad X 1.8.7 s.v. *soluta* (88v).

was clearly searching for a criterion to explain the selection of pallium days found in privileges. Hostiensis criticized Sinibaldo's reasoning; he noted that Honorius's text said nothing about "solemnities," but only "days." Thus all that really mattered was what days were listed in one's privileges. Masses for the dead, Hostiensis remarked, were not customarily included in such lists, but if one found them there, "let the will of the one taking God's place on earth, that is, the pope, be done." But the papal will was only discernible "by seeing and reading the privileges carefully."[137]

Some decretalists inserted examples of these lists into their works. When they did so, they frequently alluded to other lists present in the canonical tradition, including the *dies feriandi* proclaimed by a council of Lyon, the list that Raymond of Penyafort had omitted from Innocent III's letter to the Bulgarian archbishops, and a list of holidays on which Gregory IX had ordered judicial activity to cease.[138] Nevertheless, they followed none of these. Instead, Hostiensis and Bernard of Parma offered variations on a list that the former attributed to Vincentius Hispanus.[139] In the form it took in the *Summa Aurea*, it comprised Christmas, the feasts of St. Stephen and St. John the Evangelist, the feast of Christ's circumcision, the Epiphany, Palm Sunday, Maundy Thursday, Holy Saturday, Easter and the next two days, the feast of Christ's ascension, Pentecost, the birth of St. John the Baptist, the feasts of the apostles, the feasts of the Virgin Mary, the feast of St. Michael, All Saints' day, "the chief festivities of the church adorned with the pallium," the dedications of churches, the consecrations of bishops, the ordinations of clerics, and the anniversary of the palliger's consecration. It was a fairly customary array of occasions, but Hostiensis commented that some chose to follow Gregory IX's decretal instead, a less traditional and much broader list that even included all Sundays.[140] Bernard's version of Hostiensis's list (probably

---

137. *HostLect* ad X 1.8.7 s.v. *soluta* et *pro defunctis* (1:90r).
138. De cons. D.3 c.1, Friedberg, *Corpus*, 1:1353; X 1.8.4, ibid., 2:101; and X 2.9.5, ibid., 2:272–73.
139. As ever, such lists were often ambiguous and subject to manipulation and corruption in transmission.
140. *HostAurea* ad X 1.8 s.v. *et quibus diebus utendum sit pallio* (124–25).

unintentionally) dropped the Ascension and Michaelmas.[141] The version in the *Lectura* also left out Michaelmas, but inserted the consecrations of virgins. Here, when Hostiensis mentioned the "chief festivities of the church of the palliated man," he added the gloss, "You should also understand that any church of his province is included." If this idea were implemented, it would have dramatically increased the number of pallium days, since potentially every parish church's patron saint's feast would have been included. In any event, Hostiensis called this list "general," for a palliger might receive even more days, as could be discovered in "the tenor of the granted privilege."[142]

How was the authority of the recipient dependent on the pallium?

While the decretists had often looked to *Quoniam quidam* to probe the effect of the pallium on the palliger's power, the decretalists more often looked to the epithet that had become so crucial to conceptualizing the vestment's import: "the fullness of the pontifical office." For Sinibaldo, the phrase meant "full execution in those things which belong to order, and also in those things which belong to jurisdiction, if they are very great affairs, as is convoking a council."[143] *Plena executio* implied that an archbishop could only partly carry out certain matters of order and jurisdiction before receiving the pallium. A cross-reference to Innocent III's letter to Cardinal John suggested that *maxima negotia* included the solemn acts of consecration listed there, which were reserved to bishops. Similarly, Bernard of Parma thought that the standard epithet accounted for the unpalliated archbishop's deficient abilities—which included doing anything *tamquam archiepiscopus*.[144] Elsewhere he glossed the pallium, "the insigne of the fullness of the pontifical office," as "the sign of the fullness of the power of the pastoral office," shifting the meaning from the office *per se* to its faculties. If one wore the emblem, one had the power.[145]

---

141. BernParm ad X 1.8.4 s.v. *ad honorem* (221). Cf. BernParm ad X 1.8.7 s.v. *privilegiis* (223). The omission of these two pallium days, both of long tradition, makes little sense except by oversight.

142. *HostLect* ad X 1.8.4 (1:89r).

143. Sinibaldo ad X 1.8.3 s.v. *plenitudo* (88v).

144. BernParm ad X 1.6.28 s.v. *sine pallio* et *tamquam* (153).

145. BernParm ad X 5.33.23 (1825–26).

Hostiensis's *Lectura* borrowed the term "full execution" from Sinibaldo and specified that it applied to "any things that belong to the episcopal order."[146] Earlier in his career, however, in his *Summa Aurea*, he had considered a more nuanced approach. Besides the consecratory acts listed by Innocent III (convoking synods, confecting chrism, dedicating churches, ordaining clerics, and consecrating bishops), Hostiensis wondered about other episcopal tasks, such as confirmations, consecrations of virgins, reconciliations of penitents and churches, and blessings of abbots.[147] Since an unpalliated metropolitan would be seen to do anything "not as a bishop, but as an archbishop," was he also forbidden from these episcopal functions? His solution was to differentiate those acts that required a Mass, such as consecrations and ordinations, from those that required "only a stole" (and not a chasuble, and thus not a Mass), such as performing a confirmation, blessing a cemetery, or consecrating a chalice. The former required the pallium, but the latter did not.[148] Perhaps his rationale hinged on the fact that the pallium was a Mass vestment; therefore, it would be missed at the former functions, but not at the latter.

Johannes Teutonicus claimed that there were two exceptions to the prohibition of episcopal functions: an unpalliated archbishop could ordain another bishop's clerics if he was invited to do so in a different province, and he could commission his own suffragans to consecrate in his own province.[149] Regarding the first case, Sinibaldo vacillated between agreeing, based on the comparable circumstance of celebrating Mass outside one's province, on the one hand, and on the other preferring a "perhaps better" opinion that papal permission alone sufficed for one to exercise the *episcopale officium* in such a situation.[150] His

---

146. *HostLect* ad X 1.8.3 s.v. *plenitudo* et *archiepiscopalis nominis* (1:88v).

147. Also in this list he included "maioris inquisitionis discussio" and "ministerii consecratio" (or "ministerium consecrationis," as X 1.6.15, which he cited, put it).

148. *HostAurea* ad X 1.8 s.v. *quid sit pallium* (122–23). In this passage Hostiensis seems to have misunderstood the term "uiduatis ecclesiis" in the Johannine law to mean, not churches without pastors, but churches without the possibility for certain sacred acts to be performed in them. He also made clear that the prohibition of these acts extended not just to elected archbishops, but also to translated ones, though already bishops formerly capable of such acts.

149. JohTeut ad 3Comp 1.6.13 s.v. *sine pallio* et *simplex episcopus* (1:73).

150. Sinibaldo ad X 1.6.28 s.v. *pallio* et *sed tamquam archiepiscopus* (60r).

approach to the second case appeared tenuous. Because the pallium contained the fullness of the pontifical office, Sinibaldo said, an unpalliated archbishop could not perform any matters of order. But commanding "what belongs to himself" or "what he wishes to be done on his behalf" was a matter of jurisdiction—in this case, allowing his suffragans to perform his *officium*. Because he had been elected and confirmed, he could exercise such rights of jurisdiction, even before palliation. Yet one might object that it was his *officium* itself that was in doubt without the vestment, for he lacked the fullness of office; further, a command to consecrate seemed to pertain to order, not jurisdiction. In the end, Sinibaldo offered a simpler alternative: if the three-month deadline had not yet passed, delegating the performance of consecrations was allowed, but not afterwards.[151] Bernard of Parma differed. Because *Quoniam quidam* assumed that no consecrations would be happening at all in the province of an unpalliated metropolitan, some believed that Alexander III's words to the archbishop of Rouen on this topic were not a legal judgment, but a *provisio* or administrative act to remedy a particular situation. Could it not be generalized, however, as long as the archbishop was not yet *in mora petendi pallium*? No, Bernard said: if he could not do something, he could not give authority for others to do it, especially others of "lower order."[152]

How was the pallium prepared?

Significasti, Paschal II's letter to Lawrence of Esztergom, had made part of its argument the fact that pallia were "taken up only from the body of blessed Peter." What exactly did this Petrine connection involve? Bernard of Parma explained that the vestment was "blessed and consecrated by the pope upon the altar of blessed Peter," and once placed there, the candidate or his representative subsequently received it from that altar.[153] In this view, "body" referred metaphor-

---

151. Sinibaldo ad X 1.6.11 s.v. *ad mandatum* (45r–v).
152. BernParm ad X 1.6.11 s.v. *pallium* (120) et ad X 1.6.28 s.v. *sine pallio* (153).
153. BernParm ad X 1.6.4 s.v. *corpore assumuntur* (112). In the second half of the twelfth century, Albinus (*Digesta Pauperis Scholaris*, in Fabre and Duchesne, *Liber censuum*, 2.6:109) and Peter Mallius and Romanus of St. Peter's (*Descriptio Basilicae Vaticanae*, in Valentini and Zucchetti, *Codice*, 3:385–86) described a rite of invigilation over the pallia in St. Peter's Basilica.

ically to an altar dedicated to the saint, which in St. Peter's Basilica had been erected upon the tomb where his remains were supposed to rest. In the *Summa Aurea,* however, Hostiensis supplied reasons for broadening this idea. For him, the pallium was taken "from an altar consecrated in honor of blessed Peter—or from whatever you wish by the lord pope's command." Thus it did not have to take place at Peter's tomb or in the Vatican basilica at all, for as he contended, with the support of both canon and Roman law, *ubi papa, ibi Roma.* In addition, he claimed to have the eyewitness support of someone who had received the vestment "from the altar of the lord pope's chapel."[154] Innocent IV, who was pope when Hostiensis was writing, spent a number of years in Lyon. Indeed, since the eleventh century several popes had spent periods of their pontificates without access to Peter's relics. Thus, relying on both theory and fact, Hostiensis disconnected the pallium from its traditional home and anchored it, not to Rome, but to the pope's person (and an appropriately dedicated chapel).

What other rights and duties accompanied the pallium?

Echoing the thoughts of the decretists, Hostiensis upheld two expectations expressed through pallium documents: with the vestment should come the grant of a new privilege or the renewal of an old one, and with the "increase in honor" should come an increased "care of pastoral responsibility." Thus the ornaments of one's actions—namely, good works—should parallel the ornaments of one's clothing, even if such an ideal, sadly, was not always attained. A palliger "ought to increase the authority of dignity by his character ... and usefulness ought to be increased through dignity."[155] For many

---

154. *HostAurea* ad X 1.8 s.v. *cui concedendum sit* (123–24). When he mentioned the eyewitness, Hostiensis altered Jn 21:24 to say, "He who *has seen and received it* gives testimony, and we know that his testimony is true" (emphasis added). Was he referring to his own reception of the pallium? If so, he may have gone personally to the papal court in Lyon when he became archbishop of Embrun in 1250, and there received the vestment from a papal official (cf. the *formula traditionis* he provided, which mentioned Embrun). As far back as in 1104, Diego of Compostela had received his pallium from the altar of San Lorenzo, the pope's private chapel in Rome (*Historia Compostellana,* in CCCM 70:40).

155. *HostAurea* ad X 1.8 s.v. *et a quo* (124), *HostLect* ad X 1.8.4 s.v. *pallium* (1:89v).

decretalists, however, the documents accompanying pallia were primarily occasions not for bestowing rights or offering admonitions, but for providing details of the vestment's permitted use, chiefly through lists of pallium days.

Still, these canonists were aware of the pallium's potential to puff up its wearer, and a pallium privilege could address this problem. Sinibaldo noted that "an ambitious privilege must be restricted."[156] He may have meant a privilege that allowed its beneficiary to appear to gain a higher position than he had or to lord it over his peers; the restrictions, such as those commonly imposed on the vestment's use, served to check the palliger's pride. Hostiensis in his *Lectura* agreed that any privilege "sought from a certain arrogance" should be restricted.[157] While restrictions formed a juridical approach to keeping a palliger humble, Hostiensis seemed to favor the traditional spiritual and hortatory approach. Into this same work he incorporated an extended discussion of the pallium's etymology and allegorical meaning, more typical of a liturgical commentary than a canonical treatise. According to his scheme, "pallium" was related to "pallor," the "color befitting a lover," since the palliger was meant to excel others in love of God and neighbor and to labor to exhaustion in discipline and good works.[158] The vestment's black crosses signaled the mortification of vices, so that the palliger was crucified to the world.[159] They were paired with the four affections (joy, grief, hope, and fear) or the four cardinal virtues (justice, fortitude, prudence, and temperance), and each one's placement, along with the presence or absence of a pin, carried symbolic import that taught the palliger how to live a virtuous life.[160]

Conclusion

The treatment of the pallium in the *Liber Extra* differed sharply from that in Gratian's *Decretum*. The decretals chosen for inclusion

156. Sinibaldo ad X 1.8.5 s.v. *permittat* (88v).
157. *HostLect* ad X 1.8.5 s.v. *id permittat* (1:89v–90r).
158. Cf. John of Avranches, in Delamare, *De Officiis Ecclesiasticis*, 51.
159. Cf. Rabanus Maurus, in Zimpel, *De Institutione*, 315.
160. *HostLect* ad X 1.8.1 s.v. *pallei* (1:88r–v).

in the collections of the *ius novum*, especially in the titles dedicated to the vestment, concentrated on its meaning, its proper use, and the restrictions to its use that bound its recipient. As a result, the decretalists paid far less attention to such matters as prerequisites for receiving the pallium, simoniacal complications, and the Johannine law—which Hostiensis claimed was overly harsh and falling into desuetude—and more attention to such matters as the pallium's limits to person, place, time, and context, questions of competing jurisdictions, and the nature of the privilege of wearing it. In keeping with the growing sophistication of jurisprudence, the canonists frequently turned to unusual circumstances and seeming subtleties—from what to do if an archbishop was invited to ordain outside his province, to how to bury multiple pallia with their recipient—in order to elucidate underlying principles. As with their decretist predecessors, however, their love of the law sometimes impeded their grasp of the nature of the conferred pallium as a gift, only loosely bound by the rights and norms central to other legal matters.

The thoroughness of the decretalists, as well as a certain fascination that they manifested with the customs surrounding the pallium, resulted in a wealth of detail that previous pallium law had by and large lacked. Now scholars of canon law investigated the deeper significance of the epithet *plenitudo pontificalis officii* and its relationship to the dyad *plenitudo potestatis/pars sollicitudinis*. Now they delved into liturgical matters, such as the formula to be recited at the vestment's bestowal or the typical list of pallium days (and the rationales for it). Now they even looked into the blessing of the pallium at the altar of Peter and asked questions spurred by the events of their era—for example, how a pope not resident in Rome could perform this blessing. Most interestingly, the creative and voluminous contributions of a canonist who was himself a palliger, Hostiensis, offered new insights, sometimes startling opinions, and personal testimonies to how the Western church of his day handled the vestment. While he might bristle under its obligation and occasionally question its value, the pallium was an undeniable part of the canonical corpus he studied and a significant facet of his relationship to the pope and the rest of the episcopate.

CONCLUSION

Conclusion

The centuries of development examined in this study witnessed a dramatic transformation in the use and understanding of the pallium. In late antiquity the popes had begun sharing this insigne occasionally with other bishops as a sign of a special relationship with the Roman church. This intermittent and honorary practice had no appreciable impact on the wider church at first. But thanks to the English experiment of Gregory the Great, which penetrated the continental church through missionaries, the papacy took advantage of a new opportunity that the vestment provided during the Carolingian era. Through its conferral and its usual connection to metropolitan office, the apostolic see was able to assume a more involved and effective role in the Western church and to implement its theoretical primacy in a more comprehensive, systematic fashion. In this endeavor the pallium became a regular, juridically defined feature of ecclesiastical government.

The ways in which the pallium functioned were partly derived from its nature as a gift, but were also overlaid with paradoxes that became visible during its evolution. The gift was an act of gracious favor, which also controlled the recipient. It offered confirmation, but demanded scrutiny. It was sought, and yet imposed; freely given, and yet required. It increased the palliger's standing, and simultaneously the donor's influence. It provoked collaboration and competition, gratitude and resentment. It was a personal privilege, but bound up with an office. It became an archbishop's insigne, tied to metropolitan powers, although simple bishops received it too. It straddled the blurry border between declarative emblem and constitutive *sine qua non*. It bestowed honor, while subordinating its wearer, and authority, while making him dependent.

These seeming contradictions reveal two important truths. First, the popes themselves did not always see the pallium's role clearly. They had no consistent master plan to be executed over the centuries. Rather, they made practical decisions and adjusted their use of the vestment according to specific circumstances and individual strokes of genius—and blunders. When the popes faltered, prelates and churches outside Rome often provided the initiative, seeking links with the apostolic see that offered them legitimization and prominence. Second, its very ambiguity made the pallium a more flexible instrument. It could respond to a variety of problems and adapt to a variety of situations because there was no single way of interpreting it and its effects. When one aspect did not succeed or sparked resistance, another was emphasized. Like scripture itself, this part of the church's tradition enjoyed a polysemy that, far from being a drawback, made it a more agile tool.

Although the basic model was worked out during the first period studied here, its possibilities could not be fully brought to fruition before Carolingian society went into decline. In the next period, papal prestige sank into the morass of strife-ridden Roman politics. The custom of conferring the pallium endured, however, and helped keep the papacy actively involved in the larger church's affairs. Still, the apostolic see's chaotic fortunes resulted in an inconsistent approach to its handling of the vestment, with both thoughtlessness and imagination operating side by side. It required a vigorous, goal-oriented papacy to reharness the pallium's potential and employ it in realizing a new vision of the church.

The reform popes of the eleventh and twelfth centuries provided that ambitious drive and sense of purpose. For them, the pallium, when astutely applied to influence ecclesiastical relationships frequently, universally, and innovatively, was a ready-made tool, well suited to the interventions and reorganization needed for church-wide renewal. Once received, it forged bonds of both fidelity and subjection to the Roman pontiff, through which the hierarchy could be induced to conform to the new ideals. Reform was the context and motivation, but the product was an unprecedented practical fulfillment of the notion of papal primacy. With the pallium's help, the Roman church achieved a dominance over the other churches of the West—which, to a certain extent, they welcomed and helped bring about—that has often been called a papal monarchy. During its ascendance the customs surrounding the vestment were elaborated and enshrined in the newly systematized corpus of canon law.

The development thus charted draws attention to several ingredients in this success story. One was the necessity of laying groundwork over the centuries. The reform papacy could not have exploited the pallium's use so thoroughly unless it had long been an accepted part of ecclesiastical law and politics. And those customs could not have lasted so long without the fruitful ventures of the Carolingian age, which wove the vestment into the church's constitution. That evolution, in turn, could not have happened without the reforms of Anglo-Saxon missionaries relying on the traditions of their homeland. And that English situation resulted from the papacy's newfound focus on the Germanic peoples in the early Middle Ages.

Another ingredient in this story was the historical role of significant individuals. Again and again it was visionary figures who made headway. Pride of place goes to Gregory the Great. The extent to which succeeding generations looked back to his examples and drew lessons from them can hardly be exaggerated. His decision to attach the pallium to metropolitan functions was crucial, but his impact went beyond his own plans. His legacy (especially his letters) provided the raw materials from which the principles and practices surrounding the vestment were fashioned. Indeed, his importance in this saga was primarily as a source, an authority. Others did the building thereon. Boniface repatterned the Frankish church on Gregory's English model. Nicholas I and John VIII transformed customs into canonical requirements. John XII saw the promise in manipulating pallium days. Clement II set a new tone in interpreting the vestment. Alexander II promoted innovations such as personal reception and the oath of fidelity. John of Gaeta rewrote the book on pallium privileges. And Urban II knew how to stretch pallium law without tearing it.

Yet another ingredient was the relevance of political and cultural context. Just as the relative stability and creative ferment of the first and last periods permitted important advances, so the comparative disorder of the middle period prevented the pursuit of coherent policies. That time too may have had popes of genius, who were nevertheless unable to act extensively upon a far-sighted agenda.

A final ingredient was the nature of the artifact itself. The pallium became an instrument that the popes used to help achieve their ends. What made it an effective instrument? The papacy had other instruments at its disposal, including legates and synods. What made this one different? Its character as a gift has been explored, but other objects could have served as gifts. What made this particular gift potent?

The pallium was a papal insigne, even *the* papal insigne, and its fundamental meaning was thus connected to the highest office in the Western church. This fact affected gift-giving, because it made the gift desirable. The garb communicated widely recognized power and prestige, and would not lightly be ignored. In some sense it remained papal even after its bestowal, and, just as other relic-gifts, it tangibly reminded recipients in every land of its donor's importance, to whom they were bound by "ties created in the distribution."[1]

In addition, the pallium, as a contact relic, shared the widespread appeal enjoyed by relics in the Middle Ages. It too was seen as charged with sacred *virtus*, forming a link between heaven and earth, a sort of sacrament that incarnated divine realities and helped to bring about what it signified. As was generally true of relics, moreover, this woolen band was relatively neutral in itself, with little fixed meaning as an object; other than a specific material and form, with minimal decorations, it was a rather plain textile. It re-

---

1. See Geary, "Sacred Commodities," 183.

quired shared cultural values, imposed from outside, to render it significant, and to a great degree it passively reflected the meaning given it.[2] Rather than limiting its significance, its simplicity allowed for an enormous variety of symbolic interpretations.

In order to become such a relic, before it was given to churchmen, the pallium was laid upon and then taken from Peter's tomb. However invisible the effect of this incubation, it was essential to papal control of the insigne. Without a unique mode of production firmly under the popes' direction, this gift might have gone the way of the miter and escaped their management.[3] As when relics were shared from a central sanctuary, the spread of pallia did not diffuse the significance of Peter's shrine but enhanced it, along with the stature of its keeper, who acted as gift-giver and patron.[4]

Finally, the pallium was a liturgical vestment, and so a sign for public display. An archbishop's flock knew if he had received it or not, and thus if he had Rome's stamp of approval or not. It was worn only at sacred times and in sacred places, that is, in symbolically intense contexts, which not only heightened its import but also made its indispensability for certain sacerdotal functions seem natural. The faithful came to see it as wrapped up with the pastoral office—and the conduct expected of a good shepherd.

As an instrument of power, this modest garment was surprisingly effective, but not flawless. Since so much significance was vested in a material object, the popes lost a measure of control as soon as it left Rome. They were still important as its source, but could not always direct how it would be used or perceived, and had to struggle to keep charge of it. A similar problem bedeviled the use of papal legates, who extended papal oversight, but also placed it in other hands. Legates did not always fulfill what the popes hoped they would.

Further, the crux of the gift was the transaction itself, when

---

2. See Patrick J. Geary, *Furta Sacra: Thefts of Relics in the Central Middle Ages*, rev. ed. (Princeton, N.J.: Princeton University Press, 1990), 5–9.

3. By the thirteenth century, when evidence suggested that the popes were blessing pallia outside of Rome (*HostAurea* ad X 1.8 s.v. *cui concedendum sit* [123–24]), the papacy had become powerful enough that there was little danger of losing control of the vestment.

4. See Geary, "Sacred Commodities," 183.

the Roman pontiffs could dictate conditions and directly impact ecclesio-political relationships. Once given, however, the pallium's efficacy waned, and although abuse or other offenses could merit its deprivation, that threat was far more theoretical than practiced. The synodal activity favored by the reform popes faced a similar predicament: councils were useful when they happened, but needed additional measures to have lasting effects.

And since much of the vestment's meaning was not readily apparent from looking at it, the accompanying document that defined its proper use and understanding was a necessary adjunct (somewhat as a certificate of authentication was for a relic). As the papacy grew in strength during the high Middle Ages, the authority conveyed through the pallium came to seem the result rather of papal *fiat*, as pronounced in the privilege, than of possessing the garment itself.[5] In a sense, this kind of direct papal empowerment had often been the goal of the pallium's use since the ninth century. It had done its job so well that, from the twelfth century onward, the papacy relied on it less and less, until it was reduced to a simple symbol lacking real jurisdictional force.[6]

---

5. At this time, too, close personal bonds, which had once held society together and created public authority, were to some extent being replaced by more legal, impersonal connections (Bijsterveld, *Do ut des*, 35, 38). Further, in the wake of the reform's war against simony, the modern notion that the only genuine gift is a "free gift," without strings attached, was evolving (Reuter, "Gifts," 166).

6. Although the current Code of Canon Law in the Catholic church retains a metropolitan's obligation to request the pallium within three months of his accession, it has dropped any restrictions on exercising archiepiscopal functions before acquiring it, "to avoid giving the impression that the pallium itself conferred power." See John P. Beal, James A. Coriden, and Thomas J. Green, eds., *New Commentary on the Code of Canon Law* (New York: Paulist, 2000), 575–77. It remains a declarative sign of authority, but no longer a constitutive one.

Selected Bibliography

Editions of Primary Sources

Academia das Ciências de Lisboa. *Portugaliae Monumenta Historica: Scriptores*. 3 vols. Lisbon: Typis Academicis, 1856–61.

Acta Sanctorum. 68 vols. Antwerp/Brussels: Société des Bollandistes, 1643–1940.

Aimone, Petrus V., ed. *Summa in Decretum Simonis Bisinianensis*. Fribourg: University of Fribourg, 2007. http://www.unifr.ch/cdc/fr/document

Alberigo, G., J. A. Dossetti, P.-P. Joannou, C. Leonardi, and P. Prodi, eds. *Conciliorum Oecumenicorum Decreta*. 3rd ed. Bologna: Istituto per le Scienze Religiose, 1973.

Andrieu, Michel, ed. *Les Ordines romani du haut moyen âge*. 5 vols. Spicilegium Sacrum Lovaniense, études et documents 11, 23–24, 28–29. Louvain: Spicilegium Sacrum Lovaniense, 1931–61.

———, ed. *Le pontifical romain au moyen-âge*. 4 vols. Studi e testi 86–88, 99. Vatican City: Biblioteca Apostolica Vaticana, 1938–41.

Baker, Peter S., ed. *The Anglo-Saxon Chronicle: A Collaborative Edition*. Vol. 8. Cambridge: Brewer, 2000.

Barbier, J., ed. "La vie de saint Monon." *Analectes pour servir à l'histoire ecclésiastique de la Belgique* 5 (1868): 410–14.

Barlow, Frank, ed. *The Life of King Edward Who Rests at Westminster, Attributed to a Monk of Saint-Bertin*. 2nd ed. Oxford: Clarendon, 1992.

Bately, Janet M., ed. *The Anglo-Saxon Chronicle: A Collaborative Edition*. Vol. 3. Cambridge: Brewer, 1986.

Bautier, Robert-Henri, and Monique Gilles, eds. *Odorannus de Sens: Opera Omnia*. Sources d'histoire médiévale 4. Paris: Centre National de la Recherche Scientifique, 1972.

Bautier, Robert-Henri, and Gillette Labory, eds. *L'abbaye de Fleury en l'an mil*. Sources d'histoire médiévale 32. Paris: Centre National de la Recherche Scientifique, 2004.

———, eds. *André de Fleury: Vie de Gauzlin, abbé de Fleury*. Sources d'histoire médiévale 2. Paris: Centre National de la Recherche Scientifique, 1969.

Behrends, Frederick, ed. *The Letters and Poems of Fulbert of Chartres*. Oxford Medieval Texts. Oxford: Clarendon, 1976.

Benedict XVI, Pope. "Sollemne Initium Ministerii Summi Ecclesiae Pastoris." *Acta Apostolicae Sedis* 97 (2005): 705–12.

Bernhard, Jean, ed. "La collection en deux livres (Cod. Vat. lat. 3832): la forme primitive de la collection en deux livres, source de la collection en 74 titres et de la collection d'Anselme de Lucques." *Revue de droit canonique* 12 (1962): 1–601.

Berto, Luigi Andrea, ed. *Giovanni Diacono: Istoria Veneticorum*. Fonti per la storia dell'Italia medievale 2. Bologna: Zanichelli, 1999.

Besse, J. C., ed. "Collectionis *Anselmo Dedicata* Liber Primus." *Revue de droit canonique* 9 (1959): 207–96.

Brett, Martin, ed. *Ivo, Decretum*. https://ivo-of-chartres.github.io/decretum.html, date / revision stamp 2015-09-23 / 898fb.

———, ed. "Some New Letters of Popes Urban II and Paschal II." *Journal of Ecclesiastical History* 58 (2007): 75–96.

———, ed. *Tripartita*. https://ivo-of-chartres.github.io/tripartita.html, date / revision stamp 2015-09-23 / 898fb.

Brett, Martin, and Bruce Brasington, eds. *Panormia*. https://ivo-of-chartres.github.io/panormia.html, date / revision stamp 2015-09-23 / 898fb.

Castiglioni, Carlo, ed. *Landulphi Junioris sive de Sancto Paulo Historia Mediolanensis ab anno MXCV usque ad annum MCXXXVII*. Rerum Italicarum Scriptores 5.3. Bologna: Zanichelli, 1934.

Cavallo, Guglielmo, and Giovanni Orlandi, eds. *Rodolfo il Glabro: cronache dell'anno mille (storie)*. Milan: Mondadori, 1996.

Cessi, Roberto, ed. *Documenti relativi alla storia di Venezia anteriori al mille*. 2 vols. Testi e documenti di storia e di letteratura latina medioevale 1, 3. Padua: Gregoriana, 1940–42; reprinted in Venice: Deputazione di Storia Patria per le Venezie, 1991.

Chibnall, Marjorie, ed. *The* Historia Pontificalis *of John of Salisbury*. Rev. ed. Oxford Medieval Texts. Oxford: Clarendon, 1986.

Clover, Helen, and Margaret Gibson, eds. *The Letters of Lanfranc, Archbishop of Canterbury*. Oxford Medieval Texts. Oxford: Clarendon, 1979.

Colgrave, Bertram, ed. *The Earliest Life of Gregory the Great, by an Anonymous Monk of Whitby*. Lawrence: University of Kansas Press, 1968.

Commentaria Innocentii Quarti Pontificis Maximi super Libros Quinque Decretalium. Frankfurt, 1570.

Conn, Marie A., ed. "The Dunstan and Brodie (Anderson) Pontificals: An Edition and Study." PhD diss., University of Notre Dame, 1993.

Coppens, E. C., ed. *Animal est substantia*. http://medcanonlaw.nl/Animal_est_substantia/Introduction.html

Corpus Christianorum: Continuatio Mediaevalis. 267 vols. Turnhout: Brepols, 1966–.

Corpus Christianorum: Series Latina. 194 vols. Turnhout: Brepols, 1953–.

Corpus Iuris Canonici [*Editio Romana*]. Vol. 1, *Decretum Gratiani*, and vol. 2, *Decretales Domini Gregorii Papae IX*. Rome: Aedes Populi Romani, 1582.

Coustant, Pierre, ed. *Epistolae Romanorum Pontificum*. Vol. 1. Paris: Delatour and Coustelier, 1721.

Selected Bibliography 491

Cubbin, G. P., ed. *The Anglo-Saxon Chronicle: A Collaborative Edition.* Vol. 6. Cambridge: Brewer, 1996.
Curschmann, Fritz, ed. *Die älteren Papsturkunden des Erzbistums Hamburg: eine diplomatische Untersuchung.* Hamburg: Voss, 1909.
D'Acunto, N., and L. Saraceno, eds., based on the edition of Kurt Reindel. *Petri Damiani Epistulae / Pier Damiani lettere.* Vol. 4. Opere di Pier Damiani 1. Rome: Città Nuova, 2005.
Darlington, R. R., and P. McGurk, eds. *The Chronicle of John of Worcester.* 3 vols. Oxford Medieval Texts. Oxford: Clarendon, 1995–98.
Davis, R. H. C., and Marjorie Chibnall, eds. *The* Gesta Guillelmi *of William of Poitiers.* Oxford Medieval Texts. Oxford: Clarendon, 1998.
Delamare, R., ed. *Le De Officiis Ecclesiasticis de Jean d'Avranches, archevêque de Rouen (1067–1079): étude liturgique et publication du texte inédit.* Paris: Picard, 1923.
Dopsch, Heinz, ed. "Papst Leo III. schreibt an die Bischöfe Bayerns, daß er auf ihre Bitte den Bischof Arn von Salzburg zum Erzbischof der bayerischen Kirchenprovinz bestellt und ihm das Pallium verliehen habe (798 April)." In *1200 Jahre Erzbistum Salzburg: Dom und Geschichte,* edited by Johannes Neuhardt, 25–26. Salzburg: Dom und Metropolitankapitel von Salzburg, 1998.
———, ed. "Papst Leo III. schreibt an König Karl den Großen, daß er in dessen Auftrag den Bischof Arn von Salzburg zum Erzbischof und Metropoliten der bayerischen Kirchenprovinz erhoben und ihm das Pallium verliehen habe (798 April)." In *1200 Jahre Erzbistum Salzburg: Dom und Geschichte,* edited by Johannes Neuhardt, 23–24. Salzburg: Dom und Metropolitankapitel von Salzburg, 1998.
———, ed. "Papst Leo III. verleiht Arn, dem Erzbischof und Metropoliten der bayerischen Kirchenprovinz, das Pallium (798 April 20)." In *1200 Jahre Erzbistum Salzburg: Dom und Geschichte,* edited by Johannes Neuhardt, 17–22. Salzburg: Dom und Metropolitankapitel von Salzburg, 1998.
Duchesne, Louis, ed. *Le Liber pontificalis.* 3 vols. Bibliothèque des écoles françaises d'Athènes et de Rome, ser. 2, 3. Paris: Thorin, 1886–1957.
Duine, F., ed. *La métropole de Bretagne: chronique de Dol composée au XIe siècle et catalogues des dignitaires jusqu'à la révolution.* La Bretagne et les pays celtiques 12. Paris: Champion, 1916.
Dümmler, Ernst, ed. *Gesta Berengarii Imperatoris: Beiträge zur Geschichte Italiens im Anfänge des zehnten Jahrhunderts.* Halle: Waisenhaus, 1871.
Eckhart, Johann Georg von, ed. *Corpus Historicum Medii Aevi.* 2 vols. Leipzig: Gleditsch, 1723.
Erdmann, Carl, ed. *Papsturkunden in Portugal.* Abhandlungen der Gesellschaft der Wissenschaften zu Göttingen, philologisch-historische Klasse, neue Folge, 20.3. Berlin: Weidmann, 1927; reprinted in Göttingen: Vandenhoeck and Ruprecht, 1970.
Ewald, Paul, ed. "Die Papstbriefe der brittischen Sammlung." *Neues Archiv der Gesellschaft für ältere deutsche Geschichtskunde* 5 (1880): 275–414, 503–96.
———, ed. "Reise nach Italien im Winter von 1876 auf 1877." *Neues Archiv der Gesellschaft für ältere deutsche Geschichtskunde* 3 (1878): 139–81.

Fabre, P., and L. Duchesne, eds. *Le Liber censuum de l'église romaine*. 3 vols. Bibliothèque des écoles françaises d'Athènes et de Rome, ser. 2, 6. Paris: Fontemoing, 1889–1952.

Fleming, John, ed. *Gille of Limerick (c. 1070–1145): Architect of a Medieval Church*. Dublin: Four Courts, 2001.

Foerster, Hans, ed. *Liber Diurnus Romanorum Pontificum*. Bern: Francke, 1958.

Fransen, Gérard, and Stephan Kuttner, eds. *Summa "Elegantius in iure divino" seu Coloniensis*. 4 vols. Monumenta Iuris Canonici, ser. A, Corpus Glossatorum 1. Vatican City: Biblioteca Apostolica Vaticana, 1969–90.

Fransen, Gérard, and Theo Kölzer, eds. *Burchard von Worms: Decretorum Libri XX*. Supplemented reprint of the *editio princeps* of 1548. Aalen: Scientia, 1992.

Friedberg, Emil, ed. *Corpus Iuris Canonici*. 2 vols. Leipzig: Tauchnitz, 1879–81; reprinted in Graz: Akademische Druck- und Verlagsanstalt, 1959.

———, ed. *Quinque Compilationes Antiquae nec non Collectio Canonum Lipsiensis*. Leipzig: Tauchnitz, 1882; reprinted in Graz: Akademische Druck- und Verlagsanstalt, 1956.

Fuhrmann, Horst, and Uwe Horst, eds. *Die Sammlung "Policarpus" des Kardinals Gregor von S. Grisogono*. http://www.mgh.de/fileadmin/Downloads/pdf/polycarp.pdf

García y García, Antonio, ed. *Constitutiones Concilii Quarti Lateranensis una cum Commentariis Glossatorum*. Monumenta Iuris Canonici, ser. A, Corpus Glossatorum 2. Vatican City: Biblioteca Apostolica Vaticana, 1981.

Gargano, G. I., and N. D'Acunto, eds., based on the edition of Kurt Reindel. *Petri Damiani Epistulae / Pier Damiani lettere*. Vol. 2. Opere di Pier Damiani 1. Rome: Città Nuova, 2001.

Gassó, Pius M., and Columba M. Batlle, eds. *Pelagii I Papae: Epistulae quae Supersunt (556–561)*. Scripta et Documenta 8. Montserrat: Abbatia Montisserrati, 1956.

Giesebrecht, Wilhelm von, ed. *Geschichte der deutschen Kaiserzeit*. 5th ed. 6 vols. Leipzig: Duncker and Humblot, 1877–95.

Ginther, James R., and Tomás O'Sullivan, eds. *Electronic Norman Anonymous Project*. http://normananonymous.org/ENAP/landing.jsp

Glanvell, Victor Wolf von, ed. *Die Kanonessammlung des Kardinals Deusdedit*. Paderborn: Schöningh, 1905; reprinted in Aalen: Scientia, 1967.

Godman, Peter, ed. *Alcuin: The Bishops, Kings, and Saints of York*. Oxford Medieval Texts. Oxford: Clarendon, 1982.

Haddan, Arthur West, and William Stubbs, eds. *Councils and Ecclesiastical Documents relating to Great Britain and Ireland*. 3 vols. Oxford: Clarendon, 1869–78.

Hamman, Adalbert, ed. *Patrologiae Cursus Completus: Series Latina, Supplementum*. 5 vols. Paris: Garnier, 1958–74.

Hanssens, Ioannes Michael, ed. *Amalarii Episcopi Opera Liturgica Omnia*. 3 vols. Studi e testi 138–40. Vatican City: Biblioteca Apostolica Vaticana, 1948–50.

Harting-Correa, Alice L., ed., based on the edition of Victor Krause. *Walahfrid Strabo's* Libellus de exordiis et incrementis quarundam in observationibus ecclesiasticis rerum: *A Translation and Liturgical Commentary.* Mittellateinische Studien und Texte 19. Leiden: Brill, 1996.

Hauthaler, Willibald, and Franz Martin, eds. *Salzburger Urkundenbuch.* 4 vols. Salzburg: Gesellschaft für Salzburger Landeskunde, 1910–33.

Henrici de Segusio Cardinalis Hostiensis Summa Aurea. Basel: Guarini, 1573.

Hiestand, Rudolf, ed. *Papsturkunden für Kirchen im Heiligen Lande: Vorarbeiten zum Oriens Pontificius III.* Abhandlungen der Akademie der Wissenschaften in Göttingen, philologisch-historische Klasse, ser. 3, 136. Göttingen: Vandenhoeck and Ruprecht, 1985.

Hlawitschka, Eduard, ed. "Textkritisches zur Series abbatum Flaviniacensium." In *Landschaft und Geschichte: Festschrift für Franz Petri zu seinem 65. Geburtstag,* edited by Georg Droege et al., 250–65. Bonn: Röhrscheid, 1970.

Irvine, Susan, ed. *The Anglo-Saxon Chronicle: A Collaborative Edition.* Vol. 7. Cambridge: Brewer, 2004.

Jaffé, Philippus, ed. *Bibliotheca Rerum Germanicarum.* 6 vols. Berlin: Weidmann, 1864–73; reprinted in Aalen: Scientia, 1964.

Joannis, Georg Christian, ed. *Rerum Moguntiacarum.* 3 vols. Frankfurt: Sande, 1722–27.

Johnson, Charles, ed., revised by M. Brett, C. N. L. Brooke, and M. Winterbottom. *Hugh the Chanter: The History of the Church of York, 1066–1127.* Oxford Medieval Texts. Oxford: Clarendon, 1990.

Kehr, Paul Fridolin, ed. *Papsturkunden in Italien: Reiseberichte zur Italia Pontificia.* 6 vols. Acta Romanorum Pontificum 1–6. Vatican City: Biblioteca Apostolica Vaticana, 1977.

Lapidge, Michael, André Crépin, Pierre Monat, and Philippe Robin, eds. *Bède le Vénérable: histoire ecclésiastique du peuple anglais (Historia ecclesiastica gentis Anglorum).* 3 vols. Sources chrétiennes 489–91. Paris: Cerf, 2005.

Laspeyres, Ern. Ad. Theod., ed. *Bernardi Papiensis Faventini Episcopi Summa Decretalium.* Regensburg: Manz, 1860; reprinted in Graz: Akademische Druck- und Verlagsanstalt, 1956.

Lauer, Philippe, ed. *Les annales de Flodoard.* Collection de textes pour servir à l'étude et à l'enseignement de l'histoire 39. Paris: Picard et Fils, 1905.

Leclercq, Jean, ed. *Yves de Chartres: correspondance.* Vol. 1. Les classiques de l'histoire de France au moyen âge 22. Paris: Belles Lettres, 1949.

Lectura sive Apparatus Domini Hostiensis super Quinque Libris Decretalium. 2 vols. Strasbourg, 1512.

Lehmann, Paul, ed. *Holländische Reisefrüchte I–III.* Sitzungsberichte der bayerischen Akademie der Wissenschaften, philosophisch-philologische und historische Klasse 13. Munich: Bayerische Akademie der Wissenschaften, 1921.

Lesne, Emile, ed. "La lettre interpolée d'Hadrien I à Tilpin et l'eglise de Reims au IXe siècle." *Le moyen âge* 26 (1913): 325–51, 389–413.

Lindsay, W. M., ed. *Isidori Hispalensis Episcopi Etymologiarum sive Originum Libri XX.* 2 vols. Oxford: Clarendon, 1911.

Loewenfeld, S., ed. *Epistolae Pontificum Romanorum Ineditae.* Leipzig: Veit, 1885; reprinted in Graz: Akademische Druck- und Verlagsanstalt, 1959.

Lošek, Fritz, ed. *Die* Conversio Bagoariorum et Carantanorum *und der Brief des*

Erzbischofs Theotmar von Salzburg. Monumenta Germaniae Historica Studien und Texte 15. Hannover: Hahn, 1997.

Mansi, Joannes Dominicus, ed. *Sacrorum Conciliorum Nova et Amplissima Collectio.* 31 vols. Florence and Venice, 1759–93.

Mansilla, Demetrio, ed. *La documentación pontificia hasta Inocencio III (965–1216).* Monumenta Hispaniae Vaticana, registros 1. Rome: Instituto Español de Estudios Eclesiasticos, 1955.

Marsina, Richard, ed. *Codex Diplomaticus et Epistolaris Slovaciae.* 2 vols. Bratislava: Academia Scientiarum Slovaca, 1971–87.

Martí i Bonet, Josep M., ed., with the collaboration of Anna Rich i Abad and Joan Bellés i Sallent. *Oleguer, servent de les esglésies de Barcelona i Tarragona: comentaris als documents de sant Oleguer.* Barcelona: Claret, 2003.

McLaughlin, Terence P., ed. *The Summa Parisiensis on the Decretum Gratiani.* Toronto: Pontifical Institute of Mediaeval Studies, 1952.

Meyendorff, Paul, ed. and trans. *St. Germanus of Constantinople: On the Divine Liturgy.* Crestwood, N.Y.: St. Vladimir's Seminary Press, 1984.

Migne, J.-P., ed. *Patrologiae Cursus Completus: Series Graeca.* 161 vols. Paris: J.-P. Migne, 1857–66.

———, ed. *Patrologiae Cursus Completus: Series Latina.* 221 vols. Paris: J.-P. Migne, 1844–65.

Monticolo, Giovanni, ed. *Cronache veneziane antichissime.* Vol. 1. Fonti per la storia d'Italia 9. Rome: Forzani, 1890.

Monumenta Germaniae Historica: Auctores Antiquissimi. Berlin: Weidmann, etc., 1877–.

Monumenta Germaniae Historica: Briefe der deutschen Kaiserzeit. Weimar: Böhlau, etc., 1949–.

Monumenta Germaniae Historica: Capitularia Regum Francorum. Hannover: Hahn, etc., 1883–.

Monumenta Germaniae Historica: Concilia. Hannover: Hahn, etc., 1893–.

Monumenta Germaniae Historica: Constitutiones et Acta Publica Imperatorum et Regum. Hannover: Hahn, etc., 1893–.

Monumenta Germaniae Historica: Diplomata Regum et Imperatorum Germaniae. Hannover: Hahn, etc., 1879–.

Monumenta Germaniae Historica: Epistolae. Berlin: Weidmann, etc., 1891–.

Monumenta Germaniae Historica: Epistolae Selectae. Berlin: Weidmann, etc., 1916–.

Monumenta Germaniae Historica: Fontes Iuris Germanici Antiqui in usum scholarum separatim editi. Hannover: Hahn, etc., 1869–.

Monumenta Germaniae Historica: Formulae Merowingici et Karolini Aevi. Hannover: Hahn, etc., 1886–.

Monumenta Germaniae Historica: Libelli de Lite Imperatorum et Pontificum. Hannover: Hahn, etc., 1891–.

Monumenta Germaniae Historica: Poetae Latini Medii Aevi. Berlin: Weidmann, etc., 1881–.

Monumenta Germaniae Historica: Scriptores. Hannover: Hahn, etc., 1826–.

Monumenta Germaniae Historica: Scriptores Rerum Germanicarum in usum scholarum separatim editi. Hannover: Hahn, etc., 1841–.

Selected Bibliography 495

Monumenta Germaniae Historica: Scriptores Rerum Germanicarum, nova series. Berlin: Weidmann, etc., 1922–.
Monumenta Germaniae Historica: Scriptores Rerum Langobardicarum et Italicarum. Hannover: Hahn, etc., 1878–.
Monumenta Germaniae Historica: Scriptores Rerum Merovingicarum. Hannover: Hahn, etc., 1885–.
Motta, Joseph, ed. *Collectio Canonum Trium Librorum, Pars Prior (Liber I et II).* Monumenta Iuris Canonici, ser. B, Corpus Collectionum 8. Vatican City: Biblioteca Apostolica Vaticana, 2005.
Mynors, R. A. B., R. M. Thomson, and M. Winterbottom, eds. *William of Malmesbury:* Gesta Regum Anglorum, *The History of the English Kings.* Oxford Medieval Texts. Oxford: Clarendon Press, 1998.
Nauerth, Claudia, ed., based on the edition of O. Holder-Egger. *Agnellus von Ravenna: Bischofsbuch.* Fontes Christiani 21. Freiburg: Herder, 1996.
Orchard, Nicholas, ed. *The Leofric Missal.* 2 vols. Henry Bradshaw Society 113–14. London: Boydell, 2002.
———, ed. *The Sacramentary of Ratoldus (Paris, Bibliothèque nationale de France, lat. 12052).* Henry Bradshaw Society 116. London: Boydell, 2005.
Ordeig i Mata, Ramon, ed. *Catalunya carolíngia.* Vol. 4, *Els comtats d'Osona i Manresa.* Memòries de la secció històrico-arqueològica 53. Barcelona: Institut d'Estudis Catalans, 1999.
"Passio S. Mononis." *Analecta Bollandiana* 5 (1886): 193–208.
Pennington, Kenneth, ed. *Johannis Teutonici Apparatus Glossarum in Compilationem Tertiam.* Vol. 1. Monumenta Iuris Canonici, ser. A, Corpus Glossatorum 3. Vatican City: Biblioteca Apostolica Vaticana, 1981.
Perels, Ernst, ed. *Bonizo: Liber de Vita Christiana.* Hildesheim: Weidmann, 1998.
Pflugk-Harttung, J. von, ed. *Acta Pontificum Romanorum Inedita.* 3 vols. Tübingen: Fues, 1881, and Stuttgart: Kohlhammer, 1884–88; reprinted in Graz: Akademische Druck- und Verlagsanstalt, 1958.
Picasso, Giorgio, ed. *Collezioni canoniche milanesi del secolo XII.* Milan: Vita e Pensiero, 1969.
Prologo, Arcangelo di Gioacchino, ed. *Le carte che si conservano nello archivio del capitolo metropolitano della città di Trani (dal IX secolo fino all'anno 1266).* Barletta: Vecchi, 1877.
Rački, Fr., ed. *Documenta Historiae Chroaticae Periodum Antiquam Illustrantia.* Monumenta Spectantia Historiam Slavorum Meridionalium 7. Zagreb: Academia Scientiarum et Artium, 1877.
Ramackers, Johannes, ed. *Papsturkunden in Frankreich: neue Folge.* Vol. 5. Abhandlungen der Akademie der Wissenschaften in Göttingen, philologisch-historische Klasse, 3. Folge, 35. Göttingen: Vandenhoeck and Ruprecht, 1956.
Rau, Reinhold, ed., based on the editions of Michael Tangl and Wilhelm Levison. *Briefe des Bonifatius, Willibalds Leben des Bonifatius: nebst einigen zeitgenössischen Dokumenten.* Ausgewählte Quellen zur deutschen Geschichte des Mittelalters 4b. Darmstadt: Wissenschaftliche Buchgesellschaft, 1968.
Reischmann, Hans-Joachim, ed., based on the edition of W. Levison. *Willi-*

brord, Apostel der Friesen: seine Vita nach Alkuin und Thiofrid. Sigmaringendorf: Glock and Lutz, 1989.

Rerum Britannicarum Medii Aevi Scriptores (Rolls Series). 99 vols. London: Longman, etc., 1858–96.

Reynolds, Roger E., ed. *The* Collectio Canonum Casinensis Duodecimi Seculi (Codex Terscriptus), *a Derivative of the South-Italian Collection in Five Books: An Implicit Edition with Introductory Study*. Monumenta Liturgica Beneventana III, Studies and Texts 137. Toronto: Pontifical Institute of Mediaeval Studies, 2001.

Richard, M., ed. *Histoire des diocèses de Besançon et de Saint-Claude*. 3 vols. Besançon: Cornu, 1847–51.

Riché, Pierre, and Jean-Pierre Callu, eds. *Gerbert d'Aurillac: correspondance*. 2nd ed. Les classiques de l'histoire de France au moyen âge 45. Paris: Belles Lettres, 2008.

Richter, Michael, ed. *Canterbury Professions*. Canterbury and York Society 67. Torquay: Devonshire, 1973.

Rommel, Floribert, Bruno Judic, and Charles Morel, eds. *Grégoire le Grand: règle pastorale*. 2 vols. Sources chrétiennes 381–82. Paris: Cerf, 1992.

Santifaller, Leo, ed. *Quellen und Forschungen zum Urkunden- und Kanzleiwesen Papst Gregors VII*. Part 1. Studi e testi 190. Vatican City: Biblioteca Apostolica Vaticana, 1957.

Schaller, Dieter, ed. "Philologische Untersuchungen zu den Gedichten Theodulfs von Orléans." *Deutsches Archiv für Erforschung des Mittelalters* 18 (1962): 13–91.

Schimmelpfennig, Bernhard, ed. "Ein bisher unbekannter Text zur Wahl, Konsekration und Krönung des Papstes im 12. Jahrhundert." *Archivum Historiae Pontificiae* 6 (1968): 43–70.

———, ed. "Ein Fragment zur Wahl, Konsekration und Krönung des Papstes im 12. Jahrhundert." *Archivum Historiae Pontificiae* 8 (1970): 323–31.

Schmidt, Gustav, ed. *Urkundenbuch des Hochstifts Halberstadt und seiner Bischöfe*. 4 vols. Publicationen aus den Königlichen Preussischen Staatsarchiven 17, 21, 27, 40. Leipzig: Hirzel, 1883–89.

Schmitt, Franciscus Salesius, ed. *S. Anselmi Cantuariensis Archiepiscopi Opera Omnia*. 2nd ed. 2 vols. Stuttgart: Frommann, 1984.

Schmitz, Gerhard, ed. *Edition der falschen Kapitularien des Benedictus Levita*. http://www.benedictus.mgh.de/edition/edition.htm, version 2014-12-10.

Schon, Karl-Georg, and Klaus Zechiel-Eckes, eds. *Projekt Pseudoisidor: Text der falschen Dekretalen*. 2010. http://www.pseudoisidor.mgh.de/html/text.html

Schulte, Johann Friedrich von, ed. *Stephan von Doornick (Étienne de Tournai, Stephanus Tornacensis): Die Summa über das Decretum Gratiani*. Giessen: Roth, 1891; reprinted in Aalen: Scientia, 1965.

———, ed. *Die Summa [des Paucapalea] über das Decretum Gratiani*. Giessen: Roth, 1890; reprinted in Aalen: Scientia, 1965.

Sdralek, Max, ed. *Die Streitschriften Altmanns von Passau und Wezilos von Mainz*. Paderborn: Schöningh, 1890.

Singer, Heinrich, ed. *Summa Decretorum*. Paderborn: Schöningh, 1902; reprinted in Aalen: Scientia, 1963.

Selected Bibliography 497

Somerville, Robert, ed., in collaboration with Stephan Kuttner. *Pope Urban II, the* Collectio Britannica, *and the Council of Melfi (1089)*. Oxford: Clarendon, 1996.
Sot, Michel, Guy Lobrichon, Monique Goullet, and Pierre Bonnerue, eds. *Les gestes des évêques d'Auxerre*. Les classiques de l'histoire de France au moyen âge 42. Paris: Belles Lettres, 2002.
Southern, R. W., ed. *The Life of St. Anselm, Archbishop of Canterbury, by Eadmer*. Oxford Medieval Texts. Oxford: Clarendon, 1979.
Stimming, Manfred, ed. *Mainzer Urkundenbuch*. Vol. 1. Darmstadt: Historischer Verein für Hessen, 1932; reprinted in Darmstadt: Hessische Historische Kommission, 1972.
Thaner, Friedrich, ed. *Anselmi Episcopi Lucensis Collectio Canonum una cum Collectione Minore*. 2 vols. Innsbruck: Wagner, 1906–15.
———, ed. *Summa Magistri Rolandi*. Innsbruck: Wagner, 1874; reprinted in Aalen: Scientia, 1973.
Trillmich, Werner, ed., based on the edition of Robert Holtzmann. *Thietmar von Merseburg: Chronik*. Ausgewählte Quellen zur deutschen Geschichte des Mittelalters 9. Darmstadt: Wissenschaftliche Buchgesellschaft, 1974.
Turner, Andrew J., and Bernard J. Muir, eds. *Eadmer of Canterbury: Lives and Miracles of Saints Oda, Dunstan, and Oswald*. Oxford Medieval Texts. Oxford: Clarendon, 2006.
Valentini, Roberto, and Giuseppe Zucchetti, eds. *Codice topografico della città di Roma*. 4 vols. Fonti per la storia d'Italia 81, 88, 90–91. Rome: Tipografia del Senato, 1940–53.
Vogel, Cyrille, and Reinhard Elze, eds. *Le pontifical romano-germanique du dixième siècle*. 3 vols. Studi e testi 226–27, 269. Vatican City: Biblioteca Apostolica Vaticana, 1963–72.
Weidemann, Margarete, ed. *Geschichte des Bistums Le Mans von der Spätantike bis zur Karolingerzeit: Actus Pontificum Cenomannis in Urbe Degentium und Gesta Aldrici*. 3 vols. Römisch-germanisches Zentralmuseum Forschungsinstitut für Vor- und Frühgeschichte Monographien 56. Mainz: Römisch-germanisches Zentralmuseum, 2002.
Weigand, Rudolf, Peter Landau, and Waltraud Kozur, eds. *Magistri Honorii Summa "De iure canonico tractaturus."* 3 vols. Monumenta Iuris Canonici, ser. A, Corpus Glossatorum 5. Vatican City: Biblioteca Apostolica Vaticana, 2004–10.
———, eds. *Summa "Omnis qui iuste iudicat" sive Lipsiensis*. 2 vols. Monumenta Iuris Canonici, ser. A, Corpus Glossatorum 7. Vatican City: Biblioteca Apostolica Vaticana, 2007–12.
Whitelock, Dorothy, trans. *English Historical Documents, c. 500–1042*. 2nd ed. Vol. 1. English Historical Documents 1. London: Eyre Methuen, 1979.
Whitelock, D., M. Brett, and C. N. L. Brooke, eds. *Councils and Synods with Other Documents relating to the English Church*. Vol. 1. Oxford: Clarendon, 1981.
Wiederhold, Wilhelm, ed. *Papsturkunden in Frankreich: Reiseberichte zur Gallia Pontificia*. 2 vols. Acta Romanorum Pontificum 7–8. Vatican City: Biblioteca Apostolica Vaticana, 1985.
Winterbottom, M., ed., with the assistance of R. M. Thomson. *William of*

Malmesbury: Gesta Pontificum Anglorum, *the History of the English Bishops.* 2 vols. Oxford Medieval Texts. Oxford: Clarendon, 2007.
Winterbottom, M., and R. M. Thomson, eds. *William of Malmesbury, Saints' Lives: Lives of SS. Wulfstan, Dunstan, Patrick, Benignus and Indract.* Oxford Medieval Texts. Oxford: Clarendon, 2002.
Wisplinghoff, Erich, ed. *Rheinisches Urkundenbuch: Ältere Urkunden bis 1100.* Vol. 2. Publikationen der Gesellschaft für Rheinische Geschichtskunde 57. Düsseldorf: Droste, 1994.
Zimmermann, Harald, ed. *Papsturkunden, 896–1046.* 3 vols. Österreichische Akademie der Wissenschaften, philosophisch-historische Klasse, Denkschriften 174, 177, 198, Veröffentlichungen der historischen Kommission 3–5. Vienna: Österreichische Akademie der Wissenschaften, 1984–89.
Zimpel, Detlev, ed. *Hrabanus Maurus: De Institutione Clericorum Libri Tres.* Frankfurt: Lang, 1996.

Secondary Works

Abel, Ch. "Étude sur le pallium et le titre d'archevêque jadis portés par les évêques de Metz." *Mémoires de la Société d'archéologie et d'histoire de la Moselle* 9 (1867): 53–129.
Algazi, Gadi. "Introduction: Doing Things with Gifts." In *Negotiating the Gift: Pre-Modern Figurations of Exchange,* edited by Gadi Algazi, Valentin Groebner, and Bernhard Jussen, 9–27. Veröffentlichungen des Max-Planck-Instituts für Geschichte 188. Göttingen: Vandenhoeck and Ruprecht, 2003.
Alraum, Claudia. "Pallienprivilegien für Apulien zwischen 1063 und 1122." *Specimina Nova Pars Prima Sectio Mediaevalis* 6 (2011): 11–32.
Althoff, Gerd. *Otto III.* Translated by Phyllis G. Jestice. University Park: Pennsylvania State University Press, 2003.
Amory, Frederic. "Whited Sepulchres: The Semantic History of Hypocrisy to the High Middle Ages." *Recherches de théologie ancienne et médiévale* 53 (1986): 5–39.
Arduini, Maria Lodovica. *Rupert von Deutz (1076–1129) und der "Status Christianitatis" seiner Zeit: symbolisch-prophetische Deutung der Geschichte.* Beihefte zum Archiv für Kulturgeschichte 25. Cologne: Böhlau, 1987.
Arnold, Dorothee. *Johannes VIII.: päpstliche Herrschaft in den karolingischen Teilreichen am Ende des 9. Jahrhunderts.* Europäische Hochschulschriften, ser. 23, 797. Frankfurt: Lang, 2005.
Austin, Greta. "Secular Law in the *Collectio Duodecim Partium* and Burchard's *Decretum.*" In *Bishops, Texts and the Use of Canon Law around 1100: Essays in Honour of Martin Brett,* edited by Bruce C. Brasington and Kathleen G. Cushing, 29–44. Aldershot: Ashgate, 2008.
———. *Shaping Church Law around the Year 1000: The* Decretum *of Burchard of Worms.* Farnham: Ashgate, 2009.
Beal, John P., James A. Coriden, and Thomas J. Green, eds. *New Commentary on the Code of Canon Law.* New York: Paulist, 2000.

Selected Bibliography 499

Becker, Alfons, and Dietrich Lohrmann. "Ein erschlichenes Privileg Papst Urbans II. für Erzbischof Guido von Vienne (Calixt II.)." *Deutsches Archiv für Erforschung des Mittelalters* 38 (1982): 66–111.
Benson, Robert L. *The Bishop-Elect: A Study in Medieval Ecclesiastical Office.* Princeton, N.J.: Princeton University Press, 1968.
———. "Plenitudo Potestatis: Evolution of a Formula from Gregory IV to Gratian." *Studia Gratiana* 14 (1967): 193–217.
Berger, Rupert. "Liturgische Gewänder und Insignien." In *Gottesdienst der Kirche: Handbuch der Liturgiewissenschaft,* vol. 3, *Gestalt des Gottesdienstes: sprachliche und nichtsprachliche Ausdrucksformen,* edited by Hans Bernhard Meyer et al., 309–46. Regensburg: Pustet, 1987.
Bertram, Martin. "Die Dekretalen Gregors IX.: Kompilation oder Kodifikation?" In *Magister Raimundus,* edited by Carlo Longo, 61–86. Dissertationes Historicae 28. Rome: Istituto Storico Domenicano, 2002.
Bethurum, Dorothy. "A Letter of Protest from the English Bishops to the Pope." In *Philologica: The Malone Anniversary Studies,* edited by Thomas A. Kirby and Henry Bosley Woolf, 97–104. Baltimore: Johns Hopkins University Press, 1949.
Betz, Karl-Ulrich. *Hinkmar von Reims, Nikolaus I., Pseudo-Isidor: fränkisches Landeskirchentum und römischer Machtanspruch im 9. Jahrhundert.* Bonn: Rheinische Friedrich-Wilhelms-Universität, 1965.
Beulertz, Stefan. *Das Verbot der Laieninvestitur im Investiturstreit.* Monumenta Germaniae Historica Studien und Texte 2. Hannover: Hahn, 1991.
Beumann, Helmut. "Das Kaisertum Ottos des Grossen: ein Rückblick nach tausend Jahren." In Beumann, *Wissenschaft vom Mittelalter: ausgewählte Aufsätze,* 411–58. Cologne: Böhlau, 1972.
———. "Das Rationale der Bischöfe von Halberstadt und seine Folgen." In *Kirche und Reich: Beiträge zur früh- und hochmittelalterlichen Kloster-, Bistums- und Missionsgeschichte,* edited by Irmgard Fees, 235–68 (39–70). Bibliotheca Eruditorum 33. Goldbach: Keip, 2004.
———. *Theutonum nova metropolis: Studien zur Geschichte des Erzbistums Magdeburg in ottonischer Zeit.* Edited by Jutta Krimm-Beumann. Quellen und Forschungen zur Geschichte Sachsen-Anhalts 1. Cologne: Böhlau, 2000.
———. "Zu den Pontifikalinsignien und zum Amtsverständnis der Bischöfe von Halberstadt im hohen Mittelalter." In *Kirche und Reich: Beiträge zur früh- und hochmittelalterlichen Kloster-, Bistums- und Missionsgeschichte,* edited by Irmgard Fees, 329–69 (9–49). Bibliotheca Eruditorum 33. Goldbach: Keip, 2004.
Bigott, Boris. *Ludwig der Deutsche und die Reichskirche im Ostfränkischen Reich (826–876).* Historische Studien 470. Husum: Matthiesen, 2002.
Bijsterveld, Arnoud-Jan A. *Do ut des: Gift Giving, Memoria, and Conflict Management in the Medieval Low Countries.* Middeleeuwse studies en bronnen 104. Hilversum: Verloren, 2007.
Blaauw, Sible de. *Cultus et decor: liturgia e architettura nella Roma tardoantica e medievale: Basilica Salvatoris, Sanctae Mariae, Sancti Petri.* 2 vols. Studi e testi 355–56. Vatican City: Biblioteca Apostolica Vaticana, 1994.

Blumenthal, Uta-Renate. *The Investiture Controversy: Church and Monarchy from the Ninth to the Twelfth Century.* Philadelphia: University of Pennsylvania Press, 1988.

———. "The Papacy, 1024–1122." In *The New Cambridge Medieval History,* edited by David Luscombe and Jonathan Riley-Smith, 4.2:8–37. Cambridge: Cambridge University Press, 2004.

———. "Rom in der Kanonistik." In Blumenthal, *Papal Reform and Canon Law in the 11th and 12th Centuries,* part 5. Aldershot: Ashgate Variorum, 1998.

Booker, Courtney M. *Past Convictions: The Penance of Louis the Pious and the Decline of the Carolingians.* Philadelphia: University of Pennsylvania Press, 2009.

Boshof, Egon. *Das Erzstift Trier und seine Stellung zu Königtum und Papsttum im ausgehenden 10. Jahrhundert: der Pontifikat des Theoderich.* Cologne: Böhlau, 1972.

Braun, Joseph. *Die liturgische Gewandung im Occident und Orient: nach Ursprung und Entwicklung, Verwendung und Symbolik.* Freiburg: Herder, 1907.

Brooks, Nicholas. *The Early History of the Church of Canterbury: Christ Church from 597 to 1066.* Leicester: Leicester University Press, 1984.

Brown, Barton. "*Enigmata Figurarum*: A Study of the Third Book of the *Rationale Divinorum Officiorum* of William Durandus and its Allegorical Treatment of the Christian Liturgical Vestments." PhD diss., New York University, 1983.

Brundage, James A. "The Teaching and Study of Canon Law in the Law Schools." In *The History of Medieval Canon Law in the Classical Period, 1140–1234: From Gratian to the Decretals of Pope Gregory IX,* edited by Wilfried Hartmann and Kenneth Pennington, 98–120. Washington, D.C.: The Catholic University of America Press, 2008.

Buck, Thomas Martin. *Admonitio und Praedicatio: zur religiös-pastoralen Dimension von Kapitularien und kapitulariennahen Texten (507–814).* Freiburger Beiträge zur mittelalterlichen Geschichte 9. Frankfurt: Lang, 1997.

Büttner, Heinrich. "Erzbischof Willigis von Mainz (975–1011)." In *Zur frühmittelalterlichen Reichsgeschichte an Rhein, Main und Neckar,* edited by Alois Gerlich, 301–13. Darmstadt: Wissenschaftliche Buchgesellschaft, 1975.

———. "Mission und Kirchenorganisation des Frankenreiches bis zum Tode Karls des Großen." In *Karl der Große: Lebenswerk und Nachleben,* vol. 1, *Persönlichkeit und Geschichte,* edited by Helmut Beumann, 454–87. Düsseldorf: Schwann, 1965.

Callahan, Daniel. "Adémar of Chabannes, Apocalypticism and the Peace Council of Limoges of 1031." *Revue bénédictine* 101 (1991): 32–49.

Chazelle, Celia. "Amalarius's *Liber Officialis*: Spirit and Vision in Carolingian Liturgical Thought." In *Seeing the Invisible in Late Antiquity and the Early Middle Ages,* edited by Giselle de Nie, Karl F. Morrison, and Marco Mostert, 327–57. Utrecht Studies in Medieval Literacy 14. Turnhout: Brepols, 2005.

———. "Archbishops Ebo and Hincmar of Reims and the Utrecht Psalter." *Speculum* 72 (1997): 1055–77.

Chydenius, Johan. *Medieval Institutions and the Old Testament.* Societas Scien-

Selected Bibliography 501

tiarum Fennica: Commentationes Humanarum Litterarum 37.2. Helsinki: Helsingfors, 1965.

Claude, Dietrich. *Geschichte des Erzbistums Magdeburg bis in das 12. Jahrhundert.* 2 vols. Mitteldeutsche Forschungen 67.1. Cologne: Böhlau, 1972–75.

Claussen, M. A. *The Reform of the Frankish Church: Chrodegang of Metz and the Regula canonicorum in the Eighth Century.* Cambridge: Cambridge University Press, 2004.

Clay, John-Henry Wilson. "Gift-giving and Books in the Letters of St. Boniface and Lul." *Journal of Medieval History* 35 (2009): 313–25.

Congar, Y. M.-J. *L'ecclésiologie du haut moyen âge: de Saint Grégoire le Grand à la désunion entre Byzance et Rome.* Paris: Cerf, 1968.

Constable, Giles. "Les listes de propriétés dans les privilèges pour Baume-les-Messieurs aux XIe et XIIe siècles." *Journal des savants* (1986): 97–131.

Cowdrey, H. E. J. "Archbishop Thomas I of York and the *Pallium.*" *Haskins Society Journal* 11 (1998): 31–41.

———. *Pope Gregory VII, 1073–1085.* Oxford: Clarendon, 1998.

Cubizolles, Pierre. "Les évêques du Puy honorés jadis du *pallium.*" *Cahiers de la Haute-Loire* (1999): 23–38.

Curta, Florin. "Merovingian and Carolingian Gift-giving." *Speculum* 81 (2006): 671–99.

Cushing, Kathleen G. "Polemic or Handbook? Recension Bb of Anselm of Lucca's *Collectio Canonum.*" In *Bishops, Texts and the Use of Canon Law around 1100: Essays in Honour of Martin Brett,* edited by Bruce C. Brasington and Kathleen G. Cushing, 69–77. Aldershot: Ashgate, 2008.

———. *Reform and Papacy in the Eleventh Century: Spirituality and Social Change.* Manchester: Manchester University Press, 2005.

D'Abadal i de Vinyals, Ramon. *Dels visigots als catalans.* Edited by Jaume Sobrequés i Callicó. 2nd ed. 2 vols. Col·lecció estudis i documents 13–14. Barcelona: Edicions 62, 1974.

Dahlhaus, Joachim. "Zum Privileg Alexanders II. für Burchard II. von Halberstadt." In *Von Sacerdotium und Regnum: geistliche und weltliche Gewalt im frühen und hohen Mittelalter,* edited by Franz-Reiner Erkens and Harmut Wolff, 637–73. Passauer historische Forschungen 12. Cologne: Böhlau, 2002.

D'Alteroche, Bernard. "Le statut du pallium dans le droit canonique classique de Gratien à Hostiensis (vers 1140–1270)." *Revue historique de droit français et étranger* 83 (2005): 553–85.

Darlington, R. R. "Ecclesiastical Reform in the Late Old English Period." *The English Historical Review* 51 (1936): 385–428.

Delbrueck, Richard. *Die Consulardiptychen und verwandte Denkmäler.* Studien zur spätantiken Kunstgeschichte 2. Berlin: de Gruyter, 1929.

Delivré, Fabrice. "The Foundations of Primatial Claims in the Western Church (Eleventh-Thirteenth Centuries)." *Journal of Ecclesiastical History* 59 (2008): 383–406.

Deswarte, Thomas. "Rome et la spécificité catalane: la papauté et ses relations avec la Catalogne et Narbonne (850–1030)." *Revue historique* 294 (1995): 3–43.

Devisse, Jean. *Hincmar, archevêque de Reims, 845–882*. 3 vols. Travaux d'histoire ethico-politique 29. Geneva: Droz, 1975–76.

Dubois, Jacques. *Les martyrologes du moyen âge latin*. Typologie des sources du moyen âge occidental 26. Turnhout: Brepols, 1978.

Du Cange, Charles Du Fresne, supplemented by Léopold Favre. *Glossarium Mediae et Infimae Latinitatis*. 2nd ed. 10 vols. Niort: Favre, 1883–87; reprinted in Graz: Akademische Druck- und Verlagsanstalt, 1954.

Duchesne, L. *Fastes épiscopaux de l'ancienne Gaule*. 2nd ed. 3 vols. Paris: Fontemoing, 1907–15.

———. *Origines du culte chrétien: étude sur la liturgie latine avant Charlemagne*. 5th ed. Paris: de Boccard, 1925.

Duggan, Anne J. "Making Law or Not? The Function of Papal Decretals in the Twelfth Century." In *Proceedings of the Thirteenth International Congress of Medieval Canon Law*, edited by Peter Erdö and Sz. Anzelm Szuromi, 41–70. Monumenta Iuris Canonici, ser. C, Subsidia 14. Vatican City: Biblioteca Apostolica Vaticana, 2010.

———. "Master of the Decretals: A Reassessment of Alexander III's Contribution to Canon Law." In *Pope Alexander III (1159–81): The Art of Survival*, edited by Peter D. Clarke and Anne J. Duggan, 365–417. Farnham: Ashgate, 2012.

Dümmler, Ernst. *Auxilius und Vulgarius: Quellen und Forschungen zur Geschichte des Papsttums im Anfange des zehnten Jahrhunderts*. Leipzig: Hirzel, 1866.

Dvornik, Francis. *The Photian Schism: History and Legend*. Cambridge: Cambridge University Press, 1948.

Eidenschink, John Albert. *The Election of Bishops in the Letters of Gregory the Great: With an Appendix on the Pallium*. The Catholic University of America Canon Law Studies 215. Washington, D.C.: The Catholic University of America Press, 1945.

Elliott, Dyan. "Dressing and Undressing the Clergy: Rites of Ordination and Degradation." In *Medieval Fabrications: Dress, Textiles, Clothwork, and Other Cultural Imaginings*, edited by E. Jane Burns, 55–69. New York: Palgrave Macmillan, 2004.

Engels, Odilo. "Der Pontifikatsantritt und seine Zeichen." In *Segni e riti nella chiesa altomedievale occidentale*, 2:707–66. Settimane di studio del Centro italiano di studi sull'alto medioevo 33. Spoleto: Sede del Centro, 1987.

Falkenstein, Ludwig. *La papauté et les abbayes françaises aux XIe et XIIe siècles: exemption et protection apostolique*. Bibliothèque de l'École des hautes études, sciences historiques et philologiques 336. Paris: Champion, 1997.

———. "Zu verlorenen päpstlichen Privilegien und Schreiben: Palliumverleihungen an die Erzbischöfe von Reims (8.–12. Jahrhundert)." In *Eloquentia copiosus: Festschrift für Max Kerner zum 65. Geburtstag*, edited by Lotte Kéry, 181–224. Aachen: Thouet, 2006.

Fenske, Lutz. *Adelsopposition und kirchliche Reformbewegung im östlichen Sachsen: Entstehung und Wirkung des sächsischen Widerstandes gegen das salische Königtum während des Investiturstreits*. Veröffentlichungen des Max-Planck-Instituts für Geschichte 47. Göttingen: Vandenhoeck and Ruprecht, 1977.

Fichtenau, Heinrich. *Arenga: Spätantike und Mittelalter im Spiegel von Urkundenformeln*. Mitteilungen des Instituts für österreichische Geschichtsforschung, Ergänzungsband 18. Graz: Böhlau, 1957.
———. *Living in the Tenth Century: Mentalities and Social Orders*. Translated by Patrick J. Geary. Chicago: University of Chicago Press, 1991.
———. "Zu den Urkundenfälschungen Pilgrims von Passau." In Fichtenau, *Beiträge zur Mediävistik: ausgewählte Aufsätze*, 2:157–79. Stuttgart: Hiersemann, 1977.
Fleckenstein, Josef. *Die Hofkapelle der deutschen Könige*. 2 vols. Monumenta Germaniae Historica Schriften 16. Stuttgart: Hiersemann, 1959–66.
———. "Zum Begriff der ottonisch-salischen Reichskirche." In *Geschichte, Wirtschaft, Gesellschaft*, edited by Erich Hassinger, J. Heinz Müller, and Hugo Ott, 61–71. Berlin: Duncker and Humblot, 1974.
Floryszczak, Silke. *Die* Regula Pastoralis *Gregors des Großen: Studien zu Text, kirchenpolitischer Bedeutung und Rezeption in der Karolingerzeit*. Studien und Texte zu Antike und Christentum 26. Tübingen: Mohr Siebeck, 2005.
Fougerolles, Paula de. "Pope Gregory VII, the Archbishopric of Dol and the Normans." *Anglo-Norman Studies* 21 (1998): 47–66.
Fournier, Paul, and Gabriel Le Bras. *Histoire des collections canoniques en occident dépuis les Fausses Décrétales jusqu'au Décret de Gratien*. 2 vols. Paris: Sirey, 1931–32; reprinted in Aalen: Scientia, 1972.
Fowler-Magerl, Linda. *Clavis Canonum: Selected Canon Law Collections before 1140*. Monumenta Germaniae Historica Hilfsmittel 21. Hannover: Hahn, 2005.
Frech, Karl Augustin. *Papstregesten, 1024–1058*. 2 vols. J. F. Böhmer, Regesta Imperii 3.5.1–2. Cologne: Böhlau, 2006–11.
Freeman, Ann, and Paul Meyvaert. "The Meaning of Theodulf's Apse Mosaic at Germigny-des-Prés." *Gesta* 40 (2001): 125–39.
Fried, Johannes. Donation of Constantine *and* Constitutum Constantini: *The Misinterpretation of a Fiction and its Original Meaning*. Millennium-Studien 3. Berlin: de Gruyter, 2007.
Frutaz, Amato Pietro. *Il complesso monumentale di Sant'Agnese*. 6th ed. Rome: Nova Officina Poligrafica Laziale, 2001.
Fuhrmann, Horst. *Einfluß und Verbreitung der pseudoisidorischen Fälschungen: von ihrem Auftauchen bis in die neuere Zeit*. 3 vols. Monumenta Germaniae Historica Schriften 24. Stuttgart: Hiersemann, 1972–73.
———. "Studien zur Geschichte mittelalterlicher Patriarchate." *Zeitschrift der Savigny-Stiftung für Rechtsgeschichte, kanonistische Abteilung* 39 (1953): 112–76; 40 (1954): 1–84; 41 (1955): 95–183.
Fürst, Carl Gerold. *Cardinalis: Prolegomena zu einer Rechtsgeschichte des römischen Kardinalskollegiums*. Munich: Fink, 1967.
Gallia Pontificia. Regesta Pontificum Romanorum. Göttingen: Vandenhoeck and Ruprecht, 1998–.
Gamber, Klaus. "Das Superhumerale der Regensburger Bischöfe in seiner liturgiegeschichtlichen Entwicklung." In Gamber, *Ecclesia Reginensis: Studien zur Geschichte und Liturgie der Regensburger Kirche im Mittelalter*, 184–98. Studia Patristica et Liturgica 8. Regensburg: Pustet, 1979.

Gaudemet, Jean. *L'église dans l'empire romain (IVe–Ve siècles)*. Histoire du droit et des institutions de l'église en occident 3. Paris: Sirey, 1958.

Geary, Patrick J. *Furta Sacra: Thefts of Relics in the Central Middle Ages*. Rev. ed. Princeton, N.J.: Princeton University Press, 1990.

———. "Gift Exchange and Social Science Modeling: The Limitations of a Construct." In *Negotiating the Gift: Pre-Modern Figurations of Exchange*, edited by Gadi Algazi, Valentin Groebner, and Bernhard Jussen, 129–40. Veröffentlichungen des Max-Planck-Instituts für Geschichte 188. Göttingen: Vandenhoeck and Ruprecht, 2003.

———. "Sacred Commodities: The Circulation of Medieval Relics." In *The Social Life of Things: Commodities in Cultural Perspective*, edited by Arjun Appadurai, 169–91. Cambridge: Cambridge University Press, 1986.

Germania Pontificia. Regesta Pontificum Romanorum. Berlin: Weidmann, and Göttingen: Vandenhoeck and Ruprecht, 1911–.

Gilchrist, John T. "'Simoniaca heresis' and the Problem of Orders from Leo IX to Gratian." In *Proceedings of the Second International Congress of Medieval Canon Law*, edited by Stephan Kuttner and J. Joseph Ryan, 209–35. Monumenta Iuris Canonici, ser. C, Subsidia 1. Vatican City: Sacra Congregatio de Seminariis et Studiorum Universitatibus, 1965.

———. "Was There a Gregorian Reform Movement in the Eleventh Century?" In Gilchrist, *Canon Law in the Age of Reform, 11th–12th Centuries*, part 7. Aldershot: Ashgate Variorum, 1993.

Glenn, Jason. *Politics and History in the Tenth Century: The Work and World of Richer of Reims*. Cambridge: Cambridge University Press, 2004.

Godman, Peter. *Poets and Emperors: Frankish Politics and Carolingian Poetry*. Oxford: Clarendon, 1987.

Goffart, Walter. *The Le Mans Forgeries: A Chapter from the History of Church Property in the Ninth Century*. Harvard Historical Studies 76. Cambridge, Mass.: Harvard University Press, 1966.

Gordon, Stewart. "A World of Investiture." In *Robes and Honor: The Medieval World of Investiture*, edited by Stewart Gordon, 1–19. New York: Palgrave Macmillan, 2001.

Gottlob, Theodor. *Der kirchliche Amtseid der Bischöfe*. Kanonistische Studien und Texte 9. Bonn: Röhrscheid, 1936; reprinted in Amsterdam: Schippers, 1963.

Grégoire, Réginald. *Bruno de Segni: exégète médiéval et théologien monastique*. Centro italiano di studi sull'alto medioevo 3. Spoleto: Panetto and Petrelli, 1965.

Gresser, Georg. *Clemens II.: der erste deutsche Reformpapst*. Paderborn: Schöningh, 2007.

———. *Die Synoden und Konzilien in der Zeit des Reformpapsttums in Deutschland und Italien von Leo IX. bis Calixt II., 1049–1123*. Paderborn: Schöningh, 2006.

Grierson, Philip. "Rostagnus of Arles and the Pallium." *The English Historical Review* 49 (1934): 74–83.

Grisar, H. "Das römische Pallium und die ältesten liturgischen Schärpen." In *Festschrift zum elfhundertjährigen Jubiläum des deutschen Campo Santo in Rom*, edited by Stephan Ehses, 83–114. Freiburg: Herder, 1897.

Guttenberg, Erich Freiherr von. *Die Regesten der Bischöfe und des Domkapitels von*

Bamberg. Veröffentlichungen der Gesellschaft für fränkische Geschichte 6. Würzburg: Schöningh, 1963.

Hacke, Curt-Bogislav Graf von. *Die Palliumverleihungen bis 1143: eine diplomatisch-historische Untersuchung.* Marburg: Elwert, 1898.

Hamilton, Louis I. *A Sacred City: Consecrating Churches and Reforming Society in Eleventh-Century Italy.* Manchester: Manchester University Press, 2010.

Häring, N. M. "The Augustinian Maxim: *Nulli Sacramento Injuria Facienda Est.*" *Mediaeval Studies* 16 (1954): 87–117.

Hartmann, Ludo Moritz. *Geschichte Italiens im Mittelalter.* 4 vols. Leipzig: Wigand, 1897–1915.

Hartmann, Wilfried. *Die Synoden der Karolingerzeit im Frankenreich und in Italien.* Paderborn: Schöningh, 1989.

Hartmann, Wilfried, and Kenneth Pennington, eds. *The History of Medieval Canon Law in the Classical Period, 1140–1234: From Gratian to the Decretals of Pope Gregory IX.* Washington, D.C.: The Catholic University of America Press, 2008.

Healy, Patrick. *The Chronicle of Hugh of Flavigny: Reform and the Investiture Contest in the Late Eleventh Century.* Aldershot: Ashgate, 2006.

Heidecker, Karl. *The Divorce of Lothar II: Christian Marriage and Political Power in the Carolingian World.* Translated by Tanis M. Guest. Ithaca, N.Y.: Cornell University Press, 2010.

Hen, Yitzhak. *The Royal Patronage of Liturgy in Frankish Gaul to the Death of Charles the Bald (877).* Henry Bradshaw Society Subsidia 3. London: Boydell, 2001.

Herbers, Klaus. *Leo IV. und das Papsttum in der Mitte des 9. Jahrhunderts: Möglichkeiten und Grenzen päpstlicher Herrschaft in der späten Karolingerzeit.* Päpste und Papsttum 27. Stuttgart: Hiersemann, 1996.

———. *Papstregesten, 844–872.* 2 vols. J. F. Böhmer, Regesta Imperii 1.4.2.1–2. Cologne and Vienna: Böhlau, 1999–2012.

Herrmann, Klaus-Jürgen. *Das Tuskulanerpapsttum (1012–1046): Benedikt VIII., Johannes XIX., Benedikt IX.* Päpste und Papsttum 4. Stuttgart: Hiersemann, 1973.

Heydenreich, Johanne. *Die Metropolitangewalt der Erzbischöfe von Trier bis auf Baldewin.* Marburger Studien zur älteren deutschen Geschichte 2.5. Marburg: Elwert, 1938.

Hirsch, E. "Der Symoniebegriff und eine angebliche Erweiterung desselben im elften Jahrhundert." *Archiv für katholisches Kirchenrecht* 86 (1906): 3–19.

Histoire de l'église depuis les origines jusqu'a nos jours. 21 vols. Paris: Bloud and Gay, 1934–64.

Hoff, Erwin. *Pavia und seine Bischöfe im Mittelalter: Beiträge zur Geschichte der Bischöfe von Pavia unter besonderer Berücksichtigung ihrer politischen Stellung.* Pavia: Fusi, 1943.

Hoffmann, Hartmut, and Rudolf Pokorny. *Das Dekret des Bischofs Burchard von Worms: Textstufen, frühe Verbreitung, Vorlagen.* Monumenta Germaniae Historica Hilfsmittel 12. Munich: Monumenta Germaniae Historica, 1991.

Holtzmann, Walther. *Walther-Holtzmann-Kartei.* 2012. http://www.kuttner-institute.jura.uni-muenchen.de/holtzmann_formular.htm

Honselmann, Klemens. *Das Rationale der Bischöfe*. Paderborn: Verein für Geschichte und Altertumskunde Westfalens, 1975.
Howe, John. "The Nobility's Reform of the Medieval Church." *American Historical Review* 93 (1988): 317–39.
Italia Pontificia. 10 vols. Regesta Pontificum Romanorum. Berlin and Zurich: Weidmann, 1906–75.
Jaeger, C. Stephen. *The Envy of Angels: Cathedral Schools and Social Ideals in Medieval Europe, 950–1200*. Philadelphia: University of Pennsylvania Press, 1994.
Jaffé, Philippus. *Regesta Pontificum Romanorum ab Condita Ecclesia ad Annum post Christum Natum MCXCVIII*. Edited by Gulielmus Wattenbach, S. Loewenfeld, F. Kaltenbrunner, and P. Ewald. 2nd rev. ed. 2 vols. Leipzig: Veit, 1885–88; reprinted in Graz: Akademische Druck- und Verlagsanstalt, 1956.
Jank, Dagmar. "Bemerkungen zu einigen Trierer Palliumurkunden des 11. Jahrhunderts (JL 4010, JL 4151, JL 4646)." *Kurtrierisches Jahrbuch* 22 (1982): 13–22.
Jarnut, Jörg. "Bonifatius und die fränkischen Reformkonzilien (743–748)." *Zeitschrift der Savigny-Stiftung für Rechtsgeschichte, kanonistische Abteilung* 66 (1979): 1–26.
Jarrett, Jonathan A. "Archbishop Ató of Osona: False Metropolitans on the Marca Hispanica." *Archiv für Diplomatik* 56 (2010): 1–41.
Jasper, Detlev, and Horst Fuhrmann. *Papal Letters in the Early Middle Ages*. Washington, D.C.: The Catholic University of America Press, 2001.
Jenal, Georg. *Erzbischof Anno II. von Köln (1056–75) und sein politisches Wirken: ein Beitrag zur Geschichte der Reichs- und Territorialpolitik im 11. Jahrhundert*. 2 vols. Monographien zur Geschichte des Mittelalters 8.1–2. Stuttgart: Hiersemann, 1974–75.
Kehr, P. *Das Papsttum und der katalanische Prinzipat bis zur Vereinigung mit Aragon*. Abhandlungen der preussischen Akademie der Wissenschaften, philosophisch-historische Klasse 1926.1. Berlin: de Gruyter, 1926.
Kempf, Friedrich. "Die Eingliederung der überdiözesanen Hierarchie in das Papalsystem des kanonischen Rechts von der gregorianischen Reform bis zu Innocenz III." *Archivum Historiae Pontificiae* 18 (1980): 57–96.
———. "Primatiale und episkopal-synodale Struktur der Kirche vor der gregorianischen Reform." *Archivum Historiae Pontificiae* 16 (1978): 27–66.
Kéry, Lotte. *Canonical Collections of the Early Middle Ages (ca. 400–1140): A Bibliographical Guide to the Manuscripts and Literature*. Washington, D.C.: The Catholic University of America Press, 1999.
Klauser, Theodor. *Der Ursprung der bischöflichen Insignien und Ehrenrechte*. Bonner akademische Reden 1. Krefeld: Scherpe, 1948.
Knibbs, Eric. *Ansgar, Rimbert and the Forged Foundations of Hamburg-Bremen*. Farnham: Ashgate, 2011.
Kopczynski, Maria. *Die Arengen der Papsturkunden nach ihrer Bedeutung und Verwendung bis zu Gregor VII*. Bottrop: Postberg, 1936.
Kortüm, Hans-Henning. *Zur päpstlichen Urkundensprache im frühen Mittelalter: die päpstlichen Privilegien, 896–1046*. Beiträge zur Geschichte und Quellenkunde des Mittelalters 17. Sigmaringen: Thorbecke, 1995.

Kottje, Raymund, and Harald Zimmermann, eds. *Hrabanus Maurus: Lehrer, Abt und Bischof.* Akademie der Wissenschaften und der Literatur, Abhandlungen der geistes- und sozialwissenschaftlichen Klasse 4. Wiesbaden: Steiner, 1982.

Koziol, Geoffrey. *Begging Pardon and Favor: Ritual and Political Order in Early Medieval France.* Ithaca, N.Y.: Cornell University Press, 1992.

Krohn, Richard. *Der päpstliche Kanzler Johannes von Gaëta (Gelasius II.).* Berlin: Ebering, 1918.

Kuttner, Stephan. *Harmony from Dissonance: An Interpretation of Medieval Canon Law.* Latrobe, Pa.: Archabbey Press, 1960. Reprinted in Kuttner, *The History of Ideas and Doctrines of Canon Law in the Middle Ages,* part 1. London: Variorum, 1980.

———. "Raymond of Peñafort as Editor: The 'Decretales' and 'Constitutiones' of Gregory IX." *Bulletin of Medieval Canon Law* 12 (1982): 65–80. Reprinted in Kuttner, *Studies in the History of Medieval Canon Law,* part 12. Aldershot: Ashgate Variorum, 1990.

———. "The Revival of Jurisprudence." In *Renaissance and Renewal in the Twelfth Century,* edited by Robert L. Benson and Giles Constable with Carol D. Lanham, 299–323. Medieval Academy Reprints for Teaching 26. Toronto: University of Toronto Press, 1991.

Lambert, Malcolm. *Medieval Heresy: Popular Movements from the Gregorian Reform to the Reformation.* 3rd ed. Malden, Mass.: Blackwell, 2002.

Landau, Peter. "Gefälschtes Recht in den Rechtssammlungen bis Gratian." In *Fälschungen im Mittelalter,* part 2, *Gefälschte Rechtstexte; der bestrafte Fälscher,* 11–49. Monumenta Germaniae Historica Schriften 33.2. Hannover: Hahn, 1988.

———. "Gratian and the *Decretum Gratiani.*" In *The History of Medieval Canon Law in the Classical Period, 1140–1234: From Gratian to the Decretals of Pope Gregory IX,* edited by Wilfried Hartmann and Kenneth Pennington, 22–54. Washington, D.C.: The Catholic University of America Press, 2008.

———. *Die Kölner Kanonistik des 12. Jahrhunderts: ein Höhepunkt der europäischen Rechtswissenschaft.* Kölner rechtsgeschichtliche Vorträge 1. Badenweiler: Bachmann, 2008.

———. "Rodoicus Modicipassus: Verfasser der Summa Lipsiensis?" *Zeitschrift der Savigny-Stiftung für Rechtsgeschichte, kanonistische Abteilung* 92 (2006): 340–54.

Landes, Richard. *Relics, Apocalypse, and the Deceits of History: Ademar of Chabannes, 989–1034.* Harvard Historical Studies 117. Cambridge, Mass.: Harvard University Press, 1995.

Lanzani, Vittorio. "'Gloriosa confessio': lo splendore del sepolcro di Pietro da Costantino al Rinascimento." In *La confessione nella basilica di San Pietro in Vaticano,* edited by Alfredo Maria Pergolizzi, 11–41. Milan: Silvana, 1999.

Lapidge, Michael. "B. and the *Vita S. Dunstani.*" In *St. Dunstan: His Life, Times and Cult,* edited by Nigel Ramsay, Margaret Sparks, and Tim Tatton-Brown, 247–59. Woodbridge: Boydell, 1992.

La Plante, Michael F. "A Deperditum for Mainz in 962?" *Archiv für Diplomatik* 25 (1979): 21–36.

Larrainzar, Carlos. "La formazione del Decreto di Graziano per tappe." In *Proceedings of the Eleventh International Congress of Medieval Canon Law*, edited by Manlio Bellomo and Orazio Condorelli, 103–18. Monumenta Iuris Canonici, ser. C, Subsidia 12. Vatican City: Biblioteca Apostolica Vaticana, 2006.

Larson, Atria A. "Gratian's *De penitentia* in Twelfth-Century Manuscripts." *Bulletin of Medieval Canon Law* 31 (2014): 57–110.

Laudage, Johannes. *Priesterbild und Reformpapsttum im 11. Jahrhundert.* Beihefte zum Archiv für Kulturgeschichte 22. Cologne: Böhlau, 1984.

Leclercq, Jean. "Simoniaca Haeresis." *Studi Gregoriani* 1 (1947): 523–30.

Legg, J. Wickham. "The Blessing of the Episcopal Ornament called the Pall." *Record Series (Yorkshire Archaeological Society)* 15 (1899): 121–41.

Lehr, Waldemar. *Piligrim, Bischof von Passau, und die Lorcher Fälschungen.* Berlin: Schade, 1909.

Lesne, Emile. *La hiérarchie épiscopale: provinces, métropolitains, primats en Gaule et Germanie depuis la réforme de saint Boniface jusqu'à la mort d'Hincmar, 742–882.* Mémoires et travaux des facultés catholiques de Lille 1. Lille: Facultés Catholiques, 1905.

Levison, Wilhelm. *England and the Continent in the Eighth Century.* Oxford: Clarendon, 1946.

Lewis, Charlton T., and Charles Short. *A Latin Dictionary.* Oxford: Clarendon, 1879.

Leyser, K. J. "Concepts of Europe in the Early and High Middle Ages." *Past and Present* 137 (1992): 25–47.

Lohrmann, Dietrich. "Formen der Enumeratio bonorum in Bischofs-, Papst- und Herrscherurkunden (9.–12. Jahrhundert)." *Archiv für Diplomatik* 26 (1980): 281–311.

———. *Das Register Papst Johannes' VIII. (872–882): neue Studien zur Abschrift Reg. Vat. 1, zum verlorenen Originalregister und zum Diktat der Briefe.* Bibliothek des deutschen historischen Instituts in Rom 30. Tübingen: Niemeyer, 1968.

Loud, G. A. *The Latin Church in Norman Italy.* Cambridge: Cambridge University Press, 2007.

Maassen, Friedrich. "Eine römische Synode aus der Zeit von 871 bis 878." *Sitzungsberichte der philosophisch-historischen Classe der kaiserlichen Akademie der Wissenschaften* 91 (1878): 773–92.

Maccarrone, Michele. "La teologia del primato romano del secolo XI." In *Le istituzioni ecclesiastiche della 'societas christiana' dei secoli XI–XII: papato, cardinalato ed episcopato*, 21–122. Miscellanea del Centro di studi medioevali 7. Milan: Vita e Pensiero, 1974.

Madoz, Joseph. *Le symbole du XIe concile de Tolède: ses sources, sa date, sa valeur.* Spicilegium Sacrum Lovaniense, études et documents 19. Louvain: Spicilegium Sacrum Lovaniense, 1938.

Mann, Gareth. "The Development of Wulfstan's Alcuin Manuscript." In *Wulfstan, Archbishop of York: The Proceedings of the Second Alcuin Conference*, edited by Matthew Townend, 235–78. Studies in the Early Middle Ages 10. Turnhout: Brepols, 2004.

Mansilla, Demetrio. "Formación de la provincia bracarense después de la invasión árabe." *Hispania Sacra* 14 (1961): 5–25.

Marckhgott, Gerhart. "Bischof Pilgrim (971–991): Realpolitik und 'Lorcher Legende.'" In *Kirche in Oberösterreich: 200 Jahre Bistum Linz*, edited by Helga Litschel, 51–62. Linz: Land Oberösterreich, 1985.

Martí Bonet, José María. *El palio: insignia pastoral de los papas y arzobispos*. Madrid: Biblioteca de Autores Cristianos, 2008.

———. *Roma y las iglesias particulares en la concesión del palio a los obispos y arzobispos de occidente, año 513–1143*. Colectánea San Paciano 21. Barcelona: Herder, 1976.

Martínez Llorente, Félix J. "El palio: consideraciones histórico-canónicas en torno a un emblema pontificio." *Anales Melitenses* 1 (2004): 379–440.

Matthews, Stephen. *The Road to Rome: Travel and Travellers between England and Italy in the Anglo-Saxon Centuries*. BAR International Series 1680. Oxford: Archaeopress, 2007.

Mauss, Marcel. *The Gift: The Form and Reason for Exchange in Archaic Societies*. Translated by W. D. Halls. London: Routledge, 1990.

May, Georg. "Die Organisation der Erzdiözese Mainz unter Erzbischof Willigis." In *Willigis und sein Dom: Festschrift zur Jahrtausendfeier des Mainzer Domes, 975–1975*, edited by Anton Ph. Brück, 31–92. Mainz: Gesellschaft für Mittelrheinische Kirchengeschichte, 1975.

Mayr-Harting, Henry. *Church and Cosmos in Early Ottonian Germany: The View from Cologne*. Oxford: Oxford University Press, 2007.

McCrank, Lawrence J. "Restoration and Reconquest in Medieval Catalonia: The Church and Principality of Tarragona, 971–1177." PhD diss., University of Virginia, 1974.

McCulloh, John M. "The Cult of Relics in the Letters and 'Dialogues' of Pope Gregory the Great: A Lexicographical Study." *Traditio* 32 (1976): 145–84.

McKitterick, Rosamond. *The Frankish Church and the Carolingian Reforms, 789–895*. London: Royal Historical Society, 1977.

Meijer, Johan. *A Successful Council of Union: A Theological Analysis of the Photian Synod of 879–880*. Analecta Vlatadon 23. Thessaloniki: Patriarchal Institute for Patristic Studies, 1975.

Merlin, Karine. "La concession du pallium dans la correspondance de Grégoire le Grand." In *Correspondances: documents pour l'histoire de l'antiquité tardive*, edited by Roland Delmaire, Janine Desmulliez, and Pierre-Louis Gatier, 349–57. Collection de la maison de l'orient et de la Méditerranée 40, série littéraire et philosophique 13. Lyon: Maison de l'Orient et de la Méditerranée, 2009.

Miller, Maureen C. *Clothing the Clergy: Virtue and Power in Medieval Europe, c. 800–1200*. Ithaca, N.Y.: Cornell University Press, 2014.

———. "The Crisis in the Investiture Crisis Narrative." *History Compass* 7 (2009): 1570–80.

Mordek, Hubert. "Proprie auctoritates apostolice sedis: ein zweiter Dictatus Papae Gregors VII.?" *Deutsches Archiv für Erforschung des Mittelalters* 28 (1972): 105–32.

Mordek, Hubert, and Gerhard Schmitz. "Papst Johannes VIII. und das Konzil von Troyes (878)." In *Geschichtsschreibung und geistiges Leben im Mittelalter*, edited by Karl Hauck and Hubert Mordek, 179–225. Cologne: Böhlau, 1978.

Morin, G. "Le pallium." *Le messager des fidèles (Revue bénédictine)* 6 (1889): 258–66.

Mühlbacher, E. "Die Datirung der Urkunden Lothar I." *Sitzungsberichte der philosophisch-historischen Klasse der kaiserlichen Akademie der Wissenschaften Wien* 85 (1877): 463–544.

Müller, Jörg. *Untersuchungen zur Collectio Duodecim Partium.* Abhandlungen zur rechtswissenschaftlichen Grundlagenforschung 73. Ebelsbach: Gremer, 1989.

Müller, Richard. *Erzbischof Aribo von Mainz, 1021–1031.* Historische Studien 3. Leipzig: Veit, 1881.

Niermeyer, J. F., completed by C. Van de Kieft. *Mediae Latinitatis Lexicon Minus.* Leiden: Brill, 2001.

Nightingale, John. *Monasteries and Patrons in the Gorze Reform: Lotharingia c. 850–1000.* Oxford: Clarendon, 2001.

Noonan, John T. "Gratian Slept Here: The Changing Identity of the Father of the Systematic Study of Canon Law." *Traditio* 35 (1979): 145–72.

Ortenberg, Veronica. "The Anglo-Saxon Church and the Papacy." In *The English Church and the Papacy in the Middle Ages*, edited by C. H. Lawrence, 29–62. Rev. ed. Phoenix Mill: Sutton, 1999.

Oswald, Josef. "St. Altmanns Leben und Wirken nach der Göttweiger Überlieferung: 'Vita Altmanni.'" In *Der heilige Altmann, Bischof von Passau: sein Leben und sein Werk,* 142–66. Göttweig: Abtei Göttweig, 1965.

Oxtoby, Willard G. "Holy, Idea of the." In *The Encyclopedia of Religion,* edited by Mircea Eliade, 6:431–38. New York: Macmillan, 1987.

Pater, Januarius. *Die bischöfliche visitatio liminum ss. apostolorum: eine historisch-kanonistische Studie.* Görres-Gesellschaft zur Pflege der Wissenschaft im katholischen Deutschland Veröffentlichungen der Sektion für Rechts- und Sozialwissenschaft 19. Paderborn: Schöningh, 1914.

Patzold, Steffen. *Episcopus: Wissen über Bischöfe im Frankenreich des späten 8. bis frühen 10. Jahrhunderts.* Mittelalter-Forschungen 25. Ostfildern: Thorbecke, 2008.

Pellens, Karl. *Die Texte des normannischen Anonymus.* Veröffentlichungen des Instituts für europäische Geschichte Mainz 42. Wiesbaden: Steiner, 1966.

Pennington, Kenneth. "The Biography of Gratian, the Father of Canon Law." *Villanova Law Review* 59 (2014): 679–706.

———. "Decretal Collections 1190–1234." In *The History of Medieval Canon Law in the Classical Period, 1140–1234: From Gratian to the Decretals of Pope Gregory IX,* edited by Wilfried Hartmann and Kenneth Pennington, 293–317. Washington, D.C.: The Catholic University of America Press, 2008.

———. "The Decretalists 1190–1234." In *The History of Medieval Canon Law in the Classical Period, 1140–1234: From Gratian to the Decretals of Pope Gregory IX,* edited by Wilfried Hartmann and Kenneth Pennington, 211–45. Washington, D.C.: The Catholic University of America Press, 2008.

———. *Pope and Bishops: The Papal Monarchy in the Twelfth and Thirteenth Centuries.* Philadelphia: University of Pennsylvania Press, 1984.

Pennington, Kenneth, and Wolfgang P. Müller. "The Decretists: The Italian School." In *The History of Medieval Canon Law in the Classical Period, 1140–1234: From Gratian to the Decretals of Pope Gregory IX*, edited by Wilfried Hartmann and Kenneth Pennington, 121–73. Washington, D.C.: The Catholic University of America Press, 2008.

Perels, Ernst. *Papst Nikolaus I. und Anastasius Bibliothecarius: ein Beitrag zur Geschichte des Papsttums im neunten Jahrhundert.* Berlin: Weidmann, 1920.

Pokorny, Rudolf. "Ein unerkanntes Brieffragment Argrims von Lyon-Langres aus den Jahren 894/95 und zwei umstrittene Bischofsweihen in der Kirchenprovinz Lyon, mit Textedition und Exkurs." *Francia* 13 (1985): 602–22.

Poole, Reginald L. *Lectures on the History of the Papal Chancery down to the Time of Innocent III.* Cambridge: Cambridge University Press, 1915; reprinted in Clark, N.J.: Lawbook Exchange, 2005.

Potthast, Augustus. *Regesta Pontificum Romanorum inde ab Anno post Christum Natum MCXCVIII ad Annum MCCCIV.* 2 vols. Berlin: Decker, 1874–75.

Quentin, Henri. *Les martyrologes historiques du moyen âge: étude sur la formation du martyrologe romain.* Paris: Lecoffre/Gabalda, 1908; reprinted in Aalen: Scientia, 1969.

Quiter, Eduard. *Untersuchungen zur Entstehungsgeschichte der Kirchenprovinz Magdeburg: ein Beitrag zur Geschichte des kirchlichen Verfassungsrechtes im zehnten Jahrhundert.* Paderborn: Bonifacius, 1969.

Rabikauskas, Paul. *Diplomatica Pontificia (Praelectionum Lineamenta).* 6th rev. ed. Rome: Pontificia Università Gregoriana, 1998.

Ramseyer, Valerie. *The Transformation of a Religious Landscape: Medieval Southern Italy, 850–1150.* Ithaca, N.Y.: Cornell University Press, 2006.

Rasmussen, Niels Krogh, with the assistance of Marcel Haverals. *Les pontificaux du haut moyen âge: genèse du livre de l'évêque.* Spicilegium Sacrum Lovaniense, études et documents 49. Louvain: Spicilegium Sacrum Lovaniense, 1998.

Rathsack, Mogens. *Die fuldaer Fälschungen: eine rechtshistorische Analyse der päpstlichen Privilegien des Klosters Fulda von 751 bis ca. 1158.* Translated by Preben Kortnum Mogensen, with the assistance of Harald Zimmermann. 2 vols. Päpste und Papsttum 24. Stuttgart: Hiersemann, 1989.

Rennie, Kriston R. *The Foundations of Medieval Papal Legation.* Basingstoke: Palgrave Macmillan, 2013.

Reno, Edward A. "Gregory IX and the *Liber Extra*." In *Pope Gregory IX (1227–41)*, edited by Christoph Egger and Damian J. Smith. New York, Routledge, forthcoming.

Reuter, Timothy. "A Europe of Bishops: The Age of Wulfstan of York and Burchard of Worms." In *Patterns of Episcopal Power: Bishops in Tenth and Eleventh Century Western Europe / Strukturen bischöflicher Herrschaftsgewalt im westlichen Europa des 10. und 11. Jahrhunderts*, edited by Ludger Körntgen and Dominik Waßenhoven, 17–38. Prinz-Albert-Forschungen 6. Berlin: de Gruyter, 2011.

———. "Gifts and Simony." In *Medieval Transformations: Texts, Power, and Gifts in Context*, edited by Esther Cohen and Mayke B. de Jong, 157–68. Cultures,

Beliefs and Traditions: Medieval and Early Modern Peoples 11. Leiden: Brill, 2001.

———. "The 'Imperial Church System' of the Ottonian and Salian Rulers: A Reconsideration." *Journal of Ecclesiastical History* 33 (1982): 347–74.

———. "*Pastorale pedum ante pedes apostolici posuit*: Dis- and Reinvestiture in the Era of the Investiture Contest." In *Belief and Culture in the Middle Ages*, edited by Richard Gameson and Henrietta Leyser, 197–210. Oxford: Oxford University Press, 2001.

Reynolds, Roger E. "Liturgical Scholarship at the Time of the Investiture Controversy: Past Research and Future Opportunities." *The Harvard Theological Review* 71 (1978): 109–24.

———. "The Organisation, Law and Liturgy of the Western Church, 700–900." In *The New Cambridge Medieval History*, edited by Rosamond McKitterick, 2:587–621. Cambridge: Cambridge University Press, 1995.

———. "Rites of Separation and Reconciliation in the Early Middle Ages." In *Segni e riti nella chiesa altomedievale occidentale*, 1:405–37. Settimane di studio del Centro italiano di studi sull'alto medioevo 33. Spoleto: Sede del Centro, 1987.

Riché, Pierre. *The Carolingians: A Family Who Forged Europe*. Translated by Michael Idomir Allen. Philadelphia: University of Pennsylvania Press, 1993.

Riches, Theo. "The Changing Political Horizons of *gesta episcoporum* from the Ninth to Eleventh Centuries." In *Patterns of Episcopal Power: Bishops in Tenth and Eleventh Century Western Europe / Strukturen bischöflicher Herrschaftsgewalt im westlichen Europa des 10. und 11. Jahrhunderts*, edited by Ludger Körntgen and Dominik Waßenhoven, 51–62. Prinz-Albert-Forschungen 6. Berlin: de Gruyter, 2011.

Robinson, I. S. *Authority and Resistance in the Investiture Contest: The Polemical Literature of the Late Eleventh Century*. Manchester: Manchester University Press, 1978.

———. *The Papacy, 1073–1198: Continuity and Innovation*. Cambridge: Cambridge University Press, 1990.

Rohault de Fleury, Ch., continued by his son. *La messe: études archéologiques sur ses monuments*. 8 vols. Paris: Morel, 1883–89.

Rolker, Christof. *Canon Law and the Letters of Ivo of Chartres*. Cambridge: Cambridge University Press, 2010.

———. "History and Canon Law in the *Collectio Britannica*: A New Date for London, BL Add. 8873." In *Bishops, Texts and the Use of Canon Law around 1100: Essays in Honour of Martin Brett*, edited by Bruce C. Brasington and Kathleen G. Cushing, 141–52. Aldershot: Ashgate, 2008.

Rosenthal, Jane. "The Pontifical of St. Dunstan." In *St. Dunstan: His Life, Times and Cult*, edited by Nigel Ramsay, Margaret Sparks, and Tim Tatton-Brown, 143–63. Woodbridge: Boydell, 1992.

Rosenwein, Barbara H. *Negotiating Space: Power, Restraint, and Privileges of Immunity in Early Medieval Europe*. Ithaca, N.Y.: Cornell University Press, 1999.

Salmon, Pierre. *Étude sur les insignes du pontife dans le rit romain: histoire et liturgie*. Rome: Officium Libri Catholici, 1955.

Santifaller, Leo. *Liber Diurnus: Studien und Forschungen.* Edited by Harald Zimmermann. Päpste und Papsttum 10. Stuttgart: Hiersemann, 1976.

———. "Saggio di un elenco dei funzionari, impiegati e scrittori della Cancelleria Pontificia dall'inizio all'anno 1099." *Bullettino dell'Istituto storico italiano per il medio avo e archivio muratoriano* 56 (1940): 1–473.

Schieffer, Rudolf. *Die Entstehung des päpstlichen Investiturverbots für den deutschen König.* Monumenta Germaniae Historica Schriften 28. Stuttgart: Hiersemann, 1981.

———. "Die Romreise deutscher Bischöfe im Frühjahr 1070: Anno von Köln, Siegfried von Mainz und Hermann von Bamberg bei Alexander II." *Rheinische Vierteljahrsblätter* 35 (1971): 152–74.

Schieffer, Theodor. *Winfrid-Bonifatius und die christliche Grundlegung Europas.* Freiburg: Herder, 1954.

Schilling, Beate. *Guido von Vienne: Papst Calixt II.* Monumenta Germaniae Historica Schriften 45. Hannover: Hahn, 1998.

———. "Wilchar von Vienne und das Pallium." In *Inquirens Subtilia Diversa*, edited by Horst Kranz and Ludwig Falkenstein, 23–36. Aachen: Shaker, 2002.

Schimmelpfennig, Bernhard. "Vestments, Pope's Liturgical: Pallium." In *The Papacy: An Encyclopedia*, edited by Philippe Levillain, 3:1607–8. New York: Routledge, 2002.

Schmeidler, Bernhard. *Hamburg-Bremen und Nordost-Europa vom 9. bis 11. Jahrhundert: kritische Untersuchungen zur hamburgischen Kirchengeschichte des Adam von Bremen, zu Hamburger Urkunden und zur nordischen und wendischen Geschichte.* Leipzig: Dieterich, 1918.

Schmid, Paul. *Der Begriff der kanonischen Wahl in den Anfängen des Investiturstreits.* Stuttgart: Kohlhammer, 1926.

Schmidinger, Heinrich. "Die Palliumverleihung Benedikts VIII. für Ragusa." *Mitteilungen des Instituts für österreichische Geschichtsforschung* 58 (1950): 31–49.

———. *Patriarch und Landesherr: die weltliche Herrschaft der Patriarchen von Aquileja bis zum Ende der Staufer.* Publikationen des österreichischen Kulturinstituts in Rom, Abhandlungen 1. Graz: Böhlau, 1954.

Schneider, Fedor. "Ein interpolierter Brief Papst Nikolaus' I. und der Primat von Bourges." *Neues Archiv der Gesellschaft für ältere deutsche Geschichtskunde* 32 (1907): 476–92.

Schneider, Gerhard. *Erzbischof Fulco von Reims (883–900) und das Frankenreich.* Münchener Beiträge zur Mediävistik und Renaissance-Forschung 14. Munich: Arbeo-Gesellschaft, 1973.

Scholz, Sebastian. *Transmigration und Translation: Studien zum Bistumswechsel der Bischöfe von der Spätantike bis zum hohen Mittelalter.* Kölner historische Abhandlungen 37. Cologne: Böhlau, 1992.

Schramm, Percy Ernst. "Von der Trabea triumphalis des römischen Kaisers über das byzantinische Lorum zur Stola der abendländischen Herrscher: ein Beispiel für den Wandel von Form und Bedeutung im Laufe der Jahrhunderte und bei der Übertragung von einem Land in das andere." In

Herrschaftszeichen und Staatssymbolik: Beiträge zu ihrer Geschichte vom dritten bis zum sechszehnten Jahrhundert, edited by Percy Ernst Schramm, 1:25–50. Monumenta Germaniae Historica Schriften 13. Stuttgart: Hiersemann, 1954.

Schrör, Matthias. *Metropolitangewalt und papstgeschichtliche Wende.* Historische Studien 494. Husum: Matthiesen, 2009.

Schrörs, Heinrich. *Hinkmar, Erzbischof von Reims: sein Leben und seine Schriften.* Freiburg: Herder, 1884.

Schulte, J. Friedrich. "Die Rechtshandschriften der Stiftsbibliotheken von Göttweig Ord. S. Bened., Heiligenkreuz Ord. Cisterc., Klosterneuburg Can. Regul. Lateran., Melk Ord. S. Ben., Schotten in Wien Ord. S. Ben." *Sitzungsberichte der kaiserlichen Akademie der Wissenschaften, philosophisch-historische Classe* 57 (1867): 559–616.

Schüssler, Heinz Joachim. "Die fränkische Reichsteilung von Vieux-Poitiers (742) und die Reform der Kirche in den Teilreichen Karlmanns und Pippins: zu den Grenzen der Wirksamkeit des Bonifatius." *Francia* 13 (1985): 47–112.

Seckel, Emil. "Studien zu Benedictus Levita (Studie VII, Teil I)." *Neues Archiv der Gesellschaft für ältere deutsche Geschichtskunde* 34 (1909): 319–81.

Semmler, Josef. "Bonifatius, die Karolinger und 'die Franken.'" In *Mönchtum, Kirche, Herrschaft, 750–1000,* edited by Dieter R. Bauer, Rudolf Hiestand, Brigitte Kasten, and Sönke Lorenz, 3–49. Sigmaringen: Thorbecke, 1998.

Smith, Julia M. H. "The 'Archbishopric' of Dol and the Ecclesiastical Politics of Ninth-Century Brittany." In *Religion and National Identity,* edited by Stuart Mews, 59–70. Studies in Church History 18. Oxford: Blackwell, 1982.

Somerville, Robert. "Mercy and Justice in the Early Months of Urban II's Pontificate." In Somerville, *Papacy, Councils and Canon Law in the 11th–12th Centuries,* part 4. Aldershot: Ashgate Variorum, 1990.

Somerville, Robert, and Bruce C. Brasington. *Prefaces to Canon Law Books in Latin Christianity: Selected Translations, 500–1245.* New Haven, Conn.: Yale University Press, 1998.

Sommar, Mary E. "Hincmar of Reims and the Canon Law of Episcopal Translation." *The Catholic Historical Review* 88 (2002): 429–45.

Southern, R. W. "The Canterbury Forgeries." *The English Historical Review* 73 (1958): 193–226.

Speck, Paul. "Artabasdos, Bonifatius und die drei Pallia." *Zeitschrift für Kirchengeschichte* 96 (1985): 179–95.

Steck, Wolfgang. *Der Liturgiker Amalarius: eine quellenkritische Untersuchung zu Leben und Werk eines Theologen der Karolingerzeit.* Münchener theologische Studien, historische Abteilung 35. St. Ottilien: EOS, 2000.

Story, Joanna. "Bede, Willibrord and the Letters of Pope Honorius I on the Genesis of the Archbishopric of York." *English Historical Review* 127 (2012): 783–818.

Szabó-Bechstein, Brigitte. *Libertas ecclesiae: ein Schlüsselbegriff des Investiturstreits und seine Vorgeschichte, 4.–11. Jahrhundert.* Studi gregoriani 12. Rome: Ateneo Salesiano, 1985.

Taft, Robert F. "The Case of the Missing Vestment: The Byzantine Omophorion Great and Small." *Bollettino della Badia Greca di Grottaferrata*, ser. 3, 1 (2004): 273–301.
Thacker, Alan. "Gallic or Greek? Archbishops in England from Theodore to Ecgberht." In *Frankland: The Franks and the World of Early Medieval Europe*, edited by Paul Fouracre and David Ganz, 44–69. Manchester: Manchester University Press, 2008.
Thümmel, Hans Georg. *Die Memorien für Petrus und Paulus in Rom: die archäologischen Denkmäler und die literarische Tradition*. Arbeiten zur Kirchengeschichte 76. Berlin: de Gruyter, 1999.
Thurston, Herbert. "The Pallium." In *Historical Papers*, edited by John Morris, 1:85–124. London: Catholic Truth Society, 1892.
Tinti, Francesca. "The Archiepiscopal Pallium in Late Anglo-Saxon England." In *England and Rome in the Early Middle Ages: Pilgrimage, Art, and Politics*, edited by Francesca Tinti, 307–42. Studies in the Early Middle Ages 40. Turnhout: Brepols, 2014.
Toynbee, Jocelyn, and John Ward Perkins. *The Shrine of St. Peter and the Vatican Excavations*. New York: Pantheon, 1957.
Ullrich, Günther. "Die Kölner Bischofswahl von 870 und die Praxis der Bistumsbesetzung im Karolingerreich." *Rheinische Vierteljahrsblätter* 11 (1941): 254–62.
Unger, Veronika. *Papstregesten, 872–882*. J. F. Böhmer, Regesta Imperii 1.4.3. Cologne: Böhlau, 2013.
Van Engen, John H. *Rupert of Deutz*. Berkeley: University of California Press, 1983.
Vehse, Otto. "Bistumsexemtionen bis zum Ausgang des 12. Jahrhunderts." *Zeitschrift der Savigny-Stiftung für Rechtsgeschichte, kanonistische Abteilung* 26 (1937): 86–160.
Vlasto, A. P. *The Entry of the Slavs into Christendom: An Introduction to the Medieval History of the Slavs*. Cambridge: Cambridge University Press, 1970.
Vogel, Cyrille. *Medieval Liturgy: An Introduction to the Sources*. Revised and translated by William G. Storey and Niels Krogh Rasmussen, with the assistance of John K. Brooks-Leonard. Washington, D.C.: Pastoral, 1986.
Vregille, Bernard de. "Besançon et Lausanne: métropolitains et suffragants des origines au XIe siècle." *Zeitschrift für schweizerische Kirchengeschichte* 82 (1988): 77–88.
———. *Hugues de Salins: archevêque de Besançon, 1031–1066*. Besançon: Cêtre, 1981.
Wallace-Hadrill, J. M. *The Frankish Church*. Oxford: Clarendon, 1983.
Weigand, Rudolf. "The Development of the *Glossa ordinaria* to Gratian's *Decretum*." In *The History of Medieval Canon Law in the Classical Period, 1140–1234: From Gratian to the Decretals of Pope Gregory IX*, edited by Wilfried Hartmann and Kenneth Pennington, 55–97. Washington, D.C.: The Catholic University of America Press, 2008.
———. "The Transmontane Decretists." In *The History of Medieval Canon Law in the Classical Period, 1140–1234: From Gratian to the Decretals of Pope Gregory IX*,

edited by Wilfried Hartmann and Kenneth Pennington, 174–210. Washington, D.C.: The Catholic University of America Press, 2008.
Weinfurter, Stefan. *Heinrich II. (1002–1024): Herrscher am Ende der Zeiten.* Regensburg: Pustet, 1999.
Weinrich, Lorenz. "Laurentius-Verehrung in ottonischer Zeit." *Jahrbuch für die Geschichte Mittel- und Ostdeutschlands* 21 (1972): 45–66.
Werminghoff, Albert. "Ein neuer Text des Apologeticum Ebonis." *Neues Archiv der Gesellschaft für ältere deutsche Geschichtskunde* 25 (1900): 361–78.
White, Stephen D. "The Politics of Exchange: Gifts, Fiefs, and Feudalism." In *Medieval Transformations: Texts, Power, and Gifts in Context,* edited by Esther Cohen and Mayke B. de Jong, 169–88. Cultures, Beliefs and Traditions: Medieval and Early Modern Peoples 11. Leiden: Brill, 2001.
Wilhelmi, Hans-Albert. *Die "Vita Gregorii Magni" des Johannes Diaconus: Schwerpunkte ihrer Wirkungsgeschichte.* Deutsche Hochschuledition 76. Neuried: Ars Una, 1998.
Williams, George Huntston. *The Norman Anonymous of 1100 A.D.: Toward the Identification and Evaluation of the so-called Anonymous of York.* Harvard Theological Studies 18. Cambridge, Mass.: Harvard University Press, 1951.
Wilpert, Joseph. "Das 'Pallium discolor' der 'Officiales' im Kleidergesetz vom Jahre 382." *Bessarione,* ser. 2, 9 (1905): 215–18.
Winroth, Anders. *The Making of Gratian's Decretum.* Cambridge: Cambridge University Press, 2000.
——— . "Where Gratian Slept: The Life and Death of the Father of Canon Law." *Zeitschrift der Savigny-Stiftung für Rechtsgeschichte, kanonistische Abteilung* 99 (2013): 105–28.
Wood, Ian. *The Missionary Life: Saints and the Evangelisation of Europe, 400–1050.* Harlow: Longman, 2001.
Zimmermann, Harald. *Papstregesten, 911–1024.* 2nd ed. J. F. Böhmer, Regesta Imperii 2.5. Cologne: Böhlau, 1998.
——— . "Der Streit um das Lütticher Bistum vom Jahre 920/921: Geschichte, Quellen und kirchenrechtshistorische Bedeutung." *Mitteilungen des Instituts für österreichische Geschichtsforschung* 65 (1957): 15–52.
Zotz, Thomas. "*Pallium et alia quaedam archiepiscopatus insignia:* zum Beziehungsgefüge und zu Rangfragen der Reichskirchen im Spiegel der päpstlichen Privilegierung des 10. und 11. Jahrhunderts." In *Festschrift für Berent Schwineköper,* edited by Helmut Maurer and Hans Patze, 155–75. Sigmaringen: Thorbecke, 1982.

Index of Papal Letters

Note: Arranged chronologically according to the entries in JK, JE, JL, and Potthast

JK †4: 110
JK †90: 115
JK †250: 182
JK 255: 141
JK 369: 141, 176
JK 450: 111
JK 495: 124
JK 583: 62–63
JK 764: 1, 9
JK *766: 9
JK †767: 196, 206, 255, 266, 268
JK 829: 159
JK 913: 9
JK 918: 9
JK 944: 9
JK 945: 9
JK 979: 159
JK 1000: 9, 333, 351
JK 1041: 9, 11
JK †1064: 326
JK — (Felix IV to Roman clergy and people, 530): 9

JE 1074: 12
JE 1092: 265
JE 1096: 12
JE 1164: 10, 329, 335, 405
JE 1165: 12
JE 1173: 11
JE 1174: 11

JE 1175: 11, 57, 350, 402
JE 1259: 11, 58, 63, 134, 180, 296, 363, 404, 406
JE 1272: 10, 180
JE 1302: 159
JE 1326: 10, 59, 63, 91, 129, 134, 200, 262
JE 1330: 11, 134, 255
JE 1374: 10, 47, 81, 106, 133, 329, 404
JE 1376: 12
JE 1377: 10, 63, 134
JE 1378: 10, 170, 288, 292, 329, 335, 406
JE 1379: 12
JE 1387: 10, 329, 335, 405
JE 1388: 10, 454
JE 1397: 10
JE 1411: 11, 91, 134, 186
JE 1444: 380
JE 1491: 11, 28, 35, 180, 199, 329, 404
JE 1694: 11, 134
JE 1703: 11, 59, 64, 76, 91, 122, 231, 351
JE 1743: 12
JE 1748: 11, 57, 99, 296, 404
JE 1749: 11, 37, 49, 57
JE 1751: 11, 35, 57, 59, 99, 114, 180, 199, 210, 405
JE 1756: 10, 104, 128, 157, 166, 329

JE 1757: 12, 91, 104, 158
JE 1761: 10, 167, 180, 382
JE 1824: 49, 58
JE 1829: 11, 29, 105, 122, 147, 318, 329, 442
JE 1843: 12, 104, 144, 405
JE 1905: 10, 63, 171, 180, 186
JE 2001: 12, 265
JE 2002: 12
JE 2006: 13, 245
JE 2010: 12
JE 2016: 12
JE 2019: 13
JE 2020: 13, 245, 248
JE 2030: 182
JE *2123: 12
JE 2133: 13
JE †2146: 23, 77, 159
JE 2166: 13, 59
JE 2167: 59
JE *2231: 13
JE 2239: 13, 132
JE 2240: 13
JE 2243: 13
JE *2269: 39
JE 2270: 30, 39, 122, 126, 171, 174
JE 2271: 30, 75, 92, 122, 166, 170, 288, 290–91
JE 2286: 13, 85
JE 2291: 31, 170, 288
JE *2314: 109, 154
JE *2410: 92
JE 2411: 33, 40, 48, 51, 85, 92, 139, 156
JE †2412: 112
JE *2456: 120
JE 2475: 33–34, 37, 48, 68, 92, 103
JE 2494: 96, 141, 176
JE 2495: 142, 155
JE 2496: 33, 92–94, 145, 155, 174
JE 2498: 40, 68, 128, 169
JE 2510: 141, 153
JE 2512: 41, 70, 120, 169
JE 2549: 35, 119, 124, 170, 235
JE †2558: 35, 119–20
JE †2566: 196, 240

JE 2574: 94, 121, 169
JE 2580: 41, 59, 67, 70, 120, 131, 134, 225, 270, 297
JE 2586: 86
JE *2596: 61
JE 2603: 35, 56, 98, 218, 351–52
JE 2607: 86, 99, 107, 135, 153, 224
JE 2608: 106–7, 132, 135–37, 159, 224
JE 2616: 41, 59
JE 2618: 61
JE 2619: 61
JE 2647: 79, 91, 122, 125, 296, 426
JE 2664: 88
JE 2672: 41, 60, 131
JE 2681: 41, 60
JE 2693: 27, 36, 42, 57
JE 2720: 88, 146
JE 2753: 54–55
JE 2758: 185
JE 2759: 27, 42, 62, 67, 94, 121, 169, 341
JE 2765: 125, 133, 256, 295, 406
JE 2789: 27, 37, 43, 56, 65–66, 99, 125, 218
JE 2798: 41, 60, 120
JE 2806: 23, 27, 31, 36–37, 112, 140
JE 2807: 99, 112
JE 2809: 27, 48, 52–53, 156
JE 2810: 23, 27, 49, 53, 100, 127
JE 2812: 148, 370
JE 2822: 61
JE 2823: 27, 62–63, 107, 117, 122, 130, 136, 167, 176, 187, 437
JE 2876: 111
JE 2878: 37, 66, 168
JE 2894: 53, 66, 167
JE 2902: 23, 69, 100, 115–16, 121, 125–26, 153, 161, 172
JE 2903: 67
JE 2904: 62, 89, 115, 120–21, 126, 128, 130, 133, 161
JE *2922: 54
JE 2930: 54
JE 2932: 54, 57
JE †2950: 315

Index of Papal Letters 519

JE 2982: 38, 43, 55, 57, 71, 101, 351–52
JE 2986: 23, 38, 44, 50, 54, 57, 71, 148, 153, 352, 372, 404, 431, 456
JE 2988: 54, 71, 78, 101, 126, 159, 172, 174
JE 3063: 49, 69, 102, 155
JE 3111: 306
JE 3114: 100, 172
JE 3115: 81, 87, 102, 173
JE 3148: 47, 49, 70, 81, 84, 87, 106, 122, 133, 149, 373
JE 3149: 150, 373
JE 3183: 60, 70, 111, 121, 129, 160, 171, 312
JE 3262: 56, 70, 81, 122, 153, 158
JE 3271: 82, 101, 130, 153
JE 3273: 82
JE 3276: 82

JL 3416: 242
JL 3448: 200, 231, 242, 333, 351
JL 3457: 199, 206, 255
JL 3458: 174, 185
JL †3462: 300
JL *3508: 371
JL 3527: 200, 230, 232, 371
JL †3549: 206, 255
JL 3550: 199–200, 206, 255
JL 3554: 208, 231
JL *3566: 201, 232
JL 3568: 186
JL 3579: 231
JL †3602: 196, 199, 202, 206, 256–57, 259, 262
JL 3612: 202, 206, 255
JL 3641: 210
JL †3644: 196, 207, 210
JL *3658: 224
JL 3668: 198
JL 3682: 133, 199–200, 206, 225, 256
JL 3687: 202, 205–6, 244, 254, 263, 268
JL 3689: 187, 198, 225, 257, 259, 263

JL 3691: 198, 202, 206, 225, 254, 260, 263
JL 3701: 202, 205–6, 255
JL 3717: 187, 200
JL 3728: 202–3, 207–8, 211, 222, 225, 240, 257, 261
JL 3737: 202–3, 207, 259–60
JL 3738: 207–8, 223, 241, 257–58
JL 3747: 202, 207, 240, 254, 263
JL 3748: 208
JL 3749: 208
JL 3767: 197, 216, 304
JL †3771: 196, 210, 318
JL 3784: 202–4, 206–7, 258–59, 261, 269
JL 3808: 203, 230, 252
JL 3822: 202, 207, 258, 262
JL †3823: 204, 253
JL 3833: 241
JL 3835: 205, 207, 220, 255, 259, 261, 263
JL 3851: 202, 207, 257–58, 262–63
JL 3852: 207, 242
JL 3883: 207, 211, 255, 268
JL 3884: 199, 207, 209
JL 3908: 195, 211, 217
JL 3954: 233
JL 3957: 195, 202, 207, 211, 259
JL 3970: 199–200, 207, 211, 258, 262–63, 268
JL 3988: 242
JL 3989: 204, 207, 219, 251, 253, 259, 261, 269
JL 3990: 207, 251, 256–57, 259, 269
JL *3994: 233
JL 4005: 199, 207, 211, 262
JL 4010: 207, 251, 259, 262, 266–67, 386
JL 4011: 242
JL 4027: 242, 255
JL 4032: 202, 205, 209, 242, 255
JL 4042: 200, 202, 208, 242, 254
JL 4058: 207, 251
JL 4068: 208, 268
JL 4074: 196, 208, 251, 254, 257, 259, 262

JL 4085: 196, 206–7, 209, 253, 257
JL 4089: 193, 201–2, 207, 212, 228, 239, 257–58, 262, 264
JL 4095: 215
JL 4098: 196, 202, 207, 227, 251, 254, 258, 262, 280
JL †4119a: 347
JL 4143: 281, 285, 385
JL 4146: 261, 353
JL 4151: 279, 294, 297, 378, 386
JL 4188: 271, 364, 366, 379, 384
JL 4225: 286, 314
JL 4265: 282, 306, 308
JL 4281: 353
JL 4287: 308, 365
JL 4290: 261, 342, 353–54
JL 4299: 281
JL 4305: 301
JL 4369: 281, 387
JL 4383: 281
JL 4386: 281–82
JL *4389: 358
JL 4425–30: 298
JL 4463: 321, 330, 348, 374, 379
JL 4498: 308, 310, 353, 374, 379
JL 4501: 287
JL 4504: 287, 330, 333, 351
JL 4507: 330, 333, 351, 367
JL 4514: 270, 287, 296, 365
JL 4515: 208, 268
JL 4529: 331, 333, 351
JL 4628: 287, 365
JL 4646: 261, 287, 289, 316, 365
JL 4647: 287, 365
JL 4693: 365
JL 4795: 306, 331
JL 5004: 315, 375
JL 5021: 285, 315, 353
JL 5061: 300, 348
JL 5112: 300
JL 5131: 348, 354
JL 5155: 315
JL 5204: 1, 323, 334, 345, 367, 370
JL 5258: 294, 365, 367, 380
JL *5321: 359
JL 5352: 331

JL 5359: 333, 338, 351, 370
JL 5366: 367, 375
JL 5367: 376
JL 5385: 298, 327, 331, 333, 351
JL 5386: 283, 351–52, 367
JL 5412: 338, 365
JL 5414: 365
JL 5415: 195, 204, 331, 375, 380, 391
JL 5440: 339, 353
JL 5450: 367, 375, 383
JL 5464: 282, 355, 368, 375, 381
JL 5465: 318
JL 5475: 315, 332, 375
JL 5519: 315, 381–82
JL 5520: 316
JL 5548: 339, 355
JL 5569: 368, 375, 381
JL 5600: 318, 349
JL 5688: 263, 381
JL 5707: 318, 376
JL 5858: 383
JL 5885: 376
JL 5886: 368, 376, 381
JL 5904: 295, 368, 376, 381
JL 5914: 295, 368, 376, 381–82
JL 5948: 368, 376, 381
JL 5986: 307–8, 356, 369, 376, 381
JL 6013: 305, 369
JL 6016: 307–8, 368–69, 376, 381
JL 6056: 295, 368, 376, 381
JL 6057: 356, 368
JL 6088: 368, 376, 381
JL 6175: 332
JL 6224: 261, 316, 365
JL 6225: 316, 369
JL *6249: 307
JL 6291: 295, 309, 356, 369, 381
JL 6314: 295, 368, 376, 381
JL *6482: 338
JL 6528: 368, 376
JL 6570: 340, 346–47, 356, 368, 370, 442
JL 6596: 381
JL 6626: 360
JL 6632: 345

Index of Papal Letters

JL 6635: 345
JL 6636: 369, 376, 381
JL 6642: 345
JL 6647: 369, 376, 381
JL 9941: 448
JL 11308: 442
JL 11619: 448
JL 12377: 447
JL 14109: 448–49
JL 14198: 447
JL 17049: 447
JL 17657: 447
JL — (Alexander II to Ralph I of Tours, 1073): 261, 296, 316, 365
JL — (Alexander III to Nicholas of Messina, 1166): 454
JL — (Benedict IX to Hugh I of Besançon, 1037): 202, 207, 255, 270–71, 286, 384
JL — (Paschal II to Adalgot of Magdeburg, 1107): 284, 340, 345, 348
JL — (Paschal II to Geoffrey of Rouen, 1112): 324, 332, 349
JL — (Paschal II to Lawrence of Esztergom, after 1105): 340, 356
JL — (Paschal II to Raymond of Galicia, 1103): 360
JL — (Paschal II to William of Brindisi, 1104): 369, 376, 381
JL — (Urban II to Guy of Vienne, 1094): 381
JL — (Urban II to Peter of Grado, 1093): 303, 339, 355, 368, 383
JL — (Urban II to Raymond of Auch, 1097): 381
JL — (Urban II to Thomas I of York, 1094): 319, 345
JL — (Urban II to William of Rouen, 1094): 345, 348

Potthast 1112: 444
Potthast 1647: 444
Potthast 1735: 444
Potthast 1902: 444
Potthast 2138: 444
Potthast 2145: 444
Potthast 2588: 444
Potthast 2837: 444
Potthast 3692: 444
Potthast 5034: 449
Potthast 7455: 451

Index of Canonical Works

Animal est substantia (ca. 1206–10), 407, 409–16, 418–19, 421–22, 425–26, 428–35, 437–38, 469n114
Apparatus Glossarum in Compilationem Tertiam of Johannes Teutonicus (1216–18), 452
Apparatus in Quinque Libros Decretalium of Sinibaldo Fieschi (Innocent IV) (ca. 1245), 452

Breviarium Canonum of Atto of S. Marco (ca. 1075), 291n44
Breviarium Extravagantium. See Compilatio Prima

Candela of Gerland of Besançon (ca. 1130), 184n16
Capitularies of Benedict the Deacon (847–57), 144
Casus Fuldenses on Fourth Lateran Council (1215–20), 452, 455
Casus Parisienses on Fourth Lateran Council (1215–20), 452, 455
Code of Canon Law, 488n6
Collectio II Librorum vel VIII Partium (after 1089/after 1100), 291n44, 292n48, 296
Collectio III Librorum (after 1111), 291n44, 292n48, 326, 403
Collectio IV Librorum (1076–85), 291n44, 292n48
Collectio V Librorum (after 1014), 231n9

Collectio V Librorum in Vat. lat. 1348 (1083–85), 403
Collectio VII Librorum in Turin D.IV.33 (s. xi ex.), 291n44, 292n48
Collectio VII Librorum in Vienna 2186 (1112–20), 285n22, 286n24, 291n44, 327n23
Collectio IX Librorum in Vat. lat. 1349 (912–30), 186n24, 188n30
Collectio IX Voluminum (Sangermanensis) (1094–99), 291n44
Collectio X Partium (1123–31), 184n16, 372n35
Collectio X Partium in Cologne 199 (s. xii in.), 291n44, 372–73
Collectio XII Partium (augmented version) (ca. 1039), 183–84, 197, 267, 304n89
Collectio XII Partium (original version) (ca. 1022), 183
Collectio XIII Librorum in Savigny 3 (ca. 1089), 291n44, 292n48, 293n50
Collectio LXXIV Titulorum (Diversorum Patrum Sententiae) (1073–75), 291n44, 292n48
Collectio CLXXXIII Titulorum (S. Mariae Novellae) (1063–73), 291n44
Collectio Ambrosiana I (1090–1100), 325, 350n116
Collectio Anselmo Dedicata (882–96), 130n60, 180, 183, 186n25, 199n22, 210, 324, 381n68

Index of Canonical Works 523

Collectio Ashburnhamensis (ca. 1085), 291n44, 292n48
Collectio Atrebatensis (1093?), 291n44
Collectio Britannica (ca. 1090), 106, 283n15, 290n42, 296, 325, 330, 332n46, 333, 335, 344, 351
Collectio Brugensis (s. xi ex.), 291n44
Collectio Burdegalensis (after 1079), 291n44
Collectio Casinensis (after 1110), 297n64
Collectio Herovalliana (754–800), 104n110
Collectio Lanfranci (after 1059), 291n44
Collectio S. Hilarii Pictaviensis (XVII Librorum) (1061–74), 291n44
Collectio Sinemuriensis (Remensis) (after 1067), 285n22
Collectio Tarraconensis: version 1 (1080–90), 291n44, 292n48; version 2 (ca. 1097), 291n44, 292n48
Collectio Tripartita A (1093–94), 291n44, 326, 372
Collectio Tripartita B (s. xi ex.), 295
Collection in Arsenal 713 (early s. xii), 351n123
Collection in Arsenal 721 (after 1110), 403
Collection in BNF lat. 13368 (late s. xi–early s. xii?), 291n44
Collection in BNF lat. 13658 (s. xii), 292n48
Collection in BNF lat. 3858C (1050–75), 291nn44–45, 292n48
Collection in BNF n.a.l. 326 (ca. 1065), 291n44, 292n48
Collection in Celle C.8 (late s. xi), 291n44, 292n48
Collection in Turin E.V.44 (ca. 1100), 350n116
Collection in Vallicelliana B.89 (s. xii), 285n22
Collection in Vat. lat. 3829 (1118–19), 291n44, 292n48, 293n51, 350nn116–17

Collection in Vat. lat. 3830 (after 1054), 291n44, 292nn46.48
Collection of Abbo of Fleury (995–96), 230, 285n22
Collection of Anselm of Lucca (ca. 1083), 236n23, 291n44, 292, 293n50, 324, 350
Collection of Deusdedit of SS. Apostoli (1083–87), 12n43, 46n62, 236n23, 298n70, 324–25, 342–44, 347n101, 350n116, 352n123
Commentum super Decretalibus. See *Lectura*
Compilatio Prima of Bernard of Pavia (1189–92), 441–43, 447
Compilatio Secunda of John of Wales (1210–15), 447–49
Compilatio Tertia of Peter of Benevento (1209–10), 443–47
Compilatio Quarta of Johannes Teutonicus (1216), 449–50
Compilatio Quinta of Tancred of Bologna (1226), 451
Compilationes Antiquae (Old Compilations), 441, 444, 450–51
Concordia Discordantium Canonum. See *Decretum* of Gratian
Constitutiones of Oda of Canterbury (942–46), 270

Decretales Domini Innocentii Papae. See *Compilatio Tertia*
Decretals of Gregory IX. See *Liber Extra*
Decretals of Pseudo-Isidore (847–52), 90n60, 91n63, 103, 104n109, 105n115, 106n118, 110n135, 115n155, 128, 144n101, 157, 166
Decretum attributed to Ivo of Chartres (after 1095), 291n44, 295, 326, 351n123
Decretum of Burchard of Worms (1012–22), 46n62, 180, 182–83, 323
Decretum of Gratian (ca. 1140), 19, 327, 350n116, 397–98, 401–2, 404, 406–7, 408n22, 418, 420, 429, 452, 468, 479

524 Index of Canonical Works

De iure canonico tractaturus. See General Index, Honorius of Kent

Elegantius in iure divino (ca. 1169), 407, 408n22, 417

Glossa Ordinaria on *Decretum* by Johannes Teutonicus (ca. 1215) and Bartholomew of Brescia (ca. 1240–45), 407, 411, 413–19, 421–23, 426–32, 434–36, 438, 468, 469n114
Glossa Ordinaria on *Liber Extra* by Bernard of Parma (ca. 1266), 452, 453n46

Lectura of Hostiensis (ca. 1271), 397, 452–53, 454n50, 455, 457, 461, 462n78, 463–64, 466, 469n111, 470–73, 475–76, 479
Liber de Vita Christiana of Bonizo of Sutri (1089–95), 303, 325, 335, 381n68, 388
Liber Extra of Raymond of Penyafort (1234), 19, 400, 428–29, 435, 440–42, 444, 447–49, 451–52, 453n46, 462, 465, 470, 473, 479

Magister G. in hoc opere (ca. 1170), 407, 411–13, 415, 417, 420, 424–25, 429–31, 436–37

Omnis qui iuste iudicat (ca. 1186), 407, 408n22, 409–14, 418–19, 421–24, 426–30, 433–35, 471

Panormia of Ivo of Chartres (after 1095), 184n16, 326, 403
Polycarpus of Gregory of S. Grisogono (1104–13), 285n22, 286, 291n44, 292n48, 307n101, 327n23, 444
Propriae Auctoritates Apostolicae Sedis (*Dictatus* of Avranches) (1075–85), 297, 445

Stroma of Roland (ca. 1150), 407
Summa Aurea of Hostiensis (ca. 1253), 452, 454, 455n54, 457, 459, 463–65, 467, 469, 471, 473–74, 476, 478, 487n3
Summa Bambergensis. See Animal est substantia
Summa Coloniensis. See Elegantius in iure divino
Summa de Electione of Bernard of Pavia, 442
Summa Lipsiensis. See Omnis qui iuste iudicat
Summa of Honorius of Kent (ca. 1188). *See General Index*, Honorius of Kent
Summa of Huguccio (ca. 1188–90). *See General Index*, Huguccio
Summa of Paucapalea (ca. 1144–50). *See General Index*, Paucapalea
Summa of Rufinus (ca. 1164). *See General Index*, Rufinus
Summa of Simon of Bisignano (ca. 1177–79). *See General Index*, Simon of Bisignano
Summa of Stephen of Tournai (1165–66). *See General Index*, Stephen of Tournai
Summa Parisiensis. See Magister G. in hoc opere
Summa Titulorum Decretalium of Bernard of Pavia, 442

General Index

Aachen, 205n44, 223n108; Council of (*816*), 162
Aaron (high priest), 6, 163, 165, 174n100, 390, 392
Abbo of Fleury, 217, 230, 231n10, 237, 249, 285n22
Abel of Reims, 30n12, 31n15
Acerenza, 318, 376. *See also its bishops* Arnold; Peter
Acta Lanfranci, 378
Actard of Nantes/Tours, 62, 66–67, 69, 89, 115–16, 120–21, 126n38, 128, 130n60, 133, 161, 171–72
Adalbero II of Metz, 221n101, 311n113
Adalbert (antipope), 358
Adalbert of Bamberg, 308nn103.105
Adalbert of Hamburg, 261n111, 334, 342, 353
Adalbert of Magdeburg, 189n34, 202n34, 203n37, 207n51, 208n54, 210, 222n105, 225n113, 239–40, 257n96, 260
Adalbert of Mainz, 340
Adaldag of Hamburg, 202n34, 206n50, 210n64, 255n91
Adalgar of Autun, 49, 69, 101, 155
Adalgot of Magdeburg, 284, 340, 345, 348
Adalram of Salzburg, 35, 69, 83, 93, 120, 123, 147
Adalwin of Salzburg, 41, 60n115
Adam of Bremen, 4n6, 283, 334

Ademar of Chabannes, 225–26
Ado of Vienne, 23n2, 27n2, 36, 41–42, 57, 77, 111, 139, 159, 299n72
Adventius of Metz, 313
Aelfric of Canterbury, 249
Aelfsige of Canterbury, 243, 287
Aethelhard of Canterbury, 114, 120n11, 140n90, 142n94, 145, 147n113, 153n9, 174
Aethelnoth of Canterbury, 237, 245n55, 250
Afra (martyr), 354
Africa, 15n49, 301. *See also its bishops* John; Peter
Agapitus II (pope), 195, 198n16, 207n51, 210, 221–22
Agius of Narbonne, 208, 231
Agnellus of Ravenna, 7n17, 70, 78, 79n21, 91n62, 97, 98n87, 122n18, 134n69, 143, 155
Agnes (martyr), 3n4
Agnes of Poitou (empress), 298, 311n114, 328, 359n155, 366n13
Aiglibert of Le Mans, 110–11, 154
Aimoin of Fleury, 188n31, 217, 231n10
Aix. *See its bishop* Peter
Alban (martyr), 258, 300
Albano. *See its bishops* Albinus; Boniface; Walter
Alberic II (patrician), 213, 214n74, 224

525

Albinus of Albano, 156n23, 445n17, 462n81, 465n90, 477n153
Alcherius of Palermo, 294n55, 365, 367n16, 379
Alcuin of York, 13nn46–47, 32–33, 64–65, 68n144, 83, 84n41, 91, 108n128, 114–15, 120n11, 122, 129, 141–42, 145, 147, 151, 154, 158, 165–67, 173, 176, 178, 245, 249n68, 264
Alexander II (pope), 208n53, 261n111, 268n139, 270n148, 271, 286–89, 296, 308n104, 310–11, 316, 330–31, 332n45, 343, 353, 365, 367, 374, 377–79, 486
Alexander III (pope), 156n23, 428, 435, 441–43, 447–49, 451, 466, 469n111, 477
Alexandria, 450
Alfanus I of Benevento, 199, 207n51, 209
Alfanus II of Benevento, 199, 207nn51–52, 209, 211, 258n99, 262nn113.115, 263n116, 268n139
Alfanus I of Salerno, 281n4, 282
Alfanus II of Salerno, 318n142, 376n52
Alfonso VI of Spain, 376n52
All Saints (feast), 257, 353, 384n78, 474
Alo of Benevento, 202n33, 207nn51–52, 258n99, 262n113
Alphege of Canterbury, 249
Alps, 47, 86n47, 107, 176, 243, 287, 331n43
Altheus of Autun, 35–36, 56, 98, 218n91, 352
Altmann of Passau, 338–39, 353
Amalar of Metz, 140, 163–65, 264–65, 270n146, 389–90, 392, 410n29
Amatus I of Salerno, 241
Amatus II of Salerno, 242n44, 255n90
Amatus III of Salerno, 202n34, 205n45, 209, 242n44, 255n90

Ambrose of Milan, 164n51
Anacletus I (pope), 110n135
Anastasius III (pope), 199n23, 200, 206n50, 255n91
Anastasius IV (pope), 448n33
Anastasius of Antioch, 12n39
Anastasius the Librarian, 50, 56n100, 91n61, 137n77, 138n80, 148
Andrew of Bari, 208n53, 268n139
Andrew of Fleury, 232
Andrew of Nicopolis, 10n31
Angilram of Metz, 312n118
Anglo-Saxon Chronicle, 237, 243n49, 249–50, 268n138, 288, 321n1, 336n59, 338n68, 358n152, 378, 409n27, 445
Anglo-Saxons, 21, 269, 347, 485
Annales Hildesheimenses, 14n48
Annales Iuvavenses Antiqui, 68n142, 69n147
Annales Romani, 358
Annalista Saxo, 14n48
Annals of Xanten, 54n92, 78, 126n38
Anno II of Cologne, 4n6, 288–89, 310n110, 311n114, 330, 332n45, 367n14
Annunciation of Mary (feast), 257
Ansegis of Sens, 105
Anselm of Canterbury, 281, 319, 327, 336–37, 340n78, 348–49, 357–58, 376
Anselm of Laon, 388
Anselm of Lucca, 236n23, 291n44, 292, 293n50, 324, 350
Anselm II of Milan, 180n2
Anselm III of Milan, 283, 333, 338, 344, 352, 367n17, 370
Ansgar (missionary), 27n3, 42, 43n51, 62, 67, 86n47, 94, 121n16, 169n73, 174n97, 184–85, 341
Antioch, 450, 460n72. *See also its bishop* Anastasius
Antiquam patrum, 290
Antoninus (papal official), 11n38
Antoninus of Grado, 13n45, 77n12

General Index   527

Apollinaris of Ravenna, 134
Apostolicae sedis, 75, 119, 123, 126n38, 127, 170n81, 171, 211, 296n62, 365
Aquileia, 12, 33n22, 69n148, 94–95, 103, 196n10, 205–6, 242. *See also its bishops* Calixtus; Henry; Poppo; Ravenger; Rodwald; Serenus; Ulric
Aquitaine, 33, 145
Arbeo of Freising, 14n47, 84n40, 108n128, 159, 174n97
Aregius of Gap, 11n36, 404
Argrim of Lyon/Langres, 200, 230, 232, 371, 373
Aribo of Mainz, 64n126, 189–91, 196n10, 200, 218n91, 227–28, 244n51, 253, 254n87
Arles, 4n6, 9–10, 12, 33n22, 37n35, 47n64, 49, 84n39, 87n52, 104, 106, 144, 300, 405. *See also its bishops* Aurelian; Auxanius; Caesarius; Florian; Rostagnus; Sapaudus; Virgilius
Arno of Salzburg, 33, 40, 68–70, 91n61, 92, 94, 123, 128, 141n92, 142, 145, 147, 151, 154n12, 155, 169, 173, 174n98, 176
Arnold of Acerenza, 287, 365
Arnulf of Jerusalem, 368, 376
Arnulf of Reims, 195n4, 211n67, 216–17, 237, 249
Arnulf of Tours, 212, 218
Artold of Reims, 215, 223
Ascension (feast), 133, 255, 474–75
Assumption of Mary (feast), 131, 255, 257n96
Athens, 85n42, 142–43
Atto of San Marco, 291n44
Atto of Vic/Tarragona, 202n33, 207n51, 240, 254n89, 263n116
Auch. *See its bishop* Raymond
Augsburg. *See its bishops* Bruno; Ulric
Augustine of Canterbury, 11, 12n39, 13, 29, 45, 85n42, 104–6, 122n20, 140–41, 144, 148n117, 270n145, 303n83, 363, 405

Aurelian of Arles, 9n25
Aureus and Justina, 258
Autun, 36, 113, 454n53. *See also its bishops* Adalgar; Altheus; Syagrius; Wala
Auxanius of Arles, 9n25
Auxerre, 57. *See also its bishops* Desiderius; Hugh
Azecho of Worms, 191n42

"B." (author), 243, 269
Baldric of Dol, 261n111, 316, 332n47, 365n6, 369
Bamberg, 209, 233, 267n134, 286n26, 307–9, 317. *See also its bishops* Eberhard; Gunther; Hartwig; Herman; Otto; Suidger
Bar. *See its bishop* Peter
Barcelona. *See its bishop* Oleguer
Bardo of Mainz, 196n10, 202n34, 207n51, 227, 251, 254n89, 258, 262n114, 280n2
Bari, 338, 465; Council of (*1098*), 465. *See also its bishops* Andrew; Bisantius; Elijah; Risus
Bartholomew (apostle), 258
Bartholomew of Brescia, 408, 419
Bartholomew of Narbonne, 60
Basel Ordo, 445n17, 465n90
Basil I (emperor), 82n31, 101n103, 130n59, 153n9
Bavaria, 33, 87, 94, 142, 145, 155, 197, 267, 386n82
Beauvais: Council of (*845*), 51
Bec, 377
Bede, 13n46, 162n45, 164n50, 245, 248n66
Belgians, 106
Belisarius (general), 9
Benedict III (pope), 41, 59n115, 88n54, 131n62, 146
Benedict IV (pope), 200n26, 230, 232, 371n32
Benedict V (pope), 188–89
Benedict VI (pope), 196–97, 202n35, 215, 240

528   General Index

Benedict VII (pope), 202n34, 203, 204n44, 205, 207n51, 229, 230n7, 252, 258n100, 259n103, 261, 269n143
Benedict VIII (pope), 190–91, 199, 200n23, 202n34, 204, 207nn51–52, 208n53, 211, 219, 233, 237n28, 242, 250–52, 254n89, 255n90, 256n92, 257n96, 259n103, 261, 262nn113–14, 266–67, 269, 383, 386n82
Benedict IX (pope), 202n34, 205n45, 207n51, 209, 242n44, 255n90, 270, 286, 349n111, 384nn77–78
Benedict X (antipope), 358
Benedict XVI (pope), 267n135
Benedict of Porto, 267n134
Benedict of Salerno, 242n44
Benedict of St. Peter's, 445n17
Benedict the Deacon, 144
Benevento, 208n54, 223, 241, 258, 262n113, 263n116. *See also its bishops* Alfanus I; Alfanus II; Alo; Landulf; Ulric
Berengar I of Italy, 200
Berengar of Vic/Tarragona, 317, 367n17, 375, 382
Bernard of Braga, 332n46, 360n158
Bernard of Halberstadt, 221n101
Bernard of Hildesheim, 360–61
Bernard of Parma, 452–53, 455–57, 459–63, 466–71, 473–75, 477
Bernard of Pavia, 441–43
Bernard of Toledo, 332n46, 344, 367n17, 375, 383
Bernard of Vienne, 35, 119n7, 123, 170, 235
Bernold of Constance, 298, 350, 355n138, 424
Bertald of Besançon, 366
Berther of Vienne, 111
Berthold (Bertram) of Metz, 408n22
Bertichram of Le Mans, 110n139
Bertrand of Narbonne, 263n119, 381n69
Bertulf of Trier, 37, 38n37, 43, 55, 57, 70, 101, 313, 352

Bertwald of Canterbury, 113n147, 243n49
Besançon, 33n22, 305n92, 384. *See also its bishops* Bertald; Hugh I; Hugh III; Pontius
Birth of Mary (feast), 255
Bisantius of Bari, 208n53, 268n139
Bisantius of Trani, 270n148, 286, 296n62, 365
Bologna, 399, 401–2
Boniface (missionary), 12n42, 13–15, 21, 29–33, 36n30, 38–40, 51, 73, 75, 84–85, 92, 108–9, 122n18, 126, 132n64, 141, 144, 146, 160, 166, 170–71, 174n98, 178, 185n21, 198n16, 222n102, 288n34, 290n42, 291n43, 301, 303n83, 342, 424, 485; Bonifacian reform synod (747), 32, 38, 39n42, 75, 85, 144, 160
Boniface II (pope), 9
Boniface IV (pope), 12, 265n126
Boniface V (pope), 13n46, 245
Boniface VIII (pope), 4n6
Boniface of Albano, 328
Bonizo of Sutri, 265n126, 286, 289, 303, 304n88, 309, 325, 332n45, 335, 338, 381n68, 388, 390
Bordeaux, 33n22. *See also its bishop* Frothar
Borrell II of Barcelona, 240
Bourges, 33, 66, 126, 145, 225, 229. *See also its bishops* Ermenbert; Frothar; Gauzlin; Ralph; Wulfhad
Braga, 360. *See also its bishops* Gerald; Maurice; Peter
Braun, Joseph, 3, 6, 85n46
breastplate. *See* rational
Bremen, 184–86, 205n45
Brindisi. *See its bishop* William
Britain, 65, 85n42, 113n147, 288n34
Brittany, 36, 43, 65, 69, 99, 112, 113n147, 284, 286, 314–16, 332n46, 353, 375
Brunhild (queen), 11, 12n39, 28n5, 35–36, 329, 404
Bruno of Augsburg, 267n134

General Index   529

Bruno of Cologne, 187, 197–98, 204n40, 208, 221, 224, 225n113, 234–35
Bruno of Querfurt (missionary), 239n34
Bruno of Segni, 165n57, 175n102, 265n126, 380, 388, 391–94
Bruno of Trier, 284, 348, 371, 383
Bruno of Verona, 306, 331
Bulgaria, 81–82, 101, 147, 370n28, 444–45, 474
Burchard II of Halberstadt, 289n38, 308n104, 310–11, 353, 374, 379
Burchard of Worms, 46n62, 180–83, 323–26
Burgundy, 246
Byzantine Empire, 7, 9, 80n26, 81–82, 101, 127n43, 188, 241–42

Caesarea, 113, 114n150
Caesarius of Arles, 1, 9n25, 120n12
Caesarius of Santa Cecília de Montserrat, 333n47
Calixtus II (pope), 311–12, 395
Calixtus of Aquileia, 13n45
Candidus (papal official), 329
Candlemas (feast). *See* Purification of Mary
Canterbury, 13, 95–96, 104, 113n147, 114–15, 140–41, 147, 205, 243–44, 246–49, 263n116, 281, 288, 303n83, 318–19, 336, 338, 345, 349, 357–58, 445, 460n72, 465. *See also its bishops* Aelfric; Aelfsige; Aethelhard; Aethelnoth; Alphege; Anselm; Augustine; Bertwald; Cuthbert; Dunstan; Honorius; Jaenbert; Justus; Lanfranc; Lyfing; Oda; Ralph; Robert of Jumièges; Stigand; Theodore; Wulfhelm
Canute of England, 199, 245–46
Carlisle, 446, 459
Carloman of Austrasia, 30, 31n15, 32n18, 92
Carloman of Bavaria, 100, 102, 172
Carolingians, 16–18, 21, 26, 33n22, 37n35, 42n50, 50n75, 75, 92, 97–98, 99n94, 109, 111, 161, 162n45, 163, 165, 166nn60–61, 173n94, 174, 177–80, 192, 194–95, 201, 203, 218n89, 226, 228, 232, 254, 264, 267, 272–73, 317, 341, 362, 385n80, 390n96, 395, 399, 483–85

Carthage, 301. *See also its bishop* Dominic
Castorius (papal official), 11n35
Catalonia, 208n54, 240
Celestine I (pope), 141, 176
Celestine III (pope), 294n53, 429, 447, 462, 469
Cencius Savelli, 445n17, 462nn79.81, 465n90. *See also* Honorius III
Cenwulf of Mercia, 95–96, 140–41, 176n105
Chalcedon, Council of (*451*), 42n50, 45, 431n144
Charlemagne (emperor), 32–34, 37n35, 48n67, 65, 68, 92–94, 103n106, 111n142, 113, 145, 155, 174n98
Charles the Bald, 23n2, 27n2, 44n57, 46n60, 48–49, 53, 54n92, 69, 86, 93n69, 99–101, 110n137, 115, 121n14, 125n37, 126n38, 127, 145, 153n9, 155, 161n42, 172, 312n118
Charles the Fat, 198
Chartres. *See its bishops* Fulbert; Ivo; John of Salisbury
Childebert (king), 12n39
Christmas (feast), 130–31, 136, 255, 263n119, 309n109, 384, 474
Chrodegang of Metz, 109–10, 121, 154, 312–13, 409n27
Chronica de Singulis Patriarchis Novae Aquileiae, 13n45, 59, 77, 95n79, 103, 123n22
Chronica Pontificum Ecclesiae Eboracensis, 321n1
Chronicon Breve Bremense, 283n13
Chronicon Gradense, 95n79, 229n3, 242

General Index

Chur. *See its bishop* Guy
Cikedor, 444
Cinthius (cardinal), 444, 453
Circumcision (feast), 474
Cividale del Friuli, 94–95
Clement I (pope), 165n58
Clement II (pope), 261n111, 267, 271–72, 279, 281, 285, 294nn53–54, 297, 307–9, 353, 378, 385–86, 486
Clement III (pope), 447
Clement III (antipope), 336, 338, 343, 357–61
Clermont, Council of (*1095*), 318
Cluny, 215n78, 395
Cologne, 4n6, 30n12, 33n22, 37, 43, 54–55, 59, 66, 70, 83, 108nn127.129, 130, 159n38, 168, 181, 184–86, 198n15, 203–4, 221, 223, 225n113, 253, 303n83, 310n110, 311n114, 372, 398. *See also its bishops* Anno II; Bruno; Gunther; Heribert; Herman I; Hilduin; Pilgrim; Willibert
Compostela, 317–18, 444–45, 453, 462, 472. *See also its bishop* Diego
Conon of Palestrina, 340, 345
Conrad of Luxembourg, 299
Constance. *See its bishop* Gebhard
Constans II (emperor), 79n21
Constantine (antipope), 188
Constantine I (emperor), 90, 157n24
Constantinople, 79, 82nn31–32.34, 91, 114n150, 142, 213, 214n74, 450; First Council of (*381*), 42n50; Second Council of (*553*), 42n50; Third Council of (*680–81*), 42n50; Fourth Council of (*869–70*), 55, 80n26, 91n61, 127, 130, 137; Council of (*879–80*;"Photian Synod"), 80. *See also its bishops* Germanus; Ignatius; Photius
Constantius of Milan, 10n31
Conversio Bagoariorum et Carantanorum, 68n142, 147, 174n98

Corbinian (missionary), 14n47, 84, 108, 159, 174n97
Corinth, 10, 335n57. *See also its bishop* John
Corsica, 282, 355
Cosenza, 318, 376
Cremona. *See its bishops* Liutprand; Sicard
Crescens (missionary), 303n83
Crescentius of Split, 295n56, 368n21, 376, 381n69, 382
Csanád, 444
Cunigund (empress), 190, 191n43, 253
Cuthbert of Canterbury, 32, 39n42, 75n6, 85n44, 141, 144n102, 146, 160

Daimbert of Pisa, 282, 355, 368, 375, 381
Dalmatia, 11n38, 56, 69, 70n151, 81, 122n18, 153n9, 158, 231n11, 242
Dalmatius of Narbonne, 299
Damasus I (pope), 181, 324–26, 329
Danes, 42, 347
Dante Alighieri, 172
Desiderius of Auxerre, 57
Desiderius of Vienne, 11, 37n35, 49, 57–58
Deusdedit (cardinal), 12n43, 46n62, 236n23, 298n70, 324–25, 342–44, 347n101, 350n116, 352n123
Die. *See its bishop* Hugh
Diego of Compostela, 307, 308n104, 343n89, 356, 369, 376n53, 381, 478n154
Dionysius of Paris, 142, 308
Dionysius the Areopagite, 142
Dol, 27, 36, 43, 65, 67, 99, 112–13, 140, 284–86, 314–17, 369, 382n70. *See also its bishops* Baldric; Evan; Festinian; Juthael; Juthinael; Restwald; Roland
Dominic of Carthage, 380
Donation of Constantine, 7, 90
Donatus of Grado, 103

General Index 531

Donus of Messina, 10n30, 454n53
Dorchester. *See its bishop* Remigius
Douzy, Council of (*871*), 89n57, 105n113, 116n156, 172n86
Drogo of Metz, 60n117, 86, 93, 98, 110–11, 113, 114n150, 121, 129n55, 154n11, 312n118
Dubrovnik, 243n48, 300, 348, 446, 459. *See also its bishop* Vitalis
Duchesne, Louis, 7, 188n32
Dunstan of Canterbury, 202n34, 205, 206n50, 236, 244, 248n66, 254n89, 263n116, 268–70

Eadmer of Canterbury, 152n2, 287n33, 327n26, 336, 337n64, 357, 460n72, 465
Ealdred of Worcester/York, 321–22, 330, 348, 374, 379
Eanbald I of York, 65
Eanbald II of York, 32, 65n131, 83, 129, 158n32
Easter (feast), 130–31, 255, 257, 308, 313, 354, 384n78, 445, 474
Eberhard of Bamberg, 267n134
Eberhard of Trier, 279, 294n54, 297, 299, 378, 386
Ebo of Reims/Hildesheim, 22, 51–53, 60–61, 69, 86n47, 96–98, 100, 129, 154n11
Ebremar of Jerusalem, 332n46
Egbert of York, 13n46, 243n49
Egilbert of Freising, 267n134
Egilbert of Trier, 359, 372
Egilo of Sens, 27n2, 48, 52–53, 99, 127, 156
Eichstätt. *See its bishop* Gebhard
Ekkehard of Aura, 276
Elbe, 205n45
Elijah of Bari, 338, 365
Ember Saturdays, 262
Embrun, 33n22, 281, 461, 478n154. *See also its bishops* Hostiensis; Winiman
Engelberga (empress), 101n100
England, 11, 13–14, 29–30, 32–33,
  45, 64–65, 85n42, 85n45, 93, 95, 104–5, 110n135, 139–40, 145, 147, 148n117, 199n21, 237n28, 239, 243–48, 250, 268, 270n145, 289, 318–19, 321–22, 327, 336–37, 345, 358, 408n22, 416, 483, 485
Ephesus, Council of (*431*), 42n50
ephod. *See* superhumeral
Epiphany (feast), 255, 474
Epirus, 10n31, 405
Ermenbert of Bourges, 33, 48, 68, 92, 102–3
Ermenfrid of Sion, 349n112
Esztergom, 442–44, 446, 460, 468. *See also its bishop* Lawrence
Eugene II (pope), 35, 69n147, 83, 93n68, 120, 123n23, 154
Eugene III (pope), 454n53
Evan of Dol, 314–15, 353, 374
Exodus (book), 388
Expositio Divinorum Officiorum, 392n105

Fécamp, 316n138
Felix IV (pope), 9
Festinian of Dol, 23n2, 27n1, 31n17, 36n33, 37n34, 56–57, 99, 112, 140n86, 218n91
Flodoard of Reims, 34n24, 52n83, 60n117, 89n55, 92n65, 186n23, 198, 209, 213, 215n79, 223–24, 229, 313nn121–22
Florence, 292n46, 298, 328
Florian of Arles, 12n42, 265n126
Florus of Lyon, 163n49
Folcuin of Lobbes, 201, 210n65, 232, 239n34, 250
Formosus (pope), 213, 230, 361, 371
Fortunatus of Grado, 41n45, 70, 77n12, 120, 169
France, 289, 291, 296, 325, 331, 350–51, 364n2
Francia, 26, 47, 91n61, 109, 139, 149, 314. *See also* Franks
Francis (pope), 341n81

Frankfurt, Council of (794), 111n142
Franks, 11, 12n42, 14n47, 15, 21, 26–27, 29, 31, 32nn18–19, 33, 35, 36n32, 47, 57, 92, 98, 99n94, 109, 112, 170–71, 177, 220n96, 313, 329, 485
Frechulf of Lisieux, 93, 105n112, 139
Frederick of Hamburg, 220n97
Frederick of Salzburg, 187, 196–98, 215, 216n81, 225n113, 257, 259, 263n117
Freising, 183, 197, 267. See also its bishop Egilbert
Frisia, 109
Friuli, 94–95
Frothar of Bordeaux/Bourges, 229
Fulbert of Chartres, 211–12, 218
Fulda, 85n46
Fulk of Reims, 198, 209, 213, 216, 229, 234

Gap. See its bishop Aregius
Gaul, 1, 9, 11, 14, 15n49, 29, 30n12, 32n19, 47, 61n119, 70n149, 84n39, 86n47, 87, 104–6, 109n133, 130, 144, 148–49, 163, 205, 206n48, 213, 230nn7–8, 232, 233n16, 253n85, 264, 265n126, 301, 306, 345, 371n32, 373n41, 405, 416
Gauzlin of Bourges, 232–33
Gebhard of Constance, 356n145, 368
Gebhard of Eichstätt. See Victor II
Gebuin of Lyon, 335, 342
Gehon, 389
Gelasius II (pope), 278, 345–46, 366, 369, 376, 381n69, 395, 399
Genesis (book), 164, 389
Geoffrey of Bourges, 233
Geoffrey of Rouen, 323, 332, 349
Gerald of Braga, 332n46, 360
Gerald of Mt. Tabor, 368n21, 376n53, 381n69
Gerard of Lorch, 210
Gerard of Narbonne (pretender), 231
Gerard of York, 281, 337, 368n21, 376n53, 381n69

Gerbert of Aurillac/Reims/Ravenna, 207nn51–52, 211, 216, 217n87, 255n90, 268n139. See also Sylvester II
Gerland of Besançon, 184n16
Germanus of Constantinople, 163n49
Germany, 13–14, 40, 73, 105–6, 148, 198, 203–5, 206n48, 222, 230n7, 233n16, 252–53, 261, 263, 267n134, 276, 280, 293, 301, 306, 310, 316n136, 323, 331, 339, 343n89, 354, 359, 385, 416, 485
Gero of Magdeburg, 207n51, 251, 256n92, 257n96, 259n103, 269
Gesta Episcoporum Mettensium, 312nn117–19
Gesta Pontificum Autissiodorensium, 57, 305, 391n100
Gesta Treverorum, 111n141, 267n134, 284, 299, 312n117, 312n119, 313, 348n107, 359, 371, 373, 383
Gilbert of Limerick, 340, 374
Girona. See its bishop Peter
Giselher of Merseburg/Magdeburg, 229–30, 252
Gloria in excelsis Deo, 132, 406
Good Friday, 445n17
Gordon, Stewart, 25
Goscelin of St.-Bertin, 319n146, 363, 437
Goswin of Mainz, 300–301
Grado, 12, 33n22, 59, 69n148, 77, 94–95, 103, 123, 206, 242. See also its bishops Antoninus; Donatus; Fortunatus; Peter; Primogenius; Victor; Vitalis
Gratian of Bologna, 19, 327, 350n116, 397–402, 407–8, 410, 429, 431n140, 436–37, 440–41, 448, 451–52, 468, 470, 479; "Gratian 1," 402–5, 420, 431, 438, 443, 457; "Gratian 2," 402, 404–6, 415, 428–29, 438
Greece, 10, 12n39, 80n24, 81–82, 91n61, 114, 213–14
Gregorian Reform, 16, 179, 275, 277

General Index   533

Gregory I (the Great; pope), 10–14, 17, 21, 28, 29nn6–7, 33, 35–36, 37n35, 38n37, 45, 47–49, 50n75, 57–61, 63–65, 70n148, 76, 84n39, 87, 91, 93, 95, 99n95, 104–6, 110n135, 113, 122, 128–29, 133–35, 138–41, 144, 147, 148n117, 149, 151n2, 157–58, 159n35, 161, 162n45, 166–67, 170, 171n83, 175, 180, 186, 210, 231, 255n91, 270n145, 285, 288, 290, 292, 301, 303n83, 318–19, 324, 329nn30–31, 335n57, 350, 363, 373, 380–81, 382n71, 392n102, 393, 402–5, 406n18, 409, 411, 415, 417–19, 423, 426–27, 429–30, 436–37, 442, 448, 454n53, 457, 483, 485
Gregory II (pope), 13n45, 14n47, 59, 84, 103, 342
Gregory III (pope), 12–13, 73, 77n12, 132n64, 301
Gregory IV (pope), 41, 59, 67, 70n149, 94, 120, 121n16, 131–33, 169n73, 199, 202n33, 206n50, 225n118, 255, 270n145, 297n65
Gregory V (pope), 199, 207nn51–52, 209, 211, 217, 231n10, 237, 249, 255n90, 268n139
Gregory VII (pope), 1, 277, 282–86, 292, 294, 297–98, 300, 306, 312n117, 314–18, 323, 331, 334–36, 338, 342, 343n89, 344, 345n93, 348, 350, 353–54, 357, 359–60, 365, 367–70, 372n34, 374, 379, 424
Gregory VIII (antipope), 345
Gregory IX (pope), 397, 400, 441, 453n46, 461, 474
Gregory of San Grisogono, 285n22, 286, 291n44, 292n48, 307n101, 327n23, 443–44
Gregory of Tours, 159n35
Grenoble, 355
Grimo of Rouen, 30n11, 31n15
Grimwald of Salerno, 207n51, 242n44

Guastalla, Council of (1106), 284, 371, 383
Guibert of Nogent, 388–89
Guibert of Ravenna, 343, 347n101, 359–60. See also Clement III (antipope)
Gunther of Bamberg, 308–9, 359
Gunther of Cologne, 38n37, 50, 53–54, 58n111, 77–78, 83, 185
Guy of Chur, 360
Guy of Pavia, 305, 369
Guy of Vienne, 339, 355, 381n69, 395. See also Calixtus II

Hadamar of Fulda, 221–22
Hadrian I (pope), 17n52, 33, 37n35, 39–40, 48, 51, 68, 85, 92, 96, 102–3, 111–12, 113n147, 139, 156n21
Hadrian II (pope), 23n2, 38n37, 43, 49, 50n76, 53–54, 57–59, 62, 66–67, 69, 77–78, 83n37, 89, 100, 101n100, 108n127, 115–16, 120, 121n14, 125, 126n38, 128–30, 133, 153, 156, 159n38, 161, 167, 171
Hadrian III (pope), 229
Halberstadt, 221n101, 222n102, 310–11, 317. See also its bishops Bernard; Burchard II; Hildeward
Hamburg, 94, 184–86, 199n18, 203n38, 205n45, 210n64, 220, 255n91, 283, 342n85. See also its bishops Adalbert; Adaldag; Frederick; Hoger; Humbert; Libentius I; Liemar; Rimbert
Harold of Salzburg, 64n126, 187–88, 191, 200
Hartbert of Sens, 30n12, 31n15
Hartwig of Bamberg, 307, 309, 365
Hartwig of Salzburg, 202n34, 207n51, 257, 258n98, 262n114, 263n116
Hebrews. See Jews
Heiligenstadt, 258
Henry I of England, 337, 340
Henry II of Germany, 199, 208, 233, 261n112, 267, 308n103

Henry III of Germany, 192, 272, 275, 307
Henry IV of Germany, 283, 328, 334, 356, 359
Henry V of Germany, 276, 356
Henry of Aquileia, 343n89, 348, 354
Henry of Susa. *See* Hostiensis
Henry of Trier, 133n65, 198, 199n23, 202n33, 206n50, 225, 254n89, 255, 260, 263n117
Henry of Würzburg, 208, 233
Heribert of Cologne, 4n6, 181, 183n11, 223, 239n34, 387n86
Herman of Bamberg, 286, 287n32, 289, 309, 332n45
Herman I of Cologne, 174n97, 184–87, 191, 199n23, 201, 206n50, 255n91
Herman of Metz, 312n117
Herminus, 138n79
Higbert of Lichfield, 115, 120n11
Hildesheim, 14n48, 52. *See also its bishop* Ebo
Hildeward of Halberstadt, 221n101, 311n113
Hilduin of Cologne (pretender), 54n92
Hilduin of Liège (pretender), 201, 232
Hilduin of St.-Denis, 142
Himerius of Tarragona, 141n92
Hincmar of Laon, 105, 114
Hincmar of Reims, 21, 27n3, 40n43, 41–42, 51–53, 60n117, 61–62, 63n125, 67, 86, 88, 92n65, 93, 98, 103, 104n110, 105–8, 109n135, 113–14, 117, 122n18, 124–25, 130, 132, 135–39, 143, 146, 155, 159, 167, 176, 178, 186, 187n26, 204n44, 205, 224, 312n118, 313n121, 317, 437n177
Historia Compostellana, 343n89, 356n141, 381n67, 478n154
Höchst, Council of (*1024*), 190, 200n24
Hoger of Hamburg, 4n6, 206n50, 255n91

Holy Saturday, 257, 354, 474
Honoratus of Salona, 402
Honorius I (pope), 12, 13n46, 77, 182, 245, 248, 324
Honorius II (antipope), 309n107, 310, 353n131, 359
Honorius III (pope), 344n91, 451, 473–74
Honorius Augustodunensis, 387n86
Honorius of Canterbury, 13n46, 245n56, 248
Honorius of Kent, 407, 411, 413–15, 417–19, 422–23, 427–35
Hormisdas (pope), 159n35, 303n83
Hostiensis (canonist), 303n86, 397, 452–55, 457–61, 462n78, 463–67, 469–76, 478–80
Hugh I of Besançon, 202n34, 207n51, 255n90, 270, 271n150, 286n28, 323n4, 366, 378, 384nn77–78
Hugh III of Besançon, 368, 375, 381n69
Hugh Capet of France, 216
Hugh of Auxerre, 305
Hugh of Cluny, 330
Hugh of Die/Lyon, 318n143, 327, 335, 342, 349n113, 357
Hugh of Flavigny, 54n92, 215n78, 312–13, 371, 373
Hugh of Reims, 215n80
Hugh the Chanter, 319n145, 337n64, 345n94
Huguccio (canonist), 397, 407, 409–27, 429–38
Humbert of Hamburg, 220n97
Humbert of Silva Candida, 291n44, 292, 328
Humphrey of Magdeburg, 207n51, 251
Hungary, 241, 340, 346, 356, 444, 446, 460
Hypatius of Nicopolis, 12

Ignatius of Constantinople, 79–80, 91n61, 122n18, 125n34, 296, 426n112

Ingelheim: Council of (*840*), 22, 97, 129, 154; Council of (*948*), 215
Innocent (martyr), 260, 261n108
Innocent I (pope), 373
Innocent III (pope), 195n4, 314, 443–47, 449, 453, 454n52, 456, 459–60, 469n111, 470, 472, 474–76
Innocent IV (pope), 452, 461, 478.
  See also Sinibaldo Fieschi
Invectiva in Romam, 256n92, 361n163
Invention of the Holy Cross (feast), 354
Investiture Contest, 220n97, 275, 277–78, 301, 354, 395
Irmingard of Hammerstein, 189–90
Isidore of Pelusion, 138n79
Isidore of Seville, 85n46, 109n135
Israelites. *See* Jews
Istria, 59, 242
Italy, 10, 12, 14, 34, 69–70, 78, 94, 98, 180n2, 182n6, 200, 205–6, 209n62, 239, 241–43, 246, 247n63, 262n113, 282n10, 291, 292n46, 293, 296, 305–6, 324–26, 338, 339n73, 340, 342–44, 350, 416
Ivo of Chartres, 291n44, 295, 326, 337–38, 349, 351

Jaenbert of Canterbury, 95
James of Albenga, 472
James the Greater, 307, 356
James the Just, 409
James the Less, 409
Jerusalem, 113, 114n150, 332n46, 368n23, 376, 381n67, 409, 450.
  See also its bishops Arnulf; Ebremar
Jews, 162n45, 163n49, 164–65, 253n85, 264, 265n126, 311, 380, 381n67, 389–91, 394, 470n119
Johannes Teutonicus, 408, 419, 449, 452, 456, 468, 470, 476
Johannine legislation (*875/77*), 44–48, 87n52, 180, 183, 322–23, 325, 327, 420–23, 425, 431, 434, 436, 439, 446, 448, 457–59, 476n148, 480
John (cardinal), 444, 446, 475

John (papal official), 9n28
John III (pope), 9, 11n35
John VIII (pope), 21, 23n2, 28, 37, 38n37, 43–45, 47, 49–50, 54–57, 60n115, 63, 69–71, 78n17, 80–82, 84n39, 87, 100–102, 104, 106n120, 107, 111, 121, 122n18, 126n38, 129–30, 133n67, 138, 148–49, 153, 155, 158–59, 161, 171n82, 172, 174n99, 177, 180, 182, 186n25, 229n5, 271, 297n65, 306, 312n118, 313, 323–25, 329, 352, 362, 372n37, 373n41, 403–4, 410, 418, 420, 424, 431n141, 456–57, 459, 485
John X (pope), 186, 201, 208, 231
John XI (pope), 224
John XII (pope), 133n65, 187, 189n34, 198, 199–200n23, 202nn33–34, 205, 206n50, 225n113, 225n118, 236, 244, 254n89, 255–57, 259, 263nn116–17, 268, 485
John XIII (pope), 187, 188n30, 200n24, 202nn33–34, 203, 206, 207n51, 208, 210, 222, 225n113, 239–41, 254n89, 257, 258n99, 259n103, 260, 263n116
John XIV (pope), 202n33, 207nn51–52, 258n99, 262n113
John XV (pope), 202n34, 205n45, 207nn51–52, 220, 241, 242n44, 255n90, 257n97, 258n98, 259n103, 261, 262n114, 263nn116–17
John XVIII (pope), 195, 202n34, 204n39, 207n51, 211, 233, 249, 259n103
John XIX (pope), 191n45, 193–94, 196, 201n31, 202n34, 206, 207n51, 208n53, 209, 212, 214, 227–28, 239n34, 251, 253n85, 254n89, 257nn96–97, 258nn101–2, 259n103, 262nn113–14, 263–64, 268n139, 280n2
John at the Latin Gate (feast), 384n78

John of Africa, 301n79
John of Avranches, 388–89, 392, 479n158
John of Corinth, 10n31, 170, 292, 406n18
John of Faenza, 413
John of Gaeta, 278, 345, 366–67, 369n24, 375–76, 378, 380–81, 395, 486. *See also* Gelasius II
John of Gorze, 109n133, 312n118
John of Palermo, 10n30, 63n125, 171n83
John II of Pavia, 306
John of Prima Justiniana, 10n31, 84n39, 405, 426–27
John I of Ravenna, 63, 143, 155
John II of Ravenna, 10n30, 11n35, 58–59, 63, 91, 129n52, 134–35, 175, 255n91, 301, 363n1, 404, 429, 437
John of Salerno, 281, 285, 385, 386n83
John of Salisbury, 298n71, 305n92, 454n53
John of St. Arnulf, 86n47
John of Syracuse, 10n30
John of Trondheim, 448n33
John of Venice, 95n79, 103n107
John of Wales, 447–48
John of Worcester, 321n1, 460n72
John Paul II (pope), 341n81
John the Baptist, 131, 134, 255, 474
John the Deacon, 17, 49, 50n75, 57, 58n109, 64, 76, 84n39, 91n63, 99n95, 104, 122, 134, 147n112, 151n2, 170, 175, 186n24, 231n9, 288n34, 318n144, 448n29
John the Evangelist, 474
John the Lamb (of Tongeren), 201n31
Justinian I (emperor), 399, 435
Justus of Canterbury, 13n46, 245n56
Juthael of Dol, 314
Juthinael of Dol, 112, 113n147

Kalocsa, 446, 468
Klauser, Theodor, 8

Knechtsteden, 372n38
Kyustendil. *See* Valebud

Lambert (saint), 258
Lambert of Deutz, 223, 239n34, 387n86
Lambert of Hersfeld, 289, 309–10, 311n114, 332n45, 353
lamina, 163, 165, 264–65, 390
Landulf of Benevento, 207n51, 208n54, 223n106, 241, 257n95, 258n99
Landulf the Younger, 152n2, 237n27, 460n72
Lanfranc of Canterbury, 250n73, 318, 358n151, 377–78
Langres, 200, 230, 232, 371. *See also its bishop* Argrim
Laon, 454n53. *See also its bishop* Hincmar
Lateran, 157, 271n149; Fourth Council (*1215*), 449–50, 452, 455, 463; synod (*769*), 32n19, 188; synod (*900*), 230; synod (*964*), 188
Lausanne, 305n92, 323n4, 454n53
Lawrence (martyr), 259–61, 316n136
Lawrence of Esztergom, 339–40, 346, 356, 368n21, 370, 442, 477
Leander of Seville, 10, 91, 128, 157–58, 166
Lechfeld, Battle of (*955*), 260
Le Mans, 110, 154. *See also its bishops* Aiglibert; Bertichram
Leo I (the Great; pope), 111n142, 124, 303, 304n88
Leo II (pope), 12, 291n44
Leo III (pope), 33nn20, 33n23, 40, 65n131, 68, 70, 77n12, 83n35, 92, 94n74, 95–96, 120, 128, 140–42, 145, 153, 154n12, 155, 169, 174n98, 176
Leo IV (pope), 35, 41, 51–52, 56, 59n115, 61, 67, 79, 86, 91n61, 93, 98, 106, 122n18, 124n28, 125, 132n64, 135–36, 137n76, 146, 153, 159, 218n91, 224, 296, 352, 426n112

General Index 537

Leo VI (pope), 231n11
Leo VII (pope), 199n23, 202nn33–34, 206n50, 255n91
Leo VIII (pope), 188–89, 202n34, 205, 206n50, 255n90
Leo IX (pope), 261n111, 271n150, 281–82, 286, 301, 306–8, 314, 342, 349n111, 353, 364n2, 365–67, 378, 384n78
Leoderic of Sens, 332n47
Leofric Missal, 246, 247n59
Leopold of Mainz, 353
Le Puy, 282, 317–18, 454. See also its bishops Pontius; Stephen
Libentius I of Hamburg, 205n45, 207nn51–52, 220, 255n90, 259n103, 261, 263n117
Liber Diurnus, 34, 35n26, 39, 42n50, 59, 60n115, 75, 119, 123, 126, 156n23, 157, 159n35, 160, 166n61, 168–69, 183, 201, 206, 207n51, 255n90, 268–69, 292, 342, 364–65, 438
Liber Pontificalis, 8, 9n24, 12nn42.44, 32n19, 37n34, 60, 98, 109, 113n147, 128, 140n88, 154, 188nn31–32, 291n44, 298, 299n72, 312n118, 409n27
Liber Quare, 388–89, 390n96
Lichfield, 95–96, 114–15, 142, 147. See also its bishop Higbert
Liège, 200, 232, 250, 303. See also its bishops Hilduin; Richer
Liemar of Hamburg, 283, 334
Limoges, 181, 225; Second Council of (*1031*), 225
Liudbert of Mainz, 38n37, 43, 50n76, 53, 54n95, 57n105, 77, 130n57, 156n22
Liudpram of Salzburg, 41, 59n115, 67n140, 70n149, 120, 131n62, 134n68, 225n118, 270n145, 297n65
Liutprand of Cremona, 188, 213–14
Lombardy, 14, 94–95, 399
London, 29, 104–6, 122, 140–42, 176, 349n109

London Ordo, 465n90
Lorch, 195–96, 210, 216, 240, 263n115. See also its bishop Gerard
lorum, 7, 90, 91n61
Lothar I (emperor), 35, 51, 56n102, 60, 61n119, 67, 86, 93, 97–98, 124–25, 129, 135, 153n9, 154, 218n91, 224n110, 352
Lothar II (king), 37, 43, 53, 54n92, 55, 66, 70, 78, 101, 168
Lotharingia, 225
Lothar of Segni, 175n102, 265n126, 266n130. See also Innocent III
Louis II (emperor), 54n92, 55n99, 71, 98, 101, 130
Louis the German, 38n37, 53–54, 55n99, 58, 83, 94, 101, 129, 156, 185n20
Louis the Pious, 33n22, 60, 69n147, 83, 86n47, 88, 93–94, 96–97, 113, 123, 142, 154, 162
Lull of Mainz, 39–42, 48, 51, 85, 341
Lund, 451
Lyfing of Canterbury, 245n55
Lyon, 33n22, 113, 200, 214, 230, 318, 332n47, 349, 371, 373, 451, 453, 465, 474, 478. See also its bishops Argrim; Gebuin; Hugh

Mâcon, Council of (*581/83*), 15
Magdeburg, 198n18, 203–4, 208n54, 219n94, 221–22, 225n113, 229–30, 239, 252–53, 260. See also its bishops Adalbert; Adalgot; Gero; Giselher; Humphrey; Tagino; Walthard
Mainz, 33n22, 108n129, 182–84, 190n39, 191n42, 196n10, 198n16, 199n18, 203–4, 205n44, 225n113, 233, 247, 254n87, 258, 259n103, 261, 303n83, 308–10, 311n114, 340, 359; Council of (*1049*), 271n150, 366. See also its bishops Adalbert; Aribo; Bardo; Leopold; Liudbert; Lull; Rabanus Maurus; Riculf; Ruthard; Siegfried; Wezilo; William; Willigis

Manegold of Lautenbach, 301–2
Marinian of Ravenna, 10n30, 63n125, 91, 135, 301
Marinus I (pope), 229
Mark (evangelist), 445n17
Mark (pope), 8, 298
Marozia (patrician), 224
Martial (missionary), 225
Martin of Tours, 133, 257–58
Mary, Blessed Virgin, 131, 255, 257n96, 306, 461, 474. *See also her feasts* Annunciation; Assumption; Birth; Purification
Maternus (missionary), 303n83
Mauger of Rouen, 218n91, 349
Maundy Thursday, 125, 132, 133n65, 255, 256n92, 295, 406, 429, 474
Maurice (emperor), 329
Maurice (martyr), 252, 259–61, 316n136
Maurice of Braga, 345–46. *See also* Gregory VIII
Maurus of Ravenna, 70, 79, 98
Mauss, Marcel, 23n3, 74
Maximin of Trier, 234, 238
Maximus of Salona, 10n31, 11n38, 58, 64, 76, 91, 122, 167n68, 231, 285, 329, 350, 381
Meingaud of Trier, 195, 202n34, 207n51, 211, 259n103
Meinhard I of Würzburg, 190, 218n91, 244n51
Melfi: Council of (*1089*), 406n18
Mercia, 96
Merovingians, 110
Merseburg, 229, 260. *See also its bishops* Giselher; Thietmar
Messina, 10, 454. *See also its bishop* Donus
Metz, 109–10, 121, 311–13, 317. *See also its bishops* Adalbero II; Adventius; Angilram; Chrodegang; Drogo; Herman; Robert; Stephen; Theoderic I; Urbicius; Wala
Michael (archangel), 257–58, 474–75
Michael of Salerno, 242n44

Michael of Zeta, 300, 348
Milan, 10, 33n22, 69n148, 338, 460n72. *See also its bishops* Ambrose; Anselm II; Anselm III; Constantius
Milo of Reims/Trier, 31n15
Monte Cassino, 247n63, 297n64
Monte Gargano, 258
Mt. Tabor. *See its bishop* Gerald
Muslims, 193, 240, 375, 383

Nantes. *See its bishop* Actard
Narbonne, 208, 231, 240, 263, 299–300. *See also its bishops* Agius; Bartholomew; Bertrand; Dalmatius; Gerard
Narratio Clericorum Remensium, 52n84, 61n119, 86n47, 93n71
Natalis of Salona, 11n38, 57, 350, 402, 409, 423
New Covenant (Testament), 165, 388
Nicaea: First Council of (*325*), 42n50, 113–14, 264n120; Second Council of (*787*), 42n50
Nicholas I (pope), 23n2, 27, 31n17, 36–37, 41–44, 48, 52–53, 54n92, 55n98, 56–57, 60n115, 61–63, 65–67, 78, 86, 88, 89n55, 93n69, 94, 99–100, 107, 110n137, 111n142, 112–13, 117, 120n10, 121n16, 122n18, 124–25, 127, 130, 132, 135–37, 140, 143, 145–48, 155, 156n21, 167–68, 169n73, 176, 185n20, 187n26, 204n44, 218n91, 256n92, 295, 312n118, 341n83, 370, 406, 437, 485
Nicholas II (pope), 287n29, 298, 321–22, 328, 330, 348, 374, 379
Nicholas of Myra, 338
Nicopolis, 10, 12, 335n57. *See also its bishops* Andrew; Hypatius
Nin, 200, 242. *See also its bishop* Theodosius
Norman Anonymous, 319, 334–36, 364n2
Norman Conquest, 246n57, 318
Normandy, 289, 323, 349

General Index 539

Northumbria, 322
Notker the Stammerer, 299n72
Novit fraternitas, 292

Oda of Canterbury, 248, 265, 267, 270
Odilo of Cluny, 214–15
Odorannus of Sens, 332n47
Offa of Mercia, 64, 95–96, 114, 245n56
Officium sacerdotis, 39–40, 68, 119–20, 127–28, 169, 201, 269, 292
Old Covenant (Testament), 6, 120n9, 162n45, 164–65, 380, 388, 390
Oleguer of Barcelona/Tarragona, 369, 376n53, 381n69
Omnibonus (canonist), 407n21, 436
omophorion, 6, 9–10, 14–15, 79n22, 80n24, 81, 91n61, 127n43, 137n77, 142n96, 214, 455
Ordo Romanus: I, 129n54; VIII, 128, 130–31, 220n96; XXXIV, 127; XXXV, 128n44; XXXVI, 156n23, 157n25, 235; XXXVII A, 157n25; XL A, 156n23, 157n26; XL B, 156n23, 157n26
Orléans. *See its bishop* Theodulf
Osbern of Canterbury, 249, 287n33
Ostia, 8, 157, 298, 299n72, 305n92, 397, 452, 454, 459. *See also its bishops* Hostiensis; Peter Damian
Othlo of St. Emmeram, 31n16
Otto of Bamberg, 295n57, 309, 356, 369, 381n69
Otto I (the Great) of Germany, 187–88, 198, 213, 221–22, 259–61
Otto II of Germany, 261
Otto III of Germany, 199, 205n44, 223, 305

Palermo, 10. *See also its bishops* Alcherius; John
Palestrina. *See its bishop* Conon
Pallii usum, 35, 75, 119–20, 123, 124n26, 127, 160, 170, 171n82, 206n50
Palm Sunday, 474

Paris, 349; Council of (*829*), 93n72. *See also its bishop* Dionysius
Paschal I (pope), 35, 119n7, 123, 170, 235
Paschal II (pope), 156n23, 261n111, 276, 281, 284, 294, 304–7, 308n104, 309, 316, 319, 323, 331, 332n46, 337, 339–40, 345–50, 356–58, 360, 365n6, 368, 370–71, 376, 381–83, 392n102, 442, 463, 477
Passau, 195, 199n23, 202n33, 206n50, 207n51, 210, 241, 255n90, 256n92, 257nn96–97, 259n103, 262nn113–14, 263n115, 267, 268n139, 318n144, 373. *See also its bishops* Altmann; Pilgrim
Paucapalea (canonist), 407, 411n38, 433
Paul (apostle), 77, 87n51, 124n26, 159–60, 162–64, 256n93, 303, 308, 343, 347, 386, 390, 461
Paulinus of York, 13n46
Pavia, 306n95, 317, 454. *See also its bishops* Guy; John II
Pécs, 446, 456, 467
Pelagius I (pope), 9, 159n35, 326, 333, 351n122, 403
Pentecost (feast), 255, 309n109, 384n78, 474
Peter (apostle), 5–6, 14, 21, 32, 38, 41, 43, 69, 76–77, 81, 83–84, 87n51, 88, 124n26, 131, 134, 153, 156–60, 165, 177, 196–98, 217, 220, 227–29, 235–38, 248–50, 256n93, 263, 272, 280, 282, 285, 288, 292, 300, 302–3, 308, 322, 338, 341n81, 343, 346–47, 358, 363, 378, 385, 456, 460–61, 463, 477–78, 480, 487
Peter Damian, 298, 311n114, 328, 330, 359n155, 366–67, 387–88, 390
Peter Mallius of St. Peter's, 156n23, 462, 477n153
Peter of Acerenza, 368n21, 376n53, 381n69

Peter of Africa, 301n79
Peter of Aix, 295n56, 368n21, 376n53, 381n69
Peter of Bar, 286–87, 365
Peter of Benevento, 443–44, 447, 449
Peter of Braga, 359–60
Peter of Girona, 193, 201n31, 202n34, 207n51, 212, 228n2, 239n34, 257n97, 258, 262n113, 263
Peter of Grado, 303, 339, 355, 368, 383
Peter of Ravenna, 9, 11n35
Peter of Silva Candida (Santa Rufina), 271
Pharisees, 172
Photius of Constantinople, 80–82, 101
Pilgrim of Cologne, 191, 253, 254n87
Pilgrim of Passau, 195–97, 202n35, 210, 215, 240, 256n94, 262n115, 266–67
Pippin the Short, 30, 31n15, 92, 109
Pisa, 282n10, 355. *See also its bishop* Daimbert
plate. *See lamina*
Poitiers, 293n50
Ponthion, Council of (*876*), 105n114
Pontifical of St. Dunstan, 236, 246n56, 248, 265
Pontius of Besançon, 295n57, 368n21, 376n53, 381
Pontius of Le Puy, 307, 308n104, 368n21, 369n24, 376n53, 381n69
Poppo of Aquileia, 196n10, 206, 207n51, 209, 253n85, 257n96
Poppo of Trier, 207n51, 251, 259n103, 262n114, 266, 267n134, 383, 386n82
Porto. *See its bishop* Benedict
Portugal, 360
Premonstratensians, 372n38
Prima Justiniana, 10, 335n57. *See also its bishop* John
Primogenius of Grado, 12n45, 77
Provence, 399
Pseudo-Alcuin, 264–65, 389–90, 410
Pseudo-Germanus, 162n45, 265n126

Pseudo-Isidore, 54n96, 90n60, 91n63, 103, 104n109, 105n115, 106n118, 110n135, 115n155, 128, 144, 157, 166
Pseudo-Liutprand, 47n62, 291n44
Purification of Mary (feast), 255, 445n17

Quicumque sane, 63n123, 182, 186n25, 297n65
Quisquis metropolitanus, 45, 325nn12–13, 325n16
Quoniam quidam, 44, 180, 182–83, 296n60, 324–27, 403, 420–21, 425, 431–32, 436, 438, 448, 457–58, 475, 477

Rabanus Maurus (of Mainz), 85–86, 109n135, 140, 162, 174n96, 184, 197, 264, 267, 304n89, 367n18, 390, 479n159
Radbod of Trier, 234, 238
Ragimbert of Vercelli, 199n23, 200, 206n50, 255n91
Rainald of Reims, 195n4, 204n44, 298, 327n25, 331, 333, 375, 380, 381n67, 391n101
Ralph de Diceto, 460n72
Ralph Glaber, 214, 215n76
Ralph of Bourges, 125n35, 132, 256n92, 295n59
Ralph of Canterbury, 281, 337–38
Ralph I of Tours, 261n111, 285n19, 285n21, 287n32, 296, 315, 316n136, 353n132, 365
Ralph II of Tours, 315n133, 381n69, 382n70
rational, 15n49, 221n101, 222n102, 253n85, 264–65, 310–11, 380, 390–92, 470, 471n120
Ravenger of Aquileia, 287, 330
Ravenna, 7, 10–12, 33n22, 46, 69n148, 78–79, 91, 97–98, 129, 134, 138, 143, 186nn24–25, 211, 325, 329, 342–43, 426, 430, 438, 447–48; Council of (*877*), 45, 47, 63, 87, 107, 121, 122n18,

138, 149, 161, 180, 325; Council of (*967*), 187. *See also its bishops* Apollinaris; Gerbert; Guibert; John I; John II; Marinian; Maurus; Peter; Walter
Raymond of Auch, 381n69
Raymond of Galicia, 360n158
Raymond of Penyafort, 400, 441–42, 444, 447–51, 460, 474
Reccared (king), 10, 12n39, 91, 158
Reims, 30–31, 33n22, 52n83, 61, 75, 86n47, 92, 97–98, 103, 124, 126, 129, 137, 139, 143, 146, 166–67, 170, 174n98, 195n4, 209, 224, 249, 303n83. *See also its bishops* Abel; Arnulf; Artold; Ebo; Fulk; Gerbert; Hincmar; Hugh; Milo; Rainald; Remigius; Seulf; Tilpin
Remigius of Dorchester, 358n151
Remigius of Reims, 303n83, 349
Restwald of Dol, 112, 113n147
Rhine, 206n48, 372n38
Richard of Syracuse, 448n33
Richer of Liège, 186n22, 200–201, 210n65, 232, 239n34, 250
Richer of Sens, 330–31, 349
Riculf of Mainz, 91n61, 173
Rimbert of Hamburg, 41, 43n51, 60n115, 94n75, 120n10
Risan. *See its bishop* Sebastian
Risus of Bari, 295n57, 368n21, 376n53, 381n69
Robert Guiscard, 343n89
Robert of Jumièges (of Canterbury), 358
Robert of Metz, 312n118
Rockingham, Council of (*1095*), 357
Rodoicus Modicipassus, 408n22
Rodrigo Jiménez de Rada (of Toledo), 4n6
Rodwald of Aquileia, 202n34, 205, 206n50, 255n90
Roland (canonist), 407
Roland of Dol, 315, 332n46, 375
Roman law, 399, 402, 414, 459, 466, 468, 478
Romano-Germanic Pontifical, 156n23, 157n26, 235n22, 236n23, 247, 390
Roman Pontifical of the Twelfth Century, 156n23
Romanus of St. Peter's, 156n23, 477n153
Rome: Council of (*595*), 12, 104n109, 290, 403, 406n18, 442; Council of (*800*), 68; Council of (*875*), 44, 46n60, 63, 87, 107, 121, 122n18, 138, 149, 161, 180, 182, 296n60, 324, 403n6; Council of (*1046*), 272; Council of (*1061*), 321; Council of (*1068*), 289n37; Council of (*1080*), 315
Rostagnus of Arles, 47, 49, 70n149, 81, 84n39, 87, 106n120, 122n18, 133n67, 149, 373n41
Rothad of Soissons, 113, 146
Rothrud of Rouen, 447n26
Rouen, 30, 33n22, 75, 92, 126, 166, 170, 174n98, 318, 334, 349, 388, 447–48, 477. *See also its bishops* Geoffrey; Grimo; Mauger; Rothrud; Victricius; William
Rudolf of Germany, 283, 334
Rufinus (canonist), 407, 431, 433, 436
Rupert of Deutz, 302, 388–89
Rupert of Salzburg, 257, 259–60
Rutger of Cologne, 161n44, 187, 197, 208, 224, 234
Ruthard of Mainz, 304, 356–57, 368

Sacramentary of Ratold, 237n28, 247
Saintes, Council of (*1081*), 315–16
Salerno, 205n45, 207n51, 209n62, 241, 242n44, 255n90, 281, 318, 376, 386n83. *See also its bishops* Alfanus I; Alfanus II; Amatus I; Amatus II; Amatus III; Benedict; Grimwald; John; Michael
Salona, 10–11, 70n148, 122. *See also its bishops* Maximus; Natalis; *and also* Split
Salzburg, 33n22, 147, 184, 196n10, 197, 203n38, 216, 225n113, 257,

Salzburg *(cont.)*
    260, 263n116, 304n89. *See also its bishops* Adalram; Adalwin; Arno; Frederick; Harold; Hartwig; Liudpram; Rupert; Thietmar I; Thietmar II; Tiemo
San Lorenzo (papal chapel), 478n154
Sapaudus of Arles, 9n25
Saracens. *See* Muslims
Saturninus (missionary), 258
Saxons. *See* Anglo-Saxons
Schimmelpfennig, Bernhard, 8
Scotland, 289, 376n53
Sebastian of Risan, 12n39
Secundus of Taormina, 9, 333
Seguin of Sens, 332n47
Seligenstadt, 191n41; Council of (*1023*), 190, 196n10
Sens, 27, 30–31, 32n19, 33n22, 52, 75, 92, 100, 126, 166, 170, 174n98, 184n16, 318, 332n47, 349. *See also its bishops* Ansegis; Egilo; Hartbert; Leoderic; Richer; Seguin; Wilchar
Septimania, 399
Serenus of Aquileia, 13n45, 59, 95, 103
Sergius I (pope), 13, 84, 113n147, 165, 167, 257, 303n83
Sergius II (pope), 60, 86, 98
Sergius III (pope), 206n50, 255n91
Sergius IV (pope), 199–200n23, 207nn51–52, 211, 242n44, 258n99, 262n113, 262n115, 263n116, 268n139
Sergius and Bacchus, 258
Seulf of Reims, 209, 229n3
Severinus (pope), 112, 113n147
Seville, Second Council of (*619*), 188n30. *See also its bishops* Isidore; Leander
Sicard of Cremona, 175n102
Sicily, 9–10, 75, 76n8, 123
Siegfried of Mainz, 298, 309–11, 328–29, 330n33, 359, 366
Sigebert of Gembloux, 311n113, 312
Sigehard of St. Maximin, 234, 238

Sigloard of Reims, 234
Significasti frater, 346, 370, 442–43, 477
Silva Candida. *See its bishops* Humbert; Peter
Silverius (pope), 9, 188
Simeon of Durham, 321n1
Simon Magus, 285, 289
Simon of Bisignano, 407, 409, 418, 421, 423, 426, 430–31, 433–35
Simplicius (pope), 62–63
Sinibaldo Fieschi, 452–54, 456, 463, 466–67, 469, 471, 473–77, 479. *See also* Innocent IV
Sion. *See its bishop* Ermenfrid
Si pastores ovium, 39–40, 59, 60n115, 67, 119–21, 127–28, 131–33, 136n75, 168, 169n73, 170n81, 171n82, 199, 200n23, 201, 202n33, 206n50, 207n51, 252n80, 254n89, 255, 268–70, 316, 365, 379–80, 382n71, 384n77, 385, 389n90
Siricius (pope), 141n92
Soissons: Council of (*744*), 30; Council of (*853*), 51, 139; Council of (*866*), 52, 61n118; Council of (*868*), 67n137. *See also its bishop* Rothad
Solomon of Brittany, 27n1, 36, 37n34, 56n103, 99, 112, 125n36, 218n91
Spain, 15n49, 104n109, 193, 258, 317, 344, 382–83, 445, 470, 473
Split, 70, 200, 242n46, 300, 348. *See also its bishops* Crescentius; Theodosius; *and also* Salona
St.-Basle, Council of (*991*), 216, 217n86
Stephen (martyr), 257, 261n111, 354, 384n78, 474
Stephen II (pope), 109, 154
Stephen V (pope), 174n97, 185, 199n23, 200nn24–25, 206n50, 231n11, 242, 255n91, 299, 333, 371
Stephen IX (pope), 281n4, 282

General Index   543

Stephen of Le Puy, 282, 306, 308n104
Stephen of Metz, 312n117, 312n119
Stephen of Tournai, 407, 412, 414, 423, 430
St.-Florent, 316n138, 369
Stigand of Winchester/Canterbury, 358
St. Peter's Basilica, 156–57, 160, 165n58, 233, 236, 237n27, 358, 462, 477n153, 478
Suidger of Bamberg. *See* Clement II
superhumeral, 90, 91n61, 137, 165, 173, 176, 265, 310, 380, 391–92
Sutri, Council of (*1046*), 192, 272. *See also its bishop* Bonizo
Syagrius of Autun, 11, 35, 57–58, 113, 114n150, 199, 329, 405, 419
Sylvester I (pope), 90
Sylvester II (pope), 181, 195n4, 211n67, 217, 223
Symmachus (pope), 1, 9n25, 206n50
Syracuse, 10. *See also its bishops* John; Richard

Tagino of Magdeburg, 203, 252
Tancred of Bologna, 451
Taormina, 333n48. *See also its bishop* Secundus
Tarentaise, 33n22, 111–12
Tarnovo, 444
Tarragona, 208n54, 240, 299–300, 318, 333n47, 369, 375, 382. *See also its bishops* Atto; Berengar; Himerius; Oleguer
Thangmar of Hildesheim, 14n48
Theban Legion, 260, 261n108
Thegan of Trier, 96–97
Theodore of Canterbury, 13n46, 29n6, 85n42, 110n135
Theoderic III (king), 110
Theoderic I of Metz, 312
Theoderic of Trier, 202n34, 203n37, 207n51, 259n103, 260
Theodosius I (emperor), 7
Theodosius of Nin/Split, 200, 231n11, 242, 333

Theodulf of Orléans, 68, 88, 92n65, 109–10, 113, 114n150, 153–54, 173–75, 265n128
Theoger of St. George, 340n79
Thietgaud of Trier, 78
Thietmar of Merseburg, 208, 219, 233, 239n34
Thietmar I of Salzburg, 80–81, 87, 100, 102, 172
Thietmar II of Salzburg, 196n10, 208n53, 251, 254n89, 257n97, 259n103, 262n114
Thomas I of York, 318, 319n145, 345, 365
Thomas II of York, 319, 340, 349
Three Chapters, 77n13, 94
Tiemo of Salzburg, 339, 353
Tilpin of Reims, 33, 39, 48, 51, 85, 92, 139, 156
Toledo, 317–18, 360, 375; Fourth Council of (*633*), 216; Eleventh Council of (*675*), 202n35. *See also its bishops* Bernard; Rodrigo Jiménez de Rada
Tongeren. *See its bishop* John the Lamb
Tours, 33n22, 89n57, 99, 112–13, 116n156, 133, 261n111, 284–85, 314–16, 318, 382n70. *See also its bishops* Actard; Arnulf; Gregory; Martin; Ralph I; Ralph II
Trani. *See its bishop* Bisantius
Trier, 33n22, 37, 43, 55, 66, 70, 109, 168, 195, 203–4, 211, 225n113, 238, 256, 299, 303n83, 312–13, 372–73. *See also its bishops* Bertulf; Bruno; Eberhard; Egilbert; Henry; Maximin; Meingaud; Milo; Poppo; Radbod; Theoderic; Thietgaud; Udo
Trinity, 43, 130, 448, 449n33
Trondheim, 448, 449n33. *See also its bishop* John
Troyes: Council of (*867*), 53, 66, 167n65; Council of (*878*), 47
Tuscany, 399

544   General Index

Udo of Trier, 261n111, 287–89, 316n136, 332n45, 365
Ulric of Aquileia, 360
Ulric of Augsburg, 354
Ulric of Benevento, 281n4
Uppsala, 449, 470
Urban II (pope), 195n4, 204n44, 263n119, 282–83, 289, 294n53, 298, 303, 315, 317–18, 319n145, 327, 331, 332n46, 333, 336, 338–39, 344–45, 348–49, 352–53, 355–59, 365, 367–68, 370, 375–76, 380–83, 391n101, 465, 486
Urbicius of Metz, 312n118
Utrecht, 303n83
Utrecht Psalter, 22, 51n81, 97n85

Valebud, 444
Valentinian III (emperor), 97, 143, 155
Vatican. *See* St. Peter's Basilica
Vercelli. *See its bishop* Ragimbert
Vermandois, 215
Verona, 306, 317. *See also its bishop* Bruno
Versus de Romana Avaritia, 290n40
Vic, 208n54, 240, 263n116. *See also its bishops* Atto; Berengar
Victor (bishop), 373
Victor II (pope), 267, 281, 386–87
Victor III (pope), 298
Victor (saint), 258
Victor of Grado, 41, 59n115
Victricius of Rouen, 373
Vienne, 12, 27, 32n19, 33n22, 36n31, 37n35, 77, 111–12, 124, 382n69. *See also its bishops* Ado; Bernard; Berther; Desiderius; Guy; Wilchar
Vigilius (pope), 9n25
Vincent (saint), 384n78
Vincentius Hispanus, 452, 462, 474
Virgilius of Arles, 10n30, 47, 106n120, 133n67, 404
Visigoths, 10, 91, 158
Vita Leonis IX, 281n5

Vitalis of Dubrovnik, 200n23, 202n34, 208n53, 242–43, 254n89
Vitalis of Grado, 41, 59n115, 131n62

Walafrid Strabo, 140, 154, 164–65
Wala of Autun, 371
Wala of Metz, 60n115, 70n149, 111, 121, 129, 159, 171n82, 312n118, 313–14
Walter of Albano, 336, 358n149
Walter of Ravenna, 369, 376, 381n69
Walter of Thérouanne, 372n35
Walthard of Magdeburg, 204, 207n51, 219, 251–52, 259n103, 261, 269
Wenric of Trier, 283, 334
Wezilo of Mainz, 359
Wilchar of Vienne/Sens, 12n42, 32n19
William Durandus, 152n2, 175n102, 265n126, 370n30, 462
William of Brindisi, 369n24, 376n53, 381n69
William of Mainz, 198n16, 221–22
William of Malmesbury, 96n81, 140n90, 321n1, 337n64, 358, 460n72, 465
William of Poitiers, 218n91, 349, 385
William of Rouen, 1, 323, 334, 344, 345n93, 348, 367n15, 369
William of St. Benedict, 331n40
William of Tyre, 460n72
William Rufus of England, 327, 336, 357
Willibald of Mainz, 73, 84n42
Willibert of Cologne, 23n2, 37, 38n37, 43, 45n58, 50, 53–54, 55nn98–99, 57–58, 71, 77–78, 83, 101, 108n127, 126n38, 129–30, 148, 153n9, 156, 159, 172, 174n99, 352, 372n37, 404, 424, 431n141
Willibrord (missionary), 13, 29n7, 84, 108, 165, 167, 248n66, 303n83
Willigis of Mainz, 202n34, 203n37,

204n44, 205, 207n51, 258, 259n103, 261, 269
Winchester, 358. *See also its bishop* Stigand
Winiman of Embrun, 281, 386
Winroth, Anders, 401, 402n3
Wolfherr of Hildesheim, 14n48, 261n112
Worcester, 321–22. *See also its bishop* Ealdred
Worms, 182–83, 191n42. *See also its bishops* Azecho; Burchard
Wulfhad of Bourges, 49, 53, 66, 100, 125, 145, 167
Wulfhelm of Canterbury, 248n66
Wulfstan II of York, 237n28, 245, 246n57

Würzburg, 209, 233. *See also its bishops* Henry; Meinhard I

York, 11, 13, 29, 91, 104–6, 122–23, 141, 205, 243–44, 248, 319, 321–22, 365, 444, 446. *See also its bishops* Ealdred; Eanbald I; Eanbald II; Egbert; Gerard; Paulinus; Thomas I; Thomas II; Wulfstan II

Zachary (pope), 13n46, 21, 29n8, 30–31, 39, 75, 85n42, 92n65, 122n18, 126, 166, 170–71, 174n98, 288n34, 290n42, 291n43, 301, 424

Also in the Studies in Medieval and
Early Modern Canon Law Series

Kenneth Pennington, General Editor

Gratian's Tractatus de penitentia
Edited and translated by Atria A. Larson

Gratian the Theologian
John C. Wei

Liberty and Law: The Idea of Permissive Natural Law, 1100–1800
Brian Tierney

*Gratian and the Development of Penitential Thought and
Law in the Twelfth Century*
Atria A. Larson

Marriage on Trial: Late Medieval German Couples at the Papal Court
Ludwig Schmugge
Translated by Atria A. Larson

Medieval Public Justice
Massimo Vallerani
Translated by Sarah Rubin Blanshei

A Sacred Kingdom: Bishops and the Rise of Frankish Kingship, 300–850
Michael Edward Moore

*A Sip from the "Well of Grace": Medieval Texts from the
Apostolic Penitentiary*
Kirsi Salonen and Ludwig Schmugge

*"A Pernicious Sort of Woman": Quasi-Religious Women and
Canon Lawyers in the Later Middle Ages*
Elizabeth Makowski

Canon Law and Cloistered Women: Periculoso *and Its
Commentators, 1298–1545*
Elizabeth Makowski

The Common Legal Past of Europe, 1000–1800
Manlio Bellomo

www.ingramcontent.com/pod-product-compliance
Lightning Source LLC
Chambersburg PA
CBHW030249010526
44107CB00053B/1644